Colorado's Fourteeners

From Hikes to Climbs

Third Edition

Gerry Roach

FULCRUM
GOLDEN, COLORADO

Climbing is an inherently dangerous activity and requires good decision making and safe climbing technique. The information contained in this book is based upon the experiences of the author and might not be perceived as accurate by other persons. This book is not a substitute for sound judgment. Extreme care should be taken when following any of the routes or techniques described in this book. It is intended for use by hikers and climbers who have requisite training, experience, and knowledge. It is not intended to be used as an instructional guide. Proper clothing and equipment are essential when attempting to climb any of the routes described in this book. Failure to have the requisite experience, equipment, and conditioning may subject you to extreme physical danger, including injury and death. The safety of the routes described in this book, as well as any associated dangers, may have changed since the book's publication. Maps pictured in this book are based on USGS quadrangles and are for route definition only; use updated, full-scale USGS quadrangles for actual climbs. Neither Fulcrum Publishing nor the author assume any liability for injury, damage to property, or violation of the law that may arise from the use of this book.

There are no warranties, either express or implied, that the information contained within this book is reliable. There are no implied warranties of merchantability as to this book. There are no warranties that extend beyond the description on the face hereof. Use of this book indicates the user's assumption of risk that it may contain errors, as well as acknowledgment that the user is solely accountable for his or her own abilities to climb in a safe and responsible manner.

A few of the trailheads and trails contained in this book are on private property. These routes are noted in the book with a disclaimer "Private Property, Permission Required." Prior to using any of these trailheads or trails, the reader must get permission from the property owner; to do otherwise can be considered trespassing. The publisher and the author hereby disclaim any responsibility for utilization of any of these private trails without first obtaining permission.

The coordinates given in this book are based on the new WGS84 horizontal datum. These coordinates are derived from online map sources and may not be accurate. Do not rely on any coordinate in this book, especially for a matter involving safety.

For updates on the information contained in this guidebook, please refer to www.climb.mountains.com.

Library of Congress Cataloging-in-Publication Data
Roach, Gerry.
  Colorado's fourteeners : from hikes to climbs / Gerry Roach. -- 3rd ed.
     p. cm.
  Includes index.
  ISBN 978-1-55591-746-3 (pbk.)
  1. Mountaineering--Colorado--Guidebooks. 2.
Hiking--Colorado--Guidebooks. 3. Backpacking--Colorado--Guidebooks. 4.
Colorado--Guidebooks. I. Title.
  GV199.42.C6R63 2011
  796.52'209788--dc22

                              2010035868

Book and map design: Jack Lenzo
Cover image: Mount Sneffels © Shutterstock| Mike Norton

Printed in China

0 9 8 7 6 5 4 3 2

Fulcrum Publishing
4690 Table Mountain Drive, Suite 100
Golden, Colorado 80403
800-992-2908 • 303-277-1623
www.fulcrumbooks.com

Contents

List of Maps

Mount of the Holy Cross and Angelica couloir.

Preface

Colorado's Fourteeners: From Hikes to Climbs is a celebration of the joys that come from climbing Colorado's highest peaks. Colorado's 14,000-foot peaks offer the hiker and mountaineer one of the finest arrays of alpine challenges in the Rocky Mountains. You can be in the heart of Colorado's Fourteener country in a few hours from its metropolitan areas, and the proximity of these peaks to population centers makes them even more precious. A lifetime of adventures is waiting for you in Colorado's mountains. Climbing Fourteeners has become increasingly popular in recent years, and the challenge of climbing all the Fourteeners captures many people. The elevation celebration continues.

This guide offers a broad view of Colorado's Fourteeners. Besides the often-climbed standard routes, it describes many alternate routes on the easier Fourteeners and, also, several technical routes. Most of the routes on Colorado's Fourteeners are walk-ups (Class 1, Class 2, Easy Snow) or scampers (Class 2+), but there are many wonderful scrambles (Class 3, Moderate Snow) and technical climbs (Class 4, Class 5, Steep Snow) on these peaks. For the best routes, regardless of difficulty, I use the designation *Classic*, and have given 49 routes this accolade. Most climbers on Colorado's Fourteeners climb the standard routes, and these routes are becoming crowded. However, you can still spend days climbing Fourteeners and never see another person. If you are tired of crowded routes, try Longs' Loft Route, Democrat's North Ridge Route, Yale's East Ridge Route, or El Diente's South Slopes Route. Colorado is still full of wilderness!

Over the years, I have cherished the easy routes as much as the harder ones, and I have included a mixture of routes that will titillate the senses of almost anybody. All the routes described in this guide lead to the summit of a peak.

This is a guidebook, pure and simple. It describes where to climb but not how to climb. No book can make judgments for you, but there are several good instructional books that can aid the process of learning the fundamentals. For an introduction to the sport of mountaineering, I recommend *Mountaineering: The Freedom of the Hills* by The Mountaineers book staff (Seattle: The Mountaineers, 2010).

The trailheads I describe are places most vehicles can reach. Sometimes these places are well-marked parking lots at the end of a road, and sometimes they are just places along a continuing road where the road becomes too rough for low-clearance vehicles. Four-wheel-drive vehicles can shorten many of the ascents in Colorado, but I have never felt like this aid was necessary. I need more mountain, not less.

Unlike most guidebooks, which are compilations of many people's route descriptions, this book is the result of one man's labor of love. I started climbing

Mount Massive from the southwest.

in Colorado in 1955 and have spent the last seven decades climbing Colorado's Fourteeners. I have not rushed through my Fourteeners. I spent a leisurely 20 years climbing them all for the first time. Then I leisurely climbed them all again. I climbed many routes specifically for this guide and documented them immediately after each climb. I continue to field check this guide extensively. Because one person has climbed and reported on these routes, the descriptions are consistent. I believe climbing is a very personal activity, and I seldom give opinions that might intrude on yours. Still, my bias creeps in from time to time.

This guide is not comprehensive in its coverage of the routes on the Four-teeners. I have not revealed all the secrets of these special peaks. There are many more routes that I could have included. For every route I climbed, I saw two more! Never lose your spirit of discovery. You should finish each climb and each book wanting more.

I welcome route information and constructive criticism from readers. E-mail your comments to gerryroach@mac.com.

Anyone who climbs all the Colorado Fourteeners deserves the title Dr. Colorado. Anyone who climbs every route in this guide has graduated Summit Cum Laude! Climb safely and don't forget to have fun.

Introduction

Safety First

Climbing is dangerous, and each individual should approach these peaks with caution. Conditions can vary tremendously depending on time of day and time of year. The route descriptions in this book assume good summer conditions. Lightning is always a serious hazard in Colorado during the summer months. Snow conditions and cornices vary from year to year. Spring and early summer avalanches can be a function of winter storms that occurred months earlier. The previous winter's snowfall determines snow conditions in August.

Before charging forth with your city energy and competitive urges, take some time to understand the mountain environment you are about to enter. Carefully study your chosen route and don't be afraid to retreat if your condition, or the mountain's, is unfavorable. Better yet, do an easier climb nearby to become familiar with the area. When both you and the mountain are ready, come back and do your dream climb.

Lightning

Colorado is famous for apocalyptic lightning storms that threaten not just your life, but your soul as well. This section will have special meaning if you have ever been trapped by a storm that endures for more than an hour and leaves no gap between one peal of thunder and the next. The term *simultaneous flash-boom* has a very personal meaning for many Colorado climbers.

Dangers

- Lightning is dangerous!
- Lightning is the greatest external hazard to summer mountaineering in Colorado.
- Lightning kills people every year in Colorado's mountains.
- Direct hits are usually fatal.

Precautions

- Start early! Be off summits by noon and back in the valley by early afternoon.
- Observe thunderhead buildup carefully, noting speed and direction; towering thunderheads with black bottoms are bad.
- When lightning begins nearby, count the seconds between flash and thunder, then divide by 5 to calculate the distance to the flash in miles. Repeat to determine if lightning is approaching.
- Try to determine if the lightning activity is cloud-to-cloud or ground strikes.
- Get off summits and ridges.

Protection

- You cannot outrun a storm; physics wins.
- When caught, seek a safe zone in the 45-degree cone around an object 5 to 10 times your height.
- Be aware of ground currents; the current from a ground strike disperses along the ground or cliff, especially in wet cracks.
- Wet ropes are good conductors.
- Snow is not a good conductor.
- Separate yourself from metal objects.
- Avoid sheltering in potential spark gaps under boulders and trees.
- Disperse the group. Survivors can revive one who is hit.
- Crouch on boot soles, ideally on dry insulating material such as moss or grass. Dirt is better than rock. Avoid water.
- Do not put your hands down. Put elbows on knees and hands on head. This gives current a short path through your arms rather than the longer path through your vital organs.
- Do not lie down; current easily goes through your vital organs.

First Aid

- Know and give CPR. CPR has revived many lightning-strike victims.
- Treat for burns.
- Evacuate.

Avalanche
Hazard Forecasting

- Avalanches are the greatest external hazard to winter mountaineering in Colorado; gravity never sleeps.
- Loose-snow avalanches start at a single point and fan out downward; the danger is highest after new snowfall.
- Slab avalanches occur when an entire slope of snow starts in motion at once.
- Consistent winds of more than 15 miles per hour can build up soft slabs.
- Consistent winds of 25 to 50 miles per hour can build up hard slabs.
- Hard slabs develop more rapidly at low temperatures and are sensitive to temperature changes.
- Most avalanches occur on slopes of 30 to 45 degrees.
- Most avalanches that trap people are triggered by the victims themselves.
- Most avalanches that trap skiers are relatively small.
- Avalanches occur on open slopes, in gullies, and in open stands of trees. Ridges, outcrops, and dense stands of trees (too dense to ski through comfortably) are safer.
- Beware of avalanche danger during and after heavy winter storms. The danger factor decreases with time. The rate of decrease depends strongly on temperature. Near 32°F, the danger may persist for only a few hours. Below 0°F, it may last for many days or even weeks.
- Deep snow smooths out terrain irregularities and promotes avalanching.
- Warm snow will bond to a warm surface much better than cold snow will bond to a cold surface. Therefore, monitor the temperature at the start of a storm.
- It generally takes 10 to 12 inches of new snow to produce serious avalanche danger.

- Prolonged snowfalls of 1 inch or more per hour should always be viewed with suspicion.
- Snowfalls that begin warm and then cool off tend to be more stable than those with the opposite trend.
- Extensive sloughing after a fresh snowfall is evidence of stability.
- Sunballs (balls of snow rolling down a slope on a sunny day) are indicators of rapid changes taking place in the snow. The danger is not high if the sunballs are small and penetrate only a few inches into the surface layer. If these balls grow in size during the day and eventually achieve the form of large snow wheels that penetrate deeply into the snow, wet-snow avalanching may be imminent.
- "Talking snow," a hollow drumlike sound under your footsteps or skis, or a booming sound with or without a drop in the snow level is a sign of serious avalanche hazard.
- Other things being equal, convex slopes offer more slab-avalanche danger than concave slopes. However, many avalanches do start on concave profiles.

Precautions

- Never travel alone. Your best chance of surviving a burial is to have unburied companions.
- Avoid avalanche areas and times of high danger. The probability of being caught in an avalanche is directly proportional to the time you spend in the danger zone.
- Carry at least one shovel and avalanche beacons if possible.

If you must cross an avalanche slope:

- Travel through the danger zone one person at a time. If you are buried, your rescue depends on your unburied companions.
- Remove the wrist loops of your ski poles from your wrists.
- Unhitch any ski safety straps.
- Put on hat and mittens, and close your parka.
- Loosen pack straps.

If you are caught in an avalanche:

- Discard poles, skis, and pack.
- Attempt to stay on the surface with a swimming motion.
- Attempt to work to the side of the avalanche.
- Grab trees.
- Close your mouth.
- As the avalanche slows, cover your face with your hands.
- Make an air space.
- Don't shout when buried. Sound goes into but not out of snow.

Rescue

- Don't panic. A buried person only has a 30 percent chance of survival after 30 minutes. Organized rescue in most backcountry situations is at least one hour from the scene. The lives of your buried companions depend largely on what you do.
- Assess any additional avalanche hazard and plan escape routes.
- Mark the last-seen point.

- If equipped with avalanche beacons, the entire unburied party must turn their beacons to "receive." Search in a pattern that zeros in on the strongest signal. Turn down the volume and pinpoint the victim's exact position, then dig.
- Do a quick search below the last-seen point. Scruff around. Look for any clues and mark their location. Search likely areas near trees, on benches, and near the end of the debris.
- Start a thorough search. Search the most likely area first. Use ski poles as probes if that's all you have. Do a coarse probe, making probe holes about 2 feet apart. Have all searchers form a straight line and move uphill. A coarse probe has a 70 percent chance of finding a victim buried in the probe area. Repeat a coarse probe of the most likely area several times, then move to the next most likely area.
- Go for help. Determining when to send some of your party for additional help is a judgment call that depends on the size of your group, how far into the backcountry you are, and the availability of trained rescue groups.

Longs Peak from the south, showing the upper part of the Kieners Route.

Leave No Trace

If you use the wilderness resource, it is your responsibility to help protect it from environmental damage. The old adage "Take nothing but pictures; leave nothing but footprints" is no longer good enough. The footprints of thousands of visitors can cause extensive damage to fragile alpine areas. The ground plants above treeline are especially vulnerable because they cling to a tenuous existence. If you destroy a patch of tundra with a careless step, it may take a hundred years for the plants to recover. In some cases, they may never recover.

The routes in this book all pass through the alpine zone. Tread lightly. Stay on the trails. Where trails do not exist, travel on durable surfaces like rock and snow. Walk on rocks in the tundra, not on the tundra itself. If traveling over tundra is the only option, be sure to disperse use over a wide area. Let your eyes do the walking sometimes. You do not have to explore every inch on foot. Respect the environment you are entering. If you don't show respect, you are an intruder, not a visitor.

Leave No Trace (LNT), a national nonprofit organization dedicated to educating people about responsible use of the outdoors, recommends a few simple techniques for minimum-impact travel through fragile alpine environments. Learn them. Abide by them. For more information about LNT and minimum-impact outdoor ethics, call 800-332-4100 or visit the LNT website at www.LNT .org. The seven tenets of the LNT movement are:

1. Plan Ahead and Prepare
- Know the regulations and special concerns for the area you'll visit.
- Prepare for extreme weather, hazards, and emergencies.
- Schedule your trip to avoid times of high use.
- Visit in small groups when possible. Consider splitting larger groups into smaller groups.
- Repackage food to minimize waste.
- Use a map, compass, or GPS to eliminate the use of marking paint, rock cairns, or flagging.

2. Travel and Camp on Durable Surfaces
- Durable surfaces include established trails and campsites, rock, gravel, dry grasses, or snow.
- Protect riparian areas by camping at least 200 feet from lakes and streams.
- Good campsites are found, not made. Altering a site is not necessary.

In popular areas:
- Concentrate use on existing trails and campsites.
- Walk single file in the middle of the trail, even when wet or muddy.
- Keep campsites small. Focus activity in areas where vegetation is absent.

In pristine areas:
- Disperse use to prevent the creation of campsites and trails.
- Avoid places where impacts are just beginning.

3. Dispose of Waste Properly
- Pack it in, pack it out. Inspect your campsite and rest areas for trash or spilled foods. Pack out all trash, leftover food, and litter.
- Deposit solid human waste in catholes dug 6 to 8 inches deep at least 200 feet from water, camp, or trails. Cover and disguise the cathole when finished.
- Pack out toilet paper and hygiene products.
- To wash yourself or your dishes, carry water 200 feet away from streams or lakes and use small amounts of biodegradable soap. Scatter strained dishwater.

4. Leave What You Find

- Preserve the past: examine, but do not touch, cultural or historic structures and artifacts.
- Leave rocks, plants, and other natural objects as you find them.
- Avoid introducing or transporting nonnative species.
- Do not build structures, furniture, or dig trenches.

5. Minimize Campfire Impacts

- Campfires can cause lasting impacts to the backcountry. Use a lightweight stove for cooking and enjoy a candle lantern for light.
- Where fires are permitted, use established fire rings, fire pans, or mound fires.
- Keep fires small. Only use sticks from the ground that can be broken by hand.
- Burn all wood and coals to ash, put out campfires completely, then scatter cool ashes.

6. Respect Wildlife

- Observe wildlife from a distance. Do not follow or approach them.
- Never feed animals. Feeding wildlife damages their health, alters natural behaviors, and exposes them to predators and other dangers.
- Protect wildlife and your food by storing rations and trash securely.
- Control pets at all times, or leave them at home.
- Avoid wildlife during sensitive times: mating, nesting, raising young, or in winter.

7. Be Considerate of Other Visitors

- Respect other visitors and protect the quality of their experience.
- Be courteous. Yield to other users on the trail.
- Step to the downhill side of the trail when encountering pack stock.
- Take breaks and camp away from trails and other visitors.
- Let nature's sounds prevail. Avoid loud voices and noises.

The Rating System

I have used an extended Yosemite Decimal System (YDS) to rate each route's difficulty. Each route's rating has four parts: R Points, round-trip mileage, round-trip elevation gain, Class, and Snow Steepness. I present this information right below each route name.

R Points

My R Point number denotes the effort required by a route and its difficulty, or the route's "efferculty," as I prefer to call it. A route's R Point value expresses the route's efferculty based on the peak's elevation, the length of the approach and climb viewed in both time and distance, elevation gain, and the technical difficulty of each pitch. The R Point value does not express the route's objective dangers, exposure, the probability of bad weather, or the difficulty of retreat. You can compare the R Point numbers for two routes and know which is tougher overall. You can also use the R Point number to determine how long the climb will take you. Climbers' speeds vary, but many climbers average 20 to 25 R Points per hour. For example, if you have determined that you can average 25 R Points per hour and a route has a rating of 150 R Points, then your projected time for that route is 6 hours. In this book, my R Point value can be used instead of the Yosemite Decimal System's Grade. I feel it is a better measure of efferculty. Here is a sampling of R Point numbers for several popular Colorado hikes and climbs.

Route Name	R Points
Mount Sanitas via Dakota Ridge	26
Green Mountain via Saddle Rock Trail	44
South Boulder Peak via Shadow Canyon	67
Mount Audubon Trail	120
Grays Peak Trail	147
Bison Peak Southwest Ridge	157
The Decalibron	241
Wetterhorn Peak Southeast Ridge	291
Longs Peak Keyhole Route	348
Pikes Peak via Barr Trail	419
Crestone Peak South Face from 8,770 feet	535
Evans Egis	987
"Sunlight Spire" from Needleton	1,000

At the top of the Lost Rat couloir on Grays Peak.

Mileage

The mileage is the round-trip hiking and climbing distance from the starting point to the summit and back to the starting point. The starting point is usually a trailhead, but I often list the mileage from 4WD parking places, lakes, and other important points along the route. For harder routes, I often list the mileage if you descend an easier route.

Elevation Gain

The elevation gain is the total elevation gain encountered from the starting point to the summit and back to the starting point. Where different, I include both the net gain from trailhead to the summit and the total gain, which includes any extra gain that you will encounter going over passes or false summits, both on the ascent and on the return.

Class

A route's Class is denoted by the word *Class*, followed by a number from 1 to 5.14, in ascending order of difficulty of the route's most difficult free-climbing rock pitch. Used elsewhere, a Class rating refers to a single pitch or move. Difficulties from Class 1 to Class 4 are described with a single digit only. When the difficulty reaches Class 5, the description includes decimal places. In this guide, Class 5 difficulty ranges from 5.0 to 5.10. I have made no attempt to distinguish between 5.0, 5.1, and 5.2. I indicate difficulty in this range with the rating Class 5.0–5.2. Occasionally, I also combine 5.3 and 5.4 with the rating Class 5.3–5.4.

I have not used adjectives such as *easy*, *difficult*, or *severe* to rate the rock pitches. What is easy for one person may be difficult for another, and words like this only confuse the issue. In place of adjectives, I use examples to describe difficulty. The answer to the question "Just how hard is Class 3 anyway?" is "Climb Longs' Keyhole Route, then you will know." A list of example routes follows that includes some of the classic Front Range rock climbs for comparison. I have ordered the routes roughly from easiest to hardest within each Class.

Class	Route
Class 1	Grays Peak — North Slopes
	Mount Elbert — East Ridge
	Pikes Peak — East Slopes
	Quandary Peak — East Slopes
Class 2	Mount Massive — East Slopes
	Mount of the Holy Cross — North Ridge
	Handies Peak — Grizzly Gulch
	Mount Yale — East Ridge

Class	Route
Class 2+	Windom Peak — West Ridge
	Challenger Point — North Slopes
	Mount Sneffels — South Slopes
	Mount Lindsey — North Face
Class 3	Kit Carson Peak — West Ridge
	Longs Peak — Keyhole
	Longs Peak — Loft
	Wilson Peak — West Ridge
	Crestone Needle — South Face
Class 4	Sunlight Peak — South Slopes (final summit block)
	Mount Wilson — North Slopes (final 150 feet)
	Second Flatiron — Freeway
	Crestone Peak to Crestone Needle traverse
Class 5.0–5.2	Crestone Peak — North Buttress
	Little Bear to Blanca traverse
	Third Flatiron — Standard East Face
	Longs Peak — Notch Couloir
Class 5.3–5.4	Longs Peak — North Face
	Longs Peak — Kieners
	First Flatiron — North Arête
Class 5.5	Third Flatiron — East Face Left
	Longs Peak — Keyhole Ridge
	Boulder Canyon Dome — East Slab
	Longs Peak — Alexander's Chimney
Class 5.6	First Flatiron — Direct East Face
	Eldorado Wind Tower — Calypso
	Mount Sneffels — North Buttress
Class 5.7	Crestone Needle — Ellingwood Arête
	Boulder Canyon Castle Rock — Cussin' Crack
	Third Flatiron — Friday's Folly
	Longs Peak — Stettner's Ledges
Class 5.8	Eldorado Bastille — The Bastille Crack
	Kit Carson Peak — The Prow
	Crestone Needle — North Pillar
	Eldorado Bastille — West Arête
Class 5.9	Lizard Head — West Finish
Class 5.10	"Sunlight Spire"

These difficulty ratings are for good, dry conditions. High-country rock rapidly becomes more difficult as it becomes wet, and a route becomes a different climb entirely when snow-covered. For example, the difficulty of Longs'

Keyhole Route can jump from Class 3 to Class 5 when it is wet or snow-covered.

I discuss descent routes only occasionally. You can descend by reversing the ascent route or by descending easier routes. When I include technical routes on a peak, I always discuss an easier route, and this is usually the logical descent route. There are often several easy routes to choose from. You must use good mountaineering judgment when selecting descent routes.

Because I have defined difficulty on rock by example, people unfamiliar with the YDS will have to do some climbs before they understand what the different Class ratings mean. This is particularly true for the more difficult ratings. The following descriptions can help.

Class 1 is trail hiking or any hiking across open country that is no more difficult than walking on a maintained trail. The parking lot at the trailhead is easy Class 1, groomed trails are midrange Class 1, and some of the big step-ups near the top of the Barr Trail are difficult Class 1.

Class 2 is off-trail hiking. Class 2 usually means bushwhacking or hiking on a talus slope. You are not yet using handholds for upward movement. Occasionally, I use the rating Class 2+ for a pseudo-scrambling route where you will use your hands but do not need to search very hard for handholds. Most people are able to downclimb Class 2+ terrain facing out. I use the term *scampering* for Class 2+ movement.

Class 3 is the easiest climbing category, and people usually call it "scrambling." You are beginning to look for and use handholds for upward movement. You are now using basic climbing, not walking, movements. Although you are using handholds, you don't have to look very hard to find them. Occasionally putting your hand down for balance while crossing a talus slope does not qualify as Class 3. That is still Class 2. Many people feel the need to face in while downclimbing Class 3.

Class 4 is in the realm of technical climbing. You are not just using handholds; you have to search for, select, and test them. You are beginning to use muscle groups not involved with hiking, those of the upper body and abdominals in particular. Your movement is more focused, thoughtful, and slower. Many people prefer to rappel down a serious Class 4 pitch rather than downclimb it.

Class 5 is technical climbing. You are now using a variety of climbing techniques, not just cling holds. Your movement may involve stemming with your legs, cross-pressure with your arms, pressing down on handholds as you pass them, edging on small holds, smearing, chimneying, jamming, and heel hooks. A lack of flexibility will be noticeable and can hinder your movement. Your movement usually totally occupies your mind. You have come a long way from walking across the parking lot and entertaining a million thoughts. Most people choose to rappel down Class 5 pitches.

Class ratings of individual moves and pitches are solidified by the consensus of the climbing community at large and the local climbing community who are most familiar with the area. Only when there is considerable consensus for a rating can it be used as an example of that difficulty. Therefore, Class ratings can vary from location to location; many Class 3 routes in California would be rated Class 4 in Colorado.

The Class ratings do not make any statement about how exposed a move or pitch is. Exposure is a subjective fear that varies widely from person to person. Exposure usually increases with difficulty, but there are some noticeable exceptions to this rule. Some Class 2 passages are very exposed. A good example of this is the Catwalk on Eolus' northeast ridge. The upper part of this route is Class 3, but most of the Catwalk is only Class 2. If exposure bothers you to the point where it impairs your movement, increase my ratings accordingly.

I do not define difficulty in terms of equipment that you might or might not use. Historically, Class 3 meant unroped climbing and Class 4 was roped climbing. Unfortunately, there is a lot of historical momentum behind those old definitions. Under the old definition, when people tell me that they "third-classed" a pitch, all I know is that they climbed it unroped. I do not know how hard it is. After all, the Diamond on Longs Peak (5.10) has been "third-classed." I know how hard a pitch I am willing to do unroped, but I do not know how hard a pitch you are willing to do unroped. There are many people who can free-solo up and down every route in this guide, and many more who cannot do any of the routes, with or without a rope. The decision of when to rope up must always be the individual's.

Snow Steepness

Part of the rating system used in this guide refers to the route's steepest snow or ice. The Snow Steepness rating is not part of the YDS, but I have added it to provide more information about a route. If there is no snow or ice on a route, this designation is absent. Because a slope's steepness can be measured, this part of the rating is easier to define. The following adjectives refer to a snow slope's angle:

Snow steepness adjective	Steepness
Easy	0 to 30 degrees
Moderate	30 to 45 degrees
Steep	45 to 60 degrees
Very Steep	60 to 80 degrees
Vertical	80 to 90 degrees

Climbers seldom measure a slope angle accurately. They usually estimate the angle by the slope's feel, and these feelings vary widely. Even experienced climbers are notorious for guessing a slope angle to be steeper than it is. I have kept this in mind when determining the slope angles used in this guide. When a slope angle is hovering around the critical junction between Moderate and Steep, I apply the Steep rating.

Other Rating Systems

The Yosemite Decimal System (YDS) is widely used in the United States and has evolved as the national standard. The National Climbing Classification System (NCCS) was intended to be the standard, but it has not gained wide acceptance. The difference between the YDS and NCCS numbers is confusing. The table below lists the correspondence between these two US systems and several of the popular international systems. Note that the British system started with adjectives. It became confusing with Just Very Severe (JVS), Very Severe (VS), and Hard. These adjectives have been replaced with numbers.

YDS	NCCS	UIAA	French	British	Australian	German
Class 1	F1	I		Easy		
Class 2	F1	I		Easy		
Class 3	F2	I, II		Easy		
Class 4	F3	I, II		Easy		
Class 5.0–5.2	F4	I, II	1	Moderate	10	I
Class 5.3	F5	II	2	Difficult	11	II
Class 5.4	F5	III	3	Very Difficult	12	III
Class 5.5	F6	IV	4	4a (Severe)	12, 13	IV
Class 5.6	F6	V-	5	4b (Severe)	13	V
Class 5.7	F7	V	5	4b, 4c (JVS)	14, 15	VI
Class 5.8	F8	V+, VI-	5+	4c, 5a (VS)	15, 16, 17	VIIa, VIIb
Class 5.9	F9	VI	6a	5a, 5b (VS)	17, 18	VIIb, VIIc
Class 5.10a	F10	VI+	6a+	5b (Hard)	19	VIIc
Class 5.10b	F10	VII-	6a+, 6b	5b, 5c	20	VIIIa
Class 5.10c	F11	VII-, VII	6b	5c	20, 21	VIIIa, VIIIb
Class 5.10d	F11	VII	6b+	5c	21, 22	VIIIb, VIIIc
Class 5.11a	F12	VII+	6c	5c, 6a	22, 23	VIIIc, IXa
Class 5.11b	F12	VII+, VIII-	6c+	6a	23	IXa
Class 5.11c	F13	VIII-	7a	6a	24	IXb
Class 5.11d	F13	VIII	7a+	6a, 6b	25	IXb, IXc
Class 5.12a	F14	VIII+	7b	6b	25, 26	IXc
Class 5.12b	F14	VIII+, IX-	7b+	6b	26	Xa
Class 5.12c	F15	IX-	7b+, 7c	6b, 6c	26, 27	Xb
Class 5.12d	F15	IX	7c	6c	27	Xb, Xc
Class 5.13a	F16	IX	7c+	6c	28	Xc
Class 5.13b	F16	IX+	8a	6c, 7a	29	Xc
Class 5.13c	F17	X-	8a, 8a+	7a	30, 31	XIa
Class 5.13d	F17	X	8b, 8b+	7a	31, 32	XIb
Class 5.14a	F18	X+	8c	7b	33	XIc

Datums and Coordinates

The USGS has recently switched both their horizontal and vertical datums. The horizontal datum changed from the old NAD27 to the newer WGS84, and the vertical datum changed from the old NGVD29 to the newer NAVD88. A datum is a set of reference points on the earth's surface against which position measurements are made to create a model of the shape of the earth. Horizontal datums are used for describing a point on the earth's surface, and vertical datums measure elevations.

The old datums were not wrong, just different. Datums are based on different earth shapes or ellipsoids. The old datums were based on the best technology at the time. The newer horizontal datums are stronger because all previously existing horizontal stations and newer GPS surveyed stations were adjusted simultaneously. The positions for the old NAD27 datum were adjusted in arcs as the networks progressed across the country. Errors between stations adjusted in different arcs could have been substantial.

With the changes, the elevations of Colorado's Fourteeners went up from three to seven feet. The peaks haven't changed, the new vertical datum just gives a better estimation of their height. The USGS has published a list of new elevations for the Fourteeners and determined that there are no new Fourteeners. Colorado's highest ranked Thirteener is 13,988-foot Grizzly Peak, which is 12 feet below the mark with the old datum and at least 5 feet below the mark with the new datum.

The USGS has not published new elevations for Colorado's numerous other peaks and places. All of the 7.5' quadrangles covering the Fourteeners have elevations based on the old NGVD29 vertical datum. These are the familiar numbers that climbers have been using for many decades. The new elevations from the NAVD88 datum seem strange to most climbers, and they do not appear on the USGS maps. I present the new summit elevations in the essentials table for each peak and in the lists of Fourteeners in the appendices. All other elevation references are from the old NGVD29 datum and agree with the USGS maps.

Be aware that the vertical heights displayed by your recreational GPS receiver will not agree well with USGS map elevations. The main reason for this discrepancy is the poor geometry available for vertical determinations, since the earth is always blocking some of the desired satellites, and the use of different reference surfaces for the vertical measurement. Do not use GPS elevations for critical navigation decisions.

The coordinates given in this book are based on the new WGS84 horizontal datum. These coordinates are derived from online map sources and may not be accurate. They may be inaccurate for other reasons as well. Be aware that most recreational GPS units default to the WGS84 horizontal datum. Thus, a position from your GPS set to the new datum will not accurately transfer to a USGS map constructed with the old datum. This difference can be as large as a hundred yards, which is certainly enough to cause a problem. My book coordinates should agree with GPS coordinates set to the same datum, but experience has shown that they do not match very well. This is for a variety of technical reasons, and always remember that the coordinates in this book may be wrong for other reasons. Do not rely on any coordinate in this book, especially for a matter involving safety.

Goals

Goals on Colorado's Fourteeners are as numerous as the people who climb them. Some people are content just to look at the Fourteeners. Some people are excited if they manage to climb one. Many are content to climb the Class 1 and Class 2 routes and just admire the harder Fourteeners. These people can climb two-thirds of the Fourteeners. The standard goal is to climb all the Fourteeners on some list. Choose your list. The number of people who have climbed all the Fourteeners is approaching 3,000.

Purists accept the goal of not only climbing all the Fourteeners, but gaining 3,000 feet on each one. This is a much harder goal, one that I did not achieve until recently. This goal can be harder than climbing all the Fourteeners twice. For example, consider Lincoln, Democrat, and Bross. Even if you are careful to start 1,000 feet below 12,000-foot Kite Lake on your initial climb of all three, you have only gained 3,000 feet on one of the three peaks. To gain 3,000 feet on all three, you will have to do this standard climb three times, or do alternate routes to the other two peaks on two more occasions. Then, if you want to gain 3,000 feet on unranked summits such as Cameron, you will have to make a fourth trip to the same area.

At least two groups have climbed all the Fourteeners and used human-powered transport between each group of peaks. Hard-core mountaineers climb all the Fourteeners in winter. This is a difficult goal for a single individual. Extreme skiers ski from the summit of all the Fourteeners. Lou Dawson was the first to do this, finishing in spring 1991. The record for the most times one person has climbed all the Fourteeners is now more than 12. There is a youngest and an oldest person to complete all the Fourteeners. Tyle Smith finished climbing all the Fourteeners in 1968 at age eight. Seven-year-old Megan Emmons broke his long-standing record in 1997. In recent years, it has become popular to organize events that place someone on top of each Fourteener on the same day. Ham radio enthusiasts have attempted broadcasting from all the summits simultaneously.

There is, of course, a speed record for climbing all the Fourteeners. In 1960 Cleve McCarty climbed the then recognized 52 Fourteeners in 52 days. This stately record receives my vote as the most elegant. Then the mania began. In 1974 the Climbing Smiths climbed Colorado's Fourteeners in 33 days. They went on to California and Washington and completed the then recognized 68 Fourteeners of the contiguous 48 states in 48 days. In 1976 Steve Boyer climbed Colorado's Fourteeners in a 22-day tour de force. In 1980 Dick Walters smashed the 20-day mark and climbed them all in 18 days, 15 hours, 40 minutes. This impressive record stood for a decade.

In 1990 the quest for speed intensified. With detailed knowledge of the routes, Quade and Tyle Smith ascended and descended 54 Colorado Fourteeners in an astonishing 16 days, 21 hours, 25 minutes. They were careful to ascend at least 3,000 feet on foot to the first peak of a series. After that, traverses were allowed. Then they would descend at least 3,000 feet back to their vehicle. Ah, competition. In 1992 the superbly conditioned ultramarathoner Adrian Crane took more than a day off the Smiths' time, setting the record at 15 days, 17 hours, 19 minutes. The Smiths hiked fast, but Adrian ran on the trails. Adrian was careful to observe the 3,000-foot rule set as a standard by the Smiths in 1974. In 1993 Jeff Wagener summited 55 Colorado Fourteeners in 14 days, 3 hours, but he did not observe the 3,000-foot rule.

In 1995 a powerful pair of Colorado mountain runners, Rick Trujillo of Ouray, a five-time winner of the Pikes Peak Marathon, and Ricky Denesik of Telluride, climbed the traditional 54 Colorado Fourteeners in 15 days, 9 hours, 55 minutes, taking more than 7 hours off Adrian's 1992 record. The two Ricks, or "Rick squared" as they were called during the event, were careful to observe the 3,000-foot rule. They gained a total of 156,130 feet and covered 337 miles.

Applying their experience, Rick squared went at it again in August 1997. Bad El-Niño–related weather hampered their effort on most days. Rick Trujillo dropped out of the record attempt on day nine but remained in support. Ricky Denesik continued and was on track to finish in 13 days, 16 hours when a heinous storm drove him back from the Keyhole on Longs—his last peak. A silver moon and I accompanied Ricky on his second attempt. After moonset and an icy homestretch, we reached Longs' silent summit at 1 AM. Ricky logged a time of 14 days, 16 minutes; a gain of 153,215 feet; and a distance of 314.2 miles.

In September 1999, Andrew Hamilton became the first person to observe the 3,000-foot rule and break the elusive 14-day mark. Suffering terrible weather and a flawed logistical plan, Andrew dug deep, climbed 15 peaks in darkness, and finished in 13 days, 22 hours, 48 minutes. His impressive record lasted less than a year.

In the early summer of 2000, Ricky Denesik made his third record run and, using better planning and conditioning, smashed not just the 14-day barrier, but the 13-day barrier as well. Ricky's time of 12 days, 15 hours, 35 minutes set a high bar for the ultrafit to ponder. Also in 2000, Danelle Ballengee became the fastest woman, with a time of 14 days, 14 hours, 49 minutes. Her stunning record has remained intact for more than a decade. Some thought that Ricky's record would stand for a long time as well, but it did not.

A little more than a month after Ricky raised the bar, superfit Teddy Kaiser from Breckenridge went for the record. He had scouted and planned his attempt for two years, and he executed a flawless strategy. He employed a bold nonstop tactic: when his vehicle arrived at a trailhead, he got out and started hiking. Time of day and weather made no difference—he started hiking. His conditioning, planning, and strategy worked, and Teddy vaulted the record to an astonishing 10 days, 20 hours, 26 minutes. Teddy, aka Cave Dog, finished at 10:56 PM on September 14, 2000, after dashing down the Trough on Longs—a clever finishing tactic that saved time. Cave Dog's time is so daunting that a decade has passed and no one has even attempted to best it.

When setting your goals, remember one thing: records can be broken, but a victory is yours to keep forever. In pursuit of your goals, you might choose to rely on the standard 10 essentials.

1. Map
2. Compass
3. Sunglasses and sunscreen
4. Extra food
5. Extra clothing
6. Headlamp/flashlight
7. First aid supplies
8. Firestarter
9. Matches
10. Knife

I choose to rely on my Classic Commandments of Mountaineering:

1. Never get separated from your lunch.
2. Never get separated from your sleeping bag.
3. Never get separated from your primal urges.
4. Carefully consider where your primal urges are leading you.
5. Expect to go the wrong way some of the time.
6. First aid above 26,000 feet consists of getting below 26,000 feet.
7. Never step on the rope.
8. Never bivouac.
9. Surfer Girl is not in the mountains.
10. Never pass up a chance to pee.
11. Don't eat yellow snow.
12. Geologic time includes now.
13. Experience does not exempt you from danger; physics wins.
14. Have fun and remember why you started.

¡Vaya con Dios!

Colorado's Fourteeners

Ranking and Key to Map on page xxiv

1	14,433'	Mt Elbert		28	14,148'	Mt Democrat
2	14,421'	Mt Massive		29	14,130'	Capitol Pk
3	14,420'	Mt Harvard		30	14,110'	Pikes Pk
4	14,345'	Blanca Pk		31	14,092'	Snowmass Mtn
5	14,336'	La Plata Pk		32	14,087'	Windom Pk
6	14,309'	Uncompahgre Pk		33	14,084'	Mt Eolus
7	14,294'	Crestone Pk		34	14,081'	Challenger Point
8	14,286'	Mt Lincoln		35	14,073'	Mt Columbia
9	14,270'	Grays Pk		36	14,067'	Missouri Mtn
10	14,269'	Mt Antero		37	14,064'	Humboldt Pk
11	14,267'	Torreys Pk		38	14,060'	Mt Bierstadt
12	14,265'	Castle Pk		U3	14,060'	Conundrum Pk
13	14,265'	Quandary Pk		39	14,059'	Sunlight Pk
14	14,264'	Mt Evans		40	14,048'	Handies Pk
15	14,255'	Longs Pk		41	14,047'	Culebra Pk
16	14,246'	Mt Wilson		42	14,042'	Mt Lindsey
U1	14,238'	Mt Cameron		43	14,042'	Ellingwood Point
17	14,229'	Mt Shavano		44	14,037'	Little Bear Pk
18	14,197'	Mt Princeton		45	14,036'	Mt Sherman
19	14,197'	Mt Belford		46	14,034'	Redcloud Pk
20	14,197'	Crestone Needle		47	14,018'	Pyramid Pk
21	14,196'	Mt Yale		48	14,017'	Wilson Pk
22	14,172'	Mt Bross		49	14,015'	Wetterhorn Pk
23	14,165'	Kit Carson Pk		50	14,014'	San Luis Pk
U2	14,159'	El Diente Pk		U4	14,014'	North Maroon Pk
24	14,156'	Maroon Pk		51	14,005'	Mt of the Holy Cross
25	14,155'	Tabeguache Pk		52	14,003'	Huron Pk
26	14,153'	Mt Oxford		53	14,001'	Sunshine Pk
27	14,150'	Mt Sneffels				

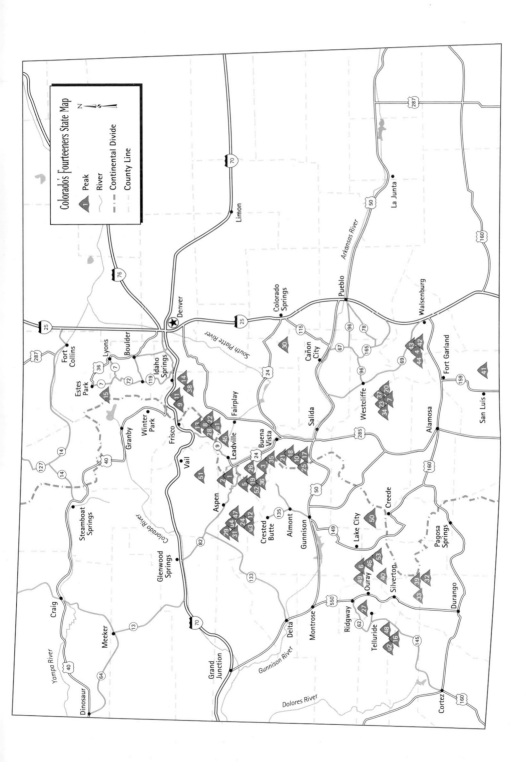

Chapter One

Front Range

Introduction

Colorado's Front Range extends from the Wyoming border southward for 175 miles to the Arkansas River Valley west of Pueblo. It is Colorado's longest range. When you approach the Rocky Mountains from the east, the Front Range provides an abrupt scenery change. The land is flat, then roars up like crazy!

The Front Range contains six Fourteeners, and because most of Colorado's population lives in the urban corridor east of the Front Range, these peaks are easily reached. You can climb any of these Fourteeners in one day from most Front Range cities. People climb Front Range Fourteeners more often than any of the other Fourteeners scattered across the state.

1. Longs Peak 14,255 feet

Longs Peak is unquestionably the monarch of the Front Range and northern Colorado. It dominates all within sight of it. Longs is the highest peak in Rocky Mountain National Park and Boulder County. It is also Colorado's northernmost Fourteener and the Rocky Mountains' only Fourteener north of 40 degrees north latitude. Its summit attracts thousands of people each year, and it is one of the most popular peaks in the western United States. The reason for its popularity is obvious. Longs enraptures all but the most heartless soul.

Longs has a tremendous east face, and its great sweep has struck emotion into many hearts. Emotions range from awe to terror. Longs' closest neighbor, Mount Meeker, has a huge, sweeping north face, and these two faces combine to form Colorado's greatest mountain cirque. Beautiful Chasm Lake nestles at the base of Longs' east face. Ships Prow, a large promontory, separates Longs' east face and Meeker's north face. Ships Prow rises directly above Chasm Lake's south side to the Loft, which is the broad, 13,450-foot saddle between Longs and Meeker.

Longs' slabby north face rises above the Boulder Field, which you can reach by the popular East Longs Peak Trail. Longs' northwest ridge contains the famous Keyhole, which allows easy access between the peak's east and west sides. Longs' large west face sweeps above Glacier Gorge with the well-named Keyboard of the Winds on its south edge. Longs' broken south side rises above Wild Basin and contains the Palisades' west-facing cliffs. The Notch is prominent on the ridge above the Palisades and is easily seen above Longs' east face.

Indians called Longs and Meeker *Nesotaieux*, meaning "the two guides," and indeed these peaks are siren sentinels when seen from the plains to the east.

Longs has more than 100 routes, but most are serious technical climbs on the great east face. I only include a dozen of Longs' easier routes in this guide. Somehow, Longs' popularity makes people feel safer, but the opposite is the case. Many people believe the greatest climbing hazard today is being below other people. With or without other people, any route on Longs is a serious undertaking.

1E – Longs Peak Essentials

Elevations	14,255' (NGVD29) 14,261' (NAVD88)
Rank	Colorado's 15th highest ranked peak
Location	Northern Boulder County, Colorado, USA
Range	Northern Front Range
Summit Coordinates	40.2457° -105.6153° (WGS84)
Ownership/Contact	Rocky Mountain National Park – Public Land
	National Park Service – 970-586-1206
Prominence and Saddle	2,940' from 11,315' Berthoud Pass
Isolation and Parent	43.71 miles to Torreys Peak
USGS Maps	Longs Peak, McHenrys Peak, Isolation Peak, Allens Park
USFS Map	Arapaho and Roosevelt National Forest
Trails Illustrated Maps	Map #200 Rocky Mountain National Park
	Map #301 Longs Peak/Bear Lake/Wild Basin
Book Map	See Map 1 on page 3
Nearest Town	Estes Park – Population 6,000 – Elevation 7,522'
Longs Peak ⚡ Easiest Route	1R1 – Keyhole – Class 3
	A long Class 1 trail approach, a Class 2 boulder hop to the Keyhole, then a
	Class 3 scramble to the top
Longs' Accolades	Longs is the highest peak in Rocky Mountain National Park and Boulder
	County. Longs is also Colorado's northernmost Fourteener and the Rocky
	Mountain's only Fourteener north of 40° north latitude.

1T – Longs Peak Trailheads

1T1 – Longs Peak Trailhead 9,400 feet 40.2724° -105.5572°

This trailhead provides access to the East Longs Peak Trail. This major trail serves all sides of Longs Peak. The trailhead is west of Colorado 7, and you can reach it from either the north or south.

If you are approaching from the north, measure from the junction of US 36 and Colorado 7 east of Estes Park and go 9.2 miles south on Colorado 7. If you are approaching from the south, measure from the junction of Colorado 7 and Colorado 72 on the Peak to Peak Highway and go 10.5 miles north on Colorado 7. Turn west onto a paved road signed for the Longs Peak Area (40.2720° -105.5425°) and go 1.0 mile west uphill to the trailhead and the Longs Peak Ranger Station. Overnight parking in the trailhead parking lot is not allowed without a permit. This trailhead is accessible in winter.

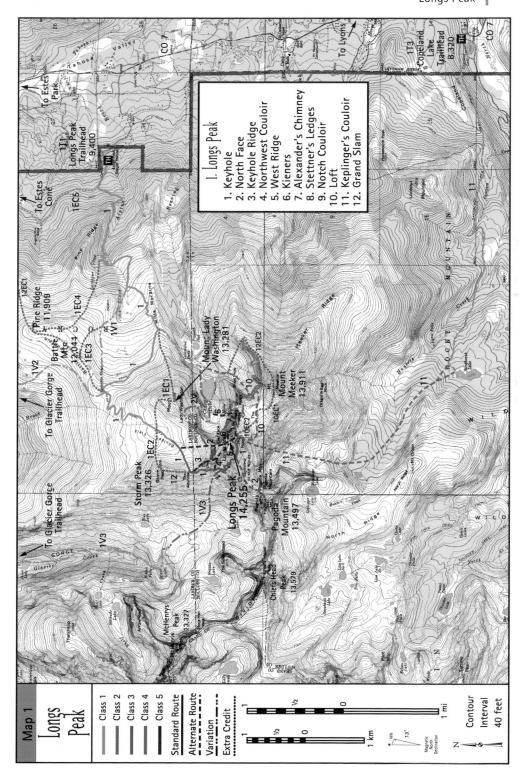

Map 1

Longs Peak

Class 1
Class 2
Class 3
Class 4
Class 5

Standard Route
Alternate Route
Variation
Extra Credit

Contour Interval 40 feet

1. Longs Peak

1. Keyhole
2. North Face
3. Keyhole Ridge
4. Northwest Couloir
5. West Ridge
6. Kieners
7. Alexander's Chimney
8. Stettner's Ledges
9. Notch Couloir
10. Loft
11. Keplinger's Couloir
12. Grand Slam

1T2 — Glacier Gorge Trailhead 9,240 feet 40.3103° -105.6373°

This trailhead provides access to Longs' north and west sides. From Rocky Mountain National Park Headquarters on US 36, go 1.2 miles west to the Beaver Meadows Entrance Station into the park. Continue 0.2 mile west on US 36 to Bear Lake Road. Turn south (left) onto Bear Lake Road (paved) and go 8.1 miles to the large trailhead, which is on the south side of the road. You can take the Bear Lake shuttle bus to this trailhead in summer, and this trailhead is usually accessible in winter with your own vehicle.

Another alternative is to park at Bear Lake and follow a trail 0.4 mile southeast from Bear Lake to the Glacier Gorge Trail near a switchback in the road. This switchback used to be the Glacier Gorge Trailhead, but with little space here and increasing use, the trailhead was moved a half mile down the road.

1T3 — Copeland Lake Trailhead 8,320 feet 40.2198° -105.5358°

This trailhead provides access to Longs' south side. The trailhead is west of Colorado 7, and you can reach it from either the north or south.

If you are approaching from the north, measure from the junction of US 36 and Colorado 7 east of Estes Park. Go 13.1 miles south on Colorado 7 to Wild Basin Road. If you are approaching from the south, measure from the junction of Colorado 7 and Colorado 72 on the Peak to Peak Highway. Go 6.6 miles north on Colorado 7 to Wild Basin Road.

From the Wild Basin Road–Colorado 7 junction, go 0.4 mile west on the old highway to another turnoff for Wild Basin and Copeland Lake. Turn west (right) and pass through the Rocky Mountain National Park entrance fee station. The trailhead is immediately north of the entrance. This trailhead is accessible in winter.

1R — Longs Peak Routes

1R1 — Longs Peak — Keyhole *Classic*

From Longs Peak TH at 9,400'	348 RP	14.4 mi RT	4,855' net; 5,255' total	Class 3
From Boulder Field at 12,750'	154 RP	2.6 mi RT	1,505' net; 1,905' total	Class 3

This is the easiest route on Longs. People climb it more than any other route in this guide. Climbing the Keyhole Route on a late summer weekend is like walking on a crowded city sidewalk through a construction zone. Queues form on the Homestretch, one going up and the other going down. At midday, there can be more than 100 people on the summit. The Keyhole Route attracts several thousand people each summer.

This is a long, arduous ascent on a high, real mountain. The route's difficulty increases dramatically when conditions are bad, and many people have died here. Sudden summer storms can turn the Homestretch into a bobsled run. The Trough usually contains snow until mid-July, and an ice ax is useful until then. The Keyhole Route spirals almost completely around the mountain, and any escape from the route takes you down into Wild Basin or Glacier Gorge.

Your return to the Longs Peak Trailhead from these drainages can assume epic proportions. Even when conditions are good, the route is crowded, which does not make your ascent safer. Understand current conditions before attempting an ascent. Don't be misled by someone else's energy. Stay true to yourself and mountaineering's fundamentals.

From the Longs Peak Trailhead at 9,400 feet, follow the well-marked East Longs Peak Trail to the Boulder Field. En route, stay left at the Eugenia Mine–Storm Pass junction (9,680 feet) at 0.5 mile (40.2750° -105.5646°), pass the Goblins Forest campsite (10,240 feet) at 1.5 miles, and cross to Alpine Brook's south side at 10,690 feet (40.2731° -105.5802°). Pass treeline, enjoy your first views of Longs, turn left at the Jims Grove junction (10,960 feet) at 2.5 miles (40.2707° -105.5846°), and reach the Chasm Lake junction on Mills Moraine (11,540 feet) after 3.5 miles (40.2658° -105.5929°). Do not go to Chasm Lake, but take a moment to marvel at Longs' east face. There is a solar-powered toilet east of this trail junction. Turn right at the Chasm Lake junction and hike northwest on the trail to 12,080-foot Granite Pass (40.2740° -105.6054°) on Mount Lady Washington's north side, where you can look north to many peaks. Turn left at the North Longs Peak Trail junction in Granite Pass at 4.5 miles, and continue southwest up into the expansive Boulder Field below Longs' slabby north face. There are campsites at 12,660 feet (permit required), and there are solar-powered toilets north of the campsites (40.2642° -105.6158°). The trail continues 200 yards beyond the campsites to end at 12,750 feet, 5.9 miles from the trailhead.

From the Boulder Field, continue southwest over large boulders toward the Keyhole, which you can see on Longs' northwest ridge. The Keyhole consists of a large overhanging rock jutting out to the north. The Keyhole allows easy access between Longs' east and west sides and is indeed the key to the route.

There is a small, open, conical-topped stone shelter 100 feet southeast of the Keyhole. This shelter memorializes Agnes Vaille, who died near here in January 1925 along with a would-be rescuer during a prodigious winter storm. Agnes and Walter Kiener had just made the first winter ascent of Longs' east face. Walter survived, but suffered severe frostbite. The route beyond the Keyhole is more serious in any season, and if conditions warrant a retreat, this is a good place to turn around.

After you scramble up the rocks into the Keyhole at 13,150 feet (40.2609° -105.6213°), you will have a great view of Glacier Gorge to the west. The Thirteeners ringing the head of the gorge, Pagoda, Chiefs Head, and McHenrys, are sure to spark your attention. Scramble through the Keyhole to the ridge's west side and traverse south on a series of ledges. The route is marked with painted bull's-eyes on the rock, so it is hard to become lost. This part of the route is appropriately called the Ledges. Climb above west-facing boilerplate slabs and negotiate a nifty V-slot in this section. Traverse above the boilerplate slabs, descend south of the slabs, then climb gently and reach the large couloir called the Trough (40.2558° -105.6207°), which is 0.3 mile south of the Keyhole. The route gains very little elevation between the Keyhole and the Trough. This section of the route is exposed to the west wind, but the views of Glacier Gorge are excellent.

The Trough is a long couloir extending all the way from Glacier Gorge to a point high on Longs' west side. Climb the Trough from 13,300 feet to the top of the couloir on Longs' west ridge at 13,850 feet. When the Trough has snow in it, try to avoid it by staying on the rocks north of the couloir. Just below the ridge, at 13,850 feet, you must pass a chockstone; this may be the route's hardest move. You can climb around either side of the chockstone; either side is Class 3.

On the small platform at the top of the Trough (40.2543° -105.6187°), you are close to the summit, but steep cliffs rise above you on both the west and south faces of the peak. A new vista appears to the south, and this is a dramatic place. Cross to Longs' south side and traverse east across Longs' south face along a convenient exposed ledge called the Narrows. At one point, you have a choice of either wiggling between a block and the wall above or stepping neatly around the exposed outside of the block.

Beyond the Narrows, go east, climb up a 10-foot slot, then scamper up ledges to the base of the Homestretch. It is 250 yards from the top of the Trough to the bottom of the Homestretch. The Homestretch is the weakness in the summit cliffs that the route has circled all the way around the peak to find. It consists of some parallel cracks angling up to the northeast across low-angled slabs. The Homestretch is easy Class 3 when it is dry, but more difficult rock lurks nearby. People have encountered trouble on the smooth slabs near the cracks. At the top of the Homestretch, scramble through a short cleft, then Longs' large, flat summit appears abruptly. The highest point is a boulder 100 feet north (40.2547° -105.6153°).

In the 1930s, guides would tell their clients that if they looked sharp they could just see the recently completed Empire State Building, and people would stare intently to the east. Today, there is cell service on the summit, and while you can't even see Kansas, you can see into Wyoming and Nebraska. Looking east from the summit on a clear day, you can see over 130 miles. You can see Pikes Peak 102 miles to the south and Mount Massive 86 miles to the southwest. The monarch is yours! Scan the sky for storms and remember that the summit is only halfway.

1R1 V1 – Variation – Jims Grove Trail

From Longs Peak TH at 9,400'   343 RP   *13.9 mi RT*   *4,855' net; 5,255' total*   Class 3

At 10,960 feet (40.2707° -105.5846°), 2.5 miles above the Longs Peak Trailhead, you have a choice of two trails. The East Longs Peak Trail climbs southwest to Mills Moraine, then takes a long tack northwest to reach Granite Pass. The Jims Grove Trail goes north from the junction, climbs west past the Jims Grove trees, then switchbacks north around an enduring snowfield in a small basin west of Jims Grove. The trail then climbs steeply west to rejoin the East Longs Peak Trail at 11,920 feet (40.2720° -105.6033°), just below Granite Pass.

The Jims Grove Trail is 0.25 mile shorter one way and provides different scenery. You miss the spectacular view of Longs' east face from Mills Moraine, but you will pass through wind-twisted trees and can enjoy the little basin above Jims Grove. Perhaps you can go up one trail and down the other.

1R1 V2 – Variation – North Longs Peak Trail

From Glacier Gorge TH at 9,240'   391 RP   18.1 mi RT   5,015' net; 5,415' total   Class 3

From the Glacier Gorge Trailhead at 9,240 feet, follow the North Longs Peak Trail for 6.35 miles to Granite Pass and join the East Longs Peak Trail and the Keyhole Route there. This approach to Longs is significantly longer but provides expansive views of the Mummy Range to the north and allows the possibility of a circle tour.

1R1 V3 – Variation – The Trough

From Glacier Gorge TH at 9,240'   385 RP   13.8 mi RT   5,015' total   Class 3, Mod Snow

With descent of North Longs Peak Trail   410 RP   16.0 mi RT   5,015' net; 5,215' total   Class 3, Mod Snow

From the Glacier Gorge Trailhead at 9,240 feet, follow the Glacier Gorge Trail for 5.0 miles to Black Lake at 10,620 feet (40.2661° -105.6404°). Hike southeast above the lake, enter the bottom of the Trough at 11,600 feet (40.2578° -105.6289°), then climb it to the west ridge at 13,850 feet (40.2543° -105.6187°). Follow the Keyhole Route to the summit. This good, early summer snow climb can provide more than 2,000 vertical feet of moderate snow.

When it is in good condition, this is one of Colorado's longest snow climbs. As summer progresses, so does the probability of rockfall from the large number of people climbing in or near the upper part of the Trough. By August this is an undesirable route. Going up this way and down the North Longs Peak Trail makes a long but wonderful Tour de Longs.

1R1 EC1 – Extra Credit – Mount Lady Washington 13,281 feet 40.2634° -105.6072°

From Longs Peak TH at 9,400'   194 RP   8.6 mi RT   3,881' total   Class 2

From Mills Moraine at 11,540'   91 RP   1.6 mi RT   1,741' total   Class 2

From Boulder Field at 12,660'   40 RP   1.0 mi RT   621' total   Class 2

One of Longs' major buttress peaks, Mount Lady Washington is 0.8 mile northeast of Longs. Lady Washington's rounded mass interferes with your view of Longs' east face from many viewpoints, including Battle Mountain and Estes Cone. To eliminate this obstacle, climb it. The view from Lady Washington is impeccable.

If you are at the Mills Moraine trail junction (40.2658° -105.5929°), climb 0.8 mile west up talus directly to the summit. If you are in the Boulder Field near the campsites at 12,660 feet, hike 500 yards east, then 300 yards south up blocky talus to the summit, which is the eastern of two highpoints. By swinging east, you avoid some troublesome talus on Lady Washington's northwest face directly above the Boulder Field. Lady Washington's talus is tedious, but you will never tire of the view from her summit.

Longs Peak's north face.

1R1 EC2 – Extra Credit – Storm Peak 13,326 feet 40.2656° -105.6205°

From Longs Peak TH at 9,400'	*202 RP*	*12.4 mi RT*	*3,926' total*	*Class 2*
From Boulder Field at 12,750'	*32 RP*	*0.6 mi RT*	*576' total*	*Class 2*
From Keyhole at 13,150'	*20 RP*	*0.7 mi RT*	*180' total*	*Class 2+*

Another of Longs' major buttress peaks, Storm Peak is 0.8 mile northwest of Longs. Storm Peak provides a superlative view of Longs' north face and the Glacier Gorge sanctuary.

From the end of the trail in the Boulder Field, go northwest up blocky, sometimes loose talus directly to the summit. In early season, this slope holds snow that the winds of winter have packed rock-hard. You can avoid this snow by climbing north-northwest from the Boulder Field onto Storm's north ridge. From the Keyhole, scamper north over large blocky talus on the east side of the ridge. Don't cut up for the summit too soon, because Storm's highpoint is the farthest point north.

1R1 EC3 – Extra Credit – Battle Mountain 12,044 feet 40.2781° -105.5987°

From Longs Peak TH at 9,400'	*112 RP*	*7.8 mi RT*	*2,644' total*	*Class 2*
From East Longs Peak Trail at 11,600'	*28 RP*	*1.0 mi RT*	*444' total*	*Class 2*
From Granite Pass at 12,080'	*24 RP*	*1.0 mi RT*	*300' total*	*Class 2+*

Battle Mountain is a minor highpoint on the ridge northeast of Granite Pass and the East Longs Peak Trail. As you walk up the trail on a warm summer morning, you may wonder why such an innocuous area received this contentious name. Come back in winter. This ridge catches winds the Continental Divide couldn't handle. Never mind Longs Peak; Battle Mountain provides a tough test on occasion.

If you are hiking from the Longs Peak Trailhead, take the Jims Grove Trail above the signed trail junction at 10,960 feet (40.2707° -105.5846°). Switchback above Jims Grove, hike west to 11,600 feet, leave the trail and hike 0.5 mile north up talus to the rocky summit (Class 2). If you are descending from the Boulder Field, leave the East Longs Peak Trail at Granite Pass (40.2740° -105.6054°) and scamper 0.5 mile northeast over two other highpoints to reach Battle Mountain's summit (Class 2+).

1R1 EC4 – Extra Credit – Pine Ridge 11,909 feet 40.2852° -105.5936°

From Longs Peak TH at 9,400'	*114 RP*	*5.6 mi RT*	*2,509' total*	*Class 2*
From East Longs Peak Trail at 10,500'	*73 RP*	*2.2 mi RT*	*1,409' total*	*Class 2*

This unranked summit is at the junction of Pine Ridge, which rises from the southeast above the East Longs Peak Trail, and a long ridge running northeast from Granite Pass below Mount Lady Washington. Overlooked by millions and minions alike, Pine Ridge provides many stout viewpoints of its surrounding giants. This humble summit makes a good winter outing.

From the Longs Peak Trailhead at 9,400 feet, hike 1.5 miles up the East Longs Peak Trail to the crossing of Larkspur Creek at 10,260 feet (40.2744° -105.5771°). From here, continue another 0.2 mile to the fourth switchback beyond the crossing. Do not confuse the crossing of Larkspur Creek with the crossing of Alpine Creek, which is farther up the trail. Leave the East Longs Peak Trail here, at 10,500 feet (40.2748° -105.5793°), and hike 0.15 mile west-northwest up through open trees to the south of Larkspur Creek to reach treeline at 10,700 feet. Continue 0.5 mile west-northwest up sweeping, open slopes to a break in the slope angle at 11,720 feet (40.2788° -105.5917°). From here, you will be able to see both summits of Pine Ridge to the north as well as the summit ramparts of Battle Mountain to the west. Continue 0.25 mile north to Pine Ridge's first rocky summit, with the extrapolated elevation of 11,940 feet (40.2824° -105.5927°), then continue 0.2 mile north to the second rocky summit, with the given elevation of 11,909 feet (40.2852° -105.5936°). This is the summit of Pine Ridge.

The map indicates that the summit with the extrapolated elevation of 11,940 feet is the summit of Pine Ridge, but I carefully hand leveled from both these summits and determined that the northern, 11,909-foot summit is indeed higher than the alleged 11,940-foot summit. Thus, the map is wrong. Since the northern summit has a given elevation, it is reasonable to assume that the highest contour line on the 11,940-foot summit is spurious, and that it is less than 11,909 feet. Accordingly, I use 11,909 feet for the elevation of Pine Ridge.

1R1 EC5 – Extra Credit – Estes Cone 11,006 feet 40.2951° -105.5673°

From Longs Peak TH at 9,400'	*66 RP*	*6.4 mi RT*	*1,606 net; 1,826' total*	*Class 2*
From East Longs Peak Trail at 9,680'	*56 RP*	*5.4 mi RT*	*1,326 net; 1,546' total*	*Class 2*

Estes Cone is the symmetrical, craggy-topped peak 1.7 miles northwest of the Longs Peak Trailhead. You can see it north of the trailhead above the road.

From Estes Cone's summit, you have a sweeping view of Meeker, Longs, Lady Washington, and Storm Peak.

From the Eugenia Mine–East Longs Peak Trail junction at 9,680 feet (40.2750° -105.5646°), 0.5 mile northwest of the Longs Peak Trailhead, go 0.9 mile north to Eugenia Mine. Descending gently, go 0.6 mile east, passing the Moore Park campsites en route to a signed trail junction just east of Moore Park at 9,780 feet (40.2877° -105.5653°). Turn north (left) and hike 0.5 mile north to Storm Pass at 10,260 feet (40.2928° -105.5745°). Turn east (right) and hike 0.7 mile east on the Estes Cone summit trail to the west side of the rocky summit. Scamper up a break in the cliff (Class 2) and continue to the highest point, 100 feet farther east.

1R2 – Longs Peak – North Face

From Longs Peak TH at 9,400'	410 RP	13.0 mi RT	4,855' total	Class 5.3
With descent of Keyhole	433 RP	13.7 mi RT	4,855' net; 5,055' total	Class 5.3

This is the old Cables Route that used to be the standard route up Longs. In 1973 the National Park Service removed the cables, and this route reverted to its original difficulty. The eyebolts for some cables remain and provide solid belay or rappel anchors. The route is often used as a descent route. One 140-foot or two 70-foot rappels overcome the difficulties.

Follow the Keyhole Route (1R1) to the Boulder Field. From the Boulder Field, hike south up toward the eastern quarter of the north face. Do not go to the exposed eastern edge, as this is the top of the vertigo-inducing east face. The route exploits a series of small west-facing corners and slabs for one long or two short Class 5.3 pitches to reach easier ground. This is where the old cables used to be. Once you are above the slabs, angle southeast (left) up through broken ledges on the upper part of the north face, then climb south to the summit.

1R2 V – Variation – The Camel

Class 2+

The Camel is a hidden gully that provides easy passage from the basin west of Chasm Lake to the Boulder Field. It lets you enjoy an excursion into the sanctuary below Longs' great east face before escaping from it at the last moment. It offers a sporting start to your ascent of Longs' North Face Route. Climbers often use the Camel as a descent route after a technical ascent on Longs.

Hike up the East Longs Peak Trail to the Mills Moraine trail junction, 3.5 miles from the trailhead. Instead of hiking northwest on the trail up to Granite Pass, hike 0.6 mile west to Chasm Meadows and scramble 200 yards west up a small gully to the east end of Chasm Lake at 11,800 feet. The west-facing Camel Couloir is hidden from here; don't despair. Hike around Chasm Lake's north side and look northwest to spot the namesake Camel Rock high on Lady Washington's southwest ridge. Camel Rock is a miniature keyhole overhanging to the west. To some it appears as a kneeling camel. It is distinctive in any case. Camel Rock is visible from Chasm Lake and the Boulder Field, and is the landmark that guides you to the hidden passage.

From Chasm Lake's west end, hike 300 yards west to 12,000 feet (40.2584° -105.6099°), turn around and look up Camel Couloir, now east of you. Scramble east up the couloir on steep grass and talus (Class 2+) to 12,400 feet (40.2598° -105.6083°). The already overpowering view only improves as you make your escape from the basin. In winter the couloir holds hard-packed snow. As you approach the top of the couloir, stay north (left) and swing 100 feet west to dodge a higher cliff band. Camel Rock will be visible above you. Climb directly northwest up talus to Camel Rock at 13,060 feet. Your escape is complete.

From Camel Rock, hike 180 yards down to the southwest to the 12,980-foot saddle between Longs and Lady Washington. Continue 0.25 mile southwest up talus to join the North Face Route below its crux slabs.

1R2 EC – Extra Credit – Chasm View 13,500 feet 40.2574° -105.6156°

Class 2+

The small detour required to go to the famous Chasm View is worth it for the world-class view that awaits there. When approaching the north face, stay east (left) of some lower slabs and scamper into the small 13,500-foot notch just below the north face's northeast edge. This vantage offers an awesome near-profile view of the Diamond on the east face, and you might be able to spot climbers inching their way up the wall. While the rocks near the edge are solid, this is a bad place to suddenly become spastic. As proof, there is a hole near the edge through which you can look down 800 feet. Slabs make it inconvenient to traverse directly west from Chasm View to rejoin the North Face Route. To minimize difficulties, go down and around the slabs.

1R3 – Longs Peak – Keyhole Ridge

From Longs Peak TH at 9,400'	553 RP	13.8 mi RT	4,855' total	Class 5.5
With descent of North Face	559 RP	13.4 mi RT	4,855' total	Class 5.5
With descent of Keyhole	561 RP	14.1 mi RT	4,855' net; 5,055' total	Class 5.5

This is an excellent technical route in a spectacular setting. The exposed route is on or near Longs' northwest ridge. Follow the Keyhole Route (1R1) to the Keyhole. Stay on the east side of the northwest ridge and scramble 200 yards up a Class 3 ramp to a higher notch in the ridge known as the False Keyhole. This takes you past the first tower on the ridge.

Continue up the ridge to the steep part of the second tower (Class 4), then follow a ramp east of the ridge (Class 4). At the end of the ramp, climb to the top of the second tower (Class 5.4). Descend 10 feet west to a ledge and follow it south to the notch south of the second tower. Scramble up yet another ramp to a belay below and east of a steep face. Angle 75 feet up to the left onto this face, then climb up excellent rock to regain the ridge (Class 5.5). This face is the route's crux. You can pass any further difficulties by staying just off the ridge crest; near the summit, stay on the ridge. This route provides a unique approach to Longs' sizable summit plateau.

1R4 – Longs Peak – Northwest Couloir

From Longs Peak TH at 9,400'	392 RP	13.9 mi RT	4,855' net; 5,255' total	Class 5.0
With descent of North Face	408 RP	13.7 mi RT	4,855' net; 5,055' total	Class 5.0
With descent of Keyhole	405 RP	14.3 mi RT	4,855' net; 5,255' total	Class 5.0

This short, obscure route has gained in popularity in recent years. Its modest technical difficulty combined with mostly solid rock make it a scintillating way to summit Longs. Follow the Keyhole Route (1R1) to the Keyhole. Pass through to the west side of the Keyhole, go two-thirds of the distance south toward the Trough, and look up to the east for the last big gully before the Trough. A distinguishing feature to help you identify the Northwest Couloir is a spire high above the south side of the couloir that looks like a horse's head or the knight chess piece. The horse head is facing north. Also, there is a series of four overhang-studded throne-room towers north of the Northwest Couloir.

Leave the Keyhole Route (40.2573° -105.6209°), scamper up toward the throne-room towers, and get into the bottom of the couloir (Class 2+). Scramble up the narrowing Class 3 gully, taking great care not to knock any loose rocks down on the Keyhole climbers below you. After a few hundred feet of thoughtful scrambling, you will see the crux of the route above you, which is a stack of pancake-shaped rocks wedged above a chimney. Climb up toward the stack, angle right up a 20-foot Class 5.0 slab past an old fixed piton, and wiggle into a hole below the largest pancake rock, which is now overhanging above you. Crawl to the back of the hole, make a U-turn, and escape the cave onto the top of the large pancake rock. Go a few exposed feet north and climb around the upper pancake rock.

The route from here to the summit is much easier. Scamper up Class 2+ rocks to reach the Keyhole Ridge at 13,960 feet (40.2567° -105.6182°). Scamper and sing 250 yards southeast up joyous rocks to reach the northwest corner of Longs' summit plateau and stroll to the capstone.

1R5 – Longs Peak – West Ridge

From Longs Peak TH at 9,400'	480 RP	14.3 mi RT	4,855' net; 5,255' total	Class 5.4

First climbed in 1924 by J. Alexander, this historic route provides a fine technical finish to the Keyhole Route, and your airy ascent is bound to attract a lot of attention. Follow the Keyhole Route (1R1) to the platform at 13,850 feet above the Trough (40.2543° -105.6187°). The route ascends the west ridge above this point. To get started, scramble up 40 feet and belay behind a large flake. Pitch 1: Climb left up ledges and flake systems on the north side of the ridge, then angle back right up a tiny, steep gully to a stance on the ridge crest. Pitch 2: Climb up the ridge, overcome a small overhang, and continue up the ridge to an exposed stance. Pitch 3: Scramble up broken ledges and pass a final steep section on the south side of the ridge. Arrive abruptly at the southwest corner of Longs' summit plateau and strut to the capstone.

1R6 – Longs Peak – Kieners *Classic*

From Longs Peak TH at 9,400'	607 RP	11.4 mi RT	4,855' total	Class 5.3–5.4, Mod Snow/Ice
With descent of North Face	623 RP	12.2 mi RT	4,855' total	Class 5.3–5.4, Mod Snow/Ice
With descent of Keyhole	619 RP	12.8 mi RT	4,855' net; 5,055' total	Class 5.3–5.4, Mod Snow/Ice

This is the finest mountaineering route on Longs Peak and, perhaps, the finest mountaineering route in Colorado. First climbed in 1924 by Walter Kiener, it is the easiest route on Longs' east face and is a mixed climb involving both snow and rock climbing. Kieners is a serious undertaking, and you should not tackle it lightly. It is a difficult route to escape from. Above Broadway, the best retreat is a forward one over Longs' summit. This can be very difficult in bad weather. I recommend an ice ax, crampons, and helmet for this route.

From the Longs Peak Trailhead at 9,400 feet, follow the East Longs Peak Trail for 4.5 miles to Chasm Meadows below Chasm Lake. Scramble 200 yards west up a small gully to the east end of Chasm Lake at 11,800 feet. The view of the east face from here is world-renowned.

You can see the upper part of the route from Chasm Lake. Study it carefully. Broadway is the large ledge system traversing completely across the face at half height. The vertical Diamond forms the upper, northern part of the face. The Notch is on the skyline south of the summit. The Notch Couloir rises from Broadway to the Notch. The upper part of Kieners crosses the broken face between the Notch Couloir and the Diamond. The Kieners Route is sometimes called the Mountaineers Route.

Go west around Chasm Lake's north side and continue 0.25 mile west toward the base of the great face. Mills Glacier is a permanent snowfield at the base of the lower face. Lambs Slide is a north-facing couloir connected to Mills Glacier that rises along the south side of the lower east face. You cannot see all the way up Lambs Slide until you reach the bottom of the face. There is permanent snow in Lambs Slide. It is prone to avalanching in early June; as August progresses, the snow turns to ice.

Climb Lambs Slide to 13,000 feet, where Broadway's multiple ledges intersect Lambs Slide. Leave Lambs Slide, climb to the highest ledge, and traverse 250 yards north (right) along Broadway. The scrambling is easy initially, but the exposure increases rapidly as you traverse out over the lower face. Just as the exposure reaches a maximum, Broadway narrows and you must make a delicate, exposed, Class 5.1 traverse around a block. Many parties rope up at this point.

The bottom of the Notch Couloir is a short distance north of the block. Go north across the bottom of the couloir to the rock just north of the couloir; this often requires crossing snow or ice. The Notch Couloir begins at Broadway

The upper east face of Longs Peak.

above 800 feet of nearly vertical rock. The prospect of being flushed out of the couloir is something to consider carefully and avoid. This is an exciting place.

There are two ways to proceed from your stance on the north side of the couloir. Option 1 is a point easier, but may require snow or ice climbing up the couloir, and has north-facing rock. Option 2 is a point harder, but is rock only.

Option 1 (Class 5.3): Climb 40 feet west up the north (right) side of the couloir to an alcove. Traverse 20 feet back east (hard right) on a ledge to the base of a short wall. Climb the wall and go up a dihedral that becomes a chimney. Climb to the top of the chimney and reach a ledge on the right side of the chimney.

Option 2 (Class 5.4): Just north of the Notch Couloir, leave Broadway and climb onto the rocks north of the couloir. The rock is steep here but not as difficult as it looks. Climb a Class 5.4 pitch by zigzagging up steep rock. Climb a second, Class 5.0 pitch up a wide chimney to a ledge on the right side of the chimney.

From the ledge on the right side of the chimney, escape north through an unexpected slot, traverse north (right) across a long ledge, climb back (left) up steps and corners (Class 5.0), and reach the broken upper part of Kieners. From here, scramble 700 feet northwest, angling right, up gullies and open slopes. When the rock is dry, the difficulty here does not exceed Class 3.

There are several steep cliffs above this broken section that bar easy access to the summit. Climb a series of steep steps called the Staircase, traverse north (right), go behind a flake just below the summit cliffs, and traverse north (right) below the summit cliffs to reach a spectacular point above the Diamond. Step north around an exposed corner, climb up a slot through the cliffs, and scamper up steep talus to the summit. The flat summit provides an abrupt scenery change.

1R7 — Longs Peak — Alexander's Chimney

From Longs Peak TH at 9,400'	*793 RP*	*11.2 mi RT*	*4,855' total*	*Class 5.5*
With descent of North Face	*813 RP*	*12.1 mi RT*	*4,855' total*	*Class 5.5*
With descent of Keyhole	*816 RP*	*12.8 mi RT*	*4,855' net; 5,055' total*	*Class 5.5*

First climbed in 1922 by J. Alexander, this is a time-tested rock route on the south side of the lower east face. It is one of the easiest rock routes on the east face. Alexander's Chimney ends on Broadway and, by itself, is not a summit route, but it is often used as a more technical start to Kieners. This option avoids the snow and ice in Lambs Slide. To descend from the top of Alexander's Chimney, traverse south on Broadway and descend Lambs Slide. This option usually requires crampons and an ice ax. The bottom of Alexander's Chimney is often wet in early summer. Also, beware rockfall from climbers traversing Broadway above you. Leave early.

Start at the Longs Peak Trailhead at 9,400 feet and follow the Kieners Route (1R6) to the base of Lambs Slide. Alexander's Chimney is the first major break in the lower face north of Lambs Slide. When you are standing at the bottom of Lambs Slide, the route is above and to the south (left). Go 200 feet up Lambs Slide, climb onto the rock, and do an ascending traverse back (right) across a Class 4 slab to reach the bottom of the chimney. To avoid as much snow as possible, cross the bottom of Lambs Slide and do a longer ascending traverse left across the Class 4 slab to reach the chimney.

You can do the route in four long pitches. Pitch 1 (150 feet): From the highest ledge below the chimney, climb an often-wet wall to the left (Class 5.0) or a crack to the right (Class 5.6) to a sloping ledge. Stem up the chimney above, then angle up to the right (Class 5.5). Belay 20 feet below a huge chockstone. Pitch 2 (150 feet): Move right to escape the chockstone, then do an ascending traverse to the right on a convenient ledge system called Alexander's Traverse (Class 4). Belay behind the northernmost of several flakes called the Dog Ear Flakes. Pitch 3 (130 feet): Climb 40 feet up a right-facing dihedral (Class 5.5), then angle 80 feet up to the left (Class 5.5) to a large ledge. This is very enjoyable climbing on clean rock. Pitch 4 (160 feet): Traverse 75 feet left into a recessed area known as the Yellow Bowl (Class 4) and climb the left side of the bowl (Class 5.4) to Broadway.

1R8 — Longs Peak — Stettner's Ledges *Classic*

From Longs Peak TH at 9,400'	*1,030 RP*	*11.2 mi RT*	*4,855' total*	*Class 5.7+*
With descent of North Face	*1,055 RP*	*12.2 mi RT*	*4,855' total*	*Class 5.7+*
With descent of Keyhole	*1,051 RP*	*12.8 mi RT*	*4,855' net; 5,055' total*	*Class 5.7+*

First climbed in 1927 by Paul and Joe Stettner, this remained the hardest climb in Colorado for 20 years. It remains a classic climb today. The route is on a small buttress flanked by right-facing dihedrals on the south part of the lower east face. The bottom of Stettner's Ledges is 300 feet north of the bottom of Alexander's Chimney. When looking at the east face from a distance, Stettner's Ledges is below and south (left) of the bottom of the Notch Couloir. The climb is normally done in six pitches. As with Alexander's Chimney, you can continue on Kieners or traverse south on Broadway to Lambs Slide.

Follow the Kieners Route (1R6) to Mills Glacier. Climb the south tongue of Mills Glacier and scramble up broken rock to the highest ledge below some right-facing dihedrals. Pitch 1 (150 feet): Climb a corner (Class 5.4), move right, and climb a right-facing dihedral (Class 5.6) to a ledge. Pitch 2 (90 feet): Go around the right side of a flake, then climb another right-facing dihedral (Class 5.4) to a large ledge. Pitch 3 (140 feet): From an alcove formed by a flake, climb a steep corner with fixed pins (Class 5.7+). This corner is called the Piton Ladder and it is often wet. Continue up a shallow dihedral (Class 5.6) to a large ledge called Lunch Ledge.

Pitch 4: From the south end of Lunch Ledge, climb a corner (Class 5.5) and continue up and left (Class 5.4) to another ledge. Pitch 5: Climb up and left to a ledge system (Class 5.4). Traverse left on the ledges, then climb up and left to join the Alexander's Chimney Route (1R7) and its last pitch. Pitch 6 (160 feet): Traverse 75 feet left into the Yellow Bowl (Class 4) and climb the left side of the bowl (Class 5.4) to Broadway.

1R8 V – Variation – Hornsby's Direct

Class 5.8

This direct finish replaces the last two pitches with steeper, harder climbing. Pitch 5 (120 feet): From the top of pitch 4, climb shallow dihedrals (Class 5.6) to a ledge below a steep section. Pitch 6 (140 feet): Climb a right-facing dihedral and pass a roof (Class 5.8) to reach Broadway.

1R9 – Longs Peak – Notch Couloir *Classic*

From Longs Peak TH at 9,400'	548 RP	11.4 mi RT	4,855' total	Class 5.2, Steep Snow/Ice
With descent of North Face	564 RP	12.2 mi RT	4,855' total	Class 5.2, Steep Snow/Ice
With descent of Keyhole	567 RP	12.9 mi RT	4,855' net; 5,055' total	Class 5.2, Steep Snow/Ice

When it is in good condition, this is the most spectacular snow climb in the park. The Notch Couloir rises from Broadway to the Notch on Longs' east face. Prior to mid-June, the couloir may still be avalanching. It is in the best condition for snow climbing from mid-June to mid-July. By August the snow melts and the couloir no longer provides a snow climb, but often an intermittent ice climb. Conditions vary greatly in this couloir, so you should study it carefully before undertaking an ascent.

Follow the Kieners Route (1R6) to the bottom of the Notch Couloir. Climb the couloir as it twists up the face to the Notch. The couloir is not consistent in its steepness, and there are short, steep sections along the way. In particular, there is a narrow crux halfway up. There are several places where you can escape north (right) onto the upper part of the Kieners Route. The angle in the couloir eases as you approach the Notch and, once past the narrow crux, it is best to continue all the way into the Notch.

From the Notch, scramble 150 feet north (right) up Class 3 ledges, then climb 100 feet up an east-facing chimney to Longs' upper southeast ridge (Class 5.2). Once you are on the ridge, the difficulty eases considerably. Scramble 100 yards north along the ridge to the summit. This is a dramatic approach to Longs' flat summit.

1R10 – Longs Peak – Loft *Classic*

From Longs Peak TH at 9,400'	*351 RP*	*12.0 mi RT*	*4,855' net; 5,155' total*	*Class 3, Mod Snow*
From Chasm Meadows at 11,580'	*210 RP*	*3.0 mi RT*	*2,675' net; 2,975' total*	*Class 3, Mod Snow*
With descent of Keyhole	*369 RP*	*13.2 mi RT*	*4,855' net; 5,355' total*	*Class 3, Mod Snow*

In August, when the snow slopes have melted, this route is only slightly harder than the Keyhole Route (1R1). It is also shorter and much less traveled. This route allows you to climb both Longs and Meeker. The Loft Route ascends the broad trough between Ships Prow and Meeker to the Loft, then skirts below the west side of the Palisades to the Homestretch. This route is dangerous when snow covers the ledges below the Loft. By August the route becomes a Class 3 scramble.

From the Longs Peak Trailhead at 9,400 feet, follow the East Longs Peak Trail for 4.5 miles to Chasm Meadows, below Chasm Lake. From Chasm Meadows, don't go to Chasm Lake but hike straight south toward Meeker's huge, sweeping north face. Once you are past the bottom of Ships Prow, turn southwest (right) and hike up the wide slope between Ships Prow and Meeker's north face. A moderate snow slope fills this trough in June and part of July. The slope narrows, and a large, sweeping cliff band blocks simple passage to the Loft.

Scramble up 100 feet of broken, Class 3 rock to the base of the cliff band. Turn south (left) and climb onto a 10-foot-wide ledge angling up to the south across the cliff band. You must find this ledge for the easiest ascent. Follow the ledge 150 yards south past an awkward step until it merges into the broken upper part of the cliff band (Class 3). Switchback 100 feet north on a 2-foot-wide grass-covered ledge and scramble up to the talus below the Loft (Class 3). From the switchback point, you can climb straight up, but this is more difficult.

Cross the Loft's large expanse to its northwest edge. Contour northwest and look sharp for some cairns. Descend slightly and find the top of a gully leading down to the scree-filled couloirs on Longs' south side. Downclimb 10 feet, then traverse east into the gully with a clever 20-foot up-and-down Class 3 sequence that avoids harder climbing. Scramble 100 feet down the gully (Class 3) until you can easily exit it to the north. Look up and you should see Clark's Arrow, an old painted arrow pointing south. It is on a smooth west-facing slab just north of the bottom of the gully. Clark's Arrow is visible for a long distance when descending from Longs to the Loft, but it is not visible until you come immediately upon it when using this route to ascend Longs. The old painted arrow has faded badly over the years, so don't rely on finding it.

From Clark's Arrow, scramble north and descend slightly to a position below the Palisades, which are the beautiful west-facing slabs soaring above you. The total elevation loss from the Loft to the low point below the Palisades is 150 vertical feet.

From the low point below the Palisades, route finding becomes simpler. Scramble north up the scree-filled couloir below the Palisades. There is some loose rock in this couloir, so you should be careful if there are other people on the route. At 13,560 feet (40.2529° -105.6145°), the couloir broadens and Longs' upper south face directly above you blocks easy ascent. The Notch is prominent up to the northeast.

Do a 250-yard ascending traverse northwest (left) on some Class 3 ledges and join the Keyhole Route (1R1) at 13,920 feet (40.2538° -105.6161°), just below the Homestretch. Follow that route to the summit. On the ascending traverse, from 13,650 feet to 13,920 feet, you are below the Homestretch and should be on the lookout for falling objects.

1R10 V – Variation – The Notch

Class 5.2

At 13,560 feet, turn east (right) instead of west (left) and climb into the Notch. This requires 30 feet of Class 5.0–5.2 climbing just below the Notch. Once you are into the Notch, finish the climb by following the upper part of the Notch Couloir Route (1R9, Class 5.2). This variation provides a technical finish to the already interesting Loft Route and avoids the crowds on the Homestretch.

1R10 EC1 – Extra Credit – Mount Meeker 13,911 feet 40.2484° -105.6050°

From Longs Peak TH at 9,400'	*318 RP*	*11.4 mi RT*	*4,511' total*	*Class 3, Mod Snow*
From Chasm Meadows at 11,580'	*184 RP*	*2.4 mi RT*	*2,331' total*	*Class 3, Mod Snow*
From the Loft at 13,460'	*33 RP*	*0.6 mi RT*	*451' total*	*Class 3*

From the Loft, hike 0.25 mile south then southeast up talus and climb to the ridge above. From here, you can see Meeker's dramatic summit block 50 yards to the east. Scramble east along the narrow, exposed ridge to the base of the summit block (Class 3), a landmark that has stirred many souls. Climb the summit block on its northwest side via an exposed, committing Class 3 move and revel on the highest point of one of Colorado's finest centennial Thirteeners.

1R10 EC2 – Extra Credit – "Southeast Longs" 14,060 feet 40.2539° -105.6134°

From the Loft at 13,460'	*36 R*	*0.6 mi RT*	*600' total*	*Class 2*

From the Loft, hike 0.3 mile northwest up steepening talus to the 14,060-foot summit of "Southeast Longs." Sometimes called "the Beaver," this spectacular summit overlooks the near-vertical south wall of the Notch high on Longs east face. With 240 feet of prominence, "Southeast Longs" doesn't rank, but is still worth a visit because of its airy vantage. A descent to the Notch from here requires a 210-foot rappel. To continue your ascent of the Loft Route, return to the Loft.

1R11 – Longs Peak – Keplinger's Couloir

From Copeland Lake TH at 8,320'   454 RP   15.2 mi RT   5,935' total   Class 3, Mod Snow

This is an easy route up Longs' south side, but it is not usually climbed in one day because of its long, rough approach and large elevation gain. This route is best done with a camp at Sandbeach Lake or in cross-country zone 1G. With a high camp, the route provides a quiet alternative to the crowded Keyhole Route.

From the Copeland Lake Trailhead at 8,320 feet, follow the Sandbeach Lake Trail as it switchbacks onto the Copeland Moraine then climbs steadily west. Cross Campers Creek at 9,580 feet after 2.4 miles. Hike south out of the Campers Creek drainage, continue west to Hunters Creek at 9,780 feet after 3.2 miles, and hike west to Sandbeach Lake (40.2209° -105.6012°) at 10,283 feet after 4.2 miles. For the climb, leave the trail 200 yards northeast of the lake (40.2220° -105.5995°) at a bend in the trail, bushwhack 0.4 mile north-northwest then 1.2 miles northwest into upper Hunter Creek, and find a small, unnamed lake at 11,200 feet (40.2352° -105.6210°). From the unnamed lake, hike 0.9 mile north past treeline to 12,000 feet (40.2470° -105.6175°) in the high, boulder-strewn basin formed by Meeker, Longs, and Pagoda.

There are many couloirs and gullies on Longs' south side. All these couloirs reach the west side of the Palisades and, ultimately, the Notch. The Palisades are west-facing cliffs high on Longs' southeast side. The Notch separates the Palisades from Longs' summit. Keplinger's Couloir is the large, westernmost couloir heading toward the west side of the Notch. It usually has snow in it through June.

Enter the couloir at 12,200 feet (40.2481° -105.6168°). The slope angle in the lower couloir is on the easy side of moderate; the couloir bends east (right) at 12,800 feet, then narrows and steepens as it approaches the Palisades. Follow the couloir to its end at 13,560 feet (40.2529° -105.6145°), below the final summit cliffs on Longs' south face. From this area, the Notch is prominent up to the northeast, and you join the Loft Route (1R10) here. Do not climb into the Notch, but scramble 250 yards north then northwest (left) up Class 3 ledges to join the Keyhole Route (1R1) at 13,920 feet (40.2538° -105.6161°). This section of the route is below the Homestretch, and rockfall is a possibility. Once you are on the Keyhole Route, continue up the Homestretch to the summit.

1R12 – Longs Peak – The Grand Slam *Classic*

From Longs Peak TH at 9,400'   496 RP   14.4 mi RT   6,991' total   Class 3, Mod Snow

Climbing Longs and its four buttress peaks in one day is a five-peak project that will stir sturdy souls. Views of the endeavor range from "prohibitive" to "a half-day workout." Follow the Loft Route (1R10) to the Loft. Hike and scramble 0.3 mile southeast to Mount Meeker's dramatic summit block. Climb the summit block's northwest side (Class 3) to reach Meeker's 13,911-foot summit. Return to the Loft and continue on the Loft Route to Longs' summit. Descend the Homestretch and go west toward the Narrows. Before climbing to reach the

Narrows, descend toward Pagoda until a pesky cliff band blocks easy prog-ress. Descend a steep gully through the upper part of the cliffs (Class 3), then traverse west on a broad ledge until you are west of the lower cliffs. Descend on talus to the Longs–Pagoda saddle (40.2512° -105.6244°). Climb Pagoda's north ridge to Pagoda's 13,497-foot summit and return to the Longs–Pagoda saddle. Take a deep breath; there's more.

Climb northeast on the east side of the Keyboard of the Winds to a notch at 13,420 feet (40.2533° -105.6222°) between two keys. Go through the notch and descend a steep northwest-facing gully (Class 3) until you are below the keys. Do an ascending traverse northeast to rejoin the Keyhole Route (1R1) where it enters the Trough (Class 3). Follow the Keyhole Route north to the Keyhole. Go through the Keyhole and climb north on the east side of Storm Peak's south ridge to Storm's 13,326-foot summit (1R1 EC2). Descend east to the Boulder Field. Continue east then south to Mount Lady Washington's 13,281-foot sum-mit (1R1 EC1). Descend 0.8 mile east on talus to the Mills Moraine trail junc-tion and follow the East Longs Peak Trail back to your starting point.

In 1988 I wrote in my Rocky Mountain National Park guide that aspirants descending from the Mills Moraine trail junction should, "Go ahead, break the record. Sprint down to the trailhead!" Knowing of no record, I included Meeker's east peak (Nesotaieux's Ten Tadasanas, 1R12 EC2) and, scurrying down the trail like a schoolboy late for lunch, I finished the Slam in 10+ hours in September 1989. Elevating the Grand Slam to test-piece status, Bill Wright, Stephan Griebel, Darrin Eisman, and John Prater steadily lowered the record to 6:21:35. Then Buzz Burrell took off with Bill Wright on September 7, 2002. Fully implementing my aging sprint suggestion, Buzz arrived back at the paved parking lot in 5:19 with Wright following 10 minutes later. However, training in the wings was the ubiquitous Bill Briggs, who climbed Longs in every month of 2001. On August 12, 2003, Briggs was behind record pace on the summit of Lady Washington but, smashing my mere sprint suggestion, Bill dashed down in an astonishing 45 minutes to finish in 5:13, setting a record that has endured into the next decade.

1R12 EC1 – Extra Credit – The Radical Slam

From Longs Peak TH at 9,400'   580 RP   17.1 mi RT   8,080' total   Class 3, Mod Snow

For the handful of souls still standing, there's more. Verifying its name, the Radical Slam has been called both a "sick concoction" and a "brilliant linkup." With a longer, more polished view, it is simply the eight summits of Longs.

Do the Grand Slam to Mount Lady Washington. Descend 0.8 mile north and north-northeast to Granite Pass. Scamper 0.5 mile northeast over two minor but rocky highpoints to reach Battle Mountain's 12,044-foot summit (1R1 EC3), descend gently 0.6 mile north-northeast to Pine Ridge's small but rocky 11,909-foot summit (1R1 EC4), and descend 1.2 miles northeast into the trees to Storm Pass at 10,260 feet. Follow the trail east up to Estes Cone's

11,006-foot summit (1R1 EC5). Return to Storm Pass and follow the Eugenia Mine Trail back to the Longs Peak Trailhead. Do 50 push-ups. Collapse.

Eric Lee, Chris Gerber, and Alan Smith set a record for the Radical Slam on September 9, 2007, with a time of 13:20. Turning my joke into a command, they each did 50 push-ups in the parking lot to complete the feat.

1R12 EC2 – Extra Credit – Nesotaieux's Ten Tadasanas

From Longs Peak TH at 9,400'   621 RP   17.8 mi RT   8,720' total   Class 3, Mod Snow

There's always more. If you want the 10 summits of Longs, stand up straight; this is it. From Chasm Meadows on the Loft Route (1R10), hike straight south toward Meeker's sweeping north face, turn east (left) at 12,000 feet, and hike up a large talus field. Aim for and climb a west-facing trough between two buttresses at the eastern edge of Meeker's north face. Hike up talus in the lower part of the trough, then enjoy some easy Class 3 scrambling between the astonishing cliffs of the flanking buttresses called the Iron Gates to reach a notch in Meeker's northeast ridge at 13,000 feet (40.2529° -105.5947°). The view of Longs from here is outstanding. Hike 0.5 mile southwest up the ridge on large talus blocks to Meeker's 13,860-foot east summit (40.2487° -105.6017°). This is the summit of Meeker Ridge, and you can see this ridge and summit from many Front Range cities. From here, you can see Meeker's main summit 300 yards to the west, and this can be a sobering view for the unprepared, especially since this is only your first summit of 10.

From Meeker's east summit, scramble west along the exposed ridge toward the main summit (Class 3). If you love wind on your boot soles, stay right on the ridge. If you eschew exposure, you can traverse on some ledges below the ridge on its north side, but this option only makes life better if the ledges are snow-free. Near the low point between the summits, there is a large block on the ridge with a small keyhole in it. Pass this block on its north side. Beyond this block, pick your way through a series of large boulders to reach the top. The last Class 3 move onto Meeker's summit boulder finishes a fine scramble. Two summits down; now you can ride your breath.

From Meeker's summit, scramble and hike 0.3 mile northwest down to the Loft. From the Loft, hike 0.3 mile northwest up steepening talus to the 14,060-foot summit of "Southeast Longs" (1R10 EC2), your third summit. Return to the Loft and continue to the Radical Slam's remaining seven summits.

Go ahead, break the record. Sprint down to the trailhead! Do 100 push-ups, which is only 10 per peak. A Tadasana is yoga's Mountain Pose, a standing pose that promotes confidence, happiness, good posture, and creates space within your body. Accordingly, rise from your push-ups, stand up straight, face mighty Longs, and breathe the elixir.

2. Grays Group

Grays Peak	14,270 feet
Torreys Peak	14,267 feet

Because of their proximity to the Denver metropolitan area, these two Fourteeners are very popular. People usually climb the two peaks together. Surprisingly, Grays and Torreys are the only Colorado Fourteeners on the Continental Divide. These distinct summits are visible from many Front Range and Summit County vantage points.

Grays Peak is 4 miles south of Exit 221 on Interstate 70, and you can get a glimpse of the summit as you drive by. Grays is the highest peak in both Clear Creek and Summit counties, and the highest peak in the Front Range. Grays is the highest peak on the Continental Divide between the origin of the Pacific–Atlantic divide on Snow Dome in the Canadian Rockies and the Mexican border.

Torreys is 3.5 miles southeast of Loveland Pass and 3.5 miles south of Interstate 70. You can easily see Torreys from Exit 221 on Interstate 70 at Bakerville, and this is a dramatic view, especially in winter.

2E – Grays Group Essentials

Elevations	Grays Peak	14,270' (NGVD29) 14,279' (NAVD88)
	Torreys Peak	14,267' (NGVD29) 14,272' (NAVD88)
Ranks	Grays Peak	Colorado's 9th highest ranked peak
	Torreys Peak	Colorado's 11th highest ranked peak
Location	Clear Creek and Summit counties, Colorado, USA	
Range	Central Front Range	
Summit Coordinates	Grays Peak	39.6330° -105.8175° (WGS84)
	Torreys Peak	39.6428° -105.8212° (WGS84)
Ownership/Contact	Arapaho National Forest – Public Land – 970-295-6600	
	US Forest Service – Clear Creek District – 303-567-3000	
Prominence and Saddles	Grays Peak	2,770' from 11,500' Boreas Pass
	Torreys Peak	560' from 13,707' Grays–Torreys saddle
Isolation and Parents	Grays Peak	25.05 miles to Mount Lincoln
	Torreys Peak	0.64 mile to Grays Peak
USGS Maps	**Grays Peak**, Montezuma, Loveland Pass	
USFS Map	Arapaho and Roosevelt National Forest	
Trails Illustrated Map	Map #104 Idaho Springs/Georgetown/Loveland Pass	
Book Map	See Map 2 on page 24	
Nearest Town	Georgetown – Population 1,000 – Elevation 8,530 feet	
Grays Peak 🥾 Easiest Route	2R1 – North Slopes – Class 1	
	A Class 1 hike on a trail all the way to the top	

2E – Grays Group Essentials

Torreys Peak 🏃 + Easiest Route	2R5 – South Slopes – Class 1+
	A Class 1 approach hike on a trail and a short Class 1+ traverse and
	climb to the summit
Grays Group Accolades	Grays and Torreys are the only Colorado Fourteeners on the Continental
	Divide. Grays is the highest peak in both Clear Creek and Summit
	counties and is the highest peak on the Continental Divide between
	the origin of the Pacific–Atlantic divide on Snow Dome in the Canadian
	Rockies and the Mexican border. Torreys offers a surprising array of
	routes, many with a significant alpine flair.

2T – Grays Group Trailheads

2T1 – Grays Peak Trailhead 11,270 feet 39.6953° -105.7847°

This trailhead provides access to Torreys and the north side of Grays. It was formerly called the Stevens Gulch Trailhead. Take Exit 221 off Interstate 70 at Bakerville. This exit is 6.3 miles west of Georgetown. Cross to the south side of Interstate 70 and find a sign for Grays Peak. Switchback 1.0 mile south up through the trees on FR 189 (dirt) to a marked junction where the Stevens Gulch and Grizzly Gulch roads split (39.6801° -105.8055°). Stay east (left) and continue 2.0 miles on FR 189.1 to the parking lot at the well-marked trailhead. This road is steep and has become much rougher in recent years. You will appreciate a 4WD vehicle.

In winter FR 189 is closed. Winter access to Stevens Gulch is from the south side of the Bakerville exit at 9,780 feet. For winter climbs above the Grays Peak Trailhead, add 6 miles and 1,490 feet.

2T2 – Grizzly Gulch Trailhead 10,320 feet 39.6758° -105.0065°

This trailhead provides access to Torreys' north side. Take Exit 221 off Interstate 70 at Bakerville, 6.3 miles west of Georgetown. Cross to the south side of Interstate 70, go south onto FR 189, and switchback 1.0 mile south up through the trees to a marked junction (39.6801° -105.8055°) between the Stevens Gulch and Grizzly Gulch roads. Turn southwest (right) and continue 0.3 mile on FR 189.1C to the trailhead. Park low-clearance vehicles below some old buildings just before the road crosses to the northwest side of Quayle Creek and becomes a 4WD road. For winter climbs above the Grizzly Gulch Trailhead, add 2.6 miles and 540 feet.

2T2 4WD1 – Grizzly Gulch 4WD Trailhead1 10,730 feet 39.6630° -105.8172°

From the Grizzly Gulch Trailhead, 4WD vehicles can cross to the north side of Quayle Creek and continue up the rough road, crossing back to the southeast side of the creek after 0.9 mile. A little beyond this point, old avalanche debris flanks the road and is an impressive reminder of the power that lives here in winter. The road reaches a meadow 1.1 miles past the 2WD trailhead, at 10,730 feet; this is a good place to park 4WD vehicles.

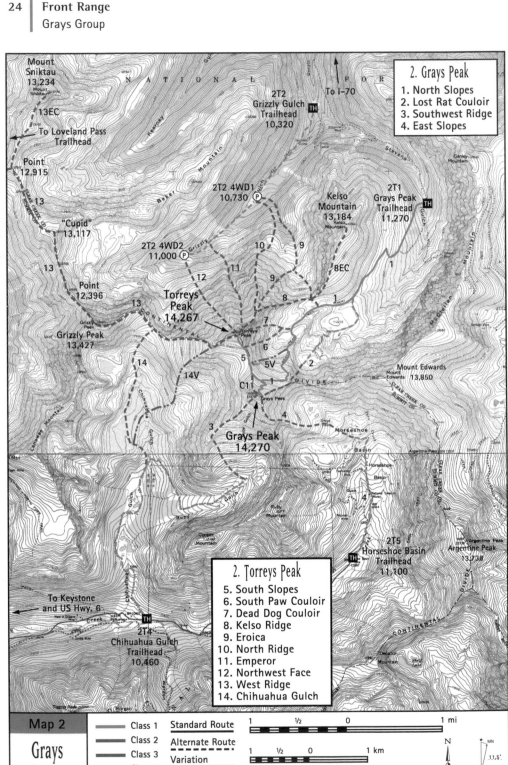

2. Grays Peak
1. North Slopes
2. Lost Rat Couloir
3. Southwest Ridge
4. East Slopes

2. Torreys Peak
5. South Slopes
6. South Paw Couloir
7. Dead Dog Couloir
8. Kelso Ridge
9. Eroica
10. North Ridge
11. Emperor
12. Northwest Face
13. West Ridge
14. Chihuahua Gulch

Map 2

Grays Group

Class 1
Class 2
Class 3
Class 4
Class 5

Standard Route
Alternate Route
Variation
Extra Credit

1   ½   0   1 mi
1   ½   0   1 km

Contour Interval 40 feet

N

MN

11.5°

Magnetic North Declination

2T2 4WD2 – Grizzly Gulch 4WD Trailhead2 11,000 feet 39.6568° -105.8269°

From 10,730 feet in Grizzly Gulch (2T2 4WD1), driving enthusiasts can cross back to the northwest side of the creek and continue 0.7 mile up the now very rough road to 11,000 feet, where the road is blocked to vehicles.

2T3 – Loveland Pass Trailhead 11,990 feet 39.6637° -105.8788°

Loveland Pass on US 6 is at an ear-popping 11,990 feet and provides easy access to the surrounding high country. If you are approaching from the east, take Exit 216 off Interstate 70 and go 4.2 miles west on US 6 to the pass. If you are approaching from the west, take Exit 205 off Interstate 70 near Dillon and go 16.2 miles east on US 6 to the pass. This trailhead is usually accessible in winter, but the pass is often closed during bad storms.

2T4 – Chihuahua Gulch Trailhead 10,460 feet 39.6005° -105.8392°

This trailhead provides access to the southwest sides of Grays and Torreys. Follow US 6 to the Keystone North Peak Ski Area Road. This road is 8.6 miles west of Loveland Pass and 7.8 miles east of Interstate 70 Exit 205 in Dillon. Leave US 6, follow the ski area road 0.1 mile south, then turn east (left) onto Montezuma Road (paved). Go 4.7 miles east on Montezuma Road, then turn left onto Peru Creek Road (dirt, unmarked). Follow Peru Creek Road 2.2 miles east to a small parking area across from the Chihuahua Gulch 4WD Road (unmarked). The Chihuahua Gulch 4WD Road is 0.1 mile east of Warden Gulch Road (marked). In winter Peru Creek Road is closed at the Montezuma–Peru Creek junction.

2T5 – Horseshoe Basin Trailhead 11,100 feet 39.6092° -105.7993°

This trailhead provides access to Grays' east side. Drive on US 6 to the Keystone North Peak Ski Area Road. This road is 8.6 miles west of Loveland Pass and 7.8 miles east of Interstate 70 Exit 205 in Dillon. Leave US 6, follow the ski area road 0.1 mile south, then turn east (left) onto Montezuma Road (paved). Go 4.7 miles east on Montezuma Road, then turn left onto Peru Creek Road (dirt). Follow Peru Creek Road 4.6 miles east to the Shoe Basin Mine at 11,100 feet. Peru Creek Road is passable for some low-clearance vehicles up to the Shoe Basin Mine, and the road is closed to motorized use above this point. In winter Peru Creek Road is closed at the Montezuma–Peru Creek junction.

2. Grays Peak 14,270 feet

2R – Grays Peak Routes
2R1 – Grays Peak – North Slopes
From Grays Peak TH at 11,270'   *147 RP*   *8.0 mi RT*   *3,000' total*   *Class 1*

Grays' lofty summit is easy to reach, and many people climb this peak each summer. In August the greatest hazard on this route may be a playful dog! Start at the Grays Peak Trailhead at 11,270 feet and cross to the west side of the creek on a large footbridge. Simply follow the Grays Peak Trail (FT 54, a National Recreation Trail) for 4.0 miles to the summit. Climb southwest below the east face of Kelso Mountain to 12,070 feet (39.6481° -105.7993°), then west into the small basin below Torreys' east face and Grays' north slopes. Move south then southeast toward a small ridge near the highest grass (39.6423° -105.8100°). Do an ascending traverse up a northwest-facing slope, and at 13,240 feet (39.6380° -105.8132°), stay left at a trail junction with a trail that angles northwest to the Grays–Torreys saddle. Do not go to the saddle; stay on the Grays Peak Trail. Climb southeast to a switchback at 13,440 feet (39.6367° -105.8117°) near a saddle with a small rock pinnacle called the Rascal to the north. With a few steps to the east, you can peer down an astonishing drop into the Lost Rat Couloir. Watch your hat if the wind is blowing. From the small saddle, switchback up Grays' broad northern slopes on the well-constructed trail that goes all the way to the summit, which is at the northwest end of a small summit ridge (39.6330° -105.8175°). From the summit, you will have expansive views of many peaks in both Summit and Clear Creek counties.

One caveat for this easy route is that it is north facing, and snowbanks can linger on the trail well into June. In nonsummer conditions, this north slope can offer a snowy, hostile, windswept experience.

2R2 – Grays Peak – Lost Rat Couloir

From Grays Peak TH at 11,270'	181 RP	7.6 mi RT	3,000' total	Class 2, Mod Snow
With descent of North Slopes	194 RP	8.8 mi RT	3,000' total	Class 2, Mod Snow

This surprising snow climb is just a short distance east of the Grays Peak Trail on Grays' small northeast face. Its steepness punctuates Grays' otherwise genial slopes. It provides a nice snow climb in late spring and early summer.

Start at the Grays Peak Trailhead at 11,270 feet and follow the Grays Peak Trail for 1.5 miles to 12,070 feet (39.6481° -105.7993°). You can see the couloir from here to the east of Grays. Leave the Grays Peak Trail before it climbs west into the basin below Torreys' east face, and follow an old road a mile south and southwest to the bottom of the couloir at 12,800 feet. From here, you can see the lower half of the Lost Rat Couloir. It is bounded on its west side by a dramatic pinnacle called the Rascal.

Climb the couloir for 400 feet to a dogleg just below the embracing Rascal. At the dogleg, turn slightly east (left) and continue for another 400 feet as the now narrower couloir steepens slightly. The steepness reaches 40 degrees as you approach the ridge. Forged by winter's winds, the snow just below the ridge can be surprisingly hard-packed, and you may appreciate crampons. The couloir ends on Grays' east ridge at 13,600 feet. Hike west on this Class 2 ridge and join the Grays Peak Trail just below the summit.

Grays Peak from the northeast.

2R2 EC – Extra Credit – The Rascal 13,420 feet 39.6369° -105.8115°

Class 4

If you descend the Grays Peak Trail, take a few steps east from the switchback at 13,440 feet (39.6367° -105.8117°) and peer over an astonishing edge into the Lost Rat Couloir. The steepness here stands in sharp contrast to the trail. For even more excitement, descend 150 yards north, then climb east to the Rascal's summit (Class 4). This is an airy perch.

2R3 – Grays Peak – Southwest Ridge

From Chihuahua Gulch TH at 10,460'	*266 RP*	*10.0 mi RT*	*3,810' total*	*Class 2*
With descent of East Slopes	*269 RP*	*9.5 mi RT*	*3,810' total*	*Class 2*

Grays' south side is easily accessible from Summit County on the west side of the Continental Divide, and this side of the peak provides a refreshing alternative to the crowded North Slopes Route (2R1). The Southwest Ridge Route winds through two valleys and ascends a scenic ridge.

Start at the Chihuahua Gulch Trailhead at 10,460 feet and follow the 4WD road north into Chihuahua Gulch. The road starts on the east side of the creek, crosses to the creek's west side, and passes a large meadow. The road then crosses back to the creek's east side and passes a second meadow. There are good views of the west side of Grays and Torreys from these meadows, but Grays' south side is hidden. From the second meadow's northern end, do not cross back to the creek's west side. The Chihuahua Gulch Road does cross the creek here, but the Ruby Gulch Road goes 100 feet *up the creek*, then climbs north on the creek's west side. Follow Ruby Gulch Road.

After climbing north of the confluence of Ruby and Chihuahua gulches to 11,370 feet, the road turns back southeast (39.6243° -105.8380°) and climbs into Ruby Gulch south of Grays. Follow the road east to its end at an old mine building at 12,120 feet (39.6213° -105.8199°). You can see the rest of the route from here. Climb northwest from the old mine building and reach Grays' southwest ridge at 13,100 feet (39.6274° -105.8266°). Follow this colorful ridge northeast to 13,800 feet (39.6325° -105.8194°), where it merges into a scree slope. Climb straight up this 470-foot scree slope to the summit. This final slope's looseness is the only detraction from an otherwise charming route. Descending the East Slopes Route (2R4) completes a southern Tour de Grays.

2R4 – Grays Peak – East Slopes

From Horseshoe Basin TH at 11,100'   152 RP   5.6 mi RT   3,170' total   Class 2

This is the shortest route on Grays. The East Slopes Route is easier than the Southwest Ridge Route (2R3) and only slightly harder than the crowded North Slopes Route (2R1). There are roads, grass slopes, and goat trails all the way. Start at the Horseshoe Basin Trailhead at 11,100 feet and follow the old road 1.3 miles north into Horseshoe Basin. Leave the road at 12,060 feet (39.6272° -105.7988°) before it turns back south. Climb west-northwest to tiny, captivating Grays Lake at 12,460 feet (39.6294° -105.8031°). Climb grass slopes west of Grays Lake and reach Grays' south ridge at 13,800 feet (39.6300° -105.8151°). Follow this ridge north to the summit.

2. Torreys Peak 14,267 feet

2R – Torreys Peak Routes
2R5 – Torreys Peak – South Slopes

From Grays Peak TH at 11,270'   147 RP   8.0 mi RT   2,997' total   Class 1+

Heather "Piper" Musmanno on Kelso Ridge. Photo by Dave Hale

This is the easiest route on Torreys. Start at the Grays Peak Trailhead at 11,270 feet. Follow the Grays Peak Trail (2R1) to 13,240 feet (39.6380° -105.8132°), leave the Grays Peak Trail, and follow a good trail 0.3 mile west up an ascending traverse across talus to the Grays–Torreys saddle at 13,707 feet (39.6380° -105.8188°). The snow slope east of this saddle persists into summer, and if possible you should stay above the snow slope's south side. You can easily see and avoid the snow slope when approaching the saddle from the Grays Peak Trail. From the Grays–Torreys saddle, hike 0.4 mile up a meandering climber's trail through the talus on Torreys' south side to the summit (39.6428° -105.8212°).

2R5 V – Variation – Saddle Direct

Steep Snow

When conditions are good (yours and the snow's), you can climb directly to the Grays–Torreys saddle on steep snow. In early summer there may be a cornice at the top.

2R6 – Torreys Peak – South Paw Couloir

From Grays Peak TH at 11,270'	*277 RP*	*7.0 mi RT*	*2,997' total*	*Class 3, Steep Snow*
With descent of South Slopes	*265 RP*	*7.5 mi RT*	*2,997' total*	*Class 3, Steep Snow*

This is the steep couloir on the south side of Torreys' east face. It is shorter but steeper than the Dead Dog Couloir. The couloir reaches Torreys' south ridge at 13,900 feet where, with a few cautious strides over to the edge, you can peer down South Paw from the South Slopes Route (2R5). This view has dissuaded many aspirants.

Start at the Grays Peak Trailhead at 11,270 feet and follow the Grays Peak Trail for 2.4 miles to a bench at 12,600 feet. The bottom of South Paw is southwest of here, 300 yards south of Dead Dog Couloir. Carefully consider conditions before attempting this climb. Even in summer, small snow slides can surprise you and take you down with them. A large, extensive cornice that persists into summer guards the top of the South Paw Couloir, and it will likely force you onto the rocks south of the couloir to finish the climb. From the top of South Paw, hike 800 feet north to Torreys' summit.

2R7 – Torreys Peak – Dead Dog Couloir

From Grays Peak TH at 11,270'	*308 RP*	*6.8 mi RT*	*2,997' total*	*Class 3, Steep Snow*
With descent of South Slopes	*293 RP*	*7.4 mi RT*	*2,997' total*	*Class 3, Steep Snow*

This is the large couloir in the center of Torreys' east face, and it reaches Kelso Ridge just below the summit. When snow conditions are good, this is the premier mountaineering route on Torreys, but after the snow melts, you should avoid this couloir. There is decent snow through June, but it melts faster here than in couloirs farther north, so don't wait too long to climb this one.

I recommend a helmet for this route, because the rock surrounding the couloir is rotten and rockfall is a hazard. The rockfall problem is compounded because a long stretch of Kelso Ridge is above the couloir, and careless climbers on that route may send rocks down upon you. Leave early.

Start at the Grays Peak Trailhead at 11,270 feet and follow the Grays Peak Trail for 2.4 miles to a bench at 12,600 feet. The couloir is directly west and easily visible. Leave the trail and climb west up the broad slope below the couloir to the start of the couloir at 13,100 feet. The couloir winds up the face, and you can't see the top until you reach halfway. The angle in the center of the couloir is 45 degrees, and the angle near the top is 50 degrees. The finish is beautiful and reaches Kelso Ridge above 14,000 feet. The summit is only 100 yards up to the south. This route can provide more than 1,000 vertical feet of snow climbing!

2R8 – Torreys Peak – Kelso Ridge *Classic*

From Grays Peak TH at 11,270'	226 RP	6.5 mi RT	2,997' total	Class 3
With descent of South Slopes	216 RP	7.3 mi RT	2,997' total	Class 3

This is Torreys' northeast ridge, and it provides a sporting alternative to the South Slopes Route (2R5). It has become quite popular in recent years. There are only a few scrambling sections on Kelso Ridge, and it looks harder than it is; however, you should treat this ridge as a climb, not a hike.

From the Grays Peak Trailhead at 11,270 feet, follow the Grays Peak Trail (2R1) 2.0 miles to a bench at 12,300 feet. Leave the trail and climb 200 yards northwest to the 12,380-foot saddle (39.6482° -105.8073°) between Torreys and 13,164-foot Kelso Mountain. Kelso is 1.6 miles northeast of Torreys and 0.9 mile west of the Grays Peak Trailhead.

From the Torreys–Kelso saddle (39.6482° -105.8073°), climb west along the gentle beginning to the ridge. The ridge soon steepens and you will meet the challenge. The Kelso Ridge sees many feet, and there is a small trail in the easier sections, but there are also some false trails. If you are uncomfortable with this initial scampering, a retreat to the Grays Peak Trail is prudent.

You must negotiate two towers between 12,800 feet and 13,200 feet. The first requires 30 feet of Class 3 scrambling up a small trough. You can pass the higher one on either side with 30 feet of exposed Class 3 scrambling. The north side is easier. Above this second tower, move to the ridge's north side and scamper up a steep dirt slope to easier ground.

Continue 0.3 mile up a strong trail on the ridge's north side. Midway along this easy stretch, at 13,600 feet, Torreys' broad north ridge rising out of Grizzly Gulch joins Kelso Ridge. The upper part of Kelso Ridge heads southwest toward the summit. Above the junction with the north ridge, do not knock rocks down the southeast (left) side of the ridge. You are above Dead Dog Couloir, and there may be climbers below you.

Just as you think you are about to walk to the top, the route's crux appears. There is a solid rock buttress on the ridge 200 yards below the summit. There are at least three ways to solve this problem. You can climb 40 feet directly up the buttress (Class 4), or you can skirt it on either side of the ridge with Class 3 scrambling.

Skirting the buttress on the north (right) side involves climbing up some loose, unpleasant rock, but you rapidly regain the ridge. Skirting the buttress on the south (left) side is easy at first, but leads into the top part of Dead Dog Couloir. In June and July, when there is steep snow here, this is not a good alternative. After the snow melts, the upper couloir becomes a steep dirt slope and this is the easiest route. You also can regain the ridge crest from partway along the south-side traverse (steep Class 3).

If you regain the ridge crest below the top of Dead Dog Couloir, there is one more interesting problem. Stay on the ridge crest and behold the notorious knife-edge of Kelso Ridge. It requires 30 feet of exposed Class 3 scrambling on

Torreys Peak from the northeast.

solid rock, and many people choose to scoot across sitting down. Fortunately, the knife is dull! The top of Dead Dog Couloir is 100 feet beyond the knife-edge, and the summit is 100 steep yards beyond that. Continue to be careful with loose rocks all the way to the summit, because any rock knocked loose will fall into Dead Dog Couloir.

2R8 EC – Extra Credit – Kelso Mountain 13,184 feet 39.6589° -105.8004°

Class 2

From the 12,380-foot Torreys–Kelso saddle (39.6482° -105.8073°), hike 0.2 mile steeply northeast to 12,700 feet, then 0.7 mile north-northeast up talus to the vista-rich summit of 13,184-foot Kelso Mountain, a ranked Thirteener.

2R9 – Torreys Peak – Eroica

From Grizzly Gulch TH at 10,320'	*406 RP*	*6.0 mi RT*	*3,947' total*	*Class 3, Steep Snow*
With descent of Northwest Face	*400 RP*	*6.2 mi RT*	*3,947' total*	*Class 3, Steep Snow*
From Grays Peak TH at 11,270'	*384 RP*	*6.8 mi RT*	*2,997' net; 3,757' total*	*Class 3, Steep Snow*
With descent of South Slopes	*347 RP*	*7.4 mi RT*	*2,997' net; 3,377' total*	*Class 3, Steep Snow*

Eroica is an eclectic climb for the erudite. It is yet another exciting climb on a peak with a reputation for being easy. Eroica is the central couloir of Torreys' tiny northeast face between the Kelso Ridge (2R8) and North Ridge (2R10) routes. With both snow and rock pitches, this is Torreys' finest mixed climb. You can approach it from either the Grizzly Gulch or Grays Peak Trailhead, and this makes several circle tours possible.

From the Grizzly Gulch Trailhead at 10,320 feet, follow the 4WD road as it climbs southwest into Grizzly Gulch. After 1.1 miles, leave the road in a meadow at 10,730 feet (39.6630° -105.8172°) and bushwhack 1.0 mile southeast into the basin between Kelso and Torreys to the base of the climb at 12,000 feet (39.6516° -105.8124°). From the Grays Peak Trailhead at 11,270 feet, follow the Grays Peak Trail for 2.0 miles to a bench at 12,300 feet. Leave the trail and climb 200 yards northwest to the 12,380-foot saddle (39.6482° -105.8073°) between Torreys and Kelso. Cross the saddle and descend 600 yards northwest into the basin to the base of the climb at 12,000 feet.

Climb southwest up the inset couloir on moderate snow to 12,800 feet. Above this point, the couloir fans open into a tiny alpine paradise where you have several steep choices. Any of the finishes can make you feel heroic and elite. You can climb south (left) and reach Kelso Ridge at 13,440 feet, or you can climb southwest and reach Torreys' north ridge at 13,400 feet. For the most aesthetic exit, climb southeast directly to the junction of Kelso Ridge and Torreys' north ridge at 13,600 feet. From here, finish on the Kelso Ridge Route (2R8) and its Class 3 crux.

2R10 – Torreys Peak – North Ridge

From Grizzly Gulch TH at 10,320'	*279 RP*	*6.0 mi RT*	*3,947' total*	*Class 3*
With descent of Northwest Face	*283 RP*	*6.2 mi RT*	*3,947' total*	*Class 3*

This route provides a less crowded, albeit steeper and less classic alternative to the Kelso Ridge Route. Start at the Grizzly Gulch Trailhead at 10,320 feet and follow the 4WD road as it climbs southwest into Grizzly Gulch. After 1.1 miles, leave the road in a meadow at 10,730 feet (39.6630° -105.8172°). Bushwhack 0.5 mile south up the hill and reach a bench just above treeline at 11,660 feet. Torreys' north ridge takes shape above this point. Hike up the increasingly distinct ridge for 1.0 mile (Class 2). You can easily pass any difficulties on the west (right). Join the Kelso Ridge Route (2R8) at 13,600 feet (39.6462° -105.8176°) and follow the upper part of that route to the summit. The upper part of Kelso Ridge includes its Class 3 crux. Ascending the North Ridge Route and descending the Northwest Face Route (2R12) provides a northern Tour de Torreys.

2R11 – Torreys Peak – Emperor

From Grizzly Gulch TH at 10,320'	*386 RP*	*6.0 mi RT*	*3,947' total*	*Class 3, Steep Snow*
With descent of Northwest Face	*389 RP*	*6.3 mi RT*	*3,947' total*	*Class 3, Steep Snow*

Torreys has a small northeast face between the north ridge and Kelso Ridge, a very small north face immediately west of the north ridge, and a larger northwest face farther west. Emperor ascends the couloirs in the center of the north face. This has been the standard tough climb on Torreys' north side for years. When it is in good condition, Emperor provides 3,000 feet of snow climbing. It is one of Colorado's longest snow climbs. You can preview Emperor's condition from Interstate 70.

From the Grizzly Gulch Trailhead at 10,320 feet, follow the 4WD road 1.1 miles southwest into Grizzly Gulch to a meadow at 10,730 feet (39.6630°

-105.8172°). Cross back to the northwest side of the creek and go 0.7 mile southwest on the road to 11,000 feet (39.6568° -105.8269°), where the road is blocked to vehicles. The route is directly above you to the south-southeast.

Leave the road, cross the creek, and bushwhack 0.4 mile south-southeast into a tiny basin. Climb steepening snow and pass through a narrow passage between black rocks at 12,100 feet. Continue up the relentless couloir to 12,800 feet, where you begin to have choices as the couloir splits. Continue up the central couloir between some more rocks to the upper basin at 13,400 feet. Do an ascending traverse to the southeast to reach Kelso Ridge near the notch at the top of the Dead Dog Couloir. Hike 100 steep yards south to the summit.

2R11 V1 – Variation – Emperor West

Steep Snow

From 12,800 feet, take the west (right) fork of the couloir, follow it to the talus at 13,400 feet and hike south to the summit. This couloir is steeper, but climbing it shortens the time you spend on snow.

2R11 V2 – Variation – Emperor Direct

Steep Snow

If snow conditions permit, you can finish your ascent by climbing south directly to the summit from 13,400 feet in the central couloir.

2R12 – Torreys Peak – Northwest Face

From Grizzly Gulch TH at 10,320'   347 RP   6.4 mi RT   3,947' total   Class 2, Mod Snow

Torreys has a small northeast face between the north ridge and Kelso Ridge, a very small north face immediately west of the north ridge, and a larger northwest face farther west. A long, wide snow couloir called the Tuning Fork splits the center of the northwest face. The eastern branch of the Tuning Fork goes directly to the summit, and the western branch reaches the west ridge 180 yards west of the summit. This is a spring or early summer route; you should carefully consider avalanche conditions before committing to this couloir. When it is in good condition, this couloir provides 2,000 feet of snow climbing and is often used as a ski descent route. Do not confuse Torreys' small, rugged north face with its larger, gentler northwest face.

Start at the Grizzly Gulch Trailhead at 10,320 feet and follow the 4WD road as it climbs southwest into Grizzly Gulch. Go 1.8 miles up the valley to 11,000 feet, where the road is blocked to vehicles. Continue 0.3 mile up the old road, now a trail, to 11,200 feet. Torreys' northwest face and its couloirs will be above you to the south-southeast.

Leave the road, cross the creek, and hike 0.4 mile south-southeast to the bottom of the Tuning Fork at 12,000 feet (39.6491° -105.8285°). The lower half of the climb is up the wide, straight couloir. At 12,700 feet (39.6469° -105.8266°), the couloir splits into two parallel couloirs. You can climb either branch, but the west (right) one is easier. The steepness approaches, but does not exceed, 40 degrees. Escape from the snow is possible at any point by moving onto the steep talus that flanks the couloirs.

Depending on the year and time of year, the snow may or may not extend all the way to Torreys' west ridge. If it does, it may be blasted hard by winter's winds, and you will appreciate crampons for this condition. You can avoid this difficulty by moving east onto the talus. Once on Torreys' west ridge at 14,100 feet, hike 180 yards east over talus to the summit.

2R13 – Torreys Peak – West Ridge

From Loveland Pass TH at 11,990'	*439 RP*	*10.0 mi RT*	*2,277' net; 5,487' total*	*Class 2*
With descent of South Slopes	*309 RP*	*9.0 mi RT*	*2,277' net; 3,882' total*	*Class 2*

You can climb Torreys from Loveland Pass on US 6. This is a longer route than those starting at the Grays Peak Trailhead, but it is a refreshing ridge route along the Continental Divide that also allows you to bag two ranked Thirteeners. Because of the multisummited roller-coaster ridge, you have to gain a whopping 5,487 feet when completing a round trip on this route, and you will be off-trail above 12,000 feet the whole time. If you can arrange a pick up at the Grays Peak Trailhead, this makes an engaging one-way ridge run.

From the Loveland Pass Trailhead at 11,990 feet, climb east up the well-traveled slope to unranked Point 12,915 (39.6672° -105.8649°). Hike south along the Continental Divide on a fair climber's trail to the rounded summit of Point 13,117, alias "Cupid" (39.6578° -105.8567°). This is one of Colorado's ranked Thirteeners, and it provides a lovely view of the rugged terrain ahead. Continue south over unranked Point 12,936 to reach noble 13,427-foot Grizzly Peak (39.6442° -105.8488°), another ranked Thirteener. In early June, there can be some dangerous cornices along this ridge. From Grizzly Peak, descend east to the grassy, 12,580-foot Grizzly–Torreys saddle (39.6436° -105.8375°) and climb Torreys' long, rounded west ridge.

2R13 EC – Extra Credit – Mount Sniktau 13,234 feet 39.6785° -105.8575°

Class 2

From Point 12,915 (39.6672° -105.8649°), hike 0.5 mile north-northeast to unranked Point 13,152, then continue 0.4 mile north-northeast to the inveigling summit of 13,234-foot Mount Sniktau, a ranked Thirteener. The fleet-footed can add Sniktau to their long West Ridge romp, but if you are feeling flat-footed, you can just do Sniktau and return to Loveland Pass.

2R14 – Torreys Peak – Chihuahua Gulch

From Chihuahua Gulch TH at 10,460'	*262 RP*	*9.8 mi RT*	*3,807' total*	*Class 2*

This is a scenic, seldom climbed route on Torreys. Start at the Chihuahua Gulch Trailhead at 10,460 feet and follow the 4WD road 2.0 miles north to 11,200 feet in Chihuahua Gulch. The road starts on the east side of the creek, crosses to the creek's west side, and passes a large meadow. The road then crosses back to the creek's east side and passes a second meadow. After one more crossing to the creek's west side, reach 11,200 feet and continue 1.4 miles north on a trail to 12,000 feet in upper Chihuahua Gulch. From the end of the trail, hike 0.4 mile northeast up a gentle slope to the 12,580-foot saddle (39.6436° -105.8375°) between Torreys and 13,427-foot Grizzly Peak. Follow Torreys' west ridge 1.1 miles along the Continental Divide to the summit (Class 2).

2R14 V – Variation – Southwest Ridge

Class 2

From 11,600 feet in Chihuahua Gulch, hike east, then climb Torreys' rounded southwest ridge to join Torreys' west ridge at 13,900 feet (39.6409° -105.8263°). This shorter, steeper alternative avoids the 12,580-foot Torreys–Grizzly saddle.

2R14 EC – Extra Credit – Grizzly Peak 13,427 feet 39.6442° -105.8488°

Class 2

From the 12,580-foot Torreys–Grizzly saddle (39.6436° -105.8375°), hike 0.8 mile northwest then west up talus to the summit of 13,427-foot Grizzly Peak, a ranked Thirteener.

2C – Grays and Torreys Combination Routes

2C1 – Grays North Slopes → Torreys South Slopes

From Grays Peak TH at 11,270'   172 RP   8.8 mi RT   3,000' net; 3,560' total   Class 2

This combination is the easiest way to climb Grays and Torreys together. Follow the Grays Peak Trail (2R1) 4.0 miles to Grays' summit, descend 0.4 mile north (Class 2) to the 13,707-foot Grays–Torreys saddle, and hike 0.4 mile up Torreys' south side (Class 1). Return to the Grays–Torreys saddle, then traverse southeast to return to the Grays Peak Trail. The snow slope below the saddle surprises some people when they approach it from above. You can do this combination in reverse, but most people climb Grays first.

2C2 – Torreys Kelso Ridge → Grays North Slopes

From Grays Peak TH at 11,270'   252 RP   8.1 mi RT   3,000' net; 3,560' total   Class 3

This popular Tour de Grays and Torreys has a mountaineering flavor. Climb the Kelso Ridge Route (2R8) to Torreys' summit, hike south to the Grays–Torreys saddle, then hike south up to Grays' summit. Descend Grays' North Slopes Route (2R1).

2C3 – Torreys Dead Dog Couloir → Grays North Slopes

From Grays Peak TH at 11,270'   329 RP   8.2 mi RT   3,000' net; 3,560' total   Class 3, Steep Snow

This combination is even more exciting. Climb the Dead Dog Couloir (2R7) to Torreys' summit, hike south to the Grays–Torreys saddle, then hike south up to Grays' summit. Descend Grays' North Slopes Route (2R1).

2C4 – Torreys West Ridge → Grays North Slopes

From Loveland Pass TH at 11,990' to Grays Peak TH at 11,270'   345 RP   9.8 mi OW   2,280' net; 4,445' total   Class 2

This lofty combination requires a vehicle shuttle but allows you to climb four ranked peaks. Start at the Loveland Pass Trailhead at 11,990 feet and follow Torreys' West Ridge Route (2R13) over 13,117-foot "Cupid" and 13,427-foot Grizzly Peak to Torreys' summit. Hike 0.4 mile south (Class 1+) to the 13,707-foot Grays–Torreys saddle, then hike 0.4 mile south (Class 2) up to Grays' summit. Descend Grays' North Slopes Route (2R1) to the Grays Peak Trailhead.

2C5 – Grays Southwest Ridge → Torreys Chihuahua Gulch

From Chihuahua Gulch TH at 10,460'   287 RP   10.7 mi RT   3,810' net; 4,370' total   Class 2

This is a scenic way to climb both Fourteeners from the south. Start at the Chihuahua Gulch Trailhead at 10,460 feet and climb Grays' Southwest Ridge Route (2R3). Hike 0.4 mile north (Class 2) to the 13,707-foot Grays–Torreys saddle, then hike 0.4 mile north (Class 1+) up to Torreys' summit. Descend Torreys' Chihuahua Gulch Route (2R14).

3. Evans Group

Mount Evans   14,264 feet
Mount Bierstadt   14,060 feet

A scant 36 miles west of Colorado's capitol building in downtown Denver, Mount Evans has the distinction of being the closest Fourteener to Denver. Evans' large massif forms the mainstay of Denver's mountain backdrop and is visible to millions of people. Evans serves as a constant reminder of why these people choose to live in Colorado. For many people, their Rocky Mountain High starts here. Evans' proximity to Denver, plus a paved road to the summit, makes it exceedingly popular. Serious cliff bands interrupt Evans' gentle slopes, and there are many adventures available on this large, complex peak.

Mount Bierstadt is 2.4 miles east of Guanella Pass and 1.4 miles west of its more famous parent, Mount Evans. Bierstadt is important because it is one of the closest Fourteeners to Denver, and one of Colorado's easiest Fourteeners. People often climb it in winter, and it is a good test piece for winter mountaineers and a training ground for spring enthusiasts. In high summer, Bierstadt welcomes hikers of all dispositions.

3E – Evans Group Essentials

Elevations	Mt Evans	14,264' (NGVD29) 14,270' (NAVD88)
	Mt Bierstadt	14,060' (NGVD29) 14,065' (NAVD88)
Ranks	Mt Evans	Colorado's 14th highest ranked peak
	Mt Bierstadt	Colorado's 38th highest ranked peak

3E – Evans Group Essentials

Location	Clear Creek County, Colorado, USA	
Range	Central Front Range	
Summit Coordinates	Mt Evans	39.5887° -105.6430° (WGS84)
	Mt Bierstadt	39.5825° -105.6887° (WGS84)
Ownership/Contact	Arapaho National Forest – Public Land – 970-295-6600	
	US Forest Service – Clear Creek District - 303-567-3000	
Prominence and Saddles	Mt Evans	2,764' from 11,500' near Guanella Pass
	Mt Bierstadt	720' from 13,340' Evans–Bierstadt saddle
Isolation and Parents	Mt Evans	9.79 miles to Grays Peak
	Mt Bierstadt	1.41 miles to Mount Evans
USGS Maps	**Mount Evans**, Georgetown, Harris Park, Idaho Springs	
USFS Maps	**Arapaho & Roosevelt National Forest**, Pike National Forest	
Trails Illustrated Map	Map #104 Idaho Springs/Georgetown/Loveland Pass	
Book Map	See Map 3 on page 38	
Nearest Town	Idaho Springs – Population 1,700 – Elevation 7,526 feet	
Mount Evans 🏃 Easiest Route	3R3 – Mount Evans Road – Class 1	
	A paved road goes close to the top, and a short trail continues to the highest point	
Mount Bierstadt 🏃 Easiest Route	3R13 – West Slopes – Class 2	
	A Class 1 trail hike most of the way, then a short Class 2 boulder hop to the top	
Evans Group Accolades	Evans and Bierstadt anchor a huge massif with multiple, long, high ridges extending over many satellite peaks. Evans is the closest Fourteener to Denver and has the highest paved road in North America. Evans is the namesake and highest peak in the Mount Evans Wilderness, and Evans' north face is home to several fine technical routes. Bierstadt is most famous for being one of Colorado's easiest Fourteeners.	

3T – Evans Group Trailheads

3T1 – Echo Lake Trailhead 10,580 feet 39.6592° -105.6065°

This trailhead provides access to Chicago Creek and the paved road up Mount Evans. Leave Interstate 70 at Exit 240 in Idaho Springs, which is signed for Mount Evans. Follow Colorado 103 13.4 miles south to Echo Lake, which is on the south side of the highway. You also can reach Echo Lake by following Colorado 103 18.5 miles west from the junction of Colorado 103 and Colorado 74 in Bergen Park. From the northwest side of Echo Lake, turn west onto a dirt road with a sign for the Echo Lake Picnic Area. Go 0.2 mile west then south to the trailhead.

There is also a parking lot east of Echo Lake at the junction of Colorado 103 and Colorado 5 (the Mount Evans Road). The road to the Echo Lake Picnic Area is 0.6 mile west of the Colorado 103–Colorado 5 junction. This trailhead is accessible in winter.

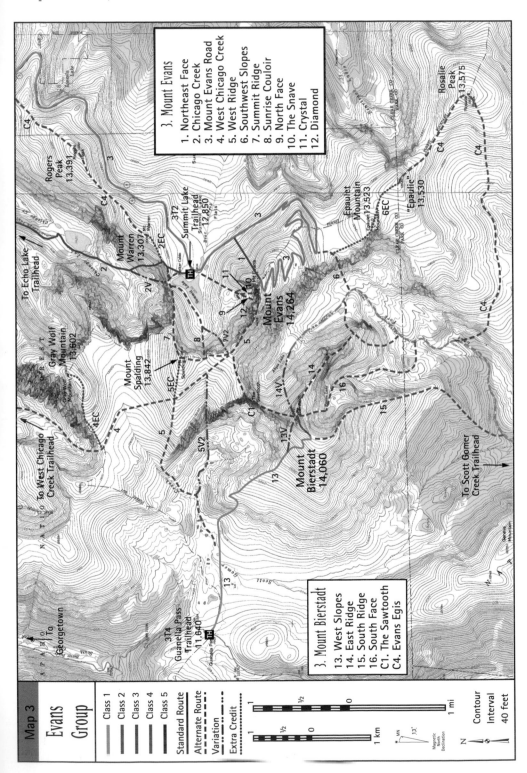

3. Mount Evans

1. Northeast Face
2. Chicago Creek
3. Mount Evans Road
4. West Chicago Creek
5. West Ridge
6. Southwest Slopes
7. Summit Ridge
8. Sunrise Couloir
9. North Face
10. The Snave
11. Crystal
12. Diamond

3. Mount Bierstadt

13. West Slopes
14. East Ridge
15. South Ridge
16. South Face
C1. The Sawtooth
C4. Evans Egis

Map 3
Evans
Group

Class 1
Class 2
Class 3
Class 4
Class 5
Standard Route
Alternate Route
Variation
Extra Credit

Contour
Interval
40 feet

Magnetic
North
Declination

N

3T2 – Summit Lake Trailhead 12,850 feet 39.5997° -105.6408°

This trailhead provides access to Evans' Northeast Face Route and the upper part of the Mount Evans Road. Leave Interstate 70 at Exit 240 in Idaho Springs, which is signed for Mount Evans. Follow Colorado 103 13.4 miles south to Echo Lake. You also can reach Echo Lake by following Colorado 103 18.5 miles west from the junction of Colorado 103 and Colorado 74 in Bergen Park.

From the east end of Echo Lake, follow Colorado 5 (the Mount Evans Road) for 9.1 miles as it climbs south to Summit Lake, which is on the west (right) side of the road. There are two additional parking areas on the road between Echo Lake and Summit Lake. The first is at 11,550 feet, 2.9 miles above Echo Lake. The second is at 12,150 feet, 4.8 miles above Echo Lake. This is the second highest trailhead in this book, and not surprisingly, the Mount Evans Road is only open in the summer.

The Forest Service took over management of Summit Lake from the city of Denver in 1998. With that change came a fee for driving up the Mount Evans Road. Rangers collect the fee on Colorado 5 at Echo Lake.

3T3 – West Chicago Creek Trailhead 9,600 feet 39.6778° -105.6582°

This trailhead provides access to the West Chicago Creek Trail. Leave Interstate 70 at Exit 240 in Idaho Springs. A sign for Mount Evans marks this exit. Follow Colorado 103 6.6 miles south to a dirt road on the south (right) side of the highway. This junction has a sign for the West Chicago Creek Campground. Leave Colorado 103 and follow the dirt road 2.8 miles southwest to the campground and the trailhead. In winter the snowplow turns around at the start of a switchback 2.0 miles above Colorado 103; you can often drive beyond this point.

3T4 – Guanella Pass Trailhead 11,640 feet 39.5960° -105.7105°

This trailhead provides access to the west sides of Evans and Bierstadt. Take Exit 228 off Interstate 70 at Georgetown and follow Guanella Pass Road 10.0 miles south, or leave US 285 at Grant and follow Guanella Pass Road 12.2 miles north. Guanella Pass Road has been recently paved and is passable for passenger cars. There are two new parking lots near the summit of the pass, one on the east side of the road just north of the pass and one on the west side of the road just west of the pass. The old Guanella Pass Trailhead has been moved from the old parking lot right on the pass to the new parking lot on the east side of the road. This change reduces the round-trip elevation gain from this trailhead by 58 feet. Arrive early at this trailhead, for once the parking lots are full, you may not be allowed to hike toward Bierstadt. Guanella Pass Road is open in winter but is the last priority for the snowplow crew. You can see Bierstadt's rounded mass east of Guanella Pass.

3T5 – Scott Gomer Creek Trailhead 9,620 feet 39.5110° -105.7112°

This trailhead provides access to the Abyss Lake Trail and the south sides of Evans and Bierstadt. Leave US 285 at Grant and follow Guanella Pass Road 5.0

miles north. You can reach the trailhead by taking Exit 228 off Interstate 70 at Georgetown, following Guanella Pass Road 10.0 miles south to Guanella Pass and continuing 7.2 miles south to the trailhead, which is adjacent to Burning Bear Campground. This trailhead is accessible in winter.

3. Mount Evans 14,264 feet

3R – Mount Evans Routes

3R1 – Mount Evans – Northeast Face

From Summit Lake TH at 12,850'   96 RP   2.8 mi RT   1,414' total   Class 2

This is a short, popular route. If you are more interested in an outing than a climb, this may be it. Start at the Summit Lake Trailhead at 12,850 feet. From the east side of Summit Lake, hike southeast on the road to 12,920 feet (39.5917° -105.6340°), below Evans' talus-covered northeast face. Leave the road, climb 0.6 mile southwest up the northeast face to the summit parking lot, and follow the short summit trail up to Evans' highest rock (39.5887° -105.6430°).

Do not confuse Evans' gentle northeast face with the steep northwest face. Many people have been involved in accidents on the northwest face when trying to descend to Summit Lake on foot after driving to the summit.

3R2 – Mount Evans – Chicago Creek

From Echo Lake TH at 10,580'   309 RP   12.5 mi RT   3,684' net; 4,834' total   Class 2

This route avoids most of the Mount Evans Road and is the normal route for mountaineers. From the Echo Lake Trailhead at 10,580 feet, walk south into the open woods near the southwest corner of the lake. You also can reach this point from the east end of Echo Lake by following a trail on the lake's south side.

Find the Chicago Lakes Trail near the slight ridge southwest of Echo Lake. Look for old blazes on the trees. Follow the Chicago Lakes Trail, cross to the west side of the ridge southwest of Echo Lake, descend south-southwest, and switchback down to reach Chicago Creek at 10,320 feet (39.6513° -105.6135°). This point is south of the private property at Shwayder Camp.

Cross to the west side of Chicago Creek and walk 0.8 mile south-southwest up the valley on an old dirt road to the northwest side of the Idaho Springs Reservoir at 10,620 feet (39.6381° -105.6191°). Continue on the road around the west side of the reservoir and enter the Mount Evans Wilderness southwest of the reservoir (39.6381° -105.6191°). Hike southwest on a trail to the southernmost Chicago Lake at 11,750 feet. From the southern end of this lake (39.6099° -105.6412°), climb 0.6 mile southeast up a broken Class 2 slope to Mount Warren's west ridge at 13,060 feet (39.6026° -105.6378°). Descend 0.25 mile southwest to the east side of Summit Lake at 12,850 feet. The Mount Evans Road passes Summit Lake, and this is a popular place in summer. Continue up the Northeast Face Route (3R1) to the summit.

3R2 V – Variation – Warren–Spalding Saddle Direct

Class 3

From the southernmost Chicago Lake at 11,750 feet, scramble up the slope directly into the 12,876-foot saddle (39.6018° -105.6424°) between Mount Warren and Mount Spalding. Do not stray onto the slope west of the saddle, because the difficulty increases rapidly in that direction.

3R2 EC – Extra Credit – Mount Warren 13,307 feet 39.6052° -105.6335°

Class 2

From Summit Lake, hike 0.5 mile northeast up talus to the 13,307-foot summit of Mount Warren, a ranked Thirteener.

3R3 – Mount Evans – Mount Evans Road

From Echo Lake TH at 10,580'	*388 RP*	*29.2 mi RT*	*3,684' total*	*Class 1*
Via Northeast Face Route	*339 RP*	*21.1 mi RT*	*3,684' total*	*Class 2*

This is the easiest route up Evans, but it is long and high. Start at the Echo Lake Trailhead at 10,580 feet and walk, run, ski, or bike up the Mount Evans Road. A significant shortcut for hikers uses the Northeast Face Route (3R1) above Summit Lake instead of following the road. People who have driven a car up Evans have told me, with evident pride, that they climbed the peak! Ahem. If you drive up, your vehicle has climbed the peak. You are awarded a nice view but no mountaineering credit at all.

3R3 V – Variation – Mount Evans Trophy Run

Class 1

There has been a sporadic Mount Evans Trophy Run up the Mount Evans Road. It is billed as the world's highest road race. The race starts at the gate just beyond the parking lot at the junction of Colorado 103 and Mount Evans Road, and finishes in the summit parking lot. The distance is 14.5 miles. Historically, any male finisher under 2 hours, 40 minutes, and any female finisher under 3 hours received a special trophy, usually a rock mounted on a plaque. Recently, cash awards have been given to the top finishers. Since the race ends in the summit parking lot, runners reveal a mountaineering appetite if they continue 300 feet above the parking lot to reach Evans' highest point.

Both the men and women's records were smashed on June 20, 2009. Ace Matt Carpenter, record holder for the Pikes Peak Marathon (ascent 2:01:06, marathon 3:16:39), ran the Mount Evans Road in 1:37:01 to eclipse the 31-year-old course record of 1:41:35 set by John Bramley in 1977. His pace was an amazing 6:42 per mile. Naoko Takahashi, the 2000 Olympic gold medalist in the marathon and former marathon world record holder (2:19:46), finished in 2:06:22—nearly a minute faster than the previous record of 2:07:14 set by J'ne Day-Lucore in 1990. For more information on the race, visit www.racingunder ground.com/mtevans/.

3R4 – Mount Evans – West Chicago Creek

From West Chicago Creek TH at 9,600'   436 RP   16.8 mi RT   4,664' total   Class 2

This long, arduous ascent ends with a traverse of Evans' high west ridge. The route is above treeline for 4 miles! Don't confuse West Chicago Creek with Chicago Creek.

From the West Chicago Creek Trailhead at 9,600 feet, follow the West Chicago Creek Trail 3.8 miles south to its end at 11,200 feet in Hells Hole (39.6322° -105.6730°). Continue 1.5 miles southeast then south up the narrow, rocky basin under the impressive northwest face of 13,602-foot Gray Wolf Mountain. There is a huge split boulder at the top of the basin. Climb 0.5 mile south to the 12,740-foot saddle (39.6115° -105.6749°) between Gray Wolf Mountain and Point 12,988. The introduction is over.

Contour 0.5 mile east-southeast, then climb 0.6 mile south to Mount Spalding's broad west ridge at 13,400 feet (39.6005° -105.6656°). Continue 0.75 mile southeast to the west end of Evans' west ridge at 13,900 feet (39.5915° -105.6553°). This route joins the West Ridge Route (3R5) here. Either hike 0.75 mile east on the trail south of the ridge crest (Class 2) or scamper 0.7 mile east along the crest of the airy, fun west ridge (Class 2+) to Evans' summit.

3R4 EC – Extra Credit – Gray Wolf Mountain 13,602 feet 39.6172° -105.6608°

Class 2

Gray Wolf Mountain is a Bi, one of Colorado's 200 highest ranked peaks. It is 0.5 mile east of this route, and you can reach its 13,602-foot summit by hiking up grass and talus.

3R5 – Mount Evans – West Ridge

From Guanella Pass TH at 11,640'   286 RP   8.9 mi RT   2,624' net; 3,104' total   Class 2

You can climb Evans by itself from Guanella Pass. Start at the Guanella Pass Trailhead at 11,640 feet and descend 1.0 mile gently southeast to the flats near Scott Gomer Creek at 11,400 feet (39.5897° -105.0338°). Leave the Mount Bierstadt Trail and hike 0.5 mile northeast across the shallow basin at the head of Scott Gomer Creek. Skirt west and north of all the cliffs that extend for a mile northwest of the Sawtooth and climb 0.5 mile northeast to 12,400 feet below the gentle, open slopes on the northwest side of 13,842-foot Mount Spalding. Climb 0.5 mile southeast, cross to the south side of Spalding's broad west ridge, and skirt south of Spalding's summit as you climb 1.0 mile southeast to reach the west end of Evans' west ridge at 13,900 feet (39.5915° -105.6553°). Move to the south (right) side of the ridge and hike 0.6 mile east on a well-defined trail that contours below the rocks of the ridge crest. When you reach Evans' summit area, hike 250 yards northeast over talus to Evans' highest summit boulder.

3R5 V1 – Variation – "West Evans" 14,256 feet 39.5887° -105.6495°

Class 2+

From the beginning of Evans' west ridge at 13,900 feet, scamper 0.7 mile east on the crest of the ridge to Evans' summit (Class 2+). Most of this airy, fun traverse is on solid, sculpted rock. The traverse stays above 14,000 feet as it crosses two false summits. The eastern false summit, known as "West Evans," reaches 14,256 feet and has 116 feet of prominence.

3R5 V2 – Variation – Gomer's Gully

From Guanella Pass TH at 11,640'   278 RP   8.5 mi RT   2,624' net; 3,104' total   Class 2

This significant and frequently used shortcut provides the shortest route up Evans that does not use the Mount Evans Road. Instead of climbing around the north end of all the cliffs extending northwest from the Sawtooth, continue straight east at 11,600 feet (39.5976° -105.6853°) and scamper up a scree gully known as Gomer's Gully (39.5963° -105.6690°) that goes through the center of the cliffs (Class 2). Rejoin the route on the slope above. You can easily see Gomer's Gully from Guanella Pass. It rarely holds snow in winter.

3R5 EC – Extra Credit – Mount Spalding 13,842 feet 39.5998° -105.6572°

Class 2

From the open slopes between Mount Spalding and the west end of Evans' west ridge, hike 0.5 mile north up talus to the summit of 13,842-foot Mount Spalding. With 262 feet of prominence, Spalding does not rank, but it is officially named and offers a superb view of Evans' north face.

3R6 – Mount Evans – Southwest Slopes

From Scott Gomer Creek TH at 9,620'   344 RP   16.4 mi RT   4,644' total   Class 2

This route is noteworthy because it is seldom climbed. Scott Gomer Creek offers an alternative approach to Evans' crowded northern slopes. The route is long, but easy for the most part. Start at the Scott Gomer Creek Trailhead at 9,620 feet and follow the Abyss Lake Trail 3.8 miles northeast to a trail junction at 10,600 feet. Stay on the Abyss Lake Trail for another 2.9 miles as it climbs east then north past treeline into the basin between Evans and Bierstadt.

Look for a keyhole-shaped pinnacle guarding the southern entrance to a steep scree gully on the east side of the valley. Leave the trail at 12,200 feet, climb northeast, and scamper up the scree gully north of the pinnacle to the low point of the broad 13,180-foot saddle (39.5770° -105.6342°) between Evans and 13,523-foot Epaulet Mountain. From this saddle, hike 1.0 mile northwest to reach Evans' summit. Use or avoid the switchbacking road as you desire.

3R6 EC – Extra Credit – Epaulet Mountain 13,523 feet 39.5705° -105.6320°

Class 2

From the 13,180-foot Evans–Epaulet saddle (39.5770° -105.6342°), hike 0.5 mile south to 13,523-foot Epaulet Mountain. For even more credit, continue 0.7 mile southeast to Point 13,530 (39.5668° -105.6232°). This unnamed summit is higher than Epaulet, and purists debate whether it is really Epaulet's summit. My opinion is that these are two separate summits, one named but unranked, and one ranked but unnamed. If you climb both summits, you have certainly climbed Epaulet and can add your voice to the debate. Because Point 13,530 is between Epaulet and 13,575-foot Rosalie, which is higher still, I have suggested the silly name "Epaulie" for Point 13,530.

3R7 – Mount Evans – Summit Ridge *Classic*

From Summit Lake TH at 12,850'	*180 RP*	*5.0 mi RT*	*1,414' net; 1,938' total*	*Class 2+*
With descent of Northeast Face	*150 RP*	*3.9 mi RT*	*1,414' net; 1,938' total*	*Class 2+*

This circular ridge walk with impressive views keeps you high and provides a unique approach to Evans' summit. Start at the Summit Lake Trailhead at 12,850 feet and walk 0.25 mile north along the east side of the lake on a good trail to the 12,876-foot saddle (39.6018° -105.6425°) between Mount Warren and Mount Spalding. Scamper 0.9 mile west up Spalding's east ridge to Spalding's 13,842-foot summit (39.5998° -105.6572°). Spalding is an officially named but unranked summit on the list of Colorado's 100 highest peaks. Spalding's sometimes rough Class 2+ east ridge offers a spectacular view of Evans' north face. From Spalding's summit descend 0.25 mile south to the 13,580-foot Evans–Spalding saddle (39.5965° -105.6577°), then climb 0.35 mile south and join Evans' West Ridge Route (3R5) at 13,900 feet. Either hike 0.75 mile east on the trail south of the ridge crest (Class 2) or scamper 0.7 mile east along the crest of the airy, fun west ridge (Class 2+) to Evans' summit. For solitude, return the same way. To complete a circle tour and considerably shorten your return, descend the Northeast Face Route (3R1).

3R7 V1 – Variation – Beyond Chicago

From Echo Lake TH at 10,580'	*382 RP*	*13.7 mi RT*	*3,684' net; 5,332' total*	*Class 2+*
With descent of Northeast Face	*358 RP*	*13.1 mi RT*	*3,684' net; 5,358' total*	*Class 2+*

Summit Ridge provides a roadless alpine finish to the Chicago Creek Route. Follow the Chicago Creek Route (3R2) to 13,060 feet on Mount Warren's west ridge. Descend 0.25 mile west to the 12,876-foot saddle Warren–Spalding saddle and continue on the Summit Ridge Route (3R7) to Evans' summit.

3R7 V2 – Variation – Snapshot

Class 2+

Use this variation if you want to enjoy Evans' upper west ridge but don't want to make the trek over Spalding. Walk around the north side of Summit Lake and hike northwest to 13,000 feet (39.5951° -105.6520°) at the base of an open slope. Hike northwest up this easy slope to 13,400 feet (39.5937° -105.6541°) then angle west-southwest to 13,780 feet (39.5930° -105.6564°) on the open slopes between the Evans–Spalding saddle and the beginning of Evans' upper west ridge. Join the Summit Ridge Route here and continue on it to Evans' summit.

3R8 – Mount Evans – Sunrise Couloir

From Summit Lake TH at 12,850'	*209 RP*	*4.8 mi RT*	*1,414' total*	*Class 3, Steep Snow*
With descent of Northeast Face	*176 RP*	*3.8 mi RT*	*1,414' total*	*Class 3, Steep Snow*

Sunrise Couloir rises 700 feet above the west end of Summit Lake to the Evans–Spalding saddle. The route is easily visible from Summit Lake, where you can preview conditions from the comfort of your car. This route will gratify those looking for a technical snow challenge with a minimal approach.

To avoid trampling tundra, walk 0.25 mile north along the east side of Summit Lake on a good trail to the 12,876-foot saddle between Mount Warren and Mount Spalding (39.6018° -105.6425°). Walk 0.5 mile southwest around the north side of the lake and hike 0.3 mile west to 13,000 feet, below the couloir. Although the couloir itself is a straightforward climb, a pesky cornice almost always caps it, even in late summer. Climb the steepening couloir and find a way to overcome the cornice. In most years, you can execute a clever climb by sneaking between the rock and snow on the north (right) side of the cornice (Class 3). Mortals will appreciate crampons and an ice ax. From the 13,580-foot Evans–Spalding saddle (39.5965° -105.6577°), continue on the Summit Ridge (3R7) and West Ridge routes (3R5) to Evans' summit.

The north face of Mount Evans

3R9 – Mount Evans – North Face

From Summit Lake TH at 12,850'	*147 RP*	*2.0 mi RT*	*1,414' total*	*Class 2, Mod Snow*
With descent of Northeast Face	*141 RP*	*2.4 mi RT*	*1,414' total*	*Class 2, Mod Snow*

Evans has a sweeping, mile-wide north face that extends west below the summit. The cliffs below the summit are the most serious, and difficulties moderate to the west. Although much of the face is broken, there are many technical treasures hidden here. Expert enthusiasts ski and snowboard the many available couloirs. The easiest route, described here, is a sweeping snowfield near the center of the face. This is a route for May or June. By August the upper part of this slope is odious rubble.

Start at the Summit Lake Trailhead at 12,850 feet, go to the east end of Summit Lake, and hike 0.5 mile southwest into the Summit Lake Bowl to a bench at 13,300 feet (Class 2). From here, the route is directly above you to the south. Climb the steepening, narrowing snowfield to Evans' west ridge. The steepness reaches 40 degrees, and the views halfway up the slope are distinctly alpine. The snow does not always reach the ridge. Depending on the year, you may have to steer around exposed rocks or scramble up talus as you approach the ridge. Reach Evans' west ridge in the 14,140-foot saddle midway between Point 14,256, aka "West Evans," and Evans' summit. Hike 0.2 mile east along the upper west ridge to the tippy-top.

3R10 – Mount Evans – The Snave

From Summit Lake TH at 12,850'	*204 RP*	*1.6 mi RT*	*1,414' total*	*Class 4, Steep Snow*
With descent of Northeast Face	*202 RP*	*2.2 mi RT*	*1,414' total*	*Class 4, Steep Snow*

The name *Snave* is Evans spelled backward, and it fits this serpentine tour. Start at the Summit Lake Trailhead at 12,850 feet, go to the east end of Summit Lake, and hike 0.5 mile southwest into the Summit Lake Bowl below Evans' rugged northwest face. This face has a lower cliff band and the summit cliffs. Bypass the lower cliff band on its north end. Do an ascending traverse south on the ramp between the lower and upper cliffs. This ramp holds good snow into June. Reach the inset couloir in the middle of the face and climb it. The snow steepens in the couloir and ends in rocks below the summit. Climb a Class 4 pitch up the upper couloir to reach a small notch and the tourist trail just north of the summit. Your arrival here is bound to attract attention.

Tourists trundling rocks from the summit could pelt this route with deadly missiles. Although this has not been a problem in recent years, leave early to beat rush hour on the summit.

3R11 – Mount Evans – Crystal

From Summit Lake TH at 12,850'	*201 RP*	*1.6 mi RT*	*1,414' total*	*Class 3, Steep Snow*
With descent of Northeast Face	*198 RP*	*2.2 mi RT*	*1,414' total*	*Class 3, Steep Snow*

This steep route on the south side of Evans' northwest face is a test piece for skiers and a nifty climb. You may be able to identify the climbing route by spotting ski tracks. Starting at the Summit Lake Trailhead at 12,850 feet, hike 0.5 mile southwest from the east end of Summit Lake into the Summit Lake Bowl, below Evans' northwest face. Crystal is a narrowing couloir south (right) of the cliffs below the summit. Start below the summit and climb south along the south side of the lower cliff band until you reach the summit cliffs on the upper end of the ramp that splits this face. This is the ramp used by the Snave Route (3R10). Escape the summit cliff by climbing south along the narrow, steep-sloped ramp and reach a small saddle and the tourist trail 100 yards south of the summit.

3R12 – Mount Evans – Diamond

From Summit Lake TH at 12,850'	*235 RP*	*2.1 mi RT*	*1,474' total*	*Class 4, Steep Snow*
With descent of Northeast Face	*228 RP*	*2.5 mi RT*	*1,474' total*	*Class 4, Steep Snow*

This mixed tour provides a sensuous snow slope capped by a rock challenge. Hike 0.5 mile southwest from the east end of Summit Lake into the Summit Lake Bowl, below Evans' northwest face. Diamond ascends the snow slope west of the first large rock buttress 350 yards west of the summit. The route is west of the North Face Route (3R9), and you may spot ski tracks on it in June. Climb the sweet, steepening snow until it ends below cliffs. Stay east (left) of some steep rock and climb two Class 4 pitches to reach Evans' west ridge just east of Point 14,256, aka "West Evans." Scamper east down to the 14,140-foot saddle between "West Evans" and Evans, and strut 0.2 mile east along the crest of the upper west ridge to Evans' crowning capstone.

3. Mount Bierstadt 14,060 feet

3R – Mount Bierstadt Routes
3R13 – Mount Bierstadt – West Slopes

From Guanella Pass TH at 11,640'   140 RP   6.9 mi RT   2,420' net; 2,900' total   Class 2

This is the easiest route on Bierstadt. Start at the Guanella Pass Trailhead at 11,640 feet and descend 1.0 mile gently southeast to the flats near Scott Gomer Creek at 11,400 feet (39.5897° -105.0338°). A controversial boardwalk trail winds through the north end of a sea of willows and makes life easy.

Before the trail appeared, hardened mountaineers took a direct line toward the summit and bashed through the heart of the willows. Clever mountaineers attempted to find a lost trail through the south end of the willows, but spent even more time thrashing around. People wearing shorts went way around the south end of the willows and spent a long time climbing Bierstadt. People without a mission went a little way into the willows and returned to the pass. So, to protect this wetland area, the proverbial powers built a boardwalk trail across it. However, there are new rumblings that the boardwalk may have to be removed since you cannot have a human construction in a wilderness area.

Mount Bierstadt from the northeast.

Always pay attention to the mountain for safety and the environment for sanity, not the human écœurement.

Once you are past the willows (39.5863° -105.6905°), continue on the Class 1 trail as it winds up Bierstadt's lower, steeper western slope to a point on Bierstadt's broad northwest ridge at 12,250 feet (39.5928° -105.6845°). From here, you can look across the upper Scott Gomer drainage at the impressive Sawtooth that separates Bierstadt and Evans. Continue southeast up the excellent trail on Bierstadt's upper northwest-facing slope to a shoulder southwest of the summit at 13,780 feet (39.5803° -105.6725°). From the shoulder, scamper 0.25 mile northeast across Class 2 boulders just north of the ridge to the summit (39.5825° -105.6887°).

On winter climbs, keep the following facts in mind. Winter's strong west winds blow freely across Guanella Pass. The wind is at your back on the ascent, but you must face it on the return. Many cold parties turn to discover that the return trip into the wind is much worse than the climb. Many parties become disoriented in whiteouts when returning across the flats near Scott Gomer Creek. Some parties have even turned south and descended into the depths of the Scott Gomer Creek drainage. This is a bad mistake, because it leaves you many miles from Guanella Pass. It is prudent to use a compass or GPS to protect your retreat. Finally, remember that the last mile back to the pass is uphill!

3R13 V – Variation – Northwest Gully

Class 2+

To add a mountaineering flair to this easy route, leave the trail at 13,200 feet (39.5831° -105.6770°) and do an ascending traverse west toward a gully just west of Bierstadt's small, steep north face. Get into the gully at 13,600 feet (39.5837° -105.6715°) and climb up it. The gully can provide a moderate snow climb in winter and spring and will be a Class 2+ talus scamper in summer. Near the summit, you can bear west (right) for the easiest route or east (left) to look for some Class 3 scrambling.

3R14 – Mount Bierstadt – East Ridge *Classic*

From Scott Gomer Creek TH at 9,620'	*371 RP*	*15.0 mi RT*	*4,440' net; 4,802' total*	*Class 3*
With descent of Northeast Face	*348 RP*	*15.8 mi RT*	*4,440' net; 4,621' total*	*Class 3*

This is the most interesting route on Bierstadt, but it is seldom climbed. The ridge is surprisingly rugged as it crosses Point 13,641. The rock is beautiful and solid. You can climb this ridge via Scott Gomer Creek or on a blitz from the Mount Evans Road. This description assumes the Scott Gomer Creek approach. See Combination 3C3 for the approach from the Mount Evans Road.

Start at the Scott Gomer Creek Trailhead at 9,620 feet and hike 5.8 miles northeast on the Abyss Lake Trail (FT 602) to 11,800 feet (39.5663° -105.6536°). From here you can see an impressive buttress forming the bottom of Bierstadt's east ridge. Leave the trail, hike 0.6 mile north up an open slope, and reach Bierstadt's east ridge at 13,100 feet (39.5741° -105.6534°), above the initial buttress.

Head 0.2 mile northwest up the ridge, scampering over and around some large blocks to reach Point 13,420 (39.5755° -105.6556°). From here you can see the next challenge, which is an improbable ridge rising up to Point 13,641. Scramble to the bottom of more difficult climbing and traverse northwest on a grassy, sloping ledge on the northeast (right) side of the ridge (Class 3). When difficulties above you relent, climb to the ridge crest (Class 3). Continue on or near the now broader ridge crest and scramble up a beautiful Class 3 slab with two parallel cracks in it to reach Point 13,641 (39.5778° -105.6577°). Scramble west over Point 13,641 and do a Class 3 descent to reach easier ground near a sybaritic 13,540-foot saddle. Sail 0.6 mile northwest on the upper east ridge to the summit.

3R14 V – Variation – Northeast Face

From Scott Gomer Creek TH at 9,620'	*304 RP*	*16.6 mi RT*	*4,440' total*	*Class 2*

If the east ridge is not to your liking, continue on the trail all the way to Abyss Lake at 12,650 feet (39.5840° -105.6566°) and climb Bierstadt's northeast face (Class 2). This route provides an easier descent after an ascent of the East Ridge Route.

3R15 – Mount Bierstadt – South Ridge

From Scott Gomer Creek TH at 9,620'   354 RP   13.7 mi RT   4,440' total   Class 2

This ridge provides another salubrious sojourn on Bierstadt's back side. Start at the Scott Gomer Creek Trailhead at 9,620 feet and hike 3.8 miles northeast on the Abyss Lake Trail (FT 602) to a trail junction at 10,620 feet (39.5495° -105.6745°). This point is at the base of Bierstadt's 3-mile-long south ridge. Stay on the Abyss Lake Trail for another 0.25 mile, leave the trail at 10,800 feet, and bushwhack 300 yards straight north to reach the rounded ridge. Bushwhack 0.6 mile northeast on the ridge to treeline at 11,840 feet (39.5602° -105.6643°). From here the route is clear. Follow the now distinct ridge 1.4 miles north to Bierstadt's south shoulder at 13,780 feet (39.5803° -105.6725°). As you approach the shoulder, you have some unique views of Frozen Lake in the basin to the north. The West Slopes Route (3R13) also reaches the south shoulder, and you are likely to meet other people here. From the shoulder, climb 0.25 mile northeast across Class 2 boulders just north of the ridge to the summit (39.5825° -105.6887°).

3R16 – Mount Bierstadt – South Face

From Scott Gomer Creek TH at 9,620'   392 RP   15.0 mi RT   4,440' total   Class 2, Steep Snow
With descent of South Ridge   386 RP   14.4 mi RT   4,440' total   Class 2, Steep Snow

This route offers industrious mountaineers a chance to visit Frozen Lake and enjoy more than 1,000 feet of fanciful snow climbing. This south face is best climbed in May or early June after a heavy-snow winter.

Start at the Scott Gomer Creek Trailhead at 9,620 feet and hike 3.8 miles northeast on the Abyss Lake Trail (FT 602) to a trail junction at 10,620 feet (39.5495° -105.6745°). Continue 2.0 miles on the Abyss Lake Trail and find a heart-shaped lake at 11,730 feet (39.5642° -105.6575°). Continue west over a small ridge and hike into the drainage below Frozen Lake. Climb 0.8 mile north up this drainage, then climb west through broken cliffs to reach Frozen Lake at 12,940 feet (39.5775° -105.6668°). Climbers seldom visit this well-named lake. From the lake's north side, climb 1,120 feet north up the consistent slope directly to Bierstadt's summit.

If snow conditions are favorable, glissade back to Frozen Lake and return as you came. If you prefer, a descent of the South Ridge Route (3R15) completes a southern Tour de Bierstadt.

3C – Evans and Bierstadt Combination Routes
3C1 – The Sawtooth *Classic*

From Guanella Pass TH at 11,640'   330 RP   10.6 mi RT   2,624' net; 4,824' total   Class 3
With descent of Evans' West Ridge   294 RP   9.8 mi RT   2,624' net; 3,964' total   Class 3

Bierstadt is 1.4 miles west of Evans, and you can climb these two peaks together by starting at Guanella Pass. The ridge connecting Evans with Bierstadt contains a step called the Sawtooth, which looks more difficult than it is. This high, wonderful ridge traverse is fun when it is dry.

Start by climbing Bierstadt's West Slopes Route (3R13). From Bierstadt's summit, descend 0.4 mile north to 13,200 feet on the east side of the 13,340-foot saddle between Bierstadt and the Sawtooth. Bypass some initial gendarmes on the ridge's east side. From a point below a second saddle, scramble up, do a rolling traverse on the ridge's east side, then scramble up a shallow, grass- and rock-studded gully to the ridge crest (Class 3). This portion of the route is usually well cairned. Cross to the ridge's west side, traverse on a large but exposed ledge below the ridge crest, cross a scree gully, and scramble up a large, sloping, diagonal ramp through the Sawtooth's cliff band to reach easier ground (some Class 3). Several cairns mark the top of the diagonal ledge to help you find it if you choose to do this traverse in the other direction.

Once you are past the Sawtooth, hike 0.5 mile east across open slopes to the beginning of Evans' west ridge at 13,900 feet. Either hike 0.75 mile east on the trail south of the ridge crest (Class 2) or scamper 0.7 mile east along the crest of the airy, fun west ridge (Class 2+) to Evans' summit. Descend Evans' West Ridge Route (3R5) to return to Guanella Pass.

3C2 – Bierstadt South Ridge → Sawtooth → Evans Southwest Slopes

From Scott Gomer Creek TH at 9,620'   471 RP   16.9 mi RT   4,644' net; 5,504' total   Class 3

This is tough. Start at the Scott Gomer Creek Trailhead at 9,620 feet and climb Bierstadt's South Ridge Route (3R15). Continue to Evans via the Sawtooth (Combination 3C1). Descend Evans' Southwest Slopes Route (3R6).

3C3 – Tour de Abyss *Classic*

From 13,300' on Mount Evans Road   269 RP   4.9 mi RT   964' net; 2,985' total   Class 3

This route maximizes excitement and minimizes walking. It traverses the best ridges Evans and Bierstadt have to offer. Start at the switchback on the Mount Evans Road at 13,300 feet (39.5795° -105.6373°) near the broad saddle between Evans and 13,523-foot Epaulet Mountain. This switchback is 11.4 miles from Echo Lake, and there is parking available at the switchback.

Hike 0.2 mile south down to the low point of the 13,180-foot Evans–Epaulet saddle, then descend west down a steep scree gully (39.5763° -105.6390°) to the lake fork of Scott Gomer Creek at 12,320 feet. Hike west across the valley near a small unnamed lake at 12,340 feet (39.5752° -105.6477°), then climb west up an open slope to reach Bierstadt's east ridge at 13,100 feet (39.5741° -105.6534°). Follow the upper part of Bierstadt's East Ridge Route (3R14) to Bierstadt's summit. Traverse to Evans via the Sawtooth (Combination 3C1). From Evans' summit, descend 0.8 mile southeast to your starting point.

3C4 – Evans Egis

From Echo Lake TH at 10,580'   987 RP   25.6 mi RT   10,200' total   Class 3

This is the big one. Because of the road, Mount Evans has a reputation for being a trivial outing, but in reality, Evans is a huge massif with multiple long, high ridges extending over many satellite peaks. This expert hiker's tour allows you to experience the real Mount Evans. It captures 11 summits and is a longer day than the Grand or Radical Slams on Longs.

Start at the Echo Lake Trailhead at 10,580 feet, hike south up the hill through the trees, cross the road three times, and reach your first summit—12,216-foot Goliath Peak. You are now launched on Evans' long northeast ridge. Hike southwest along the ridge, cross the road in a 12,152-foot saddle, hike southwest over 13,391-foot Rogers Peak, and continue southwest to 13,307-foot Mount Warren. From here, you will have a nice view of Evans' northeast and north faces, but you are just getting warmed up. From Warren, hike west down to the 12,876-foot saddle just north of Summit Lake, join Evans' Summit Ridge Route (3R7), continue west to 13,842-foot Mount Spalding, follow the ridge south then east, cross 14,256-foot "West Evans," and continue to the summit of Evans—your sixth summit. You are at your expedition's highpoint, but you are less than halfway.

From Evans, using or avoiding the road as you choose, descend southeast to the broad, 13,180-foot Evans–Epaulet saddle. Finally free of the road, continue southeast to 13,523-foot Epaulet Mountain and 13,530-foot "Epaulie." Now it gets tough. Continue southeast to 13,575-foot Rosalie Peak, which is the major summit of Evans' long east ridge. From Rosalie, descend west into an unnamed basin, do a long contour west, then descend into Scott Gomer Creek. Climb either Bierstadt's Class 2 south ridge (3R15) or Class 3 east ridge (3R14) to Bierstadt—your 10th summit. Bierstadt is the culmination of Evans' west ridge. From Bierstadt, follow Combination 3C1—the Sawtooth (Class 3)—to the open slopes where you exit the Sawtooth's difficulties. Hike north, contour below Spalding, which you have already climbed, and continue north to 13,602-foot Gray Wolf Mountain—your 11th and final peak. Gray Wolf is the major summit of Evans' sprawling, northwest massif.

From Gray Wolf, do a long descent northeast, drop into the Chicago Creek drainage, and follow the trail back to the Echo Lake Trailhead. Do 50 pushups. Collapse. On July15, 2006, Steve Nicholls did a version of this tour in 15 hours 30 minutes, but he neglected to do the 50 push-ups because I had not written this description yet. Who's next?

4. Pikes Peak 14,110 feet

Pikes Peak is the easternmost Fourteener in the United States and needs little introduction. It soars west of the Colorado Springs metropolitan area and is often the first peak seen when approaching the Rocky Mountains from the east. Its colorful history has been told many times.

Pikes is the southern Front Range's monarch and the highest peak in El Paso County. Pikes has the largest elevation gain in Colorado. The peak rises a stupendous 7,800 vertical feet above downtown Manitou Springs in a horizontal distance of 7.25 miles. No other Colorado peak can match that! Because of Pikes' direct sweep above the plains, it is not surprising that it has the lowest trailhead in this book. In an interesting twist, Pikes also has the highest trailhead in this book due to its summit road.

Each year, thousands of people reach Pikes' summit by road, rail, and trail. People run, roll, ride, bike, hike, ski, camp, stamp, stomp, and sell Pikes. In 1893, after reaching the summit of Pikes Peak and feeling "on top of the world," Katharine Lee Bates was inspired to write the opening lines of "America the Beautiful."

4E – Pikes Peak Essentials

Elevations	14,110' (NGVD29) 14,115' (NAVD88)
Rank	Colorado's 30th highest ranked peak
Location	El Paso County, Colorado, USA
Range	Southern Front Range
Summit Coordinates	38.8400° -105.0428° (WGS84)
Ownership/Contact	Pike National Forest – City of Colorado Springs inholding
	US Forest Service – Pikes Peak District – 719-636-1602
Prominence and Saddle	5,530' from 8,580' saddle south of Florissant
Isolation and Parent	60.88 miles to Mount Evans
USGS Maps	**Pikes Peak**, Manitou Springs, Woodland Park, Cascade
USFS Map	Pike National Forest
Trails Illustrated Map	Map #137 Pikes Peak/Cañon City
Book Map	See Map 4 on page 54
Nearest Towns	Manitou Springs – Population 5,000 – Elevation 6,412'
	Colorado Springs – Population 400,000 – Elevation 6,035'
Pikes Peak 🏃 Easiest Route	4R1 – East Slopes – Class 1
	A Class 1 hike on a trail all the way to the top
Pikes' Accolades	Pikes is the highest peak in El Paso County and the easternmost Fourteener
	in the United States. Pikes, an Ultra Prominent Peak, is one of only three
	Colorado peaks with more than 5,000' of prominence. There is a gravel road
	to Pikes' summit.

4T – Pikes Peak Trailheads

4T1 – Manitou Springs Trailhead 6,700 feet 38.8557° -104.9340°

This trailhead provides access to the Barr Trail on Pikes' east side. Go 0.4 mile west on the US 24 Business Loop from City Hall in the center of Manitou Springs. At a wide intersection with a roundabout, turn west (left) onto well-marked Ruxton Avenue and go 0.7 mile west to the cog railway depot. Continue 0.1 mile west past the depot, turn north (right) onto Hydro Street (paved), and go 100 steep yards north to the large parking lot at the well-marked trailhead. Although large, this parking lot fills up early on summer weekends, sometimes

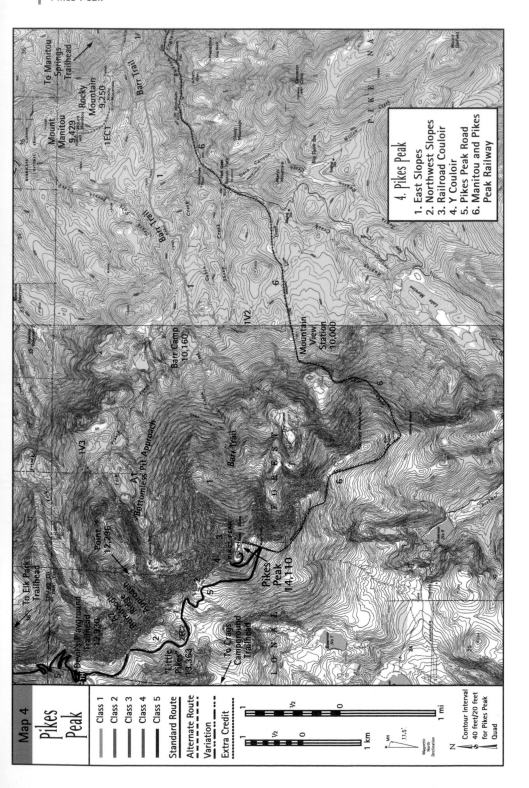

Map 4

Pikes Peak

Class 1
Class 2
Class 3
Class 4
Class 5

Standard Route

Alternate Route

Variation

Extra Credit

1 mi

1 km

Contour Interval
40 feet/20 feet
for Pikes Peak
Quad

4. Pikes Peak
1. East Slopes
2. Northwest Slopes
3. Railroad Couloir
4. Y Couloir
5. Pikes Peak Road
6. Manitou and Pikes
   Peak Railway

as early at 5:30 in the morning. Arrive earlier. By a large margin, this is the lowest trailhead in this book and it is accessible in winter.

4T2 – Crags Campground Trailhead 10,100 feet 38.8712° -105.1193°

This trailhead provides access to Pikes' northwest side. Take Exit 141 off Interstate 25 and go 18.4 miles west on US 24 to the junction of Colorado 67 and US 24 in Woodland Park. Continue 6.8 miles west on the combined Colorado 67 and US 24 to the next junction of Colorado 67 and US 24 in the small community of Divide. Leave US 24, turn south (left) onto Colorado 67, and go 4.3 miles to Teller County 62 (dirt). This poorly marked junction has two small signs, one for the Rocky Mountain Camp and the other for the Crags Campground. Turn east (left) onto Teller County 62 and go 1.6 miles to the Rocky Mountain Camp. Turn south (right) onto the main road and continue 1.6 miles to the entrance to the Crags Campground. Turn east (left) into the campground and go 0.3 mile to the well-marked trailhead on the campground's east side. Winter road closure is near the Rocky Mountain Camp.

4T3 – Elk Park Trailhead 11,900 feet 38.8755° -105.0663°

This trailhead is on the Pikes Peak Road and provides access to the Elk Park Trail and Barr Camp. Take Exit 141 off Interstate 25 and go 10.0 miles west on US 24 to Cascade. Follow good signs and turn onto the Pikes Peak Road. Follow the toll road for 13.0 miles to Glen Cove. Continue 1.0 mile to the trailhead at mile 14. The trailhead is on the road's east side, midway through a sweeping north-to-south turn. The winter road closure is at Glen Cove at 11,500 feet.

4T4 – Devil's Playground Trailhead 12,930 feet 38.8638° -105.0677°

This trailhead is on the Pikes Peak Road at 12,930 feet and provides access to Pikes' north side, including Bottomless Pit. Take Exit 141 off Interstate 25 and go 10.0 miles west on US 24 to Cascade. Follow good signs and turn onto the Pikes Peak Road. Follow the toll road for 16.0 miles past Glen Cove and the Elk Park Trailhead to the Devil's Playground in the 12,930-foot saddle between Point 13,070 and Pikes' long, ambling northwest ridge. There is ample off-road parking here.

This is the highest trailhead in this book, but there are several constraints to using it. The road is not open to Devil's Playground in winter; the winter road closure is at Glen Cove at 11,500 feet. The road above Glen Cove opens just before Memorial Day each year. Even when open, the road is closed at night, and no overnight parking is allowed along the road. The road opens at 9:30 AM each day, which negates early morning starts from this trailhead. The evening closing time varies but is never later than 10 PM; it may be much earlier in bad weather. Walking on the road or its shoulder and hitchhiking are illegal. You must walk at least 50 feet from the road; 100 feet is better. Frequent road patrols enforce these restrictions.

4A – Pikes Peak Approaches

4A1 – Pikes Peak – Bottomless Pit Trail Approach

From Manitou Springs TH at 6,700'	*189 RP*	*17.2 mi RT*	*4,940' total*	*Class 1*
From Barr Camp at 10,160'	*63 RP*	*6.0 mi RT*	*1,480' total*	*Class 1*

You can use this approach to reach the technical routes on Pikes' north face. You can reach Bottomless Pit, the dramatic bowl below the north face, by a long trail hike. Start at the Manitou Springs Trailhead at 6,700 feet and follow the Barr Trail for 5.6 miles to Barr Camp at 10,160 feet (**38.8483° -105.0070°**). Continue 1.0 mile on the Barr Trail to the prominent switchback at 10,840 feet (**38.8503° -105.0172°**). Leave the Barr Trail and hike 2.0 miles gently upward around Pikes' broad northeast slopes on the Bottomless Pit Trail into the Pit at 11,640 feet (**38.8535° -105.0468°**).

4A2 – Pikes Peak – Rumdoodle Ridge Approach

From Devil's Playground TH at 12,930'	*185 RP*	*6.0 mi RT*	*240' net; 1,770' total*	*Class 3*
From 13,100' on Pikes Peak Road	*150 RP*	*2.5 mi RT*	*70' net; 1,600' total*	*Class 3*

Rumdoodle Ridge is a shorter but much more difficult approach route to Bottomless Pit. Start at the Devil's Playground Trailhead at 12,930 feet and walk south on a trail above the road. Walking along the popular road or its shoulder and hitchhiking are illegal, so walk on the trail, not the road. Stay above the road as you skirt Point 13,190 (**38.8617° -105.0650°**) on its west side, descend slightly to a 12,925-foot saddle (**38.8572° -105.0632°**) right next to the road, and skirt Point 13,250 (**38.8546° -105.0600°**) on its west side. Cross a 13,125-foot saddle (**38.8519° -105.0603°**), then skirt Point 13,363 (**38.8494° -105.0596°**), aka "Little Pikes," on its east side; this is a good shortcut that provides brief relief from the road. Reach the 13,110-foot saddle (**38.8495° -105.0563°**) between "Little Pikes" and the small Point 13,230 to the east.

You can also park or be dropped off at 13,100 feet on the road just after it traverses around to the southeast side of 13,363-foot "Little Pikes." This point is 1.8 miles beyond Devil's Playground and just south of the 13,110-foot saddle. Remember, there is no overnight parking allowed on the Pikes Peak Road.

From the 13,110-foot saddle, go 0.2 mile northeast, skirting Point 13,230 on its west side and find the top of Rumdoodle Ridge just beyond, at 13,170 feet (**38.8516° -105.0550°**). This is the highpoint of your approach; it's downhill from here. Scramble 0.5 mile northeast down the rocky ridge (Class 3) to a 12,250-foot saddle (**38.8561° -105.0491°**). This ridge requires careful route finding to keep the difficulty at Class 3, since harder climbing lurks in the many small cliffs. From the 12,250-foot saddle, contour 0.1 mile northeast to the southeast side of the very small Point 12,296, descend 0.2 mile east to a 12,070-foot saddle (**38.8562° -105.0460°**), then descend 0.2 mile straight south to the bottom of Bottomless Pit at 11,640 feet (**38.8535° -105.0468°**). Now you are set to climb to the sky.

4R – Pikes Peak Routes

4R1 – Pikes Peak – East Slopes *Classic*

From Manitou Springs TH at 6,700'   419 RP   25.8 mi RT   7,410' total   Class 1

This is the easiest hiking route on Pikes' east side. From the Manitou Springs Trailhead at 6,700 feet, follow the Barr Trail as it winds up Pikes' eastern slopes for 12.9 miles to the summit. The elevation gain is a brutal 7,410 vertical feet, Colorado's greatest vertical rise. The excellent trail breaks naturally into four segments, each with its own personality and challenges.

The first trail segment takes you up the east slopes of Rocky Mountain and Mount Manitou. You meet their challenge immediately above the trailhead as the trail switchbacks steeply up these east slopes. The trail distance and elevation are marked with large metal signs with holes for the letters. The first sign reads "Peak 12 MI, Elev. 7,200." These signs were placed a long time ago, and you should only use the information as a general guide, because both distance and elevation are often wrong. The first sign is no exception, especially when compared with the sign at the trailhead.

After the first set of switchbacks, the trail flattens out and passes through a natural rock arch. Beyond the arch you will learn the law of the Barr Trail: a steep section quickly follows every flat section. Beyond the arch, climb steeply through two switchbacks and continue straight at the junction (38.8562° -104.9547°) with the trail leading north to the top of the old Mount Manitou incline cog railway. The trail descends briefly, then climbs to cross No Name Creek at 8,720 feet. A sign here reads "Pikes Peak Summit 9.5, Barr Camp 3.5."

The second trail segment takes you to Barr Camp. After a set of switchbacks, the trail flattens and occasionally descends as it rolls along through a Hansel and Gretel forest toward your still-distant goal. This is the easiest stretch of the Barr Trail. Enjoy it. Pass a sign that reads "Pikes Peak Summit 7.5, Top of Incline 2.5" and continue to another sign that reads "Barr Trail Elev. 9,800', Barr Camp .5, Pikes Peak Summit 6.5, Manitou Springs 6.5." Continue straight at the trail junction (38.8478° -104.9985°) near this sign. The trail heading south goes 1.5 miles to the Mountain View Station on the Manitou and Pikes Peak Cog Railway. See Variation 4R1 V2 for details on this trail.

Halfway into your ascent in both distance and elevation gain, the trail reaches Barr Camp at 10,160 feet (38.8478° -105.0067°). It is hidden in the trees just north of the trail and is operated under permit from the Forest Service. Constructed in the early 1920s by Fred Barr, the designer and builder of the Barr Trail, Barr Camp offers many amenities for weary hikers. There are two cabins, an A-frame, and two lean-to shelters for overnight stays. You might consider spending a night at Barr Camp to cut Pikes Peak down to size.

You can sleep on a bunk in the main cabin, reserve the upper cabin, which sleeps 10, or reserve the A-frame, which sleeps 4. Tent camping is also available. The cabins have propane cookstoves, mattresses, a fireplace, picnic tables, and even a well-stocked library. There is water here, which any hiker can access, but

Pikes Peak from the east.

you should purify it yourself. There are a limited number of 24-ounce bottles of spring water for sale, but not enough bottles to supply large groups. You can buy an all-you-can-eat breakfast or a dinner, but bring your own lunch. You can also buy T-shirts, sodas, and candy. Donations are appreciated. If Pikes Peak is not providing enough exercise, you can play horseshoes, badminton, and volleyball. To reserve the A-frame, lean-to shelters, and upper cabin visit www.barrcamp .com. The 20 bunks in the main cabin are rented on a first-come, first-served basis. Groups of five or more should always notify Barr Camp in advance. Refreshed by your stop at Barr Camp, you can return to the task of climbing Pikes Peak.

The third trail segment takes you to treeline. Immediately beyond Barr Camp, continue straight at the junction with the Elk Park Trail, which goes 4.5 miles north and west to the Elk Park Trailhead (4T3) at mile 14 on the toll road. See Variation 4R1 V3 for details on this trail. Pass a helicopter landing pad 200 yards beyond Barr Camp, east of the trail. Above Barr Camp, the trail finally climbs in earnest again and passes close to Cabin Creek before climbing northwest to the junction with the Bottomless Pit Trail (38.8503° -105.0173°) at 10,840 feet. The sign here reads "Pikes Peak Summit 4.8, Bottomless Pit 2.4." Do not continue straight here but switchback to the south before the rock in front of the sign.

From the switchback, climb 0.6 mile steadily southwest, then negotiate 15 switchbacks up to the A-frame shelter near treeline at 11,900 feet. Look for a sign that reads "Timberline shelter, Pike National Forest." From this sign, the A-frame shelter is down to your left. The sturdy shelter can provide a welcome respite, especially in bad weather. It is not associated with Barr Camp.

The fourth trail segment takes you to the summit. Two short switchbacks above the A-frame is a sign that reads "Barr Trail Elev 11,500', Pikes Peak

Summit 3." The elevation is wrong on this sign; it is closer to 11,950 feet. As you approach treeline, you go through a grotesque dead forest that burned in 1910. Above the trees, Pikes' upper east face, and your final challenge, sweeps up in a singular slope.

A mind-numbing 23 switchbacks above the A-frame shelter near treeline is a sign that reads "Barr Trail Elev 12,700', Pikes Peak Summit 2." These are encouraging numbers, but you may be too tired to appreciate them. A 0.7-mile ascending traverse takes you from the north edge of the east face to some teeth-like notches on the south edge, where you can peer south into Pikes' southern cirque. The trail switchbacks near the cirque's edge, past a sign that reads "Peak 1 Mi, Elev 13,300." You must be close; the sign writers no longer felt the need to remind you that the peak you are climbing is Pikes.

The trail has some rough spots as it strains for the summit, where you can see tourists watching you. Your final challenge is the 16 Golden Stairs. A Golden Stair is a switchback pair, so you have 32 switchbacks to go. Six switchbacks below the summit is a memorial plaque to Fred Barr, who constructed this amazing trail between 1914 and 1918.

At the summit (38.8400° -105.0428°), you enter another universe. You will join many people who reached this point by road or rail. As you explore the summit and, perhaps, buy refreshments in the cafeteria, you can rest with the knowledge that you have *climbed* Pikes Peak. Purists will seek out the mountain's true highpoint, which is west of the summit house where a sign atop a rock monument is the traditional place to pose for a summit photograph. Remember that from this ubiquitously known summit you can see from sea to shining sea. All you have to do is ignore the crowds and look beyond the horizon.

4R1 V1 – Variation – Englemann Canyon

Class 1

From the intersection of upper Ruxton Avenue and Hydro Street, 100 steep yards below the Manitou Springs Trailhead, continue southwest on Ruxton Avenue. Avoiding private property, stay north (right) at a V intersection (usually gated) and walk 0.4 mile southwest on a lane along the northwest side of Ruxton Creek in Englemann Canyon. The cog railway is on the other side of the creek. At 6,900 feet, where there is a short section of chain-link fence along the creek side of the lane, leave the lane, switchback to the northeast (right), and hike 200 yards northeast on a spur trail to join the Barr Trail at one of its switchbacks at 7,000 feet. This is the route used by the Pikes Peak Marathon (4R1 EC2).

4R1 V2 – Variation – Mountain View Station

Class 1

Buy a halfway ticket on the Manitou and Pikes Peak Cog Railway and get off at the Mountain View Station at 10,000 feet. Hike 1.5 miles north on a trail and join the Barr Trail at 9,820 feet (38.8478° -104.9985°). Barr Camp is 0.6 mile west of this junction. This approach greatly reduces the effort needed to reach Barr Camp, but be aware that you cannot reboard the train at Mountain View or at the summit without having purchased a ticket in advance.

4R1 V3 – Variation – Elk Park Trailhead

Class 1

This variation provides you with some interesting options. Start at the Elk Park Trailhead at 11,900 feet and descend 1.3 miles southeast on the Elk Park Trail to a trail junction at 11,150 feet. Turn east (left) at this junction, cross French Creek's north fork, and continue east then southeast on a long contour at 10,700 feet. Descend to cross French Creek's south fork at 10,200 feet and contour south to join the Barr Trail just west of Barr Camp. It is 4.5 miles from the Elk Park Trailhead to Barr Camp.

4R1 EC1 – Extra Credit – Rocky Mountain 9,250 feet 38.8597° -104.9578°
Mount Manitou 9,429 feet 38.8647° -104.9637°

Class 2

If climbing Pikes Peak is not enough for you, leave the Barr Trail at No Name Creek at 8,720 feet and hike 0.3 mile north on a Class 1 trail to Rocky Mountain's 9,250-foot summit. To complete your day, continue 0.6 mile northwest (Class 2) to Mount Manitou's 9,429-foot summit.

4R1 EC2 – Extra Credit – Pikes Peak Marathon

Class 1

If hiking up the Barr Trail leaves you fresh, run the Pikes Peak Marathon. The famous race is one of America's premier mountain runs. The race, held in mid-August each year, starts and finishes in Manitou Springs, which increases the mileage to 26.21 miles and the elevation gain to 7,815 feet. To reduce congestion on the trail, there are two races. The ascent is held on Saturday, and the round-trip marathon on Sunday. In recent years, more than 2,000 people have been finishing the two races, with the ascent being more than twice as popular as the grueling marathon. A few souls called doublers do the two races on successive days.

The male ascent record is 2:01:06, set by 29-year-old Matt Carpenter in 1993. He set this astonishing time en route to his round-trip marathon record of 3:16:39. Matt's records have endured for more than 16 years. The female ascent record is 2:33:31 seconds, set by 24-year-old Lynn Bjorklund in 1981 en route to her round-trip marathon record of 4:15:18. Lynn's impressive records have endured for more than a quarter century. There are records for each five-year age group for ages 16 to 89. For more information on the Pikes Peak Marathon, visit www.skyrunner.com.

There is also a winter record. On January 10, 2010, Steve Bremner went from the Manitou Springs Trailhead to the summit in 3:21:55 and returned to the Manitou Springs Trailhead with a round-trip time of 5:37.

4R2 – Pikes Peak – Northwest Slopes

From Crags Campground TH at 10,100'	*257 RP*	*12.8 mi RT*	*4,010' total*	*Class 2*
From Devil's Playground TH at 12,930'	*127 RP*	*5.8 mi RT*	*1,180' total*	*Class 2*

This alternative to the popular Barr Trail requires far less effort. This is also a good route to use when the Pikes Peak Road is closed for the season. Start at the Crags Campground Trailhead at 10,100 feet and go 220 yards east on the Crags Trail (FT 664) to three pipes sticking out of the ground on the north (left) side of the trail. Continue 30 yards east of the pipes to a signed trail junction. Leave the Crags Trail, angle southeast downhill on FT 753 signed for Devil's Playground, cross a log bridge to the south side of a creek, and go east on an old rocky road between two creeks. Finding this old road is the key to this route.

Follow the old road 1.0 mile east. In this mile, the road crosses to the south side of a second creek, then back to the north side at 10,900 feet under a soaring block of rock to the north. The drainage east of this point opens into a sweeping basin. Follow the old road as it climbs the slope to the east. At 11,200 feet, leave the northeast-angling road and climb east on a strong climber's trail. Switchback twice, angle southeast, and climb steeply to the highest trees at 11,800 feet.

The strong trail continues for a few hundred yards into the tundra, then slowly fades but remains discernible. To avoid trampling tundra, try to follow the trail up the lush tundra slope as you angle slightly south (right) to reach the broad 12,710-foot saddle at the top of the slope. From here, Pikes pops into view and you can see Pikes Peak Road and the upper part of the route.

From the 12,710-foot saddle (38.8633° -105.0800°), walk 0.7 mile northeast then east on an old spur road (closed to vehicles) through a small rock pass to the Devil's Playground Trailhead (4T4), which is in a 12,930-foot saddle (38.8638° -105.0677°) on Pikes Peak Road. This saddle is east of Point 13,070, aka "Devil's Playground Peak," on Pikes' long northwest ridge. You could start this route at the Devil's Playground Trailhead, but I do not recommend that choice because of the road restrictions.

Cross to the east side of Pikes Peak Road and walk south above the road on a trail. Walking along the popular road or its shoulder and hitchhiking are illegal, so walk on the trail, not the road. Stay above the road as you skirt Point 13,190 (38.8617° -105.0650°) on its west side, descend slightly to a 12,925-foot saddle (38.8572° -105.0632°) right next to the road, and skirt Point 13,250 (38.8546° -105.0600°) on its west side. Cross a 13,125-foot saddle (38.8519° -105.0603°), then skirt Point 13,363 (38.8494° -105.0596°), aka "Little Pikes," on its east side to reach the 13,110-foot saddle (38.8495° -105.0563°) between "Little Pikes" and the small Point 13,230 to the east. This is a good shortcut that provides brief relief from the road; only 1,000 feet to go! From the 13,110-foot saddle, hike 0.5 mile southeast, staying east of the road. At 13,400 feet (38.8461° -105.0505°), move away from the road and climb 0.6 mile up talus (Class 2) on Pikes' upper northwest slope to the broad summit.

4R2 EC1 – Extra Credit – "Devil's Playground Peak" 13,070 feet 38.8642° -105.0705°

Class 2

From Devil's Playground Trailhead, hike 280 yards west up talus to the summit of Point 13,070, also known as "Devil's Playground Peak." This humble summit has the distinction of being the highest point in Teller County, and you might as well bag it while you are so close.

4R2 EC2 – Extra Credit – "Little Pikes" 13,363 feet 38.8494° -105.0596°

Class 2

When you skirt Point 13,363, aka "Little Pikes," on its east side, hike 220 yards southwest up talus to this petite peak.

4R3 – Pikes Peak – Railroad Couloir

From Manitou Springs TH at 6,700'	579 RP	20.8 mi RT	7,410' total	Class 3, Steep Snow
From Devil's Playground TH at 12,930'	498 RP	8.2 mi RT	4,240' total	Class 3, Steep Snow
From Barr Camp at 10,160'	378 RP	8.2 mi RT	3,950' total	Class 3, Steep Snow
From Bottomless Pit at 11,640'	285 RP	2.2 mi RT	2,470' total	Class 3, Steep Snow

Many people are surprised to learn that Pikes has exciting technical routes. Not surprisingly, they are on Pikes' north face. The Railroad Couloir, in spite of its name, provides a titillating, sky-reaching snow climb in a rugged setting. It is the easiest route on Pikes' north face. Snow conditions are best in May and June, and the couloir is bare in August. Preview conditions from a distance before committing to this climb.

Use either the Bottomless Pit Trail Approach (4A1) or the Rumdoodle Ridge Approach (4A2) to reach Bottomless Pit at 11,640 feet (38.8535° -105.0468°). The Railroad Couloir is the easternmost couloir on the north face. Angling slightly to the east (left), climb south into the snow bowl in the center of the face at 12,600 feet. Stay to the east (left) and climb the now distinct couloir as it steepens and narrows. Pass a large rock buttress, then angle west (right) at 13,700 feet. Continue straight up for the steepest, most classic finish, or angle east (left) for an easier finish. Your climb and solitude end abruptly a few feet from the end of the cog railway line on the east side of the summit.

An unusual hazard on this climb is tourists on the summit who try to fill up Bottomless Pit by tossing rocks down your route. To minimize this risk, consider being dropped off and climbing early from a bivouac in Bottomless Pit. A very early start from Barr Camp is another good alternative. In any case, wear a helmet.

4R4 – Pikes Peak – Y Couloir *Classic*

From Manitou Springs TH at 6,700'	579 RP	20.8 mi RT	7,410' total	Class 3, Steep Snow
From Devil's Playground TH at 12,930'	498 RP	8.2 mi RT	4,240' total	Class 3, Steep Snow
From Barr Camp at 10,160'	378 RP	8.0 mi RT	3,950' total	Class 3, Steep Snow
From Bottomless Pit at 11,640'	285 RP	2.0 mi RT	2,470' total	Class 3, Steep Snow

Pikes' north face. Photo by Austin Porzak

The Y Couloir is the premier mountaineering route on Pikes' north face. It is centrally located on the north face and is slightly steeper and harder than the Railroad Couloir. The Y Couloir offers two branches near the summit. Snow conditions are best in May and June, and you can sometimes find alpine ice here in July. Preview conditions from a distance before committing to this climb.

Use either the Bottomless Pit Trail Approach (4A1) or the Rumdoodle Ridge Approach (4A2) to reach Bottomless Pit at 11,640 feet (38.8535° -105.0468°). Angling slightly to the east (left), climb south into the snow bowl in the center of the face at 12,600 feet. Curve to the west (right) and climb the well-defined couloir to 13,400 feet, where the two branches of the couloir diverge.

The west (right) branch of the Y Couloir is the easier choice. The last 600 feet provide vintage Colorado couloir climbing. The angle remains a consistent 45 degrees. You top out abruptly at 14,080 feet on the west end of the summit plateau. Use caution; you may startle a sightseer.

The east (left) branch of the Y Couloir is steeper, exceeding 50 degrees in places. It also has rock bands that can add considerable difficulty. A large rock band is almost always present at 13,500 feet, just above the junction of the two branches. Smaller rock bands will appear in the last 500 feet as the couloir melts out. When in good condition, this is a scintillating finish. The east branch ends with some Class 3 scrambling and tops out just west of the large Olympic Memorial, where many motorists mill in summer.

Summit tourists who try to fill up Bottomless Pit by tossing rocks down your route are usually unaware that there may be climbers below them. Nevertheless, the rocks are a huge hazard for climbers. Tourists are most likely to trundle from near the Olympic Memorial; the Y Couloir will catch more of these rocks than the Railroad Couloir. Consider being dropped off and climbing early from a bivouac in Bottomless Pit. A very early start from Barr Camp is another good alternative. In any case, wear a helmet.

Chapter Two

Tenmile–Mosquito Range

Introduction

This range carries the distinction and confusion of two names. The two named ranges are geographically continuous. The Continental Divide sneaks through this north–south range on an east–west line as if impatient to be elsewhere. The Tenmile Range is north of the divide, and the Mosquito Range is south of the divide.

The Tenmile Range's northern end is near Frisco on Interstate 70. The Tenmile Range has 10 numbered peaks and several imaginatively named peaks close to the Continental Divide, including one Fourteener. The Mosquito Range has four Fourteeners close to the divide and runs south over several lower peaks. The Mosquito Range's practical southern boundary is Trout Creek Pass on US 285. Colorado 9 and US 285 mark the range's eastern edge. Interstate 70, Colorado 91 and US 24 mark the range's western edge.

Access to these gentle peaks is usually from the east, and the trailheads are high. You can ascend all the Fourteeners in the Tenmile–Mosquito Range with Class 1 or easy Class 2 hiking. These are some of Colorado's easiest Fourteeners, but the range does hide a few technical challenges. Also, remember that easy peaks do not ensure good weather!

5. Quandary Peak 14,265 feet

Quandary is 6 miles southwest of Breckenridge and 3 miles northwest of Hoosier Pass on Colorado 9. It is the Tenmile Range's unquestioned monarch, since the range's lesser peaks rise in concert, each higher than the last, toward Quandary. The monolithic Quandary is justifiably popular because of its proximity to Denver and a major Summit County ski area. It is a celebrated winter ascent, and people often ski the peak. Quandary is also a good spring training climb. The west and northeast ridges offer a more technical challenge. Quandary has something for everyone.

5E – Quandary Peak Essentials

Elevations	14,265' (NGVD29) 14,270' (NAVD88)
Rank	Colorado's 13th highest ranked peak
Location	Summit County, Colorado, USA
Range	Southern Tenmile Range
Summit Coordinates	39.3972° -106.1067° (WGS84)

5E – Quandary Peak Essentials

Ownership/Contact	Arapaho National Forest – Public Land – 970-295-6600
Prominence and Saddle	1,125' from 13,140' Mt Democrat–Traver Pk saddle
Isolation and Parent	3.18 miles to Mount Lincoln
USGS Maps	Breckenridge, Copper Mountain
USFS Map	Arapaho and Roosevelt National Forest
Trails Illustrated Map	Map #109 Breckenridge/Tennessee Pass
Book Map	See Map 5 on page 66
Nearest Town	Breckenridge – Population 2,700 – Elevation 9,600'
Quandary Peak 🏃 Easiest Route	5R1 – East Slopes – Class 1
	A Class 1 hike on a trail all the way to the top
Quandary's Accolades	Quandary is the highest peak in the Tenmile
	Range and one of Colorado's easiest Fourteeners.

5T – Quandary Peak Trailheads

5T0 – Common Approach to All Quandary Peak Trailheads 39.3815° -106.0633°

If you are approaching from the north, go 7.9 miles south on Colorado 9 from the junction of Ski Hill Road, Lincoln, and Main streets in the center of Breckenridge. If you are approaching from the south, go 2.2 miles north on Colorado 9 from the summit of Hoosier Pass. Turn west onto Summit County 850. You can reach three trailheads from here.

Quandary Peak from the southeast.

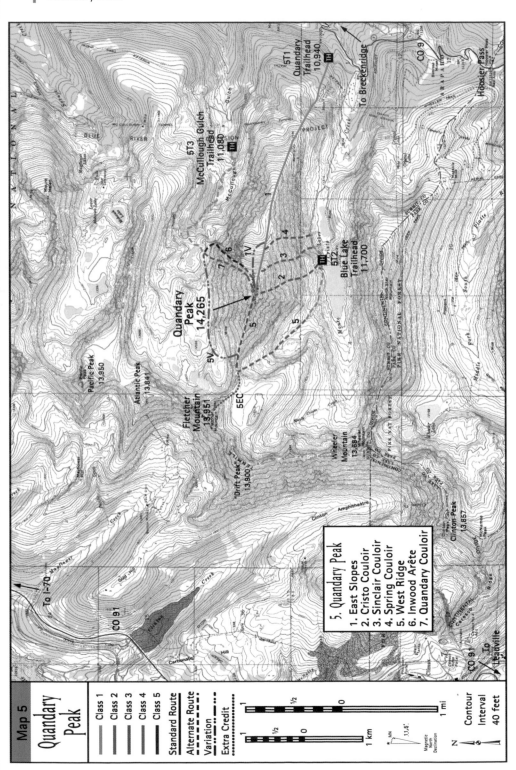

Map 5
Quandary Peak

Class 1
Class 2
Class 3
Class 4
Class 5

Standard Route
Alternate Route
Variation
Extra Credit

Contour Interval 40 feet

1 mi
1 km

Magnetic North Declination 11.5°

5. Quandary Peak
1. East Slopes
2. Cristo Couloir
3. Sinclair Couloir
4. Spring Couloir
5. West Ridge
6. Inwood Aréte
7. Quandary Couloir

5T1 – Quandary Trailhead 10,940 feet 39.3860° -106.0612°

This trailhead provides access to Quandary's east side. From the junction of Colorado 9 and Summit County 850 (see 5T0), go 0.1 mile west on Summit County 850, turn north (right) onto McCullough Gulch Road (Summit County 851), and go 0.25 mile north-northeast to the trailhead. There is a large triple signboard here. This trailhead is usually accessible in winter.

5T2 – Blue Lake Trailhead 11,700 feet 39.3867° -106.1002°

This trailhead provides access to Quandary's south and west sides. From the junction of Colorado 9 and Summit County 850 (see 5T0), go 2.2 miles west on Summit County 850 to a large parking area below the dam forming upper Blue Lake on Monte Cristo Creek.

5T3 – McCullough Gulch Trailhead 11,080 feet 39.4007° -106.0785°

This trailhead provides access to Quandary's north and west sides. From the junction of Colorado 9 and Summit County 850 (see 5T0), go 0.1 mile west on Summit County 850, turn north (right) onto McCullough Gulch Road (Summit County 851), and follow it as it curves around Quandary's east end and enters McCullough Gulch on the peak's north side. Go straight at 1.6 miles and park below a locked gate after 2.2 miles.

5R – Quandary Peak Routes

5R1 – Quandary Peak – East Slopes *Classic*

From Quandary TH at 10,940'   *128 RP*   *5.6 mi RT*   *3,325' total*   *Class 1*

This is the popular normal route on Quandary, and it is the easiest route on this complex peak. The Quandary Peak Trail (FT 39) goes all the way to the summit, and this is a good route for a first-time Fourteener hiker. Start at the Quandary Trailhead at 10,940 feet and hike west up the hillside. After crossing some old roads, the trail climbs to reach Quandary's east ridge near treeline at 11,700 feet. From treeline, follow the trail up a consistent grade for a mile to where the ridge angle moderates at 13,100 feet. From here, you can see the remaining challenge. Continue west to the summit slope and follow the now rougher trail, which stays near the south edge of a small, scooped east face to reach the summit ridge at 14,200 feet. Continue 200 yards west to the highest point (39.3972° -105.1067°). If you are lucky, goats may guide you.

5R1 V – Variation – East Face

Easy Snow

If snow conditions are favorable, you can angle northwest from 13,200 feet into the center of Quandary's small, scooped east face and climb a thousand feet of easy snow that averages 26 degrees to join the trail and summit ridge at 14,200 feet. Enthusiasts often ski this slope. You can create a simple circle tour by ascending the east face and descending the trail.

5R2 – Quandary Peak – Cristo Couloir

From Blue Lake TH at 11,700'   225 RP   2.0 mi RT   2,565' total   Class 2, Mod Snow

This route is notable because of its brevity. The Cristo Couloir is the main, shallow, south-facing couloir on Quandary's south face that rises directly toward the summit; it holds snow into June. You can use it as an early season snow climb and speedy descent route in spring. Avoid this route when avalanche danger is high and after the snow melts. Start at the Blue Lake Trailhead at 11,700 feet and climb 1.0 mile north-northwest up the steep slope to the summit. There is a climber's trail on the couloir's west side, but it is eroding badly and should be avoided.

5R3 – Quandary Peak – Sinclair Couloir

From Blue Lake TH at 11,700'   305 RP   2.4 mi RT   2,565' net; 2,685' total   Class 3, Steep Snow

With descent of Cristo Couloir   303 RP   2.2 mi RT   2,565' net; 2,625' total   Class 3, Steep Snow

The Sinclair Couloir is 400 yards east of the Cristo Couloir on Quandary's sweeping south face and is a tougher climb than the Cristo Couloir. It is named after Shawn Sinclair who proclaimed, "This is what it's all about" before perishing in 1994 at the young age of 23. Only attempt this climb when snow conditions are near perfect.

Start at the Blue Lake Trailhead at 11,700 feet and walk 400 yards northeast back down the road to 11,640 feet. Leave the road, and climb steeply north through some initial rocks to get into the bottom of the couloir (Class 3). Climb steep snow up the narrow, indented couloir until it merges with Quandary's upper southeast face at 13,600 feet. Once above the couloir, hike up a gentling slope, join the upper East Slopes Route (5R1) at 13,800 feet, and follow that route west to the summit. By ascending the Sinclair Couloir and descending the Cristo Couloir, you can enjoy a day of creative couloir climbing on a peak with a reputation for being easy.

5R4 – Quandary Peak – Spring Couloir

From Blue Lake TH at 11,700'   209 RP   3.0 mi RT   2,565' net; 2,805' total   Class 2, Mod Snow

With descent of Cristo Couloir   208 RP   2.5 mi RT   2,565' net; 2,685' total   Class 2, Mod Snow

The Spring Couloir is 300 yards east of the Sinclair Couloir on Quandary's sweeping south face. It is the shortest and easiest of Quandary's major south-facing couloirs. Like the Cristo and Sinclair couloirs, this couloir holds snow that has been blown into the depression by winter's winds, and this snow is often prone to slab avalanching. Only attempt this couloir when the snowpack has had time to stabilize, usually in late spring.

Start at the Blue Lake Trailhead at 11,700 feet and walk 0.4 mile northeast back down the road to 11,580 feet. Leave the road, and hike 200 yards north into the bottom of the couloir at 11,900 feet (Class 2). Climb consistent-angled moderate snow until the couloir reaches the upper East Slopes Route (5R1) at 13,300 feet, and follow that route 0.6 mile west to the summit.

5R5 – Quandary Peak – West Ridge

From Blue Lake TH at 11,700'	225 RP	5.4 mi RT	2,565' net; 2,685' total	Class 3
With descent of Cristo Couloir	196 RP	3.7 mi RT	2,565' net; 2,625' total	Class 3, Mod Snow
With descent of East Slopes	228 RP	7.1 mi RT	2,565' net; 2,625' total	Class 3

This route provides a scenic approach and a sporty scramble to the summit. Ascending this route and descending either the Cristo Couloir (5R2) or East Slopes Route (5R1) makes an excellent circle tour. This is not the standard route on Quandary. Sadly, a fatal accident happened to a party who thought that this was the standard hiking route. There is a big difference between Class 1 trail hiking and Class 3 scrambling on exposed, rotten rock. Please pay attention to my ratings. To be double clear, the Class 1 standard route on Quandary is the East Slopes Route (5R1).

Start at the Blue Lake Trailhead at 11,700 feet and hike north up the slope just west of the dam at upper Blue Lake. After 200 yards, angle west and follow an old mining trail through the bushes. Beyond the bushes, follow the now clear trail 0.5 mile west-northwest as it climbs to a mine site at 12,300 feet in the idyllic, embracing valley on Quandary's southwest side. Quandary's rugged southwest face is above you, and you can see the pinnacle-studded west ridge in profile.

From 12,300 feet, hike 1.0 mile northwest up the valley to reach Quandary's west ridge at 13,400 feet on the Fletcher Mountain side of the 13,340-foot Fletcher–Quandary Col (Class 2). Fletcher Mountain is the 13,951-foot peak west of Quandary. Turn east (right), descend slightly to the 13,340-foot Fletcher–Quandary Col, start toward Quandary, and pass some initial small towers on the ridge's south (right) side (Class 2). Beyond these towers, the ridge becomes a talus slope between a 13,380-foot saddle and 14,000 feet. Stay on or north of the ridge crest in this section. There is an old mining trail on the ridge's north side.

At 14,000 feet, the summit is only a few hundred yards away, but the fun has just begun. The route from here is harder than it looks, since you must negotiate several towers and notches. The route finding is challenging as you pass some towers on the north, some on the south, and climb some directly. The route never drops more than 100 feet below the ridge, so if you start to descend a steep, south-facing, rotten gully, stop, turn around, and look for a direct route up the southwest face of the tower just east of the gully. Climb this tower's short but exposed face. If you take care to find the easiest way, the difficulty will not exceed Class 3. Treat this ridge with respect. Many people have found it to be harder than they expected, and at least one fatal accident has occurred here.

The difficulties finally relent 100 yards west of the summit. You can share your adventure with the other people you are likely to find on the summit, but since they cannot see the west ridge's difficulties from the summit, your acquaintances might not understand. Descend the Cristo Couloir (5R2) or East

Slopes Route (5R1). If you descend the Cristo Couloir, carry an ice ax. If you descend the East Slopes Route, remember that you have to cover an additional 2.4 miles between the Quandary and Blue Lake trailheads.

5R5 V – Variation – Northwest Face

From McCullough Gulch TH at 11,080'	*222 RP*	*6.6 mi RT*	*3,185' total*	*Class 3*
With descent of East Slopes	*196 RP*	*6.1 mi RT*	*3,185' total*	*Class 3*

You can approach the west ridge from McCullough Gulch on Quandary's north side. Start at the McCullough Gulch Trailhead at 11,080 feet and hike 2.2 miles west on a dwindling trail up McCullough Gulch to a small, unnamed lake at 12,555 feet (Class 1). You can see your approach to the west ridge from here. Hike 0.5 mile south, using old miners' trails through the otherwise steep talus, to reach the west ridge at 13,540 feet east of the initial towers (Class 2). Hike then scramble 0.6 mile west on the upper part of the West Ridge Route to the summit (Class 3).

5R5 EC – Extra Credit – Fletcher Mountain 13,951 feet 39.4032° -106.1287°

Class 2

From the beginning of the west ridge at 13,400 feet, climb 0.5 mile northwest to 13,951-foot Fletcher Mountain, one of Colorado's 100 highest ranked peaks.

5R6 – Quandary Peak – Inwood Arête

From McCullough Gulch TH at 11,080'	*487 RP*	*4.6 mi RT*	*3,185' total*	*Class 5.4*
With descent of East Slopes	*473 RP*	*5.1 mi RT*	*3,185' total*	*Class 5.4*

The Inwood Arête is Quandary's rugged northeast ridge, and you can see it in profile when approaching the McCullough Gulch Trailhead. The ridge is named in memory of Julie Inwood, who died tragically while starting a climbing trip in Peru in 1985. The Inwood Arête is a technical rock climb of significant stature on a peak with a reputation for being easy. Climbers have gotten off-route on this ridge and found considerably harder climbing. Approach with caution and respect.

From the McCullough Gulch Trailhead at 11,080 feet, hike 1.3 mile west on a trail up McCullough Gulch to an unnamed lake at 11,900 feet. The Inwood Arête rises directly south of this lake and offers 1,500 vertical feet of climbing and scrambling. From the lake's east end, hike 0.2 mile south up to the base of the buttress at 12,100 feet (Class 2). There is a lot of rock above you at this point, and the easiest start may not be immediately obvious. A direct start up the buttress is harder than Class 5.4. To find the easiest start, drop down to the east to a slabby face reminiscent of the Flatirons above Boulder, Colorado.

Step left to climb onto the slab (Class 5.4). This opening move will remind you that this is a climb, not a hike. Climb the solid slab above for two Class 5.3 pitches to a small northeast-facing ridge. These pitches are alpine slab climbing at its best. Stay below the crest on the north side of the small knife-edge above you and climb toward some towers on the crest of the now well-formed Inwood Arête (Class 5.0–5.2). Avoid these towers on the arête's east (left) side (Class 5.4) and climb to the crest of the Inwood Arête above the towers. The major difficulties are below you at this point, but you are only halfway. As you gaze at the rock above, you may gain new respect for Quandary Peak.

The arête's upper half requires several hundred feet of fun-filled but exposed Class 3 scrambling. The difficulties end at 13,600 feet. Hike 0.4 mile west-southwest up Class 2 talus to the summit. Descend the East Slopes Route (5R1) to treeline, then descend north back to the McCullough Gulch Road.

5R7 – Quandary Peak – Quandary Couloir

From McCullough Gulch TH at 11,080'	*343 RP*	*4.6 mi RT*	*3,185' total*	*Class 4, Steep Snow*
With descent of East Slopes	*325 RP*	*5.1 mi RT*	*3,185' total*	*Class 4, Steep Snow*

Quandary's finest snow climb is just west of the Inwood Arête on the west end of Quandary's northeast face. The Inwood blocks your view, and you cannot see the Quandary Couloir from the highway or when approaching the McCullough Gulch Trailhead. This couloir's secrets are reserved for those who make an effort.

From the McCullough Gulch Trailhead at 11,080 feet, hike 1.3 mile west on a trail up McCullough Gulch to an unnamed lake at 11,900 feet. Hike 0.2 mile southwest above the lake's east end until the couloir is in full view directly to the south. As always, check conditions carefully before committing to your climb. A stable late spring snowpack is ideal. Start up steeper slopes into the couloir at 12,200 feet. Rising like an arrow, the 1,800-foot-high couloir averages 38 degrees and exceeds 45 degrees in places. Be prepared for ice and rock pitches. After the difficulties relent at 14,000 feet, stroll 0.2 mile west-southwest up talus to Quandary's summit.

6. Lincoln Group

Mount Lincoln   14,286 feet
Mount Cameron   14,238 feet
Mount Bross   14,172 feet
Mount Democrat   14,148 feet

These friendly peaks are 4 miles west of Hoosier Pass on Colorado 9 between Breckenridge and Fairplay. They are gentle, forgiving, and high. These peaks are popular as training climbs, and people usually climb them together. They are a peak bagger's delight, since nowhere else can you get so much for so little!

Mount Lincoln is the highest peak in the Tenmile–Mosquito Range and is higher than any peak in the Front Range. Lincoln is the highest peak in Park County and the eighth highest peak in Colorado.

Mount Bross challenges photographers to make it look dramatic, and people intent on checking peaks off a list love the return on investment Bross gives

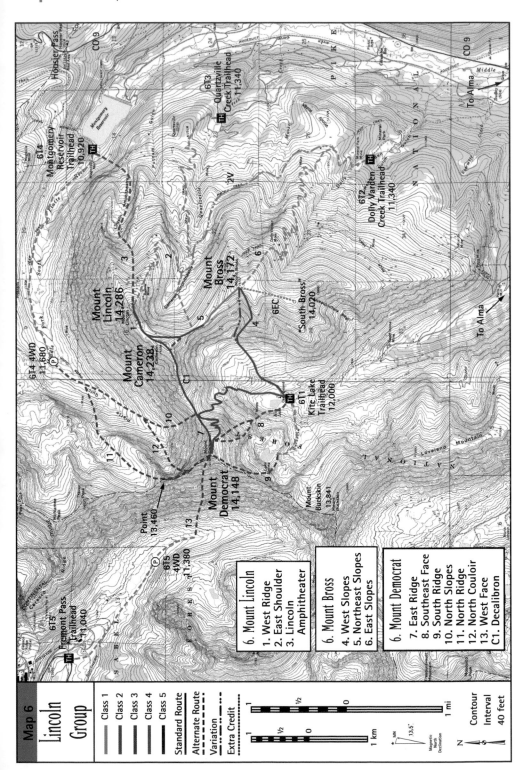

Map 6
Lincoln Group

Class 1
Class 2
Class 3
Class 4
Class 5
Standard Route
Alternate Route
Variation
Extra Credit

N

Contour
Interval
40 feet

6. Mount Lincoln
1. West Ridge
2. East Shoulder
3. Lincoln Amphitheater

6. Mount Bross
4. West Slopes
5. Northeast Slopes
6. East Slopes

6. Mount Democrat
7. East Ridge
8. Southeast Face
9. South Ridge
10. North Slopes
11. North Ridge
12. North Couloir
13. West Face
C1. Decalibron

them. Bross' flat summit is a perfect place for lounging on a clear day. Bross is sometimes jokingly called the "Aiguille du Bross."

Mount Democrat is 1.5 miles west of the collective massif of Lincoln, Cameron, and Bross. Democrat is a singular mountain and has its own unique personality. Although lower than Lincoln, Cameron, and Bross, Democrat provides the most interesting mountaineering routes on these peaks.

6E – Lincoln Group Essentials

Elevations	Mt Lincoln	14,286' (NGVD29) 14,291' (NAVD88)
	Mt Cameron	14,238' (NGVD29) 14,243' (NAVD88)
	Mt Bross	14,172' (NGVD29) 14,177' (NAVD88)
	Mt Democrat	14,148' (NGVD29) 14,152' (NAVD88)
Ranks	Mt Lincoln	Colorado's 8th highest ranked peak
	Mt Cameron	Unranked summit
	Mt Bross	Colorado's 22nd highest ranked peak
	Mt Democrat	Colorado's 28th highest ranked peak
Location	Park County, Colorado, USA	
Range	Northern Mosquito Range	
Summit Coordinates	Mt Lincoln	39.3512° -106.1117° (WGS84)
	Mt Cameron	39.3472° -106.1188° (WGS84)
	Mt Bross	39.3362° -106.1078° (WGS84)
	Mt Democrat	39.3397° -106.1403° (WGS84)
Ownership/Contact	Pike National Forest – Public Land with inholdings – 719-553-1400	
Prominence and Saddles	Mt Lincoln	3,862' from 10,424' Tennessee Pass
	Mt Cameron	138' from 14,100' Cameron–Lincoln saddle
	Mt Bross	312' from 13,860' Bross–Lincoln saddle
	Mt Democrat	768' from 13,380' Democrat–Lincoln saddle
Isolation and Parents	Mt Lincoln	22.57 miles to Mount Massive
	Mt Cameron	0.50 mile to Mount Lincoln
	Mt Bross	1.13 miles to Mount Lincoln
	Mt Democrat	1.73 miles to Mount Lincoln
USGS Maps	Alma, Climax	
USFS Maps	Pike National Forest, San Isabel National Forest	
Trails Illustrated Map	Map #109 Breckenridge/Tennessee Pass	
Book Map	See Map 6 on page 72	
Nearest Towns	Alma – Population 180 – Elevation 10,361 feet	
	Fairplay – Population 610 – Elevation 9,953 feet	
Mt Lincoln Easiest Route	6R1 – West Ridge – Class 2	
	A Class 1 trail hike much of the way, then	
	some Class 2 boulder hopping near the summit	

6E – Lincoln Group Essentials

Mt Cameron 🏃 Easiest Route	6R1 – West Ridge – Class 2	
	A Class 1 trail hike much of the way, then some Class 2 scree near the summit	
Mt Bross 🏃 Easiest Route	6R6 – East Slopes – Class 1	
	A Class 1 trail hike most of the way, then a smooth scree slope near the top	
Mt Democrat 🏃 Easiest Route	6R7 – East Ridge – Class 2	
	A Class 1 trail hike most of the way, then some Class 2 boulder hopping near the summit	
Lincoln Group Accolades	Mount Lincoln is the highest peak in the Tenmile–Mosquito Range and is higher than any peak in the Front Range. Lincoln is the highest peak in Park County and the eighth highest peak in Colorado. Bross' flat summit is a perfect place for lounging on a clear day. Democrat provides the most interesting mountaineering routes on these peaks.	

6T – Lincoln Group Trailheads

6T1 – Kite Lake Trailhead 12,000 feet 39.3277° -106.1293°

This trailhead provides access to the south sides of Democrat, Cameron, and Lincoln, and the west side of Bross. If you are approaching from the south, go 6.0 miles north on Colorado 9 from the US 285–Colorado 9 junction in Fairplay. If you are approaching from the north, go 5.8 miles south on Colorado 9 from the summit of Hoosier Pass.

Turn west onto Kite Lake Road (dirt) in the center of Alma. Park County 10 is not Kite Lake Road. The poorly marked Kite Lake Road is Park County 8, and it starts across the highway from a store. Follow Kite Lake Road for 6.0 miles northwest up Buckskin Gulch to Kite Lake at 12,000 feet. There is ample parking east of Kite Lake, and there is a pay station nearby for this fee lot. Kite Lake Road is good most of the way, but the last mile to the lake is difficult for passenger cars. Many people choose to park their passenger cars near a switchback 0.6 mile below the lake. In winter the road is closed 4.0 miles above Alma, and snowmobiles make heavy use of the road above this point.

6T2 – Dolly Varden Creek Trailhead 11,340 feet 39.3163° -106.0835°

This trailhead provides access to Bross' east side. If you are approaching from the south, go 6.0 miles north on Colorado 9 from the US 285–Colorado 9 junction in Fairplay. If you are approaching from the north, go 5.8 miles south on Colorado 9 from the summit of Hoosier Pass.

Turn west onto Kite Lake Road (dirt) in the center of Alma. Park County 10 is not Kite Lake Road. The poorly marked Kite Lake Road is Park County 8, and it starts across the highway from a store. Go 2.8 miles west on Kite Lake Road, turn north (right) onto Windy Ridge Road (FR 415), and go 2.9 miles to a parking area near the Mineral Park Mine. The road is good to this point. FR 415 is closed in winter.

6T3 – Quartzville Creek Trailhead 11,340 feet 39.3387° -106.0752°

This trailhead provides access to the east sides of Lincoln, Cameron, and Bross. If you are approaching from the south, go 8.1 miles north on Colorado 9 from the US 285–Colorado 9 junction in Fairplay. If you are approaching from the north, go 3.7 miles south on Colorado 9 from the summit of Hoosier Pass.

Turn west onto Park County 4. This is the southern of two Colorado 9–Park County 4 junctions. There is a housing subdivision west of here, and you can use several routes to reach the trailhead. The following is the most direct. Measuring from the south Colorado 9–Park County 4 junction, go west (left) at mile 0.1, south (left) at mile 0.3, hard right at mile 0.4, and follow the main road northwest as it switchbacks up the hill. Stay right at mile 2.7, and turn left onto FR 437 at mile 3.3. This point is on Quartzville Creek's north side. There is a small parking area on the west side of FR 437, just north of the subdivision road. This is the trailhead. Snowplow activity on these roads varies in the winter. The road is often plowed to the trailhead, but don't count on it, especially right after a storm.

6T4 – Montgomery Reservoir Trailhead 10,920 feet 39.3573° -106.0812°

This trailhead provides access to the north sides of Lincoln, Cameron, and Democrat. If you are approaching from the south, go 10.7 miles north on Colorado 9 from the US 285–Colorado 9 junction in Fairplay. If you are approaching from the north, go 1.1 miles south on Colorado 9 from the summit of Hoosier Pass.

Turn west onto Park County 4. This is the northern of two Colorado 9–Park County 4 junctions. Measuring from this junction, go down the hill to the west, stay right at mile 0.8, stay right at mile 1.0, go around Montgomery Reservoir's north side, and park on the reservoir's west side at mile 1.9. The road is passable for passenger cars to this point. In winter the road is plowed to the spillway road east of the reservoir.

6T4 4WD – Montgomery 4WD Trailhead 11,680 feet 39.3637° -106.1212°

Above the Montgomery Reservoir Trailhead, the road rapidly becomes rough at the Magnolia Mine, but 4WD vehicles can continue 2.4 miles west to 11,680 feet under Lincoln's north slopes.

6T5 – Fremont Pass Trailhead 11,040 feet 39.3602° -106.1797°

This trailhead provides access to Democrat's west face. If you are approaching from the south, go 12.0 miles north on Colorado 91 from Leadville. If you are approaching from the north, go 9.0 miles south on Colorado 91 from Interstate 70. The trailhead is not on top of Fremont Pass but at the lower end of the sweeping switchback 0.7 mile southeast of the pass. Park on the south side of the highway in a large pullout west of some mine buildings. This trailhead is accessible in winter.

6T5 4WD – Fremont Pass 4WD Trailhead 11,380 feet 39.3478° -106.1608°
From the Fremont Pass Trailhead, high-clearance vehicles can go 1.4 miles southeast into the valley on a fair dirt road to a closure gate at 11,380 feet. The road ends 200 yards beyond at a mine.

6. Mount Lincoln 14,286 feet

6R – Mount Lincoln Routes
6R1 – Mount Lincoln – West Ridge
From Kite Lake TH at 12,000'   175 RP   6.2 mi RT   2,286' net; 2,562' total   Class 2

This is the regular route up Lincoln; it has seen many feet. From the Kite Lake Trailhead at 12,000 feet, follow the trail 0.8 mile north to the Kentucky Belle Mine's ruins. Continue 0.8 mile northwest on the trail as it climbs above the old gold mine and switchbacks up to the 13,380-foot saddle between Democrat and Cameron (**39.3418° -106.1322°**). Turn east (right) and hike 1.0 mile up the ridge to Cameron's rounded 14,238-foot summit (**39.3472° -106.1188°**). If Cameron is beneath your dignity, you can skirt it on its north side. Lincoln is a gentle 0.5 mile northeast of Cameron. Descend northeast to the broad 14,100-foot Cameron–Lincoln saddle (**39.3499° -106.1162°**) and follow a well-worn trail east-northeast through the summit rocks to Lincoln's highest point (**39.3512° -106.1117°**).

Mount Lincoln and Mount Cameron from the east.

6R2 – Mount Lincoln – East Shoulder

From Quartzville Creek TH at 11,340' 129 RP 6.4 mi RT 2,946' total Class 1

This is a pleasant, gentle approach to Lincoln's summit that avoids the crowds ascending from Kite Lake. From the Quartzville Creek Trailhead at 11,340 feet, follow FR 437 west as it climbs along Quartzville Creek's north side. Hike into the east end of Cameron Amphitheater between Mount Lincoln to the north and Mount Bross to the south. At 13,000 feet, follow the road as it switchbacks hard east and climb onto Lincoln's east shoulder at 13,200 feet. As an alternative, you can save some distance by leaving the road and cutting straight north up the slope to reach Lincoln's east shoulder at 13,500 feet.

Once on the east shoulder, hike west on the road past several old mines. Some rusty pipes laid out across the slope mark the 14,000-foot contour line (just kidding). Leave the road before it traverses to the peak's north side and continue 300 feet west on a climber's trail to the summit. This is a good running route.

6R2 V – Variation – Varden's Way

From Dolly Varden Creek TH at 11,340' 151 RP 8.4 mi RT 2,926' total Class 1

You can approach this route from the Dolly Varden Creek Trailhead. This makes your climb of Lincoln longer but allows you to also climb Bross and make a circle tour by descending Bross' East Slopes Route (6R6). Start at the Dolly Varden Creek Trailhead at 11,340 feet, hike north onto Windy Ridge, then follow a 4WD road north and northwest into Cameron Amphitheater to join the road climbing up from the Quartzville Creek Trailhead.

6R3 – Mount Lincoln – Lincoln Amphitheater

From Montgomery Reservoir TH at 10,920' 224 RP 4.0 mi RT 3,366' total Class 2+

This is the shortest route on Lincoln. The Lincoln Amphitheater separates Lincoln's two east ridges and provides a much less traveled route up this popular peak. Start at the Montgomery Reservoir Trailhead at 10,920 feet. The crux of this route is a 400-foot headwall that bars easy access to Lincoln Amphitheater. Study it from the trailhead. Angle south up the scruffy slope and find a way through this maze of small cliffs by traversing on ledges until you find easy upward egress. In summer you may have to battle bushes as well as the route finding. In winter this is the popular Lincoln Falls ice-climbing area. Either way, be prepared for some adventure.

Leave the bushes behind and enter the Lincoln Amphitheater at 11,600 feet. Turn west and follow the curves of this gentle giant to 13,000 feet. In winter this basin is prone to avalanches; beware the giant's roar. The terrain relaxes above 13,000 feet as you hike 0.6 mile west to the summit.

6. Mount Cameron 14,238 feet

Cameron is centrally located between Democrat, Lincoln, and Bross. Cameron is named on the Alma Quadrangle but is not a ranked peak, since it rises no more than 157 feet from its connecting saddle with Lincoln. People have pooh-poohed Cameron for years; it is the official unofficial peak! If Cameron were just 50 feet higher, it would reign supreme. Nevertheless, it sits there named and waiting. The views from Cameron are better than the views of Cameron.

Cameron is not lonely. Everybody climbs it while coming from and going to the other more important peaks. It is almost always climbed with Democrat, Lincoln, or Bross. You will have an opportunity to climb Cameron when on Lincoln's West Ridge Route (6R1), the Decalibron (6C1), the Licambro (6C2), or the Lincdebro (6C3).

6. Mount Bross 14,172 feet

6R – Mount Bross Routes

6R4 – Mount Bross – West Slopes

From Kite Lake TH at 12,000'   118 RP   2.8 mi RT   2,172' total   Class 2

This is the shortest route up Bross, and well-worn climbers' trails mark the way. From the Kite Lake Trailhead at 12,000 feet, hike 0.7 mile northeast up gentle slopes to 12,700 feet at the base of Bross. From here there are two choices. Climb 0.7 mile east up the shallow basin or the ridge just south of the basin to the summit **(39.3362° -106.1078°)**. The ridge provides the best footing for the ascent and is the greener choice. Thousands of feet speeding down the basin have sent the scree elsewhere, and the basin no longer provides pleasant footing.

6R5 – Mount Bross – Northeast Slopes

From Quartzville Creek TH at 11,340'   125 RP   6.4 mi RT   2,832' total   Class 1

This is a longer, gentler approach to Bross' summit. From the Quartzville Creek Trailhead at 11,340 feet, follow FR 437 west as it climbs along Quartzville Creek's north side. At 13,000 feet, the road switchbacks hard east to climb onto Lincoln's east shoulder. Leave the road at this switchback and continue hiking west into Cameron Amphitheater. Hike southwest up gentle, grassy slopes to the elongated 13,860-foot Cameron–Bross saddle **(39.3418° -106.1156°)**. From the saddle, hike 0.6 mile southeast on roads and gentle scree to the summit **(39.3362° -106.1078°)**. This is a good running route.

6R6 – Mount Bross – East Slopes

From Dolly Varden Creek TH at 11,340'   131 RP   7.0 mi RT   2,832' total   Class 1

This is the easiest route up Bross and one of the easiest routes anywhere. As an added attraction, the route goes past the Windy Ridge Bristlecone Pine Scenic

Area. Start at the Dolly Varden Creek Trailhead at 11,340 feet, follow the road 0.2 mile west, turn north (right) onto FR 415, and switchback up to Windy Ridge. A short side trip takes you to the Bristlecone Pines.

A 4WD road switchbacks above Windy Ridge up gentle, grass-covered slopes to the Dolly Varden Mine at 13,300 feet. Either follow the road or hike straight up the gentle slopes. The road is the greener choice and the distance I give for this route assumes that you follow the road to the mine. Above the Dolly Varden Mine, leave the road and hike straight up smooth scree to Bross' flat summit. This is a good running route.

6R6 EC – Extra Credit – "South Bross" 14,020 feet 39.3269° -106.1104°

Class 2

From the summit of Bross, hike 0.6 mile south to Point 14,020, alias "South Bross." This summit does not have a lot of power, but it is a summit above 14,000 feet and it provides a good view of Democrat.

6. Mount Democrat 14,148 feet

6R – Mount Democrat Routes

6R7 – Mount Democrat – East Ridge

From Kite Lake TH at 12,000'   113 RP   4.2 mi RT   2,148' total   Class 2

This is the easiest route on Democrat. Start at the Kite Lake Trailhead at 12,000 feet and follow the well-worn trail 0.8 mile north to the Kentucky Belle Mine's ruins. Continue 0.8 mile northwest on the trail as it climbs above the old gold mine and switchbacks up to the 13,380-foot saddle between Democrat and Cameron (39.3418° -106.1322°). There are old trail remnants west of this saddle, but it is just as easy to hike 0.5 mile up Democrat's east ridge to the summit (39.3397° -106.1403°). There are building ruins in a flat area at 14,000 feet, just east of Democrat's summit; have you ever wondered how many miners were hit by lightning?

6R8 – Mount Democrat – Southeast Face

From Kite Lake TH at 12,000'   198 RP   2.4 mi RT   2,148' total   Class 2, Mod Snow

With descent of East Ridge   181 RP   2.8 mi RT   2,148' total   Class 2, Mod Snow

In May and June, this face provides a simple snow climb. Later in the summer, this is still the shortest route on Democrat. The southeast face is the face directly north of Kite Lake. Do not confuse the southeast face with the steeper south face above Lake Emma. You can preview snow conditions on the southeast face from US 285 south of Fairplay.

Start at the Kite Lake Trailhead at 12,000 feet and angle northwest up the slope on the lake's west side. Stay west of the cliffs north of Kite Lake and reach the base of the southeast face at 12,800 feet. When snow conditions are favorable, climb directly up the face to 13,900 feet on the shoulder 0.2 mile east of the summit. After the snow melts, climb the small ridge on the southeast face's west edge. This ridge separates the southeast face from the south face.

6R9 – Mount Democrat – South Ridge

From Kite Lake TH at 12,000'	*214 RP*	*3.6 mi RT*	*2,148' total*	*Class 3*
With descent of East Ridge	*195 RP*	*3.9 mi RT*	*2,148' total*	*Class 3*

The miners a hundred years ago knew more about the secrets of this ridge than today's climbers. It is seldom climbed because of its loose rock and crumbling towers. It is not a good route for a large group. Climb it if you feel compelled and are good on "junk."

Start at the Kite Lake Trailhead at 12,000 feet and follow a trail 0.8 mile west then north to Lake Emma (39.3295° -106.1396°) at 12,620 feet. This is a worthwhile hike by itself. Lake Emma nestles below Democrat's south face in a surprisingly dramatic bowl. From the south side of the lake, climb west then northwest up steepening slopes to reach Democrat's south ridge at 13,400 feet. The last 400 feet to the ridge require judicious Class 3 scrambling on loose rock. The redeeming feature of this approach to the south ridge is that it avoids most of the crumbling towers that are lower on the ridge. Once on the south ridge, scramble 0.5 mile north (Class 3) to the summit. The difficulties end at 13,800 feet.

6R10 – Mount Democrat – North Slopes

From Montgomery Reservoir TH at 10,920'	*238 RP*	*9.6 mi RT*	*3,228' total*	*Class 2*
From Montgomery 4WD TH at 11,680'	*173 RP*	*4.8 mi RT*	*2,468' total*	*Class 2*

This is the easiest way to climb Democrat from the north. Start at the Montgomery Reservoir Trailhead at 10,920 feet and go 2.4 miles west up the 4WD road along the middle fork of the South Platte. Leave this road at 11,680 feet (39.3637° -106.1212°) before it crosses the creek descending from Wheeler Lake and starts a steep climb to this lake. Hike 1.0 mile southwest on another, fainter 4WD road through the bushes to 12,000 feet (39.3521° -106.1321°). Continue 0.5 mile southwest up the main valley to 12,400 feet (39.3458° -106.1350°) and hike 0.4 mile south-southeast up steep scree to the 13,380-foot saddle between Democrat and Cameron (39.3418° -106.1322°). Join the East Ridge Route (6R7) here, and hike 0.5 mile west to Democrat's summit.

6R11 – Mount Democrat – North Ridge *Classic*

From Montgomery Reservoir TH at 10,920'	*314 RP*	*10.2 mi RT*	*3,228' total*	*Class 3*
With descent of North Slopes	*292 RP*	*9.9 mi RT*	*3,228' total*	*Class 3*
From Montgomery 4WD TH at 11,680'	*248 RP*	*5.4 mi RT*	*2,468' total*	*Class 3*
With descent of North Slopes	*226 RP*	*5.1 mi RT*	*2,468' total*	*Class 3*

This is the best mountaineering route on Democrat. This ridge is similar to the west ridge on Quandary. Some fierce-looking notches distinguish the lower part of Democrat's north ridge, but the rock is surprisingly good and the ridge is easier than it looks.

Start at the Montgomery Reservoir Trailhead at 10,920 feet and follow the 4WD road 2.4 miles west along the middle fork of the South Platte. Leave this road at 11,680 feet (39.3637° -106.1212°) before it crosses the creek descending from Wheeler Lake and starts a steep climb to this lake. Hike 0.7 mile southwest on another, fainter 4WD road through the bushes to 11,800 feet (39.3559° -106.1291°). When you are beyond the bushes, climb 0.6 mile west to 12,600 feet in the small basin southeast of 13,852-foot Traver Peak that is 1.4 miles north of Democrat. There are some old mines in this basin. From 12,600 feet in the basin, climb 0.8 mile southwest to Point 13,460 (39.3467° -106.1448°) on Democrat's north ridge.

Scramble south across Point 13,460 and engage the initial and most difficult notches on the ridge. There are two prominent notches separated by a shark-fin tower. Descend on the ridge's west side to reach the vicinity of the first notch (Class 3). Scramble around the shark-fin tower on its west (right) side just below the level of the notch (Class 3). Climb into the second notch that is graced with a conspicuous chockstone. Climb south up the ridge above the second chockstone notch (Class 3). The ridge's main difficulties are now behind you.

The ridge from here to the summit is fun. It is mostly Class 2 hiking punctuated with some Class 3 scrambling. There is more Class 3 scrambling if you adhere to the ridge crest, or if you choose, you can skirt most of the remaining towers on the ridge's west side. There is an antique mine at 13,700 feet at the top of the north couloir. There is an old trail above the mine on the ridge's west side, but it is more entertaining to continue scrambling on the ridge crest all the way to the summit. The rock becomes increasingly rotten as you approach the summit. For an easier return to the Montgomery Reservoir, descend the North Slopes Route (6R10).

6R12 – Mount Democrat – North Couloir

From Montgomery Reservoir TH at 10,920'	301 RP	9.2 mi RT	3,228' total	Class 3, Mod Snow
With descent of North Slopes	297 RP	9.4 mi RT	3,228' total	Class 3, Mod Snow
From Montgomery 4WD TH at 11,680'	235 RP	4.4 mi RT	2,468' total	Class 3, Mod Snow
With descent of North Slopes	231 RP	4.6 mi RT	2,468' total	Class 3, Mod Snow

Miners dumped tailings down this couloir a hundred years ago, but today it is seldom seen or climbed. Because the couloir is inset and protected, it can retain snow into August. Crampons are useful after June.

Start at the Montgomery Reservoir Trailhead at 10,920 feet and follow the 4WD road 2.4 miles west along the middle fork of the South Platte. Leave this road at 11,680 feet (39.3637° -106.1212°) before it crosses the creek descending from Wheeler Lake and starts a steep climb to this lake. Hike 1.0 mile southwest on another, fainter 4WD road through the bushes to 12,000 feet (39.3521°

-106.1321°) and continue 0.7 mile southwest up the main valley to 12,600 feet (39.3458° -106.1404°). The North Couloir Route is the westernmost and most pronounced couloir on Democrat's north face. The north couloir is immediately east of the lower part of the north ridge and is subject to rockfall from the steep wall above it, especially if there are climbers on the North Ridge Route (6R11).

From 12,600 feet in the head of the valley, climb south-southwest toward the north ridge and enter the couloir at 12,800 feet. Climb the couloir for 900 exciting feet to reach the antique mine on the north ridge at 13,700 feet. The couloir averages 40 degrees and approaches 45 degrees at the steepest point. Once on the north ridge, continue up that route to the summit. Descend the North Slopes Route (6R10).

6R13 – Mount Democrat – West Face

From Fremont Pass TH at 11,040'	315 RP	6.0 mi RT	3,108' total	Class 2, Mod Snow
From Fremont Pass 4WD TH at 11,380'	277 RP	3.0 mi RT	2,768' total	Class 2, Mod Snow

When snow conditions are favorable in spring and early summer, Democrat's west face provides a long snow climb. Avoid this face when it is free of snow. You can easily see this face from Colorado 91, and you should check conditions when going to and coming from other adventures. Be patient; then, when snow conditions are perfect, climb it.

Start at the Fremont Pass Trailhead at 11,040 feet and go 1.5 miles southeast on a dirt road along the west (right) side of the valley to a mine at 11,380 feet (39.3478° -106.1608°). Continue 0.5 mile on a trail beyond the mine to 11,500 feet. Democrat's 2,500-foot-high west face soars above you to the east. Cross the valley, hike up the lower slopes, do an ascending traverse to the south (right), and climb into the narrow gully that descends from near the summit. Climb the gully on the perfect snow that you have waited for and reach the top of Democrat's north ridge in a small saddle. Follow the upper north ridge to the summit. The snow steepness in the gully does not exceed 45 degrees.

6C – Lincoln, Cameron, Bross, and Democrat Combination Routes

6C1 – The Decalibron

From Kite Lake TH at 12,000'	241 RP	7.0 mi RT	3,504' total	Class 2

This is the easiest and most traveled way to climb all four peaks. Except for a short out-and-back to Lincoln, it is a perfect ring around the cirque. Start at Kite Lake Trailhead at 12,000 feet and climb Democrat's East Ridge Route (6R7). Descend east to the 13,380-foot saddle between Democrat and Cameron (39.3418° -106.1322°). Continue east on Lincoln's West Ridge Route (6R1) over Cameron and northeast to Lincoln. Return to the broad, 14,100-foot saddle between Lincoln and Cameron (39.3498° -106.1165°). Either reascend Cameron or stay below Cameron's summit on the east side. Descend southeast to the 13,860-foot saddle between Cameron and Bross (39.3418° -106.1157°), then continue 0.6 mile southeast up gentle slopes to Bross' summit. Descend Bross' West Slopes Route (6R4).

Before committing to this long, high traverse, consider that Cameron's south slopes are cliffy and that there is no easy escape back to Kite Lake between the Democrat–Cameron saddle and the Cameron–Bross saddle. This combination works in the opposite direction, but people seldom do it that way. The ease of reaching the Democrat–Cameron saddle on a trail and the quick descent down Bross' West Slopes Route at day's end prescribe the order given above.

6C2 – Licambro

From Quartzville Creek TH at 11,340'   180 RP   7.9 mi RT   3,396' total   Class 2

This combination is a quick way to collect Lincoln, Cameron, and Bross. Start at the Quartzville Creek Trailhead at 11,340 feet and climb Lincoln's East Shoulder Route (6R2). Descend southwest to the broad, 14,100-foot saddle between Lincoln and Cameron and continue southwest to Cameron's broad summit. Descend 0.4 mile southeast to the 13,860-foot saddle between Cameron and Bross, then continue 0.6 mile southeast up gentle slopes to Bross' summit. Descend Bross' Northeast Slopes Route (6R5).

6C3 – Lincdebro

From Quartzville Creek TH at 11,340'   311 RP   10.9 mi RT   5,022' total   Class 2

The Quartzville Creek Trailhead is more accessible in the winter than the Kite Lake Trailhead, and you can use this combination for winter ascents of all four peaks. Start at the Quartzville Creek Trailhead at 11,340 feet, follow the Licambro to Cameron's summit, do the long trek over to Democrat, return to Cameron's summit, and continue to Bross. Adding Democrat to the Licambro significantly increases the mileage and elevation gain.

7. Mount Sherman 14,036 feet

Mount Sherman is 9 miles west of Fairplay and 8 miles east of Leadville. You can see the mountain from US 285 in South Park, but the flat summit does not stand out. It is even less distinguished from the west side. Much of Mount Sherman, including the summit, is on private property. Please respect the permission that allows you to climb this mountain.

Some people malign Sherman because it is so easy to climb; others cherish Sherman because it is so easy to climb. It all depends on your outlook. Sherman is popular as an early season training climb, and sometimes people sleep on the summit before departing on high-altitude adventures in Earth's elevated ranges. Sherman is also the only Fourteener that has had a successful aircraft landing on its summit. Thus does Sherman touch greatness.

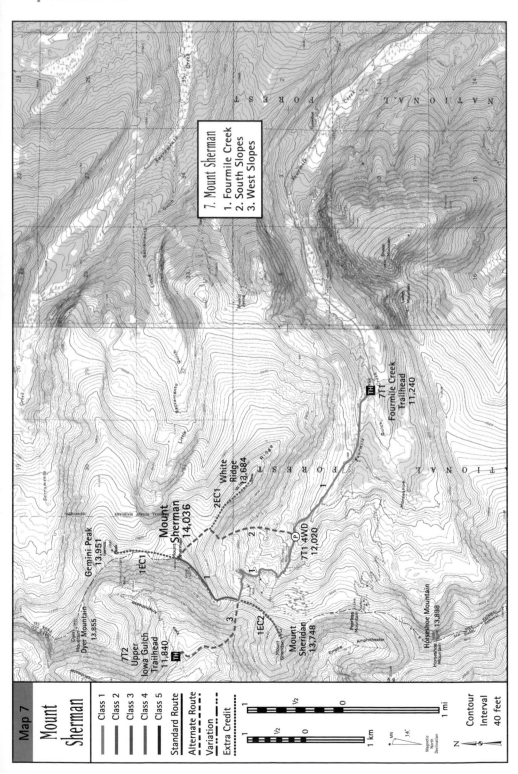

7. Mount Sherman
1. Fourmile Creek
2. South Slopes
3. West Slopes

Map 7
Mount
Sherman

Class 1
Class 2
Class 3
Class 4
Class 5
Standard Route
Alternate Route
Variation
Extra Credit

Contour
Interval
40 feet

7E – Mount Sherman Essentials

Elevations	14,036' (NGVD29) 14,040' (NAVD88)
Rank	Colorado's 45th highest ranked peak
Location	Park and Lake counties, Colorado, USA
Range	Central Mosquito Range
Summit Coordinates	39.2237° -106.1705° (WGS84)
Ownership/Contact	Pike and San Isabel national forests – 719-553-1400
	Public Land with inholdings
Prominence and Saddle	896' from 13,140' Democrat–Buckskin saddle
Isolation and Parent	8.10 miles to Mount Democrat
USGS Maps	**Mount Sherman**, Fairplay West
USFS Maps	**Pike National Forest**, San Isabel National Forest
Trails Illustrated Map	Map #110 Leadville/Fairplay
Book Map	See Map 7 on page 84
Nearest Town	Breckenridge – Population 2,700 – Elevation 9,600'
Mount Sherman 🏃 Easiest Route	7R1 – Fourmile Creek – Class 2
	A Class 1 road hike much of the way, then an easy Class 2 slope and ridge to the top
Sherman's Accolades	Surrounded by private property, Sherman is also the only Fourteener that has had a successful aircraft landing on its summit.

7T – Mount Sherman Trailheads

7T1 – Fourmile Creek Trailhead 11,240 feet 39.1952° -106.1372°

This trailhead provides access to Sherman's southeast side. From the US 285–Colorado 9 junction on Fairplay's south side, go 1.0 mile south on US 285, turn west onto Park County 18, and measure from this point. Go west on Park County 18, enter the Fourmile Creek Valley and Pike National Forest at mile 4.0, pass Fourmile Campground at mile 8.0, and park at the old Leavick town site at mile 10.5. Leavick is not marked, but there are some old mine buildings on the road's north side; this is the trailhead for passenger cars. In winter the road is often plowed as far as Leavick, and this is a popular place for snowmobilers.

7T1 4WD – Fourmile Creek 4WD Trailhead 12,020 feet 39.2072° -106.1647°

From the Fourmile Creek Trailhead at Leavick, 4WD vehicles can continue 2.0 miles west to a locked gate at 12,020 feet, below the Dauntless Mine.

7T2 – Upper Iowa Gulch Trailhead 11,840 feet 39.2248° -106.1882°

This trailhead is at 11,840 feet and provides access to Sherman's west side. Measure from the junction of US 24 (Harrison Avenue) and East Third Street in downtown Leadville. Go 0.3 mile east on East Third Street, turn south (right) onto South Toledo Street, pass East Monroe Street at mile 0.4, and continue south then east on Lake County 2 (paved). Stay north (left) at mile 4.0 on a

Mount Sherman from the east.

dirt road that passes north of an active ASARCO mine. Continue east on Iowa Gulch's north side, go under some large power lines, and park at mile 6.3. The road is passable for passenger cars to this point. Lake County 2 is open to the ASARCO mine in the winter, but not beyond.

7R – Mount Sherman Routes
7R1 – Mount Sherman – Fourmile Creek

From Fourmile Creek TH at 11,240'	*192 RP*	*8.8 mi RT*	*2,796' total*	*Class 2*
From Fourmile Creek 4WD TH at 12,020'	*135 RP*	*4.8 mi RT*	*2,016' total*	*Class 2*

This is the most popular route up Sherman. Start at the Fourmile Creek Trailhead at 11,240 feet and hike 2.0 miles northwest up the 4WD road into the upper basin of Fourmile Creek to a locked gate at 12,020 feet (**39.2072° -106.1647°**). Continue 1.3 miles northwest on the old switchbacking road past the historic Dauntless and Hilltop mines to 12,900 feet (**39.2150° -106.1752°**). Leave the road and hike 0.2 mile west (Class 2) up to the 13,140-foot saddle (**39.2325° -106.1733°**) between Sherman and 13,748-foot Mount Sheridan, the peak 1.4 miles southwest of Sherman. From the saddle, hike 0.9 mile northeast up Sherman's southwest ridge on a good trail to the highpoint (**39.2237° -106.1705°**) near the north end of the long, gentle summit ridge.

7R1 EC1 – Extra Credit – Gemini Peak 13,951 feet 39.2347° -106.1682°

From Fourmile Creek TH at 11,240'	*241 RP*	*10.2 mi RT*	*3,303' total*	*Class 2*
From Fourmile Creek 4WD TH at 12,020'	*184 RP*	*6.2 mi RT*	*2,523' total*	*Class 2*

From Sherman's summit, hike 0.7 mile north to 13,951-foot Gemini Peak. With only 171 feet of prominence, this peak does not rank, but it is officially named, which garners it a position of the list of Colorado's 100 highest peaks. As its name implies, Gemini has twin summits. The two summits are 250 yards apart and have almost equal elevations. The northeast summit (39.2347° -106.1682°) is the higher of the two summits, but purists will want to tag the top of both summits. Do not descend another way; return over Sherman's summit.

7R1 EC2 – Extra Credit – Mount Sheridan 13,748 feet 39.2090° -106.1848°

From Fourmile Creek TH at 11,240'	161 RP	8.2 mi RT	2,508' total	Class 2
From Fourmile Creek 4WD TH at 12,020'	107 RP	4.2 mi RT	1,728' total	Class 2

From the 13,140-foot saddle between Sherman and Sheridan (39.2325° -106.1733°), hike 0.6 mile southwest up a broad ridge to Mount Sheridan's 13,748-foot summit, one of Colorado's 200 highest ranked peaks.

7R2 – Mount Sherman – South Slopes

From Fourmile Creek TH at 11,240'	203 RP	7.2 mi RT	2,796' total	Class 2
From Fourmile Creek 4WD TH at 12,020'	147 RP	3.2 mi RT	2,036' total	Class 2

This is a direct route up Sherman. In winter it provides a safer route than the Fourmile Creek Route (7R1), but avoid this route in summer when unpleasant scree abounds. Start at the Fourmile Creek Trailhead at 11,240 feet and hike 2.0 miles northwest up the 4WD road to 12,000 feet (39.2073° -106.1639°) in the upper basin of Fourmile Creek (Class 1). Leave the road just before it reaches the locked gate below the Dauntless Mine and climb 0.8 mile north then northwest in or near a shallow gully on Sherman's south face. At 13,000 feet climb 0.3 mile north to the west end of the 13,500-foot saddle (39.2201° -106.1642°) between Sherman and 13,684-foot White Ridge, the summit 1.2 miles southeast of Sherman. From the saddle, hike 0.5 mile northwest up gentle slopes to Sherman's summit.

7R2 EC1 – Extra Credit – White Ridge 13,684 feet 39.2134° -106.1536°

From Fourmile Creek TH at 11,240'	188 RP	7.6 mi RT	2,444' total	Class 2
From Fourmile Creek 4WD TH at 12,020'	134 RP	3.6 mi RT	1,684' total	Class 2

From the west end of the 13,500-foot saddle (39.2201° -106.1642°), hike 0.7 mile southeast on a narrowing ridge to the craggy summit of 13,684-foot White Ridge. This is an unranked summit, but it is officially named and provides a unique view of the higher peaks.

7R2 EC2 – Extra Credit – Tour de Sherman

From Fourmile Creek TH at 11,240'	341 RP	12.0 mi RT	4,095' total	Class 2
From Fourmile Creek 4WD TH at 12,020'	284 RP	8.0 mi RT	3,335' total	Class 2

This is the big one. Start up Sherman's South Slopes Route (7R2) and bag White Ridge, Sherman, Gemini Peak, return over Sherman, then bag Sheridan. Descend the bottom of the Fourmile Creek Route (7R1). This tour will augment your opinion of Sherman.

7R3 – Mount Sherman – West Slopes

From Iowa Gulch TH at 11,840'   181 RP   4.6 mi RT   2,196' net; 2,356' total   Class 2

This is a short climb in the summer, and Sherman's west side is often used as a winter route. Start at the Iowa Gulch Trailhead at 11,840 feet (summer) or the ASARCO mine turn at 10,930 feet (winter). From the Iowa Gulch Trailhead, hike 0.2 mile east-northeast up the road until you are beyond the willows in the valley to the south. Leave the road at 12,000 feet (**39.2257° –106.1853°**), descend a little, and hike 0.5 mile south across open ground to the bottom of the shallow gully below the 13,140-foot saddle between Sherman and 13,748-foot Sheridan. Find the good trail that is visible from the trailhead and follow it east as it switchbacks 0.7 mile up to the Sherman–Sheridan saddle, where this route joins the Fourmile Creek Route (7R1). Climb 0.9 mile northeast up Sherman's southwest ridge on a good trail to Sherman's summit.

Chapter Three

Sawatch Range

Introduction

The Sawatch Range runs through the heartland of the Colorado Rockies. The range has 15 ranked Fourteeners—more than California, and more than any other Colorado range. Four of Colorado's five highest peaks are in the Sawatch.

Like most Colorado ranges, the Sawatch is a linear range that runs north and south. The northern boundary is Interstate 70 west of Vail. The southern boundary for Fourteener climbers is US 50 at Monarch Pass. Between are 80 miles of mountains, where only one paved road—Colorado 82 over Independence Pass—crosses the range. There are four wilderness areas in the Sawatch Range. All the Sawatch Fourteeners can be climbed with Class 2 talus hiking, but there are a few technical routes tucked away on these gentle peaks.

A subgrouping of Sawatch peaks has more to do with naming conventions than geography. Five of the Fourteeners in the southern half of the range carry the names of great universities, so these peaks are known as the Collegiate Peaks. Students from schools with higher namesake peaks are quick to point that out. Students from schools with lower namesake peaks have jokingly schemed the building of large summit cairns to outdo their rivals.

8. Mount of the Holy Cross 14,005 feet

Mount of the Holy Cross is one of Colorado's most beautiful Fourteeners, and the view of Holy Cross from Notch Mountain is breathtaking. A long, deep couloir on the east face and a ledge two-thirds of the way up fill with snow to form the namesake cross. Because of the snow cross, people have accorded religious significance to Holy Cross throughout the past century. Even without snow in the Cross Couloir, Holy Cross is a spectacular peak. It is the most rugged of the Sawatch Fourteeners and could well be Colorado's most famous Fourteener.

Holy Cross is also a shy peak. It is only 14 miles southwest of Vail, but Notch Mountain blocks the view and you can rarely see the cross from surrounding valleys. Distant views are afforded from the peaks of the Tenmile–Mosquito Range. Perhaps the best distant view is from the top of the Vail ski area. The spectacular close-up view from Notch Mountain is reserved for people willing to hike.

Holy Cross is the Sawatch Range's northernmost Fourteener and the highest peak in Eagle County. The Sawatch Range's southernmost Fourteener, Mount Shavano, has the Angel of Shavano on its east face. It is interesting that both the Sawatch Range's northern- and southernmost Fourteeners have snow features with religious significance. Such are the Sawatch Range boundaries.

The Eagle County sheriff's office and local search-and-rescue teams have responded to many rescue calls in recent years on Mount of the Holy Cross. They have asked me to better educate hikers about the special hazards found on this peak, and I am happy to do that. Holy Cross has three unique hazards.

First is the fact that when climbing the standard North Ridge Route (8R1), you must go over Half Moon Pass, descend 970 vertical feet to East Cross Creek, then climb the mountain. The hidden hazard is that you must reclimb the 970 feet to Half Moon Pass on your return trip. This extra climb pushes the total ascent on the North Ridge Route to over 5,600 feet. This is more gain than the standard Keyhole Route (1R1) on Longs Peak, which many people consider to be a very arduous climb.

The second unique hazard on Holy Cross is at the point where the standard North Ridge Route (8R1) reaches the lower north ridge near 11,500 feet. On descent, many hikers reach this point and continue straight down the now broad ridge instead of turning east (right) for the descent back into the East Cross Creek drainage. This is a bad error, since it is a significant departure from the route, and the error is not fail-safe. If you persist in this erroneous descent, you will encounter increasingly steep and rough terrain. Eventually, you will reach the Cross Creek Valley, which does have a trail in it, but this trail will not lead you back to the Half Moon Trailhead.

The third and most poignant hazard is not on the standard North Ridge Route (8R1) but on the much longer and more exposed Halo Ridge Route (8R5). One party of two found the length of this route to be too much for their conditioning and made the choice to separate in the saddle between 13,831-foot Holy Cross Ridge and Holy Cross. The man went to the summit of Holy Cross while the woman agreed to contour below the summit of Holy Cross near the 13,800-foot level and meet the man on the upper part of the North Ridge Route, which was their intended descent route. In spite of an enormous, lengthy search, the woman was never seen again. My personal opinion about what happened is that the woman started the contour and found it to be much longer and rougher than expected. In fact, following this contour may be more difficult than going over the summit. In general, it is very difficult to hold a strict contour, especially if you are tired. If the woman lost altitude during her attempt to contour then ran into a gully, that could easily have drawn her even lower in an attempt to cross the gully. At this point she would be in the middle of the large west face of Holy Cross and badly off route. By choice or chance, she likely descended into the trees, where the terrain steepens. There are small cliffs hidden in these trees, and any stumble or fall could have quickly left her in a life-threatening situation. Now, years later, she has still never been found. This sad story should be sufficient motivation for you to approach this mountain properly conditioned, informed, and equipped.

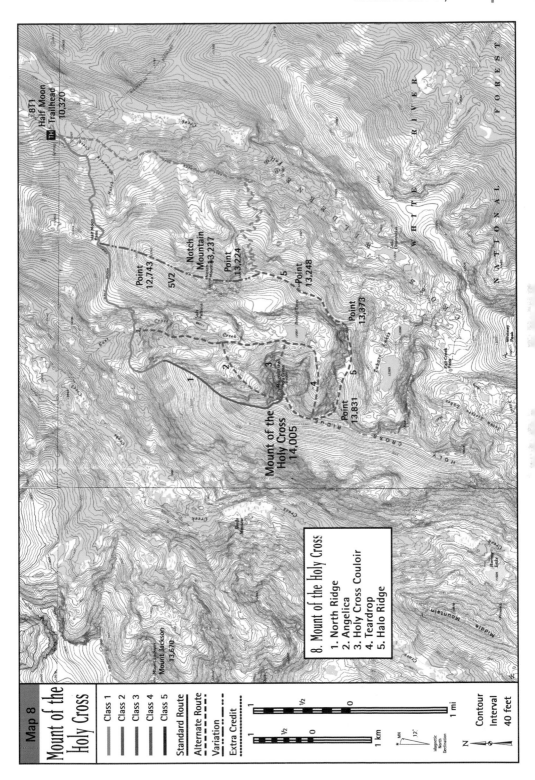

Map 8
Mount of the
Holy Cross

Class 1
Class 2
Class 3
Class 4
Class 5

Standard Route
Alternate Route
Variation
Extra Credit

1 mi
½   0

1 km
½   0

Contour
Interval
40 feet

N

MN

12°

Magnetic
North
Declination

8. Mount of the Holy Cross

1. North Ridge
2. Angelica
3. Holy Cross Couloir
4. Teardrop
5. Halo Ridge

Half Moon
Trailhead
10,320

Point
12,743

Notch
Mountain
13,237

Point
13,224

5V2

Point
13,248

Point
13,373

Point
13,831

Mount of the
Holy Cross
14,005

Mount Jackson
13,670

WHITE RIVER NATIONAL FOREST

HOLY CROSS RIDGE

8E – Mount of the Holy Cross Essentials

Elevations	14,005' (NGVD29) 14,012' (NAVD88)
Rank	Colorado's 51st highest ranked peak
Location	Eagle County, Colorado, USA
Range	Northern Sawatch Range
Summit Coordinates	39.4667° -106.4822° (WGS84)
Ownership/Contact	White River National Forest – Public Land – 970-945-2521
Prominence and Saddle	2,111' from 11,894' saddle north of Hagerman Pass
Isolation and Parent	19.93 miles to Mount Massive
USGS Maps	**Mount of the Holy Cross**, Minturn, Mount Jackson
USFS Map	White River National Forest
Trails Illustrated Map	Map #126 Holy Cross/Ruedi Reservoir
Book Map	See Map 8 on page 91
Nearest Towns	Redcliff – Population 290 – Elevation 8,750'
	Minturn – Population 1,200 – Elevation 7,861'
	Vail – Population 4,800 – Elevation 8,022'
Holy Cross 🥾 Easiest Route	8R1 – North Ridge – Class 2
	A long up-and-down Class 1 approach hike on a trail with Class 2 off-trail hiking near the top
Holy Cross' Accolades	Most famous for the snow cross on its east face, Holy Cross has attracted special attention for the last century. Holy Cross is the Sawatch Range's northernmost Fourteener and the highest peak in Eagle County.

8T – Mount of the Holy Cross Trailhead

8T1 – Half Moon Trailhead 10,320 feet 39.4905° -106.4307°

This trailhead provides access to the north, east, and south sides of Holy Cross. Don't confuse this trailhead with the North and South Half Moon Creek Trailheads described with Elbert and Massive. A few miles west of Vail, take Exit 171 off Interstate 70. From the US 24–Interstate 70 junction, go 2.0 miles south on US 24 to Main and Harrison streets in the town of Minturn. Continue 2.8 miles south on US 24, turn west onto Tigiwon Road (FR 707), and measure anew. This turn is on the north side of a bridge over the Eagle River. Tigiwon Road (dirt) climbs steadily in long sweeping switchbacks, passes the Tigiwon Campground after 6.1 miles, and reaches the Half Moon Trailhead after 8.4 miles. Tigiwon Road is rough but passable in passenger cars. Two trails start at this trailhead; make sure you follow the one you want. The Half Moon Campground is just below the trailhead. The Tigiwon road is closed in winter and usually opens in mid-June.

8R – Mount of the Holy Cross Routes

8R1 – Mount of the Holy Cross – North Ridge

From Half Moon TH at 10,320'   298 RP   10.8 mi RT   3,685' net; 5,625' total   Class 2

This is the easiest route on Holy Cross. Unfortunately, it does not provide a good view of the Cross Couloir. It is also a tough one-day climb. The route crosses Half Moon Pass and requires 970 feet of gain on your return trip. Many people choose to ameliorate this by packing in over the pass and camping near East Cross Creek. By climbing Holy Cross in one day, you will minimize your impact on this beautiful area, but you will maximize impact on yourself. Get in shape for this one!

Start at the Half Moon Trailhead at 10,320 feet and follow the Half Moon Trail (FT 2009) 1.7 miles west to Half Moon Pass at 11,640 feet (39.4940° -106.4537°). Continue over the pass and descend 1.4 miles west then southwest to East Cross Creek at 10,670 feet (39.4885° -106.4707°). There is a nice view of Holy Cross' north face and the Angelica Couloir on this descent, but you cannot see the Cross Couloir. Cross over East Cross Creek, continue 0.5 mile west on the trail, and climb north of some cliffs to reach Holy Cross' north ridge at 11,000 feet (39.4888° -106.4777°). Take note of this position for your descent, since many people have continued down the north ridge to their detriment. Stay on the trail and switchback 0.3 mile south on the west side of the ridge to reach the highest trees, at 11,700 feet (39.4837° -106.4765°). This is the end of the maintained trail. Note this position as well.

From the end of the trail, climb south up the long north ridge. The ridge is mostly talus interspersed with short sections of climber's trail. Stay on or west of the ridge crest. There are good views of Holy Cross' north face from the ridge. With a few extra steps, you can peer down the Angelica Couloir, but you still cannot see the Cross Couloir. Do not knock any rocks down Angelica, since there may be climbers below you.

The north ridge merges with the upper part of the peak at 13,440 feet (39.4683° -106.4850°). From here, climb southeast up steepening talus to a small notch at 13,720 feet (39.4668° -106.4835°). This is the top of Angelica. From here, climb east up a steep west-facing talus slope to the summit (39.4667° -106.4822°). The highest point is an angular talus block that just clears 14,000 feet. The top of the Cross Couloir is 100 feet south of the highest point, and with a few cautious steps, you can peer down the entire length of the couloir. Do not knock any rocks down the couloir, because there may be climbers below you.

8R2 – Mount of the Holy Cross – Angelica

From Half Moon TH at 10,320'   401 RP   10.7 mi RT   3,685' net; 5,625' total   Class 3, Steep Snow

With descent of North Ridge   407 RP   10.9 mi RT   3,685' net; 5,625' total   Class 3, Steep Snow

Angelica is the couloir on the west side of Holy Cross' north face. You can easily preview it when descending from Half Moon Pass to East Cross Creek. Angelica is beautiful to look at and scintillating to climb. It is not as famous

Mount of the Holy Cross
14,005

Mount of the Holy Cross from the northeast.

as the Cross Couloir but provides a shorter, simpler climb. Because of its north aspect, Angelica often holds good snow well into summer.

Start at the Half Moon Trailhead at 10,320 feet and follow the Half Moon Trail (FT 2009) 1.7 miles west to Half Moon Pass at 11,640 feet (**39.4940° -106.4537°**). Continue over the pass, descend 1.4 miles west then southwest to East Cross Creek at 10,670 feet (**39.4885° -106.4707°**), and cross to the west side of the creek. Leave the main trail 60 feet west of East Cross Creek and follow a strong side trail south to some campsites. Persevere past the campsites and find a climber's trail in the forest. This trail is worth finding. Follow the climber's trail 1.0 mile south as it winds through rock outcrops west of East Cross Creek to 11,500 feet on the bench west of beautiful Lake Patricia.

From the bench west of Lake Patricia, continue 0.2 mile south, climb 0.3 mile southwest, and reach the tiny basin below Holy Cross' north face. From 12,000 feet, climb 0.4 mile southwest up this basin toward your angelic objective. At 12,700 feet, the seraph steepens and embraces you.

Climb steepening snow to 12,900 feet, where the couloir splits. A menacing cornice often threatens the northern branch. Take the southern (left) branch. Climb south up the inset, undulating couloir for 800 fanciful feet to reach the North Ridge Route (8R1) in a small notch at 13,720 feet (**39.4668° -106.4835°**). The top of Angelica does not form a cornice, and the snow rolls placidly into the talus. Some small snow gargoyles cling under the north ridge and do threaten Angelica, so don't camp in the couloir. From 13,720 feet, hike 200 yards east up talus on the last part of the North Ridge Route (8R1) to the summit.

8R3 – Mount of the Holy Cross – Holy Cross Couloir *Classic*

From Half Moon TH at 10,320' 448 RP 11.4 mi RT 3,685' net; 5,625' total *Class 3, Steep Snow*

With descent of North Ridge 438 RP 11.1 mi RT 3,685' net; 5,625' total *Class 3, Steep Snow*

This couloir's fame has attracted many climbers over the years. When snow conditions are good, it is a classic climb. When the climber's condition or snow conditions are unfavorable, the experience can rapidly turn into a nightmare. Like most east-facing Colorado snow couloirs, the snow conditions are usually best from mid-June through mid-July. Before mid-June you should carefully consider the avalanche potential. By September the rubble- and ice-infested gully is no longer appealing for climbing. An ice ax and crampons are useful for this climb. This couloir is deeply inset and has a cliff at the bottom.

Start at the Half Moon Trailhead at 10,320 feet and follow the Half Moon Trail (FT 2009) 1.7 miles west to Half Moon Pass at 11,640 feet (39.4940° -106.4537°). Continue over the pass, descend 1.4 miles west then southwest to East Cross Creek at 10,670 feet (39.4885° -106.4707°), and cross to the west side of the creek. Leave the main trail 60 feet west of East Cross Creek and follow a strong side trail south to some campsites. Persevere past the campsites and find a climber's trail in the forest. This trail is worth finding. Follow the climber's trail 1.0 mile south as it winds through rock outcrops west of East Cross Creek to 11,500 feet on the bench west of beautiful Lake Patricia.

From the bench west of Lake Patricia, continue 1.0 mile south into the rugged, boulder-strewn basin below the Cross Couloir (Class 2). The couloir only

Skiing the Holy Cross couloir. Photo by Austin Porzak

becomes visible as you approach it. The bottom of the couloir is an ugly cliff that you can avoid. Continue south up the valley, pass below the bottom of the couloir, and go to the northwest end of the large Bowl of Tears Lake at 12,001 feet. From here, climb west up the slope well south of the couloir and angle north (right) over to the couloir's southern edge at 12,800 feet (some Class 3). The entry point into the couloir is above the cliff at the bottom of the couloir and below the steeper cliffs along the couloir's southern edge.

Test the snow conditions before committing to the couloir, since this is the last good place to turn around if a retreat is indicated. As soon as you enter the couloir, the possibility of falling over the cliff at the bottom of the couloir will pull at your heels.

If both you and the couloir are in good condition, enter and climb it for 1,205 feet to the summit. The climbing is consistent and continuous. The only good place to take a sit-down rest is on the Cross Ledge, two-thirds of the way up, and if the ledge is snow-covered, even this can be a dicey proposition. The steepest part of the couloir is between the Cross Ledge and the summit, where the angle can exceed 45 degrees. The couloir ends abruptly 100 feet south of the highest point. This is one of Colorado's most dramatic finishes, and your abrupt release from the couloir's confines onto the gentle, view-laden summit is likely to spark a song. For your continued comfort, descend the North Ridge Route (8R1).

8R4 – Mount of the Holy Cross – Teardrop

From Half Moon TH at 10,320'	*418 RP*	*13.0 mi RT*	*3,685' net; 5,625' total*	*Class 3, Steep Snow*
With descent of North Ridge	*394 RP*	*11.9 mi RT*	*3,685' net; 5,625' total*	*Class 3, Steep Snow*

This long route provides a good alternative to the Holy Cross Couloir and allows you to visit one of Colorado's reclusive alpine cirques. Teardrop is only a viable route with good snow conditions, and this slope tends to melt out early in the summer. Don't wait too long for this one.

Follow the Holy Cross Couloir Route (8R3) to Bowl of Tears Lake at 12,001 feet. Continue 0.3 mile south and hike 0.5 mile west into the narrow basin under the south face of Holy Cross to 12,800 feet. This is a special, seldom-visited place. Continue west up steepening snow to the 13,500-foot saddle southwest of Holy Cross (39.4630° -106.4870°). The last 300 feet of this slope are steep, and a cornice may guard the exit. If so, the easiest exit is north of the cornice. From the 13,500-foot saddle, hike 0.4 mile northeast up talus to the summit.

8R5 – Mount of the Holy Cross – Halo Ridge

From Half Moon TH at 10,320'	*367 RP*	*15.8 mi RT*	*3,685' net; 5,189' total*	*Class 2*
With descent of North Ridge	*319 RP*	*13.3 mi RT*	*3,685' net; 5,407' total*	*Class 2*

This route circles the Bowl of Tears Basin and provides excellent views of the Cross Couloir. The length, elevation gain, and exposed position of the Halo Ridge make it a serious undertaking and it has proven fatal. You can reduce the commitment by sleeping in the Notch Mountain shelter cabin. This shelter is not locked, but check current conditions with the Forest Service office in Minturn at 970-827-5715.

From the Half Moon Trailhead at 10,320 feet, follow the Fall Creek Trail 2.5 miles south to the bottom of the Notch Mountain Trail at 11,160 feet (39.4708° -106.4417°). Hike 2.8 miles west up the Notch Mountain Trail to the Notch Mountain shelter at 13,080 feet (39.4693° -106.4592°). Holy Cross pops into view as you crest the ridge.

At the shelter, Holy Cross' summit is less than 1,000 feet above you, but the Bowl of Tears Basin intervenes. The 2.1-mile-long Halo Ridge around the south end of the basin crosses three progressively higher summits. From the shelter, go 0.4 mile south-southwest to Point 13,248 (39.4642° -106.4625°), a ranked Thirteener, and continue 0.7 mile southwest to Point 13,373 (39.4568° -106.4712°). Turn the corner and go 0.3 mile west to a wide, flat portion of the ridge, where you can rest suspended between the summits. Continue 0.5 mile west-northwest to Point 13,831 (39.4588° -106.4858°), which is the summit of Holy Cross Ridge and one of Colorado's 100 highest ranked peaks. Descend 0.3 mile north to the 13,500-foot saddle between Holy Cross Ridge and Holy Cross, then hike 0.4 mile northeast up talus to the remaining summit—Holy Cross (39.4667° -106.4822°).

8R5 V1 – Variation – Orbital

From Half Moon TH at 10,320'   *319 RP*   *13.3 mi RT*   *3,685' net; 5,407' total*   *Class 2*

Instead of returning to the Notch Mountain shelter, descend the North Ridge Route (8R1). This descent shortens the distance and increases the total elevation gain. This tour is best done as a long day hike, because you do not retrace any steps. Remember that this route keeps you high and exposed to weather for a long time.

8R5 V2 – Variation – Notch Mountain 13,237 feet 39.4773° -106.4605°

From Half Moon TH at 10,320'	*441 RP*	*12.8 mi RT*	*3,685' net; 6,037' total*	*Class 2+*
With descent of North Ridge	*369 RP*	*11.8 mi RT*	*3,685' net; 5,811' total*	*Class 2+*
With descent of Notch Mountain Trail	*417 RP*	*14.3 mi RT*	*3,685' net; 5,593' total*	*Class 2+*

This long, scenic tour is the big one. Modify the beginning of the Halo Ridge Route (8R5) to include a traverse of Notch Mountain. Start at the Half Moon Trailhead at 10,320 feet and follow the Half Moon Trail (FT 2009) 1.7 miles west to Half Moon Pass at 11,640 feet (39.4940° -106.4537°). Leave the Half Moon Trail, and either hike 0.7 mile south-southwest up talus to Point 12,743 or follow a rough trail that swings east and ascends the east face of Point 12,743. Continue 0.7 mile south-southwest on the ridge over blocky talus to the 13,237-foot summit of Notch Mountain (39.4773° -106.4605°). The view of Holy Cross from Notch Mountain's summit is even better than the view from the shelter cabin.

The traverse across the notch between Notch Mountain's two summits requires careful route finding and some Class 2+ scampering. The north face of

Point 13,224—Notch Mountain's lower, southern summit—rises above the notch in a smooth sweep of rock. Navigating around this cliff is the crux of the route.

From Notch Mountain's 13,237-foot main summit, scamper south down broken ledges to reach the vicinity of the notch (Class 2+). Go around an unlikely corner on the west side of the ridge then scamper south on broken blocks (Class 2+). When the cliffs above relent, scamper up broken rock to Point 13,224 (39.4728° -106.4608°), one of Colorado's most favored viewpoints. From here, hike south down a trail through talus to the Notch Mountain shelter cabin (39.4693° -106.4592°) and continue on the Halo Ridge Route to Holy Cross' summit. Descend the North Ridge Route (8R1) or return to the Notch Mountain Trail.

9. Mount Massive 14,421 feet

Mount Massive is 11 miles southwest of Leadville, and its east slopes dominate the view. Massive is massive, and the mountain's name captures its essence. Massive has five summits above 14,000 feet on a 3-mile-long summit ridge. Massive is not just a peak; it is a region. No other single Fourteener carries with it such a large area above treeline. If Massive were truncated at 14,000 feet, the area of the resulting plateau would be nearly half a square mile! No other peak in the 48 contiguous states has a greater area above 14,000 feet. By this measure, Massive reigns supreme.

9E – Mount Massive Essentials

Elevations	14,421' (NGVD29) 14,428' (NAVD88)
Rank	Colorado's 2nd highest ranked peak
Location	Lake County, Colorado, USA
Range	Central Sawatch Range
Summit Coordinates	39.1878° -106.4755° (WGS84)
Ownership/Contact	San Isabel National Forest – Public Land – 719-553-1400
Prominence and Saddle	1,961' from 12,460' Massive–Elbert saddle
Isolation and Parent	5.08 miles to Mount Elbert
USGS Maps	**Mount Massive**, Mount Champion, Leadville South
USFS Map	San Isabel National Forest
Trails Illustrated Map	Map #127 Aspen/Independence Pass
Book Map	See Map 9 on page 99
Nearest Town	Leadville – Population 2,700 – Elevation 10,152 feet
Mount Massive 🎿 Easiest Route	9R1 – East Slopes – Class 2
	A long Class 1 approach hike on a trail with some Class 2 hiking along the summit ridge
Massive's Accolades	Easily visible from the Leadville area, Massive has five summits above 14,000'. Massive is massive.

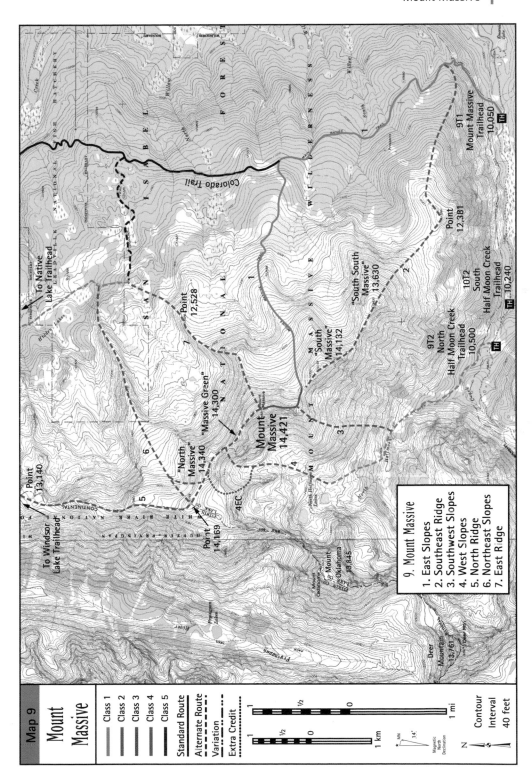

Map 9
Mount
Massive

Class 1
Class 2
Class 3
Class 4
Class 5

Standard Route
Alternate Route
Variation
Extra Credit

1 mi
½
0

1 km
½
0

Contour
Interval
40 feet

N

MN
14°

Magnetic
North
Declination

9. Mount Massive
1. East Slopes
2. Southeast Ridge
3. Southwest Slopes
4. West Slopes
5. North Ridge
6. Northeast Slopes
7. East Ridge

Mount Massive
Trailhead
10,050
9T1

Point
12,381

South
Half Moon Creek
Trailhead
10,240
10T2

North
Half Moon Creek
Trailhead
10,500
9T2

"South South
Massive"
13,630

"South
Massive"
14,132

Mount
Massive
14,421

"Massive Green"
14,300

Point
12,528

"North
Massive"
14,340

Point
13,140

To Native
Lake Trailhead

To Windsor
Lake Trailhead

Point
14,169

4EC

Mount
Oklahoma
13,845

Deer
Mountain
13,761

Colorado Trail

9T – Mount Massive Trailheads

9T1 – Mount Massive Trailhead 10,050 feet 39.1318° -106.4187°

This trailhead provides access to Massive's east side. From Third Street and US 24 (Harrison Avenue) in downtown Leadville, go 3.6 miles southwest on US 24 to Colorado 300. Turn west onto Colorado 300 (paved) and measure from this point. Go 0.7 mile and turn south (left) onto Lake County 11 (dirt). Turn southwest (right) at mile 1.8 onto another dirt road marked with signs for Half Moon Creek. Pass the San Isabel National Forest boundary at mile 3.9, Half Moon Campground at mile 5.6, Half Moon West Campground at mile 5.7, North Mount Elbert Trailhead at mile 6.6, Elbert Creek Campground at mile 6.7, and reach the well-marked Mount Massive Trailhead at mile 7.0. The road is good to this point, and there is a parking lot on the road's north side. Winter road closure varies from the start of the Half Moon Creek Road 1.8 miles from US 24 to the Half Moon Campground at mile 5.6.

9T2 – North Half Moon Creek Trailhead 10,500 feet 39.1332° -106.4580°

This trailhead provides access to Massive's south and west sides. Don't confuse this trailhead with the Half Moon Trailhead described with Mount of the Holy Cross. From the Mount Massive Trailhead (mile 7.0), continue west; pass the FR 110–1103A junction at mile 9.0, continue straight on FR 110, and reach the trailhead at mile 9.5. The road beyond the FR 110–1103A junction is 4WD, and most people park passenger cars at this junction.

9T3 – Native Lake Trailhead 10,760 feet 39.2553° -106.4313°

This trailhead provides access to Massive's northeast side. From Sixth Street and US 24 in downtown Leadville, go 4.4 miles west to the south edge of

Mount Massive from the east.

Turquoise Lake on Lake County 4. Cross the dam, go along the south side of Turquoise Lake, and continue west on Lake County 4 (the Hagerman Pass Road) for an additional 6.8 miles. The marked trailhead is on the south side of the road, just before the road curves back to the northeast and starts climbing to the pass. There is a small parking lot at the trailhead.

9T4 – Windsor Lake Trailhead 10,780 feet 39.2567° -106.4327°

This trailhead provides access to Massive's north side. From the Native Lake Trailhead, continue west for an additional 200 yards to the Windsor Lake Trailhead. There is ample parking on the north side of the road, just before the road curves back to the northeast and starts climbing to Hagerman Pass. To find the start of the Windsor Lake Trail, cross to the south side of the torrent of water coming out of the Carlton diversion tunnel; use a plank bridge to cross the concrete channel. Cross a second, small stream and find the trail sign just beyond.

9R – Mount Massive Routes

9R1 – Mount Massive – East Slopes

From Mount Massive TH at 10,050'   267 RP   13.6 mi RT   4,371' net; 4,531' total   Class 2

This long hike is mostly on a good trail, and this is the easiest way to climb Massive. Start at the Mount Massive Trailhead at 10,050 feet and follow the Colorado Trail northeast then north through the forest. Cross South Willow Creek at mile 2.4, cross Willow Creek at mile 3.0, and at mile 3.3, reach the junction with the Mount Massive Trail at 11,260 feet (**39.1847° -106.4280°**). Go 3.0 miles west on the Mount Massive Trail up Massive's vast east slopes. The Colorado Fourteener Initiative has improved and rerouted this trail to avoid wetlands. Climb to the 13,900-foot saddle (**39.1815° -106.4725°**) between 14,132-foot "South Massive" and Massive. From this saddle, climb 0.2 mile northwest up a steep slope then 0.3 mile north on a Class 2 climber's trail along Massive's south ridge to the summit (**39.1878° -106.4755°**). The size of this peak will become apparent long before you reach the summit.

9R1 EC – Extra Credit – "South Massive" 14,132 feet 39.1790° -106.4682°

Class 2

From the 13,900-foot saddle, climb 0.3 mile southeast to the 14,132-foot summit of "South Massive." The highpoint is a spectacular block perched above the others. With 232 feet of prominence, this summit garners honorable mention on Colorado's list of Fourteeners.

9R2 – Mount Massive – Southeast Ridge

From Mount Massive TH at 10,050'   459 RP   11.4 mi RT   4,371' net; 5,817' total   Class 2
With descent of East Slopes   397 RP   12.5 mi RT   4,371' net; 5,174' total   Class 2

This laconic tour collects Massive's three southern summits. If you are fit and like to wend your way above the trail and its attendant crowds, this route is for you. Start at the Mount Massive Trailhead at 10,050 feet and follow the Colorado Trail 1.0 mile northeast to 10,600 feet (39.1604 -106.4101), where the trail turns northwest. The introduction is over.

Leave the comfortable trail and climb 1.1 miles west through open trees to treeline at 11,800 feet. You've paid your dues. More than 3 miles of unfettered ridge now lie ahead of you. Continue 0.4 mile west to 12,200 feet and discover a hidden alcove. Wend your way 0.2 mile southwest through this petite parlor to Point 12,381 (39.1605° -106.4393°). If you are lucky, you may see goats here. Point 12,381 is one of Massive's least-visited summits, and it will reward you with an unobstructed view of Mount Elbert.

From Point 12,381, descend 0.2 mile northwest to a 12,180-foot saddle, then climb 1.0 mile northwest up a grassy slope to Point 13,630, alias "South South Massive" (39.1708° -106.4561°). This is another of Massive's seldom-visited summits, and no matter what your mood is, you will be isolated here. Descend 0.4 mile northwest to a 13,380-foot saddle, then climb 0.6 mile northwest up the now rougher ridge to 14,132-foot "South Massive" (39.1790° -106.4682°). The highest point of this significant summit is a spectacular block perched above its neighbors.

From "South Massive," descend 0.3 mile northwest to the 13,900-foot saddle at the top of the Mount Massive Trail. Your isolation ends here. Continue 0.5 mile northwest then north up the ridge on the top part of the East Slopes Route to Massive's lofty 14,421-foot summit (39.1878° -106.4755°). Descending the East Slopes Route (9R1) will put your ascent into perspective.

9R3 – Mount Massive – Southwest Slopes

From North Half Moon Creek TH at 10,500'   249 RP   5.8 mi RT   3,921' net; 4,001' total   Class 2

This is the shortest route up Massive, but it is much steeper than the East Slopes Route (9R1). Start at the North Half Moon Creek Trailhead at 10,500 feet and follow the North Half Moon Creek Trail 1.3 miles northwest into the Mount Massive Wilderness to a large meadow just beyond a small creek crossing. Massive's large southwest slopes and its southern subpeaks are now directly northeast of the trail. Leave the North Half Moon Creek Trail at the northwest (upper) end of the meadow at 11,200 feet (39.1678° -106.4801°) and turn north (right) onto a trail leading directly up Massive's steep southwest slopes. Many people have missed this turn.

Skirt some initial cliffs on their northwest end and climb into the bottom of a shallow, grass-filled basin between 14,132-foot "South Massive" and Massive. Follow the trail as it avoids the steep upper basin and climbs north through some rocks to reach Massive's south ridge west of and above the 13,900-foot saddle between "South Massive" and Massive. The ascent from the valley to this high perch is relentless, but compensations are wonderful wildflowers near treeline and expansive views. Climb north on a Class 2 climber's trail along Massive's south ridge to the summit (39.1878° -106.4755°).

9R4 – Mount Massive – West Slopes

From North Half Moon Creek TH at 10,500'	*266 RP*	*8.8 mi RT*	*3,921' net; 4,201' total*	*Class 2*
With descent of Southwest Slopes	*245 RP*	*7.3 mi RT*	*3,921' net; 4,121' total*	*Class 2*

This route allows you to touch the heart of the Mount Massive Wilderness. It also offers you the opportunity to traverse much of Massive's long summit ridge. Start at the North Half Moon Creek Trailhead at 10,500 feet and follow the North Half Moon Creek Trail northwest into the Mount Massive Wilderness as the trail climbs on the east side of North Half Moon Creek. At 1.3 miles, pass the meadow where the Southwest Slopes Route (9R3) leaves the valley. Continue northwest then north on the North Half Moon Creek Trail into the large basin under Massive's west slopes. The trail goes to the southern of the two North Half Moon lakes then climbs up grassy, flower-laden benches east of the lakes. The trail becomes less distinct as it climbs north into the basin above the lakes and finally disappears.

Massive's summit is on the basin's east side, and 14,340-foot "North Massive" is at the basin's north end. There is an impressive tower at the south end of a subsidiary ridge running southwest from "North Massive." Several routes are possible from the basin to Massive's summit. They all involve climbing up tedious talus and scree slopes. The route described here minimizes time spent on steep scree slopes.

Climb northeast into the upper basin between the ridge with the impressive tower on it and Massive's north ridge. This basin is under the south face of "North Massive." Stay north of some cliffs and climb steep scree to Massive's north ridge at the 14,060-foot saddle between "North Massive" and Massive (39.1928° -106.4829°). This saddle is just south of some pesky rock towers on Massive's north ridge. Stay south of these towers when approaching the ridge. From the 14,060-foot saddle, climb southeast on the gentle ridge over the rounded 14,300-foot summit of "Massive Green" (39.1909° -106.4811°) and continue on the still-gentle ridge to Massive's 14,421-foot main summit (39.1878° -106.4755°). Descend the Southwest Slopes Route (9R3).

9R4 EC – Extra Credit – "North Massive" 14,340 feet 39.1956° -106.4876°

From North Half Moon Creek TH at 10,500'	*352 RP*	*10.2 mi RT*	*3,921' net; 4,901' total*	*Class 3*
With descent of Southwest Slopes	*283 RP*	*8.0 mi RT*	*3,921' net; 4,481' total*	*Class 3*

This lofty Tour de Massive collects most of Massive's summits. From the upper basin of the West Slopes Route (9R4), climb north then northeast up a scree slope to reach the south ridge of 14,340-foot "North Massive." This is the ridge with the impressive tower on its south end. Climb north up the now easy ridge to the gentle slopes west of "North Massive's" summit. This is a notable, seldom-visited place. Climb 0.3 mile northeast to "North Massive's" surprising summit. The western of two summits is the highest, and is Colorado's fifth highest summit. With 280 feet of prominence, "North Massive" nearly qualifies for official Fourteener status; it is Colorado's only summit over 14,000 feet with a venerable soft rank.

Scramble 100 yards east, visit "North Massive's" slightly lower but spectacular east summit, then descend 200 yards southeast to a 14,100-foot saddle southeast of "North Massive." This lively descent requires careful route finding and some easy Class 3 scrambling. There are several ways to accomplish this descent. With clever, devious route finding, you can keep the difficulty at Class 2+. From the 14,100-foot saddle, scramble southeast on or below the rough ridge. This stretch of ridge also requires careful route finding and some Class 3 scrambling to pass some rock towers on their west sides. The difficulties end abruptly as you reach the 14,060-foot saddle (39.1928° -106.4829°) south of these towers and rejoin the West Slopes Route. From the 14,060-foot saddle, continue on the now gentle ridge to the broad 14,300-foot "Massive Green" (39.1909° -106.4811°). Continue on the still-gentle ridge to Massive's 14,421-foot main summit.

Descend south on the upper part of the East Slopes Route (9R1) to the junction with the Southwest Slopes Route above the 13,900-foot saddle between Massive and "South Massive" and descend the Southwest Slopes Route (9R3).

9R5 – Mount Massive – North Ridge

From Windsor Lake TH at 10,780'	*454 RP*	*12.4 mi RT*	*3,641' net; 4,679' total*	*Class 3*
With descent of East Ridge	*395 RP*	*12.3 mi RT*	*3,641' net; 4,838' total*	*Class 3*

For aficionados of the high and wild, this is it. You can spend the day above the trees walking along one of the highest stretches of the Continental Divide in North America. Start at the Windsor Lake Trailhead at 10,780 feet and follow a steep trail 1.0 mile southwest to Windsor Lake at 11,620 feet (39.2420° -106.4848°). When dawn light glances across snow slopes above the lake, this is one of Colorado's most beautiful places.

Go around the south side of the lake and hike southwest above the lake up a lush basin dotted with marsh marigolds. Angle southwest, cross a small drainage, then climb a steep slope to the 12,660-foot saddle (39.2339° -106.4978°) on the Continental Divide just south of the rocky ramparts of Point 12,740. From the saddle, you are treated to a unique view of upper Fryingpan River Valley. The introduction is over, and from just beyond the saddle, you can peer south toward Massive's main summit almost 4 miles away.

Hike south along the divide and contour below Points 13,020 and 13,140 on their west sides to a 13,020-foot saddle (39.2197° -106.4940°). These gentle slopes harbor fleets of alpine wildflowers. On Massive's north ridge, you are suspended between the Mount Massive Wilderness and the Hunter–Fryingpan Wilderness. Hike high and free for an additional 1.6 miles to Point 14,169 (39.1983° -106.4936°). This seldom-visited summit commands a massive view and has the distinction of being the highpoint of the Hunter-Fryingpan Wilderness Area. The Continental Divide continues south from here and avoids Massive's main summit. Going where the divide dares not, hike 0.4 mile southeast to 14,340-foot "North Massive" (39.1956° -106.4876°) and continue on the Northeast Slopes Route (9R6) to Massive's main summit. If the day is long and electricity-free, you may choose to return along the divide. Descending the East Ridge Route (9R7) completes a comprehensive Tour de Massive.

9R5 EC – Extra Credit – Points 13,020 and 13,140

Class 2

Go to the summits of Points 13,020 (39.2282° -106.4900°) and 13,140 (39.2207° -106.4917°) along the way.

9R6 – Mount Massive – Northeast Slopes

From Native Lake TH at 10,760'	*538 RP*	*15.2 mi RT*	*3,661' net; 5,990' total*	*Class 3, Mod Snow*
With descent of East Ridge	*458 RP*	*13.7 mi RT*	*3,661' net; 5,530' total*	*Class 3, Mod Snow*

Removed from the crowds in Half Moon Creek, this long route is suitable for a backpacking adventure, and it allows you to climb the permanent snowfield on "North Massive's" northeast flank. This snowfield is prominent from Leadville, and it graces Massive long after other snowfields melt.

Start at the Native Lake Trailhead at 10,760 feet and follow the Highline Trail 1.3 miles south to a broad saddle at 11,860 feet (39.2361° -106.4607°). Cross the saddle, descend two sweeping switchbacks, pass west of Native Lake, and 2.3 miles south of the 11,860-foot saddle, reach 11,200 feet (39.2164° -106.4536°), where the trail climbs out of the Hidden Lakes Basin. Leave the trail and hike 0.4 mile southwest to the bottom of "North Massive's" east ridge (39.2124° -106.4586°). Climb 1.2 miles west-southwest up this distinct ridge to 12,800 feet (39.2062° -106.4769°) below the basin you have worked so hard to reach. Cross the basin to 13,400 feet, choose your line on the snowfield, and climb it. From the top of the snowfield, it is easy to climb Point 14,169, Massive's northern-most 14,000-foot summit and the highpoint of the Hunter-Fryingpan Wilderness Area. Hike 0.4 mile southeast to "North Massive's" 14,340-foot summit and continue 1.0 mile east then southeast along the lively high traverse to Massive's 14,421-foot summit (Class 3). Ascending the Northeast Slopes Route and descending the East Ridge Route (9R7) makes a pithy Tour de Massive.

9R7 – Mount Massive – East Ridge

From Native Lake TH at 10,760'	*347 RP*	*12.2 mi RT*	*3,661' net; 5,037' total*	*Class 2*

This route retains the wilderness flavor of the Northeast Slopes Route (9R6) but eliminates its extra summits and difficulties. Start at the Native Lake Trailhead at 10,760 feet and follow the Highline Trail 1.3 miles south to a broad saddle at 11,860 feet (39.2361° -106.4607°). Cross the saddle, descend two sweeping switchbacks, pass west of Native Lake, and 2.3 miles south of the 11,860-foot saddle, reach 11,200 feet (39.2164° -106.4536°), where the trail climbs out of the Hidden Lakes Basin. This is the cutoff point for the Northeast Slopes Route. Continue 0.3 mile south on the trail to 11,580 feet (39.2075° -106.4511°), where the trail turns east just north of two small lakes. If you begin descending to the east along the trail, you have gone too far.

Leave the trail and hike 0.4 mile southwest past treeline to the base of a northeast-facing slope. Climb 0.4 mile up this slope to tiny Point 12,528 on the ridge above, where you can rest for a moment apart. Follow the now well-defined ridge as it curves gracefully southwest toward Massive's heights. The ridge levels briefly at 13,500 feet before turning west and merging with Massive's final face. Climb west directly to the summit.

9R8 – Mount Massive – Massive Mania

From Windsor Lake TH at 10,780'   436 RP   11.9 mi RT   4,953' total   Class 3

This is the big one. You have looked at it from Leadville for years; now climb it. Start at the Windsor Lake Trailhead at 10,780 feet and climb the North Ridge Route (9R5). Descend the Southeast Ridge Route (9R2) to the Mount Massive Trailhead at 10,050 feet and a prearranged vehicle shuttle. Along the way, you can climb all nine of Massive's summits, five of which are above 14,000 feet. At the end of this expedition, you will appreciate firsthand that Massive is massive.

10. Mount Elbert 14,433 feet

All rise. This mighty lump has received many accolades. Mount Elbert is the highest peak in Lake County, the Sawatch Range, in Colorado, and in the Rocky Mountains. Elbert is in plain view 12 miles southwest of Leadville, but many people mistake Colorado's highest peak for a Thirteener. With more intense inspection, you can see Elbert for the monarch it is. Elbert's size, not its height, fools people. Elbert is indeed a big mountain, and if by any misfortune you end up crosswise with the mountain, Elbert's size will quickly come into sharp focus.

Elbert is one of Colorado's easiest and most enjoyable Fourteener hikes. On a busy summer day, Colorado's highest summit will hold many people, and reports of more than 100 people on the summit at once are not uncommon. Because of the easy winter access to the South Mount Elbert Trailhead, Elbert has become a popular winter hike, and on one occasion, I saw 30 people on or near Elbert's summit on a less than ideal January day.

10E – Mount Elbert Essentials

Elevations	14,433' (NGVD29) 14,440' (NAVD88)
Rank	Colorado's highest ranked peak
Location	Lake County, Colorado, USA
Range	Central Sawatch Range
Summit Coordinates	39.1175° -106.4455° (WGS84)
Ownership/Contact	San Isabel National Forest – Public Land – 719-553-1400
Prominence and Saddle	9,093' from 5,340' Elbert–Whitney saddle in California

10E – Mount Elbert Essentials

Isolation and Parent	669.98 miles to Mount Whitney, California
USGS Maps	**Mount Elbert, Mount Massive,** Granite, Independence Pass
USFS Map	San Isabel National Forest
Trails Illustrated Maps	Map #127 Aspen/Independence Pass
	Map #110 Leadville/Fairplay
Book Map	See Map 10 on page 108
Nearest Town	Leadville – Population 2,700 – Elevation 10,152'
Mount Elbert 🏃 Easiest Route	10R2 – East Ridge – Class 1
	A long, undulating Class 1 hike on a trail all the way to the top
Elbert's Accolades	Mount Elbert is the highest peak in Lake County, in Colorado, and in the
	Rocky Mountains. Elbert is also Colorado's most prominent peak and one
	of only three Ultra Prominent Peaks in the state. Elbert is the highest state
	summit in 48 states, surpassed only by Whitney in CA and Denali in AK.
	Elbert is the most prominent state summit in 46 states, surpassed only by
	Whitney in CA, Rainier in WA, Mauna Kea in HI, and Denali in AK.

10T – Mount Elbert Trailheads

10T1 – North Mount Elbert Trailhead 10,040 feet 39.1420° -106.4102°

This trailhead provides access to Elbert's northeast side. From Third Street and US 24 (Harrison Avenue) in downtown Leadville, go 3.6 miles southwest on US 24 to Colorado 300. Turn west onto Colorado 300 and measure from this point. Go 0.7 mile west on Colorado 300 (paved) and turn south (left) onto Lake County 11 (dirt). Turn southwest (right) at mile 1.8 onto another dirt road marked with signs for Half Moon Creek. Pass the San Isabel National Forest boundary at mile 3.9, Half Moon Campground at mile 5.6, Half Moon West Campground at mile 5.7, and reach the signed North Mount Elbert Trailhead on the south side of the road at mile 6.6. Winter road closure varies from the start of the Half Moon Creek Road 1.8 miles from US 24 to the Half Moon Campground at mile 5.6.

10T2 – South Half Moon Creek Trailhead 10,240 feet 39.1403° -106.4532°

This trailhead provides access to Elbert's west face. Don't confuse this trailhead with the Half Moon Trailhead described with Mount of the Holy Cross. From the North Mount Elbert Trailhead (mile 6.6), continue west and reach the South Half Moon Creek Trailhead at the FR 110–1103A junction at mile 9.0. The road is good to this point.

10T3 – South Mount Elbert Trailhead 9,620 feet 39.0994° -106.3673°

This trailhead provides access to Elbert's east side and the South Mount Elbert Trail. Turn north from Colorado 82 onto Lake County 24. This turn is 4.0 miles west of the US 24–Colorado 82 junction and 2.3 miles east of the town of Twin

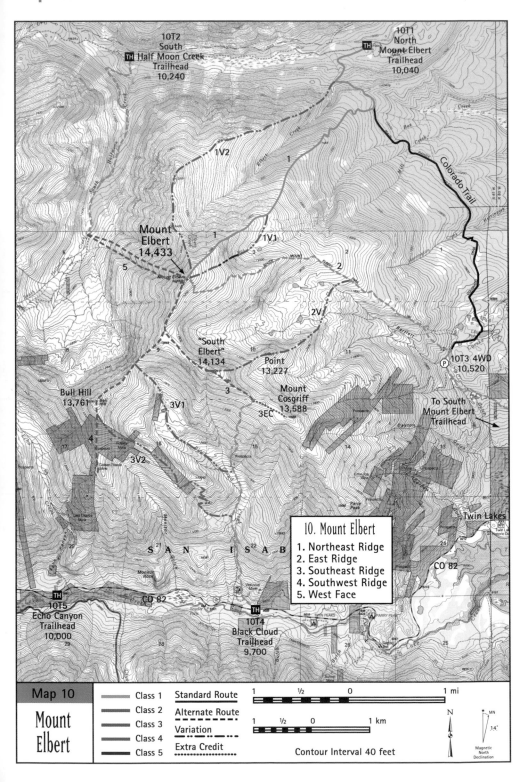

10T2
South
TH Half Moon Creek
Trailhead
10,240

10T1
North
TH Mount Elbert
Trailhead
10,040

Colorado Trail

1V2

1

Mount
Elbert
14,433

1V1

1

5

2

2V

"South
Elbert"
14,134

Point
13,227

Mount
Cosgriff
13,588

11

10T3 4WD
10,520

Bull Hill
13,761

3V1

3

3EC

To South
Mount Elbert
Trailhead

4

3V2

S A N   I S A B

Twin Lakes

CO 82

10. Mount Elbert
1. Northeast Ridge
2. East Ridge
3. Southeast Ridge
4. Southwest Ridge
5. West Face

TH
10T5
Echo Canyon
Trailhead
10,000

CO 82

TH
10T4
Black Cloud
Trailhead
9,700

Map 10		Class 1	Standard Route	1	½	0	1 mi
		Class 2	Alternate Route				
Mount		Class 3	Variation	1	½	0	1 km
Elbert		Class 4	Extra Credit				
		Class 5		Contour Interval 40 feet			

N

MN
14°

Magnetic
North
Declination

Lakes on Colorado 82. Measure from the Colorado 82–Lake County 24 junction, and go 1.0 mile west on Lake County 24 (paved) to the Lakeview Campground entrance. Continue 0.3 mile west on Lake County 24 to the trailhead, which is a pull-through parking area on the west side of the road as the road turns north. This area is accessible in winter.

10T3 4WD – South Mount Elbert 4WD Trailhead 10,520 feet 39.1055° -106.3952°

From the South Mount Elbert Trailhead, 4WD vehicles can leave Lake County 24 and go 2.0 miles west then northwest on FR 125.1B, passing the Sure Pretty overlook en route, to the end of the road just south of Corske Creek at 10,520 feet.

10T4 – Black Cloud Trailhead 9,700 feet 39.0588° -106.4295°

This trailhead provides access to Elbert's south side. The trailhead is just north of Colorado 82. The easily missed turn is 10.5 miles west of the US 24–Colorado 82 junction, 4.2 miles west of the town of Twin Lakes, and 4.0 miles east of the Colorado 82–South Fork Lake Creek Road junction. The trailhead is marked with a small sign for the Black Cloud Trail, and there is room for several vehicles to park 100 feet north of Colorado 82. The trail starts east of the parking spaces.

10T5 – Echo Canyon Trailhead 10,000 feet 39.0612° -106.4678°

This trailhead provides access to Elbert's southwest side. This trailhead is not far north of Colorado 82, but the turn is easily missed. The turn is 12.5 miles west of the US 24–Colorado 82 junction, 6.2 miles west of the town of Twin Lakes, and 2.0 miles east of the Colorado 82–South Fork Lake Creek Road junction. The trailhead is marked with a small sign for the Echo Canyon Trail. Turn north off Colorado 82 onto a dirt road in front of a cabin and go 100 feet west. There is room for one or two vehicles to park here, and passenger cars should stop here. A rough 4WD road climbs north from this spot, and this road is the start of the Echo Canyon Trail.

10R – Mount Elbert Routes

10R1 – Mount Elbert – Northeast Ridge

From North Mount Elbert TH at 10,040'   190 RP   9.0 mi RT   4,393' total   Class 1

This is the most popular summer route up Elbert. There is a good trail all the way, but you will appreciate Elbert's size long before you reach the summit. Start at the North Mount Elbert Trailhead at 10,040 feet and hike 0.3 mile southeast on a trail to the east side of Elbert Creek. Stay on the east side of Elbert Creek and hike 0.6 mile south on the Colorado Trail (FT 1776) as it climbs to 10,620 feet **(39.1459° -106.4105°)** on the lower part of Elbert's northeast ridge. Continue 0.3 mile south on the trail as it levels out then drops a little. Leave the Colorado Trail at a signed trail junction and climb southwest (right) on the North Mount Elbert Trail (FT 1484). Switchback 1.4 miles up this good but steep trail to treeline at 11,920 feet (39.1330° -106.4255°). From here, you will have a foreshortened view of the upper part of the peak; it's still 1.9 miles to the top.

Follow the trail west as it continues up lovely, moderate terrain above treeline then climbs a steeper stretch on the north side of the Box Creek Cirque to reach a flat spot on the crest of Elbert's northeast ridge at 13,900 feet (39.1220° -106.4396°). Unlike most Fourteeners, when you reach 14,000 feet on Elbert, you still have some distance to go. Being careful to not trip over the 14,000-foot contour line, continue southwest up the now lower-angled ridge to a tiny saddle at 14,340 feet, where you can peer down Elbert's steep northwest face and up at the now visible summit. Continue south then southwest up onto Elbert's long, broad summit ridge, and walk 100 yards southwest to Colorado's highest point (39.1175° -106.4455°).

10R1 V1 – Variation – Box Creek Cirque
Class 2+, Mod Snow
Instead of climbing to Elbert's northeast ridge on the trail, angle southwest into the tiny cirque at the head of Box Creek. In June there are several shallow, snow-filled couloirs in the cirque's headwall, and any of them can provide a moderate snow climb. Choose your couloir and climb it. The tops of the couloirs are at 13,800 feet, 0.5 mile east of the summit.

10R1 V2 – Variation – North–Northeast Ridge
Class 2
This seldom-climbed ridge offers an uncrowded alternative to the North Mount Elbert Trail. It is the ridge I used to first ascend Elbert in 1957. Since the route is off-trail, it is Class 2, and is environmentally incorrect for large groups. Tread lightly.

Leave the Northeast Ridge Route early, at a switchback at 10,320 feet (39.1473° -106.4157°), bushwhack west, and cross to the west side of Elbert Creek. Hike south, get onto the toe of Elbert's north-northeast ridge, and follow it southwest past treeline to minor Point 12,462 (39.1385° -106.4386°). Climb southwest up a rounded slope to a more defined ridge crest and hike south to reach Point 13,221 (39.1327° -106.4472°). From here, there is a stunning view of Mount Massive to the north. Continue south on the ridge crest to Point 13,435 (39.1256° -106.4478°), where your eyes will likely be focused on your remaining climb to Elbert. Climb south up a narrow talus ridge, join the North Mount Elbert Trail in the tiny saddle at 14,340 feet, and stroll south then southwest to the top.

10R2 – Mount Elbert – East Ridge *Classic*

From South Mount Elbert TH at 9,620'	*223 RP*	*11.2 mi RT*	*4,813' total*	*Class 1*
From South Mount Elbert 4WD TH at 10,520'	*160 RP*	*7.2 mi RT*	*3,913' total*	*Class 1*

This is the easiest route on Elbert, since it follows the excellent South Mount Elbert Trail all the way to the summit. From the South Mount Elbert Trailhead near the Lakeview Campground, this route is longer than the Northeast Ridge Route (10R1), but from the 4WD road's end at 10,520 feet, it is shorter.

Start at the South Mount Elbert Trailhead at 9,620 feet and go 2.0 miles west then northwest on FR 125.1B, passing the Sure Pretty overlook en route, to the end of the road just south of Corske Creek at 10,520 feet (39.1055° -106.3952°). Cross to the north side of Corske Creek on a good bridge, hike 30 yards northeast, turn north (left) at a signed trail junction, and continue 200 yards north on the combined Colorado and Continental Divide Trail (FT 1776) to a junction with the South Mount Elbert Trail. The 1967 Mount Elbert Quadrangle does not accurately show the trails in this area.

Leave the comfortable Colorado Trail and climb steeply west on the South Mount Elbert Trail (FT 1481) as it climbs past treeline then angles northwest to reach the crest of Elbert's broad east ridge at 12,380 feet (39.1205° -106.4190°). The view to the north opens at this point. Follow the trail up the east ridge to 13,650 feet (39.1185° -106.4364°), where the trail takes a surprising turn to the southeast and reaches the summit by switchbacking up southeast-facing slopes. The South Mount Elbert Trail joins the Northeast Ridge Route (10R1) 100 yards northeast of the summit. Enjoy Colorado's highpoint (39.1175° -106.4455°).

10R2 V – Variation – "South Elbert" 14,134 feet 39.1041° -106.4409°
Class 2

Leave the South Mount Elbert Trail at 12,000 feet and contour 0.2 mile west. Cross a branch of Bartlett Creek and contour 0.4 mile south to the main branch of Bartlett Creek. Cross this creek and climb south to the bottom of "South Elbert"'s east ridge at 12,200 feet. Climb 0.7 mile west up this ridge to Point 13,227 (39.1066° -106.4299°), where you can look northwest to the upper part of the Mount Elbert Trail and Elbert's main summit. If you are out of shape, you may wonder why you chose this circuitous route. If you are in shape, you may enjoy your solitary position.

Continue 0.6 mile west up steep talus to "South Elbert"'s 14,134-foot summit (39.1041° -106.4409°). This significant summit is 1.0 mile from Elbert's main summit and rises 234 feet above the connecting saddle. "South Elbert" is well worth climbing, and no matter what shape you are in, you should feel better here. Hike 0.5 mile northwest down a gentle, grassy slope to the broad 13,900-foot saddle (39.1090° -106.4491°) between Elbert and "South Elbert," then climb 0.7 mile north over talus to Elbert's main summit. Ascending this variation and descending the East Ridge Route (10R2) on the South Mount Elbert Trail adds 2 miles, 533 feet of gain, and makes a nifty Tour de Elbert.

10R3 – Mount Elbert – Southeast Ridge
From Black Cloud TH at 9,700'   303 RP   10.2 mi RT   4,733' net; 5,201' total   Class 2

This is a scenic alternative to the crowded trails on Elbert's east side. Surprisingly, there is a trail most of the way up this route; however, this is a tougher climb than the east-side routes. Your reward is the opportunity to climb two 14,000-foot summits. Start at the Black Cloud Trailhead at 9,700 feet and follow the excellent Black Cloud Trail (FT 1480) as it switchbacks steeply up on the east side of Black Cloud Creek. After 1.0 mile, cross to the west side of the creek at 10,860 feet (39.0802° -106.4358°) and continue up along the west side of the creek. Do not follow another trail that angles west at 11,020 feet (39.0823° -106.4364°). Higher, at 11,200 feet (39.0855° -106.4348°), cross back to the east side of Black Cloud Creek and climb to an old cabin at 11,600 feet (39.0898° -106.4365°). There are good views of La Plata Peak from Black Cloud Gulch.

Continue on the unmarked but good trail above the cabin as it climbs past a tailings pile, then switchbacks up large, southwest facing slopes to reach Elbert's long, southeast ridge at a level stretch at 13,580 feet (39.0995° -106.4316°). At this point, 2.6 miles into your hike, you may feel like you have already climbed a mountain, and the view of Elbert's summit, still 2.0 miles distant, may be discouraging. Hike 0.8 mile northwest to the 14,134-foot summit of "South Elbert" (39.1041° -106.4409°). Hike 0.5 mile northwest down a gentle, grassy slope to the broad 13,900-foot saddle (39.1090° -106.4491°) between Elbert and "South Elbert," then climb 0.7 mile north over talus to Elbert's main summit.

10R3 V1 – Variation – Upper Black Cloud Gulch

From Black Cloud TH at 9,700'   324 RP   9.4 mi RT   4,733' total   Class 2

From the old cabin at 11,600 feet, leave the trail and hike 1.0 mile northwest then north into upper Black Cloud Gulch to a small lake at 12,400 feet (39.0981° -106.4492°). Climb 0.7 mile northwest to the 13,340-foot saddle (39.1050° -106.4552°) between 13,761-foot Bull Hill and Elbert, then climb 0.5 mile northeast on a ridge, skirt minor Point 13,963, and rejoin the route in the 13,900-foot saddle between "South Elbert" and Elbert. This variation avoids the climb over South Elbert's summit. Ascending via "South Elbert's" summit and descending this variation saves 234 feet of ascent, 0.9 mile, and makes a scenic circle tour.

10R3 V2 – Variation – Bull Hill 13,761 feet 39.0995° -106.4626°

From Black Cloud TH at 9,700'   380 RP   11.2 mi RT   4,733' net; 5,575' total   Class 2

Leave the Black Cloud Trail at 11,020 feet (39.0823° -106.4364°) and follow another trail west toward Fidelity Mine. Leave this trail at 11,960 feet (39.0875° -106.4440°) and climb 100 yards north onto Bull Hill's southeast ridge. Follow this ridge 1.5 miles up to Bull Hill's 13,761-foot summit (39.0995° -106.4626°). Bull Hill has the distinction of being Colorado's highest hill and one of Colorado's 200 highest ranked peaks. From Bull Hill, descend 0.6 mile northeast to the 13,340-foot saddle (39.1050° -106.4552°) between Bull Hill and Elbert. From this saddle, climb 0.5 mile northeast on a ridge, skirt minor Point 13,963, and reach the broad, 13,900-foot saddle (39.1090° -106.4491°) between 14,134-foot "South Elbert" and Elbert. Climb 0.7 mile north along a gentle talus ridge

Mount Elbert from the southwest (photo by Steve Hoffmeyer).

to Elbert's main summit. Ascending the Southeast Ridge Route (10R3) and descending this variation makes an interesting Tour de Elbert that allows you to collect three summits.

10R3 EC – Extra Credit – Mount Cosgriff 13,588 feet 39.09/1° -106.4257°
Class 2

From 13,580 feet (39.0995° -106.4316°) on Elbert's southeast ridge, hike 0.35 mile east-southeast along the gentle ridge to 13,588-foot Mount Cosgriff. This minor ridge point was officially named in 2002 after longtime Leadville lawyer Peter Cosgriff. Since the name is new, it does not appear on the 1967 Mount Elbert Quadrangle or the 2010 USGS online map, but it does appear on the Trails Illustrated maps.

10R4 – Mount Elbert – Southwest Ridge

From Echo Canyon TH at 10,000'	*337 RP*	*10.6 mi RT*	*4,433' net; 5,275' total*	*Class 2*
With descent of Southeast Ridge	*326 RP*	*10.9 mi RT*	*4,433' net; 5,088' total*	*Class 2*

This interesting alternative route is far removed from the crowds on Elbert's eastern slopes. This route is rougher than the eastern routes, and it requires you to cross or skirt mighty Bull Hill twice. You will spend a long time on ridges above 13,000 feet.

Start at the Echo Canyon Trailhead at 10,000 feet and go 0.3 mile north up the 4WD road to an old concrete foundation at 10,200 feet. Cross to the east side of Echo Creek below the concrete foundation and hike 0.9 mile on an old road along the creek to a trail junction. Turn east (right), leave Echo Creek, and hike 1.5 miles up the old trail that switchbacks steeply up the southwest slopes of 13,761-foot Bull Hill. The road ends at the Golden Fleece Mine at 12,700 feet. Climb 100 yards northeast above the mine and reach Bull Hill's gentle upper south ridge at 12,900 feet (39.0900° -106.4621°). Climb north along this grassy ridge to 13,400 feet and either continue to Bull Hill's summit or skirt it on its south side. Bull Hill has the distinction of being Colorado's highest named hill and one of Colorado's 200 highest ranked peaks.

From Bull Hill, descend 0.6 mile northeast to the 13,340-foot saddle (39.1050° -106.4552°) between Bull Hill and Elbert. From this saddle, 0.5 mile northeast on a ridge, skirt minor Point 13,963, and reach the broad, 13,900-foot saddle (39.1090° -106.4491°) between 14,134-foot "South Elbert" and Elbert. "South Elbert" is 1 mile south of Elbert. Climb 0.7 mile north along a gentle talus ridge to Elbert's main summit. Ascending this route and descending the Southeast Ridge Route (10R3) makes an arduous Tour de Elbert that allows you to collect three summits. On Colorado 82, Black Cloud Trailhead is 2.0 miles from Echo Canyon Trailhead.

10R5 – Mount Elbert – West Face

From South Half Moon Creek TH at 10,240'   *402 RP*   *7.6 mi RT*   *4,193' total*   *Class 2, Mod Snow*

This route makes sense when it is covered with stable snow. When dry, this unrelentingly steep, rocky route is out of character with Elbert's other routes. Either way, this route provides a workout. From the South Half Moon Creek Trailhead at 10,240 feet, cross to the south side of Half Moon Creek on a broken bridge. Follow the 4WD road 1.0 mile south as it switchbacks steeply up the hill, and cross to the east side of South Half Moon Creek on another broken bridge at 10,800 feet. Continue an additional 1.5 miles south on the 4WD road to a clearing at 11,400 feet under the center of Elbert's steep west face. The introduction is over.

Elbert's summit is only 1.3 miles away but an astonishing 3,033 feet above you. There is a shallow couloir in the center of Elbert's west face that leads directly to the summit. When this couloir is full of stable snow, this is the best alternative. After the snow melts, the rounded shoulder just south of the couloir provides the best footing. Leave the road, hike east, and choose your workout.

11. La Plata Peak 14,336 feet

La Plata, Colorado's fifth highest peak, is 3 miles south of Colorado 82, about halfway between Twin Lakes and Independence Pass. The proud peak is clearly visible from Colorado 82 east of Independence Pass. *La Plata* means "silver" in Spanish. La Plata's elegant ridges and embracing cirques command a degree of respect that other Sawatch Fourteeners lack. In simple language, La Plata is steeper than its neighbors. La Plata's standard routes are easy, but it is not surprising that La Plata also offers one of the more interesting technical routes on a Sawatch Fourteener.

The 1979 photo inspection of the Mount Elbert Quadrangle designates La Plata's altitude as 14,361 feet instead of its long-standing altitude of 14,336 feet. The USGS verified that 14,361 feet is incorrect; there was an editing error during the preparation of the new map. The original altitude of 14,336 feet is still correct and will be reinstated on a future printing. Unfortunately, the Forest Service, other agencies, on-line map sites, and independent map producers are using the incorrect altitude on their maps. It will be decades before the error is fully corrected.

11E – La Plata Peak Essentials

Elevations	14,336' (NGVD29) 14,343' (NAVD88)
Rank	Colorado's 5th highest ranked peak
Location	Chaffee County, Colorado, USA
Range	Central Sawatch Range
Summit Coordinates	39.0297° -106.4733° (WGS84)
Ownership/Contact	San Isabel National Forest – Public Land – 719-553-1400
Prominence and Saddle	1,836' from 12,500' Pear Pass
Isolation and Parent	6.29 miles to Mount Elbert
USGS Maps	**Mount Elbert**, Winfield, Independence Pass
USFS Map	San Isabel National Forest
Trails Illustrated Maps	**Map #127 Aspen/Independence Pass**
	Map #129 Buena Vista/Collegiate Peaks
Book Map	See Map 11 on page 116
Nearest Towns	Leadville – Population 2,700 – Elevation 10,152'
	Buena Vista – Population 2,100 – Elevation 7,965'
La Plata Peak Easiest Route	11R3 – Southwest Ridge – Class 2
	A Class 1 approach hike on a trail, a steeper trail hike to the SW ridge, then
	an undulating Class 2 hike up the ridge
La Plata's Accolades	Easy routes from both the north and south lead to this lofty summit. La
	Plata also hosts the jagged Ellingwood Ridge.

11T – La Plata Peak Trailheads

11T1 – Lake Creek Trailhead 10,160 feet 39.0682° -106.5058°

This trailhead provides access to La Plata's north and west sides. Park at the Colorado 82–South Fork Lake Creek Road junction. This junction is 14.5 miles west of the US 24–Colorado 82 junction. Do not park on the South Fork Lake Creek Road, because the first quarter mile south of Colorado 82 is on private property. This trailhead is accessible in winter.

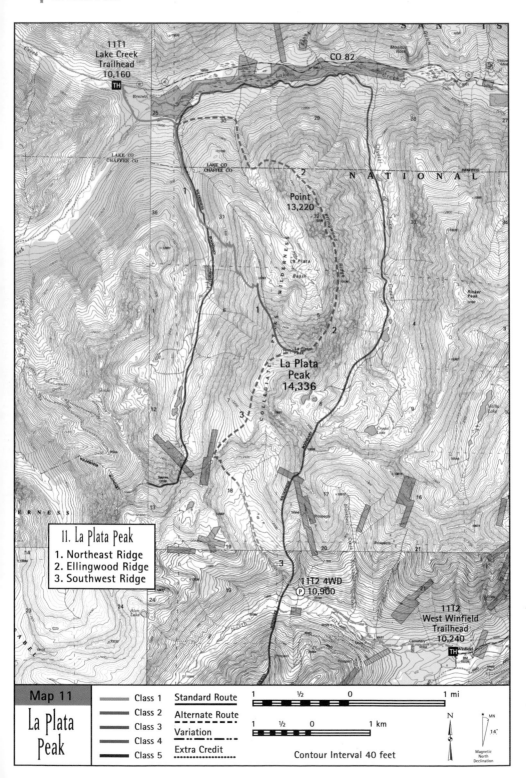

11T1
Lake Creek
Trailhead
10,160

CO 82

Point
13,220

La Plata
Peak
14,336

II. La Plata Peak

1. Northeast Ridge
2. Ellingwood Ridge
3. Southwest Ridge

11T2 4WD
10,900

11T2
West Winfield
Trailhead
10,240

Map 11

La Plata
Peak

Class 1 — Standard Route
Class 2 — Alternate Route
Class 3 — Variation
Class 4 — Extra Credit
Class 5

1   ½   0   1 mi
1   ½   0   1 km

Contour Interval 40 feet

N

MN
14°

Magnetic
North
Declination

11T2 – West Winfield Trailhead 10,240 feet 38.9850° -106.4413°

This trailhead provides access to La Plata's south side. Turn west from US 24 onto Chaffee County 390 (dirt). This junction is 14.9 miles north of the stoplight in the center of Buena Vista, 4.3 miles south of the US 24–Colorado 82 junction, and 19.3 miles south of the West Sixth–US 24 junction in the center of Leadville. Go west on Chaffee County 390 for 11.8 miles to Winfield. Park 2WD vehicles near the center of Winfield.

11T2 4WD – West Winfield 4WD Trailhead 10,900 feet 38.9943° -106.4713°

From the center of Winfield, 4WD vehicles can go north (right) for 60 yards, 0.4 mile west (left) on a rough road to the Winfield Cemetery, and continue 1.4 miles west on a rougher road to the edge of an open meadow at 10,730 feet (38.9926° -106.4687°) where the main road angles southwest. Leave the main road here and follow another 4WD road northwest (right) for 300 yards to a gate at the end of the road at 10,900 feet.

11R – La Plata Peak Routes

11R1 – La Plata Peak – Northwest Ridge

From Lake Creek TH at 10,160'   245 RP   9.4 mi RT   4,176' nct; 4,256' total   Class 2

This is the most popular route on La Plata, but it is not the shortest route on La Plata. With the trail improvements made by the Colorado Fourteener Initiative, the route is a Class 1 trail hike most of the way.

Start at the Lake Creek Trailhead at 10,160 feet, descend 0.1 mile south on the South Fork Lake Creek Road, cross the vehicle bridge over Lake Creek, and continue 0.3 mile south up the South Fork Road past all the no-trespassing

La Plata Peak from the northwest. Photo by Austin Porzak

signs. Parking is not allowed on this section of the road, so park at the trailhead. When the road angles southwest up a hill (39.0643° -106.5038°), leave it and hike 200 yards straight east on a trail through the trees to the south fork of Lake Creek. Find and cross the south fork on an exposed but solid steel bridge over a small gorge. Finding this bridge is important, because the south fork is difficult to cross on foot and there is private property just north of the bridge. The bridge is in the rocks just southeast of an old cabin. By following the directions given here, you will avoid the private property north of the bridge.

After crossing the bridge, go south (right) on a good trail along the south fork's east side, then 0.4 mile east to La Plata Gulch. Cross La Plata Gulch Creek and follow the good La Plata Peak Trail (FT 1474) 1.4 miles south (right) along the east side of the creek up La Plata Gulch to 11,040 feet (39.0473° -106.4904°).

Turn east (left), leave the comfort of the valley, and angle 1.4 miles southeast up the switchbacking La Plata Peak Trail on the steep slope above you for 1,500 feet to reach La Plata's northwest ridge at 12,740 feet (39.0388° -106.4796°). From the ridge, the view of the long, jagged Ellingwood Ridge across La Plata Basin to the east is startling and spectacular. From your airy aerie, turn south (right) and hike 1.0 mile up La Plata's rounded upper northwest ridge on a continuing trail to the summit (39.0297° -106.4733°). A snow slope lingers on the final ridge, but you can usually avoid it on its east side.

11R2 – La Plata Peak – Ellingwood Ridge *Classic*

From Lake Creek TH at 10,160'	*586 RP*	*10.0 mi RT*	*4,176' net; 5,416' total*	*Class 3*
With descent of Northwest Ridge	*464 RP*	*9.7 mi RT*	*4,176' net; 4,836' total*	*Class 3*

The Ellingwood Ridge is La Plata's long, jagged northeast ridge. Do not confuse La Plata's famous Ellingwood Ridge with the even more famous Ellingwood Arête on Crestone Needle. La Plata's Ellingwood Ridge is long and complex, but it is not as hard as its reputation implies. If you take care to find the easiest passage when faced with a problem, the difficulty will not exceed Class 3. Nevertheless, take care on this long, tiring route.

Start at the Lake Creek Trailhead at 10,160 feet and follow the Northwest Ridge Route (11R1) to La Plata Gulch. Cross La Plata Gulch Creek, go 100 feet north (left), and continue 0.6 mile east along Lake Creek's south side on a faint trail to La Plata Basin Gulch. Do not confuse La Plata Gulch with La Plata Basin Gulch. La Plata Gulch is west of the northwest ridge. You want to go to La Plata Basin Gulch, which is between the northwest ridge and the Ellingwood Ridge to the east.

There is a faint trail up the west side of La Plata Basin Gulch Creek, but even if you find it, it won't aid your approach much. Cross to the east side of La Plata Basin Gulch Creek and bushwhack south up the rugged gulch. Find and follow a small, sharp ridge east of the creek. The crest of this hidden ridge provides good passage. From the top of the ridge at 11,200 feet, you will break out of the trees and see Ellingwood Ridge's northern ramparts. From 11,200 feet, leave La Plata Basin Gulch and climb east up a long, steep, loose, tiring talus slope to reach Ellingwood Ridge's northern end at 12,600 feet (39.0561° -106.4737°). A 2-mile stretch of rugged ridge separates you from the summit. The introduction is over.

Climb southeast along the famous ridge and bypass an initial series of small summits. When faced with a difficult section, you will always find the easiest passage on the ridge's east side. You will usually have to drop down below the cliffs to keep the difficulty at Class 3, and you will spend very little time on the ridge crest. Climb to the summit of Point 13,206. The view from here is discouraging, since dozens of towers and ramparts still separate you from the summit. Descend and contour on the ridge's east side, then climb to a small, grassy 13,140-foot summit. The view from here is discouraging, since dozens of towers and ramparts still separate you from the summit, and they are closer and look more difficult. It is also clear that you will have to give up a lot of your hard-earned elevation.

Angle down from Point 13,140, then descend east down one of several available grassy gullies until you can contour south to a small but distinct dirt bench on a rib. From the bench, climb to another small but distinct dirt bench on a rib. Continue this technique. You will climb up and down a lot as you slowly solve the ridge's problems.

At 13,000 feet, contour below a flat section of ridge and engage the upper part of the peak. Climb a talus slope, then continue to use the up-and-over technique (you should be good at it by now) and bypass the next buttress on its east side. Reach a large, long, east-facing talus slope and climb it to 14,000 feet. Cross above a snow-filled gully, traverse across broken, east-facing slabs, and climb to the summit of Point 14,180, aka "East La Plata," one of Colorado's obscure low-prominence summits over 14,000 feet. From your bonus summit you have a good view of La Plata's main summit, and as you doubtless expect, several more towers. Descend west and bypass these towers on their south (left) sides. Struggle back up to the ridge one more time, then walk triumphantly 100 yards west to the summit.

11R2 V – Variation – Crest Clarity

Class 5

Climbing along Ellingwood Ridge is not an exact science. The closer you stay to the ridge crest, the greater the difficulty will be. Staying directly on the ridge crest all the way is an endeavor that requires several rappels, much Class 4 climbing, some Class 5 climbing, and possibly more than one day to complete.

11R2 EC – Extra Credit – Ellingwood Ridge 13,220 feet 39.0515° -106.4686°

Class 3

On the initial, northern part of the ridge, scramble along the crest of the ridge to Point 13,220. With 280 feet of prominence, this summit has a soft rank and is the highpoint of Ellingwood Ridge. You might as well tag it since you are so close; it will never be cheaper.

11R3 – La Plata Peak – Southwest Ridge

From West Winfield TH at 10,240'	*302 RP*	*11.4 mi RT*	*4,096' total*	*Class 2*
From West Winfield 4WD TH at 10,900'	*245 RP*	*7.4 mi RT*	*3,436' total*	*Class 2*

Many consider this to be the easiest route on La Plata. It is a gentler, scenic alternative to the more popular Northwest Ridge Route (11R1). From the 4WD parking at 10,900 feet, it is the shortest route on La Plata. This route is also south-facing and can be a drier alternative in late spring and early summer.

Start at the West Winfield Trailhead at 10,240 feet in the center of Winfield. Go north (right) for 60 yards, 0.4 mile west (left) on the rough road to the Winfield Cemetery, and continue 1.4 miles west on the 4WD road to the edge of an open meadow at 10,730 feet (38.9926° -106.4687°) where the main road angles southwest. Leave the main road and follow another 4WD road northwest (right) for 300 yards to a gate at the end of the road at 10,900 feet (38.9943° -106.4713°). 4WD vehicles can reach this point.

Cross the creek just west of the end of the road and hike 0.3 mile northwest on a trail to the east side of the creek coming from the basin between La Plata and 13,738-foot Sayers Benchmark, a ranked Thirteener southwest of La Plata. Hike 1.2 miles northwest on the continuing trail on the east side of the creek to 12,100 feet (39.0108° -106.4846°) in the beautiful basin. Hike 0.4 miles northwest up a steep, scruffy Class 2 slope to reach the 12,780-foot La Plata–Sayers Benchmark saddle (39.0139° -106.4879°), where your view opens to the north. Turn northeast (right) and hike 1.8 miles up La Plata's broad, undulating southwest ridge to the summit (39.0297° -106.4733°).

11R3 NG – Bad Idea – Sayers Benchmark 13,738 feet 39.0093° -106.4977°

Class 3

You might be tempted to climb from the 12,780-foot La Plata–Sayers Benchmark saddle to 13,738-foot Sayers Benchmark, but I do not recommend this ridge. While there is no high-end climbing involved, the route is devious, horribly rotten, and exposed. Proving its hazard, the route has produced serious accidents. You can more easily climb Sayers Benchmark's southwest flank from the North Fork Road west of Winfield, but this is a separate outing.

12. Huron Peak 14,003 feet

Huron is a shapely, shy peak hidden in the heart of the Sawatch about halfway between Buena Vista and Independence Pass. Huron just barely rises above 14,000 feet but compensates by being the Sawatch Fourteener that is farthest from a paved road. The view from Huron's summit is one of the best in the

Sawatch. A good dirt road provides easy access to Huron, and Huron's routes are simple climbs. Huron is one of the few Sawatch Fourteeners with an elevation gain of less than 4,000 feet.

12E – Huron Peak Essentials

Elevations	14,003' (NGVD29) 14,012' (NAVD88)
Rank	Colorado's 52nd highest ranked peak
Location	Chaffee County, Colorado, USA
Range	Central Sawatch Range
Summit Coordinates	38.9455° -106.4383° (WGS84)
Ownership/Contact	San Isabel National Forest – Public Land – 719-553-1400
Prominence and Saddle	1,423' from 12,580' saddle SW of Lake Ann
Isolation and Parent	3.20 miles to Missouri Mountain
USGS Map	Winfield
USFS Map	San Isabel National Forest
Trails Illustrated Map	Map #129 Buena Vista/Collegiate Peaks
Book Map	See Map 12 on page 122
Nearest Towns	Buena Vista – Population 2,100 – Elevation 7,965'
	Leadville – Population 2,700 – Elevation 10,152'
Huron Peak 🥾 Easiest Route	12R1 – Northwest Slopes – Class 1
	A Class 1 hike on a trail all the way to the top
Huron's Accolades	Huron offers a secluded, easy hike in the heartland of Colorado's highest peaks.

12T – Huron Peak Trailheads

12T1 – Rockdale Trailhead 9,940 feet 38.9904° -106.4109°

This trailhead provides access to Huron's east side and Missouri's west side. Turn west from US 24 onto Chaffee County 390 (dirt). This junction is 14.9 miles north of the stoplight in the center of Buena Vista, 4.3 miles south of the US 24–Colorado 82 junction, and 19.3 miles south of the West Sixth–US 24 junction in the center of Leadville. Go 9.8 miles west on Chaffee County 390 to Rockdale, which is at an unmarked turn on the south side of the road. Turn south (left), go past Rockdale's four cabins, and curve 0.2 mile southeast down to a parking area on the north side of Clear Creek. 2WD vehicles should park here, at 9,940 feet.

12T1 4WD – Clohesy Lake 4WD Trailhead 10,880 feet 38.9540° -106.4088°

From the Rockdale Trailhead, 4WD vehicles can ford Clear Creek and continue 3.0 miles south toward Clohesy Lake to a signed parking area at the south end of a large meadow at 10,880 feet. Reached by a trail, Clohesy Lake is 0.4 mile south of this point. The ford of Clear Creek is difficult and dangerous in high water; some vehicles have been nearly swept away.

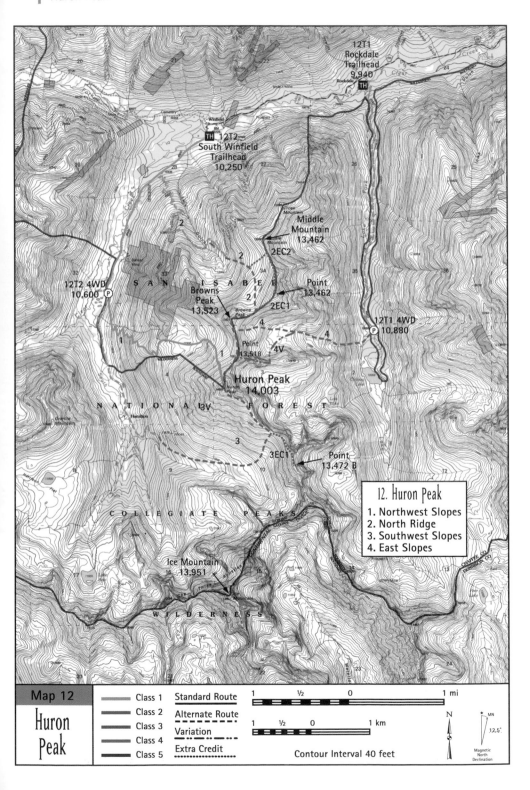

12T1
Rockdale
Trailhead
9,940

TH 12T2
South Winfield
Trailhead
10,250

Middle
Mountain
13,462

2EC2

12T2 4WD
10,600 Ⓟ

S A N   I S A B E L

2

Browns
Peak
13,523

2

Point
13,462

2EC1

4

12T1 4WD
10,880 Ⓟ

Point
13,518

4V

4

Huron Peak
14,003

N A T I O N A L 3V   F O R E S T

3

3EC1

Point
13,472 B

12. Huron Peak
1. Northwest Slopes
2. North Ridge
3. Southwest Slopes
4. East Slopes

C O L L E G I A T E   P E A K S

Ice Mountain
13,951

W I L D E R N E S S

Map 12		Class 1	Standard Route
		Class 2	Alternate Route
Huron		Class 3	Variation
Peak		Class 4	Extra Credit
		Class 5	

1   ½   0   1 mi
1   ½   0   1 km

N

★ MN

12.5°

Magnetic
North
Declination

Contour Interval 40 feet

12T2 – South Winfield Trailhead 10,250 feet 38.9825° -106.4424°

This trailhead provides access to Huron's north and west sides. From the turn to the Rockdale Trailhead at mile 9.8, continue west on Chaffee County 390 to Winfield at mile 11.8. From the center of Winfield, turn south (left) and cross to the south side of Clear Creek on a bridge. Turn west (right) and follow the road (FR 390.2B) for an additional 100 yards; here the road becomes dramatically rougher. There are parking spaces on both sides of the road, and this is the trailhead.

12T2 4WD – South Winfield 4WD Trailhead 10,600 feet 38.9590° -106.4608°

From the South Winfield Trailhead, 4WD vehicles can follow the road (FR 390.2B) 0.7 mile southwest to another 4WD road that climbs the hill south (left) of you. Do not take this road. Continue 1.0 mile south on the main 4WD road up the valley and pass the turn up to the old Banker Mine. Do not go to the Banker Mine. Continue 0.6 mile south (straight) on the main road up the valley to a Forest Service closure gate at 10,600 feet.

12R – Huron Peak Routes

12R1 – Huron Peak – Northwest Slopes

From South Winfield TH at 10,250'	*169 RP*	*9.2 mi RT*	*3,773' total*	*Class 1*
From South Winfield 4WD TH at 10,600'	*114 RP*	*4.6 mi RT*	*3,403' total*	*Class 1*

This is the shortest and standard route up Huron. Start at the South Winfield Trailhead at 10,250 feet and follow the 4WD road (FR 390.2B) 0.7 mile southwest to another 4WD road that climbs the hill south (left) of you. Do not take this road. Continue 1.0 mile south on the main 4WD road up the valley and pass the turn up to the old Banker Mine. Do not go to the Banker Mine. Continue 0.6 mile south (straight) on the main road up the valley to a Forest Service closure gate at 10,600 feet (38.9590° -106.4608°). Continue 100 yards south on the old road to 10,620 feet. From here, leave the valley trail and hike 1.2 miles steeply southeast on the Huron Peak Trail as it switchbacks into a charming basin at 12,300 feet, west of 13,523-foot Browns Peak and Huron. From the basin, continue 1.0 mile southeast on the Huron Peak Trail as it winds up a long, northwest-facing slope to Huron's summit (38.9455° -106.4383°).

12R2 – Huron Peak – North Ridge

From South Winfield TH at 10,250'	*269 RP*	*9.4 mi RT*	*3,753' net; 4,219' total*	*Class 2*
With descent of Northwest Slopes	*241 RP*	*9.3 mi RT*	*3,753' net; 4,036' total*	*Class 2*

This scenic alternative to the Northwest Slopes Route (12R1) allows you to bag two peaks. Start at the South Winfield Trailhead at 10,250 feet and follow the 4WD road (FR 390.2B) 0.7 mile southwest to another 4WD road that climbs the hill south of you (38.9779° -106.4498°). Turn south (left) onto this road and follow it as it switchbacks up the lower, northwest shoulder of 13,523-foot Browns Peak, an unranked but named summit. After 1.2 steep, switchbacking miles, the road reaches a junction at 11,393 feet (38.9687° -106.4490°). Take the east (left) fork and go east then southeast into Lulu Gulch, which is northwest of Browns Peak and 13,060-foot Middle Mountain. Stay on the deteriorating road as it crosses to the northeast side of Lulu Gulch, then climbs southeast up the gulch. The road turns sharply back to the north at 11,920 feet (38.9650° -106.4378°), 0.9 mile above the road junction at 11,393 feet. This is the end of your Class 1 approach.

Leave the road . and climb 0.3 mile southeast then 0.5 mile south up the slope at the head of Lulu Gulch to the 13,140-foot saddle (38.9569° -106.4321°) between Browns Peak and Point 13,462, which is 0.5 mile northeast of Browns Peak. All these summits are on Huron's long north ridge. From the saddle, climb 0.3 mile west-southwest to the summit of 13,523-foot Browns Peak (38.9559° -106.4367°), then follow the ridge 0.8 mile south to Huron's summit (38.9455° -106.4383°). En route, you can skirt Point 13,518 on its west side. Ascending this route and descending the Northwest Slopes Route (12R1) makes a sanguine Tour de Huron.

12R2 EC1 – Extra Credit – Point 13,462 38.9595° -106.4281°
Class 2

For a third peak, climb 0.3 mile northeast from the 13,140-foot saddle to the summit of Point 13,462, a Tri—one of Colorado's 300 highest ranked peaks.

12R2 EC2 – Extra Credit – Middle Mountain 13,060 feet 38.9678° -106.4305°
Class 2

For a fourth peak, leave the route at 12,600 feet and climb 0.25 mile northeast to the 12,940-foot saddle (38.9657° -106.4296°) between Middle Mountain and Point 13,462. Climb 300 yards northwest to 13,060-foot Middle Mountain (38.9678° -106.4305°), an unranked but named summit, and return to the saddle. Climb 0.5 mile south to the summit of Point 13,462 (38.9595° -106.4281°) and descend 0.3 mile southwest to rejoin the route in the 13,140-foot saddle (38.9569° -106.4321°).

12R3 – Huron Peak – Southwest Slopes

From South Winfield TH at 10,250'	*309 RP*	*13.0 mi RT*	*3,753' total*	*Class 2*
From South Winfield 4WD TH at 10,600'	*255 RP*	*8.4 mi RT*	*3,403' total*	*Class 2*

This is a longer, gentler route than the Northwest Slopes Route (12R1), but it is a rougher, off-trail hike near the summit. Start at the South Winfield Trailhead at 10,250 feet and follow the 4WD road 0.7 mile southwest to another 4WD road that climbs the hill south (left) of you. Do not take this road. Continue 1.0 mile south on the main 4WD road up the valley and pass the turn up to the old Banker Mine. Do not go to the Banker Mine. Continue 0.6 mile south (straight) on the main road up the valley to a Forest Service closure gate at 10,600 feet (38.9590° -106.4608°). Continue 1.4 miles south on the Lake Ann Trail (FT 1462),

Huron Peak
14,003

Huron Peak from the southwest.

entering the Collegiate Peaks Wilderness en route, to a trail junction in the Hamilton town site at 10,820 feet (38.9416° -106.4570°). Leave the Lake Ann Trail and hike 0.3 mile south-southeast above Hamilton on the Three Apostles Trail (FT 1462.2) to a trail junction at 10,960 feet (38.9386° -106.4540°). Leave the Three Apostles Trail and hike 0.2 mile east on an old trail to 11,260 feet (38.9379° -106.4506°), where the old trail cuts steeply up the hill to the north. This is the end of your Class 1 trail approach.

Leave the old trail and hike off-trail 1.1 miles east-southeast to 12,040 feet (38.9338° -106.4328°) in the basin south of Huron's steep, sweeping south face. Climb 0.5 mile northeast to the 13,060-foot saddle (38.9388° -106.4286°) between Huron and Point 13,472 B. From the saddle, climb 0.7 mile northwest along a well-defined, scenic ridge to Huron's summit (38.9455° -106.4383°). Your retrograde arrival may surprise a summit sitter.

12R3 EC1 – Extra Credit – Point 13,472 B 38.9341° -106.4246°

Class 2+

From the 13,060-foot saddle, climb 0.4 mile southeast along a rugged ridge to the summit of Point 13,472 B, a soft-ranked Thirteener.

12R3 EC2 – Extra Credit – High Five

Class 2+

Including Point 13,472 B with your ascent of Huron's Southwest Slopes Route and including Browns Peak, Point 13,462, and Middle Mountain with your descent of Huron's North Ridge Route (12R2) creates a grand, five-summit Tour de Huron.

12R4 – Huron Peak – East Slopes

From Rockdale TH at 9,940'	*260 RP*	*11.0 mi RT*	*4,063' total*	*Class 2*
From Clohesy Lake 4WD TH at 10,880'	*179 RP*	*5.0 mi RT*	*3,123' total*	*Class 2*

This is a rugged alternative to the routes starting at the South Winfield Trailhead. Start at the Rockdale Trailhead at 9,940 feet and ford Clear Creek, which can be difficult and dangerous in high water. Go 3.0 miles south toward Clohesy Lake to a signed parking area at the south end of a large meadow at 10,880 feet (38.9540° -106.4088°). It is not necessary to go all the way to Clohesy Lake.

Cross to the west side of Clear Creek's lake fork. Find and follow a faint trail 1.0 mile west to 12,200 feet (38.9538° -106.4244°) in the lower end of the small basin east of Browns Peak and Point 13,518. This is not the basin directly above Clohesy Lake and directly below Huron. From 12,200 feet, hike 0.3 mile west over large boulders, climb 0.4 mile west to the 13,340-foot saddle (38.9541° -106.4361°) between Browns Peak and Huron, and join Huron's North Ridge Route (12R2). Turn south (left) and hike 0.8 mile south up Huron's north ridge to Huron's summit. You can skirt Point 13,518 on its west side.

12R4 V – Variation – Point 13,518 38.9503° -106.4350°

Class 2+

From 12,200 feet in the basin (38.9538° -106.4244°), hike 0.3 mile southwest over large boulders to 12,400 feet (38.9515° -106.4288°). Scamper 0.2 mile south up a steep slope to the 12,860-foot saddle between Small Point 12,936 to the east and Point 13,518 to the west. Turn west (right) and scamper 0.4 mile west up the rough east ridge of Point 13,518 (38.9503° -106.4350°). Turn south (left), descend 100 yards to the 13,380-foot saddle between Point 13,518 and Huron, and climb 0.4 mile south to mighty Huron.

13. Belford Group

Mount Belford	14,197 feet
Mount Oxford	14,153 feet
Missouri Mountain	14,067 feet

Nestled in the heart of the Sawatch, these Fourteeners are 8 miles west of US 24, about one-third of the way from Buena Vista to Leadville. These peaks are not easily visible from roads, but good trails approach the peaks, and they are very popular summer hikes. The high, gentle mass of Belford and Oxford requires little more than a sturdy pair of legs, while the more rugged Missouri offers a choice of technical routes.

Belford's lofty, rounded mass sits stately between its lower companions Oxford and Missouri. There is a trail up Belford, and the peak is one of Colorado's easiest Fourteeners. Like most Sawatch Fourteeners, Belford requires more than 4,000 feet of elevation gain, but it's a manageable workout.

Mount Oxford is 1.2 miles east of Belford, and people usually climb Oxford together with Belford. Few people take the time to enjoy Oxford by itself, as it should be enjoyed. Oxford offers a choice of routes and provides more solitude than the peaks closer to popular Elkhead Pass.

Missouri Mountain is 1.3 miles southwest of Belford and 0.7 mile west of Elkhead Pass. The peak forms the southern end of Missouri Gulch, and Missouri Mountain is more of a ridge than a mountain. Missouri is harder to climb than either Belford or Oxford, and this strange peak offers some of the few technical routes on Sawatch Fourteeners.

13E – Belford Group Essentials

Elevations	Mt Belford	14,197' (NGVD29) 14,205' (NAVD88)
	Mt Oxford	14,153' (NGVD29) 14,160' (NAVD88)
	Missouri Mtn	14,067' (NGVD29) 14,073' (NAVD88)
Ranks	Mt Belford	Colorado's 19th highest ranked peak
	Mt Oxford	Colorado's 26th highest ranked peak
	Missouri Mtn	Colorado's 36th highest ranked peak
Location	Chaffee County, Colorado, USA	
Range	Central Sawatch Range	
Summit Coordinates	Mt Belford	38.9612° -106.3608° (WGS84)
	Mt Oxford	38.9647° -106.3388° (WGS84)
	Missouri Mtn	38.9467° -106.3783° (WGS84)
Ownership/Contact	San Isabel National Forest – Public Land – 719-553-1400	
Prominence and Saddles	Mt Belford	1,337' from 12,860' Belford–Harvard saddle
	Mt Oxford	653' from 13,500' Oxford–Belford saddle
	Missouri Mtn	847' from 13,220' Elkhead Pass
Isolation and Parents	Mt Belford	3.32 miles to Mount Harvard
	Mt Oxford	1.23 miles to Mount Belford
	Missouri Mtn	1.30 miles to Mount Belford
USGS Maps	**Mount Harvard, Winfield,** Harvard Lakes	
USFS Map	San Isabel National Forest	
Trails Illustrated Map	Map #129 Buena Vista/Collegiate Peaks	
Book Map	See Map 13 on page 129	
Nearest Towns	Buena Vista – Population 2,100 – Elevation 7,965'	
	Leadville – Population 2,700 – Elevation 10,152'	
Mount Belford 🥾 Easiest Route	13R1 – Northwest Ridge – Class 1	
	A Class 1 trail hike all the way to the summit	
Mount Oxford 🥾 Easiest Route	13R2 – West Ridge – Class 1	
	A Class 1 trail hike to the top of Belford, then a Class 1 hike across the connecting ridge to Oxford	

13E – Belford Group Essentials

Missouri Mtn 🏃 Easiest Route	13R5 – Northwest Ridge – Class 2
	A Class 1 trail hike into Missouri Gulch, a steeper pitch up to the
	ridge, then a bumpy Class 2 ridge to the top
Belford Group Accolades	Good trails approach these Fourteeners in the heart of the Sawatch,
	and they provide popular summer hikes. Missouri also offers some
	technical routes.

13T – Belford Group Trailheads

13T1 – Missouri Gulch Trailhead 9,640 feet 38.9981° -106.3754°

This trailhead provides access to the north sides of Missouri and Belford, and to the west ridge of Oxford. Turn west from US 24 onto Chaffee County 390 (dirt). This junction is 14.9 miles north of the stoplight in the center of Buena Vista, 4.3 miles south of the US 24–Colorado 82 junction, and 19.3 miles south of the West Sixth–US 24 junction in the center of Leadville. Go 7.7 miles west on Chaffee County 390 to Vicksburg. The large trailhead is on the south side of the road across from Vicksburg.

13T2 – Pine Creek Trailhead 8,880 feet 38.9987° -106.2304°

This trailhead provides access to Oxford's south side and Harvard's north side. Turn west from US 24 onto Chaffee County 388 (dirt). This junction is 13.2 miles north of the stoplight in the center of Buena Vista, 6.0 miles south of the US 24–Colorado 82 junction, and 21.0 miles south of the West Sixth–US 24 junction in the center of Leadville. Measure from the US 24–Chaffee County 388 junction. Go 0.3 mile west on Chaffee County 388 and continue straight on the less traveled road. Cross to Pine Creek's east side, and at mile 0.6, the road makes a sharp turn up the hill to the east (right) and becomes rougher. Park here or turn up the steep road and continue 200 yards east then south to the trailhead.

13. Mount Belford 14,197 feet

13R – Mount Belford Route

13R1 – Mount Belford – Northwest Ridge *Classic*

From Missouri Gulch TH at 9,640'   *168 RP*   *7.0 mi RT*   *4,557' net; 4,617' total*   *Class 1*

This delightful hike is the easiest route up Belford. The direct ascent is beautiful in its simplicity. Start at the Missouri Gulch Trailhead at 9,640 feet, descend a little, and cross Clear Creek on a good bridge. Beyond the bridge, you will meet Belford's challenge immediately as the excellent Missouri Gulch Trail (FT 1469) climbs steeply via a series of memorable switchbacks to enter Missouri Gulch. After the switchbacks, cross to the creek's east side on a bridge

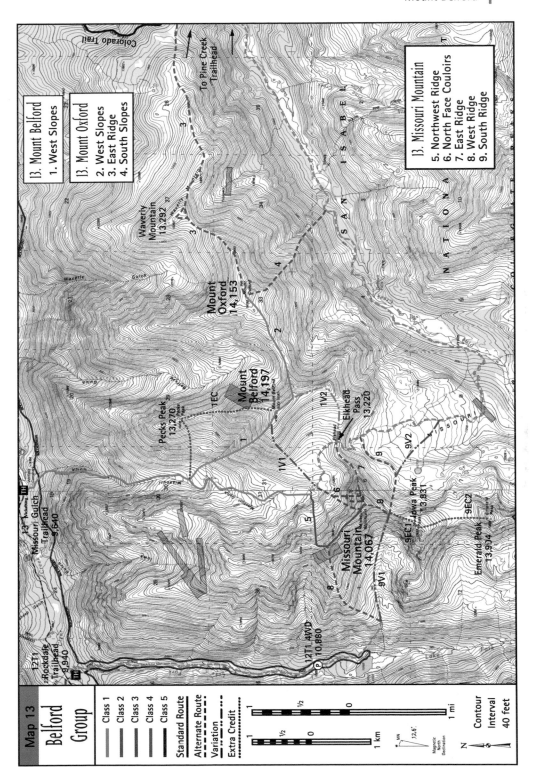

Map 13
Belford
Group

Class 1
Class 2
Class 3
Class 4
Class 5

Standard Route
Alternate Route
Variation
Extra Credit

1 mi
1 km

N

Magnetic North
Declination

Contour
Interval
40 feet

13. Mount Belford
1. West Slopes

13. Mount Oxford
2. West Slopes
3. East Ridge
4. South Slopes

13. Missouri Mountain
5. Northwest Ridge
6. North Face Couloirs
7. East Ridge
8. West Ridge
9. South Ridge

Colorado Trail

To Pine Creek Trailhead

Waverly Mountain 13,292

Mount Oxford 14,153

Mount Belford 14,197

Pecks Peak 13,270

Elkhead Pass 13,220

Missouri Gulch Trailhead 9,640

Rockdale Trailhead 9,940

Iowa Peak 13,831

Missouri Mountain 14,067

Emerald Peak 13,904

SAN ISABEL NATIONAL

P 10,880

The Belford Group from the southwest.

at 10,800 feet (38.9858° -106.3729°), then pass an old cabin just below treeline at 11,280 feet. When you break out of the trees, you will see Belford's rounded northwest ridge. As you approach, you can see the Mount Belford Trail, constructed by the Colorado Fourteener Initiative, on the northwest ridge.

Continue south on the Missouri Gulch Trail to 11,660 feet (38.9736° -106.3737°). Before the trail crosses back to the creek's west side, look sharp for the Mount Belford Trail (FT 1453) leading southeast; this is the route up Belford. Follow it as it switchbacks up the relentless, rounded, grassy ridge to 14,000 feet, then walk east-southeast up a gentle ridge to the highest point (38.9612° -106.3608°). Beautiful Belford is yours.

13R1 V1 – Variation – West Shoulder

From Missouri Gulch TH at 9,640'   230 RP   8.4 mi RT   4,557' net; 4,617' total   Class 2

For a longer, gentler hike, but one with an off-trail finish, continue on the Missouri Gulch Trail for an additional 1.2 miles into grassy upper Missouri Gulch. Leave the trail at 12,900 feet (38.9541° -106.3712°) before it begins the final climb to Elkhead Pass, hike 0.3 mile northeast, and climb 0.7 mile northeast then east up Belford's rounded, grassy west shoulder to the summit (Class 2).

13R1 V2 – Variation – Elkhead Pass

From Missouri Gulch TH at 9,640'   206 RP   10.6 mi RT   4,557' net; 4,617' total   Class 1

For an even longer, gentler hike, continue on the Missouri Gulch Trail all the way to Elkhead Pass at 13,220 feet (38.9517° -106.3664°). From the pass, climb 0.5 mile east then 0.8 mile south on a trail (FT 1454) up gentle slopes to the summit. Ascending the northwest shoulder and descending this variation allows you to see beautiful upper Missouri Gulch.

13R1 EC – Extra Credit – Pecks Peak 13,270 feet 38.9750° -106.3619°

Class 2

From Belford's summit, descend 1.0 mile north along Belford's north ridge to the gentle summit of 13,270-foot Pecks Peak. The detour to this humble summit will take you off the busy Fourteener circuit for a while. If you are lucky, you may see some goats grazing. From Pecks' summit, descend west down steep grass to the Missouri Gulch Trail.

13. Mount Oxford 14,153 feet

13R – Mount Oxford Routes

13R2 – Mount Oxford – West Ridge

From Missouri Gulch TH at 9,640'   225 RP   9.8 mi RT   4,557' net; 5,967' total   Class 1

This is the traditional and, arguably, the easiest route on Oxford. Start at the Missouri Gulch Trailhead at 9,640 feet and climb Belford's Northwest Ridge Route (13R1) to Belford's summit (38.9612° -106.3608°). Descend 0.2 mile southeast then turn east (left) onto the Mount Oxford Trail (FT 1456) and descend 0.5 mile east along the ridge to the 13,500-foot Belford–Oxford saddle (38.9599° -106.3493°). From the saddle, hike 0.7 mile east-northeast up the gentle slopes of Oxford's west ridge on the Mount Oxford Trail to Oxford's summit (38.9647° -106.3388°). To complete this long workout, return over Belford.

13R3 – Mount Oxford – East Ridge

From Pine Creek TH at 8,880'   432 RP   17.0 mi RT   5,273' net; 5,791' total   Class 2

This alternative to the standard route over Belford allows you to enjoy Oxford by itself. It is a long but enjoyable hike. Start at the Pine Creek Trailhead at 8,880 feet and go 2.2 miles west up the 4WD road to 9,200 feet, where the Pine Creek Trail starts. Follow the Pine Creek Trail (FT 1459) 2.5 miles west up the valley on Pine Creek's southeast side, entering the Collegiate Peaks Wilderness en route, to 10,400 feet, where the Colorado Trail from the south intersects the Pine Creek Trail. Turn northeast (right), cross Pine Creek and go 280 yards northwest to the intersection of the Pine Creek Trail and the Colorado Trail going north (38.9657° -106.2776°). Leave the Pine Creek Trail and follow the Colorado Trail (FT 1776) 1.5 miles northeast then north as it climbs to 11,650 feet near treeline on Oxford's long east ridge (38.9752° -106.2860°). This is the end of your Class 1 trail approach.

Leave the Colorado Trail and hike 0.4 mile west through open trees to treeline at 12,000 feet, then hike 2.0 miles up the broad, gentle ridge to Waverly Mountain's multiple summits. Waverly is an officially named but unranked Thirteener. You can easily bypass the eastern, 13,007-foot summit, but you will have to climb most of the way to the higher, 13,292-foot summit. You may as well take the few extra steps required to touch Waverly's highest point (38.9759° -106.3238°). From Waverly, follow the remaining 1.2 miles of Oxford's now better-defined northeast then east ridge to the summit (38.9647° -106.3388°).

Mount Oxford from the west. Photo by Steve Hoffmeyer

13R4 – Mount Oxford – South Slopes

From Pine Creek TH at 8,880'   397 RP   18.2 mi RT   5,273' total   Class 2

This is another Oxford alternative that can be used on a backpacking trip into upper Pine Creek. Start at the Pine Creek Trailhead at 8,880 feet and go 2.2 miles west up the 4WD road to 9,200 feet, where the Pine Creek Trail starts. Follow the Pine Creek Trail (FT 1459) 5.0 miles west up the valley, entering the Collegiate Peaks Wilderness en route, to Little Johns Cabin at 10,700 feet (38.9550° -106.3155°). Hike 300 yards southwest of the cabin, cross the side stream coming from the north, and hike another 400 yards on the trail to 10,780 feet (38.9532° -106.3224°). This is the end of your 7.4-mile Class 1 trail approach.

Leave the Pine Creek Trail and start climbing northwest through the trees. Hike up the indistinct ridge just west of the side stream. The terrain is rugged until you reach treeline at 11,800 feet. Above treeline, continue northwest up the small but relentless ridge to 13,800 feet, where the slope angle finally relents, and hike north up gentle slopes to Oxford's summit.

13. Missouri Mountain 14,067 feet

13R – Missouri Mountain Routes

13R5 – Missouri Mountain – Northwest Ridge

From Missouri Gulch TH at 9,640'   217 RP   10.2 mi RT   4,427' net; 4,487' total   Class 2

This is the traditional route up Missouri. Start at the Missouri Gulch Trailhead at 9,640 feet, descend a little, cross the bridge over Clear Creek, and stride up several memorable switchbacks into Missouri Gulch. Continue on the excellent

Missouri Gulch Trail (FT 1469) to 12,620 feet (38.9552° -106.3765°). When the trail turns east toward Elkhead Pass, leave the trail and climb 0.8 mile west on a trail up grassy slopes to a 13,700-foot saddle on Missouri's northwest ridge (38.9546° -106.3863°). Climb 0.2 mile south to Point 13,930 and continue 0.5 mile southeast to the summit (38.9467° -106.3783°). Near the summit, there are some rock towers on the ridge that you can bypass to the west on a use trail.

13R6 – Missouri Mountain – North Face Couloirs

From Missouri Gulch TH at 9,640'	*268 RP*	*9.0 mi RT*	*4,427' net; 4,487' total*	*Class 3, Mod Snow*
With descent of Northwest Ridge	*268 RP*	*9.6 mi RT*	*4,427' net; 4,487' total*	*Class 3, Mod Snow*

Missouri's craggy north face offers a choice of four couloirs that make good early summer snow climbs. When snow free, avoid these couloirs.

Follow the Northwest Ridge Route (13R5) to 12,620 feet in Missouri Gulch, continue 0.2 mile farther on the Missouri Gulch Trail to 12,720 feet (38.9546° -106.3748°), and choose your couloir. The westernmost couloir, called the C Couloir, is the easiest, and it curves gracefully up to the summit. The two central couloirs climb straight to Missouri's upper east ridge. The easternmost and most difficult couloir is not visible until you reach 12,800 feet on the Missouri Gulch Trail. This narrow couloir cuts through Missouri's steeper northeast face and is a more serious climb.

13R7 – Missouri Mountain – East Ridge

From Missouri Gulch TH at 9,640'	*353 RP*	*9.6 mi RT*	*4,427' net; 4,487' total*	*Class 4*
With descent of Northwest Ridge	*343 RP*	*9.9 mi RT*	*4,427' net; 4,487' total*	*Class 4*

This route's Class 4 rating disguises a serious and dangerous climb. What should be Missouri's premier mountaineering route is so rotten that it is relegated to this author's nightmares. This is unfortunate, because there are few technical climbs on Sawatch Fourteeners.

Start at the Missouri Gulch Trailhead at 9,640 feet and follow the Missouri Gulch Trail 4.0 miles to Elkhead Pass at 13,220 feet (38.9517° -106.3664°). As you approach the pass, you can inspect the route. The east ridge's salient feature is a band of white rock that cuts across the center of the ridge. There is a steep buttress below the band and a multifaced, flatironlike buttress above the band. These two buttresses and the white band are the ridge's cruxes. They require four Class 4 pitches.

From Elkhead Pass, hike and scramble west along the ridge to a small saddle below the first buttress. There is a significant pinnacle north of the ridge that will attract your attention, and you may see black ravens perching like a portent on the pinnacle's summit. Scramble straight up the ridge to 100 feet below the top of the first steep buttress (Class 3). Traverse under the buttress on the ridge's north side on a solid ledge (Class 3). Climb a steep wall at the end of the ledge to reach the rubble-filled gully of the white band (Class 4). Climb the gully or the broken wall to the right of the gully to a small ridge (Class 4).

These pitches are precarious because of the rubble on every hold. Climb into the large, north-facing dihedral of the upper buttress (Class 4). Climb the dihedral's east face for 100 feet on the route's only solid rock (Class 4). Above these difficulties, scramble 400 yards up Missouri's upper east ridge to the summit (Class 3). Descend another route.

13R8 – Missouri Mountain – West Ridge

From Rockdale TH at 9,940'	306 RP	11.4 mi RT	4,127' total	Class 2
From Clohesy Lake 4WD TH at 10,880'	224 RP	5.4 mi RT	3,187' total	Class 2

This alternative route up Missouri avoids the crowds at Missouri Gulch. Start at the Rockdale Trailhead at 9,940 feet (12T1; see Huron Peak), ford Clear Creek, and continue 3.0 miles south on the 4WD road toward Clohesy Lake to a signed parking area at the south end of a large meadow at 10,880 feet (38.9540° -106.4088°).

Hike 0.4 mile south up the trail beyond this parking area to a bench above the northeast side of Clohesy Lake and continue 0.2 mile south on the trail that leads around the east side of Clohesy Lake. When you are above the lake (38.9490° -106.4075°), climb 0.3 mile southeast then east on a smaller trail to treeline at 11,600 feet and continue 0.2 mile east then northeast to 12,000 feet in the basin below Missouri's steep, scree-covered southwest face. Avoid this unpleasant face by climbing 0.4 mile northeast to 12,800 feet on Missouri's broad, grassy west ridge. Climb 0.6 mile east up this ridge to 13,900 feet on Missouri's northwest ridge and follow the upper Northwest Ridge Route (13R5) from there.

13R9 – Missouri Mountain – South Ridge

From Missouri Gulch TH at 9,640'	280 RP	11.6 mi RT	4,427' net; 5,267' total	Class 2

You can use this route when coming and going on peak-bagging extravaganzas. Start at the Missouri Gulch Trailhead at 9,640 feet and follow the Missouri Gulch Trail 4.0 miles to Elkhead Pass at 13,220 feet (38.9517° -106.3664°). Continue over the pass and descend 0.4 mile south to 12,800 feet (38.9483° -106.3664°). Leave the trail, contour 0.8 mile southwest under Missouri's south face, then climb 0.3 mile west to the 13,540-foot saddle (38.9436° -106.3800°) between Missouri and 13,831-foot Iowa Peak. From the saddle, hike 0.3 mile north to Missouri's summit.

13R9 V1 – Variation – Lake Fork

From Rockdale TH at 9,940'	299 RP	11.1 mi RT	4,127' total	Class 2
From Clohesy Lake 4WD TH at 10,880'	218 RP	5.1 mi RT	3,187' total	Class 2

If you walk all the way from the Rockdale Trailhead (12T1; see Huron Peak), this is a long route. If you drive to the Clohesy Lake 4WD Parking at 10,880 feet (12T1 4WD; see Huron Peak), this is the shortest route on Missouri, but the ford of Clear Creek can make this route problematic in early summer.

Start at the Rockdale Trailhead at 9,940 feet , ford Clear Creek, and continue

3.0 miles south on the 4WD road toward Clohesy Lake to a signed parking area at the south end of a large meadow at 10,880 feet (38.9540° -106.4088°).

Hike 0.4 mile south up the trail beyond this parking area to a bench above the northeast side of Clohesy Lake and continue 0.2 mile south on the trail that leads around the east side of Clohesy Lake. When you are above the lake (38.9490° -106.4075°), climb 0.3 mile southeast then east on a smaller trail to treeline at 11,600 feet. Hike 1.1 miles east up the basin below Missouri's steep, scree-covered southwest face and climb 0.25 mile east up a steep slope to reach the 13,540-foot Missouri–Iowa Peak saddle (38.9436° -106.3800°). Hike 0.3 mile north to the summit.

13R9 V2 – Variation – Pine Creek

From Pine Creek TH at 8,880'   439 RP   26.0 mi RT   5,187' total   Class 2

You can use this remote ridge for a backpacking trip into upper Pine Creek. With its near marathon distance and vertical mile elevation gain, this approach provides a great workout for the superfit. Mortals will enjoy the pleasures of Colorado camping.

Start at the Pine Creek Trailhead at 8,880 feet and go 2.2 miles west up the 4WD road to 9,200 feet, where the Pine Creek Trail starts. Follow the Pine Creek Trail (FT 1459) 5.0 miles west up the valley, entering the Collegiate Peaks Wilderness en route, to Little Johns Cabin at 10,700 feet (38.9550° -106.3155°). Continue 3.0 miles west on the trail to the junction of the Elkhead Pass and Silver King Lake trails at 11,520 feet (38.9303° -106.3498°). Hike 1.3 miles west then north on the Elkhead Pass Trail to 12,400 feet (38.9366° -106.3624°). Leave the trail and climb 1.2 miles west to the 13,540-foot Missouri–Iowa Peak saddle (38.9436° -106.3800°). Your 12.7-mile approach is over. Now for the climb! Hike 0.3 mile north to the summit.

13R9 EC1 – Extra Credit – Iowa Peak 13,831 feet 38.9395° -106.3829°

Class 2

From the 13,540-foot Missouri–Iowa Peak saddle (38.9436° -106.3800°), climb 0.3 mile south to 13,831-foot Iowa Peak, an officially named peak with a soft rank that has honorable mention on the list of Colorado's 100 highest peaks.

13R9 EC2 – Extra Credit – Emerald Peak 13,904 feet 38.9290° -106.3813°

Class 2

For even more credit, continue 0.8 mile south from the summit of Iowa Peak to 13,904-foot Emerald Peak, an official centennial Thirteener.

13C – Belford, Oxford, and Missouri Combination Routes

13C1 – Belford Northwest Ridge → Oxford West Ridge

From Missouri Gulch TH at 9,640'   225 RP   9.8 mi RT   4,557' net; 5,967' total   Class 1

This is the standard way of climbing Belford and Oxford together; it is the same as Oxford's West Ridge Route (13R2). Start at the Missouri Gulch Trailhead at 9,640 feet and climb Belford's Northwest Ridge Route (13R1) to Belford's summit. Descend 0.2 mile southeast then turn east (left) onto the Mount Oxford Trail (FT 1456) and descend 0.5 mile east along the ridge to the 13,500-foot Belford–Oxford saddle (38.9599° -106.3493°). From the saddle, hike 0.7 mile east-northeast up the gentle slopes of Oxford's west ridge on the Mount Oxford Trail to Oxford's summit (38.9647° -106.3388°). Return over Belford and descend Missouri Gulch.

13C2 – Missouri Northwest Ridge ➜ Belford Elkhead Pass ➜ Oxford West Ridge

From Missouri Gulch TH at 9,640'   332 RP   15.0 mi RT   7,414' total   Class 2

This is the easiest way to climb Belford, Oxford, and Missouri together, but it's a tough day. Start at the Missouri Gulch Trailhead at 9,640 feet and climb Missouri's Northwest Ridge Route (13R5). Descend that route to 12,620 feet (38.9552° -106.3765°) in upper Missouri Gulch and hike the upper part of Belford's Elkhead Pass Variation (13R1 V2) to the top of Belford. Traverse to Oxford as in Combination 13C1, return over Belford, and descend Belford's Northwest Ridge Route (13R1).

14. Harvard Group

Mount Harvard   14,420 feet
Mount Columbia   14,073 feet

Mount Harvard, together with its companion Mount Columbia, forms a large, high massif 11 miles northwest of Buena Vista. Harvard is Colorado's third highest peak, but unlike the first and second highest peaks, Elbert and Massive, which are clearly seen from Leadville, Harvard does not reveal itself so easily. When you see it from neighboring peaks to the north or south, however, Harvard's bulk, height, and shape are unmistakable.

Mount Harvard is one of only three Colorado peaks to rise above 14,400 feet, and Harvard is also the highest peak in Chaffee County. Like most Sawatch Fourteeners, Harvard is easy to climb, but requires more effort than most. Many parties choose to pack in when climbing Harvard. Harvard will both test and reward you.

Columbia, 1.9 miles southeast of Harvard, is best known as Harvard's lower companion peak, but it is a fine peak by itself. Columbia's east slopes sweep up from the Arkansas River Valley, and Columbia towers over Horn Fork Basin to its west. Columbia is most often climbed with Harvard, but the traverse between the two peaks is long; some people find Columbia alone a sufficient challenge.

14E – Harvard Group Essentials

Elevations	Mt Harvard	14,420' (NGVD29) 14,427' (NAVD88)
	Mt Columbia	14,073' (NGVD29) 14,079' (NAVD88)
Ranks	Mt Harvard	Colorado's 3rd highest ranked peak
	Mt Columbia	Colorado's 35th highest ranked peak
Location	Chaffee County, Colorado, USA	
Range	Central Sawatch Range	
Summit Coordinates	Mt Harvard	38.9244° -106.3207° (WGS84)
	Mt Columbia	38.9042° -106.2978° (WGS84)
Ownership/Contact	San Isabel National Forest – Public Land – 719-553-1400	
Prominence and Saddles	Mt Harvard	2,360' from 12,060' near Independence Pass
	Mt Columbia	893' from 13,180' Harvard–Columbia saddle
Isolation and Parents	Mt Harvard	14.96 miles to Mount Elbert
	Mt Columbia	1.89 miles to Mount Harvard
USGS Maps	Mount Harvard, Mount Yale,	
	Harvard Lakes, Buena Vista West	
USFS Map	San Isabel National Forest	
Trails Illustrated Map	Map #129 Buena Vista/Collegiate Peaks	
Book Map	See Map 14 on page 138	
Nearest Town	Buena Vista – Population 2,100 – Elevation 7,965'	
Mt Harvard 🏃 Easiest Route	14R1 – South Slopes – Class 2	
	A Class 1 trail hike most of the way, then a little boulder hopping	
	near the summit	
Mt Columbia 🏃 Easiest Route	14R4 – West Slopes – Class 2	
	A Class 1 trail approach, a steep Class 2 talus slope to the ridge,	
	then a gentler Class 2 ridge walk to the top	
Harvard Group	These Fourteeners tower over the upper Arkansas River Valley.	
Accolades	Sprawling ridges offer a choice of routes, and lakes nestle in the	
	upper basins. Hiding behind its lower neighbor Columbia, Harvard	
	is the highest peak in Chaffee County.	

14T – Harvard Group Trailheads

14T1 – Harvard Lakes Trailhead 9,420 feet 38.8645° -106.2387°

This trailhead provides access to the east sides of Harvard and Columbia. From the Chaffee County 306–US 24 junction in the center of Buena Vista (stoplight), go 0.4 mile north on US 24. Turn west onto Chaffee County 350 (Crossman Avenue) and measure from this point. Go 2.1 miles west on Chaffee County 350 to a T-junction and turn north (right) onto Chaffee County 361. Chaffee County 361 turns to dirt at mile 2.4, then angles northwest. At mile 3.0, turn sharply south (left) onto Chaffee County 365, which soon turns west and enters the San Isabel National Forest at mile 5.4. Reach the Harvard Lakes Trailhead on the north side of the road at mile 6.6. The trailhead is marked

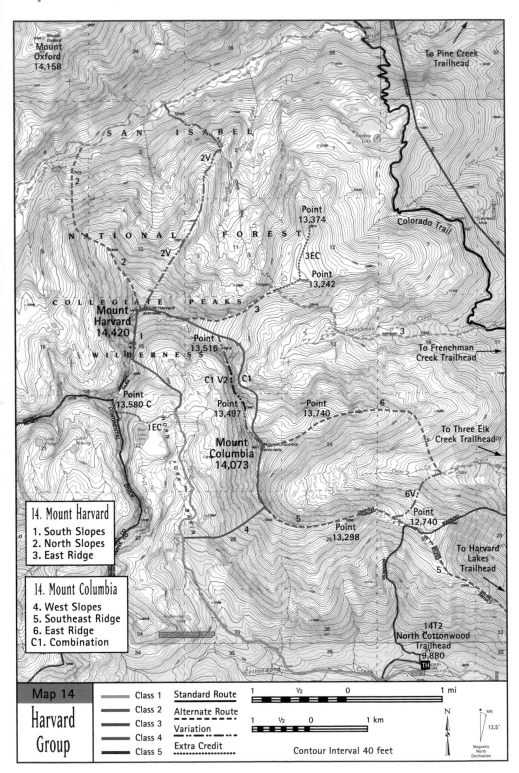

14. Mount Harvard
1. South Slopes
2. North Slopes
3. East Ridge

14. Mount Columbia
4. West Slopes
5. Southeast Ridge
6. East Ridge
C1. Combination

Map 14
Harvard
Group

Class 1
Class 2
Class 3
Class 4
Class 5

Standard Route
Alternate Route
Variation
Extra Credit

1   ½   0   1 mi
1   ½   0   1 km

Contour Interval 40 feet

N

MN
12.5°

Magnetic
North
Declination

with signs for the Colorado Trail and Harvard Lakes. The winter road closure is at the National Forest boundary, or possibly several hundred yards below the boundary at 9,000 feet.

14T2 – North Cottonwood Trailhead 9,880 feet 38.8707° -106.2667°

This trailhead provides access to the south sides of Harvard and Columbia. From the Harvard Lakes Trailhead (mile 6.6), continue west, pass the Silver Creek Trailhead (see 15T3, Mount Yale) on the south side of the road at mile 6.7, and reach the North Cottonwood Trailhead at the end of the road at mile 8.2. The winter road closure is sometimes as high as the National Forest boundary at mile 5.4, but is often at 9,000 feet several hundred yards below the National Forest boundary.

14T3 – Three Elk Creek Trailhead 9,260 feet 38.9011° -106.2232°

This trailhead provides access to Columbia's east side. From the Chaffee County 306–US 24 junction in the center of Buena Vista (stoplight), go north on US 24 for 0.4 mile. Turn west onto Chaffee County 350 (Crossman Avenue) and measure from this point. Go 2.1 miles west on Chaffee County 350 to a T-junction. Turn north (right) onto Chaffee County 361 and go 3.8 miles to Chaffee County 368 at mile 5.9. Turn west (left) onto Chaffee County 368 and go 1.2 miles to Chaffee County 368A at mile 7.1. Turn southwest onto Chaffee County 368A and go 0.1 mile to FR 368 at mile 7.2. Turn west (right) onto FR 368 and go 0.8 mile to the signed trailhead at mile 8.0. The Three Elk Creek Trail (FT 1445) goes south from here.

14T4 – Frenchman Creek Trailhead 9,300 feet 38.9369° -106.2135°

This trailhead provides access to Harvard's east side. Turn west from US 24 onto Chaffee County 386 at the tiny community of Riverside. This junction is 7.5 miles north of the stoplight in the center of Buena Vista, 11.7 miles south of the US 24–Colorado 82 junction, and 26.7 miles south of the West Sixth–US 24 junction in the center of Leadville. Go 0.3 mile west on Chaffee County 386 to FR 386 at the San Isabel National Forest boundary. There is an annual seasonal closure above this point from December 1 through April 15. Turn west (right) onto Frenchman Creek Road (FR 386) and go 1.1 miles to the trailhead area. Park 2WD vehicles here.

14T4 4WD – Frenchman Creek 4WD Trailhead 10,300 feet 38.9319° -106.2371°

From the Frenchman Creek Trailhead, 4WD vehicles can continue 1.6 miles on the Frenchman Creek Road (FR 386) to the end of the road at 10,300 feet near a ridge north of Frenchman Creek. From here, the trail goes southwest to Frenchman Creek.

14. Mount Harvard 14,420 feet

14R – Mount Harvard Routes

14R1 – Mount Harvard – South Slopes

From North Cottonwood TH at 9,880'   259 RP   12.6 mi RT   4,540' total   Class 2

This is the traditional and easiest route on Harvard. Except for some rocky terrain near the top, it is a Class 1 hike on a trail. Start at the North Cottonwood Trailhead at 9,880 feet and cross to the south side of North Cottonwood Creek on a good bridge. Follow the North Cottonwood Trail (FT 1449) 1.5 miles west to a trail junction at 10,360 feet (38.8708° -106.2929°), just after the trail returns to the creek's north side. Turn northwest (right) onto the Horn Fork Trail (FT 1449) to Horn Fork Basin and Bear Lake. Follow the Horn Fork Trail 2.2 miles northwest then north into Horn Fork Basin to reach treeline at 11,600 feet (38.8933° -106.3111°). There are several good campsites just below treeline. You can see Harvard to the north at the head of the basin, and Columbia's steep west slopes are above you to the east.

Continue 1.3 miles north on the trail into the beautiful basin to a trail junction at 12,360 feet (38.9090° -106.3140°) where a side trail goes west to Bear Lake. It is not necessary to go to Bear Lake, but the 0.3-mile side trip to this amazing lake is worth the effort if you have time. Bear Lake rests both below and above steep cliffs and offers a good view of Mount Yale to the south.

Beyond the Bear Lake Trail junction at 12,360 feet, the trail becomes steeper and rougher, but is still a discernible trail. Climb 0.5 mile north-north-west to 13,000 feet (38.9146° -106.3174°) on the poorly defined east ridge of minor Point 13,598, which is on Harvard's south ridge 0.7 mile south of Harvard. You can see the rest of the route from here. Continue 0.4 mile north-northeast on an ascending traverse and reach Harvard's south ridge at 13,600 feet (38.9194° -106.3220°), where your view to the west opens dramatically. Turn north (right) and climb 0.4 mile north just east of the ridge crest on increasingly rocky, Class 2 terrain to reach Harvard's boulder-strewn summit (38.9244° -106.3207°).

14R1 EC – Extra Credit – Point 13,580 C 38.9111° -106.3261°

From North Cottonwood TH at 9,880'   216 RP   11.8 mi RT   3,700' total   Class 2

This is a significant Extra Credit, but it gives you a decorous excuse to visit beautiful Bear Lake en route to a soft-ranked Thirteener. From the trail junction at 12,360 feet (38.9090° -106.3140°), hike 0.3 mile west to 12,400 feet on the northeast side of Bear Lake (38.9078° -106.3186°). Hike 0.4 mile west-northwest on talus, staying north of some cliffs, and reach the south ridge of Point 13,580 C at 13,200 feet (38.9090° -106.3253°). Hike 300 yards north up the rocky ridge to the summit. Soft-ranked Point 13,580 C has the dubious distinction of being the lowest peak on the list of Colorado's 200 highest peaks.

14R2 – Mount Harvard – North Slopes

From Pine Creek TH at 8,880'   *468 RP*   *21.0 mi RT*   *5,540' total*   *Class 2*

This alternative route avoids the crowds in Horn Fork Basin and allows you to combine Harvard with Belford and Oxford to the north. This long route is best done with a backpack into Pine Creek. Start at the Pine Creek Trailhead at 8,880 feet (see 13T2, Belford Group) and go 2.2 miles west up the 4WD road to 9,200 feet, where the Pine Creek Trail starts. Follow the Pine Creek Trail (FT 1459) 5.0 miles west up the valley, entering the Collegiate Peaks Wilderness en route, to Little Johns Cabin at 10,700 feet (38.9550° -106.3155°). Continue 1.0 mile west on the trail to 11,000 feet (38.9489° -106.3315°). If you pass Bedrock Falls, you have gone too far. This is the end of your 8.2 mile, Class 1 trail approach.

Leave the trail at 11,000 feet, cross to the south side of Pine Creek, steel yourself for a workout, and begin climbing Harvard's huge north slopes. Climb 1.4 miles south up these long, grassy slopes until they become a ridge at 13,400 feet (38.9338° -106.3268°). Follow this gentle ridge 0.9 mile south to the summit. Should you meet any south side trail trekkers on the summit, you can elucidate your workout for them.

14R2 V – Variation – Northeast Ridge

From Pine Creek TH at 8,880'   *428 RP*   *20.0 mi RT*   *5,540' total*   *Class 2*

This variation is easier down low, but steeper near the summit. From Little Johns Cabin at 10,700 feet, leave the Pine Creek Trail, go south, cross to the south side of Pine Creek, and find the South Pine Creek Trail (FT 1458) in the trees. Follow this trail 0.8 mile southeast past some old mines to a ridge at 11,960 feet (38.9481° -106.3049°). This ridge separates Pine Creek from South Pine Creek. Leave the South Pine Creek Trail and hike 0.3 mile south-southwest onto Harvard's broad northeast ridge. Follow the ridge 0.9 mile southwest until it merges with Harvard's broad northeast face at 12,840 feet (38.9326° -106.3137°) and climb a tedious 0.7 mile up this face to the summit.

14R3 – Mount Harvard – East Ridge

From Frenchman Creek TH at 9,300'   *328 RP*   *14.2 mi RT*   *5,120' total*   *Class 2*
From Frenchman Creek 4WD TH at 10,300'   *272 RP*   *11.0 mi RT*   *4,120' total*   *Class 2*

This route has gained in popularity in recent years; its simplicity is its charm. Start at the Frenchman Creek Trailhead at 9,300 feet and go 1.6 miles west up the 4WD Frenchman Creek Road (FR 386) to the end of the road at 10,300 feet near a ridge north of Frenchman Creek where the road becomes the Frenchman Creek Trail (FT 1457) (38.9319° -106.2371°). Hike 1.3 miles southwest on the Frenchman Creek Trail (formerly the Harvard Trail). En route, enter the Collegiate Peaks Wilderness at 10,400 feet, reach and cross to the south side of Frenchman Creek at 10,520 feet (38.9326° -106.3137°), and hike west to a junction with the Colorado Trail at 10,960 feet (38.9214° -106.2549°). Cross the Colorado Trail, continue 1.7 miles west up the Frenchman Creek Trail to a bench just

Mount Harvard and Mount Columbia from the northwest.

above treeline at 11,920 feet (**38.9209° -106.2825°**), and bask in the beautiful basin. Cross to the north side of Frenchman Creek, follow an old trail 0.9 mile north then west past a mine adit, then hike northwest to the 12,980-foot saddle between Point 13,374 and Mount Harvard (**38.9266° -106.2966°**). This is the end of your 5.5-mile Class 1 trail approach. For your peak experience, climb 1.6 miles west on Harvard's rocky upper east ridge to Harvard's summit (Class 2).

14R3 EC – Extra Credit – Point 13,374 38.9367° -106.2884°

Class 2

From the 12,980-foot saddle on Harvard's east ridge, climb 0.4 mile northeast to unranked Point 13,242 (**38.9288° -106.2900°**) and continue 0.6 mile north to Point 13,374, one of Colorado's ranked Thirteeners.

14. Mount Columbia 14,073 feet

14R – Mount Columbia Routes

14R4 – Mount Columbia – West Slopes

From North Cottonwood TH at 9,880'   274 RP   10.0 mi RT   4,193' total   Class 2

This is the standard and most direct route on Columbia. There is no trail on Columbia's steep, loose west slopes, and climbers' boots have scarred this slope in recent years. You can minimize further damage to this slope by only ascending it and descending another route, since boots skittering down the slope cause the most damage. Also, consider doing another itinerary that avoids the west slopes.

Start at the North Cottonwood Trailhead at 9,880 feet and cross to the south side of North Cottonwood Creek on a good bridge. Follow the North Cottonwood Trail (FT 1449) 1.5 miles west to a trail junction at 10,360 feet

(38.8708° -106.2929°), just after the trail returns to the creek's north side. Turn northwest (right) onto the Horn Fork Trail (FT 1449) to Horn Fork Basin and Bear Lake. Follow the Horn Fork Trail 1.9 miles northwest then north into Horn Fork Basin to reach 11,400 feet (38.8899° -106.3126°). There are several good campsites just below treeline. Columbia's steep west slopes are above you to the east. The slopes directly below Columbia's summit are especially steep and unpleasant. The easiest terrain is a mile south of the summit, so don't go too far into Horn Fork Basin before beginning your ascent.

Leave the trail just below treeline at 11,400 feet and climb 0.25 mile east to the bottom of Columbia's west slopes. Climb 0.75 mile up the long, tedious, oft-cursed slope and reach Columbia's south ridge at 13,660 feet (38.8955° -106.2974°). Hike 0.6 mile north along this gentle ridge to the summit (38.9042° -106.2978°).

14R5 – Mount Columbia – Southeast Ridge

From Harvard Lakes TH at 9,420'   394 RP   10.4 mi RT   4,653' net; 5,129' total   Class 2

This is a more challenging alternative to the standard West Slopes Route (14R4). Start at the Harvard Lakes Trailhead at 9,420 feet and follow the Colorado Trail (FT 1776) 0.5 mile north up the first steep switchbacks to Columbia's southeast ridge. Follow the trail 0.2 mile west along the ridge to 10,000 feet where the trail levels out and turns north (38.8691° -106.2411°). This is the end of your short Class 1 trail approach.

Leave the Colorado Trail and hike northwest up the ridge through open trees. Climb steadily along the ridge for 2.0 miles to Point 12,740 (38.8916° -106.2671°). From this tiny summit, follow the rocky ridge 0.8 mile west, entering the Collegiate Peaks Wilderness en route, to Point 13,298 (38.8931° -106.2817°). Continue 1.7 miles west then north along the easy ridge to Columbia's summit (38.9042° -106.2978°). At 13,600 feet, you can look down on Columbia's steep west slopes and feel noble that you chose this route.

14R6 – Mount Columbia – East Ridge

From Three Elk Creek TH at 9,260'   351 RP   11.8 mi RT   4,813' net; 5,277' total   Class 2

This is the cardinal Colorado climb. Nestled in the heart of the state's central range, it offers route finding that leads you to wilderness and, if you are lucky, wildlife. This route somehow seems to further the fantasy that every dirt road in Colorado leads to a Fourteener. The fantasy is especially rich when newly fallen aspen leaves dot the road.

Start at the Three Elk Creek Trailhead at 9,260 feet and go 300 yards south on a logging road. Leave the logging road when it turns west and continue south on the marked Three Elk Creek Trail (FT 1445). Cross several other logging roads and reach Three Elk Creek in a small gorge. Cross the creek and climb 100 yards south to an abandoned road (38.8946° -106.2254°). Go 1.0 mile southwest then west on the continuing Three Elk Trail to the Colorado Trail (FT 1776), just north of Harvard Lakes at 10,260 feet (38.8986° -106.2401°). Cross the

Colorado Trail and continue 1.5 miles northwest on the Three Elk Creek Trail to a bench just above treeline at 11,400 feet (38.9004° -106.2642°). This is the end of your 3.0-mile Class 1 trail approach.

Leave the fading trail, climb 1.0 mile northwest, and reach Columbia's east ridge near 12,440 feet (38.9093° -106.2636°). Climb 1.9 miles west along the gentle ridge over three false summits to reach Columbia's main summit.

14R6 V – Variation – Bristlecone Circle

From Three Elk Creek TH at 9,260'   349 RP   12.0 mi RT   4,813' net; 5,123' total   Class 2

To complete a beautiful circle tour, descend the Southeast Ridge Route (14R5) to 12,640 feet (38.8940° -106.2726°), then descend 1.0 mile steeply northeast through an incredible stand of bristlecone pine to rejoin the Three Elk Creek Trail.

14C – Harvard and Columbia Combination Route

14C1 – Columbia West Slopes → Harvard South Slopes

From North Cottonwood TH at 9880'   409 RP   13.7 mi RT   5,813' total   Class 2

This is the easiest way to climb Harvard and Columbia together. I describe the traverse from Columbia to Harvard so that you only ascend Columbia's fragile west slopes. Historically, people have chosen to go from Harvard to Columbia, but this leaves you descending, and further damaging, Columbia's fragile west slopes.

Start at the North Cottonwood Trailhead at 9,880 feet and climb Columbia's West Slopes Route (14R4). Even avoiding the technical ridge crest, the 2.4-mile traverse to Columbia is arduous. From Columbia's summit, descend 0.5 mile north to 13,000 feet (38.9111° -106.2981°). Stay well east of Point 13,497 on the Frenchman Creek (east) side of the ridge. Descend 0.2 mile northwest to 12,800 feet. You are now safely below the difficulties of the ridge above you to the west. Contour 0.4 mile north at the 12,800-foot level until Point 13,516 is above you to the west. When the difficulties above you relent, climb 0.8 mile northwest up a narrowing talus slope to 14,000 feet (38.9230° -106.3118°) on Harvard's east ridge. Hike 0.5 mile west up this ridge to Harvard's summit. Descend Harvard's South Slopes Route (14R1).

14C1 V1 – Variation – Circumflex

From Harvard Lakes TH at 9420'   482 RP   13.9 mi RT   6,273' total   Class 2

You can modify the beginning of this traverse by climbing Columbia's Southeast Ridge Route (14R5) from the Harvard Lakes Trailhead instead of using the West Slopes Route (14R4) from the North Cottonwood Trailhead. This increases both the distance and elevation gain but eliminates Columbia's deteriorating West Slopes Route from the itinerary. It also eliminates your ability to do the traverse from a camp in Horn Fork Basin. You also have to deal with the 1.6-mile distance between North Cottonwood and Harvard Lakes trailheads, but if you are in shape to do Circumflex, you can just hoof it down the road at the end of the day and earn an additional 17 RPs.

14C1 V2 – Variation – The Rabbits

From North Cottonwood TH at 9880'   *669 RP*   *13.4 mi RT*   *5,606' total*   *Class 5.7*

From Harvard Lakes TH at 9420'   *741 RP*   *13.6 mi RT*   *6,066' total*   *Class 5.7*

You can stay closer to the ridge crest and save 207 feet of elevation loss, but this rocky ridge is much more difficult. While descending north from Columbia's summit, stay on the ridge crest and climb or skirt Point 13,497 (Class 5.0–5.2). Descend north from Point 13,497 to a notch south of the Rabbits, several pinnacles that are the crux of the traverse. Climb 30 feet north (Class 5.7) out of the notch to a sloping ledge system on the ridge's east side. Avoid the Rabbits' multiple pinnacles by doing exposed Class 4 traverses on the east side of the ridge. Descend north along the ridge to the 13,180-foot Harvard–Columbia saddle (38.9159° -106.3038°). The major difficulties are now behind you. Scramble north to Point 13,516, then hike 1.0 mile west-northwest to Harvard's summit.

If you choose to do this traverse from Harvard to Columbia, you have the option of rappelling over the crux, Class 5.7 pitch. If you do the first part of the traverse on the ridge but change your mind either before or after the Rabbits, you can find places to descend steep scree gullies to the west and finish the traverse well below the ridge on its west side.

15. Mount Yale 14,196 feet

Mount Yale is 9 miles directly west of Buena Vista. Yale is 1 foot lower than neighboring Mount Princeton, and is not as easily seen from the Arkansas River Valley. These trivial differences with the stately Princeton only thinly disguise a great peak. Unlike Princeton, Yale is in the Collegiate Peaks Wilderness and offers a choice of several routes. Yale, like most Sawatch Fourteeners, rises abruptly from its surrounding valleys. No matter how you tackle Yale, the peak will test your legs. From Yale's summit, you are rewarded with a view of 30 of Colorado's Fourteeners.

15E – Mount Yale Essentials

Elevations	14,196' (NGVD29) 14,204' (NAVD88)
Rank	Colorado's 21st highest ranked peak
Location	Chaffee County, Colorado, USA
Range	Central Sawatch Range
Summit Coordinates	38.8441° -106.3138° (WGS84)
Ownership/Contact	San Isabel National Forest – Public Land – 719-553-1400
Prominence and Saddle	1,896' from 12,300' Yale–Harvard saddle
Isolation and Parent	5.56 miles to Mount Harvard
USGS Maps	**Mount Yale**, Buena Vista West
USFS Map	San Isabel National Forest

15E – Mount Yale Essentials

Trails Illustrated Map	Map #129 Buena Vista/Collegiate Peaks
Book Map	See Map 15 on page 147
Nearest Town	Buena Vista – Population 2,100 – Elevation 7,965'
Mount Yale 🥾 Easiest Route	15R1 – Southwest Slopes – Class 2
	A Class 1 approach hike on a trail, a sometimes steep, undulating climb to a high ridge, and a final climb along a rough, rocky ridge to the summit
Yale's Accolades	Yale is one of the dominate Collegiate Peaks and its forward position over the Arkansas River Valley makes it easily accessible, even in winter.

15T – Mount Yale Trailheads

15T1 – Denny Creek Trailhead 9,900 feet 38.8150° -106.3345°

This trailhead provides access to Yale's southwest side. From a stoplight on US 24 in the center of Buena Vista, go 11.0 miles west on Chaffee County 306 (paved) to the Collegiate Peaks Campground. Continue 1.0 mile west to the well-marked trailhead on the north side of the road. Do not confuse Denny Creek with Denny Gulch farther east. This trailhead is accessible in winter.

15T2 – Avalanche Trailhead 9,370 feet 38.8140° -106.2796°

This trailhead provides access to Yale's east side. From a stoplight on US 24 in the center of Buena Vista, go 9.1 miles west on Chaffee County 306 (paved) to the signed trailhead on the north side of the road. There is a large, paved parking lot here; the trail starts near the east end of the parking lot. This trailhead is accessible in winter.

15T3 – Silver Creek Trailhead 9,420 feet 38.8656° -106.2412°

This trailhead provides access to Yale's east side. Follow the directions for the Harvard Lakes Trailhead (see 14T1, Harvard Group). From the Harvard Lakes Trailhead on the north side of the road at mile 6.6, continue west and reach the Silver Creek Trailhead on the south side of the road at mile 6.7. The trailhead is marked with signs for the Colorado Trail.

15R – Mount Yale Routes

15R1 – Mount Yale – Southwest Slopes

From Denny Creek TH at 9,900'   *204 RP*   *8.5 mi RT*   *4,296' total*   *Class 2*

This is the standard route on Yale; it has replaced the historic route up Denny Gulch farther east. For environmental reasons, the brutally steep route up Denny Gulch is no longer used. Do not confuse Denny Creek and Denny Gulch.

Start at the Denny Creek Trailhead at 9,900 feet and walk north up the Denny Creek Trail (FT 1442). After switchbacking up the initial hill, you will enter the Collegiate Peaks Wilderness at 10,160 feet. Continue north-northwest on the west side of Denny Creek, and cross Denny Creek at 10,500 feet, 1.0

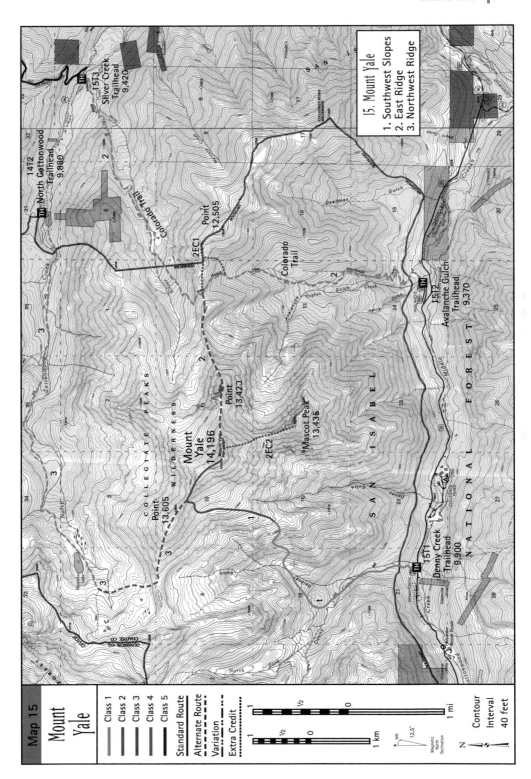

15. Mount Yale
1. Southwest Slopes
2. East Ridge
3. Northwest Ridge

Map 15
Mount
Yale

Class 1
Class 2
Class 3
Class 4
Class 5
Standard Route
Alternate Route
Variation
Extra Credit

Contour
Interval
40 feet

1   ½   0   1 mi
1   ½   0   1 km

Mount Yale from the southwest.

mile from the trailhead (38.8265° -106.3393°). Continue 0.25 mile northwest to a trail junction, leave the Denny Creek Trail, hike 0.5 mile northeast on the Mount Yale Trail (FT 1451), and cross to Delaney Creek's east side at 11,040 feet (38.8340° -106.3354°). Stay on the trail, leave the trees behind, wind 0.9 mile up the steep slope to the east (right), and reach Yale's broad southwest shoulder at 12,200 feet (38.8360° -106.3255°). Climb 1.0 mile north up this grassy shoulder, wind up another slope en route, and reach a 13,500-foot saddle on Yale's northwest ridge (38.8493° -106.3215°). Go 0.6 mile southeast along this rough, rocky ridge to the summit (38.8441° -106.3138°). You can bypass a small buttress just below the summit on its west side.

15R2 – Mount Yale – East Ridge *Classic*

From Avalanche TH at 9,370'	*300 RP*	*10.6 mi RT*	*4,826' total*	*Class 2*
From Silver Creek TH at 9,420'	*299 RP*	*10.6 mi RT*	*4,776' total*	*Class 2*

This route offers a scenic alternative to Yale's popular Southwest Slopes Route (15R1). The East Ridge Route is a little longer, but the additional effort is a small price to pay for solitude. You can approach the East Ridge Route from either the Avalanche or Silver Creek Trailhead. From the Avalanche Trailhead at 9,370 feet, climb 3.3 miles north on the Colorado Trail (FT 1776) to the 11,900-foot Silver Creek saddle (38.8473° -106.2819°) between Yale and Point 12,505, a ranked Twelver 2.4 miles east of Yale. This trail climbs steeply at first, then wanders up through delightful forest glades. If you start at the Silver Creek Trailhead at 9,420 feet, follow the Colorado Trail 3.3 miles southwest up Silver Creek to the 11,900-foot saddle.

From the 11,900-foot Silver Creek saddle, leave the Colorado Trail, hike west past treeline, then go over or around the north side of a small, 12,140-foot summit. Continue on Yale's now well-defined east ridge and climb rough boulders to a pair of small, 13,420-foot summits from which you can see Yale's summit. The remaining 0.7 mile of the ridge is less steep, and you can spy on the approaching summit long before you reach it.

Ascending the East Ridge Route from Avalanche Trailhead and descending the Southwest Slopes Route (15R1) to Denny Creek Trailhead makes a comprehensive climb. On this circle, you will have to walk, bike, or jog for 2.9 miles down the road back to the Avalanche Trailhead.

15R2 EC1 – Extra Credit – Point 12,505 38.8440° -106.2694°

Class 2

From the 11,900-foot saddle (38.8473° -106.2819°) on the Colorado Trail, leave the trail and go 0.4 mile east, skirting or going over two small summits en route, to reach a small 12,060-foot saddle (38.8471° -106.2750°). If you are coming up the Colorado Trail from the Avalanche Trailhead, you can leave the trail at 11,560 feet (38.8438° -106.2781°) and hike 0.3 mile northeast through the trees to reach the 12,060-foot saddle. From here, hike 0.4 mile east then southeast to reach Point 12,505, one of Colorado's 1,000 highest ranked peaks.

15R2 EC2 – Extra Credit – "Mascot Peak" 13,435 feet 38.8332° -106.3074°

Class 2

From Yale's summit, go 200 yards back down the east ridge, then descend 0.4 mile south to a 13,060-foot saddle (38.8378° -106.3094°). Climb 0.3 mile south up talus to Point 13,435, alias "Mascot Peak." This ranked summit is a Tri, one of Colorado's 300 highest peaks, and it provides a suspended view of Yale and Princeton. Return to the 13,060-foot saddle. From here, either climb back to Yale's east ridge at 14,040 feet or descend east down Avalanche Gulch to rejoin the Colorado Trail. Do not descend Denny Gulch to the southwest, since it is no longer politically or environmentally correct to do so.

15R3 – Mount Yale – Northwest Ridge

From North Cottonwood TH at 9,880'   333 RP   13.5 mi RT   4,316' net; 4,526' total   Class 2

This increasingly popular route is often done with a backpack to Kroenke Lake. Start at the North Cottonwood Trailhead at 9,880 feet (see 14T2, Harvard Group) and cross to the south side of North Cottonwood Creek on a good bridge. Follow the North Cottonwood Trail (FT 1449) 1.5 miles west to a trail junction at 10,360 feet (38.8708° -106.2929°), just after the trail returns to the creek's north side. Do not take the northwest (right) trail to Horn Fork Basin. Continue 2.5 miles west (straight) on the North Cottonwood Trail to Kroenke Lake near treeline at 11,500 feet (38.8658° -106.3315°). This is a classic Colorado cirque surrounded by unnamed summits, with a Fourteener hulking in the distance.

Continue on the trail around the south side of Kroenke Lake, hike to 11,960 feet (38.8628° –106.3388°), leave the trail, and climb 0.7 mile south to a 12,540-foot saddle (38.8535° –106.3372°) on Yale's distinguished northwest ridge. Climb 0.75 mile east on the ridge to unranked Point 13,605 (38.8509° –106.3243°) and behold the beauty. Continue 0.8 mile southeast to Yale's summit and behold it all.

16. Mount Princeton 14,197 feet

Princeton is a singular mountain and a true monarch because its neighbors are far lower and far away; Princeton is one of Colorado's most prominent peaks. Its summit is less than 9 miles southwest of Buena Vista, and the peak rises abruptly out of the Arkansas River Valley.

Princeton is the southernmost and most visible of the Collegiate Fourteeners. As you descend west into the Arkansas River Valley on US 285, Princeton stares you smack in the face for many miles, and you cannot ignore its gaze. When snow graces Princeton's slopes, the view is breathtaking. It always speaks for Colorado.

16E – Mount Princeton Essentials

Elevations	14,197' (NGVD29) 14,205' (NAVD88)
Rank	Colorado's 18th highest ranked peak
Location	Chaffee County, Colorado, USA
Range	Southern Sawatch Range
Summit Coordinates	38.7491° -106.2423° (WGS84)
Ownership/Contact	San Isabel National Forest – Public Land – 719-553-1400
Prominence and Saddle	2,177' from 12,020' Browns Pass
Isolation and Parent	5.21 miles to Mount Antero
USGS Maps	**Mount Antero**, St Elmo, Buena Vista West, Mount Yale
USFS Map	San Isabel National Forest
Trails Illustrated Maps	**Map #130 Salida/St Elmo/Mt Shavano**
	Map #129 Buena Vista/Collegiate Peaks
Book Map	See Map 16 on page 151
Nearest Towns	Buena Vista – Population 2,100 – Elevation 7,965'
	Salida – Population 2,100 – Elevation 7,083'
Mt Princeton 🚶 Easiest Route	16R1 – East Slopes – Class 2
	A Class 1 approach on a road and trail, a steeper climb to a high ridge, and a final hike up this talus ridge to the summit
Princeton's Accolades	Princeton is the southernmost and most visible of the Collegiate Fourteeners. Rising directly above the Arkansas River Valley, Princeton is easily accessible and very popular. There is a road leading high onto the peak's east flank.

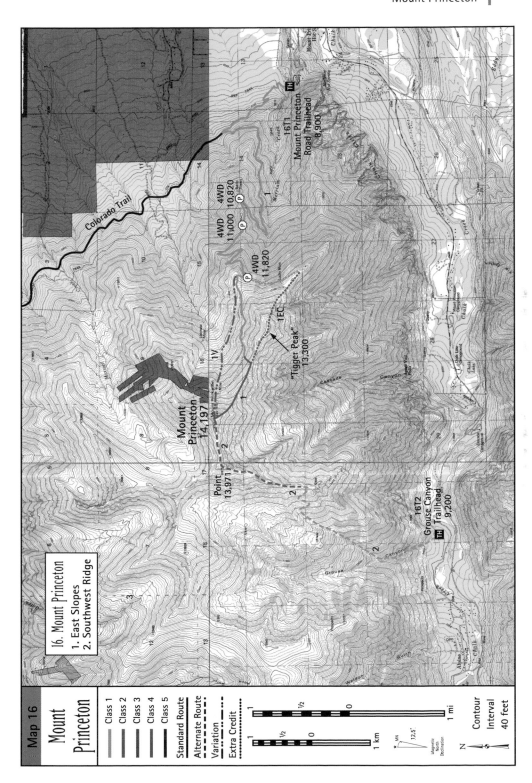

Map 16

Mount
Princeton

Class 1
Class 2
Class 3
Class 4
Class 5

Standard Route
Alternate Route
Variation
Extra Credit

N

MN

12.5°

Magnetic
North
Declination

1   ½   0   1 mi
1   ½   0   1 km

Contour
Interval
40 feet

16. Mount Princeton
1. East Slopes
2. Southwest Ridge

Colorado Trail

Mount Princeton
Road Trailhead
8,900
16T1

4WD
10,820

4WD
11,000

4WD
11,820

1EC

"Tigger Peak"
13,300

1V

Mount
Princeton
14,197

Point
13,971

Grouse Canyon
Trailhead
9,200
16T2

16T – Mount Princeton Trailheads

16T1 – Mount Princeton Road Trailhead 8,900 feet 38.7388° -106.1772°

The Mount Princeton Road starts at 8,900 feet and ends at 12,150 feet at Bristlecone Park, on Princeton's southeast side. If approaching from the north, go 5.6 miles south on US 285 from the US 24–US 285 junction just west of Johnson Village, near Buena Vista. If approaching from the south, go 15.4 miles north on US 285 from the US 50–US 285 junction in Poncha Springs.

Leave US 285 and go 4.4 miles west on Chaffee County 162 (paved) to Chaffee County 321, near Mount Princeton Hot Springs. Turn north (right) onto Chaffee County 321 (paved), go 1.3 miles, turn west (left) onto Chaffee County 322 (dirt), and go 0.9 mile to the start of the Mount Princeton Road. There is a large parking lot at the bottom of the Mount Princeton Road at 8,900 feet. If you value your vehicle, park here; this is the 2WD trailhead.

16T1 4WD – Mount Princeton 4WD Trailhead 11,000 feet 38.7449° -106.2059°

The Mount Princeton Road is continuously steep and narrow, but is passable to 11,000 feet for some medium-clearance vehicles. It is difficult to pass vehicles going the opposite direction, difficult to turn around, and difficult to park on the Mount Princeton Road. At 3.2 miles, the road reaches a ridge at 10,820 feet near some radio towers, and there is limited parking here (38.7453° -106.2006°). The road then climbs west along the ridge, and there is limited parking after 3.5 miles at 11,000 feet (38.7449° -106.2059°).

The 4WD road beyond this point climbs 1.0 mile through three switchbacks on a east-northeast slope then rounds onto a southeast slope and climbs west. If you are still driving, park where the road heads south toward Bristlecone Park near treeline at 11,820 feet (38.7444° -106.2153°). The Mount Princeton Trail climbs north from here.

16T2 – Grouse Canyon Trailhead 9,200 feet 38.7155° -106.2640°

This trailhead provides access to Princeton's southwest side. If approaching from the north, go 5.6 miles south on US 285 from the US 24–US 285 junction just west of Johnson Village, near Buena Vista. If approaching from the south, go 15.4 miles north on US 285 from the US 50–US 285 junction in Poncha Springs.

Leave US 285 and go 4.4 miles west on Chaffee County 162 (paved) to Mount Princeton Hot Springs, a favorite place for postclimb soaking. Continue 5.7 miles west on Chaffee County 162, passing under the famous Chalk Cliffs. Turn north (right) onto Chaffee County 292 and cross Chalk Creek on a bridge. Follow Chaffee County 292 0.4 mile west, turn north (right) onto an unsigned dirt road, go 100 yards north, and park. The old 4WD road beyond this point is too narrow and rough for full-size 4WD vehicles. Both Chaffee County 292 and the lower part of Grouse Creek are incorrectly marked on the St. Elmo Quadrangle in this area. Respect private property near here.

Mount Princeton from the east.

16R – Mount Princeton Routes

16R1 – Mount Princeton – East Slopes

From Mount Princeton Road TH at 8,900'	*293 RP*	*13.0 mi RT*	*5,297' total*	*Class 2*
From Mount Princeton 4WD TH at 11,000'	*176 RP*	*6.0 mi RT*	*3,197' total*	*Class 2*

This is the easiest and most popular route up Princeton. The length of the climb depends on how far you drive up the Mount Princeton Road. The lower numbers assume a start at 11,000 feet; the higher numbers assume a start at 8,900 feet.

Follow the Mount Princeton Road 3.5 miles to the 4WD parking spot at 11,000 feet (**38.7449° -106.2059°**). Continue 1.0 mile through three switchbacks on a east-northeast slope then round onto a southeast slope and climb west to treeline at 11,820 feet (**38.7444° -106.2153°**). Leave the road just as it starts to head south toward Bristlecone Park and climb 0.1 mile north on a trail to a small ridge at 11,960 feet (**38.7458° -106.2148°**). The junction of trail and road is not well marked and is easy to miss. You can see Princeton's upper slopes from the ridge.

Continue 1.0 mile on the trail as it climbs west across a north-facing slope below Point 13,300, aka "Tigger Peak." The trail is not destined for Princeton's summit but for an old mine at 13,100 feet, east of the summit. Do not follow the trail all the way to the mine, because the slope above the mine is unpleasant. Leave the trail between 12,700 feet and 12,900 feet and climb 0.2 mile southwest up Class 2 talus to reach Princeton's southeast ridge near 13,200 feet (**38.7443° -106.2336°**). The view of Mount Antero from the ridge is striking. Turn north (right) and hike 0.7 mile up Princeton's upper southeast ridge to the summit (**38.7491° -106.2423°**).

16R1 V – Variation – Line Glacier

Class 2, Mod Snow

I originally named the Line Glacier as a joke, but the name endures. The Line Glacier is a narrow snow finger that sometimes exists in the basin east of Princeton's summit. Like the perfect wave, it is rarely there. When you spot it in good condition, climb it! Leave the trail on the small ridge at 11,960 feet, traverse northwest to the snow finger, and stomp directly to the summit. After all, hotshots climb the face.

16R1 EC – Extra Credit – "Tigger Peak" 13,300 feet 38.7412° -106.2256°
Class 2

Either going to or coming from Princeton's summit, stay on the southeast ridge and hike 0.5 mile east-southeast to Point 13,300, alias "Tigger Peak." Tigger is a child's paraphrase of Princeton University's mascot, the tiger, and the name suits this suspended viewpoint.

16R2 – Mount Princeton – Southwest Ridge
From Grouse Canyon TH at 9,200'   286 RP   7.0 mi RT   4,997' net; 5,219' total   Class 2

This short, steep route provides a rough but still sanguine alternative to Princeton's crowded east side. Start at the Grouse Canyon Trailhead at 9,200 feet and follow the 4WD road for 0.25 mile to a poorly defined trail. Follow the cairned trail across flood effluent to Grouse Creek at 9,420 feet (38.7182° -106.2664°), at the bottom of Grouse Canyon. Your brief introduction is over—now for the climb.

Climb 0.5 mile north on the sometimes ill-defined trail up the east side of Grouse Canyon through embracing cliffs to 10,200 feet (38.7244° -106.2689°). Leave the main north–south branch of Grouse Canyon and follow a good trail on the slope east of and above Grouse Creek north-northeast up a side drainage. During your arduous 0.65-mile ascent up the side drainage, take time to enjoy the creek's miniature mossy mosaics. Pass treeline at 11,400 feet (38.7330° -106.2630°) and climb 0.6 mile northeast up a talus slope to reach Princeton's southwest ridge at 12,880 feet (38.7362° -106.2550°). The altruistic approach is over; now for your reward.

Climb 1.0 mile north along the studded ridge to Point 13,971 (38.7481° -106.2512°), an unranked but significant false summit. Enjoy your respite in this privileged position. The views are expansive to the north, west, and south, and the civilization to the east is mercifully hidden. When ready, continue 0.5 mile east to Princeton's stately but now pedantic summit.

17. Mount Antero 14,269 feet

Mount Antero is named after a Native American chief of the Uintah Nation. The peak is 3 miles south of Chalk Creek and is easily visible from US 285 in the Arkansas River Valley. Antero is more famous among gem collectors than it is among mountaineers, since it has produced some truly remarkable aquamarine and topaz gems and quartz crystals.

Mountaineers should keep their eyes open while hiking up Antero, because it is still possible to find a parsimonious prize. It is much more likely, though, that you will see only people—many people—looking for gems and views. Most of them drive up the 4WD road that goes up Baldwin Gulch and reaches 13,700 feet on a shoulder south of Antero's summit. On a busy summer weekend, you can hear the sounds of 4WD vehicles grinding up this road from Tabeguache Peak, 4 miles south of Antero. Antero does offer a choice of routes, but don't expect solitude in August.

17E – Mount Antero Essentials

Elevations	14,269' (NGVD29) 14,276' (NAVD88)
Rank	Colorado's 10th highest ranked peak
Location	Chaffee County, Colorado, USA
Range	Southern Sawatch Range
Summit Coordinates	38.6742° -106.2462° (WGS84)
Ownership/Contact	San Isabel National Forest – Public Land – 719-553-1400
Prominence and Saddle	2,503' from 11,766' Williams Pass
Isolation and Parent	17.77 miles to Mount Harvard
USGS Maps	**Mount Antero**, St Elmo
USFS Map	San Isabel National Forest
Trails Illustrated Map	Map #130 Salida/St Elmo/Mt Shavano
Book Map	See Map 17 on page 156
Nearest Towns	Buena Vista – Population 2,100 – Elevation 7,965' feet
	Salida – Population 2,100 – Elevation 7,083' feet
Mount Antero Easiest Route	17R1 – West Slopes – Class 2
	A long Class 1 approach on a road and a short Class 2 summit climb along a bumpy talus ridge
Antero's Accolades	Antero is famous since it has produced some truly remarkable aquamarine and topaz gems and quartz crystals; you can still find a parsimonious prize. There is a 4WD road leading high onto the peak's south side.

17T – Mount Antero Trailheads

17T1 – Cascade Trailhead 9,020 feet 38.7095° -106.2443°

This trailhead provides access to Antero's north side. If approaching from the north, go 5.6 miles south on US 285 from the US 24–US 285 junction just west of Johnson Village, near Buena Vista. If approaching from the south, go 15.4 miles north on US 285 from the US 50–US 285 junction in Poncha Springs. Leave US 285 and go 9.6 miles west on Chaffee County 162 (paved) to the Cascade Campground. The campground is the trailhead, and hikes start from the top of the campground loop road. This trailhead is accessible in winter.

17T2 – Baldwin Gulch Trailhead 9,420 feet 38.7100° -106.2918°

This trailhead provides access to Antero's west side. From the Cascade Trailhead (mile 9.6), continue 2.0 miles west on Chaffee County 162 to the Baldwin

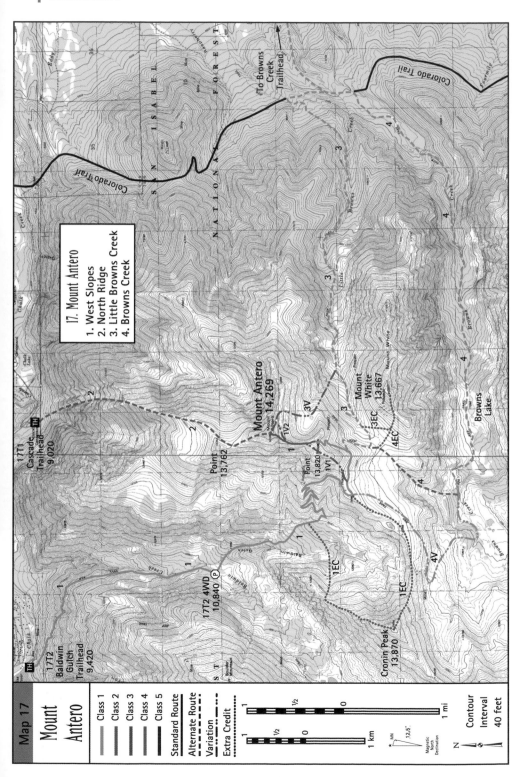

Map 17
Mount Antero

Class 1
Class 2
Class 3
Class 4
Class 5

Standard Route
Alternate Route
Variation
Extra Credit

Contour
Interval
40 feet

17. Mount Antero
1. West Slopes
2. North Ridge
3. Little Browns Creek
4. Browns Creek

17T1
Cascade
Trailhead
9,020

17T2 4WD
10,840

17T2
Baldwin
Gulch
Trailhead
9,420

Point
13,762

Mount Antero
14,269

Point
13,820

Mount White
13,667

Cronin Peak
13,870

Browns
Lake

To Browns
Creek
Trailhead

Colorado Trail

Mount Antero's south ridge. Photo by Sarah T. Meiser

Gulch Road (dirt), which is on the south side of Chaffee County 162, 11.6 miles from US 285. Park at the bottom of the Baldwin Gulch Road.

17T2 4WD – Baldwin Gulch 4WD Trailhead 10,840 feet 38.6825° -106.2728°
From the Baldwin Gulch Trailhead, 4WD vehicles can climb 3.0 miles southeast then south into Baldwin Gulch on FR 277 to a road junction at 10,840 feet. The road continues, but this is a good place to park 4WD vehicles.

17T3 – Browns Creek Trailhead 8,920 feet 38.6723° -106.1618°
This trailhead provides access to the east and south sides of Antero, and to the north side of Shavano and Tabeguache. If approaching from the north, go 8.9 miles south on US 285 from the US 24–US 285 junction just west of Johnson Village, near Buena Vista. If approaching from the south, go 12.1 miles north on US 285 from the US 50–US 285 junction in Poncha Springs. Leave US 285, turn west onto Chaffee County 270 (paved), and measure from this point. From Chaffee County 270, continue straight on Chaffee County 272 (the Browns Creek Road) at mile 1.5, enter the San Isabel National Forest at mile 2.3, turn south (left) at mile 3.5, and reach the Browns Creek Trailhead at mile 5.1. The well-marked trailhead is on the west side of the road, and there is good camping nearby.

17R – Mount Antero Routes
17R1 – Mount Antero – West Slopes

From Baldwin Gulch TH at 9,420'	*294 RP*	*16.0 mi RT*	*4,849' total*	*Class 2*
From Baldwin Gulch 4WD TH at 10,840'	*200 RP*	*10.0 mi RT*	*3,429' total*	*Class 2*

This is the easiest and most popular route up Antero, since a 4WD road goes to 13,700 feet. Start at the Baldwin Gulch Trailhead at 9,420 feet and follow the steep 4WD road (FR 277) 3.0 miles southeast then south to a road junction at 10,840 feet **(38.6825° -106.2728°)**. Leave FR 277, turn southeast (left) onto FR 278, cross Baldwin Creek, and continue 1.3 miles south into upper Baldwin Gulch to 12,000 feet (38.6670° -106.2636°). Continue 2.0 miles on the road as it switch-backs up Antero's west slopes, then angles south and finally southwest to reach a road junction on Antero's south ridge at 13,089 feet (38.6620° -106.2588°). During this 1,000-foot ascent, stay on the road and avoid any temptation to head straight up the steep, loose scree; it's hard on you and the environment.

Once on Antero's south ridge at 13,089 feet, turn hard northeast (left) onto FR 278A and hike 0.5 mile northeast then east, staying left on FR 278A at another road junction, to yet another road junction at 13,200 feet (38.6621° -106.2497°). Stay left at this junction and hike 0.6 mile north on FR 278A to where the road ends at 13,700 feet (38.6677° -106.2479°), in a small saddle just east of Point 13,820. The difficulty is Class 1 to this point. From the end of the road, hike 0.1 mile north to regain Antero's south ridge in a 13,700-foot saddle between Point 13,820 and Antero (38.6688° -106.2482°). Continue 0.25 mile north along the east side of the bumpy Class 2 ridge to 13,880 feet then climb 300 yards north-northeast up the rounded ridge to the summit (38.6742° -106.2462°).

17R1 V1 – Variation – Point 13,820 38.7412° -106.2256°
Class 2

For a shorter but slightly harder hike, go 200 yards northeast on FR 278A from the FR 278-278A junction at 13,089 feet, leave FR 278A before it heads east, and hike 0.5 mile northeast then north up a rounded talus ridge to the top of unranked Point 13,820. Some people expect this to be Antero's summit and are dismayed to see that Antero is still a half mile to the north. From Point 13,820, descend 200 yards north-northeast and rejoin the standard route in the 13,700-foot saddle between Point 13,820 and Antero.

17R1 V2 – Variation – Upper South Face
Class 2

At 13,880 feet, leave the ridge and do an ascending traverse northeast on an old miner's trail that crosses Antero's upper south face. A snow slope may cover part of this trail until late summer. Reach Antero's upper east ridge at 14,040 feet (38.6732° -106.2440°), turn west (left), and follow that ridge to the summit.

17R1 EC – Extra Credit – Cronin Peak 13,870 feet 38.6553° -106.2834°
Class 2

From 13,089 feet on Antero's south ridge, descend 1.0 mile southwest from the 4WD road on easy slopes to a 12,820-foot saddle (38.6528° -106.2705°). From the saddle, climb 0.8 mile west-northwest on a ridge to Cronin Peak, one of Colorado's 100 highest ranked peaks. For the easiest descent, reverse your ascent. For a shorter but steeper return to Baldwin Gulch, descend Cronin Peak's north ridge to 12,600 feet (38.6658° -106.2777°), leave the ridge and descend east to Baldwin Creek at 11,740 feet (38.6655° -106.2677°). Cross the stream, climb gently northeast and reach the Baldwin Gulch Road at 11,900 feet (38.6679° -106.2631°).

17R2 – Mount Antero – North Ridge

From Cascade TH at 9,020'   497 RP   6.8 mi RT   5,249' total   Class 2, Mod Snow

I do not recommend this steep, direct route for casual Fourteener hikers. When snow conditions are favorable, it does provide some good snow climbing, but the route ascends a large avalanche chute; you should carefully consider snow conditions before ascending it. The gully contains unpleasant scree when it is snow-free.

Start at the Cascade Trailhead at 9,020 feet, angle up to the southeast and enter a prominent, treeless gully at 9,600 feet (38.7053° -106.2415°). This is the western of two gullies that you can see from the Cascade Campground entrance. Climb the gully and reach Antero's north ridge at 12,200 feet (38.6959° -106.2401°). Climb south on this ridge for a long mile, pass Point 13,762 on its east side, and continue 0.5 mile south to the summit. Do not descend the unnamed basin east of the north ridge.

17R3 – Mount Antero – Little Browns Creek

From Browns Creek TH at 8,920'   310 RP   16.6 mi RT   5,349' total   Class 2

Do not confuse Little Browns Creek with Browns Creek to the south, since the two creeks drain different valleys. Little Browns Creek is in the higher, narrower valley between Mount White and Antero.

Start at the Browns Creek Trailhead at 8,920 feet and follow the Browns Creek Trail 1.3 miles west to the Colorado Trail. At this point Little Browns Creek is just 150 yards to the south. In a counterintuitive move, turn north (right) away from the creek and follow the Colorado Trail (FT 1776) 0.5 mile north to the signed Little Browns Creek Trail (FT 1430) at 9,780 feet (38.6699° -106.1831°), which is just south of the point where the Colorado Trail crosses a small, unnamed creek. The Little Browns Creek Trail starts as an old rocky road that climbs southwest up a hill. Many older maps do not show the Little Browns Creek Trail.

Leave the Colorado Trail and hike 0.7 mile southwest then 2.6 miles west on the Little Browns Creek Trail on the north side of Little Browns Creek to treeline at 11,800 feet (38.6645° -106.2283°). The climb up this enchanting valley is steep, steady, and long. Continue 1.3 miles west-southwest all the way to the broad, 12,820-foot saddle (38.6578° -106.2470°) between Antero and 13,667-foot Mount White. From here, join the 4WD road system on Antero's upper slopes, hike 0.2 mile west-northwest, 0.45 mile north-northeast, and 0.15 mile west-southwest to join the upper West Slopes Route (17R1) at 13,200 feet (38.6621° -106.2497°). Hike 0.6 mile north on FR 278A to where the road ends at 13,700 feet (38.6677° -106.2479°), in a small saddle just east of Point 13,820. This is the end of your 7.8-mile Class 1 approach.

Now for the climb. Continue 0.25 mile north along the east side of the bumpy, Class 2 ridge to 13,880 feet then climb 300 yards north-northeast up the rounded ridge to the summit (38.6742° -106.2462°).

17R3 V – Variation – Tarnacity

From Browns Creek TH at 8,920'   *328 RP*   *13.6 mi RT*   *5,349' total*   *Class 2*

This variation provides a complete escape from the 4WD roads of the West Slopes Route (17R1). It offers a shorter but steeper, rougher approach to the summit. From 0.4 mile beyond treeline at 12,080 feet (38.6640° -106.2346°), leave the Little Browns Creek Trail and hike 0.6 mile northwest (Class 2) to a small hanging basin at 13,240 feet (38.6680° -106.2429°). The 1994 Mount Antero Quadrangle shows a small, intermittent tarn in this basin, and when it actually contains water, this tarn is the highest lake in the Sawatch Range. From the tarn, hike 0.4 mile north up talus, reach Antero's upper east ridge at 13,900 feet (38.6727° -106.2415°), turn west (left), and hike 0.3 mile west up that ridge to Antero's summit (Class 2).

17R3 EC – Extra Credit – Mount White 13,667 feet 38.6561° -106.2385°

Class 2

From 12,700 feet on the Little Browns Creek Trail (38.6602° -106.2448°), leave the trail and climb 0.5 mile south then east to 13,667-foot Mount White, one of Colorado's 200 highest ranked peaks. There are two summits; the southwest summit is the highest. Little Browns Creek provides a good way to combine Mount White and Antero.

17R4 – Mount Antero – Browns Creek

From Browns Creek TH at 8,920'   *384 RP*   *19.3 mi RT*   *5,349' total*   *Class 2*

This is the longest route on Antero, and it is best done as a backpacking adventure. It is an easy route that uses trails and roads most of the way. With a camp in upper Browns Creek, you can climb Shavano, Tabeguache, Point 13,712, and Antero.

Start at the Browns Creek Trailhead down on the deck of the Arkansas River Valley at 8,920 feet and follow the Browns Creek Trail 1.3 miles west to the Colorado Trail (FT 1776). Turn south (left) on the Colorado Trail, go 150 yards south, cross Little Browns Creek, and continue 300 yards south to the upper Browns Creek Trail (FT 1429). Leave the Colorado Trail and hike 4.4 miles southwest then west up the Browns Creek Valley on FT 1429 to lower Browns Lake at 11,286 feet (38.6442° -106.2390°). From lower Browns Lake, hike 0.5 mile west to 11,370 feet and reach the end of an interminable 4WD road (FR 278) that has reached this elusive point (38.6436° -106.2489°) from Baldwin Gulch to the north. Hike 0.3 mile northwest on the 4WD road to 11,680 feet (38.6467° -106.2534°), leave the 4WD road, and hike 1.0 mile northwest, north, then northeast (Class 2) up a small side valley to reach the broad 12,820-foot saddle (38.6578° -106.2470°) between Antero and 13,667-foot Mount White. From here, join the 4WD road system on Antero's upper slopes, hike 0.2 mile west-northwest, 0.45 mile north-northeast, and 0.15 mile west-southwest to join the upper West Slopes Route (17R1) at 13,200 feet (38.6621° -106.2497°). Hike 0.6 mile north on FR 278A to the end of the road at 13,700 feet (38.6677° -106.2479°)

in a small saddle just east of Point 13,820. This is the end of your 9.15-mile approach hike.

Now for the climb. Continue 0.25 mile north along the east side of the bumpy, Class 2 ridge to 13,880 feet then climb 300 yards north-northeast up the rounded ridge to the summit (38.6742° -106.2462°).

17R4 V – Variation – Upper Browns Creek

From Browns Creek TH at 8,920'   *380 RP*   *23.1 mi RT*   *5,349' total*   *Class 2*

For a longer, easier hike, follow FR 278 then FR 278A all the way from 11,680 feet (38.6467° -106.2534°) to 13,700 feet (38.6677° -106.2479°).

17R4 EC – Extra Credit – Mount White 13,667 feet 38.6561° -106.2385°

Class 2

From the broad, 12,820-foot saddle between Antero and Mount White (38.6578° -106.2470°), climb 0.6 mile east-southeast to 13,667-foot Mount White, one of Colorado's 200 highest ranked peaks. There are two summits; the southwest summit is the highest.

18. Shavano Group

Mount Shavano   14,229 feet
Tabeguache Peak   14,155 feet

These two peaks are the southernmost Fourteeners in the Sawatch Range. They are 12 miles northwest of Poncha Springs, which is near the US 50–US 285 junction. Shavano dominates the view from US 285 north of Poncha Springs, while Tabeguache hides behind its higher neighbor. Shavano and Tabeguache are Native American names from the Ute Nation.

Mount Shavano is famous for the Angel of Shavano on its east face. The Angel is a shallow, snow-filled couloir with two diverging branches at the top. In the spring and early summer, the snow gullies resemble an angel with up-stretched arms. It is interesting that both the northernmost and southernmost Sawatch Fourteeners, Mount of the Holy Cross and Shavano, have snow features with religious significance. Shavano is also the easternmost Sawatch Fourteener.

Tabeguache is not as well known as its higher, more visible neighbor, Shavano. I do not recommend the ascent or descent of McCoy Gulch on the south side of Tabeguache. The upper part of the gulch is easy, but the lower part contains a cliffy gorge. Many parties encounter trouble trying to descend McCoy Gulch, and the Chaffee County sheriff's office, tired of rescuing people from the gulch, once placed large warning signs at both the Jennings Creek and Blank Gulch trailheads. They also yanked this book from store bookshelves and stuffed warning flyers into it. To reduce further government consternation and mischief, take it from me: do not descend McCoy Gulch.

18E – Shavano Group Essentials

Elevations	Mt Shavano	14,229' (NGVD29) 14,236' (NAVD88)
	Tabeguache Pk	14,155' (NGVD29) 14,162' (NAVD88)
Ranks	Mt Shavano	Colorado's 17th highest ranked peak
	Tabeguache Pk	Colorado's 25th highest ranked peak
Location	Chaffee County, Colorado, USA	
Range	Southern Sawatch Range	
Summit Coordinates	Mt Shavano	38.6191° -106.2394° (WGS84)
	Tabeguache Pk	38.6255° -106.2509° (WGS84)
Ownership/Contact	San Isabel National Forest – Public Land – 719-553-1400	
Prominence and Saddles	Mt Shavano	1,619' from 12,610' saddle W of Tabeguache
	Tabeguache Pk	455' from 13,700' Shavano–Tabeguache saddle
Isolation and Parents	Mt Shavano	3.82 miles to Mount Antero
	Tabeguache Pk	0.75 mile to Mount Shavano
USGS Maps	**Maysville, Garfield, St Elmo, Mount Antero**	
USFS Map	San Isabel National Forest	
Trails Illustrated Map	Map #130 Salida/St Elmo/Mt Shavano	
Book Map	See Map 18 on page 163	
Nearest Town	Salida – Population 2,100 – Elevation 7,083' feet	
Mt Shavano 🏃 Easiest Route	18R1 – East Slopes – Class 2	
	A Class 1 trail hike to a high saddle, then a short Class 2 hike up to talus to	
	the summit	
Tabeguache Pk 🏃 Easiest Route	18R4 – West Ridge – Class 2	
	A short Class 1 trail approach, an off-trail Class 2 hike up to a saddle,	
	then a Class 2 hike along a ridge to the summit	
Shavano Group	Mount Shavano is famous for the Angel of Shavano on its east face.	
Accolades	Shavano is also the easternmost Sawatch Fourteener.	

18T – Shavano Group Trailheads

18T1 – Angel of Shavano Trailhead 9,180 feet 38.5840° -106.2185°

This trailhead provides access to Shavano's south and east sides. On US 50, go 6.1 miles west of the US 50–US 285 junction in Poncha Springs. Turn north onto Chaffee County 240 and measure from this point. Chaffee County 240 is paved initially, turns to dirt at mile 2.7, and reaches the Angel of Shavano Campground and Trailhead at mile 3.8. The road is good to this point. The trailhead is on the north side of the road, and the campground is on the south side. This trailhead is accessible in winter.

18T2 – Jennings Creek Trailhead 10,540 feet 38.6006° -106.2788°

Due to environmental concerns, the Forest Service has asked that people do not start at the Jennings Creek Trailhead and climb Tabeguache via its south-west ridge but, instead, climb the peak by starting at the Blank Gulch Trailhead

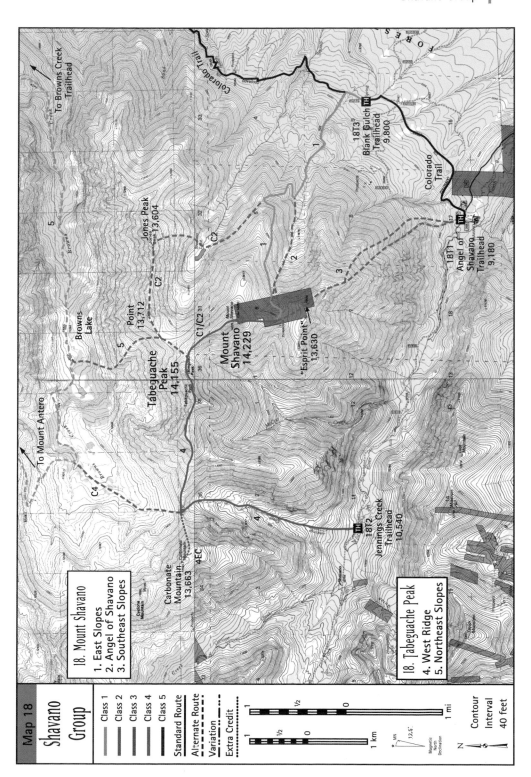

Map 18

Shavano Group

Class 1
Class 2
Class 3
Class 4
Class 5
Standard Route
Alternate Route
Variation
Extra Credit

Contour Interval 40 feet

MN 13.5° Magnetic North Declination

18. Mount Shavano
1. East Slopes
2. Angel of Shavano
3. Southeast Slopes

18. Tabeguache Peak
4. West Ridge
5. Northeast Slopes

To Browns Creek Trailhead

Colorado Trail

Blank Gulch Trailhead 9,800
18T3

Colorado Trail

Angel of Shavano Trailhead 9,180
18T1

Jones Peak 13,604

C2

C2

Point 13,712

Browns Lake

Tabeguache Peak 14,155

Mount Shavano 14,229

C1/C2

"Esprit Point" 13,630

To Mount Antero

C4

4

4EC

Carbonate Mountain 13,663

Jennings Creek Trailhead 10,540
18T2

and traversing over Mount Shavano. I include the trailhead because it is on public land and I feel that the government's route choice greatly increases dangers to climbers by forcing them to remain on a high ridge exposed to lightening for a long time. To ease environmental concerns, I have modified the route above this trailhead and hope that a sustainable trail will be constructed up Jennings Creek.

This trailhead provides access to Tabeguache's west ridge. From the Angel of Shavano Campground (mile 3.8), continue 3.8 miles west on Chaffee County 240 and reach the Jennings Creek Trailhead at mile 7.6 from US 50. The road beyond the Angel of Shavano Campground is rough but still passable for medium clearance vehicles. There are many campsites above the Angel of Shavano Campground, but none at the trailhead, and parking there is limited. The trailhead is on the north side of the road. In winter Chaffee County 240 is plowed to the Angel of Shavano Campground but not beyond.

18T3 – Blank Gulch Trailhead 9,800 feet 38.5988° -106.1976°

This trailhead provides access to Shavano's east side. On US 285, go 20.0 miles south of the US 24–US 285 junction just west of Johnson Village, near Buena Vista. Turn west onto Chaffee County 140 (paved) and measure from this point. The US 285–Chaffee County 140 junction is 1.0 mile north of the US 50–US 285 junction in Poncha Springs.

Follow Chaffee County 140 1.7 miles west, turn north (right) onto Chaffee County 250 (dirt), stay left at mile 5.7 on Chaffee County 252, cross Placer Creek at mile 6.5 (camping), go straight at mile 7.3, go straight at mile 8.7, go straight at mile 8.9 and reach the Blank Gulch Trailhead at mile 9.0. The trailhead is at the old Blank Cabin site. There is no longer a Blank Cabin, but a stone memorial marks the spot. The Colorado Trail is 100 yards west of the memorial. It is best to park low-clearance vehicles below the memorial, because the continuing road becomes rough and doesn't go very far.

18. Mount Shavano 14,229 feet

18R – Mount Shavano Routes

18R1 – Mount Shavano – East Slopes

From Blank Gulch TH at 9,800'   210 RP   8.5 mi RT   4,429' total   Class 2

This is the easiest route on Shavano, since there is a good trail all the way to the high saddle south of Shavano's summit. Start at the Blank Gulch Trailhead at 9,800 feet and go 0.25 mile north on the Colorado Trail (FT 1776) to the start of the Mount Shavano Trail (FT 1428) at 9,880 feet (38.6020° -106.1960°). Turn west (left) and hike 1.0 mile up the Mount Shavano Trail as it climbs through a beautiful forest to cross the south fork of Squaw Creek at 10,830 feet (38.6078° -106.2099). Hike 1.0 mile northwest above the creek to 11,800 feet (38.6143°

-106.2161°) near Shavano's east ridge. Hike 0.3 mile south then west to treeline at 12,200 feet (38.6132° -106.2213°), where you can look into the basin that holds the Angel of Shavano. Finally, hike 1.1 miles west on the continuing trail north of the Angel and reach the 13,380-foot saddle (38.6120° -106.2384°) south of Shavano's summit. From this saddle, turn north (right) and climb 0.6 mile north up Class 2 talus to the summit (38.6191° -106.2394°).

18R1 EC – Extra Credit – "Esprit Point" 13,630 feet 38.6079° -106.2361°

Class 2

From the 13,380-foot saddle south of the summit, hike 0.35 mile south to Point 13,630, alias "Esprit Point." This unranked but classy summit has airy views, and this is a good place to set aside the cares of the lower world for a while as you look at the Angel.

18R2 – Mount Shavano – Angel of Shavano *Classic*

From Blank Gulch TH at 9,800'	*273 RP*	*7.2 mi RT*	*4,429' total*	*Class 2, Easy Snow*
With descent of East Slopes	*265 RP*	*7.9 mi RT*	*4,429' total*	*Class 2, Easy Snow*

This is the best snow route on a Fourteener in the southern Sawatch Range. The route is not difficult, but it has personality. The Angel of Shavano is the narrow snow slope with two up-stretched arms in the center of Shavano's east slopes. It is in good condition for climbing in late May and June. You can easily check the condition of the Angel from US 285.

The Angel of Shavano spawned the colorful legend of a Native American princess who prayed for rain at the base of Shavano during a severe drought. The princess sacrificed herself to the gods and reappears every year as the Angel of Shavano. As she melts, her tears send life-giving water to the plains below.

Start at the Blank Gulch Trailhead at 9,800 feet and go 0.25 mile north on the Colorado Trail (FT 1776) to the start of the Mount Shavano Trail (FT 1428) at 9,880 feet (38.6020° -106.1960°). Turn west (left) and hike 1.0 mile up the Mount Shavano Trail as it climbs through a beautiful forest to cross the south fork of Squaw Creek at 10,830 feet (38.6078° -106.2099°). Beyond the creek crossing, hike 0.3 mile west on the trail and leave the trail at 11,100 feet (38.6089° -106.2143°) before it starts switchbacking north away from the drainage. Bushwhack 0.8 mile west up the drainage and reach the base of the Angel just above treeline at 12,000 feet (38.6112° -106.2279°).

The Angel is a gentle snow slope that does not exceed 30 degrees in steepness. An ice ax is useful, because the slope is still steep enough to produce a serious fall. Climb 0.35 mile up the body of the Angel as it rises from 12,000 feet to 12,800 feet. At the top of the body, you must choose an arm. The southern arm usually has better snow conditions and leads 0.3 mile toward the 13,380-foot saddle south of the summit. The northern arm is the preferred choice, because it leads directly toward the summit, but the northern arm melts out before the southern arm, and in some years, the northern arm is not present at all. Whichever arm you choose, you will have to leave the Angel behind and climb talus to the summit.

18R3 – Mount Shavano – Southeast Slopes

From Angel of Shavano TH at 9,180'   361 RP   6.4 mi RT   5,049' net; 5,549' total   Class 2, Mod Snow

This is the shortest route up Shavano, and it can provide a good snow climb in June. The route is in or near a shallow couloir on Shavano's southeast slopes. This is an arduous Class 2 climb up steep terrain and requires a lot of elevation gain. It is not a good choice for the casual Fourteener hiker. Do not use this route after the snow melts. The steep scree is unpleasant to ascend, and ascending or descending it is environmentally incorrect.

Start at the Angel of Shavano Trailhead at 9,180 feet and bushwhack 0.5 mile steeply north between two drainages. Continue bushwhacking 0.8 mile north-northwest along the east side of the western drainage to 12,000 feet (38.5999° -106.2254°) near treeline. From here, either climb this drainage or hike 0.5 mile northwest up the small ridge north of it. In either case, you will end up at 13,100 feet on Shavano's southeast ridge (38.6022° -106.2318°). Follow this ridge 0.5 mile north-northwest to Point 13,630, alias "Esprit Point" (38.6079° -106.2361°). Descend 0.3 mile north-northwest to the 13,380-foot saddle between "Esprit Point" and Shavano, and continue 0.6 mile north to Shavano's summit. Remember, on the return you must reascend "Esprit Point."

18. Tabeguache Peak 14,155 feet

18R – Tabeguache Peak Routes

18R4 – Tabeguache Peak – West Ridge

From Jennings Creek TH at 10,540'   294 RP   7.4 mi RT   3,615' net; 4,023' total   Class 2

The southwest ridge used to be the standard route up Tabeguache, and Shavano as well, but due to environmental concerns, the Forest Service has asked hikers to stay off the badly eroded southwest ridge trail of Tabeguache and, instead, climb the peak from the Blank Gulch Trailhead by traversing over Mount Shavano. This is a dangerous plan, since it requires hikers to reascend Shavano on their return, turning an already arduous two-peak day into a three-summit day that keeps hikers high and exposed to storms for a long time. The solution is to improve the trail on the southwest side of the peak. The West Ridge Route described here avoids the southwest ridge and is a viable option if your only goal is Tabeguache, but it does require some bushwhacking. If you want to climb Tabeguache and Shavano together, use Combination 18C1. In either case, do not descend McCoy Gulch.

Start at the Jennings Creek Trailhead at 10,540 feet and follow a trail 0.5 mile north through the trees on the east side of Jennings Creek. Just past treeline at 11,180 feet (38.6071° -106.2787°), the old eroded trail leaves the Jennings Creek drainage near a small pond and climbs steeply northeast toward

Mount Shavano and Tabeguache Peak from the southwest.

Tabeguache's southwest ridge. Do not use this trail, but continue north up Jennings Creek instead. There is no trail up Jennings Creek, and the valley is rough in spots. The easiest climbing is on a series of grassy benches on the east side of the creek, and, in compensation for the roughness, these benches support many wildflowers. Near the head of the basin, climb northwest to the west side of the 12,610-foot saddle (38.6268° -106.2764°) between Tabeguache and 13,663-foot Carbonate Mountain. From the west ridge, the view opens to the north, and you can see Mount Antero across Browns Creek, along with the rest of the Sawatch Range stretching far to the north.

Turn east (right) and climb 0.9 mile up Tabeguache's broad west ridge to unranked Point 13,936 (38.6264° -106.2612°). There is a good view of the remaining route to Tabeguache from here. Descend 0.2 mile east to a 13,820-foot saddle (38.6257° -106.2575°) and climb 0.2 mile east along the west ridge to a 14,060-foot false summit (38.6248° -106.2543°). There are some abrupt views down Tabeguache's ugly north face as you approach the false summit. The final 300 yards from the false summit to the summit (38.6255° -106.2509°) are bumpy if you stay directly on the ridge crest. The easiest route stays below the rock points on the ridge's south side.

18R4 EC – Extra Credit – Carbonate Mountain 13,663 feet 38.6267° -106.2855°

Class 2

From the 12,610-foot saddle (38.6268° -106.2764°), climb 0.5 mile west, gaining a hefty 1,050 feet of elevation to the summit of 13,663-foot Carbonate Mountain, one of Colorado's 200 highest ranked peaks.

18R5 – Tabeguache Peak – Northeast Slopes

From Browns Creek TH at 8,920'   374 RP   16.5 mi RT   5,235' total   Class 2

People seldom climb this route because of its length, but it is a good route for a backpacking excursion. A camp in upper Browns Creek allows you to climb Antero, Tabeguache, and Shavano plus their related Thirteeners on one outing.

Start at the Browns Creek Trailhead at 8,920 feet (see Mount Antero, 17T3) and follow the Browns Creek Trail 1.3 miles west to the Colorado Trail (FT 1776). Turn south (left) on the Colorado Trail, go 150 yards south, cross Little Browns Creek, and continue 300 yards south to the upper Browns Creek Trail (FT 1429). Leave the Colorado Trail and hike 4.4 miles southwest then west up the Browns Creek Valley on FT 1429 to lower Browns Lake at 11,286 feet (38.6442° -106.2390°). From lower Browns Lake, hike 0.5 mile west to 11,370 feet and reach the end of an interminable 4WD road (FR 278) that has reached this elusive point (38.6436° -106.2489°) from Baldwin Gulch to the north.

Leave the road and climb 1.2 miles southwest then south up a slope. Climb on grass at first, then talus to reach the 13,380-foot saddle (38.6303° -106.2423°) between Tabeguache and Point 13,712. It is not necessary to climb Point 13,712. From this saddle, climb 0.4 mile southwest to reach the 13,700-foot saddle (38.6261° -106.2460°) between Shavano and Tabeguache, then continue 0.25 mile west to Tabeguache's summit.

18R5 EC – Extra Credit – Point 13,712 38.6318° -106.2386°

Class 2

From the 13,380-foot saddle (38.6303° -106.2423°) between Tabeguache and Point 13,712, hike 0.25 mile east to the summit of Point 13,712. This ranked summit is a Bi, one of Colorado's 200 highest peaks.

18C – Shavano and Tabeguache Combination Routes
18C1 – Shavano East Slopes → Tabeguache East Ridge

From Blank Gulch TH at 9,800'

Via Shavano's East Slopes	292 RP	10.5 mi RT	5,413' total	*Class 2*
Via Shavano's Angel of Shavano	356 RP	9.2 mi RT	5,413' total	*Class 2, Easy Snow*

This is the most expedient way to climb Shavano and Tabeguache together. Start at the Blank Gulch Trailhead at 9,800 feet and climb either Shavano's East Slopes Route (18R1) or the Angel of Shavano Route (18R2) to Shavano's summit. Descend 0.75 mile northwest to the 13,700-foot saddle (38.6261° -106.2460°) between Shavano and Tabeguache, then climb 0.25 mile west to Tabeguache's summit.

Descend by returning back over the top of Shavano. This effort again deters many people, and they try to skirt Shavano's summit on the return or, worse yet, descend McCoy Gulch. Do not descend McCoy Gulch. Skirting Shavano's summit on either side of the ridge is unpleasant, and it is better to climb back over the top.

18C2 – Shavano East Slopes → Tabeguache → Point 13,712 → Jones Peak 13,604 feet

From Blank Gulch TH at 9,800'

Via Shavano's East Slopes	341 RP	10.6 mi RT	5,600' total	*Class 3*
Via Shavano's Angel of Shavano	372 RP	7.7 mi RT	5,600' total	*Class 3, Easy Snow*

This is a Shavano and Tabeguache climb for hardened peak baggers. Start at the Blank Gulch Trailhead at 9,800 feet and follow Combination 18C1 as far as the 13,700-foot saddle between Shavano and Tabeguache on the return from Tabeguache's summit. The good news is you don't have to reclimb Shavano; better news is that you get to climb Jones Peak instead.

Descend 0.4 mile northeast to the 13,380-foot saddle (38.6303° -106.2423°) between Tabeguache and Point 13,712, then climb 0.25 mile east to the summit of Point 13,712 (38.6318° -106.2386°). This ranked summit is a Bi, one of Colorado's 200 highest peaks. From Point 13,712, scramble 0.8 mile east to the summit of 13,604-foot Jones Peak (38.6312° -106.2251°). This difficult ridge requires some Class 3 scrambling over and around several obnoxious, rotten towers. You are committed now!

From the summit of Jones Peak, descend 0.6 south down steep, open slopes to the east end of beautiful, seldom-visited Shavano Lake (38.6236° -106.2253°) at 11,920 feet. Do a rough ascending traverse 0.2 mile south-southeast from the lake to 12,100 feet, then contour 0.6 mile southeast through dense thickets to Shavano's east ridge. Descend 0.1 mile on the south side of the ridge, find the Mount Shavano Trail near 11,800 feet (38.6143° -106.2161°), and follow it back to the Colorado Trail and the Blank Gulch Trailhead. Finding the Mount Shavano Trail near Shavano's east ridge is not a fail-safe operation, and your route-finding skills may be tested.

18C3 – Tabeguache Northeast Slopes → Shavano Northwest Ridge

From Browns Creek TH at 8,920'   *431 RP*   *18.0 mi RT*   *5,764' total*   *Class 2*

This combination avoids having to reclimb the first peak on the return, but it has a long approach. Start at the Browns Creek Trailhead at 8,920 feet (see Mount Antero, 17T3) and follow Tabeguache's Northeast Slopes Route (18R5) to Tabeguache's summit. Traverse to Shavano, return to the 13,700-foot saddle and descend Tabeguache's Northeast Slopes Route (18R5) back to Browns Creek. This combination works just as well if you climb Shavano first.

18C4 – Shavano East Slopes → Tabeguache East Ridge → Antero West Slopes

From Blank Gulch TH at 9,800' to Baldwin Gulch TH at 9,420'

Via Shavano's East Slopes	*457 RP*	*20.0 mi OW*	*7,353' total*	*Class 2*
Via Shavano's Angel of Shavano	*511 RP*	*19.3 mi OW*	*7,353' total*	*Class 2, Easy Snow*

This traverse allows you to climb Shavano, Tabeguache, and Antero together. Start at the Blank Gulch Trailhead at 9,800 feet and climb Shavano and Tabeguache using Combination 18C1. From Tabeguache's summit, descend 1.5 miles west to the 12,610-foot saddle (38.6268° -106.2764°) between Tabeguache and Carbonate Mountain. Descend 1.3 miles north-northeast to 11,800 feet upper Browns Creek (38.6353° -106.2726°), reach FR 278, and hike 2.5 miles northeast to Antero's summit on the upper part of the Upper Browns Creek Route (17R4 V). Descend Antero's West Slopes Route (17R1) to the Baldwin Gulch Trailhead (17T2) and a prearranged vehicle shuttle.

Chapter Four

Sangre de Cristo Range

Introduction

Sangre de Cristo means "blood of Christ" in Spanish, and the name suits this ancient place. The Sangre de Cristo Range is a long, linear range that starts where the Sawatch Range ends. The Sangres start south of Salida and extend 220 miles south to Santa Fe, New Mexico. The Sangre de Cristo Range is longer than any other Colorado range, and, indeed, Colorado cannot contain it!

The northern part of the range is flanked on the east by the Wet Mountain Valley and Huerfano Park. The large, flat San Luis Valley lies west of the range. The winds scouring this valley cannot carry their burden over the Sangres and have left behind 700-foot-high sand dunes. The range averages only 10 to 20 miles in width, and the high peaks rise abruptly with few foothills. Approaching the Sangres is always an awesome, neck-bending experience.

The Sangres contain 10 named Fourteeners in Colorado and all the Thirteeners in New Mexico. The Fourteeners are clustered in three groups—the Crestone Group, the Blanca Group, and the solitary Culebra Peak. Unlike the gentle summits of the Sawatch, the Sangres contain some of Colorado's most difficult Fourteeners. The Crestone Group's conglomerate rock is surprisingly good, and these peaks hold many fine technical routes.

Crestone conglomerate.

19. Crestone Group

Crestone Peak   14,294 feet
Crestone Needle   14,197 feet
Humboldt Peak   14,064 feet
Challenger Point   14,081 feet
Kit Carson Peak   14,165 feet

These peaks are the northernmost Fourteeners in the Sangre de Cristo Range. They are 12 miles southwest of Westcliffe in the Wet Mountain Valley. The Crestone Group is one of Colorado's finest collections of Fourteeners, since there is something for everybody here. There are walk-ups, moderate scrambles, and serious technical climbs. After Longs Peak, the Crestone Group has the best concentration of technical climbing on Colorado's Fourteeners.

The geology of the Crestone Group is different from other Colorado ranges, and the conglomerate rock here comes as a pleasant surprise. The rock is full of imbedded knobs. An exciting part of the Colorado Fourteener experience is tiptoeing up on these knobs. Occasionally a knob will pull out, but they are generally solid. Finding good protection on technical routes in the Crestones can be difficult, and these beautiful peaks have occasionally proven deadly.

Crestone Peak is one of Colorado's finest peaks. High and wild, it was once proclaimed unclimbable. It is now simply called "the Peak" by those who know it. The Peak draws some people like a siren but rejects others. If it draws you, approach with respect and caution. Crestone Peak's main summit is the highest point in Saguache County. Crestone Peak has two summits, and the 14,260-foot eastern summit is the highest point in Custer County. The Peak is one of Colorado's hardest Fourteeners—some people proclaim it the hardest. The Northwest Couloir Route (19R2) has been the standard route on the Peak for decades, but it is not the easiest or safest route. Today, the South Face Route (19R1) is considered the standard route. Consider choices and conditions before launching.

Beginning where Crestone Peak ends, Crestone Needle is the peak's companion. The needle is a singular summit of distinguished beauty 0.5 mile southeast of the peak. A jagged 0.5-mile-long ridge of considerable notoriety separates the two peaks. Harboring its secrets well, Crestone Needle was the last of Colorado's Fourteeners to be climbed. Crestone Needle is slightly easier to climb than Crestone Peak, but still ranks as of one of Colorado's hardest Fourteeners. The standard route is on the complex south face, while the pristine northeast face holds several fine technical routes.

The northeast face of the Needle and the Peak combine to form one of Colorado's most glorious mountain walls. The wall is a mile long, always at least 1,000 feet high, and reaches a 2,000-foot climax under Crestone Needle's summit. The most famous of the Crestone Group's technical routes is the Ellingwood Arête, which ascends the highest, steepest part of the wall directly to the Needle's summit. Crestone Needle vaulted into the international spotlight in

1979 when the Ellingwood Arête was included in the popular book *Fifty Classic Climbs of North America* by Steve Roper and Allen Steck. Crestone Needle carries the honor well.

Humble Humboldt sits by itself 1.0 mile northeast of South Colony Lakes and 1.8 miles east of Crestone Peak. It is the highpoint of a long ridge separating the South Colony Creek and North Colony Creek drainages. Humboldt's rugged north side is seldom seen; it is much better known as a shapeless hump that is easy to climb, but even humble Humboldt has proven fatal. From Humboldt's summit and western slopes, there are superb views of the northeast face of Crestone Peak and Crestone Needle. Humboldt is a great place to either nervously preview or triumphantly review Crestone climbs. For those souls who have no intention of ever climbing Crestone Peak or Crestone Needle, Humboldt offers a circumspect vantage point in the heart of this exclusive place.

Challenger Point is the west summit of Kit Carson Mountain. This summit was officially named Challenger Point in 1987 in memory of the seven-person crew of Space Shuttle *Challenger*, which exploded during liftoff on January 28, 1986. The summit rises more than 300 feet above its connecting saddle with Kit Carson's main summit, but the separation between these two summits is only 400 yards. With more than 300 feet of prominence, Challenger Point qualifies as an official Fourteener, but some people still look askance at this summit. No matter how you count, Challenger Point is officially named, and it is above 14,000 feet.

Kit Carson is on the west side of the Sangre crest, 1.3 miles northwest of Crestone Peak. When you view the Sangres from the San Luis Valley to the west, Kit Carson is more prominent than the Crestones. The Willow Creek drainage is north of Kit Carson, and the Spanish Creek drainage is south of the peak. Kit Carson Mountain is a large, complex massif with two summits above 14,000 feet and another reaching 13,980 feet. The name Kit Carson Mountain applies to all these summits. The name Kit Carson Peak applies to just the highest, 14,165-foot summit. Challenger Point is the 14,081-foot west summit of Kit Carson Mountain. Before Challenger Point was officially named, some irreverent souls called this summit "Johnny Carson." Kit Carson Mountain's 13,980-foot east summit used to carry the nickname "Kat Carson," but this summit is now officially named Columbia Point in memory of the seven-person crew of Space Shuttle *Columbia*, which disintegrated during reentry on February 1, 2003.

With its three summits of stature, Kit Carson is a magnificent mountain. Serious cliffs guard all sides of Kit Carson's summit, but Kit Carson is easier to climb than either Crestone Peak or Crestone Needle, since the easiest routes sneak through the cliffs on surprise ledges. Kit Carson supports several fine technical routes, one of which rivals anything on the Crestones. When the Great Sand Dunes National Park and Preserve land acquisition was completed, Kit Carson's summits became public, national forest land.

19E – Crestone Group Essentials

Elevations	Crestone Pk	14,294' (NGVD29) 14,298' (NAVD88)
	Crestone Needle	14,197' (NGVD29) 14,201' (NAVD88)
	Humboldt Pk	14,064' (NGVD29) 14,069' (NAVD88)
	Challenger Pt	14,081' (NGVD29) 14,084' (NAVD88)
	Kit Carson Pk	14,165' (NGVD29) 14,169' (NAVD88)
Ranks	Crestone Pk	Colorado's 7th highest ranked peak
	Crestone Needle	Colorado's 20th highest ranked peak
	Humboldt Pk	Colorado's 37th highest ranked peak
	Challenger Pt	Colorado's 34th highest ranked peak
	Kit Carson Pk	Colorado's 23rd highest ranked peak
Location	Custer and Saguache counties, Colorado, USA	
Range	Central Sangre de Cristo Range	
Summit Coordinates	Crestone Pk	37.9668° -105.5854° (WGS84)
	Crestone Needle	37.9647° -105.5765° (WGS84)
	Humboldt Pk	37.9762° -105.5552° (WGS84)
	Challenger Pt	37.9803° -105.6066° (WGS84)
	Kit Carson Pk	37.9796° -105.6026° (WGS84)
Ownership/Contact	San Isabel and Rio Grande national forests – 719-553-1400; 719-852-5941	
	Public land with private land at some west side trailheads	
Prominence and Saddles	Crestone Pk	4,554' from 9,740' Mosca Pass
	Crestone Needle	457' from 13,740' Needle–Peak saddle
	Humboldt Pk	1,204' from 12,860' Humboldt–Peak saddle
	Challenger Pt	301' from 13,780' Point–Kit Carson saddle
	Kit Carson Pk	1,025' from 13,140' Kit Carson–Peak saddle
Isolation and Parents	Crestone Pk	27.46 miles to Blanca Peak
	Crestone Needle	0.49 mile to Crestone Peak
	Humboldt Pk	1.42 miles to Crestone Needle
	Challenger Pt	0.23 miles to Kit Carson Peak
	Kit Carson Pk	1.30 miles to Crestone Peak
USGS Maps	**Crestone Peak**, Crestone, Beck Mountain	
USFS Maps	**San Isabel National Forest**, Rio Grande National Forest	
Trails Illustrated Map	Map #138 Sangre de Cristo Mountains	
Book Map	See Map 19 on page 175	
Nearest Towns	Westcliffe – Population 460 – Elevation 7,867' (east side)	
	Crestone – Population 85 – Elevation 7,923' (west side)	
Crestone Pk 🥾 Easiest Route	19R1 – South Face – Class 3, Mod Snow	
	A long approach hike to Cottonwood Lake, then a long scramble and snow climb to the summit	
Crestone Needle 🥾 Easiest Route	19R7 – South Face – Class 3, Mod Snow	
	A Class 1 approach to Lower South Colony Lake, then a seasonal snow climb to a saddle and sharp summit scramble	

19E – Crestone Group Essentials

Humboldt Pk 🏃 Easiest Route	19R12 – West Ridge – Class 2
	A Class 1 approach to Lower South Colony Lake, a trail hike to a high
	ridge, and a Class 2 hike along the ridge to reach the summit
Challenger Pt 🏃+ Easiest Route	19R14 – North Slopes – Class 2+
	A Class 1 trail approach to Willow Lake, then a devious Class 2+ scamper
	to the summit
Kit Carson Pk 🏃 Easiest Route	19R17 – West Ridge – Class 3
	A Class 2+ scamper to the top of Challenger Point,
	a down-up-down Class 2+ scamper on a wide ledge, and a
	Class 3 scramble up to the summit
Crestone Group Accolades	The Crestone Group of five Fourteeners and several Thirteeners is the
	largest, most complicated Fourteener nest in Colorado. Crestone Peak is
	the highest peak in Saguache County and its subsummit ,"East Crestone,"
	is the highest peak in Custer County. These great peaks harbor easy
	summit hikes, Class 2+ scampers, sharp Class 3 scrambles, and many fine
	technical routes on good to excellent knobby rock.

19T – Crestone Group Trailheads

19T1 – Lower South Colony Trailhead 8,770 feet 37.9935° -105.4730°

This trailhead is on the range's east side and provides access to Humboldt Peak and the east sides of Crestone Peak, Crestone Needle, and Kit Carson Peak. This is the only trailhead for the Crestone Group giving reasonable access to all five peaks. From the junction of Colorado 96 and Colorado 69 in Westcliffe, go 4.4 miles south on Colorado 69, turn south (right) onto Colfax Lane (Custer County 119), and go 5.6 miles south to a T junction. Turn west (right) onto South Colony Road (Custer County 120) and go 1.5 miles west to the trailhead, which is just before the road becomes steeper and rougher. Park lower-clearance vehicles in a parking area on the north side of the road. This trailhead is often accessible in winter.

19T1 4WD1 – Rainbow Trail 4WD Trailhead 9,810 feet 37.9816° -105.4991°

From the Lower South Colony Trailhead, 4WD vehicles can continue 1.4 miles west to the San Isabel National Forest boundary (37.9871° -105.4921°). Camping is not permitted on the private land between the trailhead and the forest boundary. 4WD vehicles can continue 0.8 mile southwest on FR 120 to the Rainbow Trail and a Forest Service parking area at 9,810 feet.

19T1 4WD2 – Upper South Colony 4WD Trailhead 11,020 feet 37.9643° -105.5459°

If the road is not gated at the Rainbow Trail Parking Area, 4WD vehicles can continue 0.5 mile west, descend, and cross to South Colony's Creek's north side (37.9761° -105.5068°). The road gets even rougher at this point, but tough 4WD

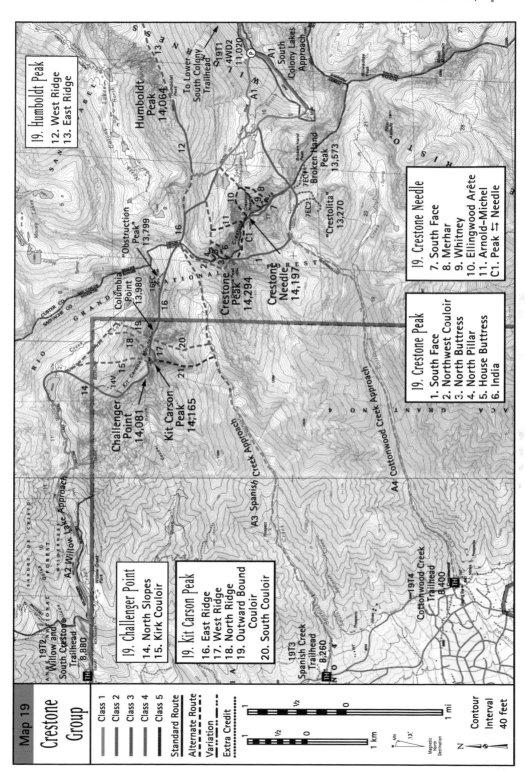

Map 19
Crestone
Group

Class 1
Class 2
Class 3
Class 4
Class 5

Standard Route
Alternate Route
Variation
Extra Credit

1 | ½ | 0 | 1 mi

1 | ½ | 0 | 1 km

MN
.13°

Magnetic
North
Declination

N

Contour
Interval
40 feet

19. Humboldt Peak
12. West Ridge
13. East Ridge

Humboldt
Peak
14,064

To Lower
South Colony
Trailhead

19T1
4WD2
11,020

A1
South
Colony Lakes
Approach

Broken Hand
Peak
13,573

"Obstruction"
Peak
13,799

"Crestolita"
13,270

19. Crestone Needle
7. South Face
8. Merhar
9. Whitney
10. Ellingwood Arête
11. Arnold–Michel
C1. Peak ⇆ Needle

Columbia
Point
13,980

Crestone
Peak
14,294

Crestone
Needle
14,197

19. Crestone Peak
1. South Face
2. Northwest Couloir
3. North Buttress
4. North Pillar
5. House Buttress
6. India

Challenger
Point
14,081

Kit Carson
Peak
14,165

A3 Spanish Creek Approach

A4 Cottonwood Creek Approach

1974
Cottonwood Creek
Trailhead
8,400

19T2
Willow and
South Crestone
Trailhead
8,880

A2 Willow Lake Approach

19. Challenger Point
14. North Slopes
15. Kirk Couloir

19. Kit Carson Peak
16. East Ridge
17. West Ridge
18. North Ridge
19. Outward Bound
    Couloir
20. South Couloir

19T3
Spanish Creek
Trailhead
8,260

vehicles can continue 2.5 miles to 11,020 feet in the South Colony Creek drainage. Either park 100 yards before the road crosses back to South Colony Creek's south side (37.9643° -105.5459°) or cross the creek and park 20 yards beyond (37.9636° -105.5462°). This road is one of Colorado's roughest, and it becomes a little rougher every year. As a consequence, the Forest Service chooses to gate the road at the Rainbow Trail rather than improve it.

19T2 – Willow and South Crestone Trailhead 8,880 feet 37.9888° -105.6626°

This trailhead is on the range's west side and provides access to Willow Lake on the north side of Kit Carson Peak and Challenger Point. If approaching from the north, go 13.8 miles south on Colorado 17 from the Colorado 17–US 285 junction. If approaching from the south, go 16.8 miles north on Colorado 17 from the Colorado 17–Colorado 112 junction in Hooper. Turn east onto a paved road 0.5 mile south of the center of Moffat. Go 12.5 miles east to the town of Crestone. The Crestones and Kit Carson loom higher and higher as you approach them.

Measuring from the Galena Avenue–Alder Street junction in the center of Crestone (37.9952° -105.6991°), go east on Galena Avenue, enter the Rio Grande National Forest at mile 1.1 (37.9890° -105.6838°), pass the old Teton Cemetery on the south side of the road (37.9887° -105.6776°), and reach the trailhead at mile 2.3. The last 1.2 miles of this road are steep in spots, and some people choose to park passenger cars at the forest boundary.

19T3 – Spanish Creek Trailhead 8,260 feet 37.9526° -105.6624°

This trailhead is on private property and access is limited to those who have permission from the landowners. The following description is intended for those with permission.

This trailhead is on the range's west side, and provides access to the south side of Kit Carson and the north side of Crestone Peak. If approaching from the north, go 13.8 miles south on Colorado 17 from the Colorado 17–US 285 junction. If approaching from the south, go 16.8 miles north on Colorado 17 from the Colorado 17–Colorado 112 junction in Hooper. Turn east onto a paved road 0.5 mile south of the center of Moffat. Go 11.8 miles east to the entrance of the Baca Grande Chalets Grants (37.9878° -105.7029°).

Turn south (right) onto Camino Baca Grande and measure from this point. Follow Camino Baca Grande (paved) through the subdivision, cross South Crestone Creek at mile 0.8 (37.9831° -105.6931°), and cross Willow Creek at mile 2.2 (37.9678° -105.6757°), where the road turns to dirt. Continue south on a dirt road to reach Spanish Creek at mile 3.5 (37.9526° -105.6624°). The road's crossing of Spanish Creek is unsigned, so look for the creek. There is a solar-powered ashram nearby on the north side of the creek. The unmarked Spanish Creek Trail starts 50 yards north of the creek and passes under (south of) the ashram.

19T4 – Cottonwood Creek Trailhead 8,400 feet 37.9342° -105.6452°

This trailhead is on private property and access is limited to those who have permission from the landowners. The following description is intended for those with permission.

This trailhead is on the range's west side and provides access to the south sides of Crestone Peak and Crestone Needle. From mile 3.5 at the Spanish Creek Trailhead (19T3), continue 1.8 miles south to reach the trailhead area at mile 5.3 (37.9342° -105.6452°). To access the Cottonwood Creek Trail, go 120 yards uphill to the east on a road past a house and water tank. The trail starts 80 feet north of Cottonwood Creek (37.9346° -105.6432°), just before the road crosses Cottonwood Creek.

19A – Crestone Group Approaches

19A1 – Crestone Group – South Colony Lakes Approach

From Lower South Colony TH at 8,770'	135 RP	13.2 mi RT	2,890' net; 2,930' total	Class 1
From Rainbow Trail 4WD TH at 9,810'	89 RP	8.8 mi RT	1,850' net; 1,890' total	Class 1
From Upper South Colony 4WD TH at 11,020'	29 RP	2.8 mi RT	640' total	Class 1

This is the standard approach to the Crestone Group. Start at the Lower South Colony Trailhead at 8,770 feet (37.9935° -105.4730°) and follow the rough 4WD road 1.4 miles west to the San Isabel National Forest boundary (37.9871° -105.4921°). Camping is not permitted on the private land between the trailhead and the forest boundary. Continue 0.8 mile southwest up FR 120 to the Rainbow Trail at 9,810 feet (37.9816° -105.4991°), go another 0.5 mile west, and cross to South Colony Creek's north side (37.9761° -105.5068°), 1.3 miles beyond the forest boundary. The road becomes rougher beyond this crossing. Continue 2.5 miles southwest to a parking area at 11,020 feet (37.9643° -105.5459°), 100 yards before the road crosses back to the creek's south side.

The approach continues on the road as it crosses back to South Colony Creek's south side. There is a sturdy, double-log footbridge at this crossing. Continue 0.7 mile southwest on the old road. There are good views of Humboldt Peak here, and the east face of Broken Hand Peak towers over you. Turn north, pass the end of the road (37.9564° -105.5570°), and continue 0.7 mile on a good trail (FT 1339) to the outlet stream below Lower South Colony Lake at 11,660 feet (37.9645° -105.5612°). There is good camping in the area, but you must camp at least 300 feet from the lake.

19A2 – Crestone Group – Willow Lake Approach

From Willow and South Crestone TH at 8,880'	95 RP	8.0 mi RT	2,700' net; 2,840' total	Class 1

This is a beautiful hike, especially when afternoon light graces the abundant cliffs soaring above you. Start at the Willow and South Crestone Trailhead at 8,880 feet, go 100 yards east, turn south (right) at a signed trail junction, cross South Crestone Creek, go 50 yards south, and turn east (left) onto the Willow Creek Trail. Follow the Willow Creek Trail (FT 865) 1.4 miles as it climbs east then switchbacks southeast up to a ridge separating the South

Crestone and Willow Creek drainages (37.9889° -105.6496°). Cross the ridge and descend slightly above a large, beautiful meadow called Willow Creek Park. Take the high (left) trail at an unmarked trail junction and enter the Sangre de Cristo Wilderness (37.9902° -105.6448°). Climb steadily, switchbacking occasionally, and cross to Willow Creek's south side at 10,880 feet (37.9925° -105.6249°). The trail on the old Crestone and Crestone Peak quadrangles is mismarked in this area. Switchback up through encroaching cliffs on the creek's south side and enter the upper basin at 11,240 feet (37.9910° -105.6228°). Contour east, descend slightly, cross back to Willow Creek's north side at 11,230 feet (37.9914° -105.6206°), and make a final climb east to a bench just above the west end of Willow Lake at 11,580 feet (37.9943° -105.6112°). The eastern end of the lake is ringed with cliffs and graced with a waterfall. This is a spectacular place. There are camping spots below the western end of the lake; you must camp at least 300 feet from the lake. The north sides of Challenger Point and Kit Carson are 1.0 mile south from the lake's eastern end.

19A3 – Crestone Group – Spanish Creek Approach

From Spanish Creek TH at 8,260'   99 RP   7.0 mi RT   2,740' total   Class 2

This trailhead is on private property and access is limited to those who have permission from the landowners. The following description is intended for those with permission.

This short but steep, difficult approach takes you to 11,000 feet in upper Spanish Creek, from which you can climb routes on the south side of Kit Carson Mountain and the north side of Crestone Peak. Since you start on the deck of the San Luis Valley, this hike can be brutally hot.

Start at the Spanish Creek Trailhead at 8,260 feet. The unmarked Spanish Creek Trail starts 50 yards north of Spanish Creek, passes under (south of) a solar-powered ashram, and climbs east into the Spanish Creek drainage. The little-used Spanish Creek Trail is rough and difficult to follow in spots. The trail is mostly on the north side of the creek, but it does cross to the south side twice. Between 9,600 feet and 10,600 feet, the trail climbs relentlessly through an old burn on the north side of the creek. Above 10,600 feet, the angle of the valley relents and there are good camping spots near treeline at 11,000 feet (37.9664° -105.6121°). From here, you can reach Kit Carson's southern routes (19R20, 19R21) and Crestone Peak's Northwest Couloir Route (19R2).

19A4 – Crestone Group – Cottonwood Creek Approach

From Cottonwood Creek TH at 8,400'   171 RP   9.2 mi RT   3,910' total   Class 2+

This trailhead is on private property and access is limited to those who have permission from the landowners. The following description is intended for those with permission.

This arduous approach leads to beautiful Cottonwood Lake, from which you can climb both Crestone Peak and Crestone Needle. If you have the energy, this is a wonderful alternative to the crowded South Colony Lakes Approach. Start at the Cottonwood Creek Trailhead at 8,400 feet. The Cottonwood Creek

Trail is initially a road that passes a house and water tank. The trail starts 80 feet north of Cottonwood Creek (37.9346° -105.6432°), just before the road crosses Cottonwood Creek. The trail stays on the north side of the creek. The Cottonwood Creek Trail is easier to follow than the Spanish Creek Trail, but there is a Class 2+ section between 10,600 feet and 11,000 feet near some boilerplate slabs that can be testy with a heavy pack.

At 11,100 feet (37.9493° -105.5887°), leave the main trail and turn northeast (left) into the side valley leading to Cottonwood Lake. A steep, rough trail climbs into this valley on the west side of the creek. At treeline, the trail fades into talus and meadows, but views of the Crestones will lure you on. Continue climbing northeast to Cottonwood Lake at 12,310 feet (37.9589° -105.5789°). This idyllic lake is nestled close under Crestone Needle's crenellated south face.

19. Crestone Peak 14,294 feet

19R – Crestone Peak Routes

19R1 – Crestone Peak – South Face *Classic*

From Lower South Colony TH at 8,770'	535 RP	17.1 mi RT	5,524' net; 6,744' total	Class 3, Mod Snow
From Lower South Colony Lake at 11,660'	336 RP	4.1 mi RT	2,634' net; 3,850' total	Class 3, Mod Snow
From Cottonwood Creek TH at 8,400'	444 RP	11.2 mi RT	5,894' total	Class 3, Mod Snow
From Cottonwood Lake at 12,310'	215 RP	2.0 mi RT	1,984' total	Class 3, Mod Snow

Depending on conditions, this may be the easiest and safest route on Crestone Peak. The approach to the south face is longer and more complicated than the approach to the Northwest Couloir Route (19R2), but you can avoid the vagaries of the Northwest Couloir, since clean scrambling and moderate snow replace the Northwest Couloir's ice and rubble. Approach the south face from Cottonwood Lake (37.9589° -105.5789°).

You can most easily reach this Elysian lake from the west by following the Cottonwood Creek Approach (19A4), but the restricted access at the Cottonwood Creek Trailhead is a complication to this approach. You also can reach Cottonwood Lake from Lower South Colony Lake, but you must cross 12,900-foot Broken Hand Pass en route. For the eastern approach to Cottonwood Lake, follow the South Colony Lakes Approach (19A1). From the trail crossing of the outlet stream below Lower South Colony Lake at 11,660 feet (37.9645° -105.5612°), hike 100 yards south on the trail and find a strong trail heading southwest through the bushes. Follow this trail 0.5 mile southwest to 12,400 feet (37.9600° -105.5694°) in the little bowl under the north face of 13,573-foot Broken Hand Peak. This bowl is south of all the difficulties on Crestone Needle's northeast face.

Hike southwest up the bowl and climb a 400-foot northeast-facing couloir to 12,900-foot Broken Hand Pass (37.9587° -105.5710°) between Crestone Needle and Broken Hand Peak. This shaded couloir can retain snow until mid-July, so be prepared for some moderate snow climbing until then. After the snow melts, the couloir requires a little Class 3 scrambling. From the pass, descend 0.4 mile west to the west end of Cottonwood Lake (Class 2).

From the west end of Cottonwood Lake (37.9589° -105.5789°), contour 0.25 mile west under the broken south face of Crestone Needle, then hike 0.25 mile north to 12,600 feet (37.9614° -105.5828°) in the basin under Crestone Peak's south face and Crestone Needle's west face. Complicated terrain is above this point, so make sure you understand it before committing to anything difficult. The entire traverse between Crestone Peak and Crestone Needle is east of you. Crestone Peak's large south face is north of you. In the center of this face, there is a long, south-facing couloir leading to the 14,180-foot red notch between Crestone Peak's main summit and the slightly lower east summit (37.9670° -105.5846°). This couloir is the key to the route.

You can climb the inset lower part of the couloir, but it's easier to avoid the lower couloir by scrambling up the rock on the couloir's east (right) side. This solid Class 3 scrambling (37.9636° -105.5837°) is fun. The terrain leads you into the couloir at 13,500 feet (37.9647° -105.5842°). Above this point, the couloir is wider and less steep. Move into the couloir and climb it for 700 feet to the red notch between the two summits (37.9670° -105.5846°). The upper part of the couloir retains snow well into July. Either climb the snow or scramble up rocks on the couloir's east (right) side. Even if you try to avoid the snow, you may find some unavoidable patches. In August the upper couloir is a Class 2+ rubble-strewn scamper.

From the red notch at the top of the couloir, scramble 250 feet west to the summit (37.9668° -105.5854°). This clean Class 3 scramble is exciting, and Crestone Peak's thrilling summit hears many spontaneous yodels.

19R1 EC – Extra Credit – "East Crestone" 14,260 feet 37.9672° -105.5841°

Class 3

From the 14,180-foot red notch between the twin summits (37.9670° -105.5846°), scramble 200 feet east to Crestone Peak's 14,260-foot east summit. This entertaining Class 3 scramble is slightly harder than the scramble to the main summit. Crestone Peak's east summit is a significant summit with dramatic views. It is also the highest point in Custer County.

It is possible to climb directly to the east summit from the upper couloir. Leave the couloir where a large ledge runs southeast from it. Climb a break in the cliffs above this ledge, reach the east summit's south-southeast ridge, and finish on this ridge. This Class 4 variation involves considerable exposure but allows you to traverse "East Crestone" on your way to the main summit.

19R2 – Crestone Peak – Northwest Couloir

From Lower South Colony TH at 8,770'	*485 RP*	*17.7 mi RT*	*5,524' net; 5,724' total*	*Class 3, Steep Snow/Ice*
From Lower South Colony Lake at 11,660'	*285 RP*	*4.7 mi RT*	*2,634' net; 2,794' total*	*Class 3, Steep Snow/Ice*
From Spanish Creek TH at 8,260'	*508 RP*	*12.5 mi RT*	*6,034' total*	*Class 3, Steep Snow/Ice*
From 11,000' in Spanish Creek	*341 RP*	*5.5 mi RT*	*3,294' total*	*Class 3, Steep Snow/Ice*

This is the historic standard route on Crestone Peak for decades, but it is not the easiest or safest route. It has been popular because it is the most expedient way to climb Crestone Peak from South Colony Lakes. The alternative South Face Route (19R1) requires an approach over a pass.

The deeply inset Northwest Couloir retains snow and ice through much of the summer. As the snow melts, it leaves water on the slabs and rubble on the ledges. The Northwest Couloir has caused at least one fatal accident. Despite its disadvantages, this is a practicable route for experienced parties, and it is the most direct route through Crestone Peak's upper difficulties.

You can approach the Northwest Couloir Route from either South Colony Lakes via the South Colony Lakes Approach (19A1) or from Spanish Creek via the Spanish Creek Approach (19A3). From Lower South Colony Lake at 11,660 feet (37.9645° -105.5612°), hike 0.5 mile northwest to Upper South Colony Lake and climb a south-facing scree gully to the long ridge connecting Humboldt Peak with Crestone Peak. Scramble west on or below this ridge to the broad, 13,140-foot Crestone Peak–Kit Carson saddle (37.9749° -105.5816°). This open area is called the Bear's Playground. If you are approaching from 11,000 feet in Spanish Creek, hike 1.9 miles east-northeast to the head of Spanish Creek and reach the Bear's Playground from the west (Class 2). There are spectacular profile views of Crestone Peak's Ellingwood Arête from here.

From the Bear's Playground, climb 0.3 mile southwest along the talus ridge toward Crestone Peak. Before you reach the steeper mass of the upper peak, leave the ridge (37.9717° -105.5846°) and traverse southwest (right) at 13,400 feet on the west side of the ridge, cross a vague couloir, and continue to the Northwest Couloir (Class 2+). The Northwest Couloir is in the center of Crestone Peak's northwest face, and the entry point into the couloir is the highest easy access near a small elbow in the couloir. Below the elbow, the couloir faces more to the northwest, then ends above a serious cliff. When descending this route, be sure to exit the couloir before you reach this cliff.

Once in the couloir, climb it for 800 feet to the 14,180-foot red notch (37.9670° -105.5846°) between Crestone Peak's main summit and the slightly lower east summit. The exact line for climbing the couloir depends on conditions. If snow conditions are good, the ascent is a simple but steep snow climb. By midsummer, the snow is no longer continuous and the ascent alternates between snow and broken, rubble-covered ledges on the couloir's sides. Helmets, ice axes, and crampons are recommended for this couloir. Short sections of ice are often unavoidable until late August.

From the red notch at the top of the couloir, scramble 250 feet west to the summit (37.9668° –105.5854°). This clean Class 3 scramble is a welcome finish after the couloir's dark confines, and the summit may feel quite airy.

19R3 – Crestone Peak – North Buttress

From Lower South Colony TH at 8,770'	529 RP	17.5 mi RT	5,524' net; 5,844' total	Class 5.0
From Lower South Colony Lake at 11,660'	330 RP	4.5 mi RT	2,634' net; 2,914' total	Class 5.0
From Spanish Creek TH at 8,260'	552 RP	12.3 mi RT	6,034' net; 6,154' total	Class 5.0
From 11,000' in Spanish Creek	386 RP	5.3 mi RT	3,294' net; 3,414' total	Class 5.0

This is a rock route on the buttress to the east of the Northwest Couloir Route (19R2). The north buttress avoids the snow and ice in the Northwest Couloir. Do not confuse the North Buttress and North Pillar (19R4) routes. Follow the Northwest Couloir Route to 13,400 feet (37.9717° –105.5846°) on the talus ridge below the steep upper portion of the peak. Instead of traversing southwest into the Northwest Couloir, continue up the buttress above you. Staying on the west side of the ridge, pass the tops of the east-facing North Pillar and House Buttress.

After 800 feet of delightful Class 3 scrambling on solid conglomerate knobs, you will reach the top of an isolated 14,260-foot tower (37.9681° –105.5845°) 200 yards northeast of 14,260-foot "East Crestone." The isolated tower, dubbed "Northeast Crestone," has the same extrapolated summit elevation as "East Crestone," but is in fact slightly lower than "East Crestone." The two summits are separated by a deep notch. A direct climb from "Northeast Crestone" to "East Crestone" would be very difficult.

The crux of this route is climbing from the summit of "Northeast Crestone" to the red notch at the top of the Northwest Couloir between the east and main summits. Do a tricky Class 5.0 downclimb on the tower's west side, then do a complicated, exposed Class 4 traverse across unprotected slabs to reach the red notch (37.9670° –105.5846°). From the notch, scramble 250 feet west to the summit (37.9668° –105.5854°).

19R4 – Crestone Peak – North Pillar *Classic*

From Lower South Colony TH at 8,770'	1,732 RP	16.4 mi RT	5,524' net; 5,684' total	Class 5.8
From Lower South Colony Lake at 11,660'	1,532 RP	3.4 mi RT	2,634' net; 2,754' total	Class 5.8

The North Pillar is the northernmost buttress on Crestone Peak's northeast face. Approach the North Pillar from Upper South Colony Lake reached via the South Colony Lakes Approach (19A1). You can easily see the North Pillar from the lake, since the pillar forms part of the northern skyline of the northeast face. The North Pillar consists of a narrow east face and a larger north face. The edge between these two faces is usually the line created where sunlight meets shadow, and it gives the pillar its dramatic appearance.

This 900-foot 10-pitch climb is beautiful, sustained and dolomite in character. The route ascends the east face near the edge between the east and north faces. It involves six sustained Class 5.7 pitches. On the seventh, crux pitch, angle south (left) to reach a weakness in a modest overhang, climb the

Crestone Peak from the north.

overhang (Class 5.8), and angle back north (right) to the edge. The angle then eases, and three more pitches (Classes 5.6, 5.4, 4) take you to the top of the pillar. Belays and protection are adequate on this climb. The top of the pillar is a small, 13,700-foot summit (37.9699° -105.5841°). From the top of the pillar, continue on the North Buttress Route (19R3).

19R5 – Crestone Peak – House Buttress

From Lower South Colony TH at 8,770'   *1,309 RP*   *16.6 mi RT*   *5,524' net; 5,724' total*   *Class 5.7*

From Lower South Colony Lake at 11,660'   *1,109 RP*   *3.6 mi RT*   *2,634' net; 2,794' total*   *Class 5.7*

The House Buttress is the large, broken buttress just south (left) of the easily identified North Pillar on the northern end of Crestone Peak's northeast face. This climb is longer and slightly easier than the North Pillar. Approach the climb from Upper South Colony Lake, reached via the South Colony Lakes Approach (19A1).

Start south of the base of the North Pillar and do an ascending traverse south (left) on a ledge cutting across the bottom of the House Buttress. Before reaching the couloir on the south edge of the buttress, climb straight up the broken south edge of the buttress. Higher up, work left into the small basin on the south side of the buttress. Climb up this basin and join the North Buttress Route (19R3) at 13,800 feet.

19R6 – Crestone Peak – India

From Lower South Colony TH at 8,770'	*1,331 RP*	*16.4 mi RT*	*5,524' net; 5,724' total*	*Class 5.8*
From Lower South Colony Lake at 11,660'	*1,131 RP*	*3.4 mi RT*	*2,634' net; 2,794' total*	*Class 5.8*

This route winds up through the center of the complex northeast face between Crestone Peak and Crestone Needle. Approach the route from Upper South Colony Lake, reached via the South Colony Lakes Approach (19A1). Start on the south (left) side of the large broken buttress in the center of the lower face. Climb slabs along the south edge of the buttress, then do an ascending traverse on a prominent ledge leading north across the buttress. Climb the upper part of the buttress along its north side and reach a lower-angled section above the buttress. Climb slabs to reach the south ridge of Crestone Peak's east summit, and follow that ridge north to 14,260-foot "East Crestone" (37.9672° -105.5841°). Scramble 200 feet west down to the 14,180-foot red notch (37.9670° -105.5846°) and 250 feet west up to the main summit (37.9668° -105.5854°) (Class 3).

19. Crestone Needle 14,197 feet

19R – Crestone Needle Routes

19R7 – Crestone Needle – South Face *Classic*

From Lower South Colony TH at 8,770'	*408 RP*	*15.6 mi RT*	*5,467' total*	*Class 3, Mod Snow*
From Lower South Colony Lake at 11,660'	*210 RP*	*2.6 mi RT*	*2,537' total*	*Class 3, Mod Snow*
From Cottonwood Creek TH at 8,400'	*399 RP*	*11.3 mi RT*	*5,797' total*	*Class 3, Mod Snow*
From Cottonwood Lake at 12,310'	*172 RP*	*2.1 mi RT*	*1,887' total*	*Class 3, Mod Snow*

This is the easiest route on Crestone Needle. It is a sharp scramble to a spectacular summit. This route's exposure and directional details have tested many modern brains, and the route remains the test piece that Albert Ellingwood and Eleanor Davis found it to be when they made the first ascent on July 24, 1916. You can approach the route from either Lower South Colony Lake reached via the South Colony Lakes Approach (19A1) or Cottonwood Lake reached via the Cottonwood Creek Approach (19A4). Prepare carefully.

From the trail crossing of the outlet stream below Lower South Colony Lake at 11,660 feet (37.9645° -105.5612°), hike 100 yards south on the trail and find a strong trail heading west through the bushes. Follow this trail 0.5 mile southwest to 12,400 feet (37.9600° -105.5694°) in the little bowl under the north face of 13,573-foot Broken Hand Peak. This bowl is south of all the difficulties on Crestone Needle's northeast face.

Hike southwest up the bowl and climb a 400-foot northeast-facing couloir to 12,900-foot Broken Hand Pass (37.9587° -105.5710°) between Crestone Needle and Broken Hand Peak. This shaded couloir can retain snow until mid-July, so be prepared for some moderate snow climbing until then. After the snow melts, the couloir requires a little Class 3 scrambling. From the west end of Cottonwood Lake (37.9589° -105.5789°), hike 0.4 mile east up to Broken Hand Pass. The western, Class 2 approach to the pass is much easier.

From Broken Hand Pass, climb northwest on the west side of Crestone Needle's southeast ridge to 13,300 feet (37.9618° -105.5741°). A good climber's trail leads you through the minor cliff bands on this section of the route. At 13,300 feet, you have neatly bypassed the difficulties of the lower part of the Needle's convoluted south face. Above 13,300 feet, the upper part of the south face rears up in earnest, and you cannot avoid it.

There are two couloirs on the eastern edge of the upper south face. Either couloir can be climbed, and it is possible to traverse between the couloirs in a few places. The Class 3 scrambling in the couloirs on solid conglomerate knobs is enjoyable.

Start up the eastern (right) couloir and, when it becomes steep, climb a steep 40-foot wall to reach the western edge of the couloir and go west through a nifty passage to reach the western (left) couloir. Many climbers miss this turn and end up climbing all the way up the eastern couloir. The upper eastern couloir works, but is more exposed and slightly harder than the upper part of the western couloir. Once in the easier western couloir, scramble up it until it merges with the eastern couloir to form a shallow bowl near the summit. From the shallow bowl above the couloirs, scramble northwest to the highest point (37.9647° -105.5765°). Crestone Needle's summit will thrill all but the most dispassionate soul.

19R7 EC1 – Extra Credit – Broken Hand Peak 13,573 feet 37.9569° -105.5668°

Class 2+

From 12,900-foot Broken Hand Pass (37.9587° -105.5710°), descend 200 feet west, traverse 100 yards south below a rock buttress, then scamper 0.3 mile south then east to the summit of 13,573-foot Broken Hand Peak. If you climb to the north ridge en route, you can view the thumb. This freestanding pinnacle gives this peak its handlike appearance when viewed from the east. The thumb has been climbed, but it's hard.

19R7 EC2 – Extra Credit – "Crestolita" 13,270 feet 37.9549° -105.5757°

Class 2+

This small but full-featured ranked Thirteener makes an ornate addition to your Crestone caper, especially if you are camped at Cottonwood Lake. The rugged "Crestolita" has two summits; the northwest summit is the highest. From the east end of Cottonwood Lake, hike 0.25 mile southeast to 12,800 feet (37.9553° -105.5739°) under the peak's broken, northeast face. From 12,900-foot Broken Hand Pass (37.9587° -105.5710°), descend 200 yards to 12,600 feet, contour 300 yards south, and climb 200 yards southwest to 12,800 feet below the face. Seeking the path of least difficulty, scamper 200 yards southwest up the convoluted face above you, reach the summit ridge, turn northwest (right), and scamper 100 yards northwest to the summit (Class 2+). Like many lower peaks near giants, "Crestolita" offers an exquisite view, and is an exclusive place to study the south face routes on both Crestone Peak and Crestone Needle.

19R8 – Crestone Needle – Merhar

From Lower South Colony TH at 8,770'	*967 RP*	*15.4 mi RT*	*5,467' total*	*Class 5.6*
From Lower South Colony Lake at 11,660'	*769 RP*	*2.4 mi RT*	*2,537' total*	*Class 5.6*

This technical climb flirts with the difficulties of Crestone Needle's great northeast face. It is well south of the Ellingwood Arête and is the southernmost route on the face. You can approach the route from the Lower South Colony Trailhead at 8,770 feet and the South Colony Lakes Approach (19A1). From the western end of Lower South Colony Lake, hike 0.3 mile west-southwest to 12,200 feet at the southern end of the face. Climb a short gully above a scree cone to avoid the lower cliffs on the face. Do an ascending traverse north on a large, sloping ledge above the lower cliffs. Climb directly up 700 feet of Class 5.6 rock on the north (right) side of a narrow couloir that is the northern of two upper extensions of the initial gully. Join the South Face Route (19R7) at 13,300 feet (37.9615° -105.5732°).

19R9 – Crestone Needle – Whitney

From Lower South Colony TH at 8,770'	*1,200 RP*	*15.1 mi RT*	*5,467' total*	*Class 5.8, Steep Snow/Ice*
From Lower South Colony Lake at 11,660'	*1,002 RP*	*2.1 mi RT*	*2,537' total*	*Class 5.8, Steep Snow/Ice*

This route starts near the bottom of the Ellingwood Arête but takes a different line on the upper part of the face. The upper part of this route is 800 feet south of the Ellingwood Arête. You can approach the route from the Lower South Colony Lake Trailhead at 8,770 feet and the South Colony Lakes Approach (19A1). From the western end of Lower South Colony Lake, hike 0.3 mile west to 12,200 feet under the center of the east-facing portion of the Needle's northeast face.

Climb through the lower cliff band (Class 3). Climb directly up the face above on the north (right) side of a narrow, cracklike couloir (Class 4). Follow a crack system in this section of the face. Move into the cracklike couloir (often snow-filled) at 13,000 feet on a lower-angled section of the face. Climb the steep upper portion of the cracklike couloir (Class 5.8, Steep Snow/Ice). This 500-foot crux couloir requires both snow and rock climbing. The top of the couloir is in the notch (37.9629° -105.5750°) between a 13,660-foot summit of some stature and the upper part of Crestone Needle. The climb to the 13,660-foot summit (37.9628° -105.5748°) is optional. From the notch, descend northwest and join the South Face Route (19R7) in its eastern couloir.

19R10 – Crestone Needle – Ellingwood Arête *Classic*

From Lower South Colony TH at 8,770'	*918 RP*	*15.4 mi RT*	*5,467' total*	*Class 5.7*
From Lower South Colony Lake at 11,660'	*720 RP*	*2.4 mi RT*	*2,537' total*	*Class 5.7*

This is one of the finest technical climbs on Colorado's Fourteeners. It has attracted climbers since 1916, when Albert Ellingwood first spied it while

Ellingwood Arête on Crestone Needle.

descending after his first ascent of Crestone Needle. Ellingwood returned in 1925 to make the first ascent of the route. When Robert Ormes made the second ascent of the route in 1937, he named it Ellingwood Ledges after his mentor. The name later evolved to Ellingwood Arête, which is misnomer, since the ridge is not sharp. Further, do not confuse Ellingwood Arête on Crestone Needle with Ellingwood Ridge on La Plata Peak.

Ellingwood Arête ascends the rounded ridge between the Needle's east and north faces. The 2,000-foot route leads directly to the summit. The lower portion of the route is straightforward, but the upper, steeper portion looks dubious from below. The sustained nature of the crux pitches so close to the summit sets this route apart.

The excellent nature of Crestone rock also sets this route apart. The conglomerate rock thrusts forth so many pink-colored knobs that sometimes you don't know which one to grab! An occasional hole testifies that the knobs can pull out, but they are generally quite firm. Tiptoeing up the knobs on this exposed route is an ethereal experience.

You can approach the route from the Lower South Colony Trailhead at 8,770 feet and the South Colony Lakes Approach (19A1). From Lower South Colony Lake, continue 0.5 mile northwest on the trail to Upper South Colony

Lake, where the route will be directly above you to the west. From the upper lake's south side, hike 0.2 mile southwest to 12,200 feet at the base of the center of the east-facing portion of the face. Your easy overture is over.

Scramble up the lower cliff band where the angle of the initial slabs relents (Class 3). Do a long, ascending traverse north (right) on broken, grassy benches to reach the arête (Class 3). The exposure gradually increases as you gain height on this initial, easy section.

Once on the arête, climb it on steepening Class 4 rock. There are still plenty of ledges, but steep steps separate them. The exposure continues to increase and the place to rope up on this route is difficult to prescribe. Use your judgment.

After 1,500 feet of climbing, you will arrive at the base of the steep upper wall. If upward progress looked dubious from below, it probably will look even worse from here. The upper wall is full of blank faces and overhanging cul-de-sacs. In particular, there is one prominent, smooth slab and, to its south, a giant overhang. The trick is to sneak up between them.

Overcome the initial part of the upper wall by ascending a 200-foot-long chimney system just north (right) of the crest of the arête. There are several chimneys here. Climb either the central or northern one. At the top of the chimneys, climb a left-angling gully to a large ledge on the crest of the arête. Continue up and go left around a corner to another ledge at the base of the famous Head Crack.

The Head Crack pitch is the route's crux, which got its name because Ellingwood actually stuck his head in the crack before stemming wildly out to the right to escape the clutch. To do it with headless aplomb, climb the awkward crack for a few feet, then move right to some small holds (Class 5.7). Continue up and slightly right to the base of a wide crack. Stem the wide crack until you can exit right. The summit is not far above this point, and your arrival there may seem abrupt.

19R10 V – Variation – Arête Direct

Class 5.4

You can do a direct start by climbing a north-facing open book just south of a point below the upper arête (Class 5.4). This start shortens the climb and replaces some of the Class 3 scrambling with quality Class 5 pitches. An even harder direct start ascends the wall directly below the arête.

19R11 – Crestone Needle – Arnold–Michel

From Lower South Colony TH at 8,770'	*1,241 RP*	*15.7 mi RT*	*5,467' total*	*Class 5.8, Steep Snow/Ice*
From Lower South Colony Lake at 11,660'	*1,043 RP*	*2.7 mi RT*	*2,537' total*	*Class 5.8, Steep Snow/Ice*

This mixed climb has an alpine flavor. The route ascends the prominent couloir on the north-facing wall on the north side of the Ellingwood Arête. You can approach the route from the Lower South Colony Trailhead at 8,770 feet and the

South Colony Lakes Approach (19A1). From Lower South Colony Lake, continue 0.5 mile northwest on the trail to Upper South Colony Lake, then hike and scamper 0.4 mile west to 12,400 feet at the base of the wall. Rack up.

Climb the rock on the west (right) side of the lower portion of the couloir. Move into the couloir near a turn in the couloir and climb it for several hundred feet. When the couloir narrows and steepens, either climb the couloir directly (difficult) or climb the rock on the right side of the couloir (easier). Higher up, move back into the couloir and follow it to the deep, 14,020-foot notch (37.9656° -105.5781°) between the Black Gendarme and the ridge leading to Crestone Peak. The 13,900-foot Black Gendarme is the most spectacular spire on the ridge connecting Crestone Needle and Crestone Peak. From the notch, descend on the southwest side of the ridge and join the Needle to Peak traverse route (Combination 19C1).

19C – Crestone Peak and Crestone Needle Combination Routes

19C1 – Crestone Peak Northwest Couloir → Crestone Needle South Face *Classic*

From Lower South Colony TH at 8,770'	622 RP	17.5 mi RT	6,321' total	Class 5.2, Steep Snow/Ice
From Lower South Colony Lake at 11,660'	422 RP	4.5 mi RT	3,391' total	Class 5.2, Steep Snow/Ice

The traverse of the Crestones is one of Colorado's four great Fourteener traverses. It is shorter but harder than the Class 4 Wilson–El Diente traverse (31C1), which is the easiest of the four. It is slightly harder and has more difficult route finding than the Class 4 Maroon Bells traverse (24C1). With only one short Class 5.2 sequence, the Crestone traverse is easier than the Little Bear–Blanca traverse (20C2), which is the hardest of the four. You can escape from the Crestone traverse by descending southwest into the basin above Cottonwood Lake. People usually climb Crestone Peak and Crestone Needle together from South Colony Lakes. Climbers debate about which peak should be climbed first, and there are trade-offs for each direction. Consider the trade-offs, then make a decision that suits you.

The most difficult part of the traverse is the 500 feet on the Needle's north side. If you climb the Needle first, you can rappel the exposed Class 4 pitch below the Needle's summit instead of climbing it. This is an advantage for some people. The traverse route is slightly easier to find when going from Needle to Peak. Because of these facts, some consider the traverse easier when going from Needle to Peak.

Weigh these advantages against some additional facts. Below the Needle's summit pitch are several hundred feet of devious Class 3 scrambling. It is not convenient to rappel these slabs and ledges, and you must downclimb some of this terrain when going from Needle to Peak. Going from Needle to Peak requires you to downclimb the Peak's Northwest Couloir Route (19R2) late in the day, when the probability of storms is greatest.

I prefer to go from Peak to Needle. I like to climb the higher Peak early in the day and prefer to ascend Class 3 to Class 4 terrain. The Needle's South Face Route (19R7) is a friendlier late-day challenge, and it leads directly to camp. I describe the traverse from Peak to Needle.

You can approach the route from the Lower South Colony Trailhead at 8,770 feet and the South Colony Lakes Approach (19A1). From Lower South Colony Lake at 11,660 feet, climb either the Northwest Couloir Route (19R2) or, for more adventure, the North Buttress Route (19R3) on Crestone Peak. The traverse to the Needle looks awesome from the summit of the Peak. The key is to stay well below the ridge on its southwest side.

Return to the 14,180-foot red notch (37.9670° –105.5846°) between Crestone Peak's main summit and "East Crestone." Descend the south-facing couloir below the notch for 300 feet. This is the top of Crestone Peak's South Face Route (19R1). Exit the couloir and scramble southeast on broken terrain. Go around a corner and descend a ledge system under a steep buttress. Pass below the 13,740-foot saddle between Crestone Peak and Crestone Needle. There is a 13,940-foot summit between the saddle and the Needle. Go well below this summit on a good ledge system on the south side of the ridge. The traverse to this point includes a lot of Class 3 scrambling. Parties who stay too high in this section end up doing much harder climbing.

The final, steep climb to the Needle is visible during most of the traverse to this point. Study it carefully as you approach the Needle, since once embroiled in the Needle's difficulties, it's hard to see the route ahead. There are three gendarmes on the Needle's northwest ridge. The traverse route passes under them on the ridge's southwest side. The northernmost 13,900-foot gendarme is an impressive tower called the Black Gendarme.

Reach the couloir below the Black Gendarme 200 feet below the bottom of the gendarme. Climb up the couloir to the base of the gendarme and enter a steep, narrow passage immediately to the east (right) of the gendarme. Climb up the passage for a few feet and climb a Class 5.2 bulge. Taken by itself, this is the hardest move on the traverse and it is also the key to unlocking the route to the Needle. Parties who miss this solution usually end up doing harder climbing somewhere else or failing on the traverse. This confusing area has produced at least one fatal accident.

Above the key bulge, scramble up the gully above, exit the gully to the right, and climb a 10-foot-long Class 4 knife-edge to a perch where you can peer south down some surprising exposure. Scramble up a Class 3 ledge and go around a corner where you can finally see the route ahead. Continue up broken Class 3 rock and cross the shallow couloir below the northern end of the central gendarme. Do an ascending traverse across a knob-studded but otherwise smooth slab (Class 3). This slab takes you to the narrow gully below the notch between the central and southern gendarmes. Climb this gully to a point near the ridge crest (Class 3). Traverse around the southernmost gendarme on a ledge and climb another knob-studded slab leading up to the ridge crest (Class 3).

The traverse between Crestone Peak and Crestone Needle.

This is an exposed place, and the dramatic summit pitch is above you.

The Class 4 summit pitch is airy and beautiful. Climb 100 feet of steep, knobby rock directly on the exposed ridge crest. This is Crestone knob climbing at its best. From the top of the pitch, scamper 100 feet up to Crestone Needle's scintillating summit. Descend Crestone Needle's South Face Route (19R7).

19C2 – Crestone Peak South Face ➔ Crestone Needle South Face *Classic*

From Cottonwood Creek TH at 8,400'	*597 RP*	*12.1 mi RT*	*6,491' total*	*Class 5.2, Mod Snow*
From Cottonwood Lake at 12,310'	*367 RP*	*2.9 mi RT*	*2,581' total*	*Class 5.2, Mod Snow*
From Lower South Colony TH at 8,770'	*671 RP*	*17.2 mi RT*	*7,341' total*	*Class 5.2, Mod Snow*
From Lower South Colony Lake at 11,660'	*471 RP*	*4.2 mi RT*	*4,411' total*	*Class 5.2, Mod Snow*

You can do the Peak to Needle traverse from Cottonwood Lake. This adds more congenial climbing to your adventure and avoids the vagaries of the Peak's Northwest Couloir Route. Climb Crestone Peak's South Face Route (19R1), traverse to the Needle as described in Combination 19C1, and descend Crestone Needle's South Face Route (19R7).

19. Humboldt Peak 14,064 feet

19R – Humboldt Peak Routes

19R12 – Humboldt Peak – West Ridge

From Lower South Colony TH at 8,770'	*318 RP*	*16.6 mi RT*	*5,334' total*	*Class 2*
From Lower South Colony Lake at 11,660'	*124 RP*	*3.6 mi RT*	*2,404' total*	*Class 2*

This is the easiest route on Humboldt. Start at the Lower South Colony Trailhead at 8,770 feet and follow the South Colony Lakes Approach (19A1). From Lower South Colony Lake, stay on the trail (FT 1339) and hike 0.6 mile northwest to 12,300 feet (37.9695° -105.5680°) above the east side of Upper South Colony Lake. Hike 0.5 mile north on the sustainable trail constructed by the Colorado Fourteener Initiative as it switchbacks up to Humboldt's west ridge near the 12,860-foot Humboldt–Crestone Peak saddle (37.9733° -105.5689°). Hike 0.7 mile east on a faint trail near the ridge through the Class 2 talus to the summit (37.9762° -105.5552°). The Crestones' majesty will be obvious long before you reach Humboldt's summit.

19R13 – Humboldt Peak – East Ridge

From Lower South Colony TH at 8,770'	*397 RP*	*12.9 mi RT*	*5,294' net; 5,394' total*	*Class 2*
From Rainbow Trail 4WD TH at 9,810'	*330 RP*	*8.5 mi RT*	*4,254' net; 4,354' total*	*Class 2*

This alternate route up Humboldt has become popular in recent years, especially as a safe winter route. While direct, the east ridge is a rugged off-trail adventure, and notorious winter winds frequently sweep the upper slopes. Start at the Lower South Colony Trailhead at 8,770 feet and follow the rough 4WD road 1.4 miles west to the San Isabel National Forest boundary (37.9871° -105.4921°). Camping is not permitted on the private land between the trailhead and the forest boundary. Continue 0.8 mile southwest up FR 120 to a parking area at 9,810 feet near the Rainbow Trail (37.9816° -105.4991°).

Leave the road, turn north onto the Rainbow Trail (FT 1336), descend 250 yards northwest, and cross to the north side of South Colony Creek on a good bridge at 9,760 feet. Follow the Rainbow Trail 0.6 mile northeast to where it crests Humboldt's lower east ridge at 9,920 feet (37.9870° -105.5001°). Turn southwest (left), leave the Rainbow Trail, enter the Sangre de Cristo Wilderness, and begin your 1.7-mile bushwhack to treeline. Hike 0.9 mile southwest through the trees along the initially narrow ridge using intermittent game trails as you find them. At 10,600 feet (37.9795° -105.5109°), go 0.8 mile straight west up a steeper slope, eventually through thinning bristlecone pines, to reach treeline at 11,840 feet (37.9790° -105.5249°). There is a solitary, distinctive, contorted bristlecone south of here.

Once free of the trees, you can see the now much simpler route ahead, although you cannot yet see the summit. Hike 0.8 mile west-northwest up a broad, rounded ridge to 13,240 feet (37.9813° -105.5382°), where you can finally see the remaining ridge to the summit. Continue 0.5 mile west-southwest on the gentle, narrowing ridge to 13,500 feet (37.9790° -105.5468°), where the ridge narrows dramatically and

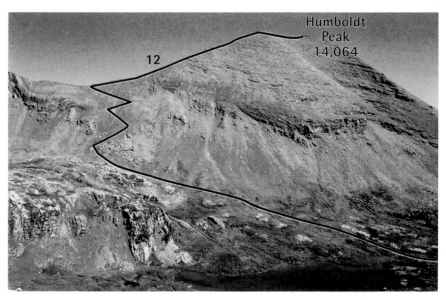

Humboldt Peak from the west.

you can peer north over a precipitous edge across the North Colony Creek drainage to 13,705-foot Colony Baldy. Continue 0.5 mile west-southwest along this dramatic but solid Class 2 ridge to the summit (37.9762° -105.5552°).

19R13 V – Variation – Proverbial Shortcut

Class 2

From the 4WD parking area at the Rainbow Trail at 9,810 feet (37.9816° -105.4991°), continue 0.5 mile southwest on FR 120, descend slightly, cross to South Colony Creek's north side (37.9761° -105.5068°), and go another 250 yards west on the road to 9,960 feet (37.9759° -105.5089°). Leave the road and bushwhack 0.9 mile west-northwest to rejoin the route at treeline at 11,840 feet (37.9790° -105.5249°). While this proverbial shortcut saves a whopping 0.9 mile, it is significantly tougher. Many parties choosing this route in winter and spring have foundered in deep snow that the notorious winds deposit on this slope. Downed trees are an additional difficulty.

19. Challenger Point 14,081 feet

19R – Challenger Point Routes

19R14 – Challenger Point – North Slopes

From Willow and South Crestone TH at 8,880'	306 RP	11.2 mi RT	5,201' net; 5,357' total	Class 2+
From Willow Lake at 11,564'	167 RP	3.2 mi RT	2,517' total	Class 2+

This is the easiest route on Challenger Point. Start at the Willow and South Crestone Trailhead at 8,880 feet and follow the Willow Lake Approach (19A2). Hike 0.4

Challenger Point from the east. Photo by Steve Hoffmeyer

mile east around the north side of Willow Lake to the benches above the waterfall at the east end of the lake. Climb 0.8 mile south up a long slope that starts as grass but steepens near its top and involves some route finding around micro-cliffs. If you take care to find the easiest route, the difficulty will not exceed Class 2+ scampering. The slope leads to Challenger Point's northwest ridge. Follow this Class 2 ridge 0.4 mile southeast to the summit (37.9803° -105.6066°).

19R14 V – Variation – Pencil Couloir

Steep Snow

There is a long, narrow couloir 200 yards east (left) of the long slope of the standard route. When filled with suitable snow, it provides a direct route to Challenger's summit ridge. The slope angle of the lower half of the couloir is moderate, but steepens in the upper half. If this is not to your liking, you can escape the couloir to the west at half height.

19R15 – Challenger Point – Kirk Couloir

From Willow and South Crestone TH at 8,880'	*406 RP*	*11.2 mi RT*	*5,201' net; 5,357' total*	*Class 2, Steep Snow*
From Willow Lake at 11,564'	*266 RP*	*3.2 mi RT*	*2,517' total*	*Class 2, Steep Snow*

This superb early season snow climb is an enticing way to climb Challenger Point. Start at the Willow and South Crestone Trailhead at 8,880 feet and follow the Willow Lake Approach (19A2). Hike 0.4 mile east around the north side of Willow Lake to the benches above the waterfall at the east end of the lake. Easily seen from here, the north-facing Kirk Couloir reaches the 13,780-foot Challenger Point–Kit Carson Peak saddle (37.9798° -105.6039°). The slopes up to 13,000 feet are easy then moderate in steepness, while the couloir's last 800 feet reach 48 degrees. From the saddle, hike 0.2 mile west to Challenger's summit. From the saddle, you can also continue on Kit Carson Peak's West Ridge Route (19R17).

19. Kit Carson Peak 14,165 feet

19R – Kit Carson Peak Routes

19R16 – Kit Carson Peak – East Ridge

From Lower South Colony TH at 8,770'	*483 RP*	*18.6 mi RT*	*5,395' net; 6,595' total*	*Class 3+*
From Lower South Colony Lake at 11,660'	*286 RP*	*5.6 mi RT*	*2,505' net; 3,665' total*	*Class 3+*
From Spanish Creek TH at 8,260'	*505 RP*	*13.4 mi RT*	*5,905' net; 6,905' total*	*Class 3+*
From 11,000' in Spanish Creek	*341 RP*	*6.4 mi RT*	*3,165' net; 4,165' total*	*Class 3+*

This is the easiest way to climb Kit Carson Peak from South Colony Lakes, but it is not the easiest route on the peak, since you can also approach the East Ridge Route from Spanish Creek. Use either the South Colony Lakes Approach (19A1) or Spanish Creek Approach (19A3).

From Lower South Colony Lake at 11,660 feet (37.9645° –105.5612°), hike 0.5 mile northwest to Upper South Colony Lake and climb a south-facing scree gully to the long ridge connecting Humboldt Peak with Crestone Peak. Scramble west on or below this ridge to the broad 13,140-foot Crestone Peak–Kit Carson saddle (37.9749° –105.5816°). This open area is called the Bear's Playground. If you are approaching from 11,000 feet in Spanish Creek, hike 1.9 miles east-northeast to the head of Spanish Creek and reach the Bear's Playground from the west (Class 2).

Hike 0.3 mile northwest across the Bear's Playground and climb to 13,500 feet. Contour 0.4 mile west below and south of the summit of Point 13,799, which carries the appropriate nickname "Obstruction Peak," and reach the 13,460-foot saddle (37.9781° –105.5941°) between "Obstruction Peak" and Kit Carson's east peak. From this saddle, climb 0.2 mile west up steep terrain to the easternmost of two summits (37.9784° –105.5968°) that compose Kit Carson's east peak. This summit carries the nickname "Kitty Kat Carson." Continue 100 yards west-northwest to the slightly higher 13,980-foot Columbia Point (37.9790° –105.5982°), the true summit of Kit Carson's east peak. The introduction is over.

Descend 0.1 mile steeply west-northwest from the summit of Columbia Point on exposed Class 3+ blocks past a shark's fin to the 13,620-foot saddle (37.9795° –105.5995°) between Columbia Point and Kit Carson's main summit. This descent is the route's crux. From this saddle, scamper 0.1 mile west on a large ledge, the lower, eastern end of Kit Carson Avenue, then scramble 0.1 mile northwest up a Class 3 gully to the summit (37.9796° –105.6026°). From the summit, there are spectacular views of Crestone Peak's north side, and you can preview Crestone Peak's Northwest Couloir Route (19R2).

19R16 EC – Extra Credit – "Obstruction Peak" 13,799 feet 37.9784° -105.5883°

Class 2

Either coming or going, take the time to climb Point 13,799, alias "Obstruction Peak." This ranked Thirteener rises 339 feet above its connecting saddle with Kit Carson, and "Obstruction Peak" is a Bi, one of Colorado's 200 highest peaks.

19R17 – Kit Carson Peak – West Ridge

From Willow and South Crestone TH at 8,880'	*394 RP*	*12.4 mi RT*	*5,285' net; 6,323' total*	*Class 3*
From Willow Lake at 11,564'	*252 RP*	*4.4 mi RT*	*2,601' net; 3,483' total*	*Class 3*

This is the easiest route on Kit Carson. This unique tour also allows you to climb Challenger Point. Start at the Willow and South Crestone Trailhead at 8,880 feet and follow the Willow Lake Approach (19A2). From here, follow Challenger Point's Class 2+ North Slopes Route (19R14).

From the 14,081-foot summit of Challenger Point, you are only 400 yards from Kit Carson's summit, but the fun has just begun. Descend 0.2 mile east from Challenger Point to the 13,780-foot Challenger Point–Kit Carson Peak saddle (37.9798° -105.6039°). From this saddle, do an ascending traverse 0.1 mile south-southeast on a large ledge called Kit Carson Avenue, go around a corner, and reach a tiny, 13,940-foot saddle (37.9786° -105.6035°) between the top of the Prow (Kit Carson's south ridge) and Kit Carson's upper cliffs.

Cross the 13,940-foot saddle and do a descending traverse 0.2 mile east on the continuing Kit Carson Avenue ledge (Class 2+). This large, remarkable ledge system is the key to this route. Avoid any temptation to leave Kit Carson Avenue too soon and head for the summit. Follow the ledge down until you are east of the summit, then scramble 0.1 mile northwest up a Class 3 gully to the summit. This is the finish used by the East Ridge Route (19R16).

19R18 – Kit Carson Peak – North Ridge *Classic*

From Willow and South Crestone TH at 8,880'	*463 RP*	*11.4 mi RT*	*5,285' net; 5,441' total*	*Class 4*
From Willow Lake at 11,564'	*321 RP*	*3.4 mi RT*	*2,601' total*	*Class 4*

This remarkable climb is easier than it looks. The route ascends Kit Carson's 1,500-foot-high north ridge directly to the summit. Start at the Willow and South Crestone Trailhead at 8,880 feet and follow the Willow Lake Approach (19A2). Hike 0.4 mile east around the north side of Willow Lake to the benches above the waterfall at the east end of the lake. Hike 1.0 mile southeast up the valley to the bottom of the north ridge at 12,600 feet (37.9844° -105.6013°).

Climb up the broken ridge 0.5 mile south then southwest to the summit. The climbing is mostly Class 3, punctuated by some Class 4 sections. There are multiple ways to navigate on this intriguing ridge, so make your own best microdecisions. The mostly solid ridge averages 45 degrees. Occasionally, one of the famous Crestone knobs will come out of its socket and you can hold it in your hand. This is not a handhold you want, so test every hold and remember that this route has proven fatal.

19R19 – Kit Carson Peak – Outward Bound Couloir

From Willow and South Crestone TH at 8,880'	*448 RP*	*11.8 mi RT*	*5,285' net; 5,441' total*	*Class 3, Steep Snow/Ice*
From Willow Lake at 11,564'	*306 RP*	*3.8 mi RT*	*2,601' total*	*Class 3, Steep Snow/Ice*

This is a captivating mixed climb. Start at the Willow and South Crestone Trailhead at 8,880 feet and follow the Willow Lake Approach (19A2). Go around the north side of Willow Lake and hike 1.1 miles southeast up the valley to 12,800 feet below the couloir (37.9817° -105.5978°). The Outward Bound Couloir is the deep couloir east of Kit Carson's north ridge, and it leads directly to the 13,620-foot saddle (37.9795° -105.5995°) between 13,980-foot Columbia Point and Kit Carson Peak's summit. The couloir gradually steepens and becomes more inset as you approach the saddle. Near the saddle, take the eastern (left) branch of the couloir. This deeply inset, north-facing couloir is often icy, and I recommend ice axes, crampons, and helmets for this route.

From the 13,620-foot saddle, scamper west on a large ledge, the lower, eastern end of Kit Carson Avenue, then scramble northwest up a Class 3 gully to the summit. This is the finish used by both the East Ridge (19R16) and West Ridge (19R17) routes.

19R20 – Kit Carson Peak – South Couloir

From Spanish Creek TH at 8,260'	*428 RP*	*10.4 mi RT*	*5,905' total*	*Class 3, Mod Snow*
From 11,000' in Spanish Creek	*264 RP*	*3.4 mi RT*	*3,165' total*	*Class 3, Mod Snow*

This is a direct way to climb Kit Carson from Spanish Creek, and when snow conditions are good, this couloir can provide a speedy descent route. The South Couloir is the deep couloir east of the Prow (19R21). Start at the Spanish Creek Trailhead at 8,260 feet and follow the Spanish Creek Approach (19A3) to reach 11,000 feet in Spanish Creek. Hike 0.7 mile east-northeast to 11,800 feet in upper Spanish Creek (37.9701° -105.6018°), then hike 0.5 mile north to 12,800 feet (37.9762° -105.6008°) below the upper couloir. Climb the couloir 0.3 mile north directly to the 13,620-foot saddle (37.9795° -105.5995°) between Columbia Point and Kit Carson Peak's summit. From the saddle, scamper 0.1 mile west on a large ledge, then scramble 0.1 mile northwest up the famous Class 3 gully to the summit.

19R21 – Kit Carson Peak – The Prow *Classic*

From Spanish Creek TH at 8,260'	*1,285 RP*	*10.4 mi RT*	*5,905' net; 6,305' total*	*Class 5.8*
From 11,000' in Spanish Creek	*1,121 RP*	*3.4 mi RT*	*3,165' net; 3,565' total*	*Class 5.8*

This is the ultimate Crestone knob climb. Start at the Spanish Creek Trailhead at 8,260 feet, then follow the Spanish Creek Approach (19A3) to reach 11,000 feet in Spanish Creek. Hike 0.7 mile east-northeast to 11,800 feet in upper Spanish Creek (37.9701° -105.6018°). The unmistakable Prow will have been visible to you for some time. Scramble 0.3 mile northwest up gentle slabs on the Prow's lower, east side and reach the ridge at 12,400 feet. Consider your future, because your commitment begins abruptly.

Kit Carson Peak
14,165

21

The Prow on Kit Carson.

The bottom of the Prow is a serious overhang, and the climb starts with its hardest move. Do a gymnastic Class 5.8 move to overcome the overhang. The rest of the first pitch is Class 5.6, and it angles slightly right to dodge a bulge. The second pitch is Class 5.6 and completes the bulge dodge. The first two pitches are on the east (right) side of the edge of the Prow.

The third pitch is Class 5.5 and ends on the now well-formed edge of the Prow. The nature of this climb is abundantly clear at this point. Escape and protection are difficult, there is tremendous exposure in every direction, and the commitment increases with every pitch. Climb the narrow edge as it arcs into the sky. You have no choice!

The numerous upper pitches average Class 5.3–5.4 in difficulty. Just when you think the angle might ease, the elegant edge sweeps up again and the climb continues. With each pitch, it becomes clearer that the best escape is to complete the climb. When you reach the top of the Prow—a small, 13,980-foot summit (37.9784° -105.6035°)—scramble north to the Kit Carson Avenue ledge of West Ridge fame. Escape is possible from here, but there is more to this route.

Descend 0.1 mile north-northwest on Kit Carson Avenue under the summit pyramid's west wall to the 13,780-foot Challenger Point–Kit Carson saddle (37.9798° -105.6039°). Scramble northeast above the saddle, then climb a long

Class 5.3–5.4 pitch into the center of the northwest wall of Kit Carson's summit pyramid. Finish your clairvoyant exercise with a long, right-angling Class 5.5 pitch on the upper wall. There is a sequence of delectable Class 5.5 moves a few feet below the summit cairn.

19R21 V – Variation – Overhang Bypass
Instead of climbing the Class 5.8 overhang at the bottom of the Prow, climb easier slabs 200 yards east (right) of this direct start. Reach the edge of the Prow higher up.

20. Blanca Group

Blanca Peak	14,345 feet
Little Bear Peak	14,037 feet
Ellingwood Point	14,042 feet
Mount Lindsey	14,042 feet

These magnificent peaks are 10 miles north of Fort Garland on US 160. They leap from the surrounding flatness even more than the Crestone Group. The Sangre de Cristo Range takes a break south of these peaks as if to honor them. You can see these peaks for long distances while driving on US 285, US 160, or Colorado 159.

Mighty Blanca carries many accolades. Blanca is Colorado's fourth highest peak, the highest peak in Colorado outside the Sawatch Range, the highest peak in the Sangre de Cristo Range, and the highest peak in Alamosa, Costilla, and Huerfano counties. Take a fresh breath. If you traveled south from Blanca, you would have to go all the way to the high volcanoes in central Mexico to find a higher peak. Blanca is one of the Navajo's four sacred peaks. It is also the highest peak in Colorado with a technical route on it; its northeast face is one of Colorado's finest mountain walls. Soaring 7,000 feet above its valleys, Blanca is one of only three Ultra Prominent Peaks in Colorado. Blanca carries its honors well. Climb it.

Little Bear is 1.0 mile southwest of Blanca and separated from its higher neighbor by a rough ridge. There is nothing little about Little Bear. This peak is steep on all sides and is one of Colorado's toughest Fourteeners. The old approach from the south into Blanca Basin is on private property and has not been used in recent years. The Lake Como Approach (20A1) is the only reliable approach.

Ellingwood Point is 0.5 mile northwest of Blanca, and this summit rests in the shadow of its higher neighbor's splendor. Ellingwood Point's sanctity as an official Fourteener has been questioned for years, and the summit was only recently named. Ellingwood Point rises 342 feet above its connecting saddle with Blanca and has 0.5 mile of separation. Although the shapely peak does not have a lot of power, it is named, ranked, and is above 14,000 feet. Together with Blanca, it crowns an amazing northeast face above the Huerfano Valley.

Overshadowed by Blanca and Ellingwood, Mount Lindsey rests quietly by itself 2.5 miles east of Blanca. You can best see the solitary Lindsey from US 160 to the south. Lindsey's southern slopes and summit are on private property, and southern approaches are not available to the public. I only describe the traditional routes from the San Isabel National Forest, north of Lindsey.

20E – Blanca Group Essentials

Elevations	Blanca Pk	14,345' (NGVD29) 14,349' (NAVD88)
	Little Bear Pk	14,037' (NGVD29) 14,040' (NAVD88)
	Ellingwood Pt	14,042' (NGVD29) 14,049' (NAVD88)
	Mt Lindsey	14,042' (NGVD29) 14,047' (NAVD88)
Ranks	Blanca Pk	Colorado's 4th highest ranked peak
	Little Bear Pk	Colorado's 44th highest ranked peak
	Ellingwood Pt	Colorado's 43rd highest ranked peak
	Mt Lindsey	Colorado's 42nd highest ranked peak
Location	Alamosa, Costilla, and Huerfano counties, Colorado, USA	
Range	Southern Sangre de Cristo Range	
Summit Coordinates	Blanca Pk	37.5777° -105.4855° (WGS84)
	Little Bear Pk	37.5666° -105.4972° (WGS84)
	Ellingwood Pt	37.5825° -105.4917° (WGS84)
	Mt Lindsey	37.5837° -105.4448° (WGS84)
Ownership/Contact	San Isabel and Rio Grande national forests to east, north, and west – Public Land – 719-553-1400; 719-852-5941	
	Sangre de Cristo Grant to south – Private Land	
Prominence and Saddles	Blanca Pk	5,326' from 9,019' Poncha Pass
	Little Bear Pk	377' from 13,660' Little Bear–Blanca saddle
	Ellingwood Pt	342' from 13,700' Ellingwood–Blanca saddle
	Mt Lindsey	1,542' from 12,500' Lindsey–Blanca saddle
Isolation and Parents	Blanca Pk	103.61 miles to Mount Harvard
	Little Bear Pk	1.00 mile to Blanca Peak
	Ellingwood Pt	0.51 mile to Blanca Peak
	Mt Lindsey	2.27 miles to Blanca Peak
USGS Maps	**Blanca Peak, Twin Peaks**, Mosca Pass	
USFS Maps	**Rio Grande National Forest**, San Isabel National Forest	
Trails Illustrated Map	Map #138 Sangre de Cristo Mountains	
Book Map	See Map 20 on page 202	
Nearest Towns	Fort Garland – Population 390 – Elevation 7,936' Alamosa – Population 8,750 – Elevation 7,543'	
	Walsenburg – Population 3,830 – Elevation 6,171'	

20E – Blanca Group Essentials

Blanca Pk 🏃 Easiest Route	20R1 – Northwest Face – Class 2
	A long Class 1 approach hike on a road to Lake Como,
	a nice walk into the upper basin,
	then a Class 2 hike up talus to the summit
Little Bear Pk 🏃 Easiest Public Route	20R4 – West Ridge – Class 4
	A long Class 1 approach hike on a road to Lake Como,
	a steep Class 2 approach to the west ridge, then a testy, dangerous
	Class 4 climb up through the confining Hourglass to reach the
	block-laden upper slopes
Ellingwood Pt 🏃 Easiest Route	20R7 – South Face – Class 2
	A Class 1 approach to Lake Como, a Class 2 hike into the basin, and
	a Class 2 boulder hop to the top
Mt Lindsey 🏃 + 🏃 Easiest Route	20R10 – North Face – Class 2+–3
	A Class 1 then Class 2 approach hike, then a thoughtful Class 2+
	scamper to the summit
Blanca Group Accolades	The Blanca Group of four Fourteeners and neighboring Thirteeners
	is a singular, almost monumental uplift that you can see for many
	miles. Blanca Peak is the highest peak in Alamosa, Costilla, and
	Huerfano counties and one of only three Ultra Prominent Peaks
	in Colorado. Little Bear is one of Colorado's most challenging
	Fourteeners. Ellingwood Point and Mount Lindsey anchor the
	corners of the extensive Huerfano Valley, one of Colorado's most
	dramatic places.

20T – Blanca Group Trailheads

20T1 – Lake Como Trailhead 8,000 feet 37.5386° -105.5759°

This trailhead provides access to the west sides of Blanca Peak, Ellingwood Point, and Little Bear. This is one of Colorado's lowest trailheads for a Fourteener. From the US 160–Colorado 150 junction 5.5 miles northwest of the town of Blanca, go 3.2 miles north on Colorado 150 to an unmarked dirt road leading northeast (37.5214° -105.6024°). Follow this rocky road 1.8 miles northeast straight toward the Blanca massif to 8,000 feet. Park here, since the road beyond becomes exceedingly rough after this point; it is prohibitive for low-clearance vehicles.

20T1 4WD – Lake Como 4WD Trailhead 11,760 feet 37.5701° -105.5156°

From 8,000 feet, ATVs and specially equipped 4WD vehicles can continue 5.2 miles northeast then east to Lake Como at 11,760 feet. This is nationally known as one of Colorado's toughest roads. There are three crux rock steps named Jaws 1, Jaws 2, and Jaws 3. Even before the Jaws, there are pitches that routinely defeat stock 4WD vehicles. A rescue from this road can quickly blow

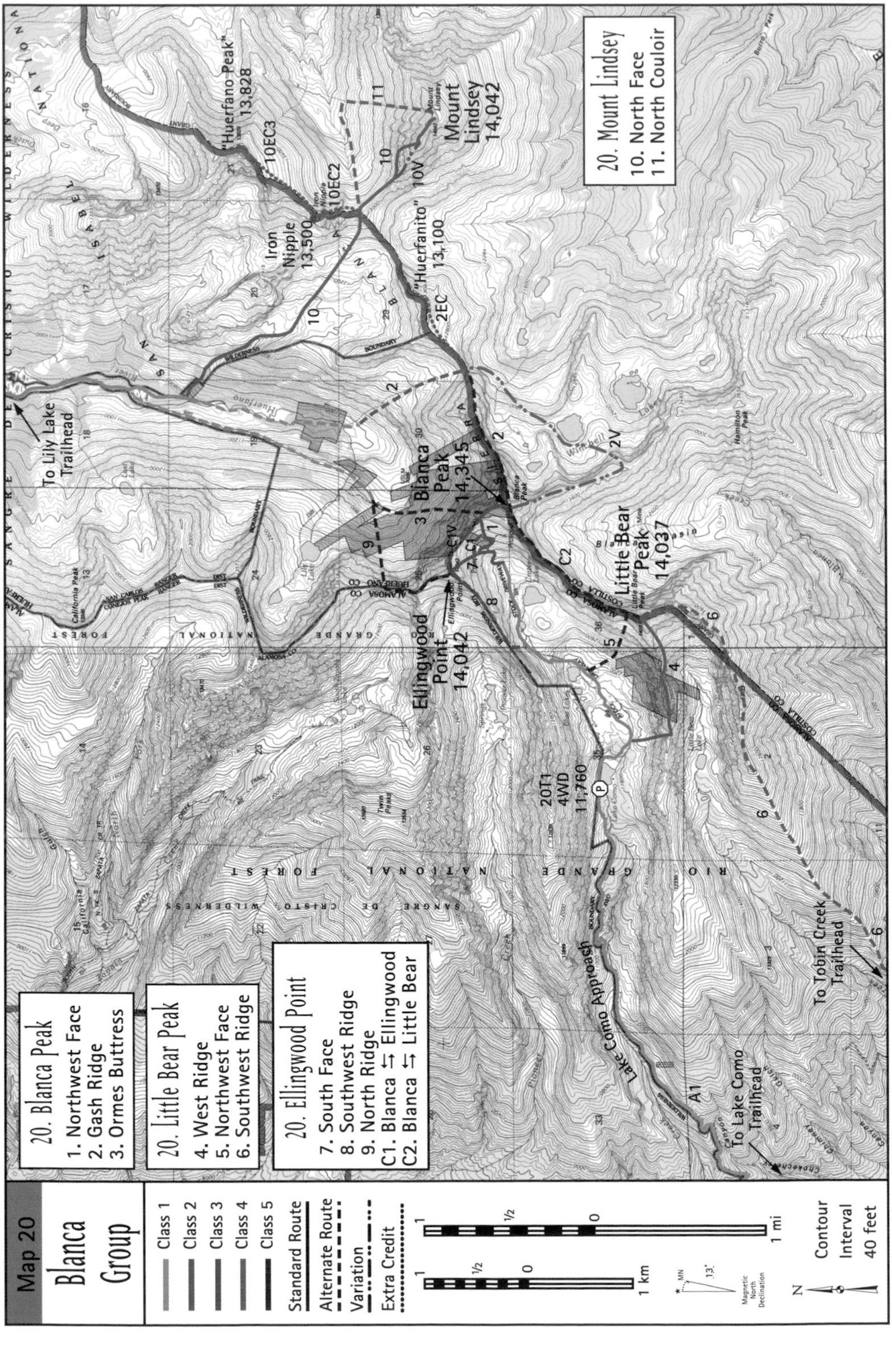

Map 20

Blanca Group

Class 1
Class 2
Class 3
Class 4
Class 5

Standard Route
Alternate Route
Variation
Extra Credit

Contour
Interval
40 feet

1   ½   0   1 mi
1   ½   0   1 km

MN
13°
Magnetic
North
Declination

N

20. Blanca Peak
1. Northwest Face
2. Gash Ridge
3. Ormes Buttress

20. Little Bear Peak
4. West Ridge
5. Northwest Face
6. Southwest Ridge

20. Ellingwood Point
7. South Face
8. Southwest Ridge
9. North Ridge
C1. Blanca ⇆ Ellingwood
C2. Blanca ⇆ Little Bear

20. Mount Lindsey
10. North Face
11. North Couloir

"Huerfano Peak"
13,828

Iron
Nipple
13,500

Mount
Lindsey
14,042

"Huerfanito"
13,100

Blanca
Peak
14,345

Little Bear
Peak
14,037

Ellingwood
Point
14,042

20T1
4WD
11,760

To Lily Lake
Trailhead

Lake Como Approach

To Lake Como
Trailhead

To Tobin Creek
Trailhead

SANGRE DE CRISTO WILDERNESS

RIO GRANDE NATIONAL FOREST

GRANDE NATIONAL FOREST

your climb and a result in a thousand-dollar bill. If you value your vehicle, leave it lower rather than higher.

20T2 – Tobin Creek 4WD Trailhead 8,820 feet 37.5344° -105.5427°

This trailhead provides access to Little Bear's Southwest Ridge Route (20R6). From the US 160–Colorado 150 junction 5.5 miles northwest of the town of Blanca, go 2.6 miles north on Colorado 150 and turn east onto Road 4.4 (dirt), leading straight east (37.5128° -105.6025°). Road 4.4 is 0.6 mile south of the unmarked road leading northeast to Lake Como; if you get to the Lake Como road, you have gone too far.

Go 2.5 miles east on the good Road 4.4 to a junction (37.5126° -105.5576°) on the Alamosa–Costilla county line. Turn 45 degrees northeast (left) and climb 1.2 miles northeast along the county line to 8,300 feet on a much rougher road. This extremely rocky road is rough enough that it is only suited to high-clearance vehicles. Enter the Rio Grande National Forest, turn 45 degrees north (left), leave the county line, and go 0.65 mile north on a slightly better road to 8,820 feet (37.5344° -105.5427°), where the road turns downhill to the west. Park at this turn; this is as close as you can drive to Little Bear and this is the trailhead. There is parking for a few vehicles at this unmarked trailhead.

20T3 – Lily Lake Trailhead 10,670 feet 37.6219° -105.4728°

This trailhead provides access to Mount Lindsey and the northeast faces of Blanca Peak and Ellingwood Point. *Huerfano* means "orphan boy" in Spanish; as you travel to this trailhead deep in the long Huerfano Valley, you will appreciate this appropriate name. Take Exit 52 from Interstate 25 north of Walsenburg and go 0.3 mile south toward Walsenburg. Turn west onto Colorado 69, go 25.1 miles to Gardner, and continue 0.7 mile to the far side of town. Turn west onto the Redwing spur of Colorado 69 (paved) and measure from this point. Go straight at mile 5.1, continue on the dirt road at mile 6.9, and go straight at mile 7.1. Do not turn left into Redwing. Turn left at a Y-junction at mile 12.0 and reach the entrance to the Singing River Ranch at mile 16.0. The road is plowed to this point in winter.

Public access is allowed from the Singing River Ranch to the San Isabel National Forest. Do not camp on the private land you are traveling through. The road becomes rougher at the Singing River Ranch but is still passable for most passenger cars. Pass the entrance to the Aspen River Ranch at mile 16.9, pass a distant view of Blanca Peak at mile 19.4, and reach the boundary of San Isabel National Forest at mile 20.4. The road becomes rougher at this point but is still passable for some passenger vehicles. Reach the end of the road and the trailhead at mile 22.5. The last mile to the trailhead is steep and may challenge low-power, low-clearance vehicles. The trailhead is at the south end of a sloping, hanging meadow above the Huerfano River; there is a good view of Blanca's northeast face from the meadow. Mount Lindsey is not visible from the trailhead.

An alternative approach to this trailhead goes 1.9 miles west of North La Veta Pass on US 160, then 12.3 miles north on Pass Creek Road (dirt) to join the route just described 2.0 miles east of the Redwing turn.

20A – Blanca Group Approach

20A1 – Blanca Group – Lake Como Approach

From Lake Como TH at 8,000'	139 RP	11.2 mi RT	3,900' total	Class 1
From Lake Como at 11,760'	8 RP	0.8 mi RT	140' total	Class 1

This is the standard approach to Blanca Peak, Little Bear, and Ellingwood Point. Start at the Lake Como Trailhead at 8,000 feet. It is 5.2 tough miles from the 8,000-foot level to Lake Como at 11,760 feet. Go up the rough then tortured 4WD road as it switchbacks toward the heights still far away. The first miles can be brutally hot in summer. The road enters the Rio Grande National Forest at 8,800 feet (37.5509° -105.5597°), steepens, climbs along Chokecherry Canyon, then angles northeast toward Holbrook Creek, which it crosses at 10,690 feet (37.5691° -105.5343°). The alleged road continues east on the north side of the creek to Lake Como at 11,760 feet (37.5701° -105.5156°). Hike 0.2 mile east around the north side of the lake and continue 0.2 mile southeast to some camping spots on the bench above the lake at 11,900 feet (37.5679° -105.5110°). Little Bear is less than a mile east of this spot, and its imposing northwest face dominates the view.

20. Blanca Peak 14,345 feet

20R – Blanca Peak Routes

20R1 – Blanca Peak – Northwest Face

From Lake Como TH at 8,000'	343 RP	15.0 mi RT	6,345' total	Class 2
From Lake Como at 11,760'	153 RP	4.6 mi RT	2,585' total	Class 2

This is the easiest route on Blanca. Because of the low-elevation trailhead, people usually do it with a backpack and camp. Start at the Lake Como Trailhead at 8,000 feet and follow the Lake Como Approach (20A1) to the camping area east of Lake Como at 11,900 feet (37.5679° -105.5110°). Still on the 4WD road, hike 0.5 mile east up the valley to the south side of Blue Lakes (37.5717° -105.5029°). There are more camping spots near Blue Lakes at 12,100 feet. When the seemingly ceaseless road finally fades, continue 0.5 mile northeast up the valley on a good trail to a point east of (beyond) Crater Lake at 12,900 feet (37.5780° -105.4925°). The connecting ridge between Blanca Peak and Ellingwood Point is at the top of the basin northeast (ahead) of you. Blanca is at the ridge's south end, and Ellingwood Point is at the north end.

Zigzag east on trail segments up a section of broken cliffs, then hike up talus to reach Blanca's north ridge at 13,800 feet (37.5802° -105.4870°). There are spectacular views down Blanca's northeast face from the ridge, but the ridge

Blanca Peak from the north.

itself is not exposed if you stay away from the edge. Follow the ridge southeast then south to Blanca's lofty, lauded summit (37.5777° -105.4855°).

The highpoint of both Alamosa and Costilla counties is at the mountain's highpoint. However, the highpoint of Costilla County is 53 feet northeast (37.5778° -105.4854°) of Blanca's summit. A vagary in where the county lines were drawn, the difference is moot for most since you climb past Costilla County's highpoint en route to Blanca's highpoint, but purists keep track of every foot.

20R2 – Blanca Peak – Gash Ridge

From Lily Lake TH at 10,670'   533 RP   8.6 mi RT   3,675' net; 4,315' total   Class 5.3–5.4

Gash Ridge is Blanca's dramatic east ridge. This ridge's classic sweep is interrupted only by its namesake gash halfway up. This aesthetic and exciting ridge is well seen from Lindsey and the Huerfano Valley. Retreat and escape are both difficult from this committing climb, and this is a route on which to exercise your craft as a mountaineer, not learn it.

Start at the Lily Lake Trailhead at 10,670 feet. Walk 1.2 miles south on the Lily Lake Trail along the west side of the Huerfano River to an often unsigned trail junction at 10,720 feet (37.6083° -105.4736°), where the Lily Lake Trail heads steeply up to the west. Don't turn west on the Lily Lake Trail but continue 1.2 miles south on the trail in the valley bottom to 10,960 feet (37.5906° -105.4777°). Blanca's sweeping northeast face soars above you, and this is one of Colorado's finest places. Gash Ridge marks the east (left) boundary of this great face. Leave the comfortable valley bottom and climb 0.5 mile steeply southeast to 12,000 feet (37.5862° -105.4724°) in a small, hanging side valley. Continue 0.4 mile south-southeast up this drainage to the 12,580-foot saddle (37.5812° -105.4712°) between Blanca and Point 13,100, aka "Huerfanito," which is 1.3 miles northeast of Blanca. Climb 0.3 mile west up the initially rounded ridge to Point 13,380 (37.5805° -105.4758°) and gaze across to the upper ridge. The introduction is over.

Descend 300 yards west to a 13,220-foot saddle and start your ascent of the upper ridge. The ridge averages 30 degrees as it gains 1,125 feet in 0.5 mile. The drops on either side of the ridge are considerably steeper, and the exposure on this climb is unrelenting. Just when you think that you are past the difficulties, you will arrive above the gash. Your best option is to rappel down the near-vertical cliff into the gash, which s a dramatic place. The climbing beyond the gash is Class 4 interspersed with Class 5.3–5.4 cruxes. Take care to find the easiest route, because more difficult climbing is never far away. The summit may surprise you.

20R2 V – Variation – South Ridge
Class 4

This important variation avoids Gash Ridge and provides the easiest route on Blanca from the Huerfano Valley. It is the easiest way to combine ascents of Blanca and Lindsey. From the 12,580-foot saddle (37.5812° -105.4712°) between Blanca and Point 13,100, aka "Huerfanito," descend 0.2 mile south to 12,100 feet (37.5786° -105.4708°). Contour 0.2 mile southwest, then climb 0.3 mile west-southwest to the north side of the northernmost of the two Winchell Lakes at 12,780 feet (37.5738° -105.4766°). Go around the east end of the lake, climb west, and climb a Class 4 ramp to reach Blanca's south ridge at 13,700 feet (37.5686° -105.4818°). Climb 0.7 mile north on this talus ridge to the summit (Class 2).

20R2 EC – Extra Credit – "Huerfanito" 13,100 feet 37.5858° -105.4632°
Class 2+

If climbing Gash Ridge is not enough, climb 0.5 mile northeast from the 12,580-foot saddle between Blanca and Point 13,081 to reach Point 13,081 (37.5846° -105.4639°), a ranked Thirteener (Class 2+). This rough little peak called "Huerfanito" provides a great view of Gash Ridge and Blanca's northeast face, and holds other surprises. A second summit 400 feet to the northeast (37.5858° -105.4632°) is a little higher and is the summit of the peak. "Huerfanito" is really 13,100 feet.

20R3 – Blanca Peak – Ormes Buttress *Classic*
From Lily Lake TH at 10,670'   706 RP   7.6 mi RT   3,675' net; 3,795' total   Class 5.6

After James Waddell Alexander II made the first ascent of his namesake Alexanders Chimney on the east face of Longs Peak in 1922 and Albert Ellingwood made the first ascent of his namesake Ellingwood Arête on Crestone Needle in 1925, the hunt was on for other great Colorado rock faces. A banner year was 1927; Paul and Joe Stettner returned to Longs and climbed their namesake Stettner's Ledges while Robert Ormes made the first ascent of Blanca's more evasive northeast face.

Blanca's northeast face is one of Colorado's largest mountain walls, but it is not easily seen from roads. Any view from civilization is a distant one, and this wall's majesty is reserved for those who hike up the Huerfano Valley. Ormes, a true pioneer, had a good eye for the natural line, and his route remains the classic and easiest way up Blanca's *Nordwand*.

Start at the Lily Lake Trailhead at 10,670 feet. Walk 1.2 miles south on the Lily Lake Trail along the west side of the Huerfano River to an often unsigned trail junction (37.6083° -105.4736°) at 10,720 feet on the south end of a meadow. Leave the valley trail, go west then north around the meadow, and find the Lily Lake Trail heading steeply up to the southwest. Continue 1.6 miles on the Lily Lake Trail to a switchback at 11,600 feet (37.5894° -105.4852°). This is the trail's closest approach to the face, and there are good campsites nestled in the trees nearby. Leave the trail and hike 0.4 mile southwest then south to the base of the face at 12,400 feet (37.5841° -105.4878°). Your approach is over.

You can now easily see the Ormes Buttress 700 feet northwest (right) of the center of Blanca's northeast face. It provides the only major break in this mile-wide face. Climb it! The lower part of the buttress is Class 4 climbing on loose rock. The rock becomes more solid as you climb higher. Several Class 5 pitches, including a Class 5.6 crux, take you up the great wall. Stay on or left of the crest. A helmet is highly recommended for this climb. Leaders, remember to protect your belayer.

The buttress reaches Blanca's north ridge at 13,860 feet (37.5800° -105.4868°). For a true mountaineer, the summit is never off-route. In the spirit of Ormes, hike 0.25 mile south up the ridge to Blanca's highest point. Revel.

20. Little Bear Peak 14,037 feet

20R – Little Bear Peak Routes
20R4 – Little Bear Peak – West Ridge

From Lake Como TH at 8,000'	402 RP	13.5 mi RT	6,037' net; 6,197' total	Class 4–5.2
From Lake Como at 11,760'	220 RP	3.1 mi RT	2,277' net; 2,437' total	Class 4–5.2

This is the most frequently climbed route on Little Bear, but it is not Little Bear's easiest route. The easiest route—from Arrowhead Ranch to the south— is not open to the public. The West Ridge Route is short and sweet, but it is also one of the most dangerous routes in this book. Loose rocks abound on the rounded ledges on the upper part of the route, and large parties can turn it into a deadly shooting gallery. I think the Hourglass (see below) is the

Little Bear Peak from Lake Como.

most dangerous spot on any of the standard routes on Colorado's Fourteeners. This route is particularly dangerous when crowds arrive on three-day holiday weekends. Avoid Little Bear's fatal attraction; climb during the week, wear a helmet, and start early.

Use the Lake Como Approach (20A1). From the east side of Lake Como, Little Bear is only a mile away, and the challenge is obvious. Little Bear's west ridge forms the wall south of Lake Como, and the connecting ridge between Little Bear and Blanca is east of the lake. These two ridges cap a single face—Little Bear's northwest face. This face is most imposing directly under Little Bear's summit.

From the campsites at 11,900 feet east of Lake Como (37.5679° -105.5110°), look straight south to see a steep, north-facing gully leading to a distinctive notch in the lower part of Little Bear's west ridge. This gully often retains some snow through July. Climb this loose scree- or snow-filled gully into the 12,580-foot notch (37.5641° -105.5057°). From the notch, go 0.25 east on the ridge crest to Point 12,980 (37.5645° -105.5110°), where you can see the rest of the route. Little Bear's west ridge steepens dramatically beyond Point 12,980, and the route avoids these difficulties by ascending the easily seen, deep gully in the center of the small face south (right) of Little Bear's west ridge.

From Point 12,980, descend 0.15 east to the 12,900-foot saddle (37.5650° -105.5038°) between Point 12,980 and Little Bear. From the saddle, leave the west ridge and follow a use trail that climbs 0.3 mile east into the center of Little Bear's small, southwest face. The trail takes you to the base of the Hourglass—a steep, deep gully.

After an initial 100 feet of Class 3 scrambling, climb 150 feet up the steep, water-polished Class 4 rock in the gully. This long pitch is the route's crux, and there is usually a sling rappel anchor at its top. If it has rained the afternoon or night before your climb, there may be water running down the center of the gully to complicate your ascent. If so, climb the rock 10 to 15 feet north (left) of the gully's center (5.0–5.2).

Above the Class 4 pitch, the angle and difficulty ease, but your responsibility increases, since any rocks knocked loose during your final climb will funnel down into the Class 4 gully. Finish the ascent with several hundred feet of Class 3 scrambling up steep sections between rubble-covered ledges. Angle slightly north (left) and arrive directly on the coveted summit (37.5666° –105.4972°).

20R5 – Little Bear Peak – Northwest Face

From Lake Como TH at 8,000'	*542 RP*	*13.0 mi RT*	*6,037' total*	*Class 4–5.2*
From Lake Como at 11,760'	*366 RP*	*3.2 mi RT*	*2,277' total*	*Class 4–5.2*

This climb flirts with the major difficulties of Little Bear's imposing northwest face but avoids them at the last minute. The scene of a fatal accident, this route is not a safer or easier alternative to the Hourglass.

Use the Lake Como Approach (20A1). From the campsites at 11,900 feet east of Lake Como (37.5679° –105.5110°), go 0.3 mile northeast. Before you reach Blue Lakes, leave the road and choose your line for climbing the sweeping, ever steepening slabs of Little Bear's northwest face. Aim for the first small, rounded notch in the ridge northeast (left) of Little Bear's summit. After an initial Class 4 headwall east of some black watermarks, several hundred feet of enjoyable Class 3 scrambling will take you to a steeper headwall below the ridge. This headwall is north (left) of the more serious face directly under Little Bear's summit.

Choose your line carefully and continue your climb. The headwall requires 400 feet of Class 4–5.2 climbing. The steepest, most exposed, and most difficult moves are just below the ridge. From the ridge, climb 300 yards south up the elegant, exposed Class 4 ridge to the summit. Ascending this route and descending the West Ridge Route (20R4) makes a stunning Tour de Little Bear.

20R6 – Little Bear Peak – Southwest Ridge

From Tobin Creek 4WD TH at 8,820'	*494 RP*	*8.0 mi RT*	*5,217' net; 6,000' total* *Class 4*

In recent years, this ridge has evolved as an alternate route up Little Bear because it avoids the dangerous Hourglass on Little Bear's West Ridge Route (20R4). However, before you lunge at this route, consider several trade-offs. This route's big advantage is that, indeed, you do not have to go up or down the Hourglass, and a minor advantage is that you can bag 14,020-foot "South Little Bear," an unranked subsummit. Another advantage of the Southwest Ridge Route is that when the Hourglass is chocked with unstable snow in June, the ridge route is likely to be mostly free of snow. The biggest disadvantage of the Southwest Ridge Route is that, unless you choose to bivouac on a waterless ridge, you must do this route in a day from your vehicle, and this requires a whopping 6,000 feet of elevation gain. All of the route requires rough off-trail bushwhacking or talus hopping, much of it exposed to the weather high on the mountain. The southwest ridge is replete with angular, obnoxious talus that extends below treeline. Like the Hourglass, the southwest ridge is also rated Class 4, since there are several places high on the southwest ridge where you must do testy traverses and downclimbs. The long southwest ridge also has a great deal of poised loose rock lurking on much of the upper ridge, and this route's loose rock hazard may be commensurate with the Hourglass. The top of the Southwest Ridge Route traverses above the Hourglass and joins the West Ridge Route for the final climb to the summit. Any rocks that you dislodge above the Hourglass could easily hurt or kill a climber who happens to be in the Hourglass. So, while you do not have to be in the Hourglass, your responsibility above it is just as great as a climber summiting the West Ridge Route. Consider these caveats, then make a route choice that best balances them. If you choose the Southwest Ridge Route, leave early and take lots of water.

From the Tobin Creek 4WD Trailhead at 8,820 feet, bushwhack 0.4 mile northeast through the trees, descend, and cross Tobin Creek near 9,100 feet (37.5384° -105.5369°). Finding a route through the thorny bushes that clog the creek is your initial obstacle, but the creek crossing itself is not difficult. Go 100 yards east of Tobin Creek to find thinner vegetation, then climb 0.5 mile steeply north over rough talus-infested terrain to reach the crest of the southwest ridge at 10,000 feet (37.5453° -105.5353°). The introduction is over; only 4,000 feet to go.

The well-defined southwest ridge is your ticket to the top. Climb 1.6 miles northeast up the ridge to Point 12,900 (37.5575° -105.5129°), a minor ridge bump from which you will have a stunning view of Little Bear's west face and the Hourglass. Continue 0.4 mile east on or near the ridge crest to Point 13,133 (37.5580° -105.5062°), a more prominent ridge bump offering a foreshortened view of the upper ridge. Staying near the ridge crest to enjoy the most stable blocks, continue scampering 0.5 mile east-northeast past several more minor ridge bumps and notches topping spectacular north-facing couloirs to 13,400 feet (37.5604° -105.4985°), where the ridge steepens. Begin your ascent of "South Little Bear" by climbing 0.2 mile northeast up the increasingly exciting ridge to a small, 13,860-foot summit (37.5624° -105.4966°) from which you will have a disheartening view of your remaining climb. Continue 200 yards north-northeast, passing below a Class 4 knife-edge on its east side en route, to reach 14,020-foot "South Little Bear" (37.5643° -105.4962°). This subsummit is important because it is over 14,000 feet, and it provides a unique view of the Little Bear–Blanca ridge. You are only 17 feet below Little Bear's summit, but 400 yards of the route's most difficult scrambling remains.

Descend north from "South Little Bear" and scramble down on the west side of the ridge to avoid a narrow, jutting fin on the ridge crest. Get back on the ridge crest and continue north near the exposed ridge crest past small but dramatic notches and more knife-edges. As summit fever grows, you will look down into the deep notch at the top of the Hourglass. To avoid the too-steep ridge crest, descend on the west face to a series of ledges that take you north across small gullies into the Hourglass' 13,940-foot notch (37.5659° -105.4967°). It is here that you must take extra care to avoid sending missiles down into the Hourglass. From the notch, join one of the finishes of the West Ridge Route (20R4), and climb north up easy but rubble-strewn ledges to Little Bear's summit (37.5666° -105.4972°).

Use extreme caution all the way to the summit, then enjoy it before facing your descent. It can take as long to descend this route as it does to ascend it, and the afternoon sun on the lower ridge can be brutally hot. Grin a little and Bear it.

20. Ellingwood Point 14,042 feet

20R – Ellingwood Point Routes

20R7 – Ellingwood Point – South Face

From Lake Como TH at 8,000'	320 RP	15.2 mi RT	6,042' total	Class 2
From Lake Como at 11,760'	138 RP	4.8 mi RT	2,282' total	Class 2

This is the easiest route on Ellingwood Point. Use the Lake Como Approach (20A1) and follow Blanca's Northwest Face Route (20R1) to 13,320 feet (37.5802° -105.4906°). From here, scamper 0.5 mile northeast then northwest up steep talus to the pointed summit (37.5825° -105.4917°).

20R8 – Ellingwood Point – Southwest Ridge *Classic*

From Lake Como TH at 8,000'	412 RP	14.5 mi RT	6,042' total	Class 3
From Lake Como at 11,760'	229 RP	4.1 mi RT	2,282' total	Class 3

This is a nifty alternative to the talus on Ellingwood's south face. Follow the South Face Route (20R7) to a tiny lake at 12,540 feet (37.5759° -105.5006°). This lake is near the junction of the Twin Peaks and Blanca Peak quadrangles, but does not appear on either map. From the lake, angle 300 yards north up a ledge system (some Class 3) to reach Ellingwood's southwest ridge at 12,940 feet (37.5773° -105.5010°).

The ascent of this elegant ridge is pure fun. The rock is solid, the Class 3 scrambling is continuous, the motion is fluid, and there are no nasty notches or other surprises on the ridge. Scramble 0.7 mile up one of Colorado's finest ridges to the summit. Ascending the southwest ridge and descending the south face makes a sporting Tour de Ellingwood. Ellingwood's southwest ridge is a good tune-up for the Little Bear–Blanca traverse (Combination 20C2).

Ellingwood Point
14,042

Ellingwood Point from the north.

20R9 – Ellingwood Point – North Ridge

From Lily Lake TH at 10,670'   549 RP   7.9 mi RT   3,372' net; 3,492' total   Class 5.0–5.2

This obtuse route is only for exposure-hardened scramblers. It has proven fatal, but for the initiated it provides a wild alternative to the crowded Lake Como routes. Start at the Lily Lake Trailhead at 10,670 feet. Walk 1.2 miles south on the Lily Lake Trail along the west side of the Huerfano River to an often unsigned trail junction at 10,720 feet (37.6083° -105.4736°) on the south end of a meadow. Leave the valley trail, go west then north around the meadow, and find the Lily Lake Trail heading steeply up to the southwest. Continue 1.6 miles on the Lily Lake Trail to a switchback at 11,600 feet (37.5894° -105.4852°). This is the trail's closest approach to Ellingwood, and there are good campsites nestled in the trees nearby.

Leave the trail and hike 0.4 mile west to 12,600 feet, below a broken rock wall 300 yards north of the base of Ellingwood's north face. Climb this 600-foot wall (Class 5.0–5.2) to the 13,220-foot saddle (37.5880° -105.4952°) between Ellingwood Point and unranked Point 13,618, which is 0.65 mile north of Ellingwood. From the saddle, climb 0.2 mile south then 0.25 mile southeast to the summit (Class 5.0–5.2). This ridge is tricky. Climb on the west (right) side of the ridge to avoid serious difficulties. The last 150 yards to the summit is the crux section of the route. Judicious Class 5.0–5.2 climbing below the ridge crest on the exposed face to the west will take you to the highest point.

20C – Blanca, Little Bear, and Ellingwood Combination Routes

20C1 – Blanca Northwest Face → Ellingwood South Face

From Lake Como TH at 8,000'   *383 RP*   *15.8 mi RT*   *6,887' total*   *Class 2*

From Lake Como at 11,760'   *192 RP*   *5.4 mi RT*   *3,127' total*   *Class 2*

This is the standard way of climbing Blanca and Ellingwood together. Follow Blanca's Northwest Face Route (20R1) to Blanca's summit. Descend Blanca's north ridge to 13,800 feet then descend west below the ridge to 13,500 feet. Contour north on the talus below the cliffs on the connecting ridge, join Ellingwood's South Face Route, and continue on that route to Ellingwood's summit. Descend Ellingwood's South Face Route (20R7).

20C1 V – Variation – High Line

Class 3

There is a high traverse near, but not quite on, the connecting ridge between Blanca and Ellingwood. Follow a cairned route that contours through the rocks 100 feet below the ridge crest on the ridge's west side. Some Class 3 scrambling is required.

20C2 – Little Bear West Ridge → Blanca East Ridge *Classic*

From Lake Como TH at 8,000'   *803 RP*   *15.4 mi RT*   *6,882' total*   *Class 5.0–5.2*

From Lake Como at 11,760'   *612 RP*   *5.0 mi RT*   *3,122' total*   *Class 5.0–5.2*

The traverse between Little Bear and Blanca is one of Colorado's four great Fourteener traverses, and it is the most difficult of the four. Simply put, this is Colorado's most astonishing connecting ridge. Escape from this doubly exposed ridge is difficult, and this ridge is an unhappy place to be during a storm. Choose your weather carefully before attempting this traverse. Time spent on the ridge varies from two to eight hours. The traverse is best done from Little Bear to Blanca.

Use the Lake Como Approach (20A1) and climb Little Bear's West Ridge Route (20R4) to Little Bear's summit. Look at Blanca 1.0 miles away and consider your future. If you like what you see, descend 300 yards north down a solid, exposed ridge (Class 4). This initial stretch of ridge is a tricky downclimb and is one of the traverse's cruxes. Continue northeast along the crest of the incredibly exposed ridge. The movement is often awkward because you must climb directly along the ridge crest—there are seldom any alternatives. There is a great deal of Class 3 scrambling, a lot of Class 4 climbing, and some Class 5.0–5.2 moves. The protection offered by using a rope on this ridge is marginal, and it will slow your progress drastically.

One-quarter of the way along the ridge, you come to a square 30-foot-high tower on the ridge that blocks easy passage. You can easily see this tower from the vicinity of Blue Lakes in the valley below, and it is a good landmark to mark your progress. Although you have stayed on the ridge crest to this point, you should pass this tower on its west (left) side via a short, exposed Class 4 traverse. This tower has been dubbed Captain Bivwacko Tower because those who climb to its summit are more likely to bivouac. Beyond Captain Bivwacko Tower, scramble back to the ridge crest and continue on or very near the still very exposed ridge crest over several more rolling summits. Slowly, the difficulty relents and you can increase your speed.

Near the halfway point, you will pass the 13,660-foot Little Bear–Blanca saddle (37.5735° -105.4921°). Beyond this saddle, the exposure eases. Two-thirds of the way across, a large gendarme (Point 13,860) blocks easy progress along the ridge crest. Bypass Point 13,860 via an easy scree slope on its south (right) side and climb into a deep notch (37.5755° -105.4901°) on the ridge crest via a loose gully. On the north side of this notch is a horrific chimney that you can see from Crater Lake. The only easy escape off this ridge is south from this notch, but this escape creates other problems because it leaves you in Blanca Basin, far from your camp.

From the notch east of Point 13,860, climb along the now easier ridge crest to yet another incredibly exposed knife-edge. Creep across this scary but solid ridge, cross a final subsummit and notch, then climb an easier but still steep ridge to Blanca's summit. Descend Blanca's Northwest Face Route (20R1).

20C3 – Little Bear West Ridge → Blanca East Ridge → Blanca North Ridge → Ellingwood South Face

From Lake Como TH at 8,000'	851 RP	16.6 mi RT	7,424' total	Class 5.0–5.2
From Lake Como at 11,760'	660 RP	6.2 mi RT	3,664' total	Class 5.0–5.2

This traverse is for the insatiable peak bagger; it collects Little Bear, Blanca, and Ellingwood Point in one swell swoop. Do the traverse from Little Bear to Blanca as described in Combination 20C2, then continue to Ellingwood as described in Combination 20C1.

20. Mount Lindsey 14,042 feet

20R – Mount Lindsey Routes
20R10 – Mount Lindsey – North Face

From Lily Lake TH at 10,670'   232 RP   8.6 mi RT   3,372' net; 3,492' total   Class 2+

This is not the easiest route on Lindsey, but it is the easiest route available to the public. It has been the standard route for many years, and it is a rewarding, scenic tour. Start at the Lily Lake Trailhead at 10,670 feet and walk south on the Lily Lake Trail, then descend 100 feet to the west side of a large meadow. Continue south on the trail on the west side of the Huerfano River, and 0.8 mile from the trailhead you'll reach an often unsigned trail junction at 10,670 feet (37.6123° -105.4748°). Stay straight, and continue 280 yards south on the trail in the valley bottom to a point where the trail reaches the Huerfano River (37.6100°

Mount Lindsey from the north.

-105.4747°) and cross to the southeast side of the river. This crossing can be difficult in June but is easy in August. After the crossing, go south on a boggy multi-threaded trail in the trees along the river's east side.

Continue on the climber's trail as it leaves the Huerfano River Valley and climbs steeply southeast along the right side of a talus field into a small side valley west of Points 12,410 and 12,915. Cross the unnamed creek in this side valley and enter a small, beautiful basin at 12,000 feet (37.5939° -105.4648°). There is a spectacular view of Blanca's northeast face from here, and you can just see Lindsey's summit pyramid poking above an intermediate, west-facing ridge. Continue on the climber's trail southeast across the basin and hike up a grassy ramp to meet the west ridge at 13,000 feet. Climb 200 yards east up this ridge to reach Lindsey's northwest ridge at 13,160 feet (37.5899° -105.4541°). Lindsey's more difficult upper slopes are plainly visible from here, and the introduction is over.

Go 0.2 mile southeast on Lindsey's northwest ridge until the ridge steepens at 13,200 feet (37.5882° -105.4521°), then follow a strong climber's trail that leaves the ridge and angles into Lindsey's north face. Climb a steep, rubble-filled chute (Class 2+) or the rock to the north (right) of the chute (Class 3) to a tiny col, then continue doing a long ascending traverse across the broken face (Class 2+). The route is steep and loose, and there is occasional exposure. Reach the crest of Lindsey's upper northwest ridge at 13,980 feet (37.5846° -105.4461°), turn southeast (left), and hike 200 yards up the easy upper ridge to the summit (37.5837° -105.4448°).

20R10 V – Variation – Northwest Ridge

Class 3

From 13,160 feet (37.5899° -105.4541°), follow the crest of the northwest ridge all the way to the summit. The ridge crest requires some exposed Class 3 scrambling on surprisingly solid rock. This airy alternative avoids the north face's loose rock. Comparing this ridge with the north face provides a good example of the difference between Class 2+ scampering and Class 3 scrambling. This comparison is also a good example of how a solid but harder route can be preferable to a looser, easier route.

20R10 EC1 – Extra Credit – "Northwest Lindsey" 14,020 feet 37.5852° -105.4472°

Class 2

From 13,980 feet on the summit ridge (37.5846° -105.4461°), hike 200 yards northwest to a tiny, 14,040-foot summit dubbed "Northwest Lindsey." The redeeming features of this summit are that it is over 14,000 feet and provides a suspended viewpoint. The Northwest Ridge Variation (20R10 V) crosses this summit.

20R10 EC2 – Extra Credit – Iron Nipple 13,500 feet 37.5938° -105.4550°

Class 2+

From 13,160 feet on Lindsey's northwest ridge (37.5899° -105.4541°), scamper 0.2 mile north to the Iron Nipple's 13,500-foot summit (Class 2+). Iron Nipple is an officially named but unranked Thirteener.

20R10 EC3 – Extra Credit – "Huerfano Peak" 13,828 feet 37.6004° -105.4477°

Class 2

For even more extra fun, traverse 0.6 mile northeast across talus from Iron Nipple to Point 13,828 known as "Huerfano Peak," one of Colorado's 100 highest ranked peaks.

20R11 – Mount Lindsey – North Couloir

From Lily Lake TH at 10,670'	*430 RP*	*9.6 mi RT*	*3,372' net; 5,412' total*	*Class 2, Mod Snow*
With descent of North Face	*367 RP*	*9.1 mi RT*	*3,372' net; 4,452' total*	*Class 2, Mod Snow*

This couloir provides an isolated spring snow climb. In most years, the couloir retains snow through June. It is best avoided after the snow melts. Follow the North Face Route (20R10) to Lindsey's northwest ridge at 13,160 feet. Descend 0.7 mile east to the bottom of the couloir at 12,200 feet. Climb 0.7 mile south up the easy then moderate couloir directly to the summit. Ascending the North Couloir Route and descending the North Face Route provides a simple Tour de Lindsey.

21. Culebra Peak 14,047 feet

Culebra is Colorado's southernmost Fourteener. The peak hides in the southern end of the Sangres only 9 miles from the New Mexico border. *Culebra* means "harmless snake" in Spanish; perhaps the peak acquired this name because of its gentle nature and long, curving, snakelike northwest ridge. This ridge is Culebra's distinguishing feature, and you can see it from Colorado 159 near the town of San Luis.

All of Culebra is privately owned. There is no public land near Culebra, and the peak is not covered on any National Forest map. As a result, the choice of routes has been limited to one in recent years. Culebra climbers should respect the landowner's wishes lest one choice becomes zero choices. The allowed access is through the Culebra Ranch west of the peak.

Culebra Ranch allows climbing by permission only during June, July, and part of August. The ranch closes to climbers in September, when preparations for hunting season begin. The ranch is closed in winter. Reservations are required, and you must call the ranch foreman at 719-672-3580 to make arrangements. The ranch does not set a limit to party size, but they do like to know how many people are in each party. The charge for climbing Culebra is $100 per person per day. Unless the road is too muddy, you will be allowed to drive a 4WD vehicle above the ranch, and this can vastly reduce the length of your climb. Camping is allowed on the peak above the ranch.

Climbers who don't like to pay a fee for climbing should consider that the ranch has invested a lot of money in road improvements, something the Forest Service rarely does. If you have suffered on the South Colony or Lake Como roads, you will find the Culebra Ranch roads refreshingly smooth. Almost half of your climbing fee is used to compensate the ranch for their road improvements to Fourway and beyond. If you walk or drive on this road, you are using what you paid for. Attempts to subvert the ranch's rules can quickly double your fee or worse, and will definitely hurt the climbing community. Don't attach your name to the demise of the permission that allows climbers to ascend Culebra. Remember that you are a guest.

21E – Culebra Peak Essentials

Elevations	14,047' (NGVD29) 14,051' (NAVD88)
Rank	Colorado's 41st highest ranked peak
Location	Costilla County, Colorado, USA
Range	Southern Sangre de Cristo Range
Summit Coordinates	37.1222° -105.1857° (WGS84)
Ownership/Contact	Culebra Ranch – Private Land – 719-672-3580
Prominence and Saddle	4,827' from 9,220' Veta Pass

21E – Culebra Peak Essentials

Isolation and Parent	35.56 miles to Blanca Peak
USGS Maps	**Culebra Peak, El Valle Creek,** Taylor Ranch
USFS Map	None
Trails Illustrated Map	Colorado 14ers Trails Illustrated Explorer
Book Map	See Map 21 on page 219
Nearest Towns	San Luis – Population 640 – Elevation 7,979'
	Fort Garland – Population 390 – Elevation 7,936'
	Alamosa – Population 8,750 – Elevation 7,543'
Culebra Peak 🎿 Easiest Route	21R1 – Northwest Ridge – Class 2
	A Class 1 approach on a road and a Class 2 summit climb along a gentle, curving ridge
Culebra's Accolades	By a large margin, Culebra is Colorado's southernmost Fourteener. Far removed from other Fourteeners, the private ranch land around the peak is steeped in history. Culebra is the highest peak in the Sangre de Cristo Range between Blanca Peak and Santa Fe, New Mexico, and Culebra is the highest peak in its namesake subrange—the Culebra Range.

21T – Culebra Peak Trailheads

21T1 – Culebra Ranch Trailhead 9,320 feet 37.1481° -105.2828°

This trailhead provides access to Culebra's west side. From the center of San Luis on Colorado 159, go southeast on road P.6 (Fourth Street) and measure from this point. Go straight at mile 2.5 when P.6 crosses road 21. There is a stop sign at this intersection. Turn east-northeast (left) at mile 4.2 onto road L.7 at a T-junction in Chama (37.1617° -105.3807°). Turn south-southeast (right) onto road 22.3 at mile 4.5 (37.1626° -105.3751°) and cross Culebra Creek. Turn east-northeast (left) onto road M.5 at mile 4.7 (37.1608° -105.3746°). Follow road M.5 as it curves east and turns to dirt, and reach the two Culebra Ranch gates at mile 8.8 (37.1710° -105.3039°). With permission, go through the southern gate and continue south and finally east to the ranch buildings at mile 10.7 (37.1498° -105.2928°). Under new ownership, this ranch is now called Culebra Ranch. Stop at the ranch buildings and check in.

From the ranch, at 9,060 feet, continue east and go east (right) at mile 11.2 at a junction (37.1485° -105.2843°) where the Whiskey Pass Road goes north. At mile 11.3, reach a large meadow on the road's south side (37.1481° -105.2828°). This is the trailhead for passenger cars, and camping is permitted here.

21T1 4WD – Culebra Ranch 4WD Trailhead 11,700 feet 37.1389° -105.2149°

The road beyond the trailhead is in good shape but is very steep. It defeats many, but not all, passenger cars. The ranch closes the road when it is muddy. From the trailhead at 9,320 feet, 4WD vehicles can continue 3.0 miles east up the steep road to a road junction called Fourway at 11,220 feet (37.1422°

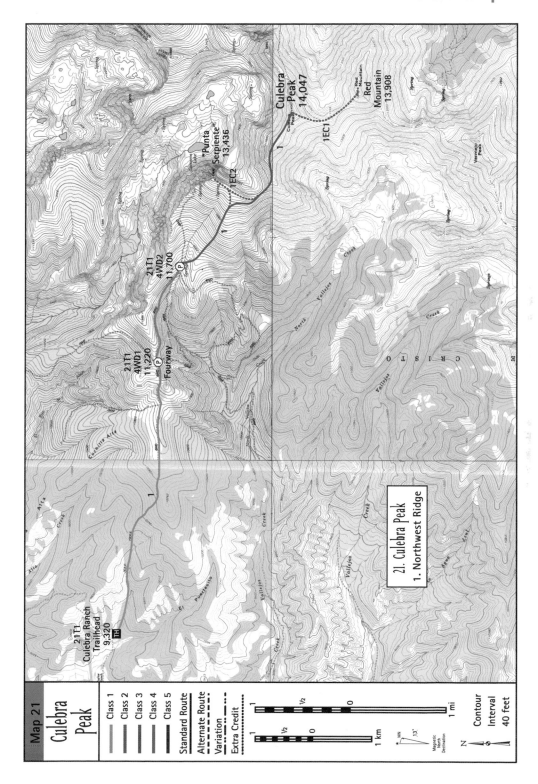

Map 21
Culebra Peak

— Class 1
— Class 2
— Class 3
— Class 4
— Class 5
— Standard Route
- - - Alternate Route
–·–·– Variation
········· Extra Credit

Contour
Interval
40 feet

21. Culebra Peak
1. Northwest Ridge

Culebra
Peak
14,047

Red
Mountain
13,908

"Punta
Serpiente"
13,436

1EC1

1EC2

2T1
4WD2
11,700

2T1
4WD1
11,220
Fourway

21T1
Culebra Ranch
Trailhead
9,320
TH

S A N G R E   D E   C R I S T O

Culebra Peak from the north.

-105.2325°). Camping is permitted here, but bring your own water. From Four-way, 4WD vehicles can continue 1.1 mile east to a parking area at the end of the road at 11,700 feet (37.1389° -105.2149°). Camping is permitted here near a small, seasonal stream.

21R – Culebra Peak Route
21R1 – Culebra Peak – Northwest Ridge

From Culebra Ranch TH at 9,320'	*325 RP*	*13.0 mi RT*	*4,727' total*	*Class 2*
From Fourway at 11,220'	*225 RP*	*7.0 mi RT*	*2,827' total*	*Class 2*
From Culebra Ranch 4WD TH at 11,700'	*192 RP*	*4.8 mi RT*	*2,347' total*	*Class 2*

This is Culebra's long, distinguishing, snakelike ridge. People sometimes malign the ridge because of its length. Taking a more distant view in either time or distance, you can view the ridge curving gracefully toward its source, Culebra's summit.

Start at the Culebra Ranch Trailhead at 9,320 feet and climb 3.0 miles east up the steep, straight, 4WD road to Fourway, a road junction in a saddle at 11,220 feet (37.1422° -105.2325°). From Fourway, continue climbing 1.1 miles east to the end of the road at 11,700 feet (37.1389° -105.2149°). There is good camping near here in a treeline meadow with a bubbling stream to serenade you.

From the end of the road, cross to the creek's south side. Climb 1.1 miles southeast up the shallow basin to 13,200 feet and contour 0.2 mile south-southeast to reach Culebra's northwest ridge in a 13,220-foot saddle (37.1269° -105.2008°) on the snake's back. From the saddle, climb the curving ridge 0.7 mile southeast then east to a 13,940-foot false summit (37.1247° -105.1912°). Continue 0.4 mile east-southeast in a gentle ascent to Culebra's coveted summit (37.1222° -105.1857°).

21R1 EC1 – Extra Credit – Red Mountain 13,908 feet 37.1122° -105.1812°

Class 2

There is an extra fee for climbing Red Mountain, so make sure you arrange this ascent with the ranch before starting up Culebra. You cannot simply pay for Red after an impromptu ascent.

From Culebra's summit, descend 0.3 mile south to a 13,500-foot saddle (37.1175° -105.1872°). Climb or skirt Point 13,599, a minor ridge bump, and descend 0.2 mile southeast to the 13,460-foot Culebra–Red saddle (37.1144° -105.1848°). From the saddle, climb 0.2 mile southeast up dirt-infested talus to 13,908-foot Red Mountain, one of Colorado's 100 highest ranked peaks.

21R1 EC2 – Extra Credit – "Punta Serpiente" 13,436 feet 37.1339° -105.1980°

Class 2

Either going to or coming from Culebra, take time to hike 0.5 mile north along the elevated arm of Culebra's curving, snakelike ridge to unranked Point 13,436, aka "Punta Serpiente." This marvelous, hallowed viewpoint allows you to survey a vast tract of Colorado's most pristine land. You may spot an elk herd grazing in the hidden Coneros Basin steeply below you to the northeast. I've often speculated that this private ranch land is better protected than the government-managed public lands.

Chapter Five

Elk Range

Introduction

The Elk Range lies south of Glenwood Springs and Interstate 70, and west of Aspen and Colorado 82. The Elk Range receives a lot of snow, and several major ski areas near Aspen take advantage of this fact. The Maroon Bells–Snowmass Wilderness embraces the range's beauty. Except for the famous views from the Maroon Lake Road, most of the Elks' high peaks are not visible from roads or towns. The Elks' exquisite beauty is reserved for those who penetrate the wilderness.

The Elks' seven Fourteeners are some of Colorado's most rugged and beautiful peaks. Often difficult and dangerous, these peaks will both inspire and challenge you. The crumbling, red sedimentary rock of the famous Maroon Bells southwest of Aspen is some of Colorado's worst rock, and it can be a nightmare to climb on for the uninitiated. While hiking in the green, lush, flower-laden valleys below, you may not understand the issue, but as soon as you cross what I call the Red Line, the flowers disappear and the rotten rock will quickly send your boots in unexpected directions. The rock on Snowmass Mountain and Capitol Peak at the northwest end of the range is better, and Capitol's north face offers some fine technical routes.

22. Capitol Peak 14,130 feet

Singular and stoic, Capitol stands supreme as the northernmost Elk Range Fourteener. Capitol leaps from its surrounding valleys, and the extensive wilderness around the peak shields it from road-bound travelers. The US Capitol building bears a faint resemblance to the stout peak, but the peak's elegant lines still challenge architects to match it.

Capitol has been called Colorado's hardest Fourteener. Many dispute that claim, but Capitol is certainly one of the hardest. Capitol's fame as a difficult peak is largely because of the northeast ridge's spectacular knife-edge. Capitol's easiest route, the Northeast Ridge Route (22R1), is Class 4, and many parties use a rope on it. Capitol's 1,800-foot-high north face is one of Colorado's highest mountain faces, and this great granite wall provides several technical climbs on fair to reasonable rock.

22E – Capitol Peak Essentials

Elevations	14,130' (NGVD29) 14,141' (NAVD88)
Rank	Colorado's 29th highest ranked peak
Location	Pitkin County, Colorado, USA
Range	Northern Elk Range
Summit Coordinates	39.1502° -107.0829° (WGS84)
Ownership/Contact	White River National Forest – Public Land – www.fs.fed.us/r2/whiteriver/ rangerdistricts/aspen_sopris/mb_scenic_site/index.shtml; 970-925-3445
Prominence and Saddle	1,750' from 12,380' Snowmass–Fravert Divide
Isolation and Parent	7.46 miles to Maroon Peak
USGS Maps	**Capitol Peak**, Highland Peak
USFS Map	White River National Forest
Trails Illustrated Map	Map #128 Maroon Bells/Redstone/Marble
Book Map	See Map 22 on page 224
Nearest Town	Aspen – Population 5,900 – Elevation 7,890'
Capitol Peak Easiest Route	22R1 – Northeast Ridge – Class 4
	A Class 1 approach on a trail to Capitol Lake, a Class 2+ hike to 13,664-foot "K2," and a Class 4 summit climb along the famous knife-edge ridge
Capitol's Accolades	Capitol, the northernmost Fourteener in the Elk Range, is widely considered to be Colorado's hardest Fourteener. The singular summit's abrupt rise and sheer north face make Capitol one of Colorado's most beautiful Fourteeners.

22T – Capitol Peak Trailhead
22T1 – Capitol Creek Trailhead 9,420 feet 39.2342° -107.0775°

This trailhead provides access to Capitol's north and east sides. Go 28.0 miles south on Colorado 82 from Glenwood Springs, or go 13.1 miles north on Colorado 82 from the roundabout on Aspen's northwest side, to the small town of Snowmass. Do not confuse the town of Snowmass with Snowmass Village. The town of Snowmass is on Colorado 82. In Snowmass, turn west onto Snowmass Creek Road (paved) and measure from this point. Turn right at a T-junction onto the Capitol Creek Road (paved) at mile 1.7, stay left at mile 1.9, straight at mile 3.2, straight at mile 4.7, and right at mile 5.9, where the road turns to dirt. Pass the Capitol Creek Guard Station at mile 8.0 and continue on the now very rough road to the trailhead at mile 9.5. The well-marked trailhead perches on a bench above Capitol Creek, and you can see Capitol Peak 6 miles to the south. In winter the Capitol Creek Road is closed 5.9 miles from Colorado 82.

22A – Capitol Peak Approaches
22A1 – Capitol Peak – Capitol Creek Approach
From Capitol Creek TH at 9,420' 129 RP 1 2.4 mi RT 2,180' net; 2,980' total *Class 1*

This is the easiest and standard approach to Capitol. Start at the Capitol Creek Trailhead at 9,420 feet, descend 0.7 mile southwest on the Capitol Creek Trail

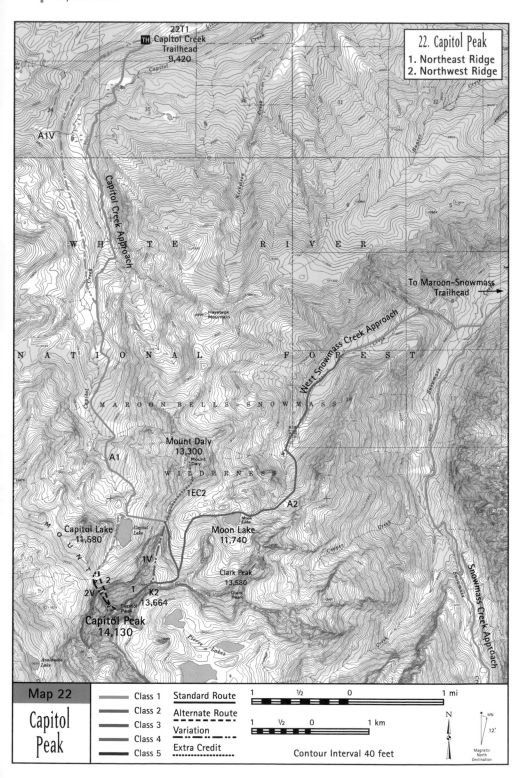

22. Capitol Peak
1. Northeast Ridge
2. Northwest Ridge

Capitol Creek Trailhead 9,420 22T1

A1V

To Maroon-Snowmass Trailhead →

W H I T E   R I V E R

Capitol Creek Approach

West Snowmass Creek Approach

N A T I O N A L   F O R E S T

M A R O O N   B E L L S   S N O W M A S S

Mount Daly 13,300

W I L D E R N E S S

1EC2

A1

A2

Capitol Lake 11,580

Moon Lake 11,740

1V

Clark Peak 13,580

2
1
K2 13,664

2V

Snowmass Creek Approach

Capitol Peak 14,130

Map 22

Capitol Peak

Class 1 — Standard Route
Class 2 — Alternate Route
Class 3 — Variation
Class 4 — Extra Credit
Class 5

1   ½   0   1 mi
1   ½   0   1 km

N

MN 12°
Magnetic North Declination

Contour Interval 40 feet

Capitol Peak from the north.

(FT 1961), and cross Capitol Creek on a good bridge at 9,020 feet (39.2270° -107.0836°). Your return trip up this 400-foot hill will compensate for your easy start. From the south side of Capitol Creek, walk 2.0 miles southwest then south up the valley on FT 1961 on Capitol Creek's east side to a trail junction with the Ditch Trail (22A1 V) and continue 0.2 mile south across a creek to another trail junction (39.2023° -107.0843°) with the West Snowmass Trail (FT 1927). Stay on the Capitol Creek Trail and hike another 3.3 arduous miles southwest then south to scenic Capitol Lake at 11,600 feet (39.1641° -107.0810°). Tantalizing peekaboo views of Capitol will accent your approach hike, and from the lake there will be no doubt about Capitol's stature. Fires are not allowed near the lake, and you cannot camp within 300 feet of the shore; there are good campsites on a tree-covered knoll 200 yards north of the lake (39.1656° -107.0825°).

22A1 V – Variation – West Side Story Approach

From Capitol Creek TH at 9,420'   124 RP   13.0 mi RT   2,180' net; 2,340' total   Class 1

There is a slightly longer, scenic trail on Capitol Creek's west side that avoids the initial 400-foot drop to Capitol Creek, and because of this, it has become

Returning across Capitol's knife edge. Photo by Austin Porzak

more popular in recent years. From the west end of the trailhead parking area, descend southwest on the signed Ditch Trail to a path paralleling a ditch. Hike 1.2 miles southwest as the Ditch Trail contours across the hillside; watch out for cows. At a junction at 9,500 feet, cross to the west side of the ditch, leave it, and continue 0.4 mile southwest on a good trail leading uphill through the trees. After crossing a side creek, enter the Maroon Bells–Snowmass Wilderness at 9,580 feet at a second creek crossing (39.2211° -107.0959°). Continue 1.2 miles south-southeast on the trail through aspens then a wonderful open area, and descend slightly to a flat meadow near Capitol Creek at 9,580 feet (39.2050° -107.0854°). You can see Capitol Peak from this meadow. Look sharp for, and take, a trail heading southeast across the meadow toward the creek. Cross Capitol Creek at 9,580 feet then climb 0.1 mile east to join the Capitol Creek Trail at 9,600 feet. Turn south (right) and continue on that trail to Capitol Lake.

22A2 – Capitol Peak – West Snowmass Creek Approach

From Maroon-Snowmass TH at 8,380'   *191 RP*   *11.2 mi RT*   *3,360' net; 3,400' total*   *Class 2*

This is a rougher, Class 2, seldom-used alternative to the popular Capitol Creek Approach that you can also use to reach Capitol's Northeast Ridge Route (22R1). It slightly shorter but has more elevation gain and a tough creek crossing. Start at the Maroon–Snowmass Trailhead (23T1; 39.2005° -106.9902°) at 8,380 feet (see Snowmass Mountain) and walk 1.4 miles west then southwest up Snowmass Creek's south then east side on the Maroon–Snowmass Trail (FT 1975) to the junction with the West Snowmass Trail (FT 1927) (39.1925° -107.0123°). Leave the Maroon–Snowmass Trail, descend west, and ford Snowmass Creek. During the spring and summer runoff, Snowmass Creek is a raging torrent that is difficult to cross, and this creek crossing can easily be the crux of your adventure. The idyllic meadow on the west side of the creek will lure you on.

Once on Snowmass Creek's west side, stroll across the meadow, rediscover the West Snowmass Trail, and hike 1.8 miles northwest then southwest on the West Snowmass Trail to the north edge of another Elysian meadow at 9,900 feet (39.1845° -107.0445°). Here, the trail descends south to the meadow and ends at a camp used by commercial horsepackers. Descend south to the meadow, leave the trail, go to the extreme southwest edge of the meadow, and get on a small trail climbing south up the open east-facing slope above the meadow. Follow this trail as it climbs several hundred feet above West Snowmass Creek to a bench, then contours south to reach the creek in another meadow at 10,400 feet (39.1733° -107.0500°). Cross to West Snowmass Creek's east side, continue on a faint trail that climbs south above the east side of the creek, then climb gently west through intermittent meadows and rocks to a final meadow at 11,400 feet (39.1649° -107.0549°). Climb west up a boulder slope to Moon Lake at 11,740 feet (39.1642° -107.0587°).

Moon Lake is rock-bound; the best camping is well below the lake in the trees. When moving beyond Moon Lake, you can go around either side of the lake, but the north side is the most expedient route.

22R – Capitol Peak Routes

22R1 – Capitol Peak – Northeast Ridge *Classic*

From Capitol Creek TH at 9,420'	*411 RP*	*16.8 mi RT*	*4,710' net; 5,610' total*	*Class 4*
From Capitol Lake at 11,600'	*220 RP*	*4.4 mi RT*	*2,530' net; 2,630' total*	*Class 4*
From Maroon-Snowmass TH at 8,380'	*530 RP*	*15.2 mi RT*	*5,750' net; 5,890' total*	*Class 4*
From Moon Lake at 11,740'	*253 RP*	*4.0 mi RT*	*2,390' net; 2,490' total*	*Class 4*

This is the easiest route on Capitol. It is most commonly approached from Capitol Creek (22A1), but you also can approach the route from West Snowmass Creek (22A2). From Capitol Lake at 11,600 feet (39.1641° -107.0810°), climb 0.7 mile steeply east on a good, switchbacking trail to the 12,500-foot saddle (39.1633° -107.0736°) between Capitol and 13,300-foot Mount Daly, a dramatic peak 1.7 miles northeast of Capitol. From the east side of the saddle, go 0.5

mile south on a strong climber's trail that crosses some gullies and talus below cliffs to reach 12,700 feet (39.1568° -107.0706°) in the basin between Mount Daly and Clark Peak, a shapely, sharp-ridged peak 1.2 miles east of Capitol. If you are approaching from West Snowmass Creek, you can easily reach this point from Moon Lake by hiking 1.0 mile west then southwest up the basin (Class 2). Once clear of the cliffs, climb 0.4 mile southwest then west up Class 2 talus toward Point 13,664—also known as "K2." It is not necessary to climb to the top of "K2." Aim for the north side of "K2"'s summit rocks, scamper around the point's north side (Class 2+), and descend west to the 13,580-foot "K2"–Capitol saddle (39.1633° -107.0736°). As you emerge from "K2"'s shadows, the view of the remaining route up Capitol is breathtaking.

The remaining climb to the summit can be time-consuming, so appraise the weather before continuing. From the notch, scramble past an initial tower then along the ridge to the notorious knife-edge, a 100-foot-long horizontal stretch of ridge. Many people scoot along the Class 4 ridge with one leg on each side, but this is actually an awkward technique. It is better to grab the edge with your hands and walk your feet along underneath you on the south side of the ridge. Well-balanced, exposure-resistant climbers can walk along the top of the knife-edge. The rock here is delightfully solid.

Beyond the knife-edge, scamper 0.2 mile southwest along the block-strewn ridge to a notch above a steep, south-facing gully (39.1519° -107.0800°). Beyond this notch do a long, ascending traverse across the face south (left) of the northeast ridge. Stay 80 to 100 feet below the ridge crest until you reach the top portion of a small southeast-facing ridge. Turn north (right) and climb up this ridge to regain the crest of the northeast ridge. Turn west (left) and scamper west to the summit (39.1502° -107.0829°).

22R1 V – Variation – "K2"'s North Ridge

Class 4

From the 12,500-foot Capitol–Daly saddle (39.1633° -107.0736°), climb directly south along the ridge crest to rejoin the route just below "K2"'s 13,664-foot summit (Class 4).

22R1 EC1 – Extra Credit – "K2" 13,664 feet 39.1539° -107.0768°

Class 3

This is a minor extra credit ascent. Instead of skirting "K2," climb it. The stunning view of Capitol from "K2"'s summit makes this extra effort worthwhile. The easiest route to the top of "K2" is on its east side, and it is best to retreat back down the east side as well. Some climbers decide to descend "K2"'s steep west, or worse, south side, but this requires Class 4 climbing on shattered rock. This choice has proven fatal.

22R1 EC2 – Extra Credit – Mount Daly 13,300 feet 39.1722° -107.0687°
Class 2+

This is a hefty extra credit ascent. From the 12,500-foot Capitol–Daly saddle (39.1633° -107.0736°), descend northeast then contour north under the ramparts of Mount Daly's south ridge. When it is feasible to do so, scamper up small, steep gullies on Daly's southeast face to reach easier-angled terrain above. Hike northwest up to Mount Daly's 13,300-foot summit. Daly is a shapely, ranked Thirteener and offers a stupendous view of Capitol Peak's north face.

22R2 – Capitol Peak – Northwest Ridge *Classic*

From Capitol Creek TH at 9,420'	1,397 RP	15.2 mi RT	5,510' total	Class 5.7, Steep Snow/Ice
From Capitol Lake at 11,600'	1,207 RP	2.8 mi RT	2,530' total	Class 5.7, Steep Snow/Ice
With descent of Northeast Ridge	1,245 RP	3.6 mi RT	2,580' total	Class 5.7, Steep Snow/Ice

Most of Colorado's great mountain faces were first climbed in the 1920s. As a testimony to its ferocity, Capitol's north face did not succumb until 1937, when a team including the pioneer Carl Blaurock climbed this route. The blunt northwest ridge is the western edge of Capitol's dramatic north face. It is the classic technical climb on this face. Use the Capitol Creek Approach (22A1). This long, deceptive climb is visible from Capitol Lake near the western skyline. The route is looser than it looks. When looking at the face from below, you cannot see the rubble that perches on hidden ledges. The ledges are welcome, but the rubble is not. Hike 0.8 mile southwest above Capitol Lake on the continuing Capitol Creek Trail (FT 1961) to just below Capitol Pass, which is the 12,060-foot saddle (39.1548° -107.0875°) below the northwest ridge.

Look for Y-shaped Slingshot Couloir on the small face east (left) of the bottom of the northwest ridge. Climb the west (right) branch of the couloir, which often contains unavoidable snow and ice. Rockfall danger in Slingshot Couloir is extreme; wear a helmet. Exit the couloir and climb up and slightly left over a series of ledges separated by short, steep rock faces that require Class 5.7 climbing. Above these steep steps, the angle of the face eases slightly. Climb to the crest of the now well-defined northwest ridge just above a feature called the Rotten Spire. Climb three 150-foot pitches near the ridge crest (Class 5.6–5.7). Use crack systems on the discontinuous face east (left) of the crest. Climb into a small saddle behind the Upper Spire, which marks the top of the steep lower ridge and the beginning of the lower-angled upper ridge. Climb along the narrow ridge (Class 4), then negotiate a loose corner punctuated by a small roof (Class 5.7). Continue up the summit pyramid with another 150-foot Class 5.7 pitch. The angle eases above this pitch, and the rest of the climb is easier. Descend the Northeast Ridge Route (22R1).

22R2 V – Variation – Slingshot Bypass
Class 5.9

The direct start to the Northwest Ridge Route is harder but avoids Slingshot Couloir with its attendant snow, ice, and rockfall hazard. Use the Capitol Creek

Approach (22A1). From Capitol Lake at 11,600 feet, hike all the way to Capitol Pass at 12,060 feet (39.1548° -107.0875°). Leave the trail and hike southeast up talus to the base of the rock wall. Traverse 30 feet east (left) to the bottom of a crack system that leads to a chimney above.

Climb a 150-foot pitch up the crack system (Class 5.9). Stem up into the chimney (Class 5.8) and climb the chimney, being careful not to knock loose rock onto your belayer. Continue for 400 feet up an easy gully and Class 4 slabs. Climb steeper slabs and grooves (Class 5.7) and reach the west (right) side of Unicorn Spire. Climb another pitch to the base of Rotten Spire. Look for loose blocks here. Do a loose but easy traverse around the east (left) side of Rotten Spire to the small saddle beyond. Continue on the upper route as described above.

23. Snowmass Mountain 14,092 feet

Rugged and remote, Snowmass reigns as one of Colorado's most spectacular Fourteeners. Snowmass is located 15 miles west of Aspen, but you cannot see the reclusive peak from towns or highways. You can see the namesake snowfield on the peak's east side from the summits of other high peaks. Snowmass' permanent snowfield is one of Colorado's largest, and ascending it is a treat. Snowmass' white rock adds to the peak's beauty.

23E – Snowmass Mountain Essentials

Elevations	14,092' (NGVD29) 14,096' (NAVD88)
Rank	Colorado's 31st highest ranked peak
Location	Pitkin and Gunnison counties, Colorado, USA
Range	Northern Elk Range
Summit Coordinates	39.1187° -107.0664° (WGS84)
Ownership/Contact	White River National Forest – Public Land
	www.fs.fed.us/r2/whiteriver/rangerdistricts/aspen_sopris/mb_scenic_site/index.shtml; 970-925-3445
Prominence and Saddle	1,152' from 12,940' Snowmass–Capitol saddle
Isolation and Parent	2.34 miles to Capitol Peak
USGS Maps	**Snowmass Mountain**, Highland Peak, Capitol Peak, Maroon Bells
USFS Map	White River National Forest
Trails Illustrated Map	Map #128 Maroon Bells/Redstone/Marble
Book Map	See Map 23 on page 232
Nearest Town	Aspen – Population 5,900 – Elevation 7,890'

23E – Snowmass Mountain Essentials

Snowmass Mtn ⚡ Easiest Route	23R1 – East Slopes – Class 3, Mod Snow
	A Class 1 approach on a trail to Snowmass Lake, a Class 2 hike and moderate snow
	slope to the summit ridge,
	and a Class 3 scramble along the ridge to the summit
Snowmass' Accolades	Famous for the namesake snowfield on its east face, Snowmass is rugged and
	remote. A trip to Snowmass takes you into the heart of the Maroon Bells–
	Snowmass Wilderness.

23T – Snowmass Mountain Trailheads

23T1 – Maroon–Snowmass Trailhead 8,380 feet 39.2005° -106.9902°

This trailhead provides access to the Snowmass Creek Approach (23A1), routes on Snowmass' east side, and the West Snowmass Creek Approach (22A2; See Capitol Peak). You can reach the trailhead via one of two roads.

For the traditional approach, go 28.0 miles south on Colorado 82 from Glenwood Springs, or go 13.1 miles north on Colorado 82 from the roundabout on Aspen's northwest side, to the small town of Snowmass. Do not confuse the town of Snowmass with Snowmass Village. The town of Snowmass is on Colorado 82. In Snowmass, turn west onto Snowmass Creek Road (paved) and measure from this point. Turn left at a T-junction at mile 1.7. The road turns to dirt at mile 7.3, crosses Snowmass Creek at mile 10.7, and reaches another T-junction at mile 10.9. Turn right at the T-junction and reach the well-marked trailhead at mile 11.3.

If starting in Aspen, the following alternative approach is shorter but rougher. From the roundabout on Aspen's northwest side, go 4.6 miles north on Colorado 82. Turn west onto the Snowmass Village Road (paved) and measure from this point. Go 5.1 miles to the junction of Brush Creek Road and Divide Road in Snowmass Village and turn right onto Divide Road (paved). At mile 6.0, turn right onto a dirt road just before you reach a lodge called The Divide at Snowmass ski area. Descend steeply on a series of switchbacks across ski runs, go straight at mile 7.6, and reach the trailhead at mile 8.0. In winter you can usually drive to within 1.0 mile of this trailhead.

23T2 – Crystal Trailhead 8,980 feet 39.0577° -107.0978°

This trailhead provides access to the Lead King Basin Approach (23A3) and routes on Snowmass' south and west sides. From Carbondale, go 22.0 miles south on Colorado 133 to the northern base of McClure Pass. Leave Colorado 133 and drive 6.0 miles east on a good paved road to the town of Marble. Continue 5.5 miles east on a rough dirt road (FR 314) to the town of Crystal. This dirt road may challenge some passenger cars. Park in a flat area 0.2 mile east of Crystal just before the road switchbacks up the hill.

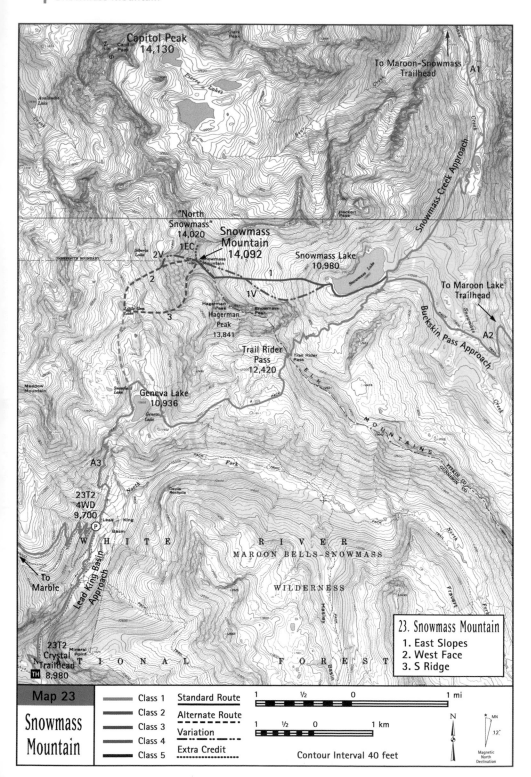

Capitol Peak
14,130

To Maroon-Snowmass
Trailhead   A1

Snowmass Creek Approach

"North
Snowmass"
14,020   Snowmass
1EC. Mountain
2V   14,092

Snowmass Lake
10,980

INDEPENDENCE BOUNDARY

2

1

1V

3

To Maroon Lake
Trailhead

A2

Buckskin Pass Approach

Hagerman Peak
Hagerman
Peak
13,841

Snowmass
Peak

Trail Rider
Pass
12,420

Trail Rider
Pass

ELK

Meadow
Mountain

Geneva Lake
10,936

MOUNTAINS

ASPEN CO. GUNNISON CO.

A3

Fork

TRAIL

23T2
4WD
9,700

North

PACK

Lead King
Basin

W H I T E   R I V E R

MAROON BELLS–SNOWMASS

WILDERNESS

Lead King Basin Approach

To
Marble

23T2
Crystal
Trailhead
8,980

TH

Mineral
Point

TIONAL   FOREST

23. Snowmass Mountain
1. East Slopes
2. West Face
3. S Ridge

Map 23		
Snowmass Mountain		

— Class 1
— Class 2
— Class 3
— Class 4
— Class 5

Standard Route
Alternate Route
Variation
Extra Credit

1   ½   0   1 mi

1   ½   0   1 km

N

MN
12°

Magnetic
North
Declination

Contour Interval 40 feet

23T2 4WD – Lead King Basin 4WD Trailhead 9,700 feet 39.0791° -107.0859°

From the Crystal Trailhead, 4WD vehicles can go 0.3 mile up the 4WD road (FR 314) to a junction (39.0594° -107.0967°) at 9,200 feet above the first switchback. Turn north (left), leave the Schofield Pass Road, and follow the rough Lead King Basin 4WD Road (FR 315) as it climbs north then northeast on the east side of Crystal River's north fork into Lead King Basin. Cross to the river's west side 1.5 miles above the trailhead (39.0733° -107.0880°). Enter the southern end of Lead King Basin and reach a marked 4WD parking area at 9,700 feet (39.0791° -107.0859°), 2.0 miles above the Crystal Trailhead and just before the road starts to switchback up the hill west of the river.

There is a longer, easier 4WD road (also FR 315) to this point that leaves the Schofield Pass Road just east of Marble and goes up Lost Trail Creek. This road can be desperately muddy when wet. In winter the road is open to Marble.

23A – Snowmass Mountain Approaches

23A1 – Snowmass Mountain – Snowmass Creek Approach

From Maroon–Snowmass TH at 8,380'   139 RP   16.8 mi RT   2,600' total   Class 1

This is the traditional backpacking approach to Snowmass Lake and routes on Snowmass' east side. It's long but worth the effort. Start at the Maroon–Snowmass Trailhead at 8,380 feet and walk 1.4 miles west then southwest up Snowmass Creek's south then east side on the Maroon–Snowmass Trail (FT 1975) to the signed junction (39.1925° -107.0123°) with the West Snowmass Trail (FT 1927). Do not take the West Snowmass Trail. Continue 3.7 miles southwest then south on the Maroon–Snowmass Trail to an exotic view of Snowmass Mountain above Bear Creek to the west.

Snowmass Mountain and Capitol Peak from the southeast.

After 6.2 miles, you reach a small lake at 10,100 feet (39.1376° -107.0110°). Go around the lake's east side and continue 0.2 mile south to the northern end of a second, larger lake and the approach's crux (39.1348° -107.0128°). You must cross Snowmass Creek to reach Snowmass Lake, and there is no bridge. Either cross a 100-foot-long logjam at the upper lake's northern end or wade the creek below the logjam. Either crossing can be dangerous in high water. Once on the creek's west side, continue 2.0 miles up the trail to the east end of Snowmass Lake at 10,980 feet (39.1174° -107.0299°).

This scenic lake is a popular destination in July and August, and fires are not permitted near the lake. The rocky bulk of Snowmass Peak and Hagerman Peak rise directly west of the lake; beyond, you can see the gentler Snowmass Mountain. Do not confuse 13,620-foot Snowmass Peak with 14,092-foot Snowmass Mountain.

23A2 – Snowmass Mountain – Buckskin Pass Approach

From Maroon Lake TH at 9,600'   209 RP   16.4 mi RT   2,862' net; 4,884' total   Class 1

With a vehicle shuttle, this route makes sense as a one-way journey. The round trip over Buckskin Pass requires more effort than the approach up Snowmass Creek, and this arduous approach is less popular than the hike up Snowmass Creek.

Start at the Maroon Lake Trailhead at 9,600 feet (see 24T1; Maroon Bells Group) and follow the main trail, Maroon–Snowmass Trail (FT 1975), 0.4 mile southwest above Maroon Lake's northwest side to the Maroon Bells–Snowmass Wilderness boundary (39.0966° -106.9488°) near Maroon Lake's west end. Continue on FT 1975 1.2 miles west-southwest to a trail junction (39.0887° -106.9658°) at 10,120 feet above Crater Lake's northeast end. Turn northwest (right) and continue on the Maroon–Snowmass Trail (FT 1975) 2.7 miles northwest to Buckskin Pass at 12,462 feet (39.1018° -106.9925°). Cross Buckskin Pass and descend 2.5 miles northwest on the trail. Cross Snowmass Creek on the edge of a meadow at 10,800 feet (39.1082° -107.0149°), then hike 1.4 miles northwest and west climbing to a highpoint of 11,040 feet before descending to Snowmass Lake at 10,980 feet (39.1174° -107.0299°).

23A3 – Snowmass Mountain – Lead King Basin Approach

From Crystal TH at 8,980'   72 RP   7.6 mi RT   1,980' total   Class 1
From Lead King Basin 4WD TH at 9,700'   34 RP   3.6 mi RT   1,260' total   Class 1

This approach is shorter but steeper than the Snowmass Creek Approach (23A1). Start at the Crystal Trailhead at 8,980 feet and go 0.3 mile up the 4WD road (FR 314) to a junction (39.0594° -107.0967°) at 9,200 feet above the first switchback. Turn north (left), leave the Schofield Pass Road, and follow the rough Lead King Basin 4WD Road (FR 315) as it climbs north then northeast on the east side of Crystal River's north fork into Lead King Basin. Cross to the river's west side 1.5 miles above the trailhead (39.0733° -107.0880°). Enter the southern end of Lead King Basin and reach a marked 4WD parking area (39.0791° -107.0859°) at

9,700 feet, 2.0 miles above the Crystal Trailhead and just before the road starts to switchback up the hill west of the river.

Follow the Geneva Lake Trail (FT 1976) 0.2 mile north-northeast, enter the Maroon Bells–Snowmass Wilderness at 9,760 feet (39.0814° -107.0846°), and continue 0.25 mile north-northeast to a trail junction at 9,900 feet (39.0849° -107.0833°). Take the west (left) trail, switchback 0.75 mile north up the steep slope at the north end of Lead King Basin to 10,640 feet (39.0911° -107.0846°), and continue 0.6 mile northeast to Geneva Lake's southwest side at 10,960 feet (39.0962° -107.0789°). There is good camping above the lake's west side, but fires are not allowed near the lake. You can see Snowmass Mountain's south and west sides rising north of the lake.

You can hike from Geneva Lake to Snowmass Lake via 12,420-foot Trail Rider Pass (39.1047° -107.0490°). This pass allows you to visit both the east side and the west side of Snowmass. You can create a beautiful backcountry experience here.

23R – Snowmass Mountain Routes

23R1 – Snowmass Mountain – East Slopes *Classic*

From Maroon-Snowmass TH at 8,380'	525 RP	21.8 mi RT	5,712' total	Class 3, Mod Snow
From Snowmass Lake at 10,980'	297 RP	5.0 mi RT	3,112' total	Class 3, Mod Snow
From Maroon Lake TH at 9,600'	565 RP	21.4 mi RT	7,956' total	Class 3, Mod Snow

This is the standard route up Snowmass' namesake snowfield; although it is long, it is the easiest route up Snowmass. Always interesting, it offers one of Colorado's finest Fourteener tours. Use either the Snowmass Creek (23A1) or Buckskin Pass (23A2) Approach to reach Snowmass Lake at 10,980 feet.

From Snowmass Lake's east end (39.1174° -107.0299°), hike 0.6 mile southwest around the lake's south side on a small trail. A steep, unpleasant scree slope rises above Snowmass Lake's west end and slows easy access to the snowfield above it. Either climb a shallow gully on the south (left) side of the scree slope (snow-filled through June) or climb grass slopes north (right) of the scree slope.

Move onto the snowfield above the scree slope and hike west up its undulating surface. The steep north wall of Snowmass Peak and Hagerman Peak are south of you, and Snowmass Mountain is to the west. Aim for a rounded protrusion below Snowmass Mountain's southeast ridge about halfway between the Snowmass Mountain–Hagerman Peak saddle and Snowmass Mountain's summit. This protrusion (39.1167° -107.0603°) provides the easiest route to the summit ridge. Climb it (Class 2+ or Moderate Snow) and reach Snowmass Mountain's southeast ridge at 13,680 feet (39.1162° -107.0631°). Scramble 0.2 mile northwest along the ridge to the summit (39.1187° -107.0664°). This ridge requires some Class 3 scrambling on surprisingly solid rock.

23R1 V – Variation – Max Snowmass

Class 3, Mod/Steep Snow

In June of a good snow year, you can stay on the snowfield longer and climb moderate snow to reach the summit ridge closer to the summit. In early June, you can sometimes climb directly to the summit on steep snow.

23R1 EC – Extra Credit – "North Snowmass" 14,020 feet 39.1211° -107.0662°

Class 3

From the summit, scramble 0.2 mile north to Snowmass Mountain's 14,020-foot north summit (Class 3). This unofficial Fourteener does not have a lot of power, but it is above 14,000 feet, is highly visible, and provides an excellent view of remote Pierre Lakes Basin and Capitol Peak. This airy summit is one of Colorado's more exotic 14,000-foot perches.

23R2 – Snowmass Mountain – West Face

From Crystal TH at 8,980'	389 RP	12.2 mi RT	5,112' total	Class 3
From Lead King Basin 4WD TH at 9,700'	333 RP	8.2 mi RT	4,392' total	Class 3
From Geneva Lake at 10,960'	270 RP	4.6 mi RT	3,132' total	Class 3

This route is a little harder than the East Slopes Route (23R1) but is much shorter. It is the most expedient way to climb Snowmass. Start at the Crystal Trailhead at 8,980 feet and follow the Lead King Basin Approach (23A3) to Geneva Lake's southwest side at 10,960 feet (39.0962° -107.0789°). Hike 0.3 mile north around Geneva Lake's west side to a trail junction (39.1001° -107.0795°), hike 0.8 mile north on a secondary trail up the valley to the east side of Little Gem Lake at 11,680 feet (39.1120° -107.0803°), and continue 0.3 mile north-north-east up the valley to 11,700 feet (39.1163° -107.0785°). If you reach Siberia Lake, you have gone too far.

From 11,700 feet, turn east (right), cross the creek, and climb 0.9 mile east-northeast up Snowmass' steep west face. This large, broken face is full of small cliff bands, and you must do some judicious route finding to keep the difficulty at Class 3. The easiest line is just south of a rib in the center of the face. The most difficult sections are between 12,600 and 12,800 feet, and near the summit. Typical of the Elk Range, there is a lot of loose rock on this face.

23R2 V – Variation – West Rib

Class 3+

Near the middle of the face, angle north (left), get onto a small rib, and climb up the rib to a point just north of the summit. The rib is a little harder, alleg-edly a little more solid, and removes you from the basin's fall line, favored by tumbling rocks. However, the rib also has its own set of angular, poised blocks.

23R3 – Snowmass Mountain – S Ridge

From Crystal TH at 8,980'	*415 RP*	*12.0 mi RT*	*5,112' net; 5,392' total*	*Class 3+*
From Lead King Basin 4WD TH at 9,700'	*358 RP*	*8.0 mi RT*	*4,392' net; 4,672' total*	*Class 3+*
From Geneva Lake at 10,960'	*296 RP*	*4.4 mi RT*	*3,132' net; 3,412' total*	*Class 3+*
With descent of West Face	*287 RP*	*4.5 mi RT*	*3,132' net; 3,272' total*	*Class 3+*

This is the shortest route on Snowmass. The S Ridge is Snowmass' southwest ridge and received its name because of its distinctive curving shape. Only the ridge's loose rock prevents it from being a classic climb. There is more exposure and harder Class 3 scrambling on this ridge than on the West Face Route (23R2).

Start at the Crystal Trailhead at 8,980 feet and follow the Lead King Basin Approach (23A3) to Geneva Lake's southwest side at 10,960 feet (39.0962° -107.0789°). You can easily see the S Ridge from the lake. Hike 0.3 mile north around Geneva Lake's west side to a trail junction (39.1001° -107.0795°) and hike 0.8 mile north on a secondary trail up the valley to the east side of Little Gem Lake at 11,680 feet (39.1120° -107.0803°). Your Class 1 approach is over.

Leave the trail, descend 200 yards east-southeast, cross the creek at 11,540 feet (39.1114° -107.0779°), and hike 0.3 mile east to 12,200 feet on the ridge's lower north side (39.1120° -107.0720°). Prepare for your climb. Scramble 180 yards southeast up broken cliffs to gain the ridge crest at 12,540 feet (39.1116° -107.0706°). Scramble 0.2 mile northwest up the ridge, move to the ridge's north side to avoid any difficulties, and reach the southern end of a flat section at 13,240 feet (39.1141° -107.0685°). This is where the ridge begins its S curve and the view of the ridge ahead may seem a bit daunting, but most of what you are seeing is Snowmass' steep south face. Scamper 200 yards north to 13,400 feet and engage the steeper upper part of the ridge (39.1157° -107.0685°). Scramble 150 yards northeast near the ridge crest to 13,600 feet. The scrambling reaches a Class 3+ crescendo near here, and you may need to make judicious detours north of the ridge crest. Your final 0.2 mile scamper northwest to the summit might peg your fun meter. Ascending the S Ridge and descending the West Face Route (23R2) makes a serpentine Tour de Snowmass.

24. Maroon Bells Group

Maroon Peak	14,156 feet
North Maroon Peak	14,014 feet
Pyramid Peak	14,018 feet

These three peaks are nestled in the heart of the Elk Range 10 miles west of Aspen. They are visible from many of the area's ski slopes, and millions of people have looked at these famous peaks. Maroon Peak and North Maroon Peak together are known as the Maroon Bells. The Maroon Bells' beauty is world renowned. Decades ago, on a climbing trip to the high Andes in Peru, I visited a small restaurant in a remote valley. On the wall above a rustic table was a picture of the Maroon Bells.

Maroon Peak is the namesake and highest peak of the Maroon Bells Group. Maroon Peak is often called South Maroon; you can see the peak together with its companion summit, North Maroon, from Maroon Lake. Thousands of people have admired the postcard view of these two peaks for centuries. On a crisp fall day, blue skies, azure lakes, and brilliant aspen trees frame the Maroon Bells. Many of Colorado's best beauties are on display here.

When you view the Maroon Bells from Maroon Lake, North Maroon appears larger and higher than Maroon Peak. In reality, North Maroon is just a northern spur of Maroon Peak. The two summits are only 650 yards apart, and North Maroon only rises 234 feet above the connecting saddle. North Maroon's status as an official Fourteener has been hotly debated for decades, but its stature is never in question. This picturesque peak is one of Colorado's most famous Fourteeners.

Well-named Pyramid Peak is 2 miles east of the Maroon Bells, and it is the first high peak you see when driving up the Maroon Lake Road. Pyramid is only 2 miles south of Maroon Lake, and the foreshortened view from the lake is neck-bending. Pyramid is at the north end of a highly convoluted, 4-mile-long ridge between West Maroon and East Maroon creeks. Pyramid is the highest point on the ridge; it carries this distinction well.

24E – Maroon Bells Group Essentials

Elevations	Maroon Pk	14,156' (NGVD29) 14,162' (NAVD88)
	N Maroon Pk	14,014' (NGVD29) 14,019' (NAVD88)
	Pyramid Pk	14,018' (NGVD29) 14,023' (NAVD88)
Ranks	Maroon Pk	Colorado's 24th highest ranked peak
	N Maroon Pk	Unranked peak
	Pyramid Pk	Colorado's 47th highest ranked peak
Location	Pitkin and Gunnison counties, Colorado, USA	
Range	Central Elk Range	
Summit Coordinates	Maroon Pk	39.0707° -106.9889° (WGS84)
	N Maroon Pk	39.0759° -106.9871° (WGS84)
	Pyramid Pk	39.0716° -106.9501° (WGS84)
Ownership/Contact	White River National Forest – Public Land	
	www.fs.fed.us/r2/whiteriver/rangerdistricts/aspen_sopris/mb_scenic_site/	
	index.shtml; 970-925-3445	
Prominence and Saddles	Maroon Pk	2,336' from 11,820' East Maroon Pass
	N Maroon Pk	234' from 13,780' N Maroon–Maroon saddle
	Pyramid Pk	1,638' from 12,380' saddle @ W Maroon Pass
Isolation and Parents	Maroon Pk	8.06 miles to Castle Peak
	N Maroon Pk	0.37 mile to Maroon Peak
	Pyramid Pk	2.08 miles to Maroon Peak
USGS Map	Maroon Bells	

24E – Maroon Bells Group Essentials

USFS Map	White River National Forest
Trails Illustrated Map	Map #128 Maroon Bells/Redstone/Marble
Book Map	See Map 24 on page 240
Nearest Towns	Aspen –Population 5,900 – Elevation 7,890'
Maroon Pk 🥾 Easiest Route	24R1 – South Ridge – Class 3
	A Class 1 approach hike on a trail, a long Class 2+ scamper up to the summit ridge, then an exacting Class 3 scramble up rotten ledges to the summit
N Maroon Pk 🥾 Easiest Route	24R4 – Northeast Ridge – Class 4
	A Class 1 approach hike on a trail, a Class 2 hike up to and over a tedious rock glacier, then a Class 3 scramble up rubble-covered ledges that is punctuated by several Class 4 moves
Pyramid Pk 🥾 Easiest Route	24R7 – Northeast Ridge – Class 4
	A short Class 1 approach on a trail, a steep Class 2 hike through a high basin, a tedious ascent up a steep slope to a high saddle, then a devious, rotten Class 4 climb to the summit
Maroon Bells Group Accolades	Beautiful, red, and rotten, these famous peaks near Aspen attract photographers, walkers, and climbers from all over the world; all are impressed. Unlike those who stay in the lush green valley, climbers quickly learn about the Red Line, where the green carpet gives way to the rotten red rock above. You can easily hold the famous beauty in you hand when a hold pulls out. Get in shape, and approach these peaks with well-considered preparation and caution.

24T – Maroon Bells Group Trailhead

24T1 – Maroon Lake Trailhead 9,600 feet 39.0992° -106.9427°

This popular trailhead provides access to the Maroon Bells and Pyramid. Go to the large roundabout on Colorado 82 northwest of Aspen, take the exit for Maroon Lake Road, and measure from this point. Go 9.4 miles west on the Maroon Lake Road to the parking area east of Maroon Lake. A postcard view of the Maroon Bells greets you here.

From mid-June through September, the Maroon Lake Road is closed from 8:30 AM to 5:00 PM. During these hours, there is a shuttle to the lake that starts at Ruby Park in downtown Aspen. For more information, call RFTA at 970-925-8484 or the White River National Forest at 970-925-3445. In winter the road is gated 3.0 miles from Colorado 82 at the T-Lazy-7 Guest Ranch.

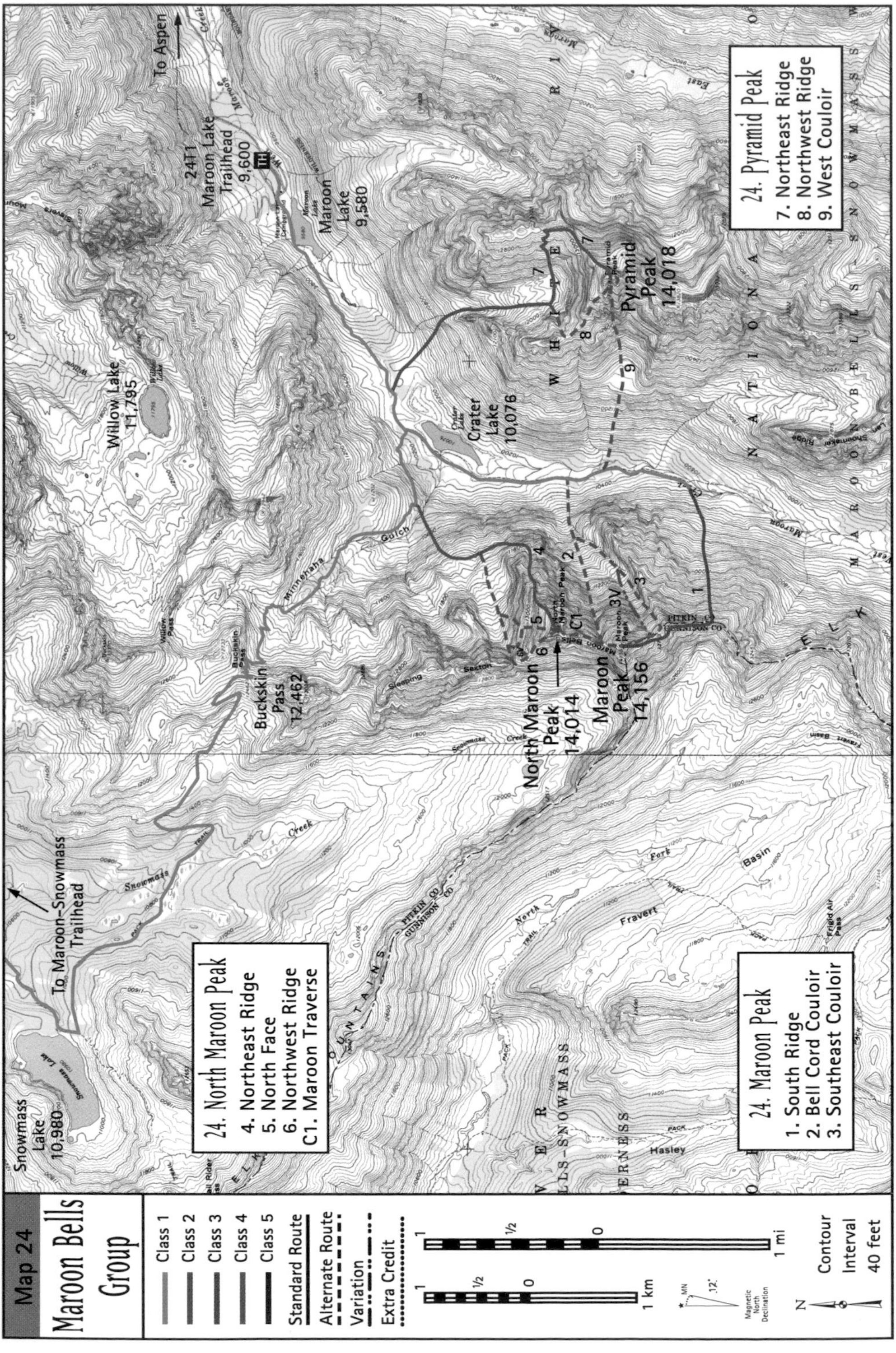

Map 24

Maroon Bells Group

Class 1
Class 2
Class 3
Class 4
Class 5

Standard Route
Alternate Route
Variation
Extra Credit

1 1/2 0 1 mi
1 1/2 0 1 km

MN 12°
Magnetic North Declination

N

Contour Interval 40 feet

24. North Maroon Peak
4. Northeast Ridge
5. North Face
6. Northwest Ridge
C1. Maroon Traverse

24. Maroon Peak
1. South Ridge
2. Bell Cord Couloir
3. Southeast Couloir

24. Pyramid Peak
7. Northeast Ridge
8. Northwest Ridge
9. West Couloir

To Aspen

Maroon Lake Trailhead
9,600

24T1

Maroon Lake
9,580

Willow Lake
11,795

Crater Lake
10,076

Pyramid Peak
14,018

WHITE

ELK-SNOWMASS

NATIONAL

Buckskin Pass
12,462

Minnehaha Gulch

Sleeping

Sexton

North Maroon Peak
14,014

Maroon Peak
14,156

PITKIN CO
GUNNISON CO

C1

Snowmass Lake
10,980

To Maroon-Snowmass Trailhead

Snowmass Creek

Fravert Basin

North Fork

West Fork

Hasley

WILDERNESS

ELK MOUNTAINS

Maroon Creek

East Snowmass Creek

24. Maroon Peak 14,156 feet

24R – Maroon Peak Routes

24R1 – Maroon Peak – South Ridge

From Maroon Lake TH at 9,600'   524 RP   10.0 mi RT   4,556' net; 4,636' total   Class 3

This is the easiest route on Maroon Peak; it is a long, arduous ascent on dangerously loose rock. From the Maroon Lake Trailhead at 9,600 feet, follow the main
trail (FT 1975) 0.4 mile southwest above Maroon Lake's northwest side to the
Maroon Bells–Snowmass Wilderness boundary (39.0966° -106.9488°) near Maroon
Lake's west end. Continue on FT 1975 1.2 miles west-southwest to a trail junction
(39.0887° -106.9658°) at 10,120 feet above Crater Lake's northeast end. Turn southwest (left) at this trail junction onto FT 1970 and walk 1.8 miles southwest around
Crater Lake then south up the valley along West Maroon Creek's west side. During
this approach hike, the Maroon Bells pass in review above you. Leave the main
trail at 10,500 feet (39.0651° -106.9716°), just before it crosses to the creek's east side.

Find a strong use trail and hike and scramble 0.9 mile west up broken Class 3
ledges to reach Maroon Peak's south ridge at 13,300 feet (39.0627° -106.9865°).
The difficult 2,800-foot ascent up this slope will test the success of your training program. The slope has several small cliff bands, but with careful route
finding, the difficulty will not exceed Class 3.

Once on the south ridge, turn north (right) and follow the well-cairned
route that starts on the ridge crest, then stays below the ridge on its west
side. At 13,340 feet, when the ridge steepens toward dramatic Point 13,753,
do a frustrating 0.25-mile up-and-down traverse northwest. Stay below the
major difficulties of Point 13,753 and at 13,400 feet, move into the couloir that
drops southwest from the 13,660-foot saddle between Maroon Peak and Point
13,753. Climb this gully on dangerously loose scree and well before you reach
the saddle, find an escape ledge to the northwest (left). Leave the couloir and
traverse on this ledge onto Maroon Peak's southwest face. Zigzag up this face,
following the path of least resistance. The exact finish to this climb is a matter
of choice. You can regain the south ridge and follow it for 400 feet to the summit, or you can choose a line farther northwest.

This climb requires careful route finding to keep the difficulty at Class 3.
Although the route has been well cairned in recent years, some cairns lead to
bad routes. Trust your judgment, not some stranger's pile of rocks. No matter
what finish you choose, the summit (39.0707° -106.9889°) will be rewarding.

24R2 – Maroon Peak – Bell Cord Couloir *Classic*

From Maroon Lake TH at 9,600'   605 RP   8.4 mi RT   4,556' total   Class 4, Steep Snow/Ice

This is the prominent couloir between Maroon Peak and North Maroon Peak.
Some people refer to it as the Bell Chord Couloir. You can preview conditions
in this couloir from the safety of your car at Maroon Lake. Preview carefully.
In winter and early spring, the couloir is prone to avalanching, and by late

summer, the snow is gone and the couloir is an undesirable scree gully speck-led with rubble-infested ice. The couloir collects rockfall in all seasons, and a helmet is recommended. In most years, late June is best for a snow climb up this classic couloir. Beware unstable snow when melting reaches its peak in early June. The couloir can present a technical ice climb in July.

From the Maroon Lake Trailhead at 9,600 feet, walk 1.6 miles west-south-west on FT 1975 to a trail junction (39.0887° -106.9658°) at 10,120 feet above Crater Lake's northeast end. Turn southwest (left) at this trail junction onto FT 1970 and walk 1.1 miles southwest around Crater Lake then south up the val-ley along West Maroon Creek's west side to an intermittent stream crossing at 10,270 feet (39.0751° -106.9711°).

Leave the trail and climb 0.8 mile west into the basin between Maroon Peak and North Maroon. Enter the straight couloir at 12,000 feet (39.0736° -106.9822°) and climb it to the 13,780-foot saddle (39.0722° -106.9888°) between Maroon Peak and North Maroon. The 1,800-foot couloir averages 42 degrees, with the steepest portions exceeding 45 degrees. An ice ax is recommended, and crampons may be useful. From the saddle, turn south (left), climb a Class 4 cleft, then climb 200 yards up broken Class 3 ledges to Maroon Peak's summit (39.0707° -106.9889°).

24R3 – Maroon Peak – Southeast Couloir

From Maroon Lake TH at 9,600'   *573 RP*   *8.4 mi RT*   *4,556' total*   *Class 3, Steep Snow/Ice*

This couloir is on Maroon Peak's southeast side and reaches a tiny 13,660-foot saddle just south of Point 13,753 on Maroon Peak's south ridge. This couloir provides a good early summer snow climb, but after the snow melts, the couloir is a bowling alley of loose rocks.

North Maroon Peak and Maroon Peak from the northeast.

Follow the Bell Cord Couloir Route (24R2) into the high basin east of Maroon Peak. Climb southwest through a huge slot called the Garbage Chute. If there is stable snow, you can climb directly up the chute. If the snow is melting, avoid rotting snow bridges over the stream by climbing on the north (right) side of the chute. Above the Garbage Chute, continue southwest through a small basin and enter Maroon Peak's southeast couloir at 12,200 feet (39.0707° -106.9826°).

The 1,500-foot couloir averages 40 degrees, with the steepest portions exceeding 45 degrees. This couloir is wider, shorter, and gentler than the Bell Cord Couloir, but it still requires careful attention. From the 13,660-foot saddle (39.0673° -106.9869°) on Maroon Peak's south ridge just south of Point 13,753, traverse on the south then west sides of Point 13,753 to the 13,660-foot saddle (39.0680° -106.9880°) just north of this summit. From here there are two choices. Either descend on the west side and finish the climb via the upper part of Maroon Peak's South Ridge Route (24R1), or do an ascending traverse from the saddle on the southwest face and finish along the upper south ridge. The southeast couloir provides a reasonable snow descent after an ascent of the Bell Cord Couloir (24R2).

24R3 V – Variation – Bell Ringer

Class 4, Steep Snow

There is a second couloir north of the one described above. It reaches the 13,660-foot saddle (39.0680° -106.9880°) just north of Point 13,753. The northern couloir is steeper, harder, and less popular than the southern one. It provides a great climb with stable snow, but avoid it if the snow is discontinuous.

24. North Maroon Peak 14,014 feet

24R – North Maroon Peak Routes

24R4 – North Maroon Peak – Northeast Ridge

From Maroon Lake TH at 9,600'   407 RP   7.2 mi RT   4,414' net; 4,494' total   Class 4

This time-honored test piece is the standard route on North Maroon. The route is complicated, loose, exposed, dangerous, and has often rendered a fatal experience. North Maroon is considered one of Colorado's toughest Fourteeners, not because it has great technical difficulty, but because it is steep enough that any fall will probably be fatal, and the rock is pathologically rotten. A rope is usually useless on this route, since there is rarely a secure anchorage, and the rope itself will dislodge rocks. Put on your cat feet for this one and climb with a light touch.

From the Maroon Lake Trailhead at 9,600 feet, follow the main trail (FT 1975) 0.4 mile southwest above Maroon Lake's northwest side to the Maroon Bells-Snowmass Wilderness boundary (39.0966° -106.9488°) near Maroon Lake's west end. Continue on FT 1975 1.2 miles west-southwest to a trail junction (39.0887° -106.9658°) at 10,120 feet above Crater Lake's northeast end. Turn west (right) at this trail junction and climb 0.5 mile west on the Maroon–Snowmass Trail (FT 1975) to a meadow at 10,700 feet (39.0883° -106.9749°). Leave the main trail at a cairn and follow a climber's trail west down to Minnehaha Creek at 10,660 feet. Ford the creek and continue on the climber's trail as it climbs west to the lower end of the basin below North Maroon's north face. The introduction is over and the challenge looms overhead. The northeast ridge is the left skyline.

Hike south at 11,700 feet across a large rock glacier in the basin and aim for a point below the northeast ridge's lowest cliffs. Find a climber's trail and do an ascending Class 2 traverse on ledges below east-facing cliffs. Near the end of the traverse, climb more steeply to a corner at 11,900 feet (39.0784° -106.9785°) on the edge of a wide gully on North Maroon's east face. When descending this route, it is important to exit the gully at this corner.

From the corner, traverse southwest into the wide gully and climb west up it via a series of grass and dirt ledges (Class 3). The gully narrows, and a 50-foot cliff band blocks easy passage at 12,800 feet. Climb a cleft near the center of the cliff band (Class 4). This crux passage is especially exciting when it is gushing with water, as it often is until the face above is completely free of snow. Above the crux cleft, angle south (left) to a small ridge at 12,900 feet between the gully you have just ascended and another gully farther south. Traverse south into the new gully and scramble up broken Class 3 ledges to reach the crest of the northeast ridge at 13,200 feet. Climb on or near the ridge crest from this point to the summit (39.0759° -106.9871°). An occasional Class 4 move is required on the ridge's steeper portions.

24R5 – North Maroon Peak – North Face *Classic*

From Maroon Lake TH at 9,600' 536 RP 7.1 mi RT 4,414' net; 4,494' total *Class 4, Steep Snow/Ice*

This classic route is seldom in good condition for climbing. Until mid-June, you can do the climb entirely on snow, but plentiful May snow tends to avalanche, June snow is often rotten, and the exposed rock bands of July and August are always rotten. Nevertheless, this sweeping north face has attracted many hardened mountaineers, and it is also a test piece for extreme skiers. Like the Eiger's *Nordwand*, this face emits a siren call for some. The 1,600-foot face averages 47 degrees and consists of a series of rock bands with steep, snow-covered ledges between them. The rock bands are the route's multiple cruxes.

Follow the Northeast Ridge Route (24R4) to the basin below the north face. Climb southwest up the basin and inspect the face carefully as you approach and pass below it. Climb to 12,400 feet high in the basin and bypass the first rock band by climbing a wide snow slope on the west (right) side of the lower face. Angle back east (left) into the center of the face on the large snow ramp above the first rock band. Climb the vague couloir in the center of the face through several smaller rock bands. Avoid the final rock band, which is called Punk Rock Band, by angling east (left) to reach the northeast ridge and follow that ridge to the summit.

24R5 V1 – Variation – Plumb Bob I

Class 4, Steep Snow/Ice

Climb the first rock band in the center of the face via a shallow couloir. The upper part of this couloir is steep, and you can best avoid it by climbing 165 feet of Class 4 rock west (right) of the couloir.

24R5 V2 – Variation – Plumb Bob II

Class 4

Climb through the center of Punk Rock Band in a narrow Class 4 cleft. Reach the northwest ridge 100 yards below the summit. Climbing directly through the first and last rock bands provides the most direct line on the north face.

24R6 – North Maroon Peak – Northwest Ridge

From Maroon Lake TH at 9,600'   431 RP   7.4 mi RT   4,414' net; 4,494' total   Class 4, Steep Snow

People seldom climb this straightforward ridge because of the difficulty in reaching the ridge. Follow the Northeast Ridge Route (24R4) to the basin below the north face. Climb west up the basin under the north face to 12,400 feet and consider your future. The complicated, 13,460-foot massif north of North Maroon is the Sleeping Sexton. The deep, 13,020-foot saddle (39.0797° -106.9908°) between Sleeping Sexton and North Maroon is called the Gunsight. It is on North Maroon's northwest ridge above the west end of the basin below North Maroon's north face. A steep, rotten, east-facing couloir called Gunsight Couloir reaches this saddle from the west end of the basin. You can see this prominent couloir from Maroon Lake.

Gunsight Couloir is best ascended when it is snow-filled, but snow melts out rapidly in this couloir. After the snow melts, the couloir is a steep shooting gallery of loose rocks. You can avoid the couloir by climbing 200 feet of Class 4 rock south (left) of the couloir. From the Gunsight, climb a Class 4 pitch to the south to exit the deep notch. Once above the Gunsight, follow a zigzag line just west of the northwest ridge. The actual ridge crest is not the best route. The upper ridge eases in difficulty and allows a ridgetop finish to the summit.

24R6 V – Variation – Trigger Finger

Steep Snow

There is a narrow, hidden couloir that ascends from the lower west end of the north face to a small, 13,260-foot notch (39.0783° -106.9899°) on the northwest ridge above the Gunsight. When filled with stable snow, this couloir provides an excellent climb that avoids the various hazards of Gunsight Couloir. The narrow couloir's steepness reaches 48 degrees.

Pyramid Peak 14,018

Pyramid Peak from the north.

24. Pyramid Peak 14,018 feet

24R – Pyramid Peak Routes
24R7 – Pyramid Peak – Northeast Ridge

From Maroon Lake TH at 9,600'   400 RP   7.0 mi RT   4,418' total   Class 4

This is the easiest route on Pyramid. Like the Maroon Bells, steep, exposed, loose rock make this a dangerous climb. Pyramid is generally considered to be one of Colorado's toughest Fourteeners, so approach this great peak with ability, conditioning, and caution. The route crosses and flirts with the upper northeast ridge, but most of the upper climbing is on Pyramid's east face, where rockfall is a hazard; wear a helmet. For the fit, Pyramid is a sprint. The peak was climbed in "an hour" most of a century ago.

Start at the Maroon Lake Trailhead at 9,600 feet and follow the main trail (FT 1975) 0.4 mile southwest above Maroon Lake's northwest side to the Maroon Bells–Snowmass Wilderness boundary (39.0966° -106.9488°) near Maroon Lake's west end. Continue 0.8 mile west on FT 1975 to a level area at 10,120 feet (39.0903° -106.9597°). Leave the main trail to Crater Lake and follow the Pyramid Trail southeast up to and across a flat, rocky area to the base of a small talus field. Climb steeply south on the recently constructed Pyramid Trail to the end of the trail at 11,300 feet (39.0828° -106.9532°) at the north end of the hanging basin below Pyramid's north face.

Beyond the trail, hike south up the center of the basin between a rock glacier to the east and a steep talus field to the west to 11,960 feet (39.0770° -106.9511°). Scamper east on a strong climber's trail up steep scree gullies to reach Pyramid's northeast ridge at a 12,980-foot saddle (39.0769° -106.9451°). Hike 0.25 mile south then southwest on a smaller trail along or near the ridge crest to a forbidding notch at 13,060 feet (39.0745° -106.9460°). Your approach is over.

Get above the broken, pale-colored wall beyond the notch by climbing up on its north (right) side, then climbing back south (left) below steeper terrain to regain the ridge crest. Move to the south side of the ridge, climb up under the ridge, cross two small rock ribs, and reach the north end of the Cliff Traverse, which is a two-foot-wide ledge going south across steep terrain. Go 100 feet south across the Cliff Traverse, which has a narrow Class 3 challenge in the middle. Continue southwest on a ledgy ascending traverse toward Pyramid's east face. Cross a small gully, then traverse south to another, larger rock rib. Cross the rib and go south to the base of the Green Wall, a steeper section of light-colored rock. Note this spot for your descent, since it is easy to miss this turn going down. Staying south of the ridge crest, climb 300 feet up the Green Wall (Class 3). Near the top of the Green Wall, climb straight up a small, steep gully (Class 4) and continue on a zigzag route up steep red rock above (Class 4).

There are several ways to climb the last 500 feet to the summit, any of which will involve an occasional Class 4 move. Take great care with your movement and route finding. If you find yourself faced with a Class 5 section, retreat to easier ground and try another route. Most of the route choices are south of the ridge crest, but if you find yourself on or near the ridge, take time to peer west across Pyramid's imposing north face. The slope angle relents above 13,900 feet, and Pyramid's scarlet summit (39.0716° -106.9501°) is one of Colorado's most rewarding.

24R8 – Pyramid Peak – Northwest Ridge

From Maroon Lake TH at 9,600'   424 RP   6.4 mi RT   4,418' total   Class 4

This ridge offers a more difficult alternative to the northeast ridge. Follow the Northeast Ridge Route (24R7) into the basin below Pyramid's north face. From 12,000 feet in the basin (39.0764° -106.9531°), climb southwest up a steep, wide couloir to a 12,700-foot saddle (39.0754° -106.9563°) on Pyramid's northwest ridge (Class 3).

The route from here to the summit is difficult to follow. You are rarely on the ridge crest as you link traverses and gullies on Pyramid's west face. From the 12,700-foot saddle, follow the northwest ridge for 300 feet then move below the ridge on its west side to the bottom of a rubble gully. Climb the gully and stay to the right near the top. At the top of the gully's left branch is the Keyhole, providing a spectacular view of Pyramid's north face. The terrain here is steep, loose, and dangerous. It is not necessary to go into the Keyhole.

Climb the steep Class 4 pitch above the top of the couloir's right branch. This is the route's technical crux, but tricky route finding remains. Beyond the crux wall, move away from the northwest ridge, traverse south on ledges, round a corner, and climb short walls when necessary. Reach a small bowl at 13,700 feet on Pyramid's upper west face. You are close. Climb the shallow couloir above the bowl to just below the summit cliff. Avoid this by traversing south to a 13,900-foot notch (39.0708° -106.9502°) on Pyramid's south ridge. You are very close. Climb 400 feet north along the rocky, exposed upper south ridge to the summit (39.0716° -106.9501°). Ascending this ridge and descending the Northeast Ridge Route (24R7) makes a spectacular Tour de Pyramid.

24R9 – Pyramid Peak – West Couloir

From Maroon Lake TH at 9,600'   448 RP   8.4 mi RT   4,418' total   Class 4, Steep Snow

This route is less popular than either the Northeast (24R7) or Northwest Ridge (24R8) routes, probably because of its length and the couloir's loose rock. Still, this is a practicable route, especially if there is good snow in the couloir. Snow usually melts out of this couloir by mid-June.

From the Maroon Lake Trailhead at 9,600 feet, follow the main trail (FT 1975) 0.4 mile southwest above Maroon Lake's northwest side to the Maroon Bells–Snowmass Wilderness boundary (39.0966° -106.9488°) near Maroon Lake's west end. Continue on FT 1975 1.2 miles west-southwest to a trail junction (39.0887° -106.9658°) at 10,120 feet above Crater Lake's northeast end. Turn southwest (left) at this trail junction onto FT 1970 and walk 1.2 miles southwest around Crater Lake then south up the valley along West Maroon Creek's west side to 10,300 feet (39.0722° -106.9704°). Your comfortable Class 1 approach is over.

Leave the trail, hike east, cross West Maroon Creek, and climb east up Pyramid's enormous west face. From 10,300 feet to 12,600 feet, the climbing is straightforward but tedious. At 12,600 feet (39.0713° -106.9551°), move into the more northerly of two major couloirs on the upper west face and climb it for 1,100 feet to 13,700 feet in a small bowl directly below the summit. The couloir has steep sections that exceed 55 degrees, and when snow free, these bulges require Class 4 climbing. Join the Northwest Ridge Route (24R8) in the small bowl at 13,700 feet and follow that route to the summit.

24C – Maroon Bells and Pyramid Combination Routes

24C1 – North Maroon Northeast Ridge ➔ South Maroon South Ridge *Classic*

From Maroon Lake TH at 9,600'   538 RP   9.0 mi RT   4,830' total   Class 4

The traverse between North Maroon and Maroon Peak is one of Colorado's four great Fourteener traverses. It rings both Bells. The rock is rotten and the traverse is dangerous, but it is a classic combination because of the spectacular positions achieved on these beautiful peaks. The traverse works equally well in either direction, and there are advantages for each direction. If going from north to south, you can rappel over the traverse's most difficult pitch and upclimb the tricky north-facing slabs on Maroon Peak. If going from south to north, you can upclimb the traverse's most difficult pitch and descend the shorter route off North Maroon. I describe the traverse from north to south.

Start at the Maroon Lake Trailhead at 9,600 feet and follow North Maroon's Northeast Ridge Route (24R4) to North Maroon's summit. Maroon Peak is only 650 yards away as the eagle soars, but you are not an eagle. The traverse can be time-consuming, so consider the weather before launching.

Descend 100 yards southwest from the summit to a small, 13,820-foot saddle (exposed Class 3). Scramble 200 yards south along the ridge to a 30-foot drop-off. Either rappel over the pitch, downclimb the pitch (Class 4), or avoid the pitch on the ridge's west side via a series of horribly rotten gullies. Continue south along the ridge to the 13,780-foot saddle (39.0722° -106.9888°) at the top of Maroon Peak's Bell Cord Couloir. Climb a Class 4 cleft above the saddle, then zigzag up a series of north-facing Class 3 ledges to Maroon Peak's summit (39.0707° -106.9889°). Descend Maroon Peak's South Ridge Route (24R1).

24C2 – The Triple Feat

From Maroon Lake TH at 9,600'   920 RP   11.1 mi RT   8,548' total   Class 4

This climb collects both of the Maroon Bells and Pyramid. Not for feeble feet, the Triple Feat requires excellent conditioning, and aficionados of the all-day workout lust after this challenge. Follow Combination 24C1 from North Maroon to Maroon Peak and descend Maroon Peak's South Ridge Route (24R1) to 10,300 feet (39.0722° -106.9704°) in West Maroon Creek. Climb Pyramid's West Couloir Route (24R9) and descend Pyramid's Northeast Ridge Route (24R7). The Triple Feat works equally well in the opposite direction.

25. Castle Group

Castle Peak   14,265 feet
Conundrum Peak   14,060 feet

These peaks are 12 miles south of Aspen and are usually climbed together. Castle is the monarch of the Elk Range, and Conundrum is really just a false summit of Castle. Conundrum receives its status on lists of Fourteeners because it is named on the Hayden Peak Quadrangle. Both peaks offer a choice of routes.

Castle is the highest peak in both Gunnison and Pitkin counties. Castle is the Elk Range's highest peak and southernmost Fourteener. After neighboring Conundrum, Castle is also the Elks' easiest Fourteener. If you are climbing in the Elk Range for the first time and are uncertain about these dangerous peaks, climb Castle as a warm-up before trying the Maroon Bells or Capitol.

Because of Conundrum's proximity to Castle, and because Conundrum rises less than 300 feet above its connecting saddle with Castle, it has not qualified as an official Fourteener on most peak lists. Nevertheless, the peak is officially named, above 14,000 feet, and it provides a worthwhile trip.

Conundrum has the distinction of being the easiest Fourteener in the Elk Range. Conundrum has two small summits, one has the given elevation of 14,022 feet, and the other has one more contour line and the extrapolated elevation of 14,060 feet. The second summit is known to be higher, and I use 14,060 feet for the elevation of Conundrum.

25E – Castle Group Essentials

Elevations	Castle Pk	14,265' (NGVD29) 14,269' (NAVD88)
	Conundrum Pk	14,060' (NGVD29) 14,064' (NAVD88)
Ranks	Castle Pk	Colorado's 12th highest ranked peak
	Conundrum Pk	Unranked peak
Location	Pitkin and Gunnison counties, Colorado, USA	
Range	Southern Elk Range	
Summit Coordinates	Castle Pk	39.0097° -106.8613° (WGS84)
	Conundrum Pk	39.0157° -106.8627° (WGS84)
Ownership/Contact	White River and Gunnison national forests – Public Land – 970-945-2521; 970-874-6600	
Prominence and Saddles	Castle Pk	2,365' from 11,900' saddle N of Taylor Pass
	Conundrum Pk	240' from 13,820' Conundrum–Castle Pass
Isolation and Parents	Castle Pk	20.91 miles to La Plata Peak
	Conundrum Pk	0.42 mile to Castle Peak
USGS Maps	**Hayden Peak**, Maroon Bells, Pearl Pass, Gothic	
USFS Maps	White River National Forest, Gunnison National Forest	
Trails Illustrated Map	Map #128 Maroon Bells/Redstone/Marble	
Book Map	See Map 25 on page 251	
Nearest Towns	Aspen – Population 5,900 – Elevation 7,890 feet	
Castle Pk 🥾 Easiest Route	25R1 – Northeast Ridge – Class 2, Easy Snow	
	A boulder hop and easy snow climb to a high saddle, then a Class 2 ridge romp to the summit	
Conundrum Pk 🥾 Easiest Route	25R8 – South Ridge – Class 2, Mod Snow	
	A boulder hop and moderate snow climb to a high saddle, then a Class 2 ridge romp to the summit	
Castle Group Accolades	One of only three Colorado summits that is the highpoint of two counties, Castle Peak is the highpoint of both Pitkin and Gunnison counties. Castle is also the Elk Range's highest peak and southernmost Fourteener. Castle and neighboring Conundrum are the easiest Fourteeners in the Elk Range.	

25T – Castle Group Trailheads

25T1 – Castle Creek Trailhead 9,800 feet 39.0223° -106.8086°

This trailhead provides access to Castle's east and north sides, and Conundrum's east and south sides. Go to the large roundabout on Colorado 82 northwest of Aspen, take the exit for Castle Creek Road to Ashcroft, and measure from this point. Pass Ashcroft at mile 11.0 and turn west (right) onto a dirt road (FR 102) at mile 13.0 (39.0292° -106.8078°) before the main road crosses to Castle Creek's east side. Go south on the dirt road as it parallels Castle Creek. There are some dispersed campsites along this stretch of road. Park at mile 13.5, before the road steepens and becomes dramatically rougher. In winter the road is open to Ashcroft.

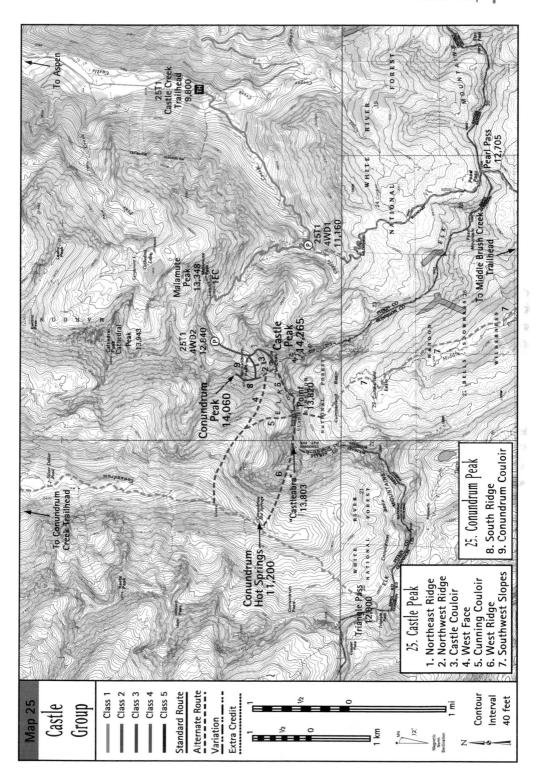

Map 25
Castle Group

Class 1
Class 2
Class 3
Class 4
Class 5
Standard Route
Alternate Route
Variation
Extra Credit

1 — 1/2 — 0 — 1 mi
1 — 1/2 — 0 — 1 km

MN
12°
Magnetic
North
Declination

N

Contour
Interval
40 feet

To Aspen

25T1
Castle Creek
Trailhead
9,800

Castle Creek

WHITE RIVER NATIONAL FOREST

Cooper Creek

Pearl Pass
12,705

To Middle Brush Creek
Trailhead

25T1
4WD1
11,160

Malamute
Peak
13,348
1EC

Cathedral
Peak
13,943

25T1
4WD2
12,840

Conundrum
Peak
14,060

Castle
Peak
14,265

9
2 1 3
8

4

5

6

"Castleabra"
13,803

Conundrum
Hot Springs
11,200

"Gibson Point"
13,880

Cumberland
Basin

7

MAROON BELLS-SNOWMASS WILDERNESS

To Conundrum
Creek Trailhead

Triangle Pass
12,900

WHITE RIVER NATIONAL FOREST

25. Castle Peak
1. Northeast Ridge
2. Northwest Ridge
3. Castle Couloir
4. West Face
5. Cunning Couloir
6. West Ridge
7. Southwest Slopes

25. Conundrum Peak
8. South Ridge
9. Conundrum Couloir

25T1 4WD1 – Castle Creek 4WD Trailhead 11,160 feet 39.0054° -106.8382°
From the Castle Creek Trailhead at 9,800 feet, 4WD vehicles can continue 0.9 mile southwest to a creek crossing at 10,180 feet (39.0149° -106.8167°). This creek crossing can be challenging for vehicles in spring and early summer, but there is a footbridge for hikers. Once safely on the creek's southeast side, continue 1.8 miles southwest up Castle Creek to a road junction at 11,160 feet (39.0054° -106.8382°) where there is parking for several vehicles.

The road heading southwest from here is the extremely rough Pearl Pass Road (FR 129). The road heading north from here is the continuing road (FR 102) up North Castle Creek that gives access to Castle and Conundrum. This road gets quite a bit rougher a mile above this junction, and parking at this junction is a good idea if you don't want to devalue your vehicle.

25T1 4WD2 – North Castle Creek 4WD Trailhead 12,840 feet 39.0187° -106.8563°
From the road junction at 11,160 feet, tough 4WD vehicles can continue on FR 102 2.2 miles north, northwest, then west to the end of the road at an astonishing 12,840 feet. There is parking for many vehicles here. This is the highest road in the Elk Range and one of the highest driving possibilities on a Colorado Fourteener. This road is excluded from the Maroon Bells–Snowmass Wilderness, so in effect, you are driving high and deep into the wilderness.

25T2 – Conundrum Creek Trailhead 8,780 feet 39.1176° -106.8575°
This trailhead provides access to Castle's west side. Go to the large roundabout on Colorado 82 northwest of Aspen, take the exit for Castle Creek Road to Ashcroft, and measure from this point. Go 4.9 miles south and turn southwest (right) onto a paved road. Descend, cross Castle Creek at mile 5.1, and turn south (left) onto a dirt road (FR 128) at a T-junction at mile 5.2. Follow this road southwest past many private driveways to the trailhead's public parking area at mile 6.0. In winter the road is open to within 0.5 mile of the trailhead, but parking is restricted; respect private property owners here and park on the Castle Creek Road.

25T3 – Middle Brush Creek Trailhead 9,180 feet 38.8970° -106.8848°
This trailhead provides access to Castle's southwest side. From the town of Crested Butte, go 2.1 miles southeast on Colorado 135. Turn north (left) onto Brush Creek Road (marked with a sign for a country club) and measure from this point. Follow Brush Creek Road northeast past the country club golf course, stay east (right) at mile 0.5, and turn east then north into the East River drainage. Cross the East River at mile 2.8 (38.8644° -106.9094°) and cross Brush Creek at mile 4.6 (38.8850° -106.9008°). Turn northeast (right) at mile 4.7 (38.8863° -106.9018°) into the Brush Creek drainage on a rougher road (FR 738). Turn east (right) at mile 5.7 (38.8961° -106.8894°) onto the Pearl Pass Road (still FR 738) and park at mile 6.0 (38.8970° -106.8848°) at a nice camping area on a broad ridge with a good view to the south.

25T3 4WD – Middle Brush Creek 4WD Trailhead 10,820 feet 38.9663° -106.8462°

Beyond the Middle Brush Creek Trailhead, the road narrows, descends northeast, and fords West Brush Creek (**38.9002° -106.8811°**). This ford stops most low-clearance 2WD vehicles. 4WD vehicles can go 2.5 miles up the 4WD road in the Middle Brush Creek drainage past another ford to a road junction at 9,480 feet (**38.9143° -106.8526°**). Turn north (left) and continue 3.2 miles north on the now much rougher Pearl Pass Road in the Middle Brush Creek drainage to a junction with the Twin Lakes Trail (**38.9533° -106.8595°**). Continue on the now even rougher Pearl Pass Road, ford Middle Brush Creek twice, and reach a meadow at 10,820 feet (**38.9663° -106.8462°**). Park 4WD vehicles here. This point is 6.9 miles from the Middle Brush Creek Trailhead. The Pearl Pass Road is well known as one of Colorado's roughest, and it can stop 4WD vehicles when it is wet. In winter the road is closed at the Cold Springs Ranch, 3.1 miles from Colorado 135.

25. Castle Peak 14,265 feet

25R – Castle Peak Routes

25R1 – Castle Peak – Northeast Ridge

From Castle Creek TH at 9,800'	*267 RP*	*11.8 mi RT*	*4,465' total*	*Class 2, Easy Snow*
From Castle Creek 4WD TH at 11,160'	*182 RP*	*6.4 mi RT*	*3,105' total*	*Class 2, Easy Snow*
From North Castle Creek 4WD TH at 12,840'	*101 RP*	*2.0 mi RT*	*1,425' total*	*Class 2, Easy Snow*

This is the standard route on Castle. The northeast ridge is similar to the northwest ridge, but the approach to the northeast ridge is easier, since it avoids the moderate snow climb and scruffy slope below the Castle–Conundrum saddle.

Castle Peak from the west.

Start at the Castle Creek Trailhead at 9,800 feet and go 0.9 mile southwest on the road to a creek crossing at 10,180 feet (39.0149° -106.8167°). This creek crossing can be challenging for vehicles in spring and early summer, but there is a footbridge for hikers. Once safely on the creek's southeast side, continue 1.8 miles southwest up Castle Creek to a road junction at 11,160 feet (39.0054° -106.8382°).

The road heading southwest from here is the Pearl Pass Road (FR 129); you do not want to follow this road. From the road junction at 11,160 feet, continue on FR 102 2.2 miles north, then northwest, pass under the ruins of the old Montezuma Mine at 12,400 feet, then go west to the end of the road at an astonishing 12,840 feet (39.0187° -106.8563°).

From the end of the road, hike 0.4 mile southwest into upper Montezuma Basin on rocks and, possibly, gentle early season snow slopes to 13,400 feet (39.0135° -106.8589°). The basin under Castle's north face is an exciting place. Don't continue up the basin, but climb 0.2 mile southeast up a good trail through an otherwise loose shale slope to a small, 13,740-foot saddle (39.0126° -106.8577°) just west of Point 13,780 on Castle's northeast ridge. From the saddle, follow a climber's trail 0.4 mile southwest along the rocky ridge to the copious summit (39.0097° -106.8613°). You can easily climb over a small step on the ridge; it's fun.

25R1 EC – Extra Credit – Malamute Peak 13,348 feet 39.0202° -106.8440°

Class 2+

Usually overlooked by eager Fourteener climbers on their way to the heights, this ranked Thirteener waits a short distance above the approach road in North Castle Creek. If after conquering mighty Castle and Conundrum you feel like you understand the Elk Range, modest Malamute can provide an attitude adjustment.

From the Montezuma Mine at 12,600 feet (39.0193° -106.8481°), leave the comfort of the road and do an ascending traverse to the east across unstable rocks near the angle of repose. You might be tempted to go straight up to the ridge to minimize your time on this loose rock, but if you do that, you will find a nasty, exposed Class 4 downclimb between you and the summit. To avoid this ridge step and keep the difficulty at Class 2+, persist with your pesky ascending traverse across two small rock ribs, then climb up to the ridge near the summit. Scamper east to Malamute's highest point and enjoy the view back to sybaritic Castle.

25R2 – Castle Peak – Northwest Ridge

From Castle Creek TH at 9,800'	*287 RP*	*11.8 mi RT*	*4,465' total*	*Class 2, Mod Snow*
From Castle Creek 4WD TH at 11,160'	*201 RP*	*6.4 mi RT*	*3,105' total*	*Class 2, Mod Snow*
From North Castle Creek 4WD TH at 12,840'	*120 RP*	*2.0 mi RT*	*1,425' total*	*Class 2, Mod Snow*

Depending on conditions, this route is similar to the Northeast Ridge Route (25R1), but the approach to the ridge is tougher, involving either a moderate snow climb, a scruffy slope where the snow has melted, or a combination of both. This used to be the standard route up Castle before the trail was built to the northeast ridge.

Start at the Castle Creek Trailhead at 9,800 feet and follow the Northeast Ridge Route (25R1) to 13,400 feet (39.0135° -106.8589°) in upper Montezuma Basin. Climb 0.3 mile west-southwest to then up a large, moderate snow slope to the 13,820-foot saddle (39.0128° -106.8637°) between Castle and 14,060-foot Conundrum Peak, which is 0.42 mile north of Castle. In late summer, the top of the snow slope melts out, revealing 200 feet of steep dirt just below the saddle. From the saddle, turn south (left) and hike 0.3 mile south-southeast on a dwindling climber's trail up increasingly loose rock near the steepening ridge to the summit (39.0097° -106.8613°). You can pass several ridge steps on the west.

25R3 – Castle Peak – Castle Couloir

From Castle Creek TH at 9,800'	287 RP	11.4 mi RT	4,465' total	Class 2, Mod Snow
From Castle Creek 4WD TH at 11,160'	202 RP	6.0 mi RT	3,105' total	Class 2, Mod Snow
From North Castle Creek 4WD TH at 12,840'	121 RP	1.6 mi RT	1,425' total	Class 2, Mod Snow

This route ascends a wide couloir on the east side of Castle's ragged north face. The couloir provides a straightforward snow climb when filled with stable snow in late spring and early summer, but is a place to avoid in August, when loose rocks replace the snow. With Castle's proximity to the ski mecca of Aspen, it's not surprising that this couloir is popular with skiers. Where expert skiers cavort, climbers may appreciate crampons; both parties can yodel.

Start at the Castle Creek Trailhead at 9,800 feet and follow the Northeast Ridge Route (25R1) to 13,400 feet (39.0135° -106.8589°) in upper Montezuma Basin. Climb 300 yards southwest on snow to the base of the couloir at 13,600 feet (39.0118° -106.8604°). Choose your line in the broad, straight couloir and climb it. If skiers or rocks are descending, you can best stay out of their way by staying on the east (left) side of the couloir. The upper part of the couloir above 14,000 feet reaches a maximum steepness of 40 degrees. After 540 vertical feet of climbing, reach a small 14,140-foot saddle on Castle's northeast ridge (39.0099° -106.8603°). From the saddle, turn west-southwest (right) and climb 100 yards up the summit pitch of the Northeast Ridge Route (25R1). To continue your snow climb all the way to the summit, you can dodge the final rock band to the south (left).

25R4 – Castle Peak – West Face

From Conundrum Creek TH at 8,780'	436 RP	18.8 mi RT	5,485' total	Class 3

This long, seldom climbed route offers a wilderness backpacking alternative to Castle's more pedestrian east side. Start at the Conundrum Creek Trailhead at 8,780 feet and walk 8.0 miles south up the scenic Conundrum Creek Trail to Conundrum Hot Springs at 11,200 feet (39.0012° -106.8910°). There are designated campsites below and above the springs, and two pools at the hot springs offer unsophisticated soaking under Castle's western ramparts.

For the ascent, backtrack 0.5 mile north down the trail to 10,800 feet (39.0203° -106.8872°), leave the trail, cross Conundrum Creek, and climb steeply east into an unnamed basin west of Castle and Conundrum. This basin is full of obnoxious talus, and this route is best done when the rocks are completely snow-covered. The broad west face between Castle and Conundrum has several scruffy cliffs below Conundrum and below the Castle–Conundrum saddle. The easiest route stays south of these cliffs. Choose a route up these steep slopes, reach Castle's northwest ridge at 13,900 feet, and follow that ridge to the summit (Class 3).

25R5 – Castle Peak – Cunning Couloir

From Conundrum Creek TH at 8,780'   460 RP   18.8 mi RT   5,485' total   Class 3, Steep Snow

This hidden couloir may excite your spirit of adventure. Follow the West Face Route (25R4) to 12,200 feet, then climb southeast to 13,000 feet (39.0079° -106.8709°) and spy the crafty couloir to the south. This north-facing couloir retains snow longer than other routes on Castle and is often a better escape from the basin than the West Face Route (25R4). Climb south up the couloir between embracing cliffs to the 13,380-foot saddle (39.0066° -106.8703°) between Point 13,803, aka "Castleabra," to the west and Castle to the east. Continue on Castle's West Ridge Route (25R6) to Castle's summit.

25R6 – Castle Peak – West Ridge

From Conundrum Creek TH at 8,780'   518 RP   20.6 mi RT   6,811' total   Class 3

This arduous ascent is best done from a camp at Conundrum Hot Springs. Start at the Conundrum Creek Trailhead at 8,780 feet and walk 8.0 miles south up the scenic Conundrum Creek Trail to Conundrum Hot Springs at 11,200 feet (39.0012° -106.8910°). There are designated campsites below and above the springs, and two pools at the hot springs. From the hot springs on Conundrum Creek's east side go 100 yards south on a trail to the snout of a large rock glacier. Leave the trail, climb east along the rock glacier's northern edge, then climb steeply east into a tiny basin west of Point 13,803, aka "Castleabra." Persevere up this tiny basin all the way to a 13,620-foot saddle (39.0059° -106.8775°) just south of "Castleabra." Early season snow can make this ascent easier. From the 13,620-foot saddle, climb 100 yards north up scree to "Castleabra"'s 13,803-foot summit (39.0072° -106.8765°). This summit has honorable mention as a Bi, one of Colorado's 200 highest peaks, and provides a lavish view of all the Elk Range Fourteeners.

From "Castleabra," descend 0.4 mile east to the 13,380-foot saddle (39.0066° -106.8703°) between "Castleabra" and the unranked Point 13,820 (Class 2) on Castle's west ridge. This saddle is at the top of the Cunning Couloir (25R5) to the north and the Southwest Slopes Route (25R7) from Cumberland Basin to the south. Climb east through two small cliff bands (Class 3) and continue up the ridge to Point 13,820 (39.0068° -106.8674°). You can see the rest of the route from here. Descend northeast to a 13,580-foot saddle (39.0077° -106.8665°) and climb Castle's upper west ridge to Castle's summit. This traverse has several scruffy cliff bands on it that require some Class 3 scrambling, but they are not sustained.

25R7 – Castle Peak – Southwest Slopes

From Middle Brush Creek TH at 9,180'	*545 RP*	*22.2 mi RT*	*5,085' net; 5,565' total*	*Class 3*
From Middle Brush Creek 4WD TH at 10,820'	*364 RP*	*8.4 mi RT*	*3,445' net; 3,925' total*	*Class 3*

This route has a long approach but takes you through Cumberland Basin, one of Colorado's private places. A 4WD vehicle can shorten the distance considerably, but even that aid can be problematic in wet conditions, since the 4WD road over Pearl Pass is well known as one of Colorado's worst. Consider using a bicycle.

Start at the Middle Brush Creek Trailhead at 9,180 feet and go 2.5 miles up the 4WD road in the Middle Brush Creek drainage to a junction at 9,480 feet (38.9143° -106.8526°). Continue 3.2 miles north (left) on the Pearl Pass Road in the Middle Brush Creek drainage to a junction with the Twin Lakes Trail (38.9533° -106.8595°). Continue on the Pearl Pass Road, ford Middle Brush Creek twice, and reach a meadow at 10,820 feet (38.9663° -106.8462°). 4WD vehicles can park here. This point is 6.9 miles from the Middle Brush Creek Trailhead.

The old trail up Cumberland Basin is now badly overgrown. The sparse trail will speed you on your way, then desert you when you need it most. It is still worth finding and will reduce your bushwhacking adventure. Walk up the road to a switchback where the road climbs southeast toward Pearl Pass. Leave the road and hike west down to the trail that is visible from here. Hike north on the trail into the Maroon Bells–Snowmass Wilderness. Your wilderness adventure begins shortly beyond the small sign marking the boundary.

The trail leads you down to Middle Brush Creek, where the trail appears to cross and continue on the creek's west side. Astute hikers will stop, check their map, and observe that the old trail stays on the creek's east side. You will wonder where as you backtrack along a wall of bushes, but the old trail does stay on the creek's east side. It is buried in the bushes near the creek. Depending on your disposition, either find the trail in the bushes or hike east then north around the initial bushes and find the trail farther up the valley. Continue north and make several similar route choices, as the bushes persist for 1.5 miles.

Break free from the bushes at 11,700 feet (38.9924° -106.8620°) and behold Cumberland Basin. In addition to the basin, you will be treated to an uninterrupted view of Castle's south ridge with its namesake turrets. Hike up through the basin on grass benches, dodging any little cliffs that intervene. Climb north to the 13,380-foot saddle (39.0066° -106.8703°) between Point 13,803, alias "Castleabra," and unranked Point 13,820 on Castle's west ridge. The slope up to the saddle is best climbed when snow-covered but provides reasonable passage on scree after the snow melts. Once on the ridge, continue on the West Ridge Route (25R6) to Castle's summit (Class 3).

25. Conundrum Peak 14,060 feet

25R – Conundrum Peak Routes

25R8 – Conundrum Peak – South Ridge

From Castle Creek TH at 9,800'	*275 RP*	*11.8 mi RT*	*4,344' total*	*Class 2, Mod Snow*
From Castle Creek 4WD TH at 11,160'	*192 RP*	*6.4 mi RT*	*2,984' total*	*Class 2, Mod Snow*
From North Castle Creek 4WD TH at 12,840'	*112 RP*	*2.0 mi RT*	*1,304' total*	*Class 2, Mod Snow*

This is the easiest route on Conundrum. Follow Castle's Northwest Ridge Route (25R2) to the 13,820-foot saddle (**39.0128° -106.8637°**) between Castle and Conundrum. When the snow melts below this saddle, the final climb to the saddle becomes an insulting effort tantamount to ascending a slope of ball bearings. Even the Elks' easiest Fourteener can provide the uninitiated with a taste of the range's woeful rock!

From the saddle, climb 0.15 mile north to Conundrum's southern summit (**39.0143° -106.8637°**). Conundrum has two summits above 14,000 feet. They are 200 yards apart. The southernmost is shown as 14,022 feet on the Hayden Peak Quadrangle. Hike northeast over this summit, descend into a 13,980-foot notch, and climb 150 feet north-northeast to the slightly higher 14,060-foot summit (**39.0157° -106.8627°**).

25R9 – Conundrum Peak – Conundrum Couloir

From Castle Creek TH at 9,800'	*323 RP*	*11.1 mi RT*	*4,260' total*	*Class 3, Steep Snow*
From Castle Creek 4WD TH at 11,160'	*239 RP*	*5.7 mi RT*	*2,900' total*	*Class 3, Steep Snow*
From North Castle Creek 4WD TH at 12,840'	*160 RP*	*1.3 mi RT*	*1,220' total*	*Class 3, Steep Snow*

Conundrum Peak from the southeast.

This is the northeast-facing couloir that reaches the notch between Conundrum's two summits. Try it in early summer when it still has continuous snow. Follow Castle's Northeast Ridge Route (25R1) to 13,400 feet (39.0135° -106.8589°) in the bowl between Castle and Conundrum. You can easily see the deeply inset Conundrum Couloir from here as it splits Conundrum's northeast face. Climb some scree to 13,500 feet below the couloir.

Climb the arrow-straight defile for 480 feet to the 13,980-foot notch (39.0153° -106.8630°) between Conundrum's two summits. The steepness reaches 47 degrees. There is usually a cornice at the top, and climbing around it is the route's crux. In the notch, Conundrum's highest point waits for you 150 feet to the north-northeast. Ascending the Conundrum Couloir and descending the South Ridge Route (25R8) is a smart Tour de Conundrum.

25C – Castle and Conundrum Combination Route
25C1 – Castle Northeast Ridge → Conundrum South Ridge

From Castle Creek TH at 9,800'	297 RP	12.4 mi RT	4,789' total	Class 2, Mod Snow
From Castle Creek 4WD TH at 11,160'	211 RP	7.0 mi RT	3,429' total	Class 2, Mod Snow
From North Castle Creek 4WD TH at 12,840'	130 RP	2.6 mi RT	1,729' total	Class 2, Mod Snow

This is the usual way of climbing Castle and Conundrum together. You can do the traverse in the opposite direction, but it is always good to get the highest peak climbed first.

Start at the Castle Creek Trailhead at 9,800 feet and climb Castle's Northeast Ridge Route (25R1) to Castle's summit. Descend 0.3 mile north on Castle's northwest ridge (see 25R2) to the 13,820-foot saddle (39.0128° -106.8637°) between Castle and Conundrum, and climb the upper part of Conundrum's South Ridge Route (25R8) to Conundrum's summit, where you can gaze back at what you have accomplished. Descend Conundrum's South Ridge Route (25R8).

Chapter Six

San Juan Range

Introduction

The San Juan Range is Colorado's finest range. Other Colorado ranges are linear, long, and narrow, and from their summits you can almost always see civilization. The San Juans are a vast mountain area in Colorado's southwest corner covering more than 4,000 square miles!

The San Juans contain 11 county summits and 13 Fourteeners. Only the Sawatch Range has more Fourteeners. San Juan peaks are both numerous and rugged, and many of Colorado's hardest Fourteeners are in the San Juans. The San Juans contain six wilderness areas, including Colorado's largest—the Weminuche Wilderness. The San Juans are less crowded than other ranges closer to the eastern slope's metropolitan areas, since it is not reasonable to climb in the San Juans on a two-day weekend from Denver. Even if you live in Durango, there are many San Juan areas that still require a multiday backpack. The San Juans are full of jagged wilderness!

One unpleasant San Juan reality is rotten rock. If you climb a dozen San Juan peaks, you are bound to find a chip-rock slope to curse. If you climb in the San Juans long enough, you will eventually find yourself on a hard-packed dirt slope covered with ball-bearing debris at the angle of repose and, if you are unlucky, there will be a cliff below you. If you keep looking, you will find diseased, knife-edge ridges with no logical means of support. Hardened San Juan veterans will run across exposed junk that can strike terror into the heart of a San Juan novice. If you stick to the standard routes on the Fourteeners, you will not encounter these extremes, but approach San Juan peaks with sharpened senses.

The large, high area of the San Juans collects a lot of winter snow, and avalanche danger is often extreme in these steep mountains. The deep snow mantle takes a long time to melt, and some areas are not easily accessible until July. Many San Juan peaks carry a lot of snow into August. You should always consider carrying an ice ax.

26. San Luis Peak 14,014 feet

San Luis is perhaps the least climbed of Colorado's Fourteeners. The shy peak is far from everywhere and offers little technical excitement. San Luis, the San Juans' easternmost Fourteener, is located in the heart of the La Garita Wilderness, 9 miles north of Creede, 20 miles east of Lake City, and 40 miles south of Gunnison. *La garita* means "the lookout" in Spanish, and the La

Garita Wilderness amplifies this name. San Luis is the highest peak and lone Fourteener in this extensive wilderness, and it is precisely San Luis' reclusive nature that makes the peak well worth climbing. Many elk live here, and your chances of seeing a large elk herd on San Luis are good. Also, moose have been reintroduced to Stewart Creek.

26E – San Luis Peak Essentials

Elevations	14,014' (NGVD29) 14,019' (NAVD88)
Rank	Colorado's 50th highest ranked peak
Location	Saguache County, Colorado, USA
Range	Eastern San Juan Range – La Garitas
Summit Coordinates	37.9868° -106.9313° (WGS84)
Ownership/Contact	Gunnison National Forest – Public Land – 970-874-6600
Prominence and Saddle	3,114' from 10,900' Spring Creek Pass
Isolation and Parent	26.93 miles to Redcloud Peak
USGS Maps	**San Luis Peak, Stewart Peak, Elk Park**, Half Moon Pass
USFS Maps	**Gunnison National Forest**, Rio Grande National Forest
Trails Illustrated Map	Map #139 La Garita/Cochetopa Hills
Book Map	See Map 26 on page 262
Nearest Towns	Creede – Population 5,460 – Elevation 8,799'
	Lake City – Population 385 – Elevation 8,661'
	Gunnison – Population 420 – Elevation 7,700'
San Luis Peak 🏂 Easiest Route	26R1 – East Slopes – Class 1
	A trail hike all the way to the top
San Luis' Accolades	San Luis is the easternmost Fourteener in the San Juans and the lone
	Fourteener and highest peak in the extensive La Garita Mountains and
	Wilderness Area.

26T – San Luis Peak Trailheads
26T1 – Stewart Creek Trailhead 10,460 feet 38.0246° -106.8412°

This trailhead provides access to San Luis' east side. There are three routes to this trailhead, and they are all long and complicated. The Forest Service maps are a big help in finding this trailhead. Winter road closures are far from this trailhead.

Route 1. If you are approaching from the north, turn south onto Colorado 114 from US 50. This junction is 33.0 miles west of Monarch Pass and 7.5 miles east of Gunnison. Go 20.0 miles south on Colorado 114 and turn right onto Saguache County NN14 (BLM 3083) along Cochetopa Creek. Go 7.0 miles south on Saguache County NN14 to Upper Dome Reservoir's south end and turn south (right) onto Saguache County 2166, which is also called the Cochetopa Road. This junction has a sign for the Stewart Creek Trailhead. If you are approaching from the south, go 7.5 miles west from the summit of Cochetopa

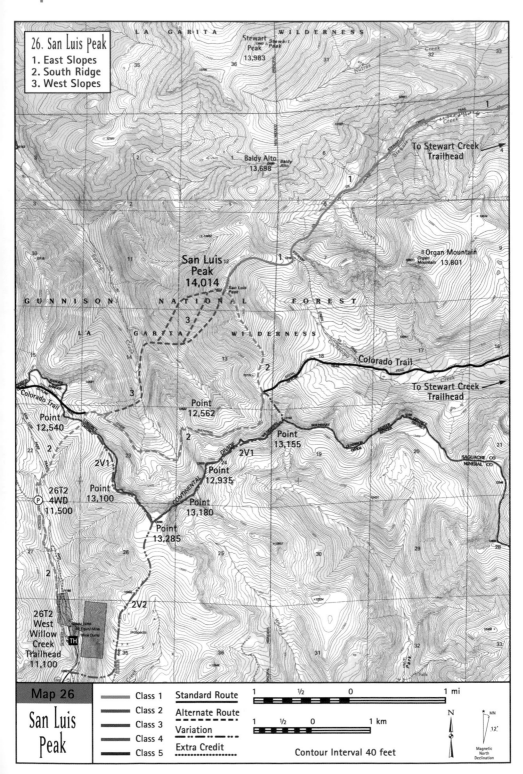

26. San Luis Peak
1. East Slopes
2. South Ridge
3. West Slopes

Map 26

San Luis Peak

	Class 1	Standard Route
	Class 2	Alternate Route
	Class 3	Variation
	Class 4	Extra Credit
	Class 5	

Contour Interval 40 feet

Pass. Measure from the junction of Saguache County NN14 and Saguache County 2166.

Go south on Saguache County 2166, straight (right) at mile 4.3, and enter the Gunnison National Forest at mile 6.9. The road is now FR 794. Cross Pauline Creek at mile 11.3 and cross Perfecto Creek at mile 13.8. Turn west (right) at mile 14.1 and stay on FR 794. Go straight (left) at mile 16.3 and stay on FR 794. Cross Chavez Creek at mile 17.1, pass the unsigned Nutras Creek Trailhead on Nutras Creek's north side at mile 18.6, and continue southeast on FR 794 to reach the Stewart Creek Trailhead at mile 20.8. The signed trailhead is south of the road before the road crosses Stewart Creek.

Route 2. From the Colorado 50–Colorado 149 junction west of Gunnison, go 45.3 miles south on Colorado 149 to Lake City. Continue south through Lake City on Colorado 149 and go another 10.0 miles southeast on Colorado 149. Just before Slumgullion Pass, turn north (left) onto Los Pinos-Cebolla Road (FR 788) and measure from this point.

Pass Slumgullion Campground at mile 0.1, Cannibal Plateau Trailhead at mile 1.0, Deer Lakes Campground at mile 2.8, Hidden Valley Campground at mile 7.3, Spruce Campground at mile 8.4, and Cebolla Campground at mile 9.3. Cross Mineral Creek at mile 12.1, Cebolla and Spring creeks at mile 15.2, and reach a three-way junction at mile 15.3. This is Cathedral.

Turn north (right) and continue on FR 788. Go straight (left) at mile 16.4, climb east, enter Gunnison National Forest at mile 19.5, cross Los Pinos Pass at mile 21.0, and turn north (right) onto FR 790 at mile 22.1 in Sage Park. Go south on FR 790, pass Groundhog Park at mile 24.5, turn east, cross Los Pinos Creek at mile 27.2, and pass the signed Cebolla Trailhead on the east side of the east fork of Los Pinos Creek at mile 28.5.

Continue east on FR 790, pass Willow Park at mile 29.6, and turn south (right) onto FR 794.28 (Perfecto Creek Road) at mile 32.1. Go south on FR 794.28, cross Pauline Creek at mile 33.0, cross Perfecto Creek at mile 34.7, and turn southwest (right) onto FR 794 at mile 36.2. Cross Chavez Creek at mile 37.0, pass the unsigned Nutras Creek Trailhead on Nutras Creek's north side at mile 38.5, and continue southeast on FR 794 to reach the Stewart Creek Trailhead at mile 40.7. The signed trailhead is south of the road before the road crosses Stewart Creek.

Route 3. If you are approaching from the north, turn south onto Colorado 114 from US 50. This junction is 33.0 miles west of Monarch Pass and 7.5 miles east of Gunnison. Go 20.0 miles south on Colorado 114 and turn right onto Saguache County NN14 (BLM 3083) along Cochetopa Creek. Go 3.5 miles south on Saguache County NN14 and turn west (right) onto BLM 3084, which continues as FR 788. **If you are approaching from the south,** go 11.0 miles west from the summit of Cochetopa Pass. Measure from the junction of Saguache County NN14 and BLM 3084.

Go south on BLM 3084, straight (left) at mile 8.8, and continue on FR 790, which is also called Big Meadows Road. Pass Blue Park, reach Big Meadows at mile 19.0, and turn south (left) onto FR 794.28 (Perfecto Creek Road). Go south on FR 794.28, cross Pauline Creek at mile 19.9, cross Perfecto Creek at mile 21.6, and turn southwest (right) onto FR 794 at mile 23.2. Cross Chavez Creek at mile 24.0, pass the unsigned Nutras Creek Trailhead on Nutras Creek's north side at mile 25.5, and continue southeast on FR 794 to reach the Stewart Creek Trailhead at mile 27.7. The signed trailhead is south of the road before the road crosses Stewart Creek.

26T2 – West Willow Creek Trailhead 11,100 feet 37.9326° -106.9599°

This trailhead provides access to San Luis' south side. From the US 160–Colorado 149 junction, go 21.4 miles north to the Willow Creek bridge just south of Creede. You also can reach Creede by driving south on Colorado 149 from Lake City via Slumgullion Pass. There are two approaches to the trailhead from Creede. Winter road closure varies but is not far above Creede.

Route 1. This approach is longer and gentler than the second approach. From the Willow Creek bridge just south of Creede, go 0.3 mile south on Colorado 149 on the west side of Willow Creek to three dirt roads leading west (right). Turn west onto the northernmost (rightmost) of the three dirt roads and measure from this point. Climb the hill southwest of Creede, pass the Creede cemetery turnoff at mile 0.5, turn west (left) at a T-junction at mile 1.2, pass the southern turnoff for the Rat Creek–West Willow Creek 4x4 Loop Road at mile 3.3, and continue on the main road to Allens Crossing over West Willow Creek at mile 6.3. Turn north (left) at a T-junction just east of Allens Crossing and go north to a parking area below the Equity Mine at mile 8.6. The road is excellent to this point, and this is the trailhead.

Route 2. This scenic approach is steep. Measure from the Willow Creek bridge just south of Creede. Go north through Creede and continue north on the dirt road out of town. Pass the Phoenix Park Road at mile 1.2 and continue north up the spectacular West Willow Creek Gorge. Pass the East Willow Creek 4x4 Loop Road at mile 3.2, pass the Nelson Mountain Road at mile 4.9, and continue north to Allens Crossing, where the first approach joins this route at mile 5.3. From Allens Crossing, go north to the trailhead parking area below the Equity Mine at mile 7.6. The trailhead parking area is 100 yards north of the northern junction with the Rat Creek–West Willow Creek 4x4 Loop Road.

26T2 4WD – West Willow Creek 4WD Trailhead 11,500 feet 37.9556° -106.9666°

From the West Willow Creek Trailhead, 4WD vehicles can continue 1.6 miles north, crossing West Willow Creek twice, to a parking spot at 11,500 feet, just before the road leaves the valley and climbs steeply up the hill to the west.

26R – San Luis Peak Routes

26R1 – San Luis Peak – East Slopes

From Stewart Creek TH at 10,460'   194 RP   12.0 mi RT   3,554' total   Class 1

This is the easiest route on San Luis. From the Stewart Creek Trailhead at 10,460 feet, hike 4.0 miles west up Stewart Creek on the Stewart Creek Trail (FT 470) through a wonderful wilderness to treeline at 12,000 feet (38.0016° -106.9076°). Climb 1.0 mile southwest on the continuing Stewart Creek Trail to the 13,107-foot saddle (37.9914° -106.9179°) between San Luis and 13,801-foot Organ Mountain, which is 2.0 miles east of San Luis. From the saddle, climb 0.5 mile west on the continuing trail through the scree below a rounded ridge toward San Luis' 13,700-foot northeast shoulder and hike 0.5 mile southwest to the summit (37.9868° -106.9313°).

26R2 – San Luis Peak – South Ridge

From West Willow Creek TH at 11,100'   216 RP   13.8 mi RT   2,914' net; 3,714' total   Class 1
From West Willow Creek 4WD TH at 11,500'   175 RP   10.6 mi RT   2,514' net; 3,314' total   Class 1

This interesting alternative route is only slightly longer than the East Slopes Route. The route is almost entirely above treeline. Start at the West Willow Creek Trailhead at 11,100 feet, go 100 yards south and 1.6 miles north on the Rat Creek–West Willow Creek 4x4 Loop Road, crossing West Willow Creek twice en route, until the road turns steeply up the hill to the west (left) at 11,500 feet (37.9556° -106.9666°). This is the West Willow Creek 4WD Trailhead.

Leave the Rat Creek–West Willow Creek 4x4 Loop Road here, go 0.3 mile north on an old 4WD road, cross back to the creek's east side (37.9589° -106.9661°), and go 100 yards northeast from the creek to 11,660 feet (37.9595°

San Luis Peak from the southwest.

−106.9651°). Do not go north-northwest toward San Luis Pass, but climb 0.7 mile north-northeast up a shoulder on an old road to the broad, 12,300-foot saddle (37.9670° −106.9582°) just southeast of Point 12,540. You can see the old road and the rocky Point 12,540 from below. You will first see San Luis when you reach the saddle, and this is a postcard view.

Cross the 12,300-foot saddle and descend 100 yards north to the excellent Colorado and Continental Divide Trail (FT 465). Follow this trail 1.8 miles east as it descends to a low point of 11,900 feet in the trees, then contours and climbs north around a basin to a 12,380-foot saddle (37.9664° −106.9386°) in the upper Spring Creek drainage. Continue 1.2 miles east on the still excellent FT 465 as it contours around a second basin, then climbs north to the 12,620-foot saddle (37.9715° −106.9240°) between San Luis and Point 13,155, a ranked Thirteener that is 1.5 miles south of San Luis. The approach is over. From this saddle, walk 1.1 miles north-northeast up San Luis' gentle, easy south ridge to the summit (37.9868° −106.9313°).

26R2 V1 – Variation – Pointfest

Class 3

This major variation allows you to stay even higher and climb three Thirteeners on your way to San Luis. From the 12,300-foot saddle (37.9670° −106.9582°) just southeast of Point 12,540, climb 0.8 mile southeast up the gentle ridge to Point 13,100 (37.9571° −106.9518°). This is a false summit, but it provides a good view of the terrain ahead. Continue 0.5 mile southeast to Point 13,285—a ranked Thirteener. Curiously, the highest point is 200 yards northeast of the rounded summit that the map marks as 13,285 (37.9523° −106.9449°). The true highpoint is at least 5 feet higher, and the map does not record this fact.

The next stretch of ridge requires some Class 3 scrambling and is out of character with the rest of this gentle hike. Descend steeply on the south side of the rough ridge leading northeast from Point 13,285 (some Class 3). Pick your way to a point near the 12,900-foot saddle between Point 13,285 and Point 13,180, then ascend Point 13,180 (37.9562° −106.9372°) via some nifty Class 3 scrambling. Point 13,180 has a soft rank and only appears on peak lists that record such minutia.

Follow the now gentle ridge northeast over or around Point 12,935 (37.9609° −106.9348°), an unranked summit, and on toward Point 13,155 (37.9674° −106.9201°), another ranked Thirteener. Another rough stretch of ridge southwest of this summit requires some Class 3 scrambling. Ascend the spectacular summit block of Point 13,155 on its north side via a solid 40-foot Class 3 scramble. Descend 0.4 mile northeast from Point 13,155 to the 12,620-foot saddle (37.9715° −106.9240°) between Point 13,155 and San Luis and continue 1.1 miles north-northeast up San Luis' gentle south ridge.

26R2 V2 – Variation – High South
Class 2

Start your climb 0.5 mile south of (below) the West Willow Creek Trailhead, where another road crosses to the creek's east side (37.9299° -106.9604°). Climb east up the steep, grassy slope above this point to yet another road on the broad ridge above. Follow this road north up the gentle ridge to the summit of Point 13,285 (37.9523° -106.9449°) and join Variation 26R2 V1 here.

26R3 – San Luis Peak – West Slopes

From West Willow Creek TH at 11,100'	*330 RP*	*10.9 mi RT*	*2,914' net; 5,114' total*	*Class 2, Easy Snow*
From West Willow Creek 4WD TH at 11,500'	*289 RP*	*7.7 mi RT*	*2,514' net; 4,714' total*	*Class 2, Easy Snow*

This used to be the standard route on San Luis, but access problems in Spring Creek have relegated it to an alternate route. Still accessible from the West Willow Creek Trailhead, this route offers an interesting approach and a seasonal snow climb. People usually do this route to experience good snow in the Yawner Gullies on San Luis' southwest face.

Start at the West Willow Creek Trailhead at 11,100 feet and follow the South Ridge Route (26R2) to the Colorado and Continental Divide Trail below the 12,300-foot saddle southeast of Point 12,540. Descend 0.35 mile east on the Colorado Trail to a switchback at 11,940 feet (37.9685° -106.9531°). Leave the Colorado Trail and boldly descend into the upper Spring Creek drainage. Descend 0.6 mile northeast to 11,200 feet and contour 0.5 mile around the north end of Point 12,562 to the base of San Luis' southwest face.

If you are here for a snow climb, choose one of the three Yawner Gullies. The northern and central gullies reach the upper part of San Luis' rounded west shoulder, while the southern Yawner follows a classic line directly to the summit. The central gully's steepness does not exceed 30 degrees. If you are here after the snow is gone, climb 1.2 miles steeply up San Luis' rounded west shoulder north of the Yawner Gullies directly to the summit. Ascending this route and descending the South Ridge Route (26R2) makes a fine Tour de San Luis.

27. Uncompahgre Group

Uncompahgre Peak   14,309 feet
Wetterhorn Peak   14,015 feet

These dramatic peaks guard the San Juans' northern edge 10 miles west of Lake City. Uncompahgre's great height and Wetterhorn's classic shape make them siren sentinels that you can see from many vantage points. Together, they provide an excellent outing.

The uncompahrable Uncompahgre Peak indeed claims many titles. It is Colorado's sixth highest peak, Colorado's sixth most prominent peak, the highest peak in the San Juans, the highest peak in Hinsdale County, and the highest peak in its namesake wilderness area. You can easily recognize its shapely size from numerous viewpoints, many quite distant.

The Uncompahgre Wilderness Area was formerly named the Big Blue Wilderness Area. *Uncompahgre* is a Native American word from the Ute Nation meaning "hot-water spring." It is pronounced un-kum-PAH-gray.

Uncompahgre is a peak of contrasts. A trail reaches the summit from the south, but the peak has a fearsome, near-vertical 700-foot-high north face. Courtly cliffs grace this compelling peak's lower ramparts, and clever routes winding past them will draw you upward.

Colorado's Wetterhorn is named after the extant Wetterhorn rising above Grindelwald in Switzerland's Bernese Alps. The Swiss Wetterhorn is the more famous of the two, and its ornamental shape dignifies many postcards. Nevertheless, Colorado's Wetterhorn has several advantages. It is higher—the Swiss Wetterhorn rises to a paltry 12,142 feet, while Colorado's Wetterhorn exceeds the magic 14,000-foot height. Also, if you live in the western United States, Colorado's Wetterhorn is more accessible. It is good to remember a peak's roots, however. *Wetterhorn* means "weather peak" in German.

Colorado's Wetterhorn is an elegant peak with four ridges and four faces. The near-vertical 800-foot-high north face gives the peak its distinctive shape, and the southeast ridge offers a more moderate approach to the summit. Even by its easiest route, Wetterhorn is a challenging peak. It has more to offer the technical mountaineer than many of Colorado's easy Fourteeners.

Both Uncompahgre and Wetterhorn are in the Uncompahgre Peak Butterfly Closure, which is designed to protect the dwindling Uncompahgre fritillary butterfly. This unremarkable-looking black and brown mottled butterfly has a one-inch wingspan. Left behind in the alpine zone when the last large glaciers retreated from the area, it's now threatened by sheep grazing, overzealous collection, and global warming. Grazing and collection are prohibited in the closure area, and climbers should stay on trails and routes as much as possible.

27E – Uncompahgre Group Essentials

Elevations	Uncompahgre Pk	14,309' (NGVD29) 14,314' (NAVD88)
	Wetterhorn Pk	14,015 (NGVD29) 14,020' (NAVD88)
Ranks	Uncompahgre Pk	Colorado's 6th highest ranked peak
	Wetterhorn Pk	Colorado's 49th highest ranked peak
Location	Hinsdale and Ouray counties, Colorado, USA	
Range	North-Central San Juan Range	
Summit Coordinates	Uncompahgre Pk	38.0716° -107.4621° (WGS84)
	Wetterhorn Pk	38.0606° -107.5109° (WGS84)
Ownership/Contacts	Uncompahgre National Forest – Public Land	
	US Forest Service – Gunnison Ranger District – 970-641-0471	
	US Forest Service – Ouray Ranger District – 970-249-3711	

27E – Uncompahgre Group Essentials

Prominence and Saddles	Uncompahgre Pk	4,242' from 10,067' Cochetopa Pass
	Wetterhorn Pk	1,635' from 12,380' Uncompahgre saddle
Isolation and Parents	Uncompahgre Pk	85.16 miles to La Plata Peak
	Wetterhorn Pk	2.75 miles to Uncompahgre Peak
USGS Maps	Uncompahgre Peak, Wetterhorn Peak, Lake City, Courthouse Mountain	
USFS Map	Uncompahgre National Forest	
Trails Illustrated Map	Map #141 Telluride, Silverton, Ouray, Lake City	
Book Map	See Map 27 on page 270	
Nearest Towns	Lake City – Population 385 – Elevation 8,661'	
	Ouray – Population 930 – Elevation 7,792'	
	Silverton – Population 520 – Elevation 9,308'	
Uncompahgre 🥾 Easiest Route	27R1 – East Slopes – Class 2	
	A good trail goes high onto the peak and a rougher trail continues to the highest point	
Wetterhorn Pk 🥾 Easiest Route	27R4 – Southeast Ridge – Class 3	
	A Class 1 trail hike into the basin, a Class 2 boulder hop to the ridge, and a Class 3 pitch to the top	
Uncompahgre Group Accolades	Uncompahgre is Colorado's sixth highest peak, Colorado's sixth most prominent peak, the highest peak in the San Juans, the highest peak in Hinsdale County, and the highest peak in the Uncompahgre Wilderness Area. Wetterhorn, named after the extant Wetterhorn in the Swiss Alps, is one of Colorado's most beautiful Fourteeners.	

27T – Uncompahgre Group Trailheads

27T1 – Nellie Creek Trailhead 9,300 feet 38.0204° -107.4007°

This trailhead provides access to Uncompahgre's east side. From the Colorado 50–Colorado 149 junction west of Gunnison, go 45.3 miles south on Colorado 149 to Lake City. Measure from the junction of Second Street and Gunnison Avenue (Colorado 149) in downtown Lake City. There is a sign here for Engineer Pass. Leave Colorado 149 and go two blocks west on Second Avenue to a T-junction at Bluff Street. Turn south (left) and follow the dirt Henson Creek Road (Hinsdale County 20) west up Henson Creek. Pass the old Henson town site at 3.9 miles and reach the signed Nellie Creek Road at 5.2 miles. Passenger cars should park here, at 9,300 feet. There is a legal campsite at Nellie Creek, but camping is not permitted elsewhere along this portion of the Henson Creek Road. In winter the Henson Creek Road is plowed to Nellie Creek.

27T1 4WD – Nellie Creek 4WD Trailhead 11,460 feet 38.0634° -107.4225°

The road up Nellie Creek above the Nellie Creek Trailhead requires a 4WD vehicle. From the Henson Creek Road, turn north and follow the Nellie Creek Road (FR 877) as it climbs along Nellie Creek's east side. The road crosses to

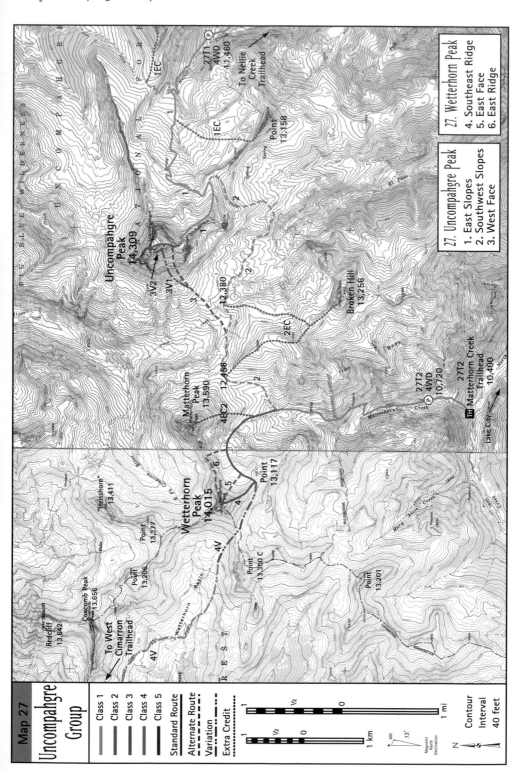

Map 27
Uncompahgre Group

Class 1
Class 2
Class 3
Class 4
Class 5

Standard Route
Alternate Route
Variation
Extra Credit

½   0   1 mi

1 km   ½   0   1

MN
13°
Magnetic
North
Declination

N

Contour
Interval
40 feet

27. Uncompahgre Peak
1. East Slopes
2. Southwest Slopes
3. West Face

27. Wetterhorn Peak
4. Southeast Ridge
5. East Face
6. East Ridge

BIG BLUE WILDERNESS

UNCOMPAHGRE

NATIONAL   FOREST

Uncompahgre
Peak
14,309

3V2
3V1

2T1 P
4WD
11,460

To Nellie
Creek
Trailhead

Point
13,158

1EC

1EC

El Paso

12,380

2

2

2

2EC

Broken Hill
13,256

Matterhorn
Peak
13,590

12,468

4EC2

2

Matterhorn   Creek

2T2 P
4WD
10,720

2T2
Matterhorn Creek
Trailhead
10,400

Lake City

"Heissehorn"
13,411

Point
13,377

Point
13,206

Coxcomb Peak
13,656

Redcliff
13,642

To West
Cimarron
Trailhead

4V

4V

6

5

Point
13,117

Wetterhorn
Peak
14,015

4

4V

Point
13,390 C

WETTERHORN   Basin

Point
13,201

Mary Alice Creek

Nellie Creek's west side at 1.9 miles (38.0428° -107.4047°). Turn west (sharp left) at 2.2 miles (38.0469° -107.4058°) and continue northwest into upper Nellie Creek to the end of the road at 9.1 miles. The road ends at 11,460 feet at the boundary of the Uncompahgre Wilderness (38.0634° -107.4225°), 3.9 miles above the Henson Creek Road. Uncompahgre's great mass dominates the view to the west.

27T2 – Matterhorn Creek Trailhead 10,400 feet 38.0231° -107.4925°

This trailhead provides access to Wetterhorn's south side and Uncompahgre's west side. From the Colorado 50–Colorado 149 junction west of Gunnison, go 45.3 south on Colorado 149 miles to Lake City. Measure from the junction of Second Street and Gunnison Avenue (Colorado 149) in downtown Lake City. There is a sign here for Engineer Pass. Leave Colorado 149 and go two blocks west on Second Avenue to a T-junction at Bluff Street. Turn south (left) and follow the dirt Henson Creek Road (Hinsdale County 20) west up Henson Creek. Pass the old Henson town site at 3.9 miles, the signed Nellie Creek Road at 5.2 miles, and El Paso Creek at 7.4 miles to reach North Henson Creek Road in the old Capitol City town site after 9.2 miles (38.0075° -107.4665°). This point is at 9,715 feet and is easily reached with passenger cars. Other than the campsite at Nellie Creek, camping is not permitted along the Henson Creek Road between Lake City and Capitol City. The road to Capitol City is often open in late April.

Leave the main Henson Creek Road and continue northwest on the North Henson Creek Road (FR 870), which is steep and rough but still passable for most passenger cars. Reach Matterhorn Creek at 11.2 miles. This point is at 10,400 feet. This is the trailhead, and most parties park here. There are some pleasant campsites between Capitol City and Matterhorn Creek.

27T2 4WD – Matterhorn Creek 4WD Trailhead 10,720 feet 38.0293° -107.4908°

From the Matterhorn Creek Trailhead, a 4WD road (FR 870.2A) goes 0.6 mile north up Matterhorn Creek's east side to 10,720 feet, where there is a small parking area below a Forest Service gate.

27T3 – West Cimarron Trailhead 10,750 feet 38.1117° -107.5533°

This trailhead provides access to Wetterhorn Basin on Wetterhorn's west side. You can reach this trailhead from either the Cimarron Creek Road or the Owl Creek Pass Road.

For the Cimarron approach: On US 50, go 2.7 miles east of Cimarron. Cimarron is 45 miles west of Gunnison and 20 miles east of Montrose. Turn south onto the well-maintained Cimarron Creek Road (FR 858) and measure from this point. Go around Silver Jack Reservoir's east side at mile 18.0, turn right at mile 20.3, turn right at mile 20.5, pass the Owl Creek Pass turnoff at mile 27.1, cross a stream at mile 30.0, and reach the trailhead at mile 30.6.

For the Owl Creek approach: On US 550, go 1.8 miles north of Ridgway. Ridgway is 26 miles south of Montrose and 11 miles north of Ouray. Drive

13.0 miles east over Owl Creek Pass (38.1579° -107.5624°) to the Cimarron Creek Road (38.1546° -107.5599°), turn south (right), and reach the trailhead after 16.5 miles. The last 2.0 miles are rough, and you may choose to park before you reach the trailhead.

27T4 – Middle Cimarron Trailhead 10,040 feet 38.1437° -107.5251°
This little-used trailhead provides access to Wetterhorn's north side. On US 50, go 2.7 miles east of Cimarron. Cimarron is 45 miles west of Gunnison and 20 miles east of Montrose. Turn south onto the well-maintained Cimarron Creek Road and measure from this point. Go around Silver Jack Reservoir's east side at mile 18.0, turn right at mile 20.3, then turn left at mile 20.5 onto the rougher Middle Fork Road (FR 861.1) and follow it to the trailhead at mile 25.2.

27. Uncompahgre Peak 14,309 feet

27R – Uncompahgre Peak Routes
27R1 – Uncompahgre Peak – East Slopes

From Nellie Creek TH at 9,300'	282 RP	16.0 mi RT	5,009' total	Class 2
From Nellie Creek 4WD TH at 11,460'	153 RP	8.2 mi RT	2,849' total	Class 2

This is the easiest route on Uncompahgre, but without a 4WD vehicle, it is long. Except for one short Class 2 section over small talus, it is a road and trail hike. From the Nellie Creek Trailhead at 9,300 feet, follow the 4WD Nellie Creek Road (FR 877) as it climbs along Nellie Creek's east side. The road crosses to Nellie Creek's west side after 1.9 miles (38.0428° -107.4047°). Turn west (sharp left) after 2.2 miles (38.0469° -107.4058°) and continue northwest into upper Nellie Creek to the end of the road at the Uncompahgre Wilderness boundary (38.0634° -107.4225°), 3.9 miles above the trailhead.

From the wilderness boundary at 11,460 feet, follow the well-worn Uncompahgre Peak Trail (FT 239) 0.9 mile west as it climbs steadily toward the peak. Go west (left) at a trail junction at 11,940 feet (38.0688° -107.4330°). Go 1.6 miles west then southwest to 12,740 feet (38.0639° -107.4527°). From here, in a counterintuitive move away from the peak, go 0.2 mile southeast then climb 0.4 mile west to reach the south ridge at 13,300 feet (38.0633° -107.4566°); stay on the trail in this section. Climb 0.4 mile northwest, then switchback 300 yards up an east-facing slope to 13,800 feet (38.0672° -107.4619°), where the trail's teeth are above you to the north. Continue climbing 200 yards north on the now fading, braided trail and dodge the route's crux cliffs between 13,800 feet and 14,000 feet (some Class 2). Find the reemerging trail above the cliffs and follow it 0.3 mile north across Uncompahgre's gentle upper south slopes to reach the summit (38.0716° -107.4621°). You can laze on flat ground near the highpoint or, with a few steps, proudly pose for a photo standing on top of Uncompahgre's sheer north face. ¡Tenga cuidado!

27R1 EC – Extra Credit – Pointification

Class 2

From the trail junction at 11,940 feet (38.0688° -107.4330°), leave the Uncompahgre Peak Trail and switchback 0.6 mile north on the Big Blue Trail (FT 232) to a 12,380-foot saddle (38.0725° -107.4316°). Leave the Big Blue Trail and hike 0.7 mile east to Point 13,106 (38.0712° -107.4210°), a ranked Thirteener. Those with grass growing between their toes can continue 2.1 miles northwest then west to Point 13,091 (38.0726° -107.3878°), another ranked Thirteener. Both of these summits have the distinction of being on the oft-snickered-at list of Colorado's lowest 100 Thirteeners.

As a separate exercise, leave the Uncompahgre Peak trail between 12,100 and 12,400 feet and hike 0.9 mile south to a 12,780-foot saddle (38.0567° -107.4424°). Hike 0.3 mile southeast up a narrow ridge to Point 13,158 (38.0542° -107.4381°), a ranked Thirteener that proudly rises above the lowest 100 list. Whatever their rankings, you will be able to pontificate about the views from these summits.

27R2 – Uncompahgre Peak – Southwest Slopes

From Matterhorn Creek TH at 10,400'	*275 RP*	*15.5 mi RT*	*3,909' net; 4,905' total*	*Class 2*
From Matterhorn Creek 4WD TH at 10,720'	*255 RP*	*14.3 mi RT*	*3,589' net; 4,585' total*	*Class 2*

This easy route is longer than the East Slopes Route if you start that route at the Nellie Creek 4WD Trailhead but allows you to climb Uncompahgre and Wetterhorn together. This route dodges all the cliffs on Uncompahgre's west side and with only one short Class 2 section, is little more than a long trail hike.

Start at the Matterhorn Creek Trailhead at 10,400 feet and go 0.6 mile north up the 4WD road on Matterhorn Creek's east side to the Forest Service gate at 10,720 feet (38.0293° -107.4908°). Continue 0.75 mile north on the old road beyond the gate. At 11,200 feet (38.0393° -107.4937°), do not follow the trail (FT 245) that continues up Matterhorn Creek. Instead, turn east (right), switchback 0.5 mile up the steep hill east of Matterhorn Creek on FT 233, and enter the Uncompahgre Wilderness at 11,580 feet (38.0433° -107.4946°). From the wilderness boundary, continue 1.5 miles north on the trail to the 12,458-foot pass (38.0606° -107.4866°) southeast of Matterhorn. You will see 13,590-foot Matterhorn Peak first, then Wetterhorn. Matterhorn is the stately peak between Uncompahgre and Wetterhorn. You will not see Uncompahgre until you reach this pass, but the view from the pass will tingle your tibia.

Cross the pass, contour 0.5 mile east on FT 233, which is the old Ridge Stock Driveway, to a low point of 12,280 feet, then climb 0.5 mile east to a broad, 12,380-foot saddle (38.0600° -107.4708°) southwest of Uncompahgre. Cross this saddle, stay on FT 233, and contour 1.0 mile southeast well below the lower cliffs on Uncompahgre's southwest side. At 12,160 feet (38.0562° -107.4619°), leave the stock driveway, stay on FT 233, and climb 1.0 mile northeast to join the Uncompahgre Peak Trail (FT 239) at 12,920 feet (38.0628° -107.4502°). Hike west then north on the Uncompahgre Peak Trail through the upper cliffs (some

Class 2) to the summit (38.0716° -107.4621°). This is the same finish as the East Slopes Route (27R1).

27R2 EC – Extra Credit – Broken Hill 13,256 feet 38.0430° -107.4718°

Class 2+

From 12,420 feet (38.0605° -107.4729°) on the route between the 12,458-foot pass and the 12,280-foot low point, leave the trail, hike 1.0 mile south across open country, and reach Broken Hill's northwest ridge at 12,900 feet (38.0471° -107.4766°). You can also reach this point by hiking 1.1 miles southeast from the 12,458-foot pass by traversing over Point 13,052, but the southeast slope of Point 13,052 holds a short, moderate snow slope well into summer. From 12,900 feet on the ridge, hike then scamper 0.4 mile southeast to Broken Hill's summit. The unbroken view of Uncompahgre from this ranked Thirteener is uncompahrable.

27R3 – Uncompahgre Peak – West Face

From Matterhorn Creek TH at 10,400'	319 RP	10.3 mi RT	3,909' net; 4,345' total	Class 2, Mod Snow
From Matterhorn Creek 4WD TH at 10,720'	299 RP	9.1 mi RT	3,589' net; 4,025' total	Class 2, Mod Snow

This route provides a direct, sporting alternative to the Southwest Slopes Route (27R2). Uncompahgre's west face provides a good snow climb in May and June of a normal snow year. Later in the summer, the scree on the west face is unpleasant, and climbing it is environmentally incorrect.

Start at the Matterhorn Creek Trailhead at 10,400 feet and go 0.6 mile north up the 4WD road Matterhorn Creek's east side to the Forest Service gate at 10,720 feet (38.0293° -107.4908°). Continue 0.75 mile north on the old road beyond the gate. At 11,200 feet (38.0393° -107.4937°), do not follow the

Uncompahgre Peak from the southwest.

trail (FT 245) that continues up Matterhorn Creek. Instead, turn east (right), switchback 0.5 mile up the steep hill east of Matterhorn Creek on FT 233, and enter the Uncompahgre Wilderness at 11,580 feet (38.0433° -107.4946°). From the wilderness boundary, continue 1.5 miles north on the trail to the 12,458-foot pass (38.0606° -107.4866°) southeast of Matterhorn Peak. From the pass, you can see three shallow gully systems on Uncompahgre's west face. Cross the pass, contour 0.5 mile east on FT 233, and descend 0.2 mile northeast to 12,240 feet (38.0609° -107.4766°). Your Class 1 trail approach is over.

Leave the trail, climb 0.6 mile northeast to 12,800 feet (38.0665° -107.4681°), and climb 0.4 mile east-northeast up the southernmost of the three gullies to reach a broad shoulder on Uncompahgre's south ridge at 13,800 feet (38.0672° -107.4619°). Join the East Slopes Route (27R1) here, get onto the Uncompahgre Peak Trail (FT 239), and follow it north through the upper cliffs and across the summit plateau to the summit.

27R3 V1 – Variation – Central Gully

Class 2, Mod Snow

Climb the central gully on the west face instead of the southernmost gully. The central gully's difficulty is the same as the southernmost gully, but the central gully is longer. The central gully ends under the final summit cliff. Angle south (right) to avoid the cliff and reach the easy upper south slopes at 14,100 feet (38.0695° -107.4620°). Stroll 250 yards north to the highest point. The central gully is a test piece for skiers.

27R3 V2 – Variation – West Direct

Class 4, Mod Snow

This dangerous variation allows a direct approach to the summit from the west. Follow Variation 27R3 V1 to the final summit cliff. Angle 200 yards north (left) under the cliff to a point close to Uncompahgre's north face. With a few more steps north you can have an air-filled view. A series of debris-covered ledges hide on the west-facing summit cliff's north end. Zigzag up these ledges, climbing short sections of rock between them, and arrive on the summit plateau 100 feet west of the highest point.

27. Wetterhorn Peak 14,015 feet

27R – Wetterhorn Peak Routes

27R4 – Wetterhorn Peak – Southeast Ridge *Classic*

From Matterhorn Creek TH at 10,400'	291 RP	8.5 mi RT	3,615' total	Class 3
From Matterhorn Creek 4WD TH at 10,720'	272 RP	7.3 mi RT	3,295' total	Class 3

This is the easiest route up Wetterhorn. It is an engaging climb with a spectacular finish to a tiny summit. This route is a good introduction to the harder

Wetterhorn Peak from the east.

Fourteeners for hikers who have climbed several easy Fourteeners and are ready to advance.

Start at the Matterhorn Creek Trailhead at 10,400 feet and go 0.6 mile north up the 4WD road on Matterhorn Creek's east side to the Forest Service gate at 10,720 feet (38.0293° -107.4908°). Continue 0.75 mile north on the old road beyond the gate. At 11,200 feet (38.0393° -107.4937°), do not follow the trail (FT 245) that continues up Matterhorn Creek. Instead, turn east (right), switchback 0.5 mile up the steep hill east of Matterhorn Creek on FT 233, and enter the Uncompahgre Wilderness at 11,580 feet (38.0433° -107.4946°). From the wilderness boundary, hike 0.7 mile north on the trail to 12,040 feet (38.0522° -107.4929°). You will see Matterhorn Peak first, then Wetterhorn. 13,590-foot Matterhorn is the stately peak between Uncompahgre and Wetterhorn.

Leave the trail at 12,040 feet, hike 0.7 mile northwest into the south-facing basin between Matterhorn and Wetterhorn, then hike 0.3 mile west under Wetterhorn's sweeping east face. Your target, the southeast ridge, soars ahead and looks impressive. Take heart, because it is easier to climb than it appears. Climb 0.2 mile southwest to the 13,060-foot saddle (38.0556° -107.5063°) on the southeast ridge between minor Point 13,117 and Wetterhorn. The introduction is over.

Turn northwest (right) and ascend the southeast ridge. The ridge is easy at first, but the difficulties increase as you approach the summit. Pass some gnarly-looking towers between 13,400 feet and 13,700 feet on the west (left) side of the ridge. The climbing in this section is mostly Class 2, with an occasional Class 3 spot. Above the initial towers is a prominent tower called the Ships Prow (38.0601° -107.5110°), just below the final summit cliff. Pass easily by the 13,900-foot Ships Prow on the ridge's east (right) side. Climb into the easternmost of two notches between the Ships Prow and Wetterhorn's summit. You can now see the west-facing summit pitch for the first time.

The summit pitch is Class 3. From the notch, traverse 15 feet north, then scramble 150 feet up near a shallow gully to the summit. The easiest route is occasionally in the gully, but is more often on the gully's north (left) side. The pitch ends abruptly a few feet north of the highest point (38.0606° -107.5109°). Although the difficulty of the summit pitch is only Class 3, it is exposed and somewhat loose. Some parties choose to use a rope on it and some do not. Use your judgment.

27R4 V – Variation – Wetterhorn Basin

From West Cimarron TH at 10,750'   370 RP   14.0 mi RT   3,265' net; 4,825' total   Class 3

You can approach this climb from Wetterhorn Basin on Wetterhorn's west side. This much longer approach is suitable for a backpacking trip or a day trip for the superfit. Lush, rolling meadow-strewn Wetterhorn Basin is one of Colorado's seldom-visited special places. The views of Wetterhorn from this basin are more dramatic than those from Matterhorn Creek since you can view Wetterhorn's steep north face in profile.

Start at the West Cimarron Trailhead at 10,750 feet and follow the West Fork Trail (FT 226) 3.5 miles south to the 12,500-foot pass (38.0798° -107.5464°) west of dramatic, 13,656-foot Coxcomb Peak. Cross the pass, descend 1.2 miles south then southeast on the trail into Wetterhorn Basin, and cross a branch of Wetterhorn Creek at a low point of 11,720 feet (38.0662° -107.5361°). Continue 0.3 mile east-southeast on the trail, cross the main branch of Wetterhorn Creek at 11,820 feet (38.0636° -107.5316°), and continue 0.3 mile southeast on the trail to 12,100 feet (38.0612° -107.5277°). Leave the trail and climb 0.7 mile east then southeast under the rugged north face of Point 13,300 C, a ranked Thirteener, to a 12,860-foot pass (38.0576° -107.5171°) between Wetterhorn and Point 13,300 C. The view of Wetterhorn from here is neck-bending. There's more.

Cross the 12,860-foot pass and contour then climb 0.5 mile east-southeast to the 13,060-foot saddle (38.0556° -107.5063°) on Wetterhorn's southeast ridge between Point 13,117 and Wetterhorn. Continue up the Southeast Ridge Route.

27R4 EC1 – Extra Credit – Ships Prow 13,900 feet 38.0601° -107.5110°

Class 3+

Climb the Ships Prow. From the westernmost notch between the summit cliff and the Ships Prow, you can reach the tower's summit with 40 feet of exposed, north-facing, Class 3+ scrambling.

27R4 EC2 – Extra Credit – Matterhorn Peak 13,590 feet 38.0652° -107.4960°

Class 3

Climb 13,590-foot Matterhorn Peak. Colorado's Matterhorn is only a faint echo of the Swiss Matterhorn, but is still one of Colorado's 200 highest ranked peaks and is well worth climbing. Colorado's Matterhorn is between Wetterhorn and Uncompahgre, and people often climb it with the Fourteeners. Matterhorn provides a good warm-up climb. The easiest route on Matterhorn is up the broad south slopes that narrow to a ridge, which requires some minor Class 3 scrambling near the summit. From Matterhorn's summit, there are airborne views of both Wetterhorn and Uncompahgre.

27R5 – Wetterhorn Peak – East Face

From Matterhorn Creek TH at 10,400'	*329 RP*	*8.0 mi RT*	*3,615' total*	*Class 3, Steep Snow*
From Matterhorn Creek 4WD TH at 10,720'	*311 RP*	*6.8 mi RT*	*3,295' total*	*Class 3, Steep Snow*

Wetterhorn's sweeping east face lies between the east ridge and the southeast ridge. It provides a direct snow climb when snow conditions permit in May and June. After the snow melts, avoid this face. Follow the Southeast Ridge Route (27R4) to 12,900 feet (38.0582° -107.5053°) in the basin between Matterhorn and Wetterhorn. Climb 0.3 mile northeast directly up the east face, dodging any rock outcroppings, to the base of the summit cliff. Skirt west (left) under the summit cliff and finish the climb with the Southeast Ridge Route's Class 3 summit pitch.

27R6 – Wetterhorn Peak – East Ridge

From Matterhorn Creek TH at 10,400'	*412 RP*	*8.9 mi RT*	*3,615' total*	*Class 4*
From Matterhorn Creek 4WD TH at 10,720'	*393 RP*	*7.7 mi RT*	*3,295' total*	*Class 4*

This ridge connects Wetterhorn with Matterhorn. It is harder and more complicated than the southeast ridge, but provides an interesting alpine challenge, especially with the addition of snow. The complete traverse from Matterhorn to Wetterhorn is arduous.

Follow the Southeast Ridge Route (27R4) to 12,600 feet (38.0600° -107.4999°) in the basin between Matterhorn and Wetterhorn. Climb 0.3 mile northwest and gain the east ridge near its low point (38.0634° -107.5013°) on the west side of a cone-shaped tower (Class 3). Follow the rocky ridge 0.6 mile west to the base of the summit tower (Class 4). Skirt the summit tower on its south side and finish the climb with the Southeast Ridge Route's Class 3 summit pitch.

27C – Uncompahgre and Wetterhorn Combination Route
27C1 – Uncompahgre Southwest Slopes → Wetterhorn Southeast Ridge

From Matterhorn Creek TH at 10,400'	*466 RP*	*18.1 mi RT*	*6,520' total*	*Class 3*
Via Uncompahgre's West Slopes	*510 RP*	*12.9 mi RT*	*5,960' total*	*Class 3, Mod Snow*
With Matterhorn Peak	*556 RP*	*19.5 mi RT*	*7,672' total*	*Class 3*
Via Uncompahgre's West Slopes	*600 RP*	*14.3 mi RT*	*7,112' total*	*Class 3, Mod Snow*

People often climb Uncompahgre and Wetterhorn together, but it is not a slam dunk, since the two peaks are 3 miles apart and Matterhorn Peak is between them. The length of the combination depends on whether you use Uncompahgre's Southwest Slopes or West Face Route.

You can do the peaks in either order, but it makes more sense to do Uncompahgre first. Start at the Matterhorn Creek Trailhead at 10,400 feet and follow either the Southwest Slopes (27R2) or West Face Route (27R3) up Uncompahgre. Return to the 12,458-foot pass below Matterhorn, contour west into the basin between Matterhorn and Wetterhorn, then continue up Wetterhorn's Southeast Ridge Route (27R4). Adding an ascent of Matterhorn en route further promotes this already senior uncompahrable tour.

28. Handies Group
Redcloud Peak   14,034 feet
Sunshine Peak   14,001 feet
Handies Peak   14,048 feet

These engaging peaks rise in moderate, complicated terrain 10 miles southwest of Lake City. They offer a variety of modest routes in a beautiful setting. These peaks are in the San Juans! This alone recommends them.

You cannot easily see well-named Redcloud Peak from surrounding valleys. Only by climbing out of the valleys and spying on it from afar or by approaching it directly will you come to know it. People usually climb Redcloud together with its southern neighbor, Sunshine.

Sunshine is 1.3 miles south of Redcloud, and people often traverse the gentle, easy ridge between these two peaks. Sunshine has one distinction its higher neighbor lacks: it is the lowest Fourteener in North America. But even the lowest Fourteener needs to be climbed!

Winsome Handies Peak stands by itself 5 miles west of Redcloud and Sunshine. The upper end of the Lake Fork of the Gunnison River embraces Handies in a wide horseshoe, and the peak lies deep in the heart of the north-central San Juans. The view from Handies' summit is famous and spectacular. On the summit, mountains embrace you as far as your eye can see, in all directions. If civilization is pressing in on you, climb Handies and spend a long hour or two on the summit.

28E – Handies Group Essentials

Elevations	Redcloud Pk	14,034' (NGVD29) 14,037' (NAVD88)
	Sunshine Pk	14,001' (NGVD29) 14,006' (NAVD88)
	Handies Pk	14,048' (NGVD29) 14,053' (NAVD88)
Ranks	Redcloud Pk	Colorado's 46th highest ranked peak
	Sunshine Pk	Colorado's 53rd highest ranked peak
	Handies Pk	Colorado's 40th highest ranked peak
Location	Hinsdale County, Colorado, USA	
Range	North-Central San Juan Range	

28E – Handies Group Essentials

Summit Coordinates	Redcloud Pk	37.9408° -107.4217° (WGS84)
	Sunshine Pk	37.9227° -107.4255° (WGS84)
	Handies Pk	37.9129° -107.5044° (WGS84)
Ownership/Contacts	Bureau of Land Management – Public Land	
	BLM – Gunnison Field Office – 970-244-3097	
Prominence and Saddles	Redcloud Pk	1,436' from 12,598' near Cinnamon Pass
	Sunshine Pk	501' from 13,500' Sunshine–Redcloud saddle
	Handies Pk	1,908' from 12,140' saddle south of Stony Pass
Isolation and Parents	Redcloud Pk	4.91 miles to Handies Peak
	Sunshine Pk	1.27 miles to Redcloud Peak
	Handies Pk	11.22 miles to Uncompahgre Peak
USGS Maps	Redcloud Peak, Handies Peak, Lake San Cristobal,	
	Lake City	
USFS Map	Uncompahgre National Forest	
Trails Illustrated Map	Map #141 Telluride, Silverton, Ouray, Lake City	
Book Map	See Map 28 on page 281	
Nearest Towns	Lake City – Population 385 – Elevation 8,661'	
	Ouray – Population 930 – Elevation 7,792'	
	Silverton – Population 520 – Elevation 9,308'	
Redcloud Pk 🏃 Easiest Route	28R1 – Northeast Ridge – Class 2	
	A good trail goes high onto the peak, and a steep, rougher trail continues to	
	the highest point	
Sunshine Pk 🏃 Easiest Route	28R4 – Southeast Ridge – Class 2	
	A Class 1 trail hike into the basin, a steep Class 2 slope up to the ridge, and a	
	Class 1+ ridge to the top	
Handies Pk 🏃 Easiest Route	28R7 – West Slopes – Class 1	
	A good trail goes to the highest point	
Handies Group Accolades	Surrounded by summits, these gentle, high peaks hide near the center of	
	the San Juan Range, and they provide popular summer hikes. Sunshine is	
	Colorado's lowest Fourteener.	

28T – Handies Group Trailheads

28T1 – Mill Creek Trailhead 9,440 feet 37.9066° -107.3918°

This trailhead provides access to Sunshine Peak's south side. From the junction of Colorado 50 and Colorado 149 west of Gunnison, go 45.3 miles south on Colorado 149 to Lake City. Measuring from the bridge over Henson Creek in downtown Lake City, go 2.2 miles south on Colorado 149 and turn right (38.0002° -107.2986°) onto the Lake San Cristobal Road (Hinsdale County 30). This is part of the Alpine Loop Scenic Byway. Go around Lake San Cristobal's west side and continue southwest up the beautiful Lake Fork of the Gunnison River. Pass the Williams Creek Campground at mile 9.1, pass the Wager

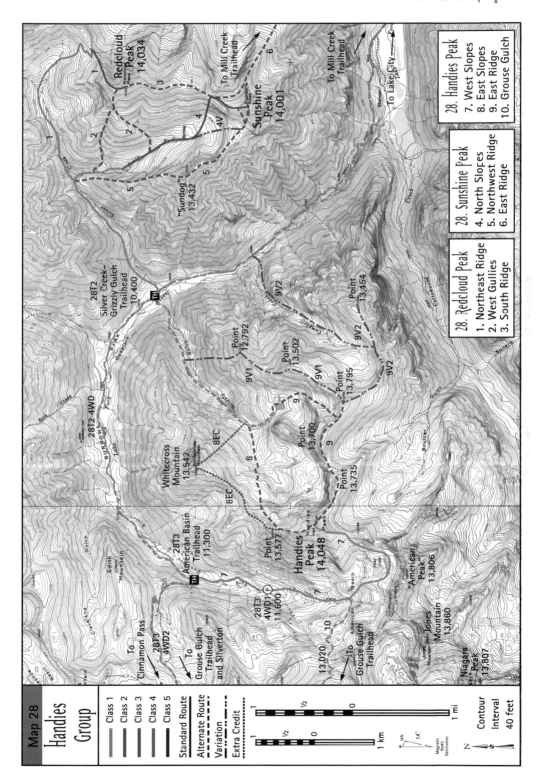

28. Handies Peak
7. West Slopes
8. East Slopes
9. East Ridge
10. Grouse Gulch

28. Sunshine Peak
4. North Slopes
5. Northwest Ridge
6. East Ridge

28. Redcloud Peak
1. Northeast Ridge
2. West Gullies
3. South Ridge

Redcloud Peak 14,034

Sunshine Peak 14,001

To Mill Creek Trailhead

To Mill Creek Trailhead

To Lake City

"Sundog" 13,432

Silver Creek–Grizzly Gulch Trailhead 10,400

28T2 4WD

BURROWS

Whitecross Mountain 13,542

Point 12,792

Point 13,502

Point 13,454

Point 13,795

Point 13,700

Point 13,735

American Basin Trailhead 11,300

To Cinnamon Pass

To Grouse Gulch Trailhead and Silverton

28T3 4WD2

28T3

28T3 4WD1 11,600

Point 13,577

Handies Peak 14,048

13,020

To Grouse Gulch Trailhead

"American Peak" 13,806

Jones Mountain 13,860

Niagara Peak 13,807

Map 28
Handies Group

Class 1
Class 2
Class 3
Class 4
Class 5

Standard Route
Alternate Route
Variation
Extra Credit

Contour Interval 40 feet

1   ½   0   1 mi

1   ½   0   1 Km

Magnetic North Declination

N

Gulch–Carson Road at mile 11.3, and reach the Mill Creek Campground at mile 13.1. Park in or near the campground. For climbs of Sunshine from here, leave the campground, cross the road, and hike north into the woods. This trailhead is often accessible in winter.

28T2 – Silver Creek–Grizzly Gulch Trailhead 10,400 feet 37.9361° -107.4596°

This trailhead provides access to the Silver Creek and Grizzly Gulch trails. The Silver Creek Trail leads to Redcloud's north side, and the Grizzly Gulch Trail leads to Handies' east side.

From the Mill Creek Campground (see 28T1; mile 13.1 from Lake City), continue west on the main road and turn northwest (right) onto Cinnamon Pass Road at mile 14.3 (37.9037° -107.4119°). Follow the Cinnamon Pass shelf road as it climbs west then northwest, and reach the trailhead at mile 18.3. The road is passable for many cars to this point, and there are camping spots at or near the trailhead. The Silver Creek Trail heads east from the parking area on the east side of the road. The Grizzly Gulch Trail starts on the west side of the road and heads west across the Lake Fork of the Gunnison River.

28T2 4WD – 4WD Approach to Silver Creek–Grizzly Gulch Trailhead

The other approach to this trailhead requires a 4WD vehicle. From Durango, go north on US 550 to Silverton. From Silverton's north end, at the junction of San Juan County 110 and San Juan County 2, turn northeast (right) onto San Juan County 2 (formerly CO 110B) and measure from this point. Follow the Animas River Road (San Juan County 2) northeast, pass Howardsville, pass Eureka, and reach Animas Forks at mile 12.3. Turn east (right) just above Animas Forks, climb steeply east to reach 12,620-foot Cinnamon Pass (37.9341° -107.5375°) at mile 15.3, cross the pass, and descend on its east side to reach the Silver Creek–Grizzly Gulch Trailhead at mile 21.1.

28T3 – American Basin Trailhead 11,300 feet 37.9309° -107.5144°

This summer trailhead provides access to American Basin and Handies' northwest side. From the Silver Creek–Grizzly Gulch Trailhead (28T2; mile 18.3 from Lake City), continue on the Cinnamon Pass Road, pass the Cooper Creek Road at mile 19.1, and reach a road junction at mile 21.9 just before a steep switchback on the Cinnamon Pass Road. This is the trailhead; parking is limited here. You will appreciate a high-clearance vehicle for the last mile of the approach to this trailhead.

28T3 4WD1 – American Basin 4WD Trailhead 11,600 feet 37.9199° -107.5166°

From the American Basin Trailhead on the Cinnamon Pass Road, 4WD vehicles can leave the Cinnamon Pass Road and go 0.9 mile south on a rough spur road to 11,600 feet and a parking area at the end of the road near an old mine. This high 4WD trailhead is under Handies' west side in lower American Basin.

28T3 4WD2 – 4WD Approach to American Basin Trailhead

The other approach to this trailhead definitely requires a 4WD vehicle. From Durango, go north on US 550 to Silverton. From Silverton's north end, at the junction of San Juan County 110 and San Juan County 2, turn northeast (right) onto San Juan County 2 (formerly CO 110B) and measure from this point. Follow the Animas River Road (San Juan County 2) northeast, pass Howardsville, pass Eureka, and reach Animas Forks at mile 12.3. Turn east (right) just above Animas Forks, climb steeply east to reach Cinnamon Pass (37.9341° -107.5375°) at mile 15.3, cross the pass, and descend on its east side to reach the American Basin Trailhead at mile 17.5.

28T4 – Grouse Gulch Trailhead 10,720 feet 37.9175° -107.5582°

This trailhead provides access to the Grouse Gulch Trail, American Basin, and Handies' west side. This trailhead is a much shorter drive when approaching from the Durango area, and you do not need a 4WD vehicle.

From Durango, go north on US 550 to Silverton. From Silverton's north end, at the junction of San Juan County 110 and San Juan County 2, turn northeast (right) onto San Juan County 2 (formerly CO 110B) and measure from this point. Go northeast on San Juan County 2 (the Animas River Road), pass the Cunningham Gulch Road (San Juan County 4) turnoff at mile 3.9, pass through Howardsville, pass the Maggie Gulch Road turnoff at mile 5.8, pass the Minnie Gulch Road turnoff at mile 6.3, and reach the bridge over the Animas River in the historic Eureka town site at mile 7.5. Cross to the Animas River's west side, continue north up the steep shelf road, pass the Picayune Gulch Road (San Juan County 9) turnoff at mile 10.2, and reach the Grouse Gulch Trailhead at mile 10.3.

Park on the road's west side immediately south of (before) a bridge over the now much smaller Animas River where the road crosses back to the river's east side. The 4WD road into Burns Gulch goes southeast 20 yards north of the bridge and the unsigned Grouse Gulch Trail heads east steeply uphill from the Animas River Road 115 yards north of the bridge. There is no decent parking at the beginning of the trail, so park below the bridge.

28. Redcloud Peak 14,034 feet

28R – Redcloud Peak Routes

28R1 – Redcloud Peak – Northeast Ridge

From Silver Creek–Grizzly Gulch TH at 10,400'   *186 RP*   *8.6 mi RT*   *3,634' total*   *Class 2*

This is the easiest route up Redcloud. The route climbs steadily as it circles the peak to reach the summit. Start at the Silver Creek–Grizzly Gulch Trailhead at 10,400 feet and hike 1.5 miles northeast up the Silver Creek Trail to 11,300 feet (37.9488° -107.4391°) and the junction with the Silver Creek South Fork Trail that

Redcloud Peak from the east.

goes up the basin northwest of Redcloud and Sunshine. Continue on the main Silver Creek Trail 1.2 miles east-northeast to 12,120 feet (37.9542° -107.4221°) in the basin north of Redcloud, go 0.7 mile southeast then more steeply south to 12,800 feet (37.9480° -107.4144°) below Redcloud's northeast ridge, then switchback 0.3 mile south up to the 13,020-foot pass (37.9460° -107.4147°) northeast of Redcloud. The trail is good to this point.

From the pass, hike 0.4 mile up a strong climber's trail on Redcloud's northeast ridge to 13,840 feet (37.9437° -107.4211°). The Class 2 trail is surprisingly steep for several hundred feet, but the slope angle relents considerably at 13,840 feet. Follow the now gentle, curving ridge 0.2 mile southwest then south to the summit (37.9408° -107.4217°).

28R2 – Redcloud Peak – West Gullies

From Silver Creek–Grizzly Gulch TH at 10,400'

Via South Gully	*308 RP*	*7.2 mi RT*	*3,634' total*	*Class 2, Mod Snow*
Via North Gully	*327 RP*	*5.9 mi RT*	*3,634' total*	*Class 2, Mod Snow*

Redcloud's west side sports several gullies that provide shorter, steeper routes than the Northeast Ridge Route (28R1). When snow conditions are good, these gullies can provide a direct ascent route or a speedy descent. Avoid the gullies when they are snow free, because the scree on this side of Redcloud is steep and unpleasant.

Start at the Silver Creek–Grizzly Gulch Trailhead at 10,400 feet and hike 1.5 miles northeast up the Silver Creek Trail to 11,300 feet (37.9488° -107.4391°) and the junction with the Silver Creek South Fork Trail that goes up the basin northwest of Redcloud and Sunshine. Leave the Silver Creek Trail, cross Silver Creek, and find the good Silver Creek South Fork Trail in the bushes south of Silver Creek and east of the south fork of Silver Creek. Follow the Silver Creek South Fork Trail on the east side of the creek into the rugged gulch under Redcloud's west face.

There are two main gullies to choose from on Redcloud's west face. The northern gully is the steepest and most direct, while the southern gully provides a slightly longer, gentler route. The bottom of the northern gully (37.9454° -107.4378°) is only 0.25 mile up the south fork from Silver Creek, and the bottom of the southern gully (37.9374° -107.4325°) is 0.9 mile up the south fork. There is a comfortable camping spot in the south fork between the two gullies at 11,950 feet (37.9393° -107.4355°), just below treeline.

Choose your gully and climb it. The gullies end below the summit, and the routes rejoin near 13,600 feet. The scree from here to the summit can be unpleasant after the snow melts.

28R3 – Redcloud Peak – South Ridge

From Silver Creek–Grizzly Gulch TH at 10,400'   231 RP   9.1 mi RT   3,634' total   Class 2, Mod Snow

Use this ridge when climbing Redcloud and Sunshine together. Follow Sunshine's Northeast Ridge Route (28R4) to the 13,500-foot saddle (37.9284° -107.4236°) between Redcloud and Sunshine. From this saddle, hike an easy mile north to Redcloud's summit. There is a Class 1 trail on the ridge that skirts several minor false summits on the ridge's west side.

28. Sunshine Peak 14,001 feet

28R – Sunshine Peak Routes

28R4 – Sunshine Peak – Northeast Ridge

From Silver Creek–Grizzly Gulch TH at 10,400'   235 RP   7.9 mi RT   3,601' total   Class 2, Mod Snow

This route has a lot to recommend it when snow conditions are good. It provides a trail approach through an enchanted forest, a picturesque cirque, and a snow climb leading to a distinctive summit.

Start at the Silver Creek–Grizzly Gulch Trailhead at 10,400 feet and hike 1.5 miles northeast up the Silver Creek Trail to 11,300 feet (37.9488° -107.4391°) and the junction with the Silver Creek South Fork Trail that goes up the basin northwest of Redcloud and Sunshine. Leave the Silver Creek Trail, cross Silver Creek, and find the good Silver Creek South Fork Trail in the bushes south of Silver Creek and east of the south fork of Silver Creek. Go 0.7 mile south on the Silver Creek South Fork Trail on the east side of the creek into the rugged gulch under Redcloud's west face. There is a comfortable camping spot in the south fork at 11,950 feet (37.9393° -107.4355°), just below treeline.

Pass treeline and continue 0.9 mile south to 12,600 feet (37.9305° -107.4305°) in the basin under Sunshine's north slopes. The Silver Creek South Fork Trail is good to this point. Climb a steep slope onto a rock glacier and continue on the climber's trail as it curves southeast. At 12,800 feet, the route steepens dramatically and ascends the scruffy slope to the 13,500-foot Sunshine–Redcloud saddle (37.9284° -107.4236°). This west-facing slope provides a nice snow climb when snow-covered, but the snow melts early on this slope. When snow free, the Class 2 trail dodges some small rock outcrops as it winds upward. Loose rocks can be a hazard on this badly eroding slope. From the 13,500-foot Sunshine–Redcloud saddle, climb 0.4 mile southwest then south up Sunshine's northeast ridge to the summit (37.9227° -107.4255°).

28R4 V – Variation – North Slopes

Class 2, Mod Snow

This is a more sporting finish. From 12,600 feet in the basin, climb southwest up a moderate snow slope to a small plateau at 13,300 feet (37.9245° -107.4296°), 0.25 mile northwest of the summit. The easiest route from the plateau to the summit follows an old trail that angles up east to join Sunshine's northeast ridge 250 feet below the summit.

28R5 – Sunshine Peak – Northwest Ridge

From Silver Creek–Grizzly Gulch TH at 10,400'   288 RP   8.2 mi RT   3,601' net; 4,265' total   Class 2+

This is an interesting route up Sunshine that allows you to bag a ranked Thirteener en route. Start at the Silver Creek–Grizzly Gulch Trailhead at 10,400 feet and hike 1.5 miles northeast up the Silver Creek Trail to 11,300 feet (37.9488° -107.4391°) and the junction with the Silver Creek South Fork Trail. Leave the Silver Creek Trail, cross Silver Creek, get on the west side of the south fork creek, and hike 0.1 mile south up onto the ridge west of the south fork. Do not hike up the bottom of the south fork gulch. The hike up onto the ridge is steep, rugged, and short.

Once on the ridge, follow it 1.4 miles up to Point 13,432, alias "Sundog" (37.9320° -107.4384°). This ranked Thirteener rises 332 feet above its connecting saddle with Sunshine and is Colorado's 300th highest ranked peak. Descend 0.5 mile southeast (Class 2+) from "Sundog" to the 13,100-foot "Sundog"–Sunshine saddle (37.9267° -107.4339°), then climb 0.3 mile southeast onto the plateau at 13,300 feet (37.9245° -107.4296°), north of Sunshine. Cross the plateau and follow an old trail angling up east to join Sunshine's northeast ridge 250 feet below the summit.

28R6 – Sunshine Peak – East Ridge

From Mill Creek TH at 9,440'   286 RP   5.2 mi RT   4,561' total   Class 2

This rugged, off-trail route has more elevation gain than others on Sunshine, but it is accessible when the road up to the Silver Creek–Grizzly Gulch Trailhead is impassable. Half of your vertical effort is a bushwhack through the trees. Start at the Mill Creek Trailhead at 9,440 feet, leave the campground, cross the road, and hike north into the woods at the base of Sunshine's vast south slopes. Hike 1.1 miles north then northwest steeply up through rough terrain to treeline at 11,900 feet (37.9176° -107.4009°). Continue 0.5 mile west-northwest up to a small plateau on Sunshine's east ridge at 12,520 feet (37.9181° -107.4076°). Cross the small plateau and climb 1.0 mile west-northwest then west up Sunshine's upper east ridge to the summit. When descending this route, be sure to head east from the summit, since descending south or even southeast from the summit will lead you into cliffs.

28C – Redcloud and Sunshine Combination Routes

28C1 – Redcloud Northeast Ridge → Sunshine Northeast Ridge

From Silver Creek–Grizzly Gulch TH at 10,400'   *230 RP*   *9.7 mi RT*   *4,135' total*   *Class 2, Mod Snow*

With reascent of Redcloud   *253 RP*   *11.4 mi RT*   *4,669' total*   *Class 2*

This is the standard way to climb Redcloud and Sunshine together. Start at the Silver Creek–Grizzly Gulch Trailhead at 10,400 feet and climb Redcloud's Northeast Ridge Route (28R1). Descend Redcloud's south ridge to the 13,500-foot Redcloud–Sunshine saddle (37.9284° -107.4236°), then hike up Sunshine's northeast ridge to Sunshine's summit. Descend Sunshine's Northeast Ridge Route (28R4). Some people choose to avoid the steep descent west from the Redcloud–Sunshine saddle and return over Redcloud's summit to descend Redcloud's Northeast Ridge Route. This choice avoids some difficulty but adds to your effort.

28C2 – Sunshine Northeast Ridge → Redcloud West Gullies

From Silver Creek–Grizzly Gulch TH at 10,400'

With descent of South Gully   *279 RP*   *9.0 mi RT*   *4,135' total*   *Class 2, Mod Snow*

With descent of North Gully   *272 RP*   *8.3 mi RT*   *4,135' total*   *Class 2, Mod Snow*

This traverse can be done in either direction, but doing Sunshine first allows you to start with the more difficult terrain and glissade down one of Redcloud's west gullies. Avoid this option if Redcloud's west gullies are snow free; you can easily preview these gullies when approaching in the south fork of Silver Creek.

Start at the Silver Creek–Grizzly Gulch Trailhead at 10,400 feet and climb Sunshine's Northeast Ridge Route (28R4). Descend Sunshine's northeast ridge to the 13,500-foot Redcloud–Sunshine saddle (37.9284° -107.4236°), then hike along Redcloud's gentle south ridge to Redcloud's summit. Descend Redcloud's West Gullies Route (28R2).

28C3 – Sunshine East Ridge → Redcloud South Ridge

From Mill Creek TH at 9,440'   *328 RP*   *7.6 mi RT*   *5,095' total*   *Class 2*

This combination provides a good way to climb both peaks when the shelf road to the Silver Creek–Grizzly Gulch Trailhead is in bad shape. Start at the Mill Creek Trailhead at 9,440 feet and climb Sunshine's East Ridge Route (28R6). Descend Sunshine's northeast ridge to the 13,500-foot Redcloud–Sunshine saddle (37.9284° -107.4236°), hike along Redcloud's gentle south ridge to Red-cloud's summit, then return to the 13,500-foot saddle. Instead of climbing Sunshine again, contour 0.5 mile south then southeast across Sunshine's northeast face to rejoin and descend Sunshine's East Ridge Route.

28. Handies Peak 14,048 feet

28R – Handies Peak Routes

28R7 – Handies Peak – West Slopes

From American Basin TH at 11,300'	121 RP	6.4 mi RT	2,748' total	Class 1
From American Basin 4WD TH at 11,600'	96 RP	4.6 mi RT	2,448' total	Class 1

Beautiful in its brevity, this is the shortest, easiest route up Handies. Start at the American Basin Trailhead at 11,300 feet and go 0.3 mile south toward American Basin on a 4WD spur road, ford the Lake Fork of the Gunnison River at 11,370 feet (37.9276° -107.5150°), and continue 0.6 mile south on the road under Handies' west face to a parking area at the end of the road at 11,600 feet (37.9199° -107.5166°) near an old mine.

From the end of the road, hike 0.9 mile south then southwest on a trail into upper American Basin to a trail junction at 12,380 feet (37.9077° -107.5182°). The Grouse Gulch Trail goes west and the Handies Peak Trail goes southeast from this junction. Turn southeast (left) onto the Handies Peak Trail, avoid any temptation to take a shortcut in this area, and climb 0.4 mile southeast on the trail to 12,900 feet (37.9048° -107.5120°) on a bench north of Sloan Lake. Stay on the trail and climb 0.4 mile east-southeast on a shelf trail, then 0.2 mile north to a point west of the 13,460-foot saddle (37.9082° -107.5058°) between Handies and Point 13,588, a minor summit on Handies' south ridge 0.5 mile south of Handies. As views open in all directions, hike 0.4 mile north on a winding trail up Handies' gentle, rounded south ridge to the vaunted summit (37.9129° -107.5044°).

28R8 – Handies Peak – East Slopes *Classic*

From Silver Creek–Grizzly Gulch TH at 10,400'	147 RP	7.0 mi RT	3,648' total	Class 1+

This is the most scenic route on Handies. From the Silver Creek–Grizzly Gulch Trailhead at 10,400 feet, go 100 yards north up the road to the start of the Grizzly Gulch Trail on the west side of the road. Leave the road, cross the Lake Fork of the Gunnison River on a bridge, and hike 1.8 miles west-southwest then southwest on the Grizzly Gulch Trail on the creek's north side to treeline at 11,800 feet (37.9238° -107.4846°). Handies' picturesque east face will lure you on.

Continue 1.0 mile west on the trail into the upper basin and switchback 0.3 mile up northeast-facing slopes to a 13,460-foot saddle (37.9184° -107.5049°) on Handies' north ridge between Handies and the minor Point 13,577. From the saddle, turn south (left) and follow the rough trail 0.5 mile south near Handies' undulating north ridge to the summit (37.9129° -107.5044°).

Handies Peak from the east. Photo by Jennifer Roach

28R8 EC – Extra Credit – Whitecross Mountain 13,542 feet 37.9306° -107.4933°

Class 2+

Adding Whitecross Mountain to this route works best on the descent from Handies. From Handies' summit, descend Handies' north ridge, cross Point 13,577 (37.9192° -107.5049°), and descend 0.6 mile northeast to the 12,980-foot saddle (37.9250° -107.4973°) between Handies and 13,542-foot Whitecross Mountain. The ridge between Point 13,577 and the 12,980-foot saddle is rough and requires some Class 2+ scampering. From the 12,980-foot saddle, climb 0.6 mile northeast to Whitecross' summit. Descend Whitecross' steep southeast slopes and regain the Grizzly Gulch Trail near treeline at 11,800 feet (37.9238° -107.4846°).

28R9 – Handies Peak – East Ridge *Classic*

From Silver Creek–Grizzly Gulch TH at 10,400'	290 RP	9.0 mi RT	3,648' net; 4,733' total	*Class 2*
With descent of East Slopes	244 RP	8.3 mi RT	3,648' net; 4,298' total	*Class 2*

This interesting route allows you to climb Point 13,795, a ranked Thirteener, en route to Handies. From the Silver Creek–Grizzly Gulch Trailhead at 10,400 feet, go 100 yards north up the road to the start of the Grizzly Gulch Trail on the west side of the road. Leave the road, cross the Lake Fork of the Gunnison River on a bridge, and hike 1.8 miles west-southwest then southwest on the Grizzly Gulch Trail on the creek's north side to treeline at 11,800 feet (37.9238° -107.4846°). Leave the Handies Peak Trail and continue 0.4 mile south up an old trail to a small, unnamed lake at 12,323 feet (37.9188° -107.4825°). Your Class 1 approach is over.

From the lake at 12,323 feet, climb 0.5 mile south-southeast then south up a steep, rocky slope to 13,000 feet (37.9134° -107.4798°) at the entrance to a miniature basin under the north slopes of Point 13,795. Hike 0.4 mile southwest up this basin to the 13,580-foot saddle (37.9095° -107.4841°) just west of Point 13,795, then walk 0.2 mile east up a gentle ridge to the summit of Point 13,795 (37.9087° -107.4810°). This ranked Thirteener rises 495 feet above its connecting saddle with Handies Peak and is a Bi, one of Colorado's 200 highest ranked peaks.

From Point 13,795, descend 0.2 mile west, contour 0.3 mile northwest on the south side of unranked Point 13,700, and descend 0.2 mile west to the 13,300-foot Point 13,795–Handies saddle (37.9110° -107.4921°). Continue 0.2 mile southwest to unranked Point 13,735, descend 0.2 mile west to a 13,580-foot saddle, and finally climb 0.3 mile northwest to Handies' summit. Ascending the East Ridge Route and descending the East Slopes Route (28R8) makes an elegant, circular Tour de Handies.

28R9 V1 – Variation – Tour de Grizzly

From Silver Creek–Grizzly Gulch TH at 10,400'	*452 RP*	*8.4 mi RT*	*3,648' net; 4,986' total*	*Class 2, Mod/Steep Snow*
With descent of East Slopes	*389 RP*	*7.8 mi RT*	*3,648' net; 4,752' total*	*Class 2, Mod/Steep Snow*
With Whitecross Mtn	*446 RP*	*8.6 mi RT*	*3,648' net; 5,431' total*	*Class 2, Mod/Steep Snow*

This variation adds a mountaineering flavor to your ascent. From the Silver Creek–Grizzly Gulch Trailhead at 10,400 feet, go 100 yards north up the road to the start of the Grizzly Gulch Trail on the west side of the road. Leave the road, cross the Lake Fork of the Gunnison River on a bridge, and follow the Grizzly Gulch Trail 1.0 mile west to a small clearing at 11,100 feet (37.9325° -107.4722°). Leave the trail, go south across Grizzly Gulch, and climb the westernmost (37.9308° -107.4728°) of three north-facing avalanche gullies to unranked Point 12,792 (37.9240° -107.4716°). When snow conditions are favorable, this gully provides more than 1,000 feet of moderate snow climbing with one steep crux. In a normal snow year, this gully is dangerous before June, in good condition in June, and snow free later in the summer. I recommend an ice ax in June, and the steep crux may require crampons.

From Point 12,792, go 0.6 mile south-southwest then south up the ridge to unranked Point 13,502 (37.9166° -107.4747°) and continue 0.7 south-southwest to Point 13,795 on the East Ridge Route. Continue west on that route to Handies' summit. Either descend the East Slopes Route (28R8) or continue over Whitecross Mountain (28R8 EC) for a veritable tour of the Grizzly Gulch Basin. There's more.

28R9 V2 – Variation – Parhelia

From Silver Creek–Grizzly Gulch TH at 10,400'	*428 RP*	*11.4 mi RT*	*3,648' net; 5,487' total*	*Class 2+*
With descent of East Slopes	*337 RP*	*9.3 mi RT*	*3,648' net; 4,872' total*	*Class 2+*
With Whitecross Mtn	*393 RP*	*10.1 mi RT*	*3,648' net; 5,551' total*	*Class 2+*

This long, off-trail variation allows you to climb two ranked Thirteeners en route to Handies. It offers a good introduction to bagging obscure Thirteeners, at the end of which you may agree with many who argue that Thirteeners are harder than Fourteeners.

From the Silver Creek–Grizzly Gulch Trailhead at 10,400 feet, go 1.1 miles south back down the Cinnamon Pass Road to a small pullout (37.9233° -107.4544°) on the road's east side. Either walk here or drive here, and plan on walking down the road to retrieve your vehicle at the end of the day, or if your party has multiple vehicles, you can arrange a shuttle. From the pullout, walk 0.1 mile southeast down the road to 10,284 feet (37.9223° -107.4534°). Your cursory Class 1 approach is over.

Leave the soporific road, plunge southwest down to the Lake Fork of the Gunnison River at 10,220 feet, and engineer a crossing to its west side. This crossing can be problematic in June. Get on the south side of Campbell Creek and climb 0.4 mile steeply west above its south side to 10,900 feet (37.9207° -107.4593°). The peak you are trying to climb, Point 13,454, is only 1.2 miles south of you, but a whopping 2,554 feet above you. Welcome to Thirteenerland. Staying on the creek's southeast (left) side and climb a relentless, tough 1.0 mile southwest up the Campbell Creek Basin to a heartening break in the slope angle at 12,440 feet (37.9100° -107.4684°). Congratulations, you have just gained 2,220 feet in 1.4 miles. There's more.

Continue 0.4 mile southwest up the basin to 12,800 feet, then climb 200 yards steeply south to the 13,060-foot Point 13,454–Point 13,795 saddle (37.9042° -107.4704°). The intense effort of your initial climb is over; now it's time to enjoy a summit ride. Turn east-northeast (hard left) and climb 0.5 mile east-northeast up a much lower-angle ridge to the summit of Point 13,454, aka "Campbell Creek Peak" (37.9066° -107.4627°). This seldom-climbed ranked Thirteener is a Tri, one of Colorado's 300 highest ranked peaks. This is just the first peak of the Parhelia. There's always more.

Return to the 13,060-foot saddle, climb 0.9 mile west then northwest on or near the rough Class 2+ ridge to Point 13,795, join the East Ridge Route there, and continue to Handies. If you include Whitecross Mountain at the other end of this memorable ridge run, you can use your four-peak story to baffle beginners.

28R10 – Handies Peak – Grouse Gulch

From Grouse Gulch TH at 10,720'   184 RP   9.0 mi RT   3,328' net; 4,608' total   Class 1

This route provides access to Handies from the south and west. When approaching from the Durango area, you do not need a 4WD vehicle and you can avoid the long drive to Lake City.

Start at the Grouse Gulch Trailhead at 10,720 feet, walk 115 yards north up the road to the start of the Grouse Gulch Trail (37.9186° -107.5581°), and hike 2.1 miles east then southeast up the Grouse Gulch Trail to the 13,020-foot pass (37.9110° -107.5297°) at Grouse Gulch's east end. From the pass, you can see Handies' west side across American Basin. Descend 0.9 mile east into American Basin on the trail to a trail junction at 12,380 feet (37.9077° -107.5182°), join the West Slopes Route (28R7) here, and follow it to Handies summit.

29. Windom Group

Windom Peak	14,087 feet
Sunlight Peak	14,059 feet
Mount Eolus	14,084 feet

These wild, rugged peaks are the most remote of Colorado's Fourteeners. They lie buried in the heart of Colorado's greatest range—the San Juans. Windom, Sunlight, and Eolus harbor the zenith of the Colorado Fourteener experience. They are the highest peaks in the Needle Mountains and in the Weminuche Wilderness. The peaks are 15 miles southeast of Silverton, far from roads, and difficult to see. They are most often seen from other high San Juan peaks, and they always seem to be far away.

The remote sanctity of such peaks is what wilderness is all about. These peaks are popular—a testimony that we need wilderness now more than ever. Knowledge of wilderness is a prerequisite for its preservation. Tread lightly on this special place as you learn about it.

Windom is the highest peak in La Plata County and the monarch of the San Juans' rugged heartland. It is the first Fourteener you see when hiking up Needle Creek, and it appears friendly. Windom is 1.7 miles east of Eolus and 0.5 mile south of Sunlight. It's easier to climb than Eolus and Sunlight. If you are looking for a Fourteener in the heart of San Juan wilderness with views and charm but only modest commitment, climb Windom.

Sunlight's luminescent summit rests in secretive splendor at Chicago Basin's extreme northeast corner, 0.5 mile north of Windom. It is 1.6 miles east of Eolus and even more difficult to see than the secluded Eolus. Sunlight supports three craggy ridges, and from certain vantage points, the view of this peak is startling. Sunlight is perhaps best known for its exposed summit block. The final move onto this block is the hardest move required to reach the summit of a Colorado Fourteener by its easiest route. If the term *hardest* hinges on the difficulty of a few moves, then Sunlight can be called Colorado's hardest Fourteener.

Reclusive Eolus carefully guards its secrets. Eolus' singular splendor forms Chicago Basin's northwest rampart. Æolus was the ruler of the winds in Greek mythology; elevated to godlike status, Æolus was seen as an embodiment of wind itself. The peak attracts its own winds, and the name fits this massive monarch. The weather here can be violent, since warm summer air from the Utah desert rises into the San Juans and creates intense thunderstorms. The storms seem to reach a climax near Eolus. In winter, moisture-laden air wraps Eolus in a deep mantle of snow.

Sharp eyes will notice that I am using elevations for Windom and Eolus that differ from the long-standing 14,083 feet for Eolus and 14,082 feet for Windom. These are the elevations of the benchmarks near the summits of these two peaks, not their precise highpoints. The USGS has verified this, and their data sheets show the difference between the benchmark and the true summit in both cases. The summit of Eolus is 1 foot higher than the nearby benchmark, but the summit of Windom is 5 feet higher than its benchmark, which is on a ledge below the highest block. Thus the true summit elevations are 14,084 feet for Eolus and 14,087 feet for Windom. This difference is important since it makes Windom higher than Eolus and dethrones Eolus as the highest peak in La Plata County; Windom is the highest peak in La Plata County.

Differences between benchmark and true summit elevations exist on other peaks, but not usually with such a consequence. For example, the benchmark on 14,059-foot Sunlight Peak is well below the highest point, perhaps as much as 20 feet below. Thus, the true summit elevation for Sunlight could be as high as 14,079 feet, but this difference, large as it is, just repositions Sunlight in the list; it does not give it additional status. The USGS does not have a data sheet for this benchmark, so I use the traditional 14,059-foot elevation for Sunlight.

29E – Windom Group Essentials

Elevations	Windom Pk	14,087' (NGVD29) 14,092' (NAVD88)
	Sunlight Pk	14,059' (NGVD29) 14,064' (NAVD88)
	Mt Eolus	14,084' (NGVD29) 14,089' (NAVD88)
Ranks	Windom Pk	Colorado's 32nd highest ranked peak
	Sunlight Pk	Colorado's 39th highest ranked peak
	Mt Eolus	Colorado's 33rd highest ranked peak
Location	La Plata County, Colorado, USA	
Range	South-Central San Juan Range	
Summit Coordinates	Windom Pk	37.6211° -107.5918° (WGS84)
	Sunlight Pk	37.6273° -107.5958° (WGS84)
	Mt Eolus	37.6218° -107.6226° (WGS84)
Ownership/Contact	San Juan National Forest – Public Land	
	San Juan Public Lands Center – Durango – 970-247-4874	
Prominence and Saddles	Windom Pk	2,187' from 11,900' N Henson–Cow Ck Divide
	Sunlight Pk	399' from 13,660' Sunlight–Windom saddle
	Mt Eolus	1,024' from 13,060' Twin Thumbs Pass
Isolation and Parents	Windom Pk	26.55 miles to Wilson Peak
	Sunlight Pk	0.47 mile to Windom Peak
	Mt Eolus	1.68 miles to Windom Peak
USGS Maps	**Columbine Pass, Storm King Peak, Mountain View Crest,**	
	Snowdon Peak, Electra Lake, Engineer Mountain,	
	Vallecito Reservoir	
USFS Map	San Juan National Forest	
Trails Illustrated Map	Map #140 Weminuche Wilderness	
Book Map	See Map 29 on page 295	
Nearest Towns	Silverton – Population 520 – Elevation 9,308'	
	Durango – Population 16,500 – Elevation 6,523'	

29E – Windom Group Essentials

Windom Pk 🐾 + Easiest Route	29R1 – West Ridge – Class 2+
	A Class 1 hike to Chicago Basin and Twin Lakes, a Class 2 approach to a
	saddle, and a Class 2+ scamper up a ridge to the summit
Sunlight Pk 🐾 Easiest Route	29R3 – South Slopes – Class 4
	A Class 1 hike to Chicago Basin and Twin Lakes, a steep Class 2+ scamper
	to a high saddle, and a Class 3 scramble up to the Class 4 summit block
Mt Eolus 🐾 Easiest Route	28R5 – Northeast Ridge – Class 3
	A Class 1 hike to Chicago Basin and Twin Lakes, an easy Class 3 scramble to
	a high saddle, and a steep, exposed Class 3 scramble to the summit
Windom Group Accolades	You can best approach Colorado's most remote Fourteeners by train.
	Buried in Colorado's largest wilderness, the Weminuche, these peaks offer
	a grand mountaineering experience. Windom is the highest peak in La
	Plata County.

29T – Windom Group Trailheads

29T1 – Needleton Trailhead 8,212 feet 37.6337° -107.6925°

This trailhead provides access to Chicago Basin from the west. Chicago Basin is the popular approach for the standard routes up Eolus, Sunlight, and Windom. Needleton is deep in the Animas River Canyon 13 miles south of Silverton. You reach Needleton by rail or foot, not by road. The Durango and Silverton Narrow Gauge Railroad runs through the canyon, but the gorge is too narrow to accommodate both tracks and a road. The nearest road, US 550, is many miles to the west and separated from the Animas River Canyon by the West Needle Mountains. Approaching these peaks behind a 100-year-old steam locomotive puffing through a wild canyon is one of the trip's charms. The greatest hazard of the approach is hanging your head out the window and getting a cinder in your eye!

The privately owned Durango and Silverton Narrow Gauge Railroad starts operation in May, runs multiple trains a day between Durango and Silverton in the summer, and continues with a reduced schedule into October. Backpackers can board trains in Durango or Silverton, but only some of the trains stop at Needleton, so plan accordingly. The train stop is the Needleton Trailhead. The Durango train depot is at 479 Main Avenue, Durango, CO 81301, and you can make reservations by calling 1-888-TRAIN-07 or visit www.durangotrain. com. Make reservations early. As of 2010, the Durango–Silverton Railroad charged $79 round-trip, no matter where you get on or off. You may also be charged $10 for your pack. Do check for a group discount.

29T2 – Purgatory Flats Trailhead 8,740 feet 37.6298° -107.8068°

This trailhead provides access to the Purgatory Trail and Animas River Trail, which offer a long trail-access to Needle Creek and Chicago Basin. This is the best alternative for those who find the train to the Needleton Trailhead too expensive.

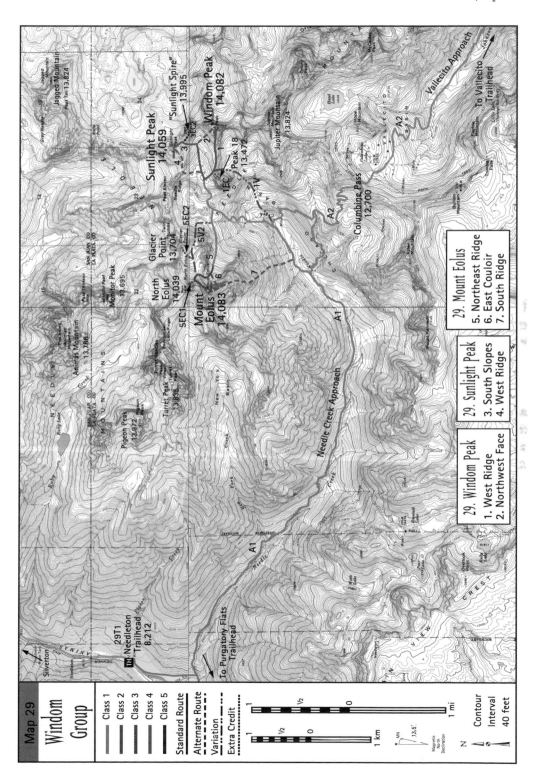

Map 29

Windom Group

Class 1
Class 2
Class 3
Class 4
Class 5

Standard Route
Alternate Route
Variation
Extra Credit

Contour Interval 40 feet

29. Windom Peak
1. West Ridge
2. Northwest Face

29. Sunlight Peak
3. South Slopes
4. West Ridge

29. Mount Eolus
5. Northeast Ridge
6. East Couloir
7. South Ridge

From Durango, go 27 miles north on US 550 and turn east (right) onto a paved road directly across the highway from the Durango Mountain Resort. Go 0.2 mile east past condos to the trailhead. The trail starts on the south side of the road, and there is a large parking area 100 yards east of the trail on the north side of the road. This trailhead is accessible in winter.

29T3 – Vallecito Trailhead 7,900 feet 37.4744° -107.5483°

This trailhead provides access to Chicago Basin from the east via a long trail hike over 12,700-foot Columbine Pass. This trailhead is seldom used to approach the Fourteeners, but it does provide a refreshing alternative for a long backpacking vacation. Go to Vallecito Reservoir, which is 13.0 miles north of Bayfield on US 160 or 20.0 miles east of Durango on Florida Road. Go 5.0 miles north around the west side of Vallecito Reservoir to a well-marked junction, stay left, and continue 3.0 miles north to the trailhead, which is just south of the Vallecito Campground.

The bridge over the Vallecito Creek 7 miles north of the trailhead washed away in 2006, and as of 2010, the Forest Service still steadfastly announced that it had "no intention" of replacing this bridge. This wily choice endangers all hikers who go up the valley.

29A – Windom Group Approaches

29A1 – Windom Group – Needle Creek Approach

From Needleton TH at 8,212'   125 RP   13.2 mi RT   2,988' net; 3,048' total   Class 1

This is the standard approach to Windom, Sunlight, and Eolus. Take the Durango and Silverton narrow gauge train from either Durango or Silverton and get off at Needleton. This is the Needleton Trailhead. Cross the good bridge to the Animas River's east side, turn south (right), and walk 0.8 mile south along the Animas River to the start of the Needle Creek Trail at 8,280 feet (37.6232° -107.6950°). The signed Needle Creek Trail is on Needle Creek's north side.

From the junction of the Animas River Trail and the Needle Creek Trail, turn east (left), enter the Weminuche Wilderness, and hike 1.6 miles east-southeast on the Needle Creek Trail (FT 504) to the bridge over New York Creek at 9,260 feet (37.6133° -107.6696°). This is a refreshing spot, since there is a waterfall just above the bridge. There are also campsites north of the trail, west of New York Creek. From the New York Creek bridge, continue 3.3 miles east-southeast, east, then east-northeast up the Needle Creek Trail past a peekaboo first view of 13,830-foot Jupiter Mountain to a sudden break in the trees (37.6046° -107.6218°) where you enter Chicago Basin at 10,960 feet and have a grander view of both Windom and Jupiter. There are a few campsites near here south of (below) the trail in the trees, and if the upper basin campsites are jammed, these sites are palatable. Continue 0.2 mile east-northeast to an unmarked trail junction with the start of the western approach trail for the Columbine Pass Trail at 11,000 feet (37.6065° -107.6191°). This trail junction is just north of the confluence of Needle Creek and a side creek emerging from a colorful gorge to the south. You do not want to go to Columbine Pass, at least not right now. Continue 0.7 mile east-northeast (straight), passing campsites both above and below the trail, to a trail junction at 11,200 feet (37.6114° -107.6106°). This is the end of the approach route. Try to camp below this junction, as sites beyond this point are sparse, sloping, or illegal.

Angling northeast (left) from the trail junction at 11,200 feet is the start of the excellent Colorado Fourteener Initiative trail on the upper creek's west then east side that climbs 1.1 miles north to Twin Lakes at 12,500 feet (37.6216° -107.6081°). Camping is not permitted around or above Twin Lakes. From the 11,200-foot trail junction, the continuing Needle Creek Trail soon turns south and climbs to Columbine Pass. Campfires are not allowed anywhere in the Needle Creek drainage.

29A1 V – Variation – Cascade Creek and Animas River Approach

From Purgatory Flats TH at 8,740'   273 RP   30.4 mi RT   2,460' net; 5,760' total   Class 1

If you choose to walk from the Purgatory Flats Trailhead at 8,740 feet, follow the Purgatory Trail (FT 511) 1.3 miles east down to Cascade Creek then 2.8 miles south down Cascade Creek on a spectacular shelf trail to the Animas River at 7,680 feet (37.5976° -107.7768°). Cross to the Animas River's southeast (far) side on a good footbridge just west-southwest (downstream) of the confluence of Cascade Creek and the Animas River. You are now just north of the Cascade Wye, and this is an interesting side trip if you have the time and energy.

To continue your approach from the footbridge, walk 220 yards east to the railroad tracks, walk north-northwest on a trail next to the tracks until you are just south of the railroad bridge over the Animas River (37.5980° -107.7735°), cross the tracks (not the bridge), and find the start of the Animas River Trail going up the hill away from the tracks. Follow the good Animas River Trail (FT 675) 5.1 miles northeast along the Animas River's southeast side (the railroad tracks are on the river's northwest side) to Needle Creek, cross Needle Creek on a sturdy bridge, go 100 yards east to the start of the Needle Creek Trail at 8,280 feet (37.6232° -107.6950°), and follow the Needle Creek Approach from there.

There are good campsites on Needle Creek's south side both above and below the Animas River Trail just south of the bridge over Needle Creek (37.6232° -107.6956°). It is 9.4 miles from the Purgatory Trailhead to the Needle Creek Trail, and if you choose to hike out via this route, you will have to gain 1,540 feet to end your expedition.

29A2 – Windom Group – Vallecito Approach

From Vallecito TH at 7,900'   407 RP   36.0 mi RT   3,300' net; 6,300' total   Class 1

This seldom-used approach requires a long backpack trip, but it avoids the train's cost and crowds. This approach is suitable for an extended trip. Consider doing a traverse and only using the train one way.

Start at the Vallecito Trailhead at 7,900 feet and, crossing Vallecito Creek three times en route, follow the Vallecito Creek Trail (FT 529) 8.8 miles north to its junction with the Johnson Creek Trail at 9,120 feet (37.5842° -107.5307°). There are many good campsites near here. Cross to Vallecito Creek's west side on a good bridge and follow the Johnson Creek Trail (FT 504) 6.7 miles west-south-west then west-northwest as it climbs steadily up Johnson Creek to Columbine Pass at 12,700 feet (37.5989° -107.6028°). Johnson Creek is beautiful and rugged, and you are deep in the wilderness here. Cross Columbine Pass and descend 2.5 miles north to the 11,200-foot trail junction in Chicago Basin (37.6114° -107.6106°). Camping is not permitted around or above Twin Lakes at 12,500 feet, and campfires are not allowed anywhere in the Needle Creek drainage.

29A EC – Extra Credit – Five Trails Run

From Purgatory Flats TH at 8,740' to Vallecito TH at 7,900'   364 RP   32.1 mi OW   5,640' total   Class 1

This point-to-point course used to be a test piece for local runners in the 1970s, when I set a standard of 6½ hours for the course. The route fell into obscurity for many years, but is now being rediscovered as a glorious way to spend a day. The route's evident charms should be sufficient motivation for runners and backpackers alike. Plan carefully, arrange a vehicle shuttle, and let 'er rip.

In brief, you start at the Purgatory Flats Trailhead at 8,740 feet and end at the Vallecito Trailhead at 7,900 feet following five major drainages en route. Go 4.1 miles down Cascade Creek, 5.3 miles along the Animas River, and 5.1 miles up Needle Creek to an unmarked trail junction with the start of the western approach trail for the Columbine Pass Trail at 11,000 feet (37.6065° -107.6191°). This trail junction is just north of the confluence of Needle Creek and a side creek emerging from a colorful gorge to the south. Now you want to go to Columbine Pass. Leave the Needle Creek Trail, cross Needle Creek, switchback southeast up through the trees, and climb along the north edge of the colorful gorge to a trail junction at 11,680 feet (37.6060° -107.6073°). There are good campsites near here. Turn south (right), cross the creek headed for the gorge, and climb to Columbine Pass at 12,700 feet (37.5989° -107.6028°). It is 2.1 miles from Needle Creek to Columbine Pass. Descend 6.7 miles down Johnson Creek and 8.8 miles down the Vallecito. Pace yourself.

29. Windom Peak 14,087 feet

29R – Windom Peak Routes

29R1 – Windom Peak – West Ridge *Classic*

From Needleton TH at 8,212'	*356 RP*	*17.6 mi RT*	*5,875' net; 5,935' total*	*Class 2+*
From 11,200' in Chicago Basin	*158 RP*	*4.4 mi RT*	*2,887' net; 2,887' total*	*Class 2+*
From Purgatory Flats TH at 8,740'	*589 RP*	*34.8 mi RT*	*5,347' net; 8,647' total*	*Class 2+*
From Vallecito TH at 7,900'	*659 RP*	*40.4 mi RT*	*6,187' net; 9,187' total*	*Class 2+*

This is the easiest route on Windom. You can see the upper part of the west ridge from treeline in Chicago Basin. I have done this surrealistic tour in the heart of Colorado's wilderness many times, and it always reminds me of why I started climbing.

Use one of the Windom Group approaches to reach Chicago Basin. From 11,200 feet (37.6114° -107.6106°) in Chicago Basin, hike 1.1 miles steeply north on the excellent Colorado Fourteener Initiative trail to Twin Lakes at 12,500 feet (37.6216° -107.6081°). From Twin Lakes, climb 0.4 mile east to 13,000 feet in the lower end of the basin between Sunlight and Windom. Look for a newly constructed trail and stay south of a waterfall on this ascent. From 13,000 feet, turn southeast (right) and ascend snow or talus to the 13,260-foot saddle (37.6213° -107.6001°) between Windom and 13,472-foot Peak Eighteen, which is the small but dramatic peak at the west end of Windom's west ridge. Peak Eighteen has a sheer west face that you can easily see from Chicago Basin, but Peak Eighteen is not named on the Columbine Pass Quadrangle.

From the Windom–Peak Eighteen saddle, turn east (left) and hike then scamper 0.5 mile up Windom's west ridge to the summit. Wilderness views rise above the surrounding peaks as you climb. The ridge is Class 2 talus hiking at first, then the ridge steepens as you approach the summit. The Class 2+ scampering over the large but solid boulders near the summit is not as hard or exposed as the Class 3 scrambling on Sunlight or Eolus. The final moves up angular blocks can make you feel like a climber is supposed to feel. From the summit (37.6211° -107.5918°), you have expansive views in all directions. In particular, you can gaze north across an existential wilderness. Welcome to Colorado.

29R1 V – Variation – Southern Shortcut

Class 3

You can reach the 13,260-foot saddle between Windom and Peak Eighteen from the south. From 11,200 feet in Chicago Basin, climb east through some cliff bands to reach the lower end of the high basin between Windom and 13,830-foot Jupiter Mountain, which is 0.6 mile south of Windom. Turn north (left) and climb a couloir to the saddle. This seldom-used shortcut is more difficult than the northern approach to the saddle and doesn't save time.

Windom Peak from the north.

29R1 EC – Extra Credit – Peak Eighteen 13,472 feet 37.6206° -107.6014°

Class 4

From the 13,260-foot saddle between Windom and Peak Eighteen, climb west to the summit of 13,472-foot Peak Eighteen. The easiest route is Class 4 on the ridge's south side.

29R2 – Windom Peak – Northwest Face

From Needleton TH at 8,212'	400 RP	17.6 mi RT	5,935' total	Class 3, Mod Snow
From 11,200' in Chicago Basin	201 RP	4.4 mi RT	2,887' total	Class 3, Mod Snow
From Purgatory Flats TH at 8,740'	633 RP	34.8 mi RT	8,647' total	Class 3, Mod Snow
From Vallecito TH at 7,900'	702 RP	40.4 mi RT	9,187' total	Class 3, Mod Snow

This face is often climbed or descended when climbing Windom together with Sunlight. From 11,200 feet (37.6114° -107.6106°) in Chicago Basin, hike 1.1 miles steeply north on the excellent Colorado Fourteener Initiative trail to Twin Lakes at 12,500 feet (37.6216° -107.6081°). From Twin Lakes, climb 0.8 mile east to 13,300 feet (37.6231° -107.5951°) in the high basin between Sunlight and

Windom. Turn southeast (right) and climb 0.3 mile southeast up Windom's northwest face to the summit (intermittent Class 3). Your exact line is a matter of choice. This face retains some snow until late in the summer, and the exposed rock slabs are often wet. Choose your line carefully.

29. Sunlight Peak 14,059 feet

29R – Sunlight Peak Routes

29R3 – Sunlight Peak – South Slopes

From Needleton TH at 8,212'	417 RP	17.4 mi RT	5,847' net; 5,907' total	Class 4
From 11,200' in Chicago Basin	219 RP	4.2 mi RT	2,859' net; 2,859' total	Class 4
From Purgatory Flats TH at 8,740'	651 RP	34.6 mi RT	5,319' net; 8,619' total	Class 4
From Vallecito TH at 7,900'	720 RP	40.2 mi RT	6,159' net; 9,159' total	Class 4

This is the easiest route on Sunlight Peak. Use one of the Windom Group approaches to reach Chicago Basin. From 11,200 feet (37.6114° -107.6106°) in Chicago Basin, hike 1.1 miles steeply north on the excellent Colorado Fourteener Initiative trail to Twin Lakes at 12,500 feet (37.6216° -107.6081°). From Twin Lakes, climb 0.7 mile east-northeast to 13,200 feet (37.6234° -107.5958°) in the high basin between Sunlight and Windom. Look for a newly constructed trail and stay south of a waterfall on this ascent. Sunlight is north of you, and the spectacular 13,995-foot "Sunlight Spire" is above you on the connecting ridge between Sunlight and Windom.

Turn north (left) toward Sunlight Peak and climb 0.2 mile up scrawny, open Class 2+ slopes flanked by small slabs to reach the westernmost (37.6261°

Sunlight Peak from the west.

-107.5947°) of two small 13,780-foot saddles between Sunlight Peak and "Sunlight Spire." This saddle is often called the Window for the awesome view it offers into the San Juan heartland. From the Window, climb northwest to a higher saddle, then do a clever Class 3 traverse west to avoid the pinnacles on the ridge above you. Climb up a series of steep Class 3 steps interspersed with easier scrambling. The south slopes narrow to a ridge before you reach the summit. Pass west of a hole in this ridge and climb to a second, higher hole, which is called the Worm Hole. Wiggle east through the Worm Hole, then scramble north up to an alcove just south of Sunlight's famous 30-foot-high summit block. Many souls have elected to stop here, but this is not the summit.

Scramble up to the summit block's east end (Class 3). The final, committing Class 4 moves onto the summit block require you to step across an exposed gap, then pull yourself up over a second gap onto the rounded, smooth block (37.6273° -107.5958°). The final move onto the summit is the harder of the two moves. If you are tall, you can avoid the final move by reaching up and touching the highest point with your hand. As you straddle the gaps, you can peer down the north face between your legs, as any wind will likely whistle where it's not wanted. Many people enjoy the protection of a rope on this summit block, but it is difficult to arrange an anchor. Sunlight's exciting summit can only accommodate one or two people at a time!

29R3 V – Variation – Gapless
Class 5.0–5.2

A less exposed but harder alternative is to climb the Class 5.0–5.2 slab on the south face of a 15-foot-high boulder leaning against the summit block, step east (right) on the top of the boulder, then make one more move to reach the highest point. This variation avoids the airy gaps a few feet to the east, and the top of the boulder offers a secure stance for a belayer. With dexterity, you can thread a sling around the 4-inch connection between the boulder and the summit block.

29R3 EC1 – Extra Credit – Standing Ovation
Class 4

Most summit shots show people sitting on the summit. Center yourself and stand on the summit (Class 4). For triple points, do a headstand on the summit (Class 5).

29R3 EC2 – Extra Credit – "Sunlight Spire" 13,995 feet 37.6255° -107.5936°

From Needleton TH at 8,212'	1,000 RP	17.4 mi RT	5,783' net; 5,843' total	Class 5.10
From 11,200' in Chicago Basin	803 RP	4.2 mi RT	2,795' net; 2,795' total	Class 5.10
From Purgatory Flats TH at 8,740'	1,231 RP	34.6 mi RT	5,255' net; 8,555' total	Class 5.10
From Vallecito TH at 7,900'	1,299 RP	40.2 mi RT	6,095' net; 9,095' total	Class 5.10

For years peak baggers have admired "Sunlight Spire" from a distance, then heaved a sigh of relief that the summit does not rank, does not have an official name, does not reach 14,000 feet, and therefore, they don't have to climb it. However, when the USGS switched to the NAVD88 vertical datum, the latter excuse was erased. Both Sunlight Peak and Windom went up 5 feet, and it is highly probable that, under the new datum, "Sunlight Spire" also goes up 5 feet, bringing it to an even 14,000 feet. With only 215 feet of prominence, the spire will not leap onto lists of official Fourteeners, but remember that El Diente and world-famous North Maroon Peak also do not rank, and they have been on the traditional list for decades.

George Bell Sr., David Michael, and John Marshall first climbed the spire with aid (A1) in July 1961 by climbing the ramp left of the crack, swinging 10 feet over to the crack via one bolt, then aiding the top 10 feet of the crack. The bolt from this first ascent is now gone, and since bolting is not allowed in a wilderness area, this strategy is no longer an option. Climbing the entire crack, Jeff Achey made the first free ascent in 1988, rating the crack 5.10C. George Bell Jr., son of the first ascensionist, and Bill Wright made a free ascent on July 4, 1998. Spectacular "Sunlight Spire" is worth a second look, and in recent years, many free climbers consider the spire a significant prize.

Follow Sunlight Peak's South Slopes Route to just below the easternmost 13,780-foot saddle between Sunlight Peak and "Sunlight Spire." Scamper southeast across increasingly blocky talus, then do an ascending traverse 200 feet east up a series of delightful ledges and upclimbs (Class 3). The rock on this approach scramble is the most solid rock that I have found in the San Juans. Secure chin-up bar holds might make you feel like you are in the Sierra, and they keep the difficulty on the steepening, increasingly exposed approach at Class 3. However, once a chin-up hold did collapse, causing a serious injury. You are still in the San Juans! Reach a highpoint where you can look up at the upper spire and see the southwest-facing crack that is the route's crux. You are not yet directly below the spire, so rappel or downclimb (Class 5.4) 15 feet south to a large, grassy ledge and walk 15 feet east to a stance directly below the remaining route. There are many anchor possibilities at this stance. There is also a lower approach scramble that climbs a short Class 5.6 pitch to reach this stance from below.

The pitch from the belay stance to the summit is 85 feet long. Climb 45 feet to the upper spire, overcoming a Class 5.7 crux midway in this stretch. The vertical 40-foot crack in the summit block is now directly above you, and your defining moment has arrived. If you want to shorten the summit pitch, you can also arrange a belay here, and a fixed anchor is nearby. The width of the unrelenting left-angling finger crack is consistent between one and two inches. The bottom two-thirds of the crack overhangs 3 or 4 degrees, and the angle relents to vertical near the top. Some free climbers have rated the crack 5.10C or even 5.10D—the hardest 5.10 ratings—while others have stated that no move is harder than 5.9+, but it is the unyielding sequence that gives the crack a 5.10 rating. All agree, however, that the altitude makes the ascent more difficult. Also, crack climbers used to doing vertical cracks in the desert find this left-angling crack onerous. The final move over the lip is also difficult, but the summit itself is flat enough to sit on comfortably. The crack continues through the summit and provides anchorage. It is still possible to aid the crack with a large rack of small nuts and cams.

29R4 – Sunlight Peak – West Ridge *Classic*

From Needleton TH at 8,212'	*429 RP*	*17.2 mi RT*	*5,847' net; 5,907' total*	*Class 4*
From 11,200' in Chicago Basin	*230 RP*	*4.0 mi RT*	*2,859' net; 2,859' total*	*Class 4*
From Purgatory Flats TH at 8,740'	*662 RP*	*34.4 mi RT*	*5,319' net; 8,619' total*	*Class 4*
From Vallecito TH at 7,900'	*731 RP*	*40.0 mi RT*	*6,159' net; 9,159' total*	*Class 4*

This is a more difficult route than the South Slopes Route. It is notable because the rock is solid (for the San Juans!), and because the positions encountered are spectacular. Ascending this route and descending the South Slopes Route makes a scintillating Tour de Sunlight.

Use one of the Windom Group approaches to reach Chicago Basin. From 11,200 feet (37.6114° -107.6106°) in Chicago Basin, hike 1.1 miles steeply north on the excellent Colorado Fourteener Initiative trail to Twin Lakes at 12,500 feet (37.6216° -107.6081°). From Twin Lakes, you can see the jagged Needle Ridge that forms the lower end of Sunlight's west ridge. The complete traverse of Needle Ridge is a difficult undertaking and is not part of the route described here.

From Twin Lakes, climb 0.4 mile east to 13,000 feet in the lower end of the basin between Sunlight and Windom. Turn north (left) and climb 0.2 mile north in a rubble-filled gully to a 13,300-foot saddle (37.6260° -107.5999°) between Needle Ridge and Sunlight. Make sure you climb to the saddle east of

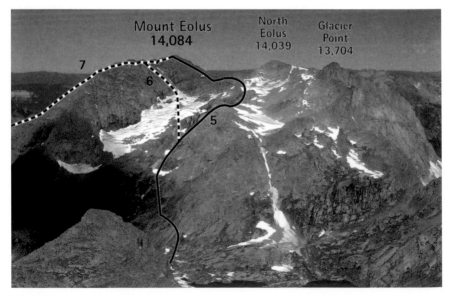

Mount Eolus from the summit of Windom Peak.

Needle Ridge. The rubble-filled gully is unpleasant, but such are the dues you must pay to reach the exciting upper scrambling.

From the 13,300-foot saddle, the west ridge looks formidable. Overcome it one step at a time. Meet the challenge immediately and climb a steep Class 4 wall. The climbing above this initial wall alternates between the broken ridge and more short Class 3 walls. One lower-angled solid wall is positively primal. The scrambling remains interesting, but the difficulties ease as you approach the summit. Join the South Slopes Route (29R3) near the Worm Hole and continue on the South Slopes Route to the tippy-top of the summit block.

29. Mount Eolus 14,084 feet

29R – Mount Eolus Routes

29R5 – Mount Eolus – Northeast Ridge

From Needleton TH at 8,212'	*367 RP*	*18.1 mi RT*	*5,872' net; 5,932' total*	*Class 3*
From 11,200' in Chicago Basin	*169 RP*	*4.9 mi RT*	*2,884' net; 2,884' total*	*Class 3*
From Purgatory Flats TH at 8,740'	*601 RP*	*35.3 mi RT*	*5,344' net; 8,644' total*	*Class 3*
From Vallecito TH at 7,900'	*670 RP*	*40.9 mi RT*	*6,184' net; 9,184' total*	*Class 3*

This is the standard route on Eolus. Use one of the Windom Group approaches to reach Chicago Basin. From 11,200 feet (37.6114° -107.6106°) in Chicago Basin, hike 1.1 miles steeply north on the excellent Colorado Fourteener Initiative trail to Twin Lakes at 12,500 feet (37.6216° -107.6081°). From the outlet of the southern Twin Lake, hike west on a climber's trail into the small basin under Eolus' steep east face.

Hike 0.7 mile west on a good climber's trail past a large, sweeping slab to the north (right) to 13,000 feet (37.6211° -107.6177°) in the basin under Eolus' east face (Class 1). Continue west-northwest, pass an initial ledge leading northeast across the slab, then turn northeast (hard right) and do an ascending traverse northeast on a higher, broader ledge (Class 2+). Reach the upper, western end of a flat area between Eolus and 13,704-foot Glacier Point. This flat area has a small lake at its lower, eastern end. This temporal paradise rests high and wild. Do an ascending traverse 200 yards northwest to 13,760 feet (37.6242° -107.6201°), turn west (left), and scramble up just north of a gully to the northernmost 13,860-foot saddle (37.6241° -107.6206°) between Eolus and North Eolus (Easy Class 3). North Eolus (14,039 feet) is a spur summit 0.25 mile north of Eolus.

From the saddle, walk and scramble southwest along a famous stretch of ridge called the Catwalk (a little Class 3). The ridge narrows to a width of 2 feet, and there is exposure on both sides of the ridge. En route you must climb over an 8-foot bump on the ridge (Class 3). Beyond the Catwalk (37.6228° -107.6218°), Eolus' northeast ridge rears up above you. Do not climb directly up the steep part of the ridge, but traverse south on a large ledge on the ridge's east side onto Eolus' east face. When the difficulties above you relent, scramble up, move south on a broken ledge, scramble up to a higher ledge, scamper south, and angle south (left) up a lower-angled weakness to reach the south ridge of Eolus. Scamper 100 feet north just west of the ridge crest to reach the summit (Class 2+).

The easiest route on this complex face can be difficult to follow, and many people have gotten off-route here, some to their considerable detriment. There are many cairns, but many of them are off the easiest line. Take your time and look before launching. If you find yourself attempting a significantly harder move than those you have been making, you are probably off-route. From the summit (37.6218° -107.6226°), you have a commanding view of a vast sea of San Juan peaks. You also can see Shiprock in New Mexico—and you may feel the desert's pull.

29R5 V1 – Variation – Upper Northeast Ridge

Class 4

From the south end of the Catwalk (37.6228° -107.6218°), climb directly up the upper northeast ridge instead of traversing onto the upper east face. This is a harder, more spectacular finish on highly fractured blocks.

29R5 V2 – Variation – Lake Couloir

Class 3, Mod Snow

From Twin Lakes, climb straight west up a steep Class 3 couloir to reach the small lake (37.6240° -107.6138°) at the eastern end of the flat area between Eolus and 13,704-foot Glacier Point. This couloir retains snow through June and can provide a refreshing, moderate snow climb. Continue west across the flat area and rejoin the Northeast Ridge Route below the Eolus–North Eolus saddle.

29R5 EC1 – Extra Credit – North Eolus 14,039 feet 37.6251° -107.6212°

Class 3

From the 13,860-foot Eolus–North Eolus saddle (37.6241° -107.6206°), scramble 200 yards north-northwest to the summit of 14,039-foot North Eolus. This modest Class 3 scramble is fun, and it is easier than the final scramble on Eolus. You can do it before you summit Eolus to tune up your technique and survey the route on Eolus. You can do it after you summit Eolus to take a photo and feel good about what you have just done. North Eolus only has 179 feet of prominence, but it is an officially named summit above 14,000 feet.

29R5 EC2 – Extra Credit – Glacier Point 13,704 feet 37.6260° -107.6144°

Class 2

From the flat area below the Eolus–North Eolus saddle, hike northeast and hike up steep talus to Glacier Point's 13,704-foot summit, a soft-ranked Thirteener. This perch gives you a spectacular view north into the Noname Creek drainage. You can easily climb Glacier Point with Eolus when you climb the Lake Couloir (29R5 V2) above Twin Lakes.

29R6 – Mount Eolus – East Couloir

From Needleton TH at 8,212'	*454 RP*	*17.8 mi RT*	*5,872' net; 5,932' total*	Class 3, Steep Snow
From 11,200' in Chicago Basin	*256 RP*	*4.6 mi RT*	*2,884' net; 2,884' total*	Class 3, Steep Snow
From Purgatory Flats TH at 8,740'	*688 RP*	*35.0 mi RT*	*5,344' net; 8,644' total*	Class 3, Steep Snow
From Vallecito TH at 7,900'	*757 RP*	*40.6 mi RT*	*6,184' net; 9,184' total*	Class 3, Steep Snow

When it is in good condition, this hidden couloir offers a nifty way to avoid the crowds on the upper Northeast Ridge Route. Avoid this couloir after the snow melts. The couloir angles to the south as it splits the east face and reaches the south ridge near the summit.

Follow the Northeast Ridge Route (29R5) to 13,400 feet in the basin under the east face. You can see the couloir from here. Leave the Northeast Ridge Route before it traverses northeast to reach the shelf under North Eolus. Hike south, enter the narrow couloir, and climb it for 600 exciting feet to a deep, spectacular notch on the south ridge. From the notch, scramble north on the west side of the ridge to the summit (37.6218° –107.6226°).

29R7 – Mount Eolus – South Ridge

From Needleton TH at 8,212'	*584 RP*	*14.6 mi RT*	*5,872' net; 5,932' total*	Class 4
From 11,080' in Chicago Basin	*400 RP*	*2.5 mi RT*	*3,004' net; 3,004' total*	Class 4
From Purgatory Flats TH at 8,740'	*818 RP*	*31.8 mi RT*	*5,344' net; 8,644' total*	Class 4
From Vallecito TH at 7,900'	*915 RP*	*39.6 mi RT*	*6,184' net; 9,242' total*	Class 4

This challenging mountaineering route is seldom climbed. The complicated ridge hides a wilderness adventure. Perhaps the ridge should be named Discovery Ridge.

If you want to discover your adventure, leave the Needle Creek Trail at 11,080 feet (37.6085° –107.6176°) in lower Chicago Basin, 0.15 mile east of the Columbine Pass Trail junction. Climb north up a long Class 2 approach slope and angle slightly west toward the ridge crest above you. The ridge steepens and narrows between 12,200 feet and 13,400 feet. Stay close to the ridge crest when you can, and leave the ridge to avoid difficulties when you need to. High on the ridge, the easiest route is on the west side of the ridge. Discover your route all the way to the summit. This ridge provides spectacular positions, but this is not a good route to be on when electric storms roll in from the desert.

29C – Eolus, Sunlight, and Windom Combination Routes

29C1 – Sunlight South Slopes ➔ Windom West Ridge

From Needleton TH at 8,212'	*481 RP*	*18.6 mi RT*	*5,875' net; 6,894' total*	Class 4
From 11,200' in Chicago Basin	*283 RP*	*5.4 mi RT*	*2,887' net; 3,846' total*	Class 4
From Purgatory Flats TH at 8,740'	*715 RP*	*34.8 mi RT*	*5,347' net; 9,606' total*	Class 4
From Vallecito TH at 7,900'	*784 RP*	*41.4 mi RT*	*6,187' net; 10,146' total*	Class 4

This is the easiest way to climb Sunlight and Windom together. Climb Sunlight's South Slopes Route (29R3) and descend that route to 13,100 feet, in the basin between Sunlight and Windom. Climb to the 13,260-foot saddle between Windom and Peak Eighteen and continue on Windom's West Ridge Route (29R1) to Windom's summit. Descend Windom's West Ridge Route. By giving up some elevation to reach Windom's west ridge, you avoid the vagaries of Windom's northwest face.

29C2 – Sunlight West Ridge ➔ Windom Northwest Face

From Needleton TH at 8,212'	514 RP	18.0 mi RT	6,694' total	Class 4, Mod Snow
From 11,200' in Chicago Basin	316 RP	4.8 mi RT	3,646' total	Class 4, Mod Snow
From Purgatory Flats TH at 8,740'	748 RP	35.2 mi RT	9,406' total	Class 4, Mod Snow
From Vallecito TH at 7,900'	817 RP	40.8 mi RT	9,946' total	Class 4, Mod Snow

This is a more exciting way to climb Sunlight and Windom together that allows you to do four different routes. Climb Sunlight's West Ridge Route (29R4) and descend Sunlight's South Slopes Route (29R3) to 13,300 feet in the basin between Sunlight and Windom. Continue up Windom's Northwest Face Route (29R2) and descend Windom's West Ridge Route (29R1).

29C3 – Eolus Northeast Ridge ➔ Sunlight South Slopes ➔ Windom West Ridge

From Needleton TH at 8,212'	624 RP	22.4 mi RT	5,875' net; 8,478' total	Class 4
From 11,200' in Chicago Basin	426 RP	9.2 mi RT	2,887' net; 5,430' total	Class 4
From Purgatory Flats TH at 8,740'	858 RP	39.6 mi RT	5,347' net; 11,190' total	Class 4
From Vallecito TH at 7,900'	927 RP	45.2 mi RT	6,187' net; 11,730' total	Class 4

This is the easiest way to climb all three peaks in one day. Climb Eolus' Northeast Ridge Route (29R5) and return to Twin Lakes. Continue with Combination 29C1. These peaks can be done in any order, but doing Eolus first puts the difficulties of Eolus behind you early. Doing Windom last allows you to descend Windom's obliging west ridge at the end of the day.

30. Mount Sneffels 14,150 feet

This stunning peak is 7 miles west of Ouray and 5 miles north of Telluride. Mount Sneffels is the highest peak in Ouray County and the highest peak in its namesake Mount Sneffels Wilderness. Sneffels rules an abrupt escarpment on the San Juans' northwest edge that is visible for great distances to the north. As you approach the range, Sneffels' distinctive shape predominates, and it becomes clear that Sneffels is the monarch of this area. As you come even closer, Sneffels' great north face looms over your head in a collar-crunching view. The views of Sneffels from the highway between Ridgway and Dallas Divide are renowned, and when the aspens change colors in the fall, this panorama represents Colorado. Sneffels is also on the cover of this book.

30E – Mount Sneffels Essentials

Elevations	14,150' (NGVD29) 14,155' (NAVD88)
Rank	Colorado's 27th highest ranked peak
Location	Ouray County, Colorado, USA
Range	Western San Juan Range – Sneffels Range
Summit Coordinates	38.0037° -107.7923° (WGS84)
Ownership/Contact	Uncompahgre National Forest – Public Land – 970-874-6600
Prominence and Saddle	3,050' from 11,100' Red Mountain Pass
Isolation and Parent	15.74 miles to Mount Wilson
USGS Maps	**Mount Sneffels, Telluride,** Ironton
USFS Maps	**Uncompahgre National Forest**
Trails Illustrated Map	Map #141 Telluride, Silverton, Ouray, Lake City
Book Map	See Map 30 on page 310
Nearest Towns	Ridgway – Population 820 – Elevation 6,985'
	Ouray – Population 930 – Elevation 7,792'Telluride – Population 2,400 – Elevation 8,750'
Mount Sneffels 🏔 + Easiest Route	30R1 – South Slopes – Class 2+
	A road and trail approach hike, a steep slope to a high saddle, a narrow couloir, and a rocky Class 2+ scamper to the summit
Sneffels' Accolades	Mount Sneffels is the highest peak in Ouray County and the highest peak in its namesake Mount Sneffels Wilderness Area and Range. Highly visible from the north, Sneffels is one of Colorado's most photographed Fourteeners.

30T – Mount Sneffels Trailheads

30T1 – Yankee Boy Basin Trailhead 10,700 feet 37.9776° -107.7574°

This trailhead provides access to Sneffels' south side. On US 550, go 0.4 mile south past Ouray's south edge. Turn south onto Ouray County 361 and measure from this point (38.0176° -107.6747°). Follow Ouray County 361 as it turns, crosses the Uncompahgre River on a high bridge, and climbs steeply west up Canyon Creek. Stay right at mile 4.7 (37.9757° -107.7218°) on FR 853.1B, continue west on a spectacular shelf road, go straight at mile 6.0, pass the historic Sneffels town site, and reach a short side road on the left after mile 6.7 (37.9776° -107.7572°). This is the trailhead, and ample parking is available on the side road. The road to this point has some rough spots, and you will appreciate a higher clearance vehicle. Amazingly, this trailhead is often accessible in winter.

30T1 4WD – Yankee Boy Basin 4WD Trailhead 12,440 feet 37.9947° -107.7847°

The road beyond the trailhead becomes rougher rapidly, but tough 4WD vehicles can continue another 2.8 miles. Measuring from the Yankee Boy Basin Trailhead at 10,700 feet, 4WD vehicles can continue northwest up the Yankee Boy Basin Road (FR 853.1B). Stay right at mile 0.2 (37.9794° -107.7592°) and continue

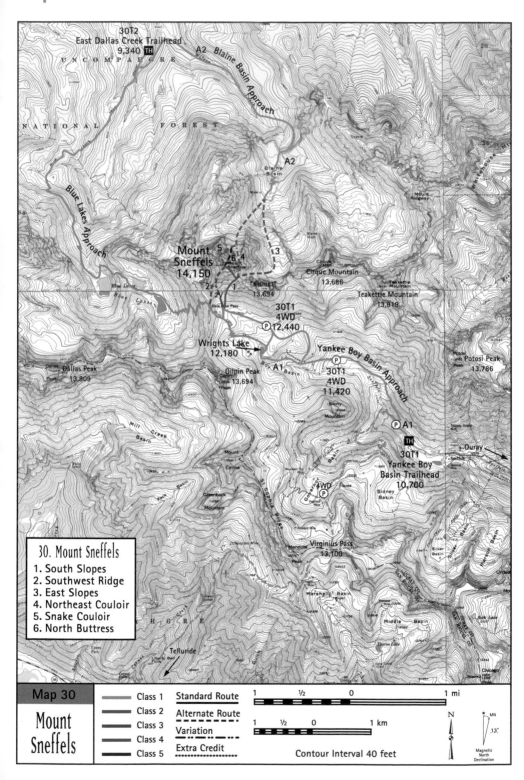

30. Mount Sneffels
1. South Slopes
2. Southwest Ridge
3. East Slopes
4. Northeast Couloir
5. Snake Couloir
6. North Buttress

Map 30

Mount Sneffels

Class 1	**Standard Route**
Class 2	**Alternate Route**
Class 3	**Variation**
Class 4	
Class 5	**Extra Credit**

Contour Interval 40 feet

N

MN

13°

Magnetic
North
Declination

1.2 miles northwest to a road junction at 11,415 feet (37.9896° -107.7714°). The road beyond this point steepens, and some people choose to park here. Tough 4WD vehicles can continue 0.4 mile west up the rough, 4WD road to another junction at 11,760 feet (37.9891° -107.7774°). This junction is between the road, which heads north, and a trail that heads west. Continue on the switchbacking road 0.7 mile north then west to a level area at 12,320 feet (37.9938° -107.7815°), north of tiny Wrights Lake. You can park here or continue on the road 0.3 mile northwest to the road's highest point at 12,440 feet. The Blue Lakes Trail (FT 201) starts here and heads west through the scree.

30T2 – East Dallas Creek Trailhead 9,340 feet 38.0344° -107.8073°

This trailhead provides access to Sneffels' north side. If approaching from the north or south, go west on Colorado 62 for 4.8 miles from the US 550–Colorado 62 junction in Ridgway. Ridgway is 26 miles south of Montrose and 11 miles north of Ouray. If approaching from the west, go east on Colorado 62 for 18.5 miles from the junction of Colorado 145 and Colorado 62.

Turn south onto Ouray County 7 (East Dallas Creek Road) and measure from this point. Stay left at mile 0.3, stay right at mile 2.0, and enter the Uncompahgre National Forest at mile 7.2 (38.0577° -107.8067°). The oft-photographed views of Sneffels from here are remarkable. Stay right and cross East Dallas Creek at mile 8.2 (38.0439° -107.8077°). Take the middle of three forks at mile 8.8 (38.0357° -107.8067°) and reach the trailhead at mile 9.0. Two trails start at this trailhead. Make sure you follow the trail you want. The road to this trailhead is not plowed in winter.

30A – Mount Sneffels Approaches

30A1 – Mount Sneffels – Yankee Boy Basin Approach

From Yankee Boy Basin TH at 10,700'   71 RP   5.4 mi RT   1,740' total   Class 1

This is the approach for Sneffels' standard South Slopes Route (30R1). Start at the Yankee Boy Basin Trailhead at 10,700 feet and go west up the Yankee Boy Basin Road (FR 853.1B). Stay right at mile 0.2 (37.9794° -107.7592°) and continue 1.2 miles northwest to a road junction at 11,415 feet (37.9896° -107.7714°). A spectacular view of 13,786-foot Potosi Peak emerges behind you as you climb. Continue 0.4 mile west up the rough, 4WD road to another junction at 11,760 feet (37.9891° -107.7774°). This junction is between the road, which heads north, and a trail that heads west. Leave the road and hike 0.6 mile west then north on the trail to the east side of tiny Wrights Lake at 12,200 feet (37.9909° -107.7845°). Hike 0.3 mile north-northwest and rejoin the road at its highest point (37.9947° -107.7847°). The Blue Lakes Trail (FT 201) starts here at 12,440 feet and heads west through the scree.

30A2 – Mount Sneffels – Blaine Basin Approach

From East Dallas Creek TH at 9,340'   63 RP   6.8 mi RT   1,760' total   Class 1

This approach gives access to all the routes on Sneffels' north and east sides. Start at the East Dallas Creek Trailhead at 9,340 feet and go straight at the trail junction just south of the road closure gate onto the Blaine Basin Trail (FT 203). Go 100 yards south, cross to East Dallas Creek's east side, go 0.3 mile north-northeast, cross to the east side of a ridge at 9,540 feet (38.0386° -107.8037°), then contour 0.5 mile southeast to reach and cross Wilson Creek at 9,580 feet (38.0344° -107.7973°). The lower part of this trail is not marked on the 1983 Mount Sneffels Quadrangle. Climb 2.0 miles southeast up Wilson Creek and reach lower Blaine Basin at 10,740 feet (38.0194° -107.7819°). The trail crosses Wilson Creek four times, and these crossings can be tricky in June. Either camp here or continue 0.5 mile south on the trail as it switchbacks up a headwall and reach a bench at 11,100 feet (38.0152° -107.7829°) that overlooks the lower basin. All of Blaine Basin's open camping spots have impressive views of Sneffels' north face.

30R – Mount Sneffels Routes

30R1 – Mount Sneffels – South Slopes *Classic*

From Yankee Boy Basin TH at 10,700'   193 RP   7.7 mi RT   3,450' total   Class 2+

From Yankee Boy Basin 4WD TH at 12,440'   101 RP   2.3 mi RT   1,710' total   Class 2+

This is the shortest and easiest route on Sneffels. It is harder than Colorado's Class 1 and Class 2 walk-up routes, but not as hard as the Class 3 routes found on the Crestones, Maroon Bells, and Wilsons. This is a good route for someone who has climbed many easy Fourteeners and wants a taste of what the harder ones are like, since the route's harder sections illustrate the difference between Class 2 and Class 2+.

Use the Yankee Boy Basin Approach (30A1). From the road's highest point at 12,440 feet (37.9947° -107.7847°), walk 0.5 mile west on the Blue Lakes Trail (FT 201) through the scree to 12,640 feet (37.9972° -107.7916°). This trail is not accurately marked on older versions of the Telluride Quadrangle, but it is worth finding because it provides easy passage through the scree. As an alternative, you can also follow the Wrights Lake Spur Trail (FT 201.1A) from Wrights Lake at 12,200 feet to reach this same point.

You cannot see the route up Sneffels until you reach 12,640 feet, so avoid any temptation to leave the trail too soon. The peak above you before you reach 12,640 feet is 13,694-foot "Kismet," and several overeager aspirants have charged up the hill only to find themselves entangled in "Kismet"'s rugged ramparts and staring at still-distant Sneffels. Remember that the most common mountaineering mistake is cutting up too soon.

Leave the trail at 12,700 feet (37.9960° -107.7929°), just before it starts switchbacking up to Blue Lakes Pass. You can see the next portion of the route from here. Climb 0.4 mile north up the eastern edge of a wide slope to 13,500-foot

Mount Sneffels from the south.

Scree Col (38.0017° -107.7899°), southeast of Sneffels' summit (Class 2). Scree Col, also called Lavender Col, is the saddle between Sneffels and "Kismet." The slope leading to Scree Col is covered with talus and laced with dirt alleys. Stay on the rocks on the east (right) side of the slope, because the eroding dirt alleys in the center of the slope are an unpleasant, environmentally incorrect option.

From Scree Col, you have a postcard view of 13,809-foot Dallas Peak to the west, and you can also see the rest of the route up Sneffels. Hike 140 yards northwest and enter an inset couloir at 13,680 feet (38.0026° -107.7908°) leading toward the summit (Class 2). This is the route. There is another inset couloir 70 yards to the east (right) that is not the route. The correct couloir retains some snow in early summer, when you may find an ice ax useful. Scamper 200 yards up the couloir to within 20 feet of the 14,020-foot notch (38.0038° -107.7915°) at its top (Class 2+). Climbing all the way into the notch is slightly off-route, but the few extra steps are worthwhile for the chance to peer down Sneffels' steep north side.

From 20 feet below the notch, climb west out of the couloir via a 30-foot exit slot (Class 2+). This celebrated slot is the route's key passage. From the top of the slot, scamper 210 feet west up broken ledges to the summit (Class 2+). This is an exciting finish leading to a wonderful summit. From the summit (38.0037° -107.7923°), you can peek down the north face, and the open view reminds you that you are on a monarch.

30R1 V – Variation – South Face

Class 2+

Instead of climbing to within 20 feet of the notch at the top of the couloir, exit the couloir 300 feet below the notch. This Class 2+ exit is one-third of the way up the couloir. Once out of the couloir, climb broken ledges on the couloir's west (left) side (Class 2+). Rejoin the regular route near the summit. This variation is snow free much earlier in the year than the couloir is. If snow conditions in the couloir are not to your liking and the ledges are dry, this alternative can offer better footing, but it is more exposed.

30R2 – Mount Sneffels – Southwest Ridge *Classic*

From Yankee Boy Basin TH at 10,700'	*228 RP*	*7.8 mi RT*	*3,450' total*	*Class 3*
With descent of South Slopes	*223 RP*	*7.8 mi RT*	*3,450' total*	*Class 3*
From Yankee Boy Basin 4WD TH at 12,440'	*136 RP*	*2.4 mi RT*	*1,710' total*	*Class 3*
With descent of South Slopes	*131 RP*	*2.4 mi RT*	*1,710' total*	*Class 3*

This is a more exciting route than the standard South Slopes Route (30R1). The southwest ridge is on the west (left) edge of Sneffels' south face, and you can easily see it from upper Yankee Boy Basin. The ridge looks ferocious, but the climb is not as hard as it looks.

Use the Yankee Boy Basin Approach (30A1). From the road's highest point at 12,440 feet (37.9947° -107.7847°), walk 0.5 mile west on the Blue Lakes Trail (FT 201) through the scree to 12,640 feet (37.9972° -107.7916°). This trail is not accurately marked on older versions of the Telluride Quadrangle, but it is worth finding because it provides easy passage through the scree. As an alternative, you can also follow the Wrights Lake Spur Trail (FT 201.1A) from Wrights Lake at 12,200 feet to reach this same point. Continue 0.2 mile west on the switchbacking Blue Lakes Trail to Blue Lakes Pass at 12,980 feet (37.9979° -107.7950°). You can also reach Blue Lakes Pass by following the Blue Lakes Trail for 4.8 miles from the East Dallas Creek Trailhead (30T2).

Leave the trail in the pass, turn north, and climb the ridge toward Sneffels. Easily bypass some jagged pinnacles low on the ridge on the ridge's west (left) side. Once you are past the pinnacles, climb into a prominent 13,500-foot notch (38.0012° -107.7943°) on the ridge crest north of the pinnacles. From the notch, climb a south-facing gully leading to the upper ridge (Class 3). Scramble north-northeast up the upper ridge directly onto or slightly east (right) of the ridge crest. There is often considerable exposure on the ridge's west side, making this a dramatic approach to Sneffels' summit. Ascending this ridge and descending the South Slopes Route (30R1) makes a canny Tour de Sneffels.

30R2 V – Variation – East Pinnacle Bypass
Class 2+, Mod Snow

When snow conditions permit, climb snow on the ridge's east side to reach the prominent 13,500-foot notch north of the pinnacles.

30R3 – Mount Sneffels – East Slopes

From East Dallas Creek TH at 9,340'	*360 RP*	*10.3 mi RT*	*4,810' total*	*Class 2+, Mod Snow*
From 11,100' in Blaine Basin	*253 RP*	*3.5 mi RT*	*3,050' total*	*Class 2+, Mod Snow*

This is the easiest route on Sneffels from Blaine Basin, north of the peak. This route provides an opportunity to experience Sneffels' wild north side without climbing it. This is also a good descent route after an ascent of a more difficult north-face route.

Use the Blaine Basin Approach (30A2). From the bench at 11,100 feet above Blaine Basin (38.0152° -107.7829°), climb 0.95 mile south under Sneffels' east face to 12,400 feet (38.0042° -107.7828°), where you can finally see the route to the west (Class 2). Climb 0.15 mile southwest to 12,500 feet (38.0025° -107.7839°), turn west (right), and climb 0.4 mile west up a wide trough to 13,500-foot Scree Col (38.0017° -107.7899°), southeast of Sneffels' summit. This trough provides a moderate snow climb early in the summer and reasonable passage later in the summer. From Scree Col, continue on the South Slopes Route (30R1) to the summit.

30R4 – Mount Sneffels – Northeast Couloir

From East Dallas Creek TH at 9,340'	*415 RP*	*9.9 mi RT*	*4,810' net; 4,970' total*	*Class 3, Steep Snow*
With descent of East Slopes	*419 RP*	*10.1 mi RT*	*4,810' net; 4,890' total*	*Class 3, Steep Snow*
From 11,100' in Blaine Basin	*312 RP*	*3.1 mi RT*	*3,050' net; 3,210' total*	*Class 3, Steep Snow*
With descent of East Slopes	*315 RP*	*3.3 mi RT*	*3,050' net; 3,130' total*	*Class 3, Steep Snow*

This improbable route provides an amicable snow climb in early summer. You can see the route from Colorado 62 west of Ridgway, and you can preview snow conditions from a distance. Ascending this route and descending the East Slopes Route (30R3) makes a northern Tour de Sneffels.

Use the Blaine Basin Approach (30A2). The broad northeast couloir is the easternmost of three major couloirs on Sneffels' north face, and you can see it from Blaine Basin. Do not mistake the northeast couloir for two other narrower couloirs in the center of the north face. From the bench at 11,100 feet above Blaine Basin (38.0152° -107.7829°), hike 0.9 mile southwest then south under the north face's eastern edge and enter the couloir at 13,000 feet (38.0057° -107.7898°). The couloir is quite wide at the bottom, then narrows and steepens near its top. Climb 0.25 mile south up the steepening couloir and climb into the eastern (38.0038° -107.7894°) of two 13,580-foot notches at the top of the couloir. The snow melts from the upper part of the couloir first, and you may have to do some Class 3 scrambling to reach the notch. Descend on the notch's south side and contour 300 yards south to reach 13,500-foot Scree Col (38.0017°

-107.7899°), southeast of Sneffels' summit (Class 2+). From Scree Col, continue on the South Slopes Route (30R1) to the summit.

30R5 – Mount Sneffels – Snake Couloir *Classic*

From East Dallas Creek TH at 9,340'	*501 RP*	*9.4 mi RT*	*4,810' total*	*Class 3, Steep Snow/Ice*
With descent of East Slopes	*512 RP*	*9.9 mi RT*	*4,810' total*	*Class 3, Steep Snow/Ice*
From 11,100' in Blaine Basin	*394 RP*	*2.6 mi RT*	*3,050' total*	*Class 3, Steep Snow/Ice*
With descent of East Slopes	*405 RP*	*3.1 mi RT*	*3,050' total*	*Class 3, Steep Snow/Ice*

When snow conditions are good, this is one of the best mountaineering routes on Colorado's Fourteeners. When snow conditions are bad, or after the snow melts, avoid this couloir. The confined couloir acts as a funnel for falling debris, and this famous route has produced epic accidents. The Snake Couloir is the westernmost of the three major couloirs on Sneffels' north face. The deeply inset Snake Couloir is well named because it snakes up through the heart of the complex north face.

The bottom of the Snake Couloir faces northeast, and the upper part faces northwest. Because of the turn in the couloir, there is no single vantage point that allows you to see the entire couloir. You can see the upper part of the couloir from Colorado 62 west of Ridgway, but the lower part is hidden. You can see the lower part of the couloir from Blaine Basin, but the upper part is hidden. The snow in this natural avalanche chute gradually turns to ice as summer progresses.

Use the Blaine Basin Approach (30A2). From the bench at 11,100 feet above Blaine Basin (38.0152° -107.7829°), hike 0.9 mile southwest toward the center of the north face and enter the couloir at 13,000 feet (38.0061° -107.7920°). The average angle of the couloir is 40 degrees, but the angle is not consistent. The steepest portion of the couloir is the 200 feet below the turn in the couloir at 13,550 feet (38.0051° -107.7934°). The angle here reaches 50 degrees.

After the turn, the couloir gradually becomes less inset until it ends below a cliff leading directly to the summit. The easiest finish does not climb this cliff but angles east (left) to the top of the north ridge. From here, do an ascending traverse east to reach a small 14,060-foot notch just west of and above the 14,020-foot notch at the top of the couloir on the South Slopes Route (30R1). Finally released from the steep face, scamper 150 feet west to the summit.

30R5 V – Variation – Uncoiled

Class 5.6

You can do a more difficult finish on rock by climbing directly to the summit from the top of the couloir.

3OR6 – Mount Sneffels – North Buttress *Classic*

From East Dallas Creek TH at 9,340'	*841 RP*	*9.3 mi RT*	*4,810' total*	*Class 5.6*
With descent of East Slopes	*854 RP*	*9.8 mi RT*	*4,810' total*	*Class 5.6*
From 11,100' in Blaine Basin	*734 RP*	*2.5 mi RT*	*3,050' total*	*Class 5.6*
With descent of East Slopes	*747 RP*	*3.0 mi RT*	*3,050' total*	*Class 5.6*

The north buttress is the large buttress forming the eastern edge of the Snake Couloir. The North Buttress and the Snake Couloir routes provide a matched pair of great climbs. The soaring north buttress is between the Snake Couloir and the seldom-climbed central couloir on Sneffels' complex north face. The north buttress was a test piece for early mountaineers and remains a test piece today.

Use the Blaine Basin Approach (30A2). From the bench at 11,100 feet (38.0152° -107.7829°) above Blaine Basin, hike 0.9 mile southwest toward the center of the north face and reach the base of the buttress at 13,000 feet (38.0060° -107.7916°). This point is just to the east of the bottom of the Snake Couloir. The direct start is difficult, but you can do an easier start by climbing 100 feet up the central couloir then moving west (right) onto the rock. The climb's greatest difficulties are on the bottom half of the buttress, where you should stay on the eastern side of the buttress. Above the turn in the Snake Couloir, follow the crest of the buttress. Either finish the climb by climbing the summit cliff directly (Class 5.6), or traverse east as described with the Snake Couloir Route.

31. Wilson Group

Wilson Peak	14,017 feet
Mount Wilson	14,246 feet
El Diente Peak	14,159 feet

These peaks are remote and rugged. They are 13 miles southwest of Telluride, and they are the sentinels of the San Miguel Mountains in the western San Juans. These are some of Colorado's most difficult Fourteeners, since they all require at least Class 3 scrambling by their easiest route, and rotten rock adds to the challenge. The traverse between Mount Wilson and El Diente (see Combination 31C1) is one of Colorado's four great Fourteener traverses. Approach these peaks with care.

Wilson Peak has the distinction of being the highest peak in San Miguel County. Wilson Peak is 1.5 miles north of Mount Wilson, and people often confuse the two peaks. Wilson Peak is lower and easier to climb than Mount Wilson and El Diente, and many people ascend Wilson Peak as a tune-up for the other two. People often photograph Wilson Peak from Colorado 145 north of Lizard Head Pass, especially in the fall when the charming aspen groves surrounding Wilson Peak change color.

Mount Wilson is the highest peak in Dolores County, the Lizard Head Wilderness, the San Miguel Mountains, and is the second highest peak in the

San Juans. The peak is in the center of the massif between Wilson Peak and El Diente. Mount Wilson is a rugged alpine peak with several permanent snowfields, but because of its many neighbors, you seldom see it to good advantage. Mount Wilson remains a reclusive test piece for mountaineers.

El diente means "the tooth" in Spanish, and the name fits this feral peak. El Diente is the Colorado Fourteener farthest from Denver and is also Colorado's westernmost Fourteener. El Diente is 0.8 mile west of Mount Wilson; a jagged ridge that drops to 13,900 feet connects the two peaks. El Diente rises only 259 feet above the low point of the ridge and, by more than one criterion, does not qualify as an official Fourteener. However, El Diente remains on most peak lists because it is officially named and it has stature as a sentimental favorite. Most people who traverse the ridge from Mount Wilson to El Diente feel like they have climbed a peak! And yes, sadly El Diente has also proven fatal.

31E – Wilson Group Essentials

Elevations	Wilson Pk	14,017' (NGVD29) 14,024' (NAVD88)
	Mt Wilson	14,246' (NGVD29) 14,250' (NAVD88)
	El Diente Pk	14,159' (NGVD29) 14,164' (NAVD88)
Ranks	Wilson Pk	Colorado's 48th highest ranked peak
	Mt Wilson	Colorado's 16th highest ranked peak
	El Diente Pk	Unranked peak
Location	San Miguel and Dolores counties, Colorado, USA	
Range	Western San Juan Range – San Miguel Mountains	
Summit Coordinates	Wilson Pk	37.8602° -107.9847° (WGS84)
	Mt Wilson	37.8393° -107.9916° (WGS84)
	El Diente Pk	37.8394° -108.0053° (WGS84)
Ownership/Contacts	Uncompahgre and San Juan National Forests – Public Land	
	Norwood Ranger District 970-327-4261	
	San Juan Public Lands Center – Durango – 970-247-4874	
Prominence and Saddles	Wilson Pk	877' from 13,140' Wilson Pk–Mt Wilson Pass
	Mt Wilson	4,024' from 10,222' Lizard Head Pass
	El Diente Pk	259' from 13,900' El Diente–Mt Wilson Pass
Isolation and Parents	Wilson Pk	1.51 miles to Mount Wilson
	Mt Wilson	33.05 miles to Uncompahgre Peak
	El Diente Pk	0.75 mile to Mount Wilson
USGS Maps	**Mount Wilson, Dolores Peak**, Little Cone, Gray Head	
USFS Maps	**San Juan National Forest**, Uncompahgre National Forest	
Trails Illustrated Map	Map #141 Telluride, Silverton, Ouray, Lake City	
Book Map	See Map 31 on page 320	
Nearest Towns	Telluride – Population 2,400 – Elevation 8,750'	
	Rico – Population 260 – Elevation 8,825'	
	Dolores – Population 920 – Elevation 6,936'	

31E – Wilson Group Essentials

Wilson Pk 🏃 Easiest Route	31R1 – West Ridge – Class 3
	A Class 1 hike to Rock of Ages saddle, a loose, Class 2+ scamper high onto the
	peak, and a Class 3 scramble to the summit
Mt Wilson 🏃 Easiest Route	31R2 – North Slopes – Class 4
	A Class 1 hike to Navajo Basin, a steep Class 2+ scamper to a high saddle, and
	a short Class 4 pitch to the highest point
El Diente 🏃 Easiest Route	31R6 – South Slopes – Class 3
	A Class 1 hike to lower Kilpacker Basin, a testy boulder hop up the basin, and
	a Class 3 scramble to the summit
Wilson Group Accolades	Mount Wilson is the highest peak in Dolores County, the Lizard Head
	Wilderness, the San Miguel Mountains, and is the second highest peak in the
	San Juans. Wilson Peak is the highest peak in San Miguel County. Unranked
	El Diente is Colorado's westernmost Fourteener and the third highest summit
	in the San Juans.

31T – Wilson Group Trailheads

31T1 – Rock of Ages Trailhead 10,340 feet 37.8822° -108.0186°

After a lengthy, contentious access hiatus, public access to the Rock of Ages saddle from the north has been restored. Please disregard earlier reports and descriptions that direct you south up through the length of Silver Pick Basin. That old route is still closed to the public, and the new public access described here is from a new trailhead in the Elk Creek drainage to the west. Starting at the new Rock of Ages Trailhead, the new Rock of Ages Approach (31A1) is the only public access to reach the Rock of Ages saddle from the north. Many people and organizations worked for years and spent considerable money to secure this access. Please do not disrespect their efforts by attempting any other approach to Rock of Ages saddle from the north.

This trailhead provides access to the north side of all three Fourteeners. If approaching from the north or west, go 6.7 miles east on Colorado 145 from the junction of Colorado 145 and Colorado 62. If approaching from the south, go 6.0 miles west on Colorado 145 from the Telluride spur junction on Colorado 145 (Society Turn).

Turn south onto San Miguel County 60M (becomes FR 622) and measure from this point (37.9677° -107.9712°). Cross the San Miguel River, stay left at mile 3.3, take the middle of three roads at mile 4.0, enter the Uncompahgre National Forest at mile 6.3, stay left at mile 6.4, stay right at mile 8.1, and reach the Wilson Mesa Trailhead at mile 8.8 at 9,960 feet (37.8941° -108.0011°). The Wilson Mesa Trail (FT 421) goes east from this trailhead.

Do not continue south up FR 622; that's the old route that is now closed to the public. Leave FR 622, turn southwest (right) onto FR 645, go south-southwest on FR 645, and cross Big Bear Creek at mile 9.8 at 10,180 feet (37.8818°

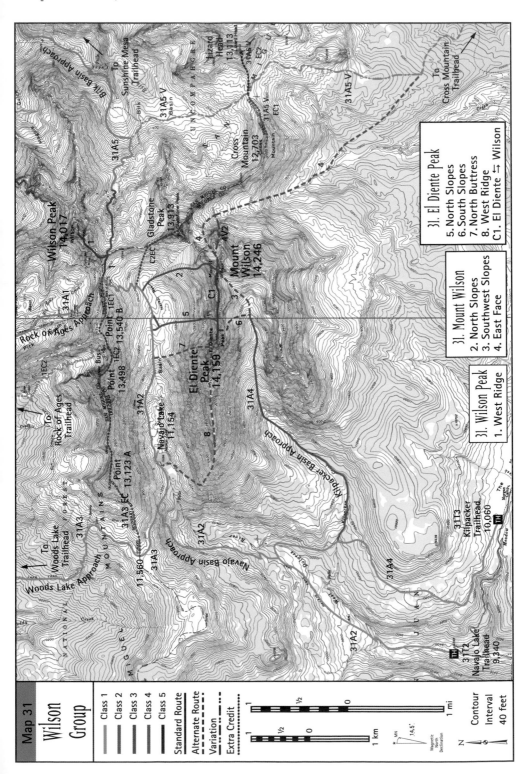

Map 31
Wilson Group

— Class 1
— Class 2
— Class 3
— Class 4
— Class 5

— Standard Route
-- Alternate Route
··· Variation
···· Extra Credit

N

Magnetic North Declination

Contour Interval 40 feet

31. Wilson Peak
1. West Ridge

31. Mount Wilson
2. North Slopes
3. Southwest Slopes
4. East Face

31. El Diente Peak
5. North Slopes
6. South Slopes
7. North Buttress
8. West Ridge
C1. El Diente ⇄ Wilson

Wilson Peak 14,017

Gladstone Peak 13,913

Mount Wilson 14,246

El Diente Peak 14,159

Navajo Lake 11,154

Point 13,540 B

Point 13,498

Point 13,123 A

Cross Mountain 12,703

Lizard Head 13,113

Kilpacker Trailhead 10,060

Navajo Lake Trailhead 9,340

To Sunshine Mesa Trailhead
To Cross Mountain Trailhead
To Rock of Ages Trailhead
To Woods Lake Trailhead

Rock of Ages Approach
Bilk Basin Approach
Kilpacker Basin Approach
Navajo Basin Approach
Woods Lake Approach

-108.0080°). Continue north-northeast (away from the peaks) on FR 645 and cross a ridge at mile 10.4 at 10,383 feet (37.8886° -108.0117°). This is the ridge separating the Big Bear Creek drainage from the Elk Creek drainage, which is the next drainage to the west. Switchback over the ridge, continue south-southwest then southwest on FR 645, and reach the new Rock of Ages Trailhead at mile 11.1 at 10,340 feet. FR 645 is rough and often wet in places, and you will appreciate a high-clearance or 4WD vehicle on this road.

The Wilson Mesa Trail (FT 421) continues west from this trailhead. The Wilson Mesa Trail and FR 645 are coincident between FR 622 and this trailhead. The Rock of Ages Trail (FT 429) goes south from this trailhead, and this is the trail that will take you to the Rock of Ages saddle. For reference, the Elk Creek Trail (FT 407) that used to go south from this trailhead still exists; it leaves the Rock of Ages Trail 0.5 mile south of the trailhead and continues south up the Elk Creek drainage. See the Rock of Ages Approach (31A1) for details on how to reach the Rock of Ages saddle from here.

31T2 – Navajo Lake Trailhead 9,340 feet 37.8047° -108.0635°

This trailhead provides access to Navajo Basin on the north side of Mount Wilson and El Diente. If approaching from the north, go 5.4 miles south on Colorado 145 from the summit of 10,222-foot Lizard Head Pass. If approaching from the south, go 6.5 miles north on Colorado 145 from the Rico Post Office.

Turn west onto Dunton Road (FR 535) and measure from this point (37.7718° -107.9814°). Continue west then northwest on Dunton Road (dirt) as it climbs above Coal Creek, crosses Coal Creek at 10,060 feet (37.7898° -108.0170°), and enters the meadows west of Coal Creek. Go straight at mile 4.2 (37.7908° -108.0207°), pass Morgan Camp (private) at mile 5.0, descend west toward the West Dolores River, turn hard north (right) at mile 7.2 (37.8029° -108.0639°), go north on a spur road, and reach the trailhead at mile 7.3. Dunton Road is passable for passenger cars, and there is ample parking at the well-marked trailhead, which is just east of the West Dolores River. Dunton Road is not plowed in winter.

31T3 – Kilpacker Trailhead 10,060 feet 37.7973° -108.0395°

This trailhead provides access to Kilpacker Basin on the southwest side of Mount Wilson and south side of El Diente. If approaching from the north, go 5.4 miles south on Colorado 145 from the summit of 10,222-foot Lizard Head Pass. If approaching from the south, go 6.5 miles north on Colorado 145 from the Rico Post Office.

Turn west onto Dunton Road (FR 535) and measure from this point (37.7718° -107.9814°). Go west then northwest on Dunton Road (dirt) as it climbs above Coal Creek, crosses Coal Creek at 10,060 feet (37.7898° -108.0170°), and enters the meadows west of Coal Creek. Go straight at mile 4.2 (37.7908° -108.0207°), pass Morgan Camp (private) at mile 5.0, turn northwest (right) onto FR 207 at mile

Mount Wilson 14,246   Wilson Peak 14,017   El Diente Peak 14,159

The Wilson Group from the northwest.

5.1 (37.7959° -108.0359°), and reach the trailhead at mile 5.3. There are pastoral camping spots in the trees near the trailhead. Dunton Road is not plowed in winter, but snowmobilers use the eastern portion.

31T4 – Cross Mountain Trailhead 10,060 feet 37.7968° -107.9389°
This trailhead provides access to Mount Wilson's east side. From the summit of 10,222-foot Lizard Head Pass, go 2.0 miles southwest on Colorado 145, turn northwest onto FR 424 (37.7961° -107.9365°), and go 0.15 mile northwest to the trailhead. There is a small parking area here, and trail signs near the trees to the north. Colorado 145 is open in winter.

31T5 – Woods Lake Trailhead 9,360 feet 37.8861° -108.0554°
This trailhead provides an alternate access to Navajo Basin and all three Four-teeners. If approaching from the north or west, go 2.8 miles east on Colorado 145 from the junction of Colorado 145 and Colorado 62. If approaching from the south, go 9.9 miles west on Colorado 145 from the Telluride spur junction on Colorado 145 (Society Turn). Turn south onto the Fall Creek Road (San Miguel County 57P, FR 618) and measure from this point (37.9939° -108.0224°). Cross the San Miguel River, go south on the Fall Creek Road, go right at mile 4.0, straight at mile 6.2, straight at mile 7.8, and arrive at the turn for the Woods Lake Campground at mile 8.9 (37.8860° -108.0546°), north of Woods Lake. Turn west (right) toward the campground and park in the large, signed trail-head parking area at mile 9.0, 200 yards east of the campground.

This is a heavily used area in summer. To reach the beginning of the Woods Lake Trail (FT 406), go 200 yards southeast from the trailhead parking area to the signed beginning of the trail on the east side of the continuing road toward Woods Lake.

31T6 – Sunshine Mesa Trailhead 9,780 feet 37.8785° -107.9248°

This trailhead provides access to Wilson Peak's east side. From Society Turn west of Telluride, go 2.7 miles west on Colorado 145 to the South Fork Road, which is 100 yards west of milepost 71. Turn south onto South Fork Road and measure from this point (37.9481° -107.9170°). Go east on South Fork Road and cross the San Miguel River (37.9442° -107.8993°) at mile 1.0. Go south, pass Ilium (37.9299° -107.8975°) at mile 2.0, turn west (right) onto the Sunshine Mesa Road (FR 623) at mile 2.2, and cross to the west side of the south fork of the San Miguel River. Climb south on the Sunshine Mesa Road, switchback southwest then south up onto Sunshine Mesa, and reach the trailhead at the end of the road at mile 7.7.

31A – Wilson Group Approaches

31A1 – Wilson Group – Rock of Ages Approach

From Rock of Ages TH at 10,340'   107 RP   6.8 mi RT   2,680' total   Class 1

You can approach Wilson Peak's West Ridge Route (31R1), Mount Wilson's North Slopes Route (31R2), and El Diente's North Slopes Route (31R5) from the north. Start at the Rock of Ages Trailhead at 10,340 feet and go 0.5 mile south on the Rock of Ages Trail (FT 429) to a trail junction at 10,580 feet (37.8762° -108.0185°), where the Elk Creek Trail (FT 407) goes south up the Elk Creek drainage and the Rock of Ages Trail climbs the hill to the east. Turn east (left), stay on the Rock of Ages Trail, and climb 0.3 mile east-southeast to another trail junction at 11,280 feet (37.8750° -108.0137°), where the Rock of Ages Trail joins an old road. Turn north (left) and hike 200 yards north-northeast to the ridge separating the Elk Creek and Big Bear Creek drainages at 11,300 feet (37.8763° -108.0127°). Cross to the ridge's east side, stay on the trail, hike 0.6 mile south-southeast on a side hill, and climb to 11,440 feet on the western edge of Silver Pick Basin (37.8695° -108.0062°).

Beyond here, the Rock of Ages Trail dodges several private mine claims as it pursues its legal access route, so stay on the well-marked trail even though it makes some counterintuitive moves. From 11,440 feet, hike 0.1 mile east-northeast, 0.2 mile south-southeast along the west side of Big Bear Creek, 0.2 mile south away from the creek, 0.2 mile south-southeast, 0.25 mile east-southeast, 0.2 mile southeast, 0.25 mile west, and 0.5 mile east-northeast on a good trail through the scree to reach Rock of Ages saddle at 13,020 feet (37.8565° -107.9927°). Whew!

After admiring the astonishing view of Mount Wilson and El Diente across Navajo Basin, take a moment to bow to the Telluride Foundation and the Trust for Public Land, who purchased a critical 220-acre parcel of land that allowed the Forest Service to build the public Rock of Ages Trail to this elusive saddle. Prepare to climb.

31A2 – Wilson Group – Navajo Basin Approach

From Navajo Lake TH at 9,340'   *135 RP*   *12.4 mi RT*   *2,560' net; 2,972' total*   *Class 1*

You can approach Wilson Peak's West Ridge Route(31R1), Mount Wilson's North Slopes Route (31R2), and El Diente's North Slopes (31R5) and West Ridge (31R8) routes from Navajo Basin. Start at the Navajo Lake Trailhead at 9,340 feet and follow the Navajo Lake Trail 5.0 miles north, northeast, then east to Navajo Lake at 11,154 feet (37.8476° -108.0287°). There are campsites here in the trees; fires are not allowed in Navajo Basin. Hike 0.1 mile around Navajo Lake's north side and follow a trail 1.1 miles east up a long scree slope to reach the grassy benches at 11,900 feet (37.8490° -108.0077°) in upper Navajo Basin. There are many open camping sites on these benches, and this is the upper end of the backpacking approach.

For El Diente's North Slopes Route (31R5), hike 0.35 mile east to 12,120 feet (37.8493° -108.0023°) in upper Navajo Basin. For Mount Wilson's North Slopes Route (31R2), hike 0.8 mile east to 12,300 feet (37.8501° -107.9966°) in upper Navajo Basin. For Wilson Peak's West Ridge Route (31R8), hike 0.9 mile east to 12,400 feet (37.8516° -107.9943°) in the upper end of Navajo Basin, then follow a good switchbacking trail 0.7 mile north to 13,020-foot Rock of Ages saddle (37.8565° -107.9927°) between Wilson Peak and Point 13,540, a ranked Thirteener 1.0 mile west of Wilson Peak. There is an old shack called the Tiltin' Hilton at 12,800 feet (37.8557° -107.9930°) just below the saddle at the Rock of Ages Mine.

31A3 – Wilson Group – Woods Lake Approach

From Woods Lake TH at 9,360'   *132 RP*   *11.2 mi RT*   *2,540' net; 3,352' total*   *Class 1*

You can approach Navajo Basin and all three Fourteeners from Woods Lake, and this shorter approach has gained in popularity in recent years. For many, the Woods Lake Trailhead on the range's north side is easier to reach than the Navajo Lake Trailhead on the range's south side, but since this approach goes over a high ridge en route, it is more exposed to the weather than the Navajo Basin Approach.

Start at the Woods Lake Trailhead parking area at 9,360 feet and go 200 yards southeast to the signed beginning of the Woods Lake Trail (FT 406) on the east side of the continuing road toward Woods Lake. Go east then south around Woods Lake, pass a trail junction with the Lone Cone Trail (FT 426), which heads west, pass another trail junction with a spur of the Wilson Mesa Trail (FT 421), which heads east, and go 2.4 miles south then east on the Woods Lake Trail (FT 406) to a trail junction with the Elk Creek Trail (FT 407) at 11,517 feet (37.8575° -108.0396°). Continue 0.6 mile southwest on the Woods Lake Trail and reach a rounded ridge just above treeline at 11,560 feet (37.8510° -108.0424°). This is the highpoint of your approach to Navajo Lake. Stroll over the rest of the ridge and behold Navajo Basin. Descend 0.6 mile east-southeast to a trail junction with the Navajo Lake Trail (FT 635) at 11,360 feet (37.8481° -108.0364°). Joining the Navajo Basin Approach (31A2) here, descend 0.5 mile east to Navajo Lake at 11,154 feet (37.8476° -108.0287°). Either camp near Navajo Lake or hike above the lake to the grassy benches 11,900 feet (37.8490° -108.0077°) in upper Navajo Basin, as described with the Navajo Basin Approach (31A2).

31A3 EC – Extra Credit – Point 13,123 A 37.8555° -108.0312°

From Woods Lake TH at 9,360'   163 RP   8.5 mi RT   3,763' total   Class 2

From the highpoint on the ridge at 11,560 feet (37.8510° -108.0424°), hike 0.55 mile east up delightful grass slopes to 12,300 feet (37.8522° -108.0359°). Continue 0.4 mile east-northeast up a steeper Class 2 rock slope to Point 13,123 A, a ranked Thirteener. From here, you have a great profile view of El Diente's west ridge and peekaboo views of the rest of Navajo Basin. Looking to the east, you might wonder about the ragged ridge between Point 13,123 A and Point 13,498 (see 31R1 EC2). It is long, loose, and testy, but goes at Class 3.

31A4 – Wilson Group – Kilpacker Basin Approach

From Kilpacker TH at 10,060'   185 RP   10.2 mi RT   2,740' total   Class 2

You can approach Mount Wilson's Southwest Slopes Route (31R3) and El Diente's South Slopes Route (31R6) from Kilpacker Basin. Start at the Kilpacker Basin Trailhead at 10,060 feet and follow the Kilpacker Trail (FT 203) 1.0 mile northwest, then 1.2 miles north into the Lizard Head Wilderness. This trail rolls through several captivating aspen groves and reminds you that you are in the San Juans.

Leave the Kilpacker Trail 200 yards south of (before) Kilpacker Creek at 10,260 feet (37.8196° -108.0428°), follow a good spur trail 0.5 mile east into Kilpacker Basin, and cross to Kilpacker Creek's north side at 10,460 feet (37.8196° -108.0333°). The trail fades into a series of large, grassy meadows. Stroll 1.1 miles northeast up the meadows as El Diente watches your progress.

Kilpacker Basin has two waterfalls near treeline, and you can see the upper one from a distance as it ornaments the already impressive view of El Diente. Trees hide the lower falls, and there is good camping below the lower falls near 10,700 feet. This is an enchanting place.

The enchantment withers as you engage upper Kilpacker Basin's scree. The wretched, sharp rock is another reminder that you are in the San Juans. Stay on the creek's north side, engage the scree, and find a faint climber's trail going straight up the west side of a patch of burly bushes north of the upper waterfall. The trail climbs east above the bushes and upper falls and soon dies into immense scree slopes. Hike 1.1 miles east up the untamed basin to 12,800 feet (37.8346° -108.0000°), where your mood may turn feral.

31A5 – Wilson Group – Bilk Basin Approach

From Sunshine Mesa TH at 9,780'   106 RP   9.4 mi RT   2,320' total   Class 1

You can approach the upper part of Wilson Peak's West Ridge Route (31R1) from Bilk Basin east of the peak. Start at the Sunshine Mesa Trailhead at 9,780 feet and contour 0.8 mile west on the Wilson Mesa Trail (FT 421) to a trail junction (37.8775° -107.9389°) at 9,900 feet. Leave the Wilson Mesa Trail and hike 1.2 miles southwest then south-southwest on FT 420 to the Morning Star Mine on Bilk Creek's west side at 10,100 feet (37.8637° -107.9487°). You can't yet see the summits, but Wilson Peak is high above you to the west and 12,930-foot Sunshine Mountain is steeply above you to the east.

From the mine, enter the Lizard Head Wilderness, hike 1.1 mile south-southwest on the Lizard Head Trail (FT 505), climbing steeply above Bilk Creek en route, and reach treeline at 11,060 feet (37.8551° -107.9611°) in lower Bilk Basin. In this stretch, you will have views of several cascades on Bilk Creek, Sunshine Mountain will gain stature to the east, and when you emerge from the trees, you can see 13,913-foot Gladstone Peak to the southwest.

The trail above this point is incorrectly marked on the old 1953 Mount Wilson Quadrangle, and other mapmakers have copied this error. Continue 0.6 mile on the Lizard Head Trail as it climbs above the lower basin's north side then climbs south to 11,400 feet (37.8523° -107.9667°) at the creek descending from upper Bilk Basin. Leave the Lizard Head Trail here and hike 1.0 mile northwest then west on a spur trail that is also mispositioned on the Mount Wilson Quadrangle. Follow this trail as it switchbacks into upper Bilk Basin to 12,100 feet (37.8546° -107.9745°) on the north side of a small lake in this enchanting place. The gray hulk of mighty Wilson Peak is 0.7 mile northwest, and Gladstone with its distinctive black rock and distinguished snowfield below its north face is 0.8 mile southwest. Prepare to climb.

31A5 V – Variation – Bilk Basin from Cross Mountain Trailhead Approach

From Cross Mountain TH at 10,060'   139 RP   12.0 mi RT   2,040' net; 3,198' total   Class 1

You can reach Bilk Basin from the Cross Mountain Trailhead. From the Cross Mountain Trailhead at 10,060 feet, hike 3.1 miles southwest then south on the Cross Mountain Trail (FT 637) to a trail junction with the Lizard Head Trail (FT 505) at 11,920 feet (37.8315° -107.9527°). Turn northwest (left) and hike 0.4 mile northwest on the Lizard Head Trail to the 11,979-foot saddle (37.8346° -107.9584°) between 13,113-foot Lizard Head to the east and 12,703-foot Cross Mountain to the west. As tough as the Wilsons are, you may still feel happy that you are headed for the Wilsons instead of climbing Lizard Head. Cross the saddle, descend 1.5 miles north on the Lizard Head Trail to the creek crossing at 11,400 feet (37.8523° -107.9667°), and join the Bilk Basin Approach here for the 1.0 mile climb into upper Bilk Basin.

31A5 V EC1 – Extra Credit – Cross Mountain 12,703 feet 37.8320° -107.9687°

From Cross Mountain TH at 10,060'   138 RP   8.4 mi RT   2,643' total   Class 2+

From the 11,979-foot Cross Mountain–Lizard Head saddle (37.8346° -107.9584°), hike and scamper 0.7 mile west to Cross Mountain, an unranked Twelver. Between 12,300 and 12,400 feet, you will have to scamper through a Class 2+

cliff band. This summit is notable for its sensational view of the surrounding giants. Mount Wilson's east face soars to the west and Lizard Head's solitary spire to the east will likely inspire a tingling stare.

31. Wilson Peak 14,017 feet

31R – Wilson Peak Route
31R1 – Wilson Peak – West Ridge

From Rock of Ages TH at 10,340'	210 RP	8.3 mi RT	3,677' net; 3,817' total	Class 3
From Navajo Lake TH at 9,340'	329 RP	17.1 mi RT	4,677' net; 5,229' total	Class 3
From Navajo Lake at 11,154'	182 RP	7.1 mi RT	2,863' net; 3,003' total	Class 3
From Woods Lake TH at 9,360'	324 RP	15.9 mi RT	4,657' net; 5,609' total	Class 3
From Sunshine Mesa TH at 9,780'	293 RP	12.3 mi RT	4,237' net; 4,317' total	Class 3
From Cross Mountain TH at 10,060'	337 RP	14.9 mi RT	3,957' net; 5,195' total	Class 3

This is the easiest route up Wilson Peak. You can approach the west ridge from Rock of Ages saddle, Navajo Basin, or Bilk Basin. The Rock of Ages Approach is shorter if reaching Wilson Peak is your only objective. A camp in Navajo Basin provides good access to all three peaks, and Bilk Basin provides a clever alternative. Use either the Rock of Ages Approach (31A1) or Navajo Basin Approach (31A2) to reach the 13,020-foot Rock of Ages saddle (37.8565° -107.9927°) between Wilson Peak and Point 13,540, a ranked Thirteener 1.0 mile west of Wilson Peak.

From the 13,020-foot Rock of Ages saddle, hike 150 yards east along the crest of the ridge, then hike 0.2 mile southeast on an ascending traverse below the cliffs on the ridge's south (right) side to a small 13,260-foot saddle (37.8556° -107.9887°) on the ridge between Wilson Peak and 13,913-foot Gladstone Peak. Do not climb too high on this ascending traverse. If you use the Bilk Basin Approach (31A5) to reach 12,100 feet (37.8546° -107.9745°) on the north side of a small lake in upper Bilk Basin, hike 1.0 mile west-northwest on the dwindling spur trail through the rocks to reach the 13,260-foot saddle. From the small saddle, the view opens and you can see the San Juans' vast expanse to the east, and Lizard Head's spire will attract your attention.

You can see the next portion of the route from the small 13,260-foot saddle. Cross to the east side of the Wilson Peak–Gladstone Peak Ridge and contour north across some broken cliffs (Class 3) or descend on the east side of the small saddle to avoid the cliffs (Class 2). Beyond the cliffs, stay below the ridge crest and scramble northeast up broken Class 2+ rock to regain the ridge at 13,500 feet (37.8579° -107.9879°). Scamper east-northeast up the ridge to a false summit at 13,900 feet (37.8595° -107.9855°). You can easily see the remaining challenge and the route's crux from here.

Descend 40 feet on the ridge's north (left) side, contour 50 feet east under the ridge crest, then scramble back to the ridge crest (Class 3). Scramble 150

Mount Wilson.

feet east to the summit (Class 3). From the summit (37.8602° -107.9847°), you have a free view of Mount Wilson, El Diente, and beyond.

31R1 EC1 – Extra Credit – Point 13,540 B 37.8568° -108.0014°

Class 2+

From the Rock of Ages saddle, scamper 0.5 mile west on or near a rough ridge to Point 13,540 B, a ranked Thirteener. This exclusive vantage offers a superb view of the Fourteeners.

31R1 EC2 – Extra Credit – Point 13,498 37.8570° -108.0117°

Class 3

If you are still feeling frisky, descend 0.45 mile west (Class 2) from Point 13,540 B to a 13,140-foot saddle (37.8553° -108.0093°). This saddle is above the seldom-appreciated School Bus Basin to the north, and if you look sharp, you can see the improbable namesake school bus in the basin below. From the saddle, scramble 0.2 mile west-northwest (Class 3) to the summit of Point 13,498, another ranked Thirteener. The upper part of this ridge requires some careful Class 3 scrambling on the ridge's south side on loose blocks. This summit's privileged position provides the best view in the San Miguels. In addition to the evident Fourteeners, you can admire Dolores and Middle peaks to the west.

Your most expedient return to the Rock of Ages Trailhead is back over the top of Point 13,540 B. If you choose to take a test and descend north into School Bus Basin, go at least 200 yards east of the 13,140-foot saddle, descend north down a steep, treacherous rock slope, check out the school bus at 12,660 feet (37.8578° -108.0069°), descend the narrow basin on old mine roads, pick up the Elk Creek Trail (FT 407) at 11,160 feet (37.8670° -108.0163°), follow it north to a trail junction at 10,580 feet (37.8762° -108.0185°) where the Elk Creek Trail meets the Rock of Ages Trail (FT 429), and follow the Rock of Ages Trail 0.5 mile north to the Rock of Ages Trailhead. If you manage all this without missing a step, you get an A.

31. Mount Wilson 14,246 feet

31R – Mount Wilson Routes
31R2 – Mount Wilson – North Slopes

From Rock of Ages TH at 10,340'	340 RP	10.3 mi RT	3,906' net; 5,346' total	Class 4
From Navajo Lake TH at 9,340'	400 RP	15.9 mi RT	4,906' net; 5,318' total	Class 4
From Navajo Lake at 11,154'	247 RP	5.9 mi RT	3,092' net; 3,092' total	Class 4
From Woods Lake TH at 9,360'	394 RP	14.7 mi RT	4,886' net; 5,698' total	Class 4

This is the easiest route on Mount Wilson. You can approach the route from either Rock of Ages saddle or Navajo Basin. Use either approach to reach 12,300 feet (37.8501° -107.9966°) in upper Navajo Basin. From here, climb 0.7 mile south up a rounded shoulder just west of a large permanent snowfield between Mount Wilson and Gladstone Peak. This snowfield is sometimes called the Navajo Glacier. By ascending the shoulder, it is not necessary to get on the glacier; however, snow persists through the summer on Mount Wilson's north side, so an ice ax is recommended for this route.

Hike up the steepening shoulder to 13,500 feet (37.8425° -107.9908°), below Mount Wilson's northeast ridge. Do not climb all the way to the ridge. From 13,600 feet, climb south-southwest up steep talus well below the ridge crest and cross several gullies, the last of which is likely to be snow-filled through the summer. If you don't want to cross any snow, stay low and get below the couloir. Beyond the last couloir, scamper south up steep blocks to a notch just north of Mount Wilson's summit. If you follow the easiest route, the climbing to this point is Class 2+. From the notch, you can look west down into Kilpacker Basin and east down a long snow slope above Slate Creek.

From the notch, climb 130 feet south on or near the ridge crest toward the summit (Class 3). The final blocks are the route's crux, and the hardest, Class 4 move is on the east (left) side of the blocks immediately below the summit. There is considerable exposure on both sides of the ridge, and some parties choose to use a rope here. From the summit (37.8393° -107.9916°) of this monarch, you command a view from Shiprock to Uncompahgre. Open to the expanse.

31R2 V – Variation – East Side Story

Class 4

You can avoid the final, crux Class 4 move to the summit, but at a price. From the high notch 150 feet north of the summit, descend 40 feet east down the top of the couloir east of the notch. Leave the couloir, traverse south, and scamper up past a slanted block. Turn west (right) and scamper up to the base of the east-facing summit wall. Angling south (left), climb 40 feet up the blocky wall (Class 4) to a fin-studded ridge, turn south (left), and scramble south to the summit. This variation is not really easier than the standard finish, and many consider it to be harder. Mount Wilson guards its summit well.

31R3 – Mount Wilson – Southwest Slopes

From Kilpacker TH at 10,060'   419 RP   11.8 mi RT   4,186' total   Class 4, Mod Snow

When snow conditions are good, this route is a refreshing alternative to the North Slopes Route. After the snow melts, the route becomes a scree-and-rubble challenge that is best avoided. Follow the Kilpacker Basin Approach (31A4), climb east into Kilpacker Basin past El Diente's summit, and continue east toward Mount Wilson. You cannot see the route up Mount Wilson until you reach 13,000 feet (37.8350° -107.9979°), and your escape from this confining basin may seem improbable.

Above 13,000 feet, stay on the basin's north side and climb northeast up a hidden trough. When snow-filled, this trough provides a straightforward snow climb. As the snow melts, rubble and dirt are exposed, but some snow and ice often remain in this trough all summer. Climb the narrow couloir leading to the notch 150 feet north of the summit. This is the high notch on the North Slopes Route. Climb 150 feet south to the summit (Class 4).

31R4 – Mount Wilson – East Face

From Cross Mountain TH at 10,060'   445 RP   10.1 mi RT   4,186' net; 4,586' total   Class 4, Mod Snow

When snow conditions are good, which for once is most of the summer, this route is one of the superlative moderate snow climbs on Colorado's Fourteeners. Unfortunately, this exceptional climb requires a heinous approach. If you have a passion for solitude and wilderness, the joys of climbing in the upper Slate Creek Basin will compensate for the bushwhack approach.

Start at the Cross Mountain Trailhead at 10,060 feet and follow the Cross Mountain Trail (FT 637) 1.25 mile north then northwest to 11,000 feet (37.8097° -107.9538°). The bushwhack begins here. Leave the trail, go 0.1 mile west over a rounded ridge, and contour 1.1 miles northwest near 11,000 feet. This high traverse keeps you from enduring the even greater misery of climbing through the dreaded slate mounds that abound in lower Slate Creek. Descend 0.3 mile northwest to Slate Creek at 10,800 feet (37.8224° -107.9726°).

Climb 1.0 mile north-northwest up the Slate Creek drainage to 12,000 feet (37.8345° -107.9799°). Continue 0.4 mile north-northwest, and at 12,400 feet

(37.8397° -107.9808°), you enter the sheltered sanctuary under Mount Wilson's east face and Gladstone Peak's south face. Climb 0.2 mile northwest to 12,800 feet (37.8415° -107.9836°) in the center of the basin that you have worked so hard to reach, and turn west. You are in a privileged position here; enjoy your passage.

Climb 0.2 mile west to 13,100 feet (37.8413° -107.9866°), where the unbroken sweep of snow on Mount Wilson's east face steepens. Climb the clean sweep directly toward the summit. As you approach the summit rocks, stay to the south (left) and climb to the end of the snow just south of the summit. Climb north up Class 4 rock to the summit. Your solitude may be broken if you meet other climbers on the summit, but if you share the joy of your ascent, you will feel even better.

31R4 V1 – Variation – Etude

Class 4, Steep Snow

For another elegant finish, stay to the north of the summit rocks and climb a short, steep couloir to reach the notch 150 feet north of Mount Wilson's summit. Join the North Slopes Route here and climb 150 feet south on that route's final, Class 4 pitch to reach the summit.

31R4 V2 – Variation – Boxcar Couloir

Class 4, Steep Snow

For even more excitement, leave the East Face Route at 12,400 feet (37.8397° -107.9808°) and climb straight west up the S-shaped Boxcar Couloir. This steep, sinuous passage splits Mount Wilson's east buttress. Exit the Boxcar Couloir at 13,600 feet (37.8394° -107.9870°) and rejoin the East Face Route. Reclusive and remote, this ascent may make you feel like an explorer from an ancient age.

31. El Diente Peak 14,159 feet

31R – El Diente Routes

31R5 – El Diente – North Slopes

From Rock of Ages TH at 10,340'	441 RP	9.5 mi RT	3,819' net; 5,619' total	Class 3, Steep Snow
From Navajo Lake TH at 9,340'	474 RP	15.1 mi RT	4,819' net; 5,231' total	Class 3, Steep Snow
From Navajo Lake at 11,154'	324 RP	5.1 mi RT	3,005' net; 3,005' total	Class 3, Steep Snow
From Woods Lake TH at 9,360'	469 RP	13.9 mi RT	4,799' net; 5,611' total	Class 3, Steep Snow

This is the most often climbed route on El Diente, but depending on conditions, it may not be the easiest route. El Diente's north side retains some snow through most of the summer, and this may aid or hinder progress depending on the climber. People climb the route because it is above Navajo Basin, and Mount Wilson and Wilson Peak can be climbed from there as well. You can approach the route from either Rock of Ages saddle or Navajo Basin. Use either approach to reach 12,120 feet (37.8493° -108.0023°) in upper Navajo Basin.

El Diente Peak from Mount Wilson.

From 12,120 feet in upper Navajo Basin, climb 0.4 mile south to 12,600 feet (37.8433° -108.0011°) at the base of a prominent couloir leading toward the El Diente–Mount Wilson Ridge, 0.25 mile east of El Diente's summit. The couloir retains some snow through the summer, so I recommend an ice ax for this route. The couloir ends in a rock face below the ridge crest. To avoid this obstacle, angle west (right) and reach the ridge crest at 13,900 feet (37.8392° -108.0014°). Cross to the ridge's south side and traverse west below the ridge crest to avoid some towers called the Organ Pipes (some Class 3). Climb back to the ridge crest via a gully, cross the ridge, and finish the climb on the ridge's north side (some Class 3). The summit (37.8394° -108.0053°) appears abruptly. From the top of the Tooth, sink your teeth into the exhibition.

31R6 – El Diente – South Slopes

From Kilpacker TH at 10,060'   353 RP   11.5 mi RT   4,099' total   Class 3

When it is snow free, this route is probably the safest and easiest route on El Diente. Unpleasant but safe scree replaces the dangerous steep snow on the North Slopes Route (31R5). Follow the Kilpacker Basin Approach (31A4) and climb east into Kilpacker Basin past El Diente's summit to 12,800 feet (37.8346° -108.0000°). Avoid the temptation to leave the basin and climb up toward the summit too soon.

From 12,800 feet, climb north up steep talus toward the low point in the El Diente–Mount Wilson Ridge. The route to the ridge is not a straight line. Climb up under a cliff at 13,500 feet, do an ascending traverse west (left) to avoid it, and reach an easier slope west of the cliff. Hike or scramble up this slope on steep scree (Class 2) or the nearby rock ribs (Class 3). Some Class 3 scrambling is required as you approach the ridge. Depending on your disposition, the scrambling may come as a welcome relief from the scree.

It is not necessary to go all the way to the ridge, since the South Slopes Route joins the North Slopes Route below the Organ Pipes on the ridge's south side. Traverse west below the Organ Pipes (some Class 3). Climb to the ridge crest via a gully, cross the ridge, and finish the climb on the ridge's north side (some Class 3). The summit appears abruptly.

31R7 – El Diente – North Buttress

From Rock of Ages TH at 10,340'	417 RP	11.6 mi RT	3,819' net; 6,059' total	Class 4
From Navajo Lake TH at 9,340'	426 RP	14.0 mi RT	4,819' net; 5,231' total	Class 4
From Navajo Lake at 11,154'	276 RP	4.0 mi RT	3,005' net; 3,005' total	Class 4
From Woods Lake TH at 9,360'	421 RP	12.8 mi RT	4,799' net; 5,611' total	Class 4

El Diente's north buttress is a diffuse rib that rises to a point on the upper west ridge very close to the summit. The route has a Class 4 crux, which makes it harder than the North Slopes Route (31R5), but it offers an adventurous alpine outing that avoids the steep snow on the North Slopes Route. However, if you climb the North Buttress and descend the North Slopes, you will still likely need an ice ax.

I climbed this route through a frosty night in 1966 after a day on which I had already climbed the three Fourteeners. The purpose of this orthogonal adventure was to rescue a hapless climber who was stuck on a ledge not far below the summit. Earlier, he had disdained the standard routes and set out alone for El Diente's proper *Nordwand*. At dusk he wildly waved his jacket, and after dark there was no mistaking his SOS signal. Thinking he was seriously injured, my group organized a massive effort, and I raced up the route with two stalwart companions. We reached him at 3 AM and discovered that he was not injured, merely scared and stuck. We flashed the good news to our waiting teammates on Rock of Ages saddle who were poised to run for the Rescue Group. At dawn I rounded the final corner to his perch, rousted him, roped him in, belayed him to safety, and short-roped him down what was for him El Colmillo. Wretched and churlish, he never thanked any of us. I hope he at least stayed out of the mountains.

You can approach the route from either Rock of Ages saddle or Navajo Basin. Use either approach to reach 11,900 feet (37.8490° -108.0077°) in upper

Navajo Basin. Your view of the route from here is highly foreshortened. Leave the trail here, climb 0.3 mile south-southeast up the initial slab-infested grass slope and boulder field to 12,400 feet (37.8450° -108.0071°), below the buttress, and get onto the buttress just above its low point. Climb Class 2+ slabs on the ridge's west (right) side, then climb back to the ridge crest over large, imbedded boulders to a small bench on the ridge. Climb up the boulders on or to the west (right) of the ridge crest above to a second bench on the ridge. The ridge above is steeper, but is easier to climb than it appears and will take you to a third, narrower bench. The narrowing ridge above requires some navigation around obstacles (Class 3) and an ascent directly up the ridge (Class 3) to the base of small tower. Go around the tower's east (left) side and reach a small saddle. From the saddle, climb blocks and slabs east (left) of the now disjoint ridge crest above. Climb up one of several available chimneys (Class 4), angle 50 feet steeply uphill to the west (loose Class 3), and reach the west ridge. Scramble 70 yards east to the summit (37.8394° -108.0053°).

31R8 – El Diente – West Ridge

From Rock of Ages TH at 10,340'	557 RP	16.8 mi RT	3,819' net; 7,551' total	Class 4
From Navajo Lake TH at 9,340'	485 RP	14.4 mi RT	4,819' net; 5,231' total	Class 4
From Navajo Lake at 11,154'	335 RP	4.4 mi RT	3,005' net; 3,005' total	Class 4
From Woods Lake TH at 9,360'	480 RP	13.2 mi RT	4,799' net; 5,611' total	Class 4

This is the westernmost route in this book, and solitude comes with that geographic distinction. This long ridge of stature has several surprises along the way. Be prepared for exacting route finding and rotten rock. Many parties have found this ridge to be far more difficult and dangerous than anticipated; however, this book-ending ridge is in a magnificent position and provides expansive views to the west.

Use either the Rock of Ages Approach (31A1), Navajo Basin Approach (31A2), or Woods Lake Approach (31A3) to reach Navajo Lake at 11,154 feet (37.8476° -108.0287°). From the west end of the lake, do an ascending traverse 0.5 mile southwest to 11,600 feet (37.8416° -108.0323°), at the bottom of the west ridge. Climb 0.7 mile east-southeast up the initial, easy but tedious ridge to Point 13,082 (37.8397° -108.0227°), from which you can survey the formidable mile that separates you from the summit. Scamper 0.35 mile east over several ridge bumps to Point 13,300 (37.8402° -108.0171°), from which you have an even more sobering view of the ridge's upper difficulties. Scramble 0.45 mile east over increasing difficulties to tiny Point 13,860 (37.8401° -108.0085°), on which you may wonder why you chose this route. The remaining 0.2 mile of ridge is the crux of the route, and there are different strategies for overcoming it. When dry, you can traverse below the ridge crest on the ridge's south side. You can also attempt to stay close to the ridge crest, an exercise in ridge scooting that has been likened with hyperbole to a half mile of Capitol Knife Edge. When the difficulties ease, you can scurry over the last 300 feet to the summit (37.8394° -108.0053°).

31C – Wilson Peak, Mount Wilson, and El Diente Combination Routes

31C1 – Wilson Peak West Ridge ➔ Mt Wilson North Slopes ➔ El Diente *Classic*

From Rock of Ages TH at 10,340'   583 RP   13.0 mi RT   7,182' total   Class 4, Steep Snow

This is the most expedient way to climb all three peaks in one day from a trailhead. Start at the Rock of Ages Trailhead at 10,340 feet and follow Wilson Peak's West Ridge Route (31R1) to Wilson Peak's summit. Return to the 13,020-foot Rock of Ages saddle, descend 0.7 mile south into Navajo Basin to 12,300 feet (37.8501° -107.9966°), and continue on Mount Wilson's North Slopes Route (31R2) to Mount Wilson's summit.

The traverse from Mount Wilson to El Diente is one of Colorado's four great Fourteener traverses. It is long and time-consuming. Time spent to complete this traverse will range from two to four hours. Escape from the ridge is difficult, and this is a bad ridge to be trapped on during an electrical storm. Consider the weather carefully before launching.

From Mount Wilson's summit, descend 150 feet north to the high saddle described with Mount Wilson's North Slopes Route (Class 4). From the high saddle, descend west down a couloir, then traverse west under the ridge crest on the south side of the Mount Wilson–El Diente Ridge. Reach the ridge crest at a 14,060-foot saddle (37.8395° -107.9931°).

From the 14,060-foot saddle, climb west on the ridge crest and traverse a narrow, exposed coxcomb (Class 3). The exposure on both sides of the coxcomb is sensational, and this is a particularly bad place to be during an electrical storm. As you approach the coxcomb's west end, the ridge drops down to a 13,980-foot saddle. If you stay on the ridge crest, you will discover that the drop becomes abrupt. A 60-foot rappel will overcome the problem.

You also can overcome the problem by doing a Class 3 downclimb on the ridge's south side. Because of its sinuous nature, the exact line of this devious downclimb is difficult to describe. Start the downclimb before you reach the end of the coxcomb. End the downclimb 100 feet southeast of and slightly below the 13,980-foot saddle. This downclimb has the traverse's most difficult climbing.

At the 13,980-foot saddle (37.8393° -107.9949°), you are one-quarter of the way along the traverse, and the enormity of your endeavor will be apparent. Take heart, because the ridge is easier for a while. Traverse west on a broader section of ridge over a 14,100-foot summit (37.8391° -107.9970°) called "West Wilson" (Class 2). The next obstacle is a series of towers near the west end of "West Wilson." These towers are not the Organ Pipes.

The easiest way around the towers is to descend 250 feet down the ridge's south side, traverse below the towers, then climb back to the ridge west of the towers. Shorter routes traverse below the towers on the ridge's south side without losing so much elevation, but these routes are harder and difficult to find.

From the west side of the towers, traverse another easy stretch of ridge and reach the 13,900-foot saddle (37.8392° -108.0014°) where El Diente's North Slopes

Route reaches the ridge. Traverse west below the ridge crest on the ridge's south side to avoid the Organ Pipes (some Class 3). Climb back to the ridge crest via a gully, cross the ridge, and climb to El Diente's summit on the ridge's north side (some Class 3). Descend El Diente's North Slopes Route (31R5) and return to the Rock of Ages Trailhead over the 13,020-foot Rock of Ages saddle west of Wilson Peak.

Consider doing El Diente first and completing the tour in the opposite direction. This will put you on the Mount Wilson–El Diente Ridge sooner rather than later, which can help you beat thunderstorms. It is easier to climb El Diente's North Slopes Route than to descend it. Doing the traverse from El Diente to Mount Wilson has trade-offs at the steep pitch just east of the 13,980-foot saddle. It is easier to climb up this Class 3 pitch than downclimb it, but you lose the option of rappelling over the pitch.

31C2 – Triple Trick

From Navajo Lake TH at 9,340'	663 RP	19.4 mi RT	7,694' total	Class 4, Steep Snow
From Navajo Lake at 11,154'	511 RP	9.4 mi RT	5,468' total	Class 4, Steep Snow
From Woods Lake TH at 9,360'	654 RP	17.9 mi RT	8,074' total	Class 4, Steep Snow

From the Navajo Lake Trailhead, this combination is longer than Combination 31C1, but from a camp at Navajo Lake, it is shorter. Start at the Navajo Lake Trailhead at 9,340 feet and hike to Navajo Lake using the Navajo Basin Approach (31A2). Hike into Navajo Basin and climb all three peaks as described in Combination 31C1. Return to Navajo Lake at the end of the day.

31C2 EC – Extra Credit – Gladstone Peak 13,913 feet 37.8451° -107.9840°

From Navajo Lake TH at 9,340'	364 RP	16.0 mi RT	4,985' total	Class 3
From Navajo Lake at 11,154'	219 RP	6.0 mi RT	2,759' total	Class 3
From Woods Lake TH at 9,360'	359 RP	14.8 mi RT	5,365' total	Class 3

Climb 13,913-foot Gladstone Peak in addition to the Fourteeners. Gladstone is the dramatic Centennial Thirteener between Wilson Peak and Mount Wilson, and people usually climb it via its north ridge. This ridge requires some Class 3 scrambling on dangerous, questionable blocks. On one occasion, a section of this ridge collapsed, killing a climber who went down with the debris. Tread lightly. Including Gladstone makes this tour a grand slam.

31C3 – El Diente South Slopes → Mt Wilson → Mt Wilson North Slopes *Classic*

From Kilpacker TH at 10,060'	587 RP	17.8 mi RT	5,611' total	Class 4
From 10,700' in Kilpacker Basin	487 RP	10.2 mi RT	4,671' total	Class 4

Now for something completely different. This combination may provide the easiest means of doing Mount Wilson and El Diente together. You can see two valleys for the price of one. Start at the Kilpacker Basin Trailhead at 10,060 feet and hike to the lower waterfall in Kilpacker Basin, where you can camp near 10,700 feet. Climb El Diente's South Slopes Route (31R6), traverse to Mount Wilson (31C1), and descend Mount Wilson's North Slopes Route (31R2) to Navajo Lake. Follow the Navajo Lake Trail 2.3 miles west then south, then turn east onto the Kilpacker Trail's upper end at 10,160 feet (37.8301° -108.0459°). Follow the Kilpacker Trail 1.0 mile south and hike back up Kilpacker Creek to your camp. The trail miles are much easier than upper Kilpacker Basin's scree.

31A5 V EC2 – Extra Credit – Lizard Head 13,113 feet 37.8358° -107.9506°

From Cross Mountain TH at 10,060'   723 RP   8.0 mi RT   3,053' total   Class 5.9

Now for something massively different. If you have climbed all the Fourteeners and are looking for a tougher challenge, tackle Lizard Head, Colorado's hardest peak over 12,500 feet. From the 11,979-foot Cross Mountain-Lizard Head saddle (see 31A5 V), hike and scamper 0.4 mile east to the base of Lizard Head's vertical west face. Hike south along the base of the wall to a point 100 feet north of the end of the wall. If there are climbers above this traverse, run. The beginning of the route is now above you. This point is memorialized by Robert Ormes terse route description in his now historic *Guide to the Colorado Mountains*, "Climb...to base of peak. Take photograph and go away."

Times have changed. Climb 80 feet up a rickety wall just south (right) of some body-sized cracks (Class 5.6) to a small stance. You can belay here, but the anchorage is suspect. Move north (left) and climb 70 feet up the upper part of the continuing body-sized crack system (Class 5.8) to a tiny, exposed notch. You can belay here, and there is a fixed rappel anchor nearby.

Climb north out of the notch via a deceptive, exposed, Class 4 sequence to reach easier ground. Scramble and climb 150 feet north up poised rubble and broken blocks to the base of the summit tower (Class 4). Rocks you dislodge on the scramble and climb to the summit tower will bombard the running climbers approaching the base of the route. Move around to an alcove on the west side of the summit tower.

Climb up the alcove to an overhang that blocks simple passage. Overcome the overhang with a Class 5.9 sequence using the 4-inch crack just north (left) of the overhang. Do a similar but slightly easier sequence above, then climb up a steep narrow rib (Class 5.6) to the south (right) to reach a stance on the summit ridge with a rappel anchor. Scramble 60 feet north on or near the exposed summit ridge to Lizard Head's highest point.

For an alternate finish up the summit tower, climb diagonally right up an incipient, sloping ledgelette on the south side of the summit tower and arrive directly at the rappel anchor (Class 5.8). While a point easier, there is no way to protect this pitch. This is the summit pitch led by Albert Ellingwood when he made the first ascent of Lizard Head in 1920. Those old guys were tough.

31A5 V EC3 — Extra Credit — Where's the Author?

Class 7.11

And this old author's fingers are tough, but tired. Tapping for twenty-two years, I've worn out five computers creating this tome. Enjoy the ride, folks. You're welcome. For me, it's time for a beer. Perhaps I'll see you out there, but remember, wherever you go, look to the highest, hardest place you can see and that's where I'll be.

Excelsior!

Appendix

In Defense of Mountaineering Guidebooks

I am always amazed when I see stumps of once large trees near treeline. They are not going to grow back, at least not until a comet hits the earth and changes the balance of nature. I am equally amazed that nothing grows on mine tailings. Even a comet may not make them fertile. We are the future generation and we have stumps and tailings to look at. Yet the mountains are not dead. We can climb them, then loll about in fields of flowers.

Ironically, we now drive up the miners' old roads in 4WD vehicles made of mined metals, hike uphill for a few hours to a summit, and claim a personal victory or conquest. Miners and loggers make physical extractions from the mountains. Climbers make mental extractions from the mountains. For now, we have driven mining and logging offshore. We no longer rush to the mountains to get the gold; we go to get their good tidings.

The debate today swirls around the opinion that even climbers' mental extractions are causing unacceptable environmental damage. We leave too many footprints. Those who choose to make an effort are being cast as pseudocriminals who are loving the mountains to death. Eh? I take a longer view. Death to a mountain is when it is mined into oblivion like Bartlett Mountain. Death to a mountain is when it commits suicide like Mount St. Helens. As violent as those actions were, we can still climb the stumps of those peaks. There are still good tidings there.

Any long view must compare the damage done by climbers' boots with that of monster trucks. Obviously, boots pale in comparison. Still, are boots too much? Sometimes, yes. What do we do? Rather than lament the lost age when we could walk unfettered by such concerns, we should strap in and solve the problem. For a government agency to shut the door and refuse entry is not a solution. Excess footprints are easily dealt with. We need sustainable trails through the fragile alpine zone. The Colorado Fourteener Initiative is creating these trails. Their efforts are a grand example of the public's ability to strap in and solve the problem. There is no environmental problem created by climbers that cannot be solved by climbers.

Our mental extractions from the mountains are going to continue to increase. So is the positive social value of these gifts. As society creaks and groans in other arenas, we need the mountain's good tidings more than ever. The gift mountains offer society is immense. Mountains give us an arena where we can lift not just our bodies, but our spirits. Without uplifted spirits, we devolve. Mountaineering is a great metaphor for life. It is worth fighting for. I view guidebooks as part of the solution, not part of the problem.

I started climbing in 1956. For nearly 20 years I could not conceive of writing a guidebook. I reasoned, like a miner, that the good tidings were hidden and, once found, should be protected by some sort of claim. I felt a proprietary ownership of the secrets I found with my efforts. I felt that sharing the secret would diminish it as a microscope can change the microbe. I dashed across the globe to discover it before it was diminished. While I had many unique climbs and experiences, this effort left me frustrated and exhausted. I could not dash fast enough. Too many people were ahead of me. After an ascent of the Matterhorn in 1973 that I shared with a hundred other people, I pointed to the heavens and started pontificating about the lost age. Then I realized no one was listening. They were just climbing the Matterhorn. Society had jumped my claim. I pondered this for many years.

Still, I did not write a guidebook. I reasoned that sharing would attract still more people and hasten the demise. I clung to this view as the population quietly doubled and mountain use increased tenfold. My pontifical finger withered. I was alone with my memories of the lost age. Then, early one morning in 1981, I sat upright in bed and started writing a guidebook. It was done in a week. At the time, I could not explain it but I knew that not sharing would hasten the demise. Finally, I just set the demise aside. I knew that what the mountains needed was love.

Approached with love, the mountains can endure our mental extractions forever. Approached with malice, greed, or ignorance, the mountains will indeed suffer. Worse, even with love, climbers may lose their access because of other interests and opinions. The government agencies and monster trucks stand ready. The best we can do is love the mountains and share this love. Climbers as a group need to evolve. We must spread our arms wide and embrace not just the mountains, but other user groups as well. The mountains need loving user groups intimate with their secrets to be their ambassadors. I offer my guidebooks from a deep love for the mountains so that future ambassadors can also share the mountain's good tidings.

In Defense of Feet

The world is in a big rush to abandon feet and replace feet with meters. Why? Let's see...my dictionary defines a meter as 39.37 inches, and an inch is one-twelfth of a foot. Aren't we trying to define meters in terms of feet here? Ah! My dictionary goes on to say that a meter was meant to be one ten-millionth of the distance along a meridian from the equator to the pole. Yeah, I can really identify with that.

But a meter isn't actually what it was meant to be. When I looked deep into my inviolable handbook of chemistry and physics, I learned that a meter is 1,553,164.13 times the wavelength of the red cadmium line in air under 760 millimeters of pressure at 15 degrees Centigrade. Now, I positively have an intrinsic feeling for that! And aren't we using millimeters in the definition of a meter?

The whole point of meters seems to be that we can divide them by 10 because we have 10 fingers. Dividing by 10 is something that scientists and engineers do all the time, but they usually have computers to help them do it. Now, sports-minded people don't usually carry computers around, nor do they need to divide by 10, so they need something they can understand—like a foot. Now, a foot was the length of some old king's foot. I can identify with that because my foot is just about the same length as his foot. The best part is that I can see my foot. It is 4 feet away when I am sitting down and 6 feet away when I am standing up. I have a foot. I do not have a meter.

A foot is a good measure to use when I am throwing, jumping, running, or climbing. In 1955 the national track and field championships were held in my hometown of Boulder, Colorado. All the kids went because it was the biggest meet ever to hit town. Back in 1955, Parry O'Brien was the only man who could shot put more than 60 feet. He came to the meet, and the officials drew a big line out at 60 feet. Parry whirled and let out a huge grunt that was heard across the stadium. The shot put flew and flew. It landed with a thud and kicked up the dust on the 60-foot line. The crowd went wild. For the next week, kids all over town were whirling and grunting. The rocks sailed. We all learned from Parry O'Brien exactly how far 60 feet is. At that time, 60 feet was over in the middle of the neighbor's yard. You need feet if you are going to have a 60-foot shot put.

Back in 1955, no one had high-jumped 7 feet. It seemed impossibly high. It was higher than me and higher than anybody I knew. Imagine jumping higher than your head! John Thomas wanted to be the first person to high-jump 7 feet, so he painted a big red line around his room at 7 feet to get used to the idea. My room was 8 feet high, and I lay in bed visualizing jumping up and over my imaginary line. You need feet if you are going to have a 7-foot high-jump.

The four-minute mile is the perfect event. Four laps, four minutes, one mile. The first four-minute mile by Roger Bannister in 1954 is as well known as the first ascent of Everest in 1953. Most of today's metric track meets still cling to the mile. Why? Because it's the perfect event. You need feet if you are going to have a four-minute mile.

I grew up with all these magic events, and they taught me how long a foot is. The essence of a foot is deeply imbedded in my soul. My trusty Scout pace measures 5 feet for two steps. I can pace off 60 feet to within a few inches, and that is good enough for anything I want to do outdoors. I still don't know how long a meter is.

When I started climbing, I quickly learned what it meant to climb a vertical foot. You had to climb 1,000 vertical feet per hour or you couldn't go on the trip. I was young and strong and could easily climb 3,000 feet per hour. If I pushed myself, I could climb 5,000 feet per hour for a while. I learned to eyeball a slope and tell just how high it was—in feet.

I learned what it felt like at 14,000 feet. I grew up in Colorado, and

Fourteeners were magic. I idolized people who had climbed them all. I climbed them too, trying to be one of the elite. I knew all the Fourteener elevations by heart and could recite them on demand. Better yet, given an elevation, I would recite the peak name. The imaginary line in the sky at 14,000 feet separated the chosen few from the rank and file. The name of the game was to get as high as possible and stay there for as long as possible. You need feet if you are going to have a Fourteener. You need feet if you are going to climb it.

The scientists and engineers are hard at work trying to impose their fingers over my feet. The USGS maps of the Sierra are already appearing in meters. Gack! In time, the memories will fade and the magic will be lost. There will be no more 70-foot shotputs, 8-foot high-jumps or four-minute miles. When they replace feet with meters, there will be no more Fourteeners. Feet—and this book—will be obsolete.

I intend to go out kicking and screaming. I hope this book will preserve the magic for a little longer. If the Colorado maps become metric, I will go into the mountains without them. I will rely on my eye and trusty Scout pace. From the high summits, the Fourteeners will still be visible.

What Is a Peak?

The question about what constitutes an official peak and what is just a false summit has plagued mountaineers for decades. Most mountaineers know all about false summits. When you reach what you think is the summit and discover that the peak you are trying to climb is still farther and higher, you are on a false summit. For many mountaineers, this is all they need to know, and the following discussion will seem banal.

The traditional list of Colorado Fourteeners has varied from 52 to 55 peaks over the years and has always been based on a healthy degree of emotionalism. Peaks have come and gone for sentimental reasons. In this high-tech peak-bagging age, however, many climbers are interested in peak lists based on a rational system. These climbers are interested in the discussion about what constitutes a peak because the answer determines a list's contents and, hence, their climbs.

For some time in Colorado, a single, simple criterion has been used to determine if a summit is a peak or a false summit: For a summit to be a peak, it must rise at least 300 vertical feet above the highest saddle connecting it to higher ground. If just one criterion is to be used, this is a good one. There is nothing sacred about 300 feet. It is just a round number that seems to make sense in Colorado. It is a criterion that serves most people most of the time, and the peak list that follows uses it.

When Is a Peak Climbed?

After grappling with the question of what is a peak, we need to think about another question: When is a peak climbed? Stated differently, What constitutes an ascent? Most people would wince if you drove a vehicle to just a few feet from the summit and then walked to the top, and most people would wince if you didn't reach the highest point at all. So, two necessary conditions seem to be that you must reach the highest point under your own power and that you must gain a certain amount of elevation. But how much? That question seems to be the crux.

An obvious answer is that, to climb a mountain, you must climb from the bottom to the top. While the top of most mountains is well defined, the bottom is not. One definition is that the bottom of all mountains is sea level. This flip definition makes little topographic sense, however, and it means that almost nobody has ever climbed anything.

In Colorado there has been a long-standing informal agreement that one should gain 3,000 feet for a "legal" ascent of a Fourteener. Of course, there is nothing sacred about the number 3,000. It is approximately equal to the vertical distance between treeline and summit, and it represents a nice workout, but other than that, it's just a one-number estimate for defining the bottom of a Colorado mountain. Even people who are careful to gain 3,000 feet on the first Fourteener of the day often hike the connecting ridge to the next Fourteener and claim a legal ascent of the second peak after an ascent of only a few hundred feet. Most people who climb Fourteeners do this.

One criterion for climbing a peak is that you should gain a vertical height under your own power equal to your peak's rise from its highest connecting saddle with a neighbor peak. If you do less than that, you are just visiting summits, not climbing mountains. Beyond this minimum gain, you are free to gain as much altitude as your peak-bagging conscience requires. The greater your elevation gain, the greater your karmic gain. Except for ridge traverses, 3,000 feet seems to satisfy most people.

There are other interesting questions. If someone rides a bicycle up the Mount Evans Road, then walks up to the highest point, have they climbed Evans? They ascended under their own power and even hauled up the bicycle's weight. Suppose someone else runs on a treadmill all winter and charges up a bank of batteries. When summer comes, they load the batteries into a battery-powered car and drive to the top of Evans in comfort. Has this person climbed Evans? This may be an "ascent," but it isn't a climb. The cyclist ascended Evans under their own power, but with considerable aid from mechanical advantage. The motorist used stored energy for propulsion. Both these activities seem to be outside the sport of mountaineering. Climbers should carry their equipment, not let their equipment carry them.

Peak and Route Lists

The following peak lists cover Colorado's Fourteeners. If you want detailed information on the Centennial Thirteeners, see my guidebook *Colorado's Thirteeners: From Hikes to Climbs.*

The USGS has changed from the very old NGVD29 vertical datum to the newer, more accurate NAVD88 vertical datum and announced new altitudes for all of Colorado's Fourteeners. The USGS adjusted the elevations for all Fourteeners upward from three to seven feet. The peaks have not instantly gained height, since this is just a mathematical adjustment. In the text, the peaks are headlined with the traditional, old elevations. The new elevations are given in the essentials section with each peak. Both the old and new elevations are given in the Fourteener lists that follow.

A peak qualifies for these lists if it is named or ranked. Named summits are on a list if they are ranked or unranked. The officially named summits include peaks, mounts, mountains, named ridges, named benchmarks if they do not have a peak name, named rocks, and named hills. Unofficial names are enclosed in quotation marks. If a summit has both a peak name and a named benchmark, the peak name takes precedence.

I list ranked summits whether they are named or not. I rank a summit if it rises at least 300 feet from the highest connecting saddle to a higher ranked summit. The closest, higher ranked summit is the "proximate parent." A fine point is that this may be a different peak from the higher ranked summit above the highest connecting saddle; that peak is the "line parent." In the rare case where there are two or more connecting saddles of the same elevation leading to different higher-ranked summits, the closer summit is the parent. My lists differ from some older lists in that I search for a higher, ranked parent, not just another peak on the list that may be lower and unranked. That would be a "neighbor." It is interesting to be on a summit and know where the nearest higher peak is. The proximate and line parents are usually the same peak, and in this case, I just list the one peak name. When they are different peaks, I list the proximate parent first and the line parent on the next line. In this case, I list the two different isolations (see below) in like manner.

I give extrapolated elevations to summits and interpolated elevations to saddles that are only shown with contour lines. Most USGS quadrangles covering Colorado have 40-foot contour intervals. Thus, I add 20 feet to the elevation of the highest closed contour for a summit without a given elevation. I give unmarked saddles an elevation halfway between the highest contour that does not go through the saddle and the lowest contour that does go through the saddle.

If, using either given or extrapolated/interpolated elevations, a summit rises at least 300 feet from its highest connecting saddle to a higher ranked summit, it has a "hard rank." A summit's elevation above its highest connecting saddle to a higher ranked summit is the peak's "prominence." Summits that do not have a hard rank but could rank if extrapolated/interpolated elevations were not used for either the summit or connecting saddle have a "soft rank." There is one soft-ranked summit on these lists: Point 14,340, alias "North Massive." This summit has a left-justified S in the Rank column. A right-justified number in this column means that the peak has a hard rank.

The Iso column shows the straight-line map distance in miles between the peak and its proximate parent; this is the peak's "isolation." Summits with the same elevation are listed in descending order of those peaks' prominence. If multiple peaks have the same elevation and the same prominence, they are listed in descending order of those peaks' "isolation." Multiple peaks with the same name get a trailing letter to distinguish them. The highest gets A, the second highest B, and so on.

The Quadrangle column gives the USGS 7.5-minute quadrangle that shows the summit of the peak. The parent(s) may be on a different quadrangle. The Rg column shows the peak's range as follows: FR for Front, TM for Tenmile-Mosquito, SW for Sawatch, SC for Sangre de Cristo, EL for Elk, and SJ for San Juan. Use the star column to track your climbs. The following abbreviations are used: Pk for Peak, Mt for Mount, Mtn for Mountain, BM for Benchmark, NE for Northeast, NW for Northwest, and SE for Southeast.

The Fourteener lists cover 73 summits, 53 of which have a hard rank, 1 of which has a soft rank, and 5 of which do not rank but have official names. This set of 59 14,000-foot summits has become a popular list to pursue. Two named and famous Fourteeners, El Diente and North Maroon, do not have a hard rank under the 300-foot criterion. The topography speaks without emotion. In compensation, a new Fourteener with a soft rank, "North Massive," appears on the Fourteener list. I also list another 14 summits with unofficial names that do not rank to bring the list total to 73. If you are a hard-core Fourteener aficionado, you will climb every summit on my extended list of 73.

The route list is unique and the first of its kind for Colorado's Fourteeners. It lists the 614 routes in this book that have been assigned R Points. Remember that R Points measure a symbiosis of distance, elevation gain, and route difficulty. I call this synthesis efferculty. I list the routes in descending R Point value, or efferculty. Simply stated, I list the routes from toughest to easiest. Granted there is some duplication of effort in these listings, but it is still a useful tool. Bt this measure, the Front Range has 47,015 R Points, the Tenmile-Mosquito 12,402, the Sawatch 36,856, the Sangre de Cristo 46,068, the Elks 21,737, and the San Juans have 65,282 R Points. Not surprisingly, the San Juan Range is efferculty king and the Tenmile-Mosquito is efferculty poor.

The total efferculty computed for this book of 229,350 R Points is enough to require a flat hike of 22,162 miles at 14,000 feet. This is nearly enough to circle the earth. If you do not want to hike around the world at 14,000 feet to earn your points, you could climb 2,286 miles up a ladder. Humm, that's well beyond earth's atmosphere and almost a tenth of the way to the moon. There's no breathable air there; maybe you should stay at 14,000 feet. If your feet hurt thinking about all that hiking and climbing, you could just do 1,139 Class 5.10 pitches, but you would have to do them at 14,000 feet. Wait, there's more. There are another 109 routes in this book for which I have not calculated R Points. And this book is just a Fourteener guide. For every ranked Fourteener in Colorado, there are 11 ranked Thirteeners. You get the idea. The adventure discussed in this book is vast, but it is just a start. You cannot do it all, but you can pursue joy where ever you go. Climbing happily into my seventh calendar decade, I leave you with the following poem.

I have not lost the magic of long days; I live them, dream them still.
Still am I master of the starry ways, and freeman of the hill.
Shattered my glass, ere half the sands had run—I hold the heights,
I hold the heights I won.

Mine still the hope that hailed me from each height, mine the unresting flame.
With dreams I charmed each doing to delight; I charm the rest the same.
Severed my skein, ere half the strands were spun—I keep the dreams,
I keep the dreams I won.

What if I live no more those kingly days? Their night sleeps with me still.
I dream my feet upon the starry ways; my heart rests in the hill.
I may not grudge the little left undone; I hold the heights,
I keep the dreams I won.

—Geoffrey Winthrop Young

Colorado's Fourteeners – Sorted by Elevation

Rank CO	NGVD29 Elev feet	NAVD88 Elev feet	Prom feet	Summit Name	Parent	Iso miles	Quadrangle	Rg	Page	✓
1	14,433	14,440	9,093	Mt Elbert	Mt Whitney, CA	669.98	Mt Elbert	SW	106	□
2	14,421	14,42w8	1,961	Mt Massive	Mt Elbert	5.08	Mt Massive	SW	98	□
3	14,420	14,427	2,360	Mt Harvard	Mt Elbert	14.96	Mt Harvard	SW	140	□
					Mt Massive	19.97				
4	14,345	14,349	5,326	Blanca Pk	Mt Harvard	103.61	Blanca Pk	SC	204	□
S1	14,340	~14,347	280	"North Massive"	Mt Massive	0.86	Mt Massive	SW	103	□
5	14,336	14,313	1,036	La Plata Pk	Mt Elbert	6.29	Mt Elbert	SW	114	□
					Mt Harvard	10.95				
6	14,309	14,314	4,242	Uncompahgre Pk	La Plata Pk	85.16	Uncompahgre Pk	SJ	272	□
					Mt Harvard	85.38				
	14,300	~14,307	120	"Massive Green"	Mt Massive	0.38	Mt Massive	SW	103	□
7	14,294	14,298	4,554	Crestone Pk	Blanca Pk	27.46	Crestone Pk	SC	179	□
8	14,286	14,291	3,862	Mt Lincoln	Mt Massive	22.57	Alma	TM	76	□
9	14,270	14,279	2,770	Grays Pk	Mt Lincoln A	25.05	Grays Pk	FR	25	□
10	14,269	14,276	2,503	Mt Antero	Mt Harvard	17.77	Mt Antero	SW	154	□
11	14,267	14,272	560	Torreys Pk	Grays Pk	0.64	Grays Pk	FR	28	□
12	14,265	14,269	2,365	Castle Pk A	La Plata Pk	20.91	Hayden Pk	EL	253	□
13	14,265	14,270	1,125	Quandary Pk	Mt Lincoln A	3.18	Breckenridge	TM	64	□
14	14,264	14,270	2,764	Mt Evans A	Grays Pk	9.79	Mt Evans	FR	40	□
	14,260	~14,264	120	"Northeast Crestone"	Crestone Pk	0.11	Crestone Pk	SC	182	□
	14,260	~14,264	80	"East Crestone"	Crestone Pk	0.08	Crestone Pk	SC	180	□
	14,256	~14,262	116	"West Evans"	Mt Evans A	0.31	Mt Evans	FR	43	□
15	14,255	14,261	2,940	Longs Pk	Torreys Pk	43.71	Longs Pk	FR	1	□
16	14,246	14,250	4,024	Mt Wilson	Uncompahgre Pk	33.05	Mt Wilson	SJ	329	□
	14,238	~14,243	138	Mt Cameron	Mt Lincoln A	0.50	Alma	TM	78	□
17	14,229	14,236	1,619	Mt Shavano	Mt Antero	3.82	Maysville	SW	164	□
18	14,197	14,205	2,177	Mt Princeton	Mt Antero	5.21	Mt Antero	SW	150	□
					Mt Harvard	12.79				
19	14,197	14,205	1,337	Mt Belford	Mt Harvard	3.32	Mt Harvard	SW	128	□
20	14,197	14,201	457	Crestone Needle	Crestone Pk	0.49	Crestone Pk	SC	184	□
21	14,196	14,204	1,896	Mt Yale	Mt Harvard	5.56	Mt Yale	SW	145	□
	14,180	~14,187	80	"East La Plata"	La Plata Pk	0.21	Mt Elbert	SW	119	□
22	14,172	14,177	312	Mt Bross A	Mt Lincoln A	1.13	Alma	TM	78	□
23	14,165	14,169	1,025	Kit Carson Pk	Crestone Pk	1.30	Crestone Pk	SC	195	□
	14,159	14,164	259	El Diente Pk	Mt Wilson	0.75	Dolores Pk	SJ	331	□
24	14,156	14,162	2,336	Maroon Pk	Castle Pk A	8.06	Maroon Bells	EL	241	□
25	14,155	14,162	455	Tabeguache Pk	Mt Shavano	0.75	Saint Elmo	SW	166	□
26	14,153	14,160	653	Mt Oxford	Mt Belford	1.23	Mt Harvard	SW	131	□
27	14,150	14,155	3,050	Mt Sneffels	Mt Wilson	15.74	Mt Sneffels	SJ	308	□
					Uncompahgre Pk	18.61				
28	14,148	14,152	768	Mt Democrat	Mt Lincoln A	1.73	Climax	TM	79	□
	14,134	~14,141	234	"South Elbert"	Mt Elbert	0.97	Mt Elbert	SW	111	□
	14,132	~14,139	232	"South Massive"	Mt Massive	0.70	Mt Massive	SW	101	□
29	14,130	14,141	1,750	Capitol Pk	Maroon Pk	7.46	Capitol Pk	EL	222	□
30	14,110	14,115	5,530	Pikes Pk	Mt Evans A	60.88	Pikes Pk	FR	52	□
					Mt Lincoln A	67.31				
	14,100	~14,104	120	"West Wilson"	Mt Wilson	0.30	Mt Wilson	SJ	335	□
31	14,092	14,096	1,152	Snowmass Mtn	Capitol Pk	2.34	Snowmass Mtn	EL	230	□
32	14,087	14,092	2,187	Windom Pk	Mt Wilson	26.55	Columbine Pass	SJ	299	□
					Uncompahgre Pk	31.86				
33	14,084	14,089	1,024	Mt Eolus	Windom Pk	1.68	Columbine Pass	SJ	305	□
34	14,081	14,084	301	Challenger Point	Kit Carson Pk	0.23	Crestone Pk	SC	193	□
35	14,073	14,079	893	Mt Columbia	Mt Harvard	1.89	Mt Harvard	SW	142	□
36	14,067	14,073	847	Missouri Mtn	Mt Belford	1.30	Winfield	SW	132	□

Rank CO	NGVD29 Elev feet	NAVD88 Elev feet	Prom feet	Summit Name	Parent	Iso miles	Quadrangle	Rg	Page	✓
37	14,064	14,069	1,204	Humboldt Pk	Crestone Needle	1.42	Crestone Pk	SC	192	☐
					Crestone Pk	1.77				
38	14,060	14,065	720	Mt Bierstadt	Mt Evans A	1.41	Mt Evans	FR	47	☐
	14,060	~14,064	240	Conundrum Pk	Castle Pk A	0.42	Hayden Pk	EL	258	☐
	14,060	~14,066	240	"Southeast Longs"	Longs Pk	0.10	Longs Pk	FR	18	☐
39	14,059	14,064	399	Sunlight Pk A	Windom Pk	0.47	Storm King Pk	SJ	301	☐
40	14,048	14,053	1,908	Handies Pk	Uncompahgre Pk	11.22	Handies Pk	SJ	288	☐
					Sunlight Pk A	20.33				
41	14,047	14,051	4,827	Culebra Pk	Blanca Pk	35.56	Culebra Pk	SC	217	☐
42	14,042	14,047	1,542	Mt Lindsey	Blanca Pk	2.27	Blanca Pk	SC	214	☐
43	14,042	14,049	342	Ellingwood Point	Blanca Pk	0.51	Blanca Pk	SC	211	☐
	14,039	~14,044	179	North Eolus	Mt Eolus	0.25	Storm King Pk	SJ	306	☐
44	14,037	14,040	377	Little Bear Pk	Blanca Pk	1.00	Blanca Pk	SC	207	☐
45	14,036	14,040	896	Mt Sherman	Mt Democrat	8.10	Mt Sherman	TM	83	☐
46	14,034	14,037	1,436	Redcloud Pk	Handies Pk	4.91	Redcloud Pk	SJ	283	☐
	14,020	~14,025	80	"South Bross"	Mt Bross A	0.61	Alma	TM	79	☐
	14,020	~14,023	80	"South Little Bear"	Little Bear Pk	0.18	Blanca Pk	SC	209	☐
	14,020	~14,024	40	"North Snowmass"	Snowmass Mtn	0.18	Snowmass Mtn	EL	236	☐
	14,020	~14,025	40	"Northwest Lindsey"	Mt Lindsey	0.17	Blanca Pk	SC	216	☐
47	14,018	14,023	1,638	Pyramid Pk A	Maroon Pk	2.08	Maroon Bells	EL	246	☐
48	14,017	14,024	877	Wilson Pk	Mt Wilson	1.51	Mt Wilson	SJ	327	☐
49	14,015	14,020	1,635	Wetterhorn Pk	Uncompahgre Pk	2.75	Wetterhorn Pk	SJ	275	☐
50	14,014	14,019	3,114	San Luis Pk A	Redcloud Pk	26.93	San Luis Pk	SJ	260	☐
					Handies Pk	31.71				
	14,014	14,019	234	North Maroon Pk	Maroon Pk	0.37	Maroon Bells	EL	243	☐
51	14,005	14,012	2,111	Mt of the Holy Cross	Mt Massive	19.93	Mt of the Holy Cross	SW	89	☐
52	14,003	14,012	1,423	Huron Pk	Missouri Mtn	3.20	Winfield	SW	120	☐
					La Plata Pk	6.10				
53	14,001	14,006	501	Sunshine Pk	Redcloud Pk	1.27	Redcloud Pk	SJ	285	☐

Colorado's Fourteeners – Sorted by Prominence

Rank CO	NGVD29 Elev feet	NAVD88 Elev feet	Prom feet	Summit Name	Parent	Iso miles	Quadrangle	Rg	Page	✓
1	14,433	14,440	9,093	Mt Elbert	Mt Whitney, CA	669.98	Mt Elbert	SW	106	☐
30	14,110	14,115	5,530	Pikes Pk	Mt Evans A	60.88	Pikes Pk	FR	52	☐
					Mt Lincoln A	67.31				
4	14,345	14,349	5,326	Blanca Pk	Mt Harvard	103.61	Blanca Pk	SC	204	☐
41	14,047	14,051	4,827	Culebra Pk	Blanca Pk	35.56	Culebra Pk	SC	217	☐
7	14,294	14,298	4,554	Crestone Pk	Blanca Pk	27.46	Crestone Pk	SC	179	☐
6	14,309	14,314	4,242	Uncompahgre Pk	La Plata Pk	85.16	Uncompahgre Pk	SJ	272	☐
					Mt Harvard	85.38				
16	14,246	14,250	4,024	Mt Wilson	Uncompahgre Pk	33.05	Mt Wilson	SJ	329	☐
8	14,286	14,291	3,862	Mt Lincoln A	Mt Massive	22.57	Alma	TM	76	☐
50	14,014	14,019	3,114	San Luis Pk A	Redcloud Pk	26.93	San Luis Pk	SJ	260	☐
					Handies Pk	31.71				
27	14,150	14,155	3,050	Mt Sneffels	Mt Wilson	15.74	Mt Sneffels	SJ	308	☐
					Uncompahgre Pk	18.61				

Rank CO	NGVD29 Elev feet	NAVD88 Elev feet	Prom feet	Summit Name	Parent	Iso miles	Quadrangle	Rg	Page	✓
15	14,255	14,261	2,940	Longs Pk	Torreys Pk	43.71	Longs Pk	FR	1	☐
9	14,270	14,279	2,770	Grays Pk	Mt Lincoln A	25.05	Grays Pk	FR	25	☐
14	14,264	14,270	2,764	Mt Evans A	Grays Pk	9.79	Mt Evans	FR	40	☐
10	14,269	14,276	2,503	Mt Antero	Mt Harvard	17.77	Mt Antero	SW	154	☐
12	14,265	14,269	2,365	Castle Pk A	La Plata Pk	20.91	Hayden Pk	EL	253	☐
3	14,420	14,427	2,360	Mt Harvard	Mt Elbert	14.96	Mt Harvard	SW	140	☐
					Mt Massive	19.97				
24	14,156	14,162	2,336	Maroon Pk	Castle Pk A	8.06	Maroon Bells	EI	241	☐
32	14,087	14,092	2,107	Windom Pk	Mt Wilson	26.55	Columbine Pass	SJ	299	☐
					Uncompahgre Pk	31.86				
18	14,197	14,205	2,177	Mt Princeton	Mt Antero	5.21	Mt Antero	SW	150	☐
					Mt Harvard	12.79				
51	14,005	14,012	2,111	Mt of the Holy Cross	Mt Massive	19.93	Mt of the Holy Cross	SW	89	☐
2	14,421	14,428	1,961	Mt Massive	Mt Elbert	5.08	Mt Massive	SW	98	☐
40	14,048	14,053	1,908	Handies Pk	Uncompahgre Pk	11.22	Handies Pk	SJ	288	☐
					Sunlight Pk A	20.33				
21	14,196	14,204	1,896	Mt Yale	Mt Harvard	5.56	Mt Yale	SW	145	☐
5	14,336	14,343	1,836	La Plata Pk	Mt Elbert	6.29	Mt Elbert	SW	114	☐
					Mt Harvard	10.95				
29	14,130	14,141	1,750	Capitol Pk	Maroon Pk	7.46	Capitol Pk	EL	222	☐
47	14,018	14,023	1,638	Pyramid Pk A	Maroon Pk	2.08	Maroon Bells	EL	246	☐
49	14,015	14,020	1,635	Wetterhorn Pk	Uncompahgre Pk	2.75	Wetterhorn Pk	SJ	275	☐
17	14,229	14,236	1,619	Mt Shavano	Mt Antero	3.82	Maysville	SW	164	☐
42	14,042	14,047	1,542	Mt Lindsey	Blanca Pk	2.27	Blanca Pk	SC	214	☐
46	14,034	14,037	1,436	Redcloud Pk	Handies Pk	4.91	Redcloud Pk	SJ	283	⊓
52	14,003	14,012	1,423	Huron Pk	Missouri Mtn	3.20	Winfield	SW	120	☐
					La Plata Pk	6.10				
19	14,197	14,205	1,337	Mt Belford	Mt Harvard	3.32	Mt Harvard	SW	128	⊓
37	14,064	14,069	1,204	Humboldt Pk	Crestone Needle	1.42	Crestone Pk	SC	192	☐
					Crestone Pk	1.77				
31	14,092	14,096	1,152	Snowmass Mtn	Capitol Pk	2.34	Snowmass Mtn	EL	230	☐
13	14,265	14,270	1,125	Quandary Pk	Mt Lincoln A	3.18	Breckenridge	TM	64	☐
23	14,165	14,169	1,025	Kit Carson Pk	Crestone Pk	1.30	Crestone Pk	SC	195	☐
33	14,084	14,089	1,024	Mt Eolus	Windom Pk	1.68	Columbine Pass	SJ	305	☐
45	14,036	14,040	896	Mt Sherman	Mt Democrat	8.10	Mt Sherman	TM	83	☐
35	14,073	14,079	893	Mt Columbia	Mt Harvard	1.89	Mt Harvard	SW	142	☐
48	14,017	14,024	877	Wilson Pk	Mt Wilson	1.51	Mt Wilson	SJ	327	☐
36	14,067	14,073	847	Missouri Mtn	Mt Belford	1.30	Winfield	SW	132	☐
28	14,148	14,152	768	Mt Democrat	Mt Lincoln A	1.73	Climax	TM	79	☐
38	14,060	14,065	720	Mt Bierstadt	Mt Evans A	1.41	Mt Evans	FR	47	☐
26	14,153	14,160	653	Mt Oxford	Mt Belford	1.23	Mt Harvard	SW	131	☐
11	14,267	14,272	560	Torreys Pk	Grays Pk	0.64	Grays Pk	FR	28	☐
53	14,001	14,006	501	Sunshine Pk	Redcloud Pk	1.27	Redcloud Pk	SJ	285	☐
20	14,197	14,201	457	Crestone Needle	Crestone Pk	0.49	Crestone Pk	SC	184	☐
25	14,155	14,162	455	Tabeguache Pk	Mt Shavano	0.75	Saint Elmo	SW	166	☐
39	14,059	14,064	399	Sunlight Pk A	Windom Pk	0.47	Storm King Pk	SJ	301	☐
44	14,037	14,040	377	Little Bear Pk	Blanca Pk	1.00	Blanca Pk	SC	207	☐
43	14,042	14,049	342	Ellingwood Point	Blanca Pk	0.51	Blanca Pk	SC	211	☐
22	14,172	14,177	312	Mt Bross A	Mt Lincoln A	1.13	Alma	TM	78	☐
34	14,081	14,084	301	Challenger Point	Kit Carson Pk	0.23	Crestone Pk	SC	193	☐
S1	14,340	~14,347	280	"North Massive"	Mt Massive	0.86	Mt Massive	SW	103	☐
	14,159	14,164	259	El Diente Pk	Mt Wilson	0.75	Dolores Pk	SJ	331	☐
	14,060	~14,064	240	Conundrum Pk	Castle Pk A	0.42	Hayden Pk	EL	258	☐
	14,060	~14,066	240	"Southeast Longs"	Longs Pk	0.10	Longs Pk	FR	18	☐
	14,134	~14,141	234	"South Elbert"	Mt Elbert	0.97	Mt Elbert	SW	111	☐
	14,014	14,019	234	North Maroon Pk	Maroon Pk	0.37	Maroon Bells	EL	243	☐

Rank CO	NGVD29 Elev feet	NAVD88 Elev feet	Prom feet	Summit Name	Parent	Iso miles	Quadrangle	Rg	Page	✓
	14,132	~14,139	232	"South Massive"	Mt Massive	0.70	Mt Massive	SW	101	☐
	14,039	~14,044	179	North Eolus	Mt Eolus	0.25	Storm King Pk	SJ	306	☐
	14,238	~14,243	138	Mt Cameron	Mt Lincoln A	0.50	Alma	TM	78	☐
	14,300	~14,307	120	"Massive Green"	Mt Massive	0.38	Mt Massive	SW	103	☐
	14,260	~14,264	120	"Northeast Crestone"	Crestone Pk	0.11	Crestone Pk	SC	182	☐
	14,100	~14,104	120	"West Wilson"	Mt Wilson	0.30	Mt Wilson	SJ	335	☐
	14,256	~14,262	116	"West Evans"	Mt Evans A	0.31	Mt Evans	FR	43	☐
	14,260	~14,264	80	"East Crestone"	Crestone Pk	0.08	Crestone Pk	SC	180	☐
	14,180	~14,187	80	"East La Plata"	La Plata Pk	0.21	Mt Elbert	SW	119	☐
	14,020	~14,025	80	"South Bross"	Mt Bross A	0.61	Alma	TM	79	☐
	14,020	~14,023	80	"South Little Bear"	Little Bear Pk	0.18	Blanca Pk	SC	209	☐
	14,020	~14,024	40	"North Snowmass"	Snowmass Mtn	0.18	Snowmass Mtn	EL	236	☐
	14,020	~14,025	40	"Northwest Lindsey"	Mt Lindsey	0.17	Blanca Pk	SC	216	☐

Colorado's Fourteeners – Sorted by Quadrangle

Rank CO	NGVD29 Elev feet	NAVD88 Elev feet	Prom feet	Summit Name	Parent	Iso miles	Quadrangle	Rg	Page	✓
8	14,286	14,291	3,862	Mt Lincoln A	Mt Massive	22.57	Alma	TM	76	☐
	14,238	~14,243	138	Mt Cameron	Mt Lincoln A	0.50	Alma	TM	78	☐
22	14,172	14,177	312	Mt Bross A	Mt Lincoln A	1.13	Alma	TM	78	☐
	14,020	~14,025	80	"South Bross"	Mt Bross A	0.61	Alma	TM	79	☐
4	14,345	14,349	5,326	Blanca Pk	Mt Harvard	103.61	Blanca Pk	SC	204	☐
42	14,042	14,047	1,542	Mt Lindsey	Blanca Pk	2.27	Blanca Pk	SC	214	☐
43	14,042	14,049	342	Ellingwood Point	Blanca Pk	0.51	Blanca Pk	SC	211	☐
44	14,037	14,040	377	Little Bear Pk	Blanca Pk	1.00	Blanca Pk	SC	207	☐
	14,020	~14,023	80	"South Little Bear"	Little Bear Pk	0.18	Blanca Pk	SC	209	☐
	14,020	~14,025	40	"Northwest Lindsey"	Mt Lindsey	0.17	Blanca Pk	SC	216	☐
13	14,265	14,270	1,125	Quandary Pk	Mt Lincoln A	3.18	Breckenridge	TM	64	☐
29	14,130	14,141	1,750	Capitol Pk	Maroon Pk	7.46	Capitol Pk	EL	222	☐
28	14,148	14,152	768	Mt Democrat	Mt Lincoln A	1.73	Climax	TM	79	☐
32	14,087	14,092	2,187	Windom Pk	Mt Wilson Uncompahgre Pk	26.55 31.86	Columbine Pass	SJ	299	☐
33	14,084	14,089	1,024	Mt Eolus	Windom Pk	1.68	Columbine Pass	SJ	305	☐
7	14,294	14,298	4,554	Crestone Pk	Blanca Pk	27.46	Crestone Pk	SC	179	☐
	14,260	~14,264	120	"Northeast Crestone"	Crestone Pk	0.11	Crestone Pk	SC	182	☐
	14,260	~14,264	80	"East Crestone"	Crestone Pk	0.08	Crestone Pk	SC	180	☐
20	14,197	14,201	457	Crestone Needle	Crestone Pk	0.49	Crestone Pk	SC	184	☐
23	14,165	14,169	1,025	Kit Carson Pk	Crestone Pk	1.30	Crestone Pk	SC	195	☐
34	14,081	14,084	301	Challenger Point	Kit Carson Pk	0.23	Crestone Pk	SC	193	☐
37	14,064	14,069	1,204	Humboldt Pk	Crestone Needle Crestone Pk	1.42 1.77	Crestone Pk	SC	192	☐
41	14,047	14,051	4,827	Culebra Pk	Blanca Pk	35.56	Culebra Pk	SC	217	☐
	14,159	14,164	259	El Diente Pk	Mt Wilson	0.75	Dolores Pk	SJ	331	☐
9	14,270	14,279	2,770	Grays Pk	Mt Lincoln A	25.05	Grays Pk	FR	25	☐
11	14,267	14,272	560	Torreys Pk	Grays Pk	0.64	Grays Pk	FR	28	☐

Rank CO	NGVD29 Elev feet	NAVD88 Elev feet	Prom feet	Summit Name	Parent	Iso miles	Quadrangle	Rg	Page	✓
40	14,048	14,053	1,908	Handies Pk	Uncompahgre Pk	11.22	Handies Pk	SJ	288	☐
					Sunlight Pk A	20.33				
12	14,265	14,269	2,365	Castle Pk A	La Plata Pk	20.91	Hayden Pk	EL	253	☐
	14,060	~14,064	240	Conundrum Pk	Castle Pk A	0.42	Hayden Pk	EL	258	☐
15	14,255	14,261	2,940	Longs Pk	Torreys Pk	43.71	Longs Pk	FR	1	☐
	14,060	~14,066	240	"Southeast Longs"	Longs Pk	0.10	Longs Pk	FR	18	☐
24	14,156	14,162	2,336	Maroon Pk	Castle Pk A	8.06	Maroon Bells	EL	241	☐
47	14,018	14,023	1,638	Pyramid Pk A	Maroon Pk	2.08	Maroon Bells	EL	246	☐
	14,014	14,019	234	North Maroon Pk	Maroon Pk	0.37	Maroon Bells	EL	243	☐
17	14,229	14,236	1,619	Mt Shavano	Mt Antero	3.82	Maysville	SW	164	☐
10	14,269	14,276	2,503	Mt Antero	Mt Harvard	17.77	Mt Antero	SW	154	☐
18	14,197	14,205	2,177	Mt Princeton	Mt Antero	5.21	Mt Antero	SW	150	☐
					Mt Harvard	12.79				
1	14,433	14,440	9,093	Mt Elbert	Mt Whitney, CA	669.98	Mt Elbert	SW	106	☐
5	14,336	14,343	1,836	La Plata Pk	Mt Elbert	6.29	Mt Elbert	SW	114	☐
					Mt Harvard	10.95				
	14,180	~14,187	80	"East La Plata"	La Plata Pk	0.21	Mt Elbert	SW	119	☐
	14,134	~14,141	234	"South Elbert"	Mt Elbert	0.97	Mt Elbert	SW	111	☐
14	14,264	14,270	2,764	Mt Evans A	Grays Pk	9.79	Mt Evans	FR	40	☐
	14,256	~14,262	116	"West Evans"	Mt Evans A	0.31	Mt Evans	FR	43	☐
38	14,060	14,065	720	Mt Bierstadt	Mt Evans A	1.41	Mt Evans	FR	47	☐
3	14,420	14,427	2,360	Mt Harvard	Mt Elbert	14.96	Mt Harvard	SW	140	☐
					Mt Massive	19.97				
19	14,197	14,205	1,337	Mt Belford	Mt Harvard	3.32	Mt Harvard	SW	128	☐
26	14,153	14,160	653	Mt Oxford	Mt Belford	1.23	Mt Harvard	SW	131	☐
35	14,073	14,079	893	Mt Columbia	Mt Harvard	1.89	Mt Harvard	SW	142	☐
2	14,421	14,428	1,961	Mt Massive	Mt Elbert	5.08	Mt Massive	SW	98	☐
S1	14,340	~14,347	280	"North Massive"	Mt Massive	0.86	Mt Massive	SW	103	☐
	14,300	~14,307	120	"Massive Green"	Mt Massive	0.38	Mt Massive	SW	103	☐
	14,132	~14,139	232	"South Massive"	Mt Massive	0.70	Mt Massive	SW	101	☐
51	14,005	14,012	2,111	Mt of the Holy Cross	Mt Massive	19.93	Mt of the Holy Cross	SW	89	☐
45	14,036	14,040	896	Mt Sherman	Mt Democrat	8.10	Mt Sherman	TM	83	☐
27	14,150	14,155	3,050	Mt Sneffels	Mt Wilson	15.74	Mt Sneffels	SJ	308	☐
					Uncompahgre Pk	18.61				
16	14,246	14,250	4,024	Mt Wilson	Uncompahgre Pk	33.05	Mt Wilson	SJ	329	☐
	14,100	~14,104	120	"West Wilson"	Mt Wilson	0.30	Mt Wilson	SJ	335	☐
48	14,017	14,024	877	Wilson Pk	Mt Wilson	1.51	Mt Wilson	SJ	327	☐
21	14,196	14,204	1,896	Mt Yale	Mt Harvard	5.56	Mt Yale	SW	145	☐
30	14,110	14,115	5,530	Pikes Pk	Mt Evans A	60.88	Pikes Pk	FR	52	☐
					Mt Lincoln A	67.31				
46	14,034	14,037	1,436	Redcloud Pk	Handies Pk	4.91	Redcloud Pk	SJ	283	☐
53	14,001	14,006	501	Sunshine Pk	Redcloud Pk	1.27	Redcloud Pk	SJ	285	☐
25	14,155	14,162	455	Tabeguache Pk	Mt Shavano	0.75	Saint Elmo	SW	166	☐
50	14,014	14,019	3,114	San Luis Pk A	Redcloud Pk	26.93	San Luis Pk	SJ	260	☐
					Handies Pk	31.71				
31	14,092	14,096	1,152	Snowmass Mtn	Capitol Pk	2.34	Snowmass Mtn	EL	230	☐
	14,020	~14,024	40	"North Snowmass"	Snowmass Mtn	0.18	Snowmass Mtn	EL	236	☐
39	14,059	14,064	399	Sunlight Pk A	Windom Pk	0.47	Storm King Pk	SJ	301	☐
	14,039	~14,044	179	North Eolus	Mt Eolus	0.25	Storm King Pk	SJ	306	☐
6	14,309	14,314	4,242	Uncompahgre Pk	La Plata Pk	85.16	Uncompahgre Pk	SJ	272	☐
					Mt Harvard	85.38				
49	14,015	14,020	1,635	Wetterhorn Pk	Uncompahgre Pk	2.75	Wetterhorn Pk	SJ	275	☐
36	14,067	14,073	847	Missouri Mtn	Mt Belford	1.30	Winfield	SW	132	☐
52	14,003	14,012	1,423	Huron Pk	Missouri Mtn	3.20	Winfield	SW	120	☐
					La Plata Pk	6.10				

Colorado's Fourteeners – Sorted by Range

Rank CO	NGVD29 Elev feet	NAVD88 Elev feet	Prom feet	Summit Name	Parent	Iso miles	Quadrangle	Rg	Page	✓
12	14,265	14,269	2,365	Castle Pk A	La Plata Pk	20.91	Hayden Pk	EL	253	☐
24	14,156	14,162	2,336	Maroon Pk	Castle Pk A	8.06	Maroon Bells	EL	241	☐
29	14,130	14,141	1,750	Capitol Pk	Maroon Pk	7.46	Capitol Pk	EL	222	☐
31	14,092	14,096	1,152	Snowmass Mtn	Capitol Pk	2.34	Snowmass Mtn	EL	230	☐
	14,060	~14,064	240	Conundrum Pk	Castle Pk A	0.42	Hayden Pk	EL	258	☐
	14,020	~14,024	40	"North Snowmass"	Snowmass Mtn	0.18	Snowmass Mtn	EL	236	☐
47	14,018	14,023	1,638	Pyramid Pk A	Maroon Pk	2.08	Maroon Bells	EL	246	☐
	14,014	14,019	234	North Maroon Pk	Maroon Pk	0.37	Maroon Bells	EL	243	☐
9	14,270	14,279	2,770	Grays Pk	Mt Lincoln A	25.05	Grays Pk	FR	25	☐
11	14,267	14,272	560	Torreys Pk	Grays Pk	0.64	Grays Pk	FR	28	☐
14	14,264	14,270	2,764	Mt Evans A	Grays Pk	9.79	Mt Evans	FR	40	☐
	14,256	~14,262	116	"West Evans"	Mt Evans A	0.31	Mt Evans	FR	43	☐
15	14,255	14,261	2,940	Longs Pk	Torreys Pk	43.71	Longs Pk	FR	1	☐
30	14,110	14,115	5,530	Pikes Pk	Mt Evans A	60.88	Pikes Pk	FR	52	☐
					Mt Lincoln A	67.31				
38	14,060	14,065	720	Mt Bierstadt	Mt Evans A	1.41	Mt Evans	FR	47	☐
	14,060	~14,066	240	"Southeast Longs"	Longs Pk	0.10	Longs Pk	FR	18	☐
4	14,345	14,349	5,326	Blanca Pk	Mt Harvard	103.61	Blanca Pk	SC	204	☐
7	14,294	14,298	4,554	Crestone Pk	Blanca Pk	27.46	Crestone Pk	SC	179	☐
	14,260	~14,264	120	"Northeast Crestone"	Crestone Pk	0.11	Crestone Pk	SC	182	☐
	14,260	~14,264	80	"East Crestone"	Crestone Pk	0.08	Crestone Pk	SC	180	☐
20	14,197	14,201	457	Crestone Needle	Crestone Pk	0.49	Crestone Pk	SC	184	☐
23	14,165	14,169	1,025	Kit Carson Pk	Crestone Pk	1.30	Crestone Pk	SC	195	☐
34	14,081	14,084	301	Challenger Point	Kit Carson Pk	0.23	Crestone Pk	SC	193	☐
37	14,064	14,069	1,204	Humboldt Pk	Crestone Needle	1.42	Crestone Pk	SC	192	☐
					Crestone Pk	1.77				
41	14,047	14,051	4,827	Culebra Pk	Blanca Pk	35.56	Culebra Pk	SC	217	☐
42	14,042	14,047	1,542	Mt Lindsey	Blanca Pk	2.27	Blanca Pk	SC	214	☐
43	14,042	14,049	342	Ellingwood Point	Blanca Pk	0.51	Blanca Pk	SC	211	☐
44	14,037	14,040	377	Little Bear Pk	Blanca Pk	1.00	Blanca Pk	SC	207	☐
	14,020	~14,023	80	"South Little Bear"	Little Bear Pk	0.18	Blanca Pk	SC	209	☐
	14,020	~14,025	40	"Northwest Lindsey"	Mt Lindsey	0.17	Blanca Pk	SC	216	☐
6	14,309	14,314	4,242	Uncompahgre Pk	La Plata Pk	85.16	Uncompahgre Pk	SJ	272	☐
					Mt Harvard	85.38				
16	14,246	14,250	4,024	Mt Wilson	Uncompahgre Pk	33.05	Mt Wilson	SJ	329	☐
	14,159	14,164	259	El Diente Pk	Mt Wilson	0.75	Dolores Pk	SJ	331	☐
27	14,150	14,155	3,050	Mt Sneffels	Mt Wilson	15.74	Mt Sneffels	SJ	308	☐
					Uncompahgre Pk	18.61				
	14,100	~14,104	120	"West Wilson"	Mt Wilson	0.30	Mt Wilson	SJ	335	☐
32	14,087	14,092	2,187	Windom Pk	Mt Wilson	26.55	Columbine Pass	SJ	299	☐
					Uncompahgre Pk	31.86				
33	14,084	14,089	1,024	Mt Eolus	Windom Pk	1.68	Columbine Pass	SJ	305	☐
39	14,059	14,064	399	Sunlight Pk A	Windom Pk	0.47	Storm King Pk	SJ	301	☐
40	14,048	14,053	1,908	Handies Pk	Uncompahgre Pk	11.22	Handies Pk	SJ	288	☐
					Sunlight Pk A	20.33				
	14,039	~14,044	179	North Eolus	Mt Eolus	0.25	Storm King Pk	SJ	306	☐
46	14,034	14,037	1,436	Redcloud Pk	Handies Pk	4.91	Redcloud Pk	SJ	283	☐
48	14,017	14,024	877	Wilson Pk	Mt Wilson	1.51	Mt Wilson	SJ	327	☐

Rank CO	NGVD29 Elev feet	NAVD88 Elev feet	Prom feet	Summit Name	Parent	Iso miles	Quadrangle	Rg	Page	✓
49	14,015	14,020	1,635	Wetterhorn Pk	Uncompahgre Pk	2.75	Wetterhorn Pk	SJ	275	☐
50	14,014	14,019	3,114	San Luis Pk A	Redcloud Pk	26.93	San Luis Pk	SJ	260	☐
					Handies Pk	31.71				
53	14,001	14,006	501	Sunshine Pk	Redcloud Pk	1.27	Redcloud Pk	SJ	285	☐
1	14,433	14,440	9,093	Mt Elbert	Mt Whitney, CA	669.98	Mt Elbert	SW	106	☐
2	14,421	14,428	1,961	Mt Massive	Mt Elbert	5.08	Mt Massive	SW	98	☐
3	14,420	14,427	2,360	Mt Harvard	Mt Elbert	14.96	Mt Harvard	SW	140	☐
					Mt Massive	19.97				
S1	14,340	~14,347	280	"North Massive"	Mt Massive	0.86	Mt Massive	SW	103	☐
5	14,336	14,343	1,836	La Plata Pk	Mt Elbert	6.29	Mt Elbert	SW	114	☐
					Mt Harvard	10.95				
	14,300	~14,307	120	"Massive Green"	Mt Massive	0.38	Mt Massive	SW	103	☐
10	14,269	14,276	2,503	Mt Antero	Mt Harvard	17.77	Mt Antero	SW	154	☐
17	14,229	14,236	1,619	Mt Shavano	Mt Antero	3.82	Maysville	SW	164	☐
18	14,197	14,205	2,177	Mt Princeton	Mt Antero	5.21	Mt Antero	SW	150	☐
					Mt Harvard	12.79				
19	14,197	14,205	1,337	Mt Belford	Mt Harvard	3.32	Mt Harvard	SW	128	☐
21	14,196	14,204	1,896	Mt Yale	Mt Harvard	5.56	Mt Yale	SW	145	☐
	14,180	~14,187	80	"East La Plata"	La Plata Pk	0.21	Mt Elbert	SW	119	☐
25	14,155	14,162	455	Tabeguache Pk	Mt Shavano	0.75	Saint Elmo	SW	166	☐
26	14,153	14,160	653	Mt Oxford	Mt Belford	1.23	Mt Harvard	SW	131	☐
	14,134	~14,141	234	"South Elbert"	Mt Elbert	0.97	Mt Elbert	SW	111	☐
	14,132	~14,139	232	"South Massive"	Mt Massive	0.70	Mt Massive	SW	101	☐
35	14,073	14,079	893	Mt Columbia	Mt Harvard	1.89	Mt Harvard	SW	142	☐
36	14,067	14,073	847	Missouri Mtn	Mt Belford	1.30	Winfield	SW	132	☐
51	14,005	14,012	2,111	Mt of the Holy Cross	Mt Massive	19.93	Mt of the Holy Cross	SW	89	☐
52	14,003	14,012	1,423	Huron Pk	Missouri Mtn	3.20	Winfield	SW	120	☐
					La Plata Pk	6.10				
8	14,286	14,291	3,862	Mt Lincoln A	Mt Massive	22.57	Alma	TM	76	☐
13	14,265	14,270	1,125	Quandary Pk	Mt Lincoln A	3.18	Breckenridge	TM	64	☐
	14,238	~14,243	138	Mt Cameron	Mt Lincoln A	0.50	Alma	TM	78	☐
22	14,172	14,177	312	Mt Bross A	Mt Lincoln A	1.13	Alma	TM	78	☐
28	14,148	14,152	768	Mt Democrat	Mt Lincoln A	1.73	Climax	TM	79	☐
45	14,036	14,040	896	Mt Sherman	Mt Democrat	8.10	Mt Sherman	TM	83	☐
	14,020	~14,025	80	"South Bross"	Mt Bross A	0.61	Alma	TM	79	☐

Routes on Colorado's Fourteeners – Sorted by R Points

Summit Name	Elev feet	Route Name	R Points	RT miles	Elev Gain feet	Class/ Snow	Page	✓
Crestone Peak	14,294	19R4 North Pillar from Lower South Colony TH	1,732	16.4	5,684	5.8	182	☐
Crestone Peak	14,294	19R4 North Pillar from Lower South Colony Lake	1,532	3.4	2,754	5.8	182	☐
Capitol Peak	14,130	22R2 Northwest Ridge from Capitol Creek TH	1,397	15.2	5,510	5.7SS	229	☐
Crestone Peak	14,294	19R6 India from Lower South Colony TH	1,331	16.4	5,724	5.8	184	☐
Crestone Peak	14,294	19R5 House Buttress from Lower South Colony TH	1,309	16.3	5,684	5.7	183	☐
Sunlight Peak	13,995	29R3 EC2 "Sunlight Spire" from Vallecito TH	1,299	40.2	9,095	5.10	302	☐
Kit Carson Peak	14,165	19R21 The Prow from Spanish Creek TH	1,285	10.4	6,305	5.8	197	☐
Capitol Peak	14,130	22R2 Northwest Ridge -> Northeast Ridge	1,245	3.6	2,580	5.7 SS	229	☐
Crestone Needle	14,197	19R11 Arnold-Michel from Lower South Colony TH	1,241	15.7	5,467	5.8 SS	188	☐

Sorted by R Points

Summit Name	Elev feet	Route Name	R Points	RT miles	Elev Gain feet	Class/ Snow	Page	✓
Sunlight Peak	13,995	29R3 EC2 "Sunlight Spire" from Purgatory Flats TH	1,231	34.6	8,555	5.10	302	☐
Capitol Peak	14,130	22R2 Northwest Ridge from Capitol Lake	1,207	2.8	2,530	5.7 SS	229	☐
Crestone Needle	14,197	19R9 Whitney from Lower South Colony TH	1,200	15.1	5,467	5.8 SS	186	☐
Crestone Peak	14,294	19R6 India from Lower South Colony Lake	1,131	3.4	2,794	5.8	184	☐
Kit Carson Peak	14,165	19R21 The Prow from 11,000' in Spanish Creek	1,121	3.4	3,565	5.8	197	☐
Crestone Peak	14,294	19R5 House Buttress from Lower South Colony Lake	1,109	3.3	2,754	5.7	183	☐
Longs Peak	14,255	1R8 Stettner's Ledges -> North Face	1,055	12.2	4,855	5.7+	15	☐
Longs Peak	14,255	1R8 Stettner's Ledges -> Keyhole	1,051	12.8	5,055	5.7+	15	☐
Crestone Needle	14,197	19R11 Arnold-Michel from Lower South Colony Lake	1,043	2.7	2,537	5.8 SS	188	☐
Longs Peak	14,255	1R8 Stettner's Ledges from Longs Peak TH	1,030	11.2	4,855	5.7+	15	☐
Crestone Needle	14,197	19R9 Whitney from Lower South Colony Lake	1,002	2.1	2,537	5.8SS	186	☐
Sunlight Peak	13,995	29R3 EC2 "Sunlight Spire" from Needleton TH	1,000	17.4	5,843	5.10	302	☐
Evans & Bierstadt	14,264	3C4 Evans Egis	987	25.6	10,200	3	51	☐
Crestone Needle	14,197	19R8 Merhar from Lower South Colony TH	967	15.4	5,467	5.6	186	☐
Windom Group	14,087	29C3 Eolus NE Ridge -> Sunlight S Slopes -> Windom W Ridge from Vallecito Flats TH	927	45.2	11,730	4	308	☐
Maroon Bells Group	14,156	24C2 The Triple Feat from Maroon Lake TH	920	11.1	8,548	4	249	☐
Crestone Needle	14,197	19R10 Ellingwood Arête from Lower South Colony TH	918	15.4	5,467	5.7	186	☐
Mount Eolus	14,084	29R7 South Ridge from Vallecito TH	915	39.6	9,424	4	307	☐
Windom Group	14,087	29C3 Eolus NE Ridge -> Sunlight S Slopes -> Windom W Ridge from Purgatory Flats TH	858	39.6	11,190	4	308	☐
Mount Sneffels	14,150	30R6 North Buttress -> East Slopes from East Dallas Creek TH	854	9.8	4,810	5.6	317	☐
Blanca Group	14,345	20C3 Little Bear W Ridge ->Blanca E Ridge -> Blanca N Ridge -> Ellingwood S Face from Lake Como TH	851	16.6	7,424	5.0–5.2	214	☐
Mount Sneffels	14,150	30R6 North Buttress from East Dallas Creek TH	841	9.3	4,810	5.6	317	☐
Mount Eolus	14,084	29R7 South Ridge from Purgatory Flats TH	818	31.8	8,644	4	307	☐
Windom Group	14,087	29C2 Sunlight W Ridge -> Windom NW Face from Vallecito TH	817	40.8	9,946	4 MS	308	☐
Longs Peak	14,255	1R7 Alexander's Chimney -> Keyhole	816	12.8	5,055	5.5	15	☐
Longs Peak	14,255	1R7 Alexander's Chimney -> North Face	813	12.1	4,855	5.5	15	☐
Blanca Group	14,345	20C2 Little Bear W Ridge -> Blanca E Ridge from Lake Como TH	803	15.4	6,882	5.0–5.2	213	☐
Sunlight Peak	13,995	29R3 EC2 "Sunlight Spire" from 11,200' in Chicago Basin	803	4.2	2,795	5.10	302	☐
Longs Peak	14,255	1R7 Alexander's Chimney from Longs Peak TH	793	11.2	4,855	5.5	15	☐
Windom Group	14,087	29C1 Sunlight S Slopes -> Windom W Ridge from Vallecito TH	784	41.4	10,146	4	307	☐
Crestone Needle	14,197	19R8 Merhar from Lower South Colony Lake	769	2.4	2,537	5.6	186	☐
Mount Eolus	14,084	29R6 East Couloir from Vallecito TH	757	40.6	9,184	3 SS	307	☐
Windom Group	14,087	29C2 Sunlight W Ridge -> Windom NW Face from Purgatory Flats TH	748	35.2	9,406	4MS	308	☐
Mount Sneffels	14,150	30R6 North Buttress -> East Slopes from 11,100' in Blaine Basin	747	3.0	3,050	5.6	317	☐
Harvard & Columbia	14,420	14C1 V2 The Rabbits from Harvard Lakes TH	741	13.6	6,066	5.7	145	☐
Mount Sneffels	14,150	30R6 North Buttress from 11,100' in Blaine Basin	734	2.5	3,050	5.6	317	☐
Sunlight Peak	14,059	29R4 West Ridge from Vallecito TH	731	40.0	9,159	4	304	☐

Summit Name	Elev feet	Route Name	R Points	RT miles	Elev Gain feet	Class/ Snow	Page	✓
Lizard Head	13,113	31A5 V EC2 Lizard Head from Cross Mountain TH	723	8.0	3,053	5.9	337	☐
Crestone Needle	14,197	19R10 Ellingwood Arête from Lower South Colony Lake	720	2.4	2,537	5.7	186	☐
Sunlight Peak	14,059	29R3 South Slopes from Vallecito TH	720	40.2	9,159	4	301	☐
Windom Group	14,087	29C1 Sunlight S Slopes -> Windom W Ridge from Purgatory TH	715	34.8	9,606	4	307	☐
Blanca Peak	14,345	20R3 Ormes Buttress from Lily Lake TH	706	7.6	3,795	5.6	206	☐
Windom Peak	14,087	29R2 Northwest Face from Vallecito TH	702	40.4	9,187	3 MS	300	☐
Mount Eolus	14,084	29R6 East Couloir from Purgatory Flats TH	688	35.0	8,644	3 SS	307	☐
Crestone Peak & Needle	14,294	19C2 Crestone Peak S Face -> Crestone Needle S Face from Lower South Colony TH	671	17.2	7,341	5.2 MS	191	☐
Mount Eolus	14,084	29R5 Northeast Ridge from Vallecito TH	670	40.9	9,184	3	305	☐
Harvard & Columbia	14,420	14C1 V2 The Rabbits from North Cottonwood TH	669	13.4	5,606	5.7	145	☐
Wilson Group	14,246	31C2 Triple Trick from Navajo Lake TH	663	19.4	7,694	4 SS	336	☐
Sunlight Peak	14,059	29R4 West Ridge from Purgatory Flats TH	662	34.4	8,619	4	304	☐
Blanca Group	14,345	20C3 Little Bear W Ridge -> Blanca E Ridge -> Blanca N Ridge -> Ellingwood S Face from Lake Como	660	6.2	3,664	5.0–5.2	214	☐
Windom Peak	14,087	29R1 West Ridge from Vallecito TH	659	40.4	9,187	2+	299	☐
Wilson Group	14,246	31C2 Triple Trick from Woods Lake TH	654	17.9	8,074	4 SS	336	☐
Sunlight Peak	14,059	29R3 South Slopes from Purgatory Flats TH	651	34.6	8,619	4	301	☐
Windom Peak	14,087	29R2 Northwest Face from Purgatory Flats TH	633	34.8	8,647	3 MS	300	☐
Windom Group	14,087	29C3 Eolus NE Ridge -> Sunlight S Slopes -> Windom W Ridge from Needleton TH	624	22.4	8,478	4	308	☐
Longs Peak	14,255	1R6 Kieners -> North Face	623	12.2	4,855	5.3–5.4 MS	13	☐
Crestone Peak & Needle	14,294	19C1 Crestone Peak NW Couloir -> Crestone Needle S Face from Lower South Colony TH	622	17.5	6,321	5.2 SS	189	☐
Longs Peak	14,255	1R12 EC2 Nesotaieux's Ten Tadasanas	621	17.8	8,720	3 MS	21	☐
Longs Peak	14,255	1R6 Kieners -> Keyhole	619	12.8	5,055	5.3–5.4 MS	13	☐
Blanca Group	14,345	20C2 Little Bear W Ridge -> Blanca E Ridge from Lake Como	612	5.0	3,122	5.0–5.2	213	☐
Longs Peak	14,255	1R6 Kieners from Longs Peak TH	607	11.4	4,855	5.3–5.4 MS	13	☐
Maroon Peak	14,156	24R2 Bell Cord Couloir from Maroon Lake TH	605	8.4	4,556	4 SS	241	☐
Mount Eolus	14,084	29R5 Northeast Ridge from Purgatory Flats TH	601	35.3	8,644	3	305	☐
Uncompahgre Group	14,309	27C1 Uncompahgre SW Slopes -> Wetterhorn SE Ridge + Matterhorn Pk via Uncompahgre W Slopes	600	14.3	7,112	3 MS	278	☐
Crestone Peak & Needle	14,294	19C2 Crestone Peak S Face -> Crestone Needle S Face from Cottonwood Creek TH	597	12.1	6,491	5.2 MS	191	☐
Windom Peak	14,087	29R1 West Ridge from Purgatory Flats TH	589	34.8	8,647	2+	299	☐
Wilson Group	14,246	31C3 El Diente S Slopes -> Mt Wilson -> Mt Wilson N Slopes from Kilpacker TH	587	17.8	5,611	4	336	☐
La Plata Peak	14,336	11R2 Ellingwood Ridge from Lake Creek TH	586	10.0	5,416	3	118	☐
Mount Eolus	14,084	29R7 South Ridge from Needleton TH	584	14.6	5,932	4	307	☐
Wilson Group	14,246	31C1 Wilson Peak W Ridge -> Mt Wilson N Slopes -> El Diente from Rock of the Ages TH	583	13.0	7,182	4 SS	335	☐
Longs Peak	14,255	1R12 EC1 Radical Slam	580	17.1	8,080	3 MS	20	☐
Pikes Peak	14,110	4R3 Railroad Couloir from Manitou Springs TH	579	20.8	7,410	3 SS	62	☐
Pikes Peak	14,110	4R4 Y Couloir from Manitou Springs TH	579	20.8	7,410	3 SS	62	☐
Maroon Peak	14,156	24R3 Southeast Couloir from Maroon Lake TH	573	8.4	4,556	3 SS	242	☐
Longs Peak	14,255	1R9 Notch Couloir -> Keyhole	567	12.9	5,055	5.2 SS	16	☐
Snowmass Mountain	14,092	23R1 East Slopes from Maroon Lake TH	565	21.4	7,956	3 MS	235	☐

Summit Name	Elev feet	Route Name	R Points	RT miles	Elev Gain feet	Class/ Snow	Page	✓
Longs Peak	14,255	1R9 Notch Couloir -> North Face	564	12.2	4,855	5.2 SS	16	☐
Longs Peak	14,255	1R3 Keyhole Ridge -> Keyhole	561	14.1	5,055	5.5	11	☐
Longs Peak	14,255	1R3 Keyhole Ridge -> North Face	559	13.4	4,855	5.5	11	☐
El Diente Peak	14,159	31R8 West Ridge from Rock of Ages TH	557	16.8	7,551	4	334	☐
Uncompahgre Group	14,309	27C1 Uncompahgre SW Slopes -> Wetterhorn SE Ridge + Matterhorn Peak	556	19.5	7,672	3	278	☐
Longs Peak	14,255	1R3 Keyhole Ridge Longs Peak TH	553	13.8	4,855	5.5	11	☐
Crestone Peak	14,294	19R3 North Buttress from Spanish Creek TH	552	12.3	6,154	5.0	182	☐
Ellingwood Point	14,042	20R9 North Ridge from Lily Lake TH	549	7.9	3,492	5.0–5.2	212	☐
Longs Peak	14,255	1R9 Notch Couloir from Longs Peak TH	548	11.4	4,855	5.2 SS	16	☐
Castle Peak	14,265	25R7 Southwest Slopes from Middle Brush Creek TH	545	22.2	5,565	3	257	☐
Little Bear Peak	14,037	20R5 Northwest Face from Lake Como TH	542	13.0	6,037	4–5.2	209	☐
Mount Massive	14,421	9R6 Northeast Slopes from Native Lake TH	538	15.2	5,990	3 MS	105	☐
Maroon Bells Group	14,156	24C1 North Maroon NE Ridge -> S Maroon S Ridge	538	9.0	4,830	4	248	☐
North Maroon Peak	14,014	24R5 North Face from Maroon Lake TH	536	7.1	4,494	4 SS	244	☐
Crestone Peak	14,294	19R1 South Face from Lower South Colony TH	535	17.1	6,744	3 MS	179	☐
Blanca Peak	14,345	20R2 Gash Ridge from Lily Lake TH	533	8.6	4,315	5.3–5.4	205	☐
Capitol Peak	14,130	22R1 Northeast Ridge from Maroon-Snowmass TH	530	15.2	5,890	4	227	☐
Crestone Peak	14,294	19R3 North Buttress from Lower South Colony TH	529	17.5	5,844	5.0	183	☐
Snowmass Mountain	14,092	23R1 East Slopes from Maroon-Snowmass TH	525	21.8	5,712	3 MS	235	☐
Maroon Peak	14,156	24R1 South Ridge from Maroon Lake TH	524	10.0	4,636	3	241	☐
Castle Peak	14,265	25R6 West Ridge from Conundrum Creek TH	518	20.6	6,811	3	256	☐
Windom Group	14,087	29C2 Sunlight W Ridge -> Windom NW Face from Needleton TH	514	18.0	6,694	4 MS	308	☐
Mount Sneffels	14,150	30R5 Snake Couloir -> East Slopes from East Dallas Creek TH	512	9.9	4,810	3 SS	316	☐
Shavano & Tabeguache	14,229	18C4 Shavano E Slopes -> Tabeguache E Ridge -> Antero W Slopes	511	19.3	7,353	2 ES OW	169	☐
Wilson Group	14,246	31C2 Triple Trick from Navajo Lake	511	9.4	5,468	4 SS	336	☐
Uncompahgre Group	14,309	27C1 Uncompahgre SW Slopes ->Wetterhorn SE Ridge via Uncompahgre W Slopes	510	12.9	5,960	3 MS	278	☐
Crestone Peak	14,294	19R2 Northwest Couloir from Spanish Creek TH	508	12.5	6,034	3 SS	181	☐
Kit Carson Peak	14,165	19R16 East Ridge from Spanish Creek TH	505	13.4	6,905	3+	195	☐
Mount Sneffels	14,150	30R5 Snake Couloir from East Dallas Creek TH	501	9.4	4,810	3 SS	316	☐
Pikes Peak	14,110	4R3 Railroad Couloir from Devil's Playground TH	498	8.2	4,240	3 SS	62	☐
Pikes Peak	14,110	4R4 Y Couloir from Devil's Playground TH	498	8.2	4,240	3 SS	62	☐
Mount Antero	14,269	17R2 North Ridge from Cascade TH	497	6.8	5,249	2 MS	159	☐
Longs Peak	14,255	1R12 Grand Slam	496	14.4	6,991	3 MS	19	☐
Little Bear Peak	14,037	20R6 Southwest Ridge from Tobin Creek 4WD TH	494	8.0	6,000	4	209	☐
Quandary Peak	14,265	5R6 Inwood Arête from McCullough Gulch TH	487	4.6	3,185	5.4	70	☐
Wilson Group	14,246	31C3 El Diente S Slopes -> Mt Wilson -> Mt Wilson N Slopes from 10,700' in Kilpacker Basin	487	10.2	4,671	4	336	☐
Crestone Peak	14,294	19R2 NW Couloir from Lower South Colony TH	485	17.7	5,724	3 SS	181	☐
El Diente Peak	14,159	31R8 West Ridge from Navajo Lake TH	485	14.4	5,231	4	334	☐
Kit Carson Peak	14,165	19R16 East Ridge from Lower South Colony TH	483	18.6	6,595	3+	195	☐
Harvard & Columbia	14,420	14C1 V1 Circumflex from Harvard Lakes TH	482	13.9	6,273	2	144	☐

Summit Name	Elev feet	Route Name	R Points	RT miles	Elev Gain feet	Class/ Snow	Page	✓
Windom Group	14,087	29C1 Sunlight S Slopes -> Windom W Ridge from Needleton TH	481	18.6	6,894	4	307	☐
Longs Peak	14,255	1R5 West Ridge from Longs Peak TH	480	14.3	5,255	5.4	12	☐
El Diente Peak	14,159	31R8 West Ridge from Woods Lake TH	480	13.2	5,611	4	334	☐
El Diente Peak	14,159	31R5 North Slopes from Navajo Lake TH	474	15.1	5,231	3 SS	331	☐
Quandary Peak	14,265	5R6 Inwood Arête -> East Slopes	473	5.1	3,185	5.4	70	☐
Evans & Bierstadt	14,264	3C2 Bierstadt S Ridge -> Sawtooth -> Evans SW Slopes	471	16.9	5,504	3	51	☐
Crestone Peak & Needle	14,294	19C2 Crestone Peak S Face -> Crestone Needle S Face from Lower South Colony Lake	471	4.2	4,411	5.2 MS	191	☐
El Diente Peak	14,159	31R5 North Slopes from Woods Lake TH	469	13.9	5,611	3 SS	331	☐
Mount Harvard	14,420	14R2 North Slopes from Pine Creek TH	468	21.0	5,540	2	141	☐
Uncompahgre Group	14,309	27C1 Uncompahgre SW Slopes -> Wetterhorn SE Ridge from Matterhorn Creek TH	466	18.1	6,520	3	278	☐
La Plata Peak	14,336	11R2 Ellingwood Ridge -> Northwest Ridge	464	9.7	4,836	3	118	☐
Kit Carson Peak	14,165	19R18 North Ridge from Willow & South Crestone TH	463	11.4	5,441	4	196	☐
Castle Peak	14,265	25R5 Cunning Couloir from Conundrum Creek TH	460	18.8	5,485	3 SS	256	☐
Mount Massive	14,421	9R2 Southeast Ridge from Mt Massive TH	459	11.4	5,817	2	101	☐
Mount Massive	14,421	9R6 Northeast Slopes -> East Ridge	458	13.7	5,530	3 MS	105	☐
Shavano & Tabeguache	14,229	18C4 Shavano E Slopes -> Tabeguache E Ridge -> Antero W Slopes	457	20.0	7,353 0W	2	169	☐
Longs Peak	14,255	1R11 Keplingers Couloir from Copeland Lake TH	454	15.2	5,935	3 MS	19	☐
Mount Massive	14,421	9R5 North Ridge from Windsor Lake TH	454	12.4	4,679	3	104	☐
Mount Eolus	14,084	29R6 East Couloir from Needleton TH	454	17.8	5,932	3 SS	307	☐
Handies Peak	14,048	28R9 V1 Tour de Grizzly from Silver Creek– Grizzly Gulch TH	452	8.4	4,986	2 MS/SS	290	☐
Mt of the Holy Cross	14,005	8R3 Holy Cross Couloir from Half Moon TH	448	11.4	5,625	3 SS	95	☐
Kit Carson Peak	14,165	19R19 Outward Bound Couloir from Willow & South Crestone TH	448	11.8	5,441	3 SS	197	☐
Pyramid Peak	14,018	24R9 West Couloir from Maroon Lake TH	448	8.4	4,418	4 SS	248	☐
Handies Peak	14,048	28R9 V1 Tour de Grizzly + Whitecross Mtn	446	8.6	5,431	2 MS/SS	290	☐
Mount Wilson	14,246	31R4 East Face from Cross Mountain TH	445	10.1	4,586	4 MS	330	☐
Crestone Peak	14,294	19R1 South Face from Cottonwood Creek TH	444	11.2	5,894	3 MS	179	☐
Mt of the Holy Cross	14,005	8R5 V2 Notch Mtn from Half Moon TH	441	12.8	6,037	2+	97	☐
El Diente Peak	14,159	31R5 North Slopes from Rock of Ages TH	441	11.3	5,619	3 SS	331	☐
Torreys Peak	14,267	2R13 West Ridge from Loveland Pass TH	439	10.0	5,487	2	34	☐
Missouri Mountain	14,067	13R9 V2 South Ridge from Pine Creek TH	439	26.0	5,187	2	135	☐
Mt of the Holy Cross	14,005	8R3 Holy Cross Couloir -> North Ridge	438	11.1	5,625	3 SS	95	☐
Mount Massive	14,421	9R8 Massive Mania from Windsor Lake TH	436	11.9	4,953	3	106	☐
Castle Peak	14,265	25R4 West Face from Conundrum Creek TH	436	18.8	5,485	3	255	☐
Longs Peak	14,255	1R2 North Face -> Keyhole	433	13.7	5,055	5.3	10	☐
Mount Oxford	14,153	13R3 East Ridge from Pine Creek TH	432	17.0	5,791	2	131	☐
Shavano & Tabeguache	14,229	18C3 Tabeguache NE Slopes -> Shavano NW Ridge	431	18.0	5,764	2	169	☐
North Maroon Peak	14,014	24R6 Northwest Ridge from Maroon Lake TH	431	7.4	4,494	4 SS	245	☐
Mount Lindsey	14,042	20R11 North Couloir from Lily Lake TH	430	9.6	5,412	2 MS	216	☐
Mount Evans	14,264	3R4 West Chicago Creek from W Chicago Creek TH	429	16.5	4,664	2	42	☐
Sunlight Peak	14,059	29R4 West Ridge from Needleton TH	429	17.2	5,907	4	304	☐

Sorted by R Points

Summit Name	Elev feet	Route Name	R Points	RT miles	Elev Gain feet	Class/ Snow	Page	✓
Mount Harvard	14,420	14R2 V Northeast Ridge from Pine Creek TH	428	20.0	5,540	2	141	❑
Kit Carson Peak	14,165	19R20 South Couloir from Spanish Creek TH	428	10.4	5,905	3 MS	197	❑
Handies Peak	14,048	28R9 V2 Parhelia from Silver Creek–Grizzly Gulch TH	428	11.4	5,487	2+	290	❑
Windom Group	14,087	29C3 Eolus NE Ridge -> Sunlight S Slopes -> Windom W Ridge from 11,200' in Chicago Basin	426	9.2	5,430	4	308	❑
El Diente Peak	14,159	31R7 North Buttress from Navajo Lake TH	426	14.0	5,231	4	333	❑
Pyramid Peak	14,018	24R8 Northwest Ridge from Maroon Lake TH	424	6.4	4,418	4	247	❑
Crestone Peak & Needle	14,294	19C1 Crestone Peak NW Couloir -> Crestone Needle S Face from Lower South Colony Lake	422	4.5	3,391	5.2 SS	189	❑
El Diente Peak	14,159	31R7 North Buttress from Woods Lake TH	421	12.8	5,611	4	333	❑
Pikes Peak	14,110	4R1 East Slopes from Manitou Springs TH	419	25.8	7,410	1	57	❑
Mount Sneffels	14,150	30R4 Northeast Couloir -> East Slopes from East Dallas Creek TH	419	10.1	4,890	3 SS	315	❑
Mount Wilson	14,246	31R3 Southwest Slopes from Kilpacker TH	419	11.8	4,186	4 MS	330	❑
Mt of the Holy Cross	14,005	8R4 Teardrop from Half Moon TH	418	13.0	5,625	3 SS	96	❑
Mt of the Holy Cross	14,005	8R5 V2 Notch Mtn -> Notch Mtn Trail	417	14.3	5,593	2+	97	❑
Sunlight Peak	14,059	29R3 South Slopes from Needleton TH	417	17.4	5,907	4	301	❑
El Diente Peak	14,159	31R7 North Buttress from Rock of Ages TH	417	11.6	6,059	4	333	❑
Snowmass Mountain	14,092	23R3 S Ridge from Crystal TH	415	12.0	5,392	3+	237	❑
Mount Sneffels	14,150	30R4 Northeast Couloir from East Dallas Creek TH	415	9.9	4,970	3 SS	315	❑
Ellingwood Point	14,042	20R8 Southwest Ridge from Lake Como TH	412	14.5	6,042	3	211	❑
Wetterhorn Peak	14,015	27R6 East Ridge from Matterhorn Creek TH	412	8.9	3,615	4	278	❑
Capitol Peak	14,130	22R1 Northeast Ridge from Capitol Creek TH	411	16.8	5,610	4	227	❑
Longs Peak	14,255	1R1 V3 Trough -> North Longs Peak Trail	410	16.0	5,215	3 MS	7	❑
Longs Peak	14,255	1R2 North Face from Longs Peak TH	410	13.0	4,855	5.3	10	❑
Harvard & Columbia	14,420	14C1 Columbia West Slopes -> Harvard South Slopes	409	13.7	5,813	2	144	❑
Longs Peak	14,255	1R4 Northwest Couloir -> North Face	408	13.7	5,055	5.0	12	❑
Crestone Needle	14,197	19R7 South Face from Lower South Colony TH	408	15.6	5,467	3 MS	184	❑
Mt of the Holy Cross	14,005	8R2 Angelica -> North Ridge	407	10.9	5,625	3SS	93	❑
North Maroon Peak	14,014	24R4 Northeast Ridge from Maroon Lake TH	407	7.2	4,494	4	243	❑
Chicago Basin	12,700	29A2 Vallecito Approach from Vallecito TH	407	36.0	6,300	1	297	❑
Torreys Peak	14,267	2R9 Eroica from Grizzly Gulch TH	406	6.0	3,947	3 SS	31	❑
Challenger Point	14,081	19R15 Kirk Couloir from Willow & South Crestone TH	406	11.2	5,357	2 SS	194	❑
Longs Peak	14,255	1R4 Northwest Couloir -> Keyhole	405	14.3	5,255	5.0	12	❑
Mount Sneffels	14,150	30R5 Snake Couloir -> East Slopes from 11,100' in Blaine Basin	405	3.1	3,050	3 SS	316	❑
Mount Elbert	14,433	10R5 West Face from South Half Moon Creek TH	402	7.6	4,193	2 MS	114	❑
Little Bear Peak	14,037	20R4 West Ridge from Lake Como TH	402	13.5	6,197	4–5.2	207	❑
Mt of the Holy Cross	14,005	8R2 Angelica from Half Moon TH	401	10.7	5,625	3 SS	93	❑
Torreys Peak	14,267	2R9 Eroica from Grizzly Gulch TH -> Northwest Face	400	6.2	3,947	3 SS	31	❑
Pyramid Peak	14,018	24R7 Northeast Ridge from Maroon Lake TH	400	7.0	4,418	4	246	❑
Windom Peak	14,087	29R2 Northwest Face from Needleton TH	400	17.6	5,935	3 MS	300	❑
Mount Eolus	14,084	29R7 South Ridge from 11,080' in Chicago Basin	400	2.5	3,004	4	307	❑

Summit Name	Elev feet	Route Name	R Points	RT miles	Elev Gain feet	Class/ Snow	Page	✓
Mount Wilson	14,246	31R2 North Slopes from Navajo Lake TH	400	15.9	5,318	4	329	☐
Crestone Needle	14,197	19R7 South Face from Cottonwood Creek TH	399	11.3	5,797	3 MS	184	☐
Mount Massive	14,421	9R2 Southeast Ridge -> East Slopes	397	12.5	5,174	2	101	☐
Mount Oxford	14,153	13R4 South Slopes from Pine Creek TH	397	18.2	5,273	2	132	☐
Humboldt Peak	14,064	19R13 East Ridge from Lower South Colony TH	397	12.9	5,394	2	192	☐
Mount Massive	14,421	9R5 North Ridge -> East Ridge	395	12.3	4,838	3	104	☐
Mt of the Holy Cross	14,005	8R4 Teardrop -> North Ridge	394	11.9	5,625	3 SS	96	☐
Mount Columbia	14,073	14R5 Southeast Ridge from Harvard Lakes TH	394	10.4	5,129	2	143	☐
Kit Carson Peak	14,165	19R17 West Ridge from Willow & South Crestone TH	394	12.4	6,323	3	196	☐
Mount Sneffels	14,150	30R5 Snake Couloir from 11,100' in Blaine Basin	394	2.6	3,050	3 SS	316	☐
Mount Wilson	14,246	31R2 North Slopes from Woods Lake TH	394	14.7	5,698	4	329	☐
Wetterhorn Peak	14,015	27R6 East Ridge from Matterhorn Creek 4WD TH	393	7.7	3,295	4	278	☐
Handies Peak	14,048	28R9 V2 Parhelia + Whitecross Mtn	393	10.1	5,551	2+	290	☐
Longs Peak	14,255	1R4 Northwest Couloir from Longs Peak TH	392	13.9	5,255	5.0	12	☐
Mount Bierstadt	14,060	3R16 South Face from Scott Gomer Creek TH	392	15.0	4,440	2 SS	50	☐
Longs Peak	14,255	1R1 V2 Keyhole via North Longs Peak Trail	391	18.1	5,415	3	7	☐
Torreys Peak	14,267	2R11 Emperor -> Northwest Face from Grizzly Gulch TH	389	6.3	3,947	3 SS	32	☐
Snowmass Mountain	14,092	23R2 West Face from Crystal TH	389	12.2	5,112	3	236	☐
Handies Peak	14,048	28R9 V1 Tour de Grizzly -> East Slopes	389	7.8	4,752	2 MS/SS	290	☐
Mount Evans	14,264	3R3 Mount Evans Road from Echo Lake TH	388	29.2	3,684	1	41	☐
Torreys Peak	14,267	2R11 Emperor from Grizzly Gulch TH	386	6.0	3,947	3 SS	32	☐
Mount Bierstadt	14,060	3R16 South Face -> South Ridge	386	14.4	4,440	2 SS	50	☐
Crestone Peak	14,294	19R3 North Buttress from 11,000' in Spanish Creek	386	5.3	3,414	5.0	182	☐
Longs Peak	14,255	1R1 V3 Keyhole via Trough	385	13.8	5,015	3 MS	7	☐
Torreys Peak	14,267	2R9 Eroica from Grays Peak TH	384	6.8	3,757	3 SS	31	☐
Mount Antero	14,269	17R4 Browns Creek from Browns Creek TH	384	19.3	5,349	2	160	☐
Blanca Group	14,345	20C1 Blanca NW Face -> Ellingwood S Face from Lake Como TH	383	15.8	6,887	2	213	☐
Mount Evans	14,264	3R7 V1 Beyond Chicago from Echo Lake TH	382	13.7	5,332	2+	44	☐
Mount Elbert	14,433	10R3 V2 Bull Hill from Black Cloud TH	380	11.2	5,575	2	112	☐
Mount Antero	14,269	17R4 V Upper Browns Creek from Browns Creek TH	380	23.1	5,349	2	161	☐
Pikes Peak	14,110	4R3 Railroad Couloir from Barr Camp	378	8.2	3,950	4	62	☐
Pikes Peak	14,110	4R4 Y Couloir from Barr Camp	378	8.0	3,950	3 SS	62	☐
Tabeguache Peak	14,155	18R5 Northeast Slopes from Browns Creek TH	374	16.5	5,235	2	167	☐
Shavano & Tabeguache	14,229	18C2 Shavano E Slopes -> Tabeguache -> Point 13,712 -> Jones Peak	372	7.7	5,600	3 SS	168	☐
Mount Bierstadt	14,060	3R14 East Ridge from Scott Gomer Creek TH	371	15.0	4,802	3	49	☐
Wetterhorn Peak	14,015	27R4 V Wetterhorn Basin from West Cimarron TH	370	14.0	4,825	3	275	☐
Longs Peak	14,255	1R10 Loft -> Keyhole	369	13.2	5,355	3 MS	17	☐
Mt of the Holy Cross	14,005	8R5 V2 Notch Mtn -> North Ridge	369	11.8	5,811	2+	97	☐
Mt of the Holy Cross	14,005	8R5 Halo Ridge from Half Moon TH	367	15.8	5,189	2	96	☐
Crestone Peak & Needle	14,294	19C2 Crestone Peak S Face -> Crestone Needle S Face from Cottonwood Lake	367	2.9	2,581	5.2	191	☐
Mount Lindsey	14,042	20R11 North Couloir -> North Face	367	9.1	4,452	2 MS	216	☐
Mount Eolus	14,084	29R5 Northeast Ridge from Needleton TH	367	18.1	5,932	3	305	☐
Little Bear Peak	14,037	20R5 Northwest Face from Lake Como	366	3.2	2,277	4-5.2	209	☐

Summit Name	Elev feet	Route Name	R Points	RT miles	Elev Gain feet	Class/ Snow	Page	✓
Castle Peak	14,265	25R7 Southwest Slopes from Middle Brush Creek 4WD	364	8.4	3,925	3	257	☐
Chicago Basin	12,700	29A EC Five Trails Run from Purgatory Flats TH	364	32.1 0W	5,640	1	298	☐
Gladstone Peak	13,913	31C2 EC Gladstone from Navajo Lake TH	364	16.0	4,985	3	336	☐
Mount Shavano	14,229	18R3 Southeast Slopes from Angel of Shavano TH	361	6.4	5,549	2 MS	166	☐
Mount Sneffels	14,150	30R3 East Slopes from East Dallas Creek TH	360	10.3	4,810	2+ MS	315	☐
Gladstone Peak	13,913	31C2 EC Gladstone from Woods Lake TH	359	14.8	5,365	3	336	☐
Mount Evans	14,264	3R7 V1 Beyond Chicago -> Northeast Face	358	13.1	5,358	2+	44	☐
Snowmass Mountain	14,092	23R3 S Ridge from Lead King Basin 4WD TH	358	8.0	4,672	3+	237	☐
Shavano & Tabeguache	14,229	18C1 Shavano E Slopes -> Tabeguache E Ridge	356	9.2	5,413	2 ES	168	☐
Windom Peak	14,087	29R1 West Ridge from Needleton TH	356	17.6	5,935	2+	299	☐
Mount Bierstadt	14,060	3R15 South Ridge from Scott Gomer Creek TH	354	13.7	4,440	2	50	☐
Missouri Mountain	14,067	13R7 East Ridge from Missouri Gulch TH	353	9.6	4,487	4	133	☐
El Diente Peak	14,159	31R6 South Slopes from Kilpacker TH	353	11.5	4,099	3	332	☐
Mount Massive	14,421	9R4 EC North Massive from North Half Moon TH	352	10.2	4,901	3	103	☐
Longs Peak	14,255	1R10 Loft from Longs Peak TH	351	12.0	5,155	3 MS	17	☐
Mount Columbia	14,073	14R6 East Ridge from Three Elk Creek TH	351	11.8	5,277	2	143	☐
Mount Columbia	14,073	14R6 V Bristlecone Circle from Three Elk Creek TH	349	12.0	5,123	2	144	☐
Longs Peak	14,255	1R1 Keyhole from Longs Peak TH	348	14.4	5,255	3	4	☐
Mount Bierstadt	14,060	3R14 East Ridge -> Northeast Face	348	15.8	4,621	3	49	☐
Torreys Peak	14,267	2R9 Eroica from Grays Peak TH -> South Slopes	347	7.4	3,377	3 SS	31	☐
Torreys Peak	14,267	2R12 Northwest Face	347	6.4	3,947	2 MS	33	☐
Mount Massive	14,421	9R7 East Ridge from Native Lake TH	347	12.2	5,037	2	105	☐
Grays & Torreys	14,270	2C4 Torreys West Ridge -> Grays North Slopes	345	9.8	4,445	2	36	☐
Mount Evans	14,264	3R6 Southwest Slopes from Scott Gomer Creek TH	344	16.4	4,644	2	43	☐
Longs Peak	14,255	1R1 V1 Keyhole via Jims Grove	343	13.9	5,255	3	6	☐
Quandary Peak	14,265	5R7 Quandary Couloir from McCullough Gulch TH	343	4.6	3,185	4 SS	71	☐
Missouri Mountain	14,067	13R7 East Ridge -> Northwest Ridge	343	9.9	4,487	4	133	☐
Blanca Peak	14,345	20R1 Northwest Face from Lake Como TH	343	15.0	6,345	2	204	☐
Mount Sherman	14,036	7R2 EC2 Tour de Sherman from Fourmile Creek TH	341	12.0	4,095	2	87	☐
Shavano & Tabeguache	14,229	18C2 Shavano E Slopes -> Tabeguache -> Point 13,712 -> Jones Peak	341	10.6	5,600	3	168	☐
Crestone Peak	14,294	19R2 NW Couloir from 11,000' in Spanish Creek	341	5.5	3,294	3 SS	181	☐
Kit Carson Peak	14,165	19R16 East Ridge from 11,000' in Spanish Creek	341	6.4	4,165	3+	195	☐
Mount Wilson	14,246	31R2 North Slopes from Rock of Ages TH	340	10.3	5,346	4	329	☐
Mount Evans	14,264	3R3 Mount Evans Road via Northeast Face	339	21.1	3,684	2	41	☐
Mount Elbert	14,433	10R4 Southwest Ridge from Echo Canyon TH	337	10.6	5,275	2	113	☐
Handies Peak	14,048	28R9 V2 Parhelia -> East Slopes	337	9.3	4,872	2+	290	☐
Wilson Peak	14,017	31R1 West Ridge from Cross Mountain TH	337	14.9	5,195	3	327	☐
Crestone Peak	14,294	19R1 South Face from Lower South Colony Lake	336	4.1	3,850	3 MS	179	☐
El Diente Peak	14,159	31R8 West Ridge from Navajo Lake	335	4.4	3,005	4	334	☐
Mount Yale	14,196	15R3 Northwest Ridge from North Cottonwood TH	333	13.5	4,526	2	149	☐

Summit Name	Elev feet	Route Name	R Points	RT miles	Elev Gain feet	Class/ Snow	Page	✓
Snowmass Mountain	14,092	23R2 West Face from Lead King Basin 4WD TH	333	8.2	4,392	3	236	☐
Belford, Oxford, Missouri	14,197	13C2 Missouri NW Ridge -> Belford Elkhead Pass -> Oxford W Ridge	332	15.0	7,414	2	136	☐
Evans & Bierstadt	14,264	3C1 The Sawtooth from Guanella Pass TH	330	10.6	4,824	3	50	☐
Crestone Peak	14,294	19R3 North Buttress from Lower South Colony Lake	330	4.5	2,914	5.0	182	☐
Humboldt Peak	14,064	19R13 East Ridge from Rainbow Trail 4WD TH	330	8.5	4,354	2	192	☐
San Luis Peak	14,014	26R3 West Slopes from West Willow Creek TH	330	10.9	5,114	2 ES	267	☐
Grays & Torreys	14,270	2C3 Torreys Dead Dog Couloir -> Grays North Slopes	329	8.2	3,560	3 SS	35	☐
Wetterhorn Peak	14,015	27R5 East Face from Matterhorn Creek TH	329	8.0	3,615	3 SS	278	☐
Wilson Peak	14,017	31R1 West Ridge from Navajo Lake TH	329	17.1	5,229	3	327	☐
Mount Harvard	14,420	14R3 East Ridge from Frenchman Creek TH	328	14.2	5,120	2	141	☐
Mount Antero	14,269	17R3 V Tarnacity from Browns Creek TH	328	13.6	5,349	2	160	☐
Redcloud & Sunshine	14,034	28C3 Sunshine East Ridge -> Redcloud South Ridge from Mill Creek TH	328	7.6	5,095	2	287	☐
Redcloud Peak	14,034	28R2 West Gullies from Silver Creek–Grizzly Gulch TH via North Gully	327	5.9	3,634	2 MS	284	☐
Mount Elbert	14,433	10R4 Southwest Ridge -> Southeast Ridge	326	10.9	5,088	2	113	☐
Quandary Peak	14,265	5R7 Quandary Coulnir -> East Slopes	325	5.1	3,185	4 SS	71	☐
Culebra Peak	14,047	21R1 Northwest Ridge from Culebra Ranch TH	325	13.0	4,727	2	220	☐
Mount Elbert	14,433	10R3 V1 Upper Black Cloud Gulch from Black Cloud TH	324	9.4	4,733	2	112	☐
Wilson Peak	14,017	31R1 West Ridge from Woods Lake TH	324	15.9	5,609	3	327	☐
Conundrum Peak	14,060	25R9 Conundrum Couloir from Castle Creek TH	323	11.1	4,260	3 SS	258	☐
Kit Carson Peak	14,165	19R18 North Ridge from Willow Lake	321	3.4	2,601	4	196	☐
Ellingwood Point	14,042	20R7 South Face from Lake Como TH	320	15.2	6,042	2	211	☐
Mt of the Holy Cross	14,005	8R5 Halo Ridge -> North Ridge	319	13.3	5,407	2	96	☐
Mt of the Holy Cross	14,005	8R5 V1 Orbital	319	13.3	5,407	2	97	☐
Uncompahgre Peak	14,309	27R3 West Face from Matterhorn Creek TH	319	10.3	4,345	2 MS	274	☐
Mount Meeker	13,911	1R10 EC1 Mount Meeker from Longs Peak TH	318	11.4	4,511	3 MS	18	☐
Humboldt Peak	14,064	19R12 West Ridge from Lower South Colony TH	318	16.6	5,334	2	192	☐
Windom Group	14,087	29C2 Sunlight W Ridge -> Windom NW Face via 11,200' in Chicago Basin	316	4.8	3,646	4 MS	308	☐
Mount Democrat	14,148	6R13 West Face from Fremont Pass TH	315	6.0	3,108	2 MS	82	☐
Mount Democrat	14,148	6R11 North Ridge from Montgomery Reservoir TH	314	10.2	3,228	3	80	☐
Mount Sneffels	14,150	30R4 Northeast Couloir -> East Slopes from 11,100' in Blaine Basin	315	3.3	3,130	3 SS	315	☐
Lincoln, Democrat, Bross	14,286	6C3 Lincdebro	311	10.9	5,022	2	83	☐
Wetterhorn Peak	14,015	27R5 East Face from Matterhorn Creek 4WD TH	311	6.8	3,295	3 SS	278	☐
Mount Antero	14,269	17R3 Little Browns Creek from Browns Creek TH	310	16.6	5,349	2	159	☐
Torreys Peak	14,267	2R13 West Ridge from Loveland Pass TH -> S Slopes	309	9.0	3,882	2	34	☐
Mount Evans	14,264	3R2 Chicago Creek from Echo Lake TH	309	12.5	4,834	2	40	☐
Huron Peak	14,003	12R3 Southwest Slopes from South Winfield TH	309	13.0	3,753	2	124	☐
Torreys Peak	14,267	2R7 Dead Dog Couloir from Grays Peak TH	308	6.8	2,997	3 SS	29	☐
Redcloud Peak	14,034	28R2 West Gullies from Silver Creek–Grizzly Gulch TH via South Gully	308	7.2	3,634	2 MS	284	☐

Summit Name	Elev feet	Route Name	R Points	RT miles	Elev Gain feet	Class/ Snow	Page	✓
Mount Sneffels	14,150	30R4 Northeast Couloir from 11,100' in Blaine Basin	312	3.1	3,210	3 SS	315	☐
Missouri Mountain	14,067	13R8 West Ridge from Rockdale TH	306	11.4	4,127	2	134	☐
Challenger Point	14,081	19R14 North Slopes from Willow & South Crestone TH	306	11.2	5,357	2+	193	☐
Kit Carson Peak	14,165	19R19 Outward Bound Couloir from Willow Lake	306	3.8	2,601	3 SS	197	☐
Quandary Peak	14,265	5R3 Sinclair Couloir from Blue Lake TH	305	2.4	2,685	3 SS	68	☐
Mount Bierstadt	14,060	3R14 V Northeast Face from Scott Gomer Creek TH	304	16.6	4,440	2	49	☐
Quandary Peak	14,265	5R3 Sinclair Couloir -> Cristo Couloir	303	2.2	2,625	3 SS	68	☐
Mount Elbert	14,433	10R3 Southeast Ridge from Black Cloud TH	303	10.2	5,201	2	111	☐
La Plata Peak	14,336	11R3 Southwest Ridge from West Winfield TH	302	11.4	4,096	2	120	☐
Mount Democrat	14,148	6R12 North Couloir from Montgomery Reservoir TH	301	9.2	3,228	3 MS	81	☐
Mount Yale	14,196	15R2 East Ridge from Avalanche TH	300	10.6	4,826	2	148	☐
Missouri Mountain	14,067	13R9 V1 Lake Fork from Rockdale TH	299	11.1	4,127	2	134	☐
Mount Yale	14,196	15R2 East Ridge from Silver Creek TH	299	10.6	4,776	2	148	☐
Uncompahgre Peak	14,309	27R3 West Face from Matterhorn Creek 4WD TH	299	9.1	4,025	2 MS	274	☐
Mt of the Holy Cross	14,005	8R1 North Ridge from Half Moon TH	298	10.8	5,625	2	93	☐
El Diente Peak	14,159	31R5 North Slopes from Navajo Lake	298	2.7	3,005	3 SS	331	☐
Mount Democrat	14,148	6R12 North Couloir Montgomery Reservoir TH -> North Slopes	297	9.4	3,228	3 MS	81	☐
Snowmass Mountain	14,092	23R1 East Slopes from Snowmass Lake	297	5.0	3,112	3 MS	235	☐
Castle & Conundrum	14,265	25C1 Castle NE Ridge -> Conundrum S Ridge from Castle Creek TH	297	12.4	4,789	2 MS	259	☐
Snowmass Mountain	14,092	23R3 S Ridge from Geneva Lake	296	4.4	3,412	3+	237	☐
Evans & Bierstadt	14,264	3C1 The Sawtooth -> Evans West Ridge	294	9.8	3,964	3	50	☐
Mount Antero	14,269	17R1 West Slopes from Baldwin Gulch TH	294	16.0	4,849	2	157	☐
Tabeguache Peak	14,155	18R4 West Ridge from Jennings Creek TH	294	7.4	4,023	2	166	☐
Torreys Peak	14,267	2R7 Dead Dog Couloir -> South Slopes	293	7.4	2,997	3 SS	29	☐
Mount Princeton	14,197	16R1 East Slopes from Mt Princeton Road TH	293	13.0	5,297	2	153	☐
Wilson Peak	14,017	31R1 West Ridge from Sunshine Mesa TH	293	12.3	4,317	3	327	☐
Mount Democrat	14,148	6R11 North Ridge Mont Res TH -> North Slopes	292	9.9	3,228	3	80	☐
Shavano & Tabeguache	14,229	18C1 Shavano E Slopes -> Tabeguache E Ridge	292	10.5	5,413	2	168	☐
Wetterhorn Peak	14,015	27R4 Southeast Ridge from Matterhorn Creek TH	291	8.5	3,615	3	275	☐
Handies Peak	14,048	28R9 East Ridge from Silver Creek–Grizzly Gulch TH	290	9.0	4,733	2	289	☐
San Luis Peak	14,014	26R3 West Slopes from West Willow Creek 4WD TH	289	7.7	4,714	2 ES	267	☐
Sunshine Peak	14,001	28R5 Northwest Ridge from Silver Creek–Grizzly Gulch TH	288	8.2	4,265	2+	286	☐
Grays & Torreys	14,270	2C5 Grays Southwest Ridge -> Torreys Chihuahua Gulch	287	10.7	4,370	2	36	☐
Snowmass Mountain	14,092	23R3 S Ridge from Geneva Lake -> West Face	287	4.5	3,272	3+	237	☐
Castle Peak	14,265	25R2 Northwest Ridge from Castle Creek TH	287	11.8	4,465	2 MS	254	☐
Castle Peak	14,265	25R3 Castle Couloir from Castle Creek TH	287	11.4	4,465	2 MS	255	☐
Mount Evans	14,264	3R5 West Ridge from Guanella Pass TH	286	8.9	3,104	2	42	☐
Mount Princeton	14,197	16R2 Southwest Ridge from Grouse Canyon TH	286	7.0	5,219	2	154	☐

Summit Name	Elev feet	Route Name	R Points	RT miles	Elev Gain feet	Class/ Snow	Page	✓
Kit Carson Peak	14,165	19R16 East Ridge from Lower South Colony Lake	286	5.6	3,665	3+	195	❏
Sunshine Peak	14,001	28R6 East Ridge from Mill Creek TH	286	5.2	4,561	2	286	❏
Pikes Peak	14,110	4R3 Railroad Couloir from Bottomless Pit	285	2.2	2,470	3 SS	62	❏
Pikes Peak	14,110	4R4 Y Couloir from Bottomless Pit	285	2.0	2,470	3 SS	62	❏
Crestone Peak	14,294	19R2 NW Couloir from Lower South Colony Lake	285	4.7	2,794	3 SS	181	❏
Mount Sherman	14,036	7R2 EC2 Tour de Sherman from Fourmile Creek 4WD	284	8.0	3,335	2	87	❏
Torreys Peak	14,267	2R10 North Ridge -> NW Face	283	6.2	3,947	3	32	❏
Mount Massive	14,421	9R4 EC North Massive -> Southwest Slopes	283	8.0	4,481	3	103	❏
Windom Group	14,087	29C1 Sunlight S Slopes -> Windom W Ridge from 11,200' in Chicago Basin	283	5.4	3,846	4	307	❏
Uncompahgre Peak	14,309	27R1 East Slopes from Nellie Creek TH	282	16.0	5,009	2	272	❏
Missouri Mountain	14,067	13R9 South Ridge from Missouri Gulch TH	280	11.6	5,267	2	134	❏
Torreys Peak	14,267	2R10 North Ridge from Grizzly Gulch TH	279	6.0	3,947	3	32	❏
Redcloud & Sunshine	14,034	28C2 Sunshine NE Ridge -> Redcloud West Gullies with descent of South Gully	279	9.0	4,135	2 MS	287	❏
Mount Evans	14,264	3R5 V2 West Ridge via Gomer's Gully	278	8.5	3,104	2	43	❏
Torreys Peak	14,267	2R6 South Paw Couloir from Grays Peak TH	277	7.0	2,997	3 SS	29	❏
Mount Democrat	14,148	6R13 West Face from Fremont Pass 4WD TH	277	3.0	2,768	2 MS	82	❏
El Diente Peak	14,159	31R7 North Buttress from Navajo Lake	276	4.0	3,005	4	333	❏
Conundrum Peak	14,060	25R8 South Ridge from Castle Creek TH	275	11.8	4,344	2 MS	258	❏
Uncompahgre Peak	14,309	27R2 Southwest Slopes from Matterhorn Creek TH	275	15.5	4,905	2	273	❏
Mount Columbia	14,073	14R4 West Slopes from North Cottonwood TH	274	10.0	4,193	2	142	❏
Mount Shavano	14,229	18R2 Angel of Shavano from Blank Gulch TH	273	7.2	4,429	2 ES	165	❏
Chicago Basin	11,200	29A1 V Cascade Creek and Animas River Approach from Purgatory Flats TH	273	30.4	5,760	1	297	❏
Mount Harvard	14,420	14R3 East Ridge from Frenchman Creek 4WD TH	272	11.0	4,120	2	141	❏
Wetterhorn Peak	14,015	27R4 Southeast Ridge from Matterhorn Creek 4WD TH	272	7.3	3,295	3	275	❏
Redcloud & Sunshine	14,034	28C2 Sunshine NE Ridge -> Redcloud West Gullies with descent of North Gully	272	8.3	4,135	2 MS	287	❏
Snowmass Mountain	14,092	23R2 West Face from Geneva Lake	270	4.6	3,132	3	236	❏
Grays Peak	14,270	2R3 Southwest Ridge -> East Slopes	269	9.5	3,810	2	27	❏
Evans & Bierstadt	14,264	3C3 Tour de Abyss	260	4.9	2,985	3	51	❏
Huron Peak	14,003	12R2 North Ridge from South Winfield TH	269	9.4	4,219	2	123	❏
Missouri Mountain	14,067	13R6 North Face Couloirs from Missouri Gulch TH	268	9.0	4,487	3 MS	133	❏
Missouri Mountain	14,067	13R6 North Face Couloirs -> Northwest Ridge	268	9.6	4,487	3 MS	133	❏
Mount Massive	14,421	9R1 East Slopes from Mt Massive TH	267	13.6	4,531	2	101	❏
Castle Peak	14,265	25R1 Northeast Ridge from Castle Creek TH	267	11.8	4,465	2 ES	253	❏
Grays Peak	14,270	2R3 Southwest Ridge from Chihuahua Gulch TH	266	10.0	3,810	2	27	❏
Mount Massive	14,421	9R4 West Slopes from North Half Moon TH	266	8.8	4,201	2	103	❏
Challenger Point	14,081	19R15 Kirk Couloir from Willow Lake	266	3.2	2,517	2 SS	194	❏
Torreys Peak	14,267	2R6 South Paw Couloir -> South Slopes	265	7.5	2,997	3 SS	29	❏
Mount Shavano	14,229	18R2 Angel of Shavano -> East Slopes	265	7.9	4,429	2 ES	165	❏
Kit Carson Peak	14,165	19R20 South Couloir from 11,000' in Spanish Creek	264	3.4	3,165	3 MS	197	❏
Torreys Peak	14,267	2R14 Chihuahua Gulch from Chihuahua Gulch TH	262	9.8	3,807	2	34	❏
Huron Peak	14,003	12R4 East Slopes from Rockdale TH	260	11.0	4,063	2	126	❏

Summit Name	Elev feet	Route Name	R Points	RT miles	Elev Gain feet	Class/ Snow	Page	✓
Mount Harvard	14,420	14R1 South Slopes from North Cottonwood TH	259	12.6	4,540	2	140	☐
Pikes Peak	14,110	4R2 Northwest Slopes from Crags Campground TH	257	12.8	4,010	2	61	☐
Mount Eolus	14,084	29R6 East Couloir from 11,200' in Chicago Basin	256	4.6	2,884	3 SS	307	☐
Huron Peak	14,003	12R3 Southwest Slopes from South Winfield 4WD TH	255	8.4	3,403	2	124	☐
Uncompahgre Peak	14,309	27R2 Southwest Slopes from Matterhorn Creek 4WD TH	255	14.3	4,585	2	273	☐
Capitol Peak	14,130	22R1 Northeast Ridge from Moon Lake	253	4.0	2,490	4	227	☐
Redcloud & Sunshine	14,034	28C1 Redcloud NE Ridge -> Sunshine NE Ridge + reascend Redcloud	253	11.4	4,669	2	287	☐
Mount Sneffels	14,150	30R3 East Slopes from 11,100' in Blaine Basin	253	3.5	3,050	2 MS	315	☐
Grays & Torreys	14,270	2C2 Torreys Kelso Ridge -> Grays North Slopes	252	8.1	3,560	3	35	☐
Kit Carson Peak	14,165	19R17 West Ridge from Willow Lake	252	4.4	3,483	3	196	☐
Mount Massive	14,421	9R3 Southwest Slopes from North Half Moon TH	249	5.8	4,001	2	102	☐
Mount Democrat	14,148	6R11 North Ridge from Montgomery 4WD TH	248	5.4	2,468	3	80	☐
Mount Wilson	14,246	31R2 North Slopes from Navajo Lake	247	5.9	3,092	4	329	☐
Mount Massive	14,421	9R4 West Slopes -> Southwest Slopes	245	7.3	4,121	2	103	☐
La Plata Peak	14,336	11R1 Northwest Ridge from Lake Creek TH	245	9.4	4,256	2	117	☐
La Plata Peak	14,336	11R3 Southwest Ridge from West Winfield 4WD TH	245	7.4	3,436	2	120	☐
Handies Peak	14,048	28R9 East Ridge -> East Slopes	244	8.3	4,298	2	289	☐
Lincoln, Democrat, Bross	14,286	6C1 The Decalibron	241	7.0	3,504	2	82	☐
Mount Sherman	14,036	7R1 EC1 Gemini Pk from Fourmile Creek TH	241	10.2	3,303	2	86	☐
Huron Peak	14,003	12R2 North Ridge -> Northwest Slopes	241	9.3	4,036	2	123	☐
Conundrum Peak	14,060	25R9 Conundrum Couloir from Castle Creek 4WD TH	239	5.7	2,900	3 SS	258	☐
Mount Democrat	14,148	6R10 North Slopes from Montgomery Reservoir TH	238	9.6	3,228	2	80	☐
Mount Evans	14,264	3R12 Diamond from Summit Lake TH	235	2.1	1,474	4 SS	47	☐
Mount Democrat	14,148	6R12 North Couloir from Montgomery 4WD TH	235	4.4	2,468	3 MS	81	☐
Sunshine Peak	14,001	28R4 Northeast Ridge from Silver Creek–Grizzly Gulch TH	235	7.9	3,601	2 MS	285	☐
Mount Lindsey	14,042	20R10 North Face from Lily Lake TH	232	8.6	3,492	2+	214	☐
Mount Democrat	14,148	6R12 North Couloir Montgomery 4WD TH -> North Slopes	231	4.6	2,468	3 MS	81	☐
Redcloud Peak	14,034	28R3 South Ridge from Silver Creek–Grizzly Gulch TH	231	9.1	3,634	2 MS	285	☐
Mount Belford	14,197	13R1 V1 West Shoulder from Missouri Gulch TH	230	8.4	4,617	2	130	☐
Redcloud & Sunshine	14,034	28C1 Redcloud NE Ridge -> Sunshine NE Ridge	230	9.7	4,135	2 MS	287	☐
Sunlight Peak	14,059	29R4 West Ridge from 11,200' in Chicago Basin	230	4.0	2,859	4	304	☐
Ellingwood Point	14,042	20R8 Southwest Ridge from Lake Como	229	4.1	2,282	3	211	☐
Mount Evans	14,264	3R12 Diamond -> Northeast Face	228	2.5	1,474	4 SS	47	☐
Quandary Peak	14,265	5R5 West Ridge -> East Slopes	228	7.1	2,625	3	69	☐
Mount Sneffels	14,150	30R2 Southwest Ridge from Yankee Boy Basin TH	228	7.8	3,450	3	314	☐
Torreys Peak	14,267	2R8 Kelso Ridge from Grays Peak TH	226	6.5	2,997	3	30	☐

Summit Name	Elev feet	Route Name	R Points	RT miles	Elev Gain feet	Class/ Snow	Page	✓
Mount Democrat	14,148	6R11 North Ridge Montgomery 4WD TH -> North Slopes	226	5.1	2,468	3	80	☐
Quandary Peak	14,265	5R2 Cristo Couloir from Blue Lake TH	225	2.0	2,565	2 MS	68	☐
Quandary Peak	14,265	5R5 West Ridge from Blue Lake TH	225	5.4	2,685	3	69	☐
Mount Oxford	14,197	13R2 West Ridge from Missouri Gulch TH	225	9.8	5,967	1	131	☐
Belford, Oxford	14,197	13C1 Belford NW Ridge -> Oxford W Ridge	225	9.8	5,967	1	135	☐
Culebra Peak	14,047	21R1 Northwest Ridge from Fourway	225	7.0	2,827	2	220	☐
Mount Lincoln	14,286	6R3 Lincoln Amphitheater from Montgomery Reservoir TH	224	4.0	3,366	2+	77	☐
Missouri Mountain	14,067	13R8 West Ridge from Clohesy Lake 4WD TH	224	5.4	3,187	2	134	☐
Mount Elbert	14,433	10R2 East Ridge from South Mount Elbert TH	223	11.2	4,813	1	110	☐
Mount Sneffels	14,150	30R2 Southwest Ridge -> South Slopes from Yankee Boy Basin TH	223	7.8	3,450	3	314	☐
Quandary Peak	14,265	5R5 V NW Face from McCullough Gulch TH	222	6.6	3,185	3	70	☐
Little Bear Peak	14,037	20R4 West Ridge from Lake Como	220	3.1	2,437	4–5.2	207	☐
Capitol Peak	14,130	22R1 Northeast Ridge from Capitol Lake	220	4.4	2,630	4	227	☐
Sunlight Peak	14,059	29R3 South Slopes from 11,200' in Chicago Basin	219	4.2	2,859	4	301	☐
Gladstone Peak	13,913	31C2 EC Gladstone from Navajo Lake	219	6.0	2,759	3	336	☐
Missouri Mountain	14,067	13R9 V1 Lake Fork from Clohesy Lake 4WD TH	218	5.1	3,187	2	134	☐
Missouri Mountain	14,067	13R5 Northwest Ridge from Missouri Gulch TH	217	10.2	4,487	2	132	☐
Torreys Peak	14,267	2R8 Kelso Ridge -> South Slopes	216	7.3	2,997	3	30	☐
Mount Harvard	13,580	14R1 EC Point 13,580 from North Cottonwood TH	216	11.8	3,700	2	140	☐
San Luis Peak	14,014	26R2 South Ridge from West Willow Creek TH	216	13.8	3,714	1	265	☐
Crestone Peak	14,294	19R1 South Face from Cottonwood Lake	215	2.0	1,984	3 MS	179	☐
Mount Democrat	14,148	6R9 South Ridge from Kite Lake TH	214	3.6	2,148	3	80	☐
Castle & Conundrum	14,265	25C1 Castle NE Ridge -> Conundrum S Ridge from Castle Creek 4WD TH	211	7.0	3,429	2 MS	259	☐
Longs Peak	14,255	1R10 Loft from Chasm Meadows	210	3.0	2,975	3 MS	17	☐
Mount Shavano	14,229	18R1 East Slopes from Blank Gulch TH	210	8.5	4,429	2	164	☐
Crestone Needle	14,197	19R7 South Face from Lower South Colony Lake	210	2.6	2,537	3 MS	184	☐
Wilson Peak	14,017	31R1 West Ridge from Rock of Ages TH	210	8.3	3,817	3	327	☐
Mount Evans	14,264	3R8 Sunrise Couloir from Summit Lake TH	209	4.8	1,414	3 SS	45	☐
Quandary Peak	14,265	5R4 Spring Couloir from Blue Lake TH	209	3.0	2,805	2 MS	68	☐
Snowmass Mountain	12,462	23A2 Buckskin Pass Approach from Maroon Lake TH	209	16.4	4,844	1	234	☐
Quandary Peak	14,265	5R4 Spring Couloir -> Cristo Couloir	208	2.5	2,685	2 MS	68	☐
Mount Belford	14,197	13R1 V2 Elkhead Pass from Missouri Gulch TH	206	10.6	4,617	1	130	☐
Mount Evans	14,264	3R10 The Snave from Summit Lake TH	204	1.6	1,414	4 SS	46	☐
Mount Yale	14,196	15R1 Southwest Slopes from Denny Creek TH	204	8.5	4,296	2	146	☐
Mount Sherman	14,036	7R2 South Slopes from Fourmile Creek TH	203	7.2	2,796	2	87	☐
Storm Peak	13,326	1R1 EC2 Storm Peak from Longs Peak TH	202	12.4	3,926	2	8	☐
Mount Evans	14,264	3R10 The Snave -> Northeast Face	202	2.2	1,414	4 SS	46	☐
Castle Peak	14,265	25R3 Castle Couloir from Castle Creek 4WD TH	202	6.0	3,105	2 MS	255	☐
Mount Evans	14,264	3R11 Crystal from Summit Lake TH	201	1.6	1,414	3 SS	46	☐
Castle Peak	14,265	25R2 Northwest Ridge from Castle Creek 4WD TH	201	6.4	3,105	2 MS	254	☐
Windom Peak	14,087	29R2 Northwest Face from 11,200' in Chicago Basin	201	4.4	2,887	3 MS	300	☐
Mount Antero	14,269	17R1 West Slopes from Baldwin Gulch 4WD TH	200	10.0	3,429	2	157	☐
Mount Evans	14,264	3R11 Crystal -> Northeast Face	198	2.2	1,414	3 SS	46	☐
Mount Democrat	14,148	6R8 Southeast Face from Kite Lake TH	198	2.4	2,148	2 MS	79	☐

Summit Name	Elev feet	Route Name	R Points	RT miles	Elev Gain feet	Class/ Snow	Page	✓
Quandary Peak	14,265	5R5 West Ridge -> Cristo Couloir	196	3.7	2,625	3 MS	69	☐
Quandary Peak	14,265	5R5 V NW Face -> East Slopes	196	6.1	3,185	3	70	☐
Mount Democrat	14,148	6R9 South Ridge -> East Ridge	195	3.9	2,148	3	80	☐
Mt Lady Washington	13,281	1R1 EC1 Mt Lady Washington from Longs Peak TH	194	8.6	3,881	2	7	☐
Grays Peak	14,270	2R2 Lost Rat Couloir -> North Slopes	194	8.8	3,000	2 MS	26	☐
San Luis Peak	14,014	26R1 East Slopes from Stewart Creek TH	194	12.0	3,554	1	265	☐
Mount Sneffels	14,150	30R1 South Slopes from Yankee Boy Basin TH	193	7.7	3,450	2+	312	☐
Mount Sherman	14,036	7R1 Fourmile Creek from Fourmile Creek TH	192	8.8	2,796	2	86	☐
Blanca Group	14,345	20C1 Blanca NW Face -> Ellingwood S Face from Lake Como	192	5.4	3,127	2	213	☐
Culebra Peak	14,047	21R1 Northwest Ridge from Culebra Ranch 4WD TH	192	4.8	2,347	2	220	☐
Conundrum Peak	14,060	25R8 South Ridge from Castle Creek 4WD TH	192	6.4	2,984	2 MS	258	☐
Capitol Peak	11,740	22A2 West Snowmass Creek Approach from Maroon-Snowmass TH	191	11.2	3,400	2	227	☐
Mount Elbert	14,433	10R1 Northeast Ridge from North Mount Elbert TH	190	9.0	4,393	1	109	☐
Pikes Peak	11,640	4A1 Bottomless Pit Approach from Manitou Springs TH	189	17.2	4,940	1	56	☐
White Ridge	13,684	7R2 EC1 White Ridge from Fourmile Creek TH	188	7.6	2,444	2	87	☐
Redcloud Peak	14,034	28R1 Northeast Ridge from Silver Creek–Grizzly Gulch TH	186	8.6	3,634	2	283	☐
Pikes Peak	13,170	4A2 Rumdoodle Ridge Approach from Devil's Playground TH	185	6.0	1,770	3	56	☐
Wilson Group	12,800	31A4 Kilpacker Basin Approach from Kilpacker TH	185	10.2	2,740	2	325	☐
Mount Meeker	13,911	1R10 EC1 Mount Meeker from Chasm Meadows	184	2.4	2,331	3 MS	18	☐
Mount Sherman	14,036	7R1 EC1 Gemini Pk from Fourmile Creek 4WD TH	184	6.2	2,523	2	86	☐
Handies Peak	14,048	28R10 Grouse Gulch from Grouse Gulch TH	184	9.0	4,608	1+	291	☐
Castle Peak	14,265	25R1 Northeast Ridge from Castle Creek 4WD TH	182	6.4	3,105	2 ES	253	☐
Wilson Peak	14,017	31R1 West Ridge from Navajo Lake	182	7.1	3,003	3	327	☐
Grays Peak	14,270	2R2 Lost Rat Couloir from Grays Peak TH	181	7.6	3,000	2 MS	26	☐
Mount Democrat	14,148	6R8 Southeast Face -> East Ridge	181	2.8	2,148	2 MS	79	☐
Mount Sherman	14,036	7R3 West Slopes from Iowa Gulch TH	181	4.6	2,356	2	88	☐
Mount Evans	14,264	3R7 Summit Ridge from Summit Lake TH	180	5.0	1,938	2+	44	☐
Lincoln, Democrat, Bross	14,286	6C2 Licambro	180	7.9	3,396	2	83	☐
Huron Peak	14,003	12R4 East Slopes from Clohesy Lake 4WD TH	179	5.0	3,123	2	126	☐
Mount Evans	14,264	3R8 Sunrise Couloir -> Northeast Face	176	3.8	1,414	3 SS	45	☐
Mount Princeton	14,197	16R1 East Slopes from Mt Princeton 4WD TH	176	6.0	3,197	2	153	☐
Mount Lincoln	14,286	6R1 West Ridge from Kite Lake TH	175	6.2	2,562	2	76	☐
San Luis Peak	14,014	26R2 South Ridge from West Willow Creek 4WD TH	175	10.6	3,314	1	265	☐
Mount Democrat	14,148	6R10 North Slopes from Montgomery Reservoir 4WD TH	173	4.8	2,468	2	80	☐
Grays & Torreys	14,270	2C1 Grays North Slopes -> Torreys South Slopes	172	8.8	3,560	2	35	☐
Crestone Needle	14,197	19R7 South Face from Cottonwood Lake	172	2.1	1,887	3 MS	184	☐
Crestone Group	12,310	19A4 Cottonwood Creek Approach from Cottonwood Creek TH	171	9.2	3,910	2+	178	☐
Huron Peak	14,003	12R1 Northwest Slopes from South Winfield TH	169	9.2	3,773	1	123	☐
Mount Eolus	14,084	29R5 Northeast Ridge from 11,200' in Chicago Basin	169	4.9	2,884	3	305	☐

Summit Name	Elev feet	Route Name	R Points	RT miles	Elev Gain feet	Class/ Snow	Page	✓
Mount Sheridan	13,748	7R1 EC2 Mt Sheridan from Fourmile Creek TH	161	8.2	2,508	2	87	☐
Mount Belford	14,197	13R1 NW Ridge from Missouri Gulch TH	168	7.0	4,617	1	128	☐
Challenger Point	14,081	19R14 North Slopes from Willow Lake	167	3.2	2,517	2+	193	☐
Mount Elbert	14,433	10R2 East Ridge from South Mount Elbert 4WD TH	160	7.2	3,913	1	110	☐
Conundrum Peak	14,060	25R9 Conundrum Couloir from N Castle Creek 4WD TH	160	1.3	1,220	3 SS	258	☐
Windom Peak	14,087	29R1 West Ridge from 11,200' in Chicago Basin	158	4.4	2,887	2+	299	☐
Point 13,123 A	13,123	31A3 EC Point 13,123 A from Woods Lake TH	163	8.5	3,763	2	325	☐
Longs Peak	14,255	1R1 Keyhole from Boulder Field	154	2.6	1,905	3	4	☐
Blanca Peak	14,345	20R1 Northwest Face from Lake Como	153	4.6	2,585	2	204	☐
Uncompahgre Peak	14,309	27R1 East Slopes from Nellie Creek 4WD TH	153	8.2	2,849	2	272	☐
Grays Peak	14,270	2R4 East Slopes from Horseshoe Basin TH	152	5.6	3,170	2	28	☐
Mount Evans	14,264	3R7 Summit Ridge -> Northeast Face	150	3.9	1,938	2+	44	☐
Mount Lincoln	14,286	6R2 V Varden's Way from Dolly Varden Creek TH	151	8.4	2,926	1	77	☐
Pikes Peak	13,170	4A2 Rumdoodle Ridge Approach from 13,100' on Pikes Road	150	2.5	1,600	3	56	☐
Grays Peak	14,270	2R1 North Slopes from Grays Peak TH	147	8.0	3,000	1	25	☐
Torreys Peak	14,267	2R5 South Slopes from Grays Peak TH	147	8.0	2,997	1+	28	☐
Mount Evans	14,264	3R9 North Face from Summit Lake TH	147	2.0	1,414	2 MS	46	☐
Mount Sherman	14,036	7R2 South Slopes from Fourmile Creek 4WD TH	147	3.2	2,036	2	87	☐
Handies Peak	14,048	28R8 East Slopes from Silver Creek–Grizzly Gulch TH	147	7.0	3,648	1	288	☐
Mount Evans	14,264	3R9 North Face -> Northeast Face	141	2.4	1,414	2 MS	46	☐
Mount Bierstadt	14,060	3R13 West Slopes from Guanella Pass TH	140	6.9	2,900	2	47	☐
Blanca Group	11,900	20A1 Lake Como Approach from Lake Como TH	139	11.2	3,900	1	204	☐
Snowmass Mountain	10,980	23A1 Snowmass Creek Approach from Maroon–Snowmass TH	139	16.8	2,600	1	233	☐
Wilson Group	12,100	31A5 V Bilk Basin Approach from Cross Mountain TH	139	12.0	3,198	1	326	☐
Ellingwood Point	14,042	20R7 South Face from Lake Como	138	4.8	2,282	2	211	☐
Cross Mountain	12,703	31A5 V EC1 Cross Mountain from Cross Mountain TH	138	8.4	2,643	2+	326	☐
Mount Sneffels	14,150	30R2 Southwest Ridge from Yankee Boy Basin 4WD TH	136	2.4	1,710	3	314	☐
Mount Sherman	14,036	7R1 Fourmile Creek from Fourmile Creek 4WD TH	135	4.8	2,016	2	86	☐
Wilson Group	11,900	31A2 Navajo Basin Approach from Navajo Lake TH	135	12.4	2,972	1	324	☐
White Ridge	13,684	7R2 EC1 White Ridge from Fourmile Creek 4WD TH	134	3.6	1,684	2	87	☐
Crestone Group	11,660	19A1 South Colony Lakes Approach from South Colony TH at 8,770'	133	13.0	2,930	1	177	☐
Wilson Group	11,900	31A3 Woods Lake Approach from Woods Lake TH	132	11.2	3,352	1	324	☐
Mount Bross	14,172	6R6 East Slopes from Dolly Varden Creek TH	131	7.0	2,832	1	78	☐
Mount Sneffels	14,150	30R2 Southwest Ridge -> South Slopes from Yankee Boy Basin 4WD TH	131	2.4	1,710	3	314	☐
Castle & Conundrum	14,265	25C1 Castle NE Ridge -> Conundrum S Ridge from N Castle Creek 4WD TH	130	2.6	1,749	2 MS	259	☐
Mount Lincoln	14,286	6R2 East Shoulder from Quartzville Creek TH	129	6.4	2,946	1	77	☐
Capitol Peak	11,600	22A1 Capitol Creek Approach from Capitol Creek TH	129	12.4	2,980	1	223	☐

Summit Name	Elev feet	Route Name	R Points	RT miles	Elev Gain feet	Class/ Snow	Page	✓
Quandary Peak	14,265	5R1 East Slopes from Quandary TH	128	5.6	3,325	1	67	□
Pikes Peak	14,110	4R2 Northwest Slopes from Devil's Playground TH	127	5.8	1,180	2	61	□
Mount Bross	14,172	6R5 Northeast Slopes from Quartzville Creek TH	125	6.4	2,832	1	78	□
Chicago Basin	11,200	29A1 Needle Creek Approach from Needleton TH	125	13.2	3,048	1	296	□
Humboldt Peak	14,064	19R12 West Ridge from Lower South Colony Lake	124	3.6	2,404	2	192	□
Capitol Peak	11,600	22A1 V West Side Story from Capitol Creek TH	124	13.0	2,340	1	223	□
Castle Peak	14,265	25R3 Castle Couloir from North Castle Creek 4WD TH	121	1.6	1,425	2 MS	255	□
Handies Peak	14,048	28R7 West Slopes from American Basin TH	121	6.4	2,748	1	288	□
Castle Peak	14,265	25R2 Northwest Ridge from N Castle Creek 4WD TH	120	2.0	1,425	2 MS	254	□
Mount Bross	14,172	6R4 West Slopes from Kite Lake TH	118	2.8	2,172	2	78	□
Pine Ridge	11,909	1R1 EC4 Pine Ridge from Longs Peak TH	114	5.6	2,509	2	9	□
Huron Peak	14,003	12R1 Northwest Slopes from South Winfield 4WD TH	114	4.6	3,403	1	123	□
Mount Democrat	14,148	6R7 East Ridge from Kite Lake TH	113	4.2	2,148	2	79	□
Battle Mountain	12,044	1R1 EC3 Battle Mountain from Longs Peak TH	112	7.8	2,644	2	8	□
Conundrum Peak	14,060	25R8 South Ridge from North Castle Creek 4WD TH	112	2.0	1,304	2 MS	258	□
Mount Sheridan	13,748	7R1 EC2 Mt Sheridan from Fourmile Creek 4WD TH	107	4.2	1,728	2	87	□
Wilson Group	13,020	31A1 Rock of Ages Approach from Rock of Ages TH	107	6.8	2,680	1	323	□
Wilson Group	12,100	31A5 Bilk Basin Approach from Sunshine Mesa TH	106	9.4	2,320	1	325	□
Castle Peak	14,265	25R1 Northeast Ridge from N Castle Creek 4WD TH	101	2.0	1,425	2 ES	253	□
Mount Sneffels	14,150	30R1 South Slopes from Yankee Boy Basin 4WD TH	101	2.3	1,710	2+	312	□
Crestone Group	11,000	19A3 Spanish Creek Approach from Spanish Creek TH	99	7.0	2,740	2	178	□
Mount Evans	14,264	3R1 Northeast Face from Summit Lake TH	96	2.8	1,414	2	40	□
Handies Peak	14,048	28R7 West Slopes from American Basin 4WD TH	96	4.6	2,448	1	288	□
Crestone Group	11,580	19A2 Willow Lake Approach from Willow and South Lakes TH	95	8.0	2,840	1	177	□
Mt Lady Washington	13,281	1R1 EC1 Mt Lady Washington from Mills Moraine	91	1.6	1,741	2	7	□
Crestone Group	11,660	19A1 South Colony Lakes Approach from Rainbow Trail 4WD TH	89	8.8	1,890	1	177	□
Pine Ridge	11,909	1R1 EC4 Pine Ridge from E Longs Peak Trail at 10,500'	73	2.2	1,409	2	9	□
Snowmass Mountain	10,960	23A3 Lead King Basin Approach from Crystal TH	72	7.6	1,980	1	234	□
Mount Sneffels	12,440	30A1 Yankee Boy Basin Approach from Yankee Boy Basin TH	71	5.4	1,740	1	311	□
Estes Cone	11,006	1R1 EC5 Estes Cone from Longs Peak TH	66	6.4	1,826	2	9	□
Pikes Peak	11,640	4A1 Bottomless Pit Approach from Barr Camp	63	6.0	1,480	1	56	□
Mount Sneffels	10,740	30A2 Blaine Basin Approach from East Dallas Creek TH	63	6.8	1,760	1	312	□
Estes Cone	11,006	1R1 EC5 Estes Cone from E Longs Peak Trail at 9,680'	56	5.4	1,546	2	9	□
Mt Lady Washington	13,281	1R1 EC1 Lady Washington from Boulder Field 12,660'	40	1.0	621	2	7	□

Summit Name	Elev feet	Route Name	R Points	RT miles	Elev Gain feet	Class/ Snow	Page	✓
Snowmass Mountain	10,960	23A3 Lead King Basin Approach from Lead King Basin 4WD TH	34	3.6	1,260	1	234	☐
"Southeast Longs"	14,060	1R10 EC2 "Southeast Longs" from Loft	36	0.6	600	2	18	☐
Mount Meeker	13,911	1R10 EC1 Mount Meeker from Loft	33	0.6	451	3	18	☐
Storm Peak	13,326	1R1 EC2 Storm Peak from Boulder Field at 12,750'	32	0.6	576	2	8	☐
Crestone Group	11,660	19A1 South Colony Lakes Approach from Upper South Colony 4WD TH	29	2.8	640	1	177	☐
Battle Mountain	12,044	1R1 EC3 Battle Mountain from 11,600'	28	1.0	444	2	8	☐
Battle Mountain	12,044	1R1 EC3 Battle Mountain from Granite Pass	24	1.0	300	2+	8	☐
Storm Peak	13,326	1R1 EC2 Storm Peak from Keyhole	20	0.7	180	2+	8	☐
Blanca Group	11,900	20A1 Lake Como Approach from Lake Como	8	0.8	140	1	204	☐

Index